# East Coast GARDENER

## A Month-by-Month Guide to Successful Gardening

MARJORIE WILLISON

NIMBUS PUBLISHING

Nimbus Publishing Limited
PO Box 9166
Halifax, NS B3K 5M8
(902) 455-4286

Cover photography: Scott Munn
Cover design: Heather Bryan
Interior design and illustration: Kathy Kaulbach, Touchstone Design

Printed and bound in Canada

Library and Archives Canada Cataloguing in Publication

Willison, Marjorie Jean Hanlon
East Coast gardener : the complete gardeners almanac / Marjorie Willison. — Updated and rev. ed.
Includes bibliographical references and index.
ISBN 1-55109-597-1

1. Gardening. I. Title.

SB453.W54 2006 635 C2006-904891-6

Canada

The Canada Council for the Arts | Le Conseil des Arts du Canada

We acknowledge the financial support of the Government of Canada through the Book Publishing Industry Development Program (BPIDP) and the Canada Council, and of the Province of Nova Scotia through the Department of Tourism, Culture and Heritage for our publishing activities.

# Contents

## January

3



## February

35

## *March/April*



## *April/May*

## *June*

207



## *July*

245

## *October/November*

## November

411



## December

435

# List of Tables

# Acknowledgements

To all of the people who helped this book grow—and grow— thank you:
the listeners of CBC Radio, with their constant enthusiasm and passion to learn, for their many gardening questions;
the readers of the *Daily News*, for helping me get straight to the point on many gardening topics;
the staff of the Halifax City Regional Library, for providing wonderful resources;
Dorothy Blythe, for suggesting that a gardener's almanac was needed and urging me to write it, and for her constant support in all that I produced;
Elizabeth Eve, experienced gardener and friend, for seeing the potential in the first draft and for her suggestions on how to make the mass of information more accessible;
Anne Webb, editor and novice gardener, for her steady flow of questions, meticulous attention to detail, and careful, thoughtful editing;
Kathy Kaulbach, creative gardener, designer and illustrator, who rose to every occasion no matter what was asked of her, for her commitment to the project and for her sense of humour;
Joanne Elliott, production editor, for her calm reassurance and help in response to all my phone calls, and for her marathon job on the index;
Martin, my husband, and Meghan and Kate, our children, who made it clear that I was needed despite my complete immersion in the book.

# Preface

For many years I have been listening to gardeners and talking to them about their plants. Each year I am struck by their passion to learn and to understand how their gardens grow. Novices and old hands alike share the joys and frustrations of working the soil, nurturing the plants, living with insects and coping with difficult climates. Repeatedly, too, I hear gardeners say that they want to work with the environment, rather than always trying to exert control over it.

I am also struck by how often a few small steps taken at the right time can reduce the frustration and increase the joy of gardening. Tending plants should be a pleasure, not a chore, and my chief aim in writing this book is to enable gardeners to put away their spades at the end of the day with a sense of satisfaction and contentment, no matter what kind of garden they have.

The book is arranged month by month, with more than enough suggestions to keep the most devoted gardener fully occupied. My hope is that each reader will pick and choose the parts that apply to his or her own garden and level of experience. By observing what is happening to certain indicator plants, by working with expected frost dates in each location, and by keeping track of various events each year, gardeners can work out a gardening schedule that is perfectly tuned to their own patch of paradise, no matter what the climate.

There are many areas of interest to gardeners. Vegetable growers need to know, for example, the different starting dates for growing vegetable transplants from seed, how to prevent seedlings from toppling over, when to sow green manures, how to rotate and interplant crops, what causes green shoulder in tomatoes, why beans and peppers drop their flowers, what are the most effective watering strategies, when to bring in the pumpkins in the autumn, and how to store the harvest over the winter.

Fruit growers want to know such things as how to prepare the soil, why immature fruit falls off trees, what to do about insects, when to prune to maximize fruit production, how to shape and train espaliered plants, how and when to propagate soft fruits, when to harvest fruits and how to store them, various strategies for managing strawberries and whether to mulch plants before or after the ground freezes.

Flower lovers require such information as the best times for setting out transplants, how to tell that perennials need dividing, when it is safe to move them, ideal annuals for window boxes and containers, good flowers for cutting, when and how to dry flowers, various methods of propagating bulbs and perennials, how to reduce the time and effort spent on roses, when to dig up tender bulbs and how to store them over the winter, and how and where to plant spring blooming bulbs in the autumn.

Herbalists need to know about soil preparation and exposure to the sun, what herbs to grow in shade, methods of extending the crop, various ways to use herbs, harvest times for maximum flavour and production, when and how to bring in tender herbs at the end of the season, and different ways to preserve herbs for winter use.

Some gardeners want information on lawn care, such as when and how often to apply lime and fertilizer, how to get rid of brown patches and weeds, when to plant or rejuvenate a lawn, and what to do about moss. Other gardeners are only too keen to know the tricks for reducing lawn upkeep, or how to get rid of lawns altogether.

Tree and shrub fanciers are concerned about pruning times, why the tree they bought in flower has not bloomed since and the shrub they planted years ago has never flowered, why their evergreens turn brown, when to move trees and shrubs, how to propagate them from cuttings, what to do about leaf miners and loopers, and how and when to fertilize.

More and more people are moving their gardening efforts indoors in the winter, or using some sort of sheltered growing space in the early spring and late autumn. Complementing the outdoor garden with herbs and vegetables grown indoors, planting flowers to bloom in the winter, and harvesting rhubarb and strawberries during the dark days of winter are treats for the palate and food for the soul. Even composting can continue through the winter with worms in the bin.

There are building projects, too, to keep gardeners busy in the winter. Gardeners find themselves wanting propagation units for their cuttings, a sundial made for their own latitude, one or more flower presses to save the colour of summer, bird houses designed to attract different birds, a strawberry barrel for indoor or outdoor use, containers for herbs, vegetables, flowers and shrubs, and a variety of cold frames for use in all seasons.

By making suggestions on a monthly basis, I hope that gardeners will use gardening methods that both harmonize with nature and will increase their chances of success. Novices will hopefully feel more comfortable with gardening routines, and experienced gardeners may feel moved to try new or advanced techniques.

# Gardening Zone Map

| USDA Zones | | Canadian Zones |
|---|---|---|
| | crocuses bloom late April to late May | 3 |
| 3 | crocuses bloom mid April to mid May | 4 |
| 4 | crocuses bloom early April to early May | 5 |
| 5 | crocuses bloom late March to late April | 6 |

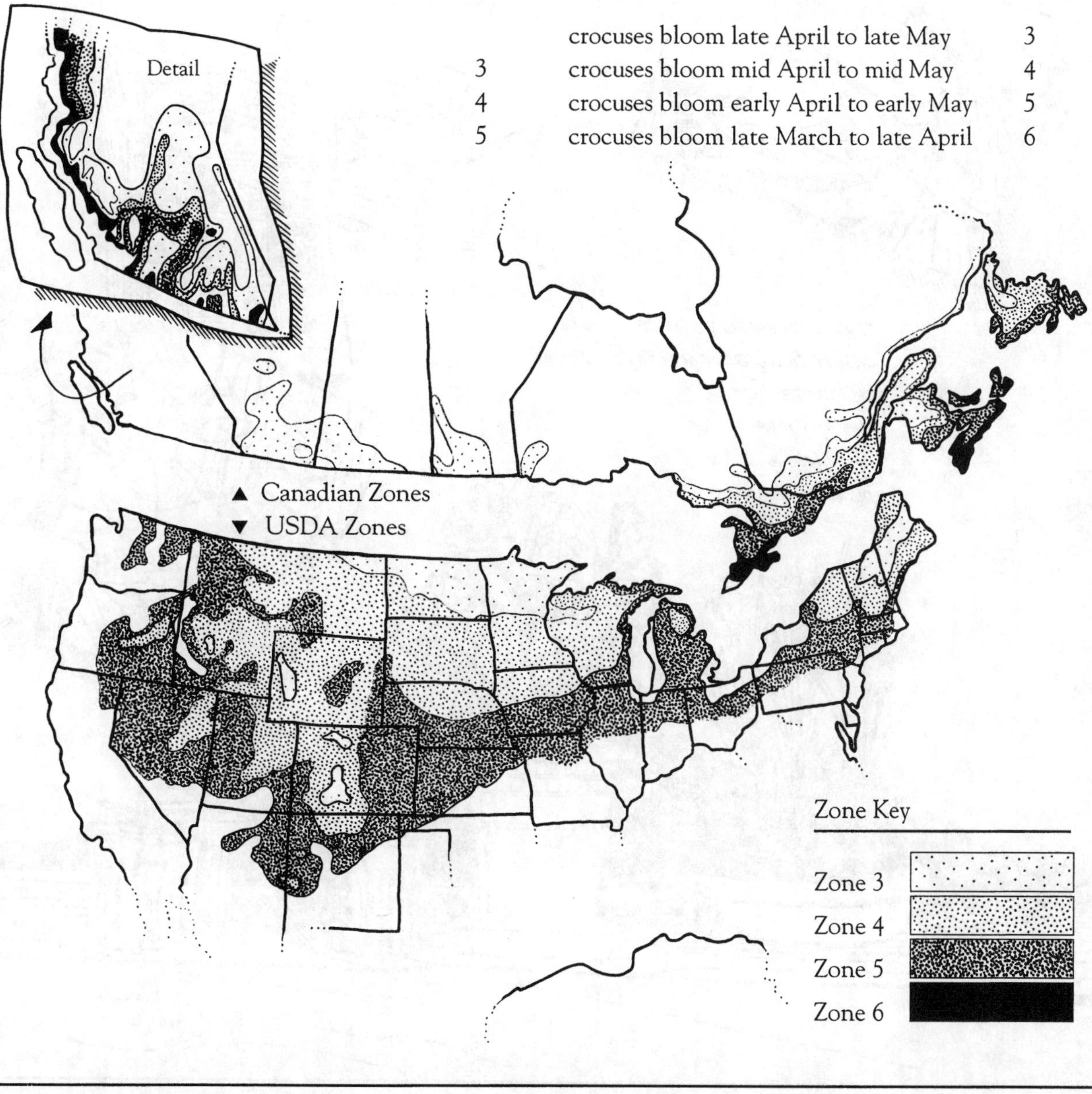

Month-by-Month

# January

# January

**Brochures and Catalogs**
*Forms of entertaining fiction published by nurseries, seedsmen, and tool manufacturers.*

*Beard and McKie*

There is a quiet bubbling of anticipation in the hearts of gardeners when the seed and nursery catalogues start arriving. Pictures of glowing vegetables, colourful flowers and fruit-laden trees start the imagination racing. The first delight is going through the catalogues and ticking off all the things one would like to have. This stage of delerium can last for several weeks. Then reality starts to set in with the realization that one's garden is not estate size, and that there is limited room in the house for starting seeds. As well, it is easy to get caught up in the details of selecting individual trees, shrubs or flowers and to forget the overall garden design. The bittersweet agony of ordering is not so much deciding what to buy, but rather deciding what not to buy.

## General Garden Planning

### Fitting it All In

If the yard is thought of as a cluster of "rooms" to be used for sitting in the sunshine, growing vegetables, playing games, drying clothes and storing various articles, the garden can be seen in a new light. For example, one wants to make sure a deck is positioned so that it is in the sunshine during the time of day it will be used most often. A vegetable garden should be in full sunshine, and both vegetables and fruits grow better when sheltered from wind. If a windbreak is to be planted, consider whether it will block a fine view or provide screening from neighbours.

Look outside and consider the position and pattern of snow accumulation in the yard. Exposed, windy places will be swept relatively clear of snow, and sheltered areas will harbour deep drifts. This information should help you determine the best position for a shelterbelt (also see page 43); erecting a temporary snow fence will clearly demonstrate the effect a hedge or windbreak would have. It is very discouraging to plant a hedge, only to discover in subsequent years that it causes snow to pile up in the driveway.

Even if a shelterbelt is not needed, it is useful to note the exposed areas so that wind-sensitive plants are not purchased for those locations. Broad-leaved evergreens, such as rhododendrons and hollies, fare poorly in winter wind and are best planted in sheltered places.

Juggle, shift and combine various "rooms" and growing areas until the desired shape of the garden is determined. Next, consider the size and shape of plantings around each room. Should the deck, for example, be completely open to the rest of the garden, partially enclosed by waist-high plants, or totally cut off from other areas by shrubs that are head-high. Maybe a tree that casts light shade would provide a corner to the deck. Its ultimate height would need to suit the size of the house and yard, and its roots should be deep enough that other things could be planted under it.

Once the choice of trees and shrubs is narrowed according to size, it's time to start thinking about how to integrate certain desirable characteristics. A mixed hedge of shrubs with berries will attract birds, for example (see pages 421-422). Perhaps certain functions could be combined, such as using fruit trees and fruiting shrubs as screens and hedges. Consider, too, how much of the garden will be visible from the house in the winter, so that plants for winter interest can be introduced.

Some gardens contain a lot of natural vegetation. Planning in this case involves deciding what plants to clear out to enable other plants to grow better. Judicious pruning, and perhaps a few purchases to augment what is already there, is a more appropriate use of natural resources than wholesale clearing to plant a manicured garden of imported ornamentals. Broad bands of natural vegetation are also important along lakes and streams to keep the waters clean. An added bonus is that native plants are less bothered by insect pests and diseases than plants which are introduced.

In general, think about how each area of the garden will be used, how various plant characteristics can be combined, and during which times of the year various areas will be viewed. On top of all that, it is essential to consider growing conditions. Either choose plants to match existing conditions (this is the best route), or change the conditions to match the chosen plants.

## *Growing Conditions*

The ideal flower, fruit or vegetable garden is in full sunshine, is not in a frost pocket, has no competition from tree roots or overhanging branches, is sheltered from strong wind, and is full of deep, rich soil that drains well. Few gardeners are blessed with the ideal; however, there are strategies for coping with just about any situation (see pages 375-382, for soil preparation, including situations where there is no soil!).

Root competition is quite a severe problem for all plants, particularly during dry summers. Raised beds are a help, or resort to containers, but the best solution is to keep gardens away from tree and shrub roots. Next to buildings can be particularly dry, so avoid those sites also, or be prepared to water frequently.

In a shady yard, root and leaf vegetables fare quite well. Carrots, turnips, onions, leeks, lettuce, Swiss chard, the brassicas (cabbage and its relatives), beets, mustard, radishes and green onions require less light than fruit and flower crops such as tomatoes, squash, corn, lima beans, pumpkins, eggplants and peppers. The sunniest corner should be reserved for these, or plant them in containers where they can get full sun. Many foliage plants are very attractive in shady flower gardens, whether or not they carry flowers, and there are herbs for sunny positions as well as for shady corners.

Soil next to old houses is often contaminated with lead from old style paints, but this tends not to be absorbed by plants. Urban gardens can be high in lead from automobile exhaust, which is absorbed by plants—a concern to food growers. Roots absorb the greatest amount of lead, but most of it stays in the skin where it can be peeled away. There is a ten-fold decrease in lead uptake in leaves, and a further ten-fold decrease in fruit. This might help in deciding which crops to grow if the soil is contaminated.

Fruiting trees and shrubs can add structure and colour to the landscape, but they require good drainage and most need full sunshine, although a few will manage to fruit in partial shade. When deciding whether or not fruiting trees and shrubs will fit into the yard, keep in mind that slight slopes improve drainage and provide some protection from frost (see Green Thumb Tip, page 43).

Almost all plants grow better in sheltered locations, and fruit trees require shelter in the winter as well (see page 43). Vegetables will have 20 to 30% greater yields if sheltered from even light winds. Greater increases are realized with protection from strong winds. This is due to the greater warmth and reduced loss of moisture experienced behind shelters. Protection from wind is also important for young plants and rooted cuttings. A little space in the vegetable garden or some other sheltered place should meet most needs for a plant nursery.

The most effective windbreaks are 50% permeable, such as a lattice of 1 inch (2.5 cm) wide slats spaced 1 inch (2.5 cm) apart. Even net and web materials will help to reduce wind in a vegetable or flower garden. Temporary shelters of corn, sunflowers or Jerusalem artichokes will also help until windbreak trees or shrubs have had time to grow. Ideally, a shelter should be placed at a distance of six to ten times its height. Fences 39 inches (1 m) high, spaced 20 feet (6 m) apart down the length of the vegetable or berry patch give good protection. Around the perimeter of the garden a 6 ½ foot (2 m) high windbreak or open fence is very effective. Some gardens, however, are so sheltered that the air barely circulates and there is a rapid buildup of diseases and pests. Raised beds help to improve air circulation, as does wider spacing of plants within each bed.

Sunflowers can act as windbreaks for wind sensitive plants such as peppers.

After considering each area of the garden, fitting the parts together to make a whole, and taking the growing conditions into account, the choice of what to plant and where to put it is much easier. You should also be able to avoid having to decide at the last minute where to plant what you have ordered. Winter dreams will have been tempered by reality in advance.

## Planning for Seasonal Interest

To take planning a step further, consider how best to use colour throughout the garden, both in terms of season and space. Planning is easiest if the garden is thought of as various areas seen more or less during various seasons.

Winter is the most difficult season to plan for, so start there. While most people spend relatively little time in their gardens when the weather is cold and miserable, they may frequently see certain areas from vantage spots indoors (such as the window above the kitchen sink). These areas are the places for plants with winter interest, such as evergreens, berried plants, plants with coloured or textured bark and those with interesting shapes (see December, page 435). If, however, such a location is ideal for summer flowers, try to include a few shrubs that provide winter interest.

Some spring days can be pretty dreary so, again, put early-blooming spring plants where they can be appreciated from indoors, or along the path between the car park and house. Little blobs of colour at the far end of the garden are okay, but spring gems such as miniature daffodils and early crocuses are best appreciated close-up. Plant late spring bloomers at the front of the house for passers-by, and along the route to the tool shed, for inspiration.

In the summer, the whole yard invites use. If there is a lot of space, fit in colour everywhere, but be more selective in smaller gardens. For example, leave room for fragrant plants close to the deck, and include a few with white flowers for evening enjoyment. Place other flowers where you will see them regularly. A solid backbone of autumn-blooming plants between storage areas and the vegetable garden or "orchard" will add considerable pleasure to the harvest.

Colour need not be restricted to flowering annuals and perennials. Groundcovers, bulbs, vegetables, herbs, fruits, trees and shrubs should also be considered. Planning colour schemes according to the location of plants and the seasons during which they are most visible will simplify the task. Predominantly green areas can enhance other jewels in bloom.

## Ordering Seeds

Once the garden is planned and the logistics of accommodating vegetables, herbs and flowers are worked out, it is time to choose and order seeds. Seeds should be ordered in January to ensure that they are available at indoor seeding time (see December, page 454, for tips on how to locate seed companies). Factors affecting the purchase of fruit trees and other woody plants are discussed in February (see pages 43-46).

Beginner gardeners may opt to purchase transplants of herbs, flowers and vegetables when spring arrives. Tomatoes, peppers and eggplants are usually set out into the garden as plants, as are some annual flowers (see Tables FEB-2, page 52; FEB-3, page 54; and FEB-4, page 56), but there are many flowers, herbs and vegetables that do not need to be started indoors.

## Seed Viability

Seed packages often contain more seeds than are required for a single planting season and gardeners often find several year's accumulation tucked away in cupboards. It is hard to know if they will still germinate. Research has shown that some seeds stay viable for longer periods than others. Most seed kept at average room temperatures in unsealed containers will be viable for about two or three years, although the germination rate will drop each year.

With vegetables, lettuce seeds will keep for up to three years; carrot and cauliflower seeds for up to six years; cabbage, rutabaga (swede) and turnip for up to nine years; and tomato and radish seeds for up to ten years. Many gardeners have first hand evidence of how long tomato seeds will last. People find them springing up in the most unlikely places, depending on where the compost was spread in previous years.

Seeds which should be ordered fresh each year include parsnip, salsify, spinach, corn, onion, leek, chives, anise and parsley. Squash seeds will keep up to four years, but do not save seed from their fruits as they are the result of cross-pollination and will not be like the parent. With flowers, seeds up to two or three years old are probably viable, and even older if they have been stored cool and dry.

Old seeds, however, will not germinate as well as new seeds under adverse conditions. For example, one study showed that under ideal germination conditions, both old and new carrot seeds showed a 95% germination rate. Under adverse conditions, however (cold, wet soil), 60% of the new seed germinated, compared to only 35% of the old seed. As well, seedlings from old seeds lose vigour; lettuce, for example, will mature later, and the yield of carrots will be reduced. All of this is not to say that fresh seeds have to be ordered every year, just be aware of the pitfalls.

### Storage conditions

It is important to store newly purchased seeds carefully. Germination rates can drop even in the short weeks between arrival and sowing if seeds are not kept cool and dry, and long-term viability can be affected. Research has shown how important cool conditions are: for each 10°F (5°C) rise above 32°F (0°C), the storage life of seeds is halved. So, if a certain type of seed is normally viable for ten years at 41°F (5°C), it will be viable for only five years at 50°F (10°C), and only one year at 70°F (21°C).

Similarly, increases in moisture content reduce seed viability. For each 1% increase in seed moisture content between 5 and 14%, the life of the seed is reduced by one half. Put another way, seed that would last ten years at 8% moisture content would last only five years at 9% moisture content. The effects of temperature and moisture content are additive. For example, seed that lasted ten years at 41°F (5°C) and 8% moisture, would last only two and a half years at 50°F (10°C) and 9% moisture content.

When successive sowings from a new seed package give poor results it is probably attributable to poor storage conditions. Put newly purchased seeds in a cool place in a glass jar with the lid screwed on tightly. It also helps to put some silica gel in the jar, the kind that is blue when dry and pink when moist. As long as the gel remains blue the moisture level is low enough.

### Germination test

When in doubt about seed viability, do a germination test. Sprinkle ten seeds from the package in question onto several layers of wet paper towel in a bowl. Cover the bowl with clear plastic, and lift the cover each day to aerate the seeds. Some seeds take longer to germinate than others so allow one week longer than the average length of time noted on the seed package. If only half germinate, plant twice as many seeds to get the desired number of plants; if only a few germinate, it is probably best to buy fresh seed. For perennial flowers, it is sometimes difficult to get the seeds to germinate at all, let alone carry out a germination test. To be safe, purchase fresh seed, but even with fresh seed 100% germination is unlikely.

### Focus on Plants

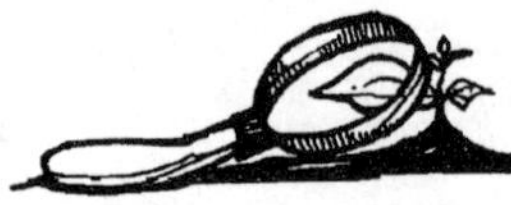

Asparagus is a perennial vegetable that takes three years to reach harvest size. Seeds can be planted close together the first year, but plants will require one square yard (1m²) for every two and one-quarter plants when transplanted in the second year to a permanent location. Allow three crowns of asparagus per person for seasonal consumption and ten to twelve crowns per person if additional amounts are required for storage.

## Minimum Germination Levels for No. 1 Seed

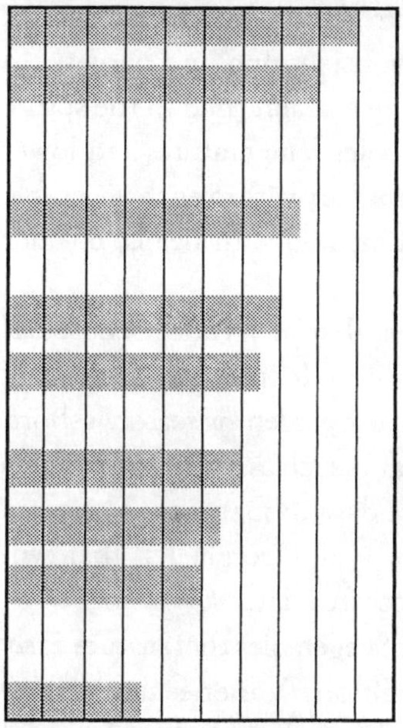

90% - corn

80% - beans, all the brassicas, radish, rutabaga (swede), turnip, melons, cucumber, pumpkin, squash, mustard

75% - pea, beet, Swiss chard, tomato, onion, asparagus, salsify, cress, chervil

70% - lettuce

65% - spinach, leek, pepper, eggplant, endive, chicory, chives

60% - carrot, parsnip, celeriac

55% - celery, parsley

50% - New Zealand spinach, dill, sage, summer savory, thyme

35% - watercress

## Selecting Varieties

### Vegetables

The first consideration when ordering vegetable seeds is the amount of space available to actually grow them. Count on roughly one to two square yards (1-2 $m^2$) per vegetable type for a family of four for a seasonal supply of fresh vegetables. Potatoes and corn will need considerably more space and root crops such as carrots will need less.

If part of the vegetable crop will be stored for winter use, the amount of space required can easily double or quadruple; allow an area of 24 by 30 feet (7.2 by 9 m), or a dozen beds of 4 by 15 feet (1.2 by 4.5 m). Interplanting and successional planting will allow more vegetables to be grown in a given space (see February, pages 37-38).

First-time vegetable growers should choose a few favourite vegetables to grow in small amounts. One seed package of each vegetable will be more than enough, even for gardeners who grow extra for winter storage. One or two plants of zucchini or summer squash are enough for most families. When choosing particular varieties of a given vegetable, remember to consider habit of growth, disease and pest resistance, and the local climate.

A vegetable garden of approximately 24' x 30' or 12 plots 4' x 15' is a workable size for a family of 4.

### Focus on Plants

Determinate or bush tomatoes, which grow as fairly tidy little bushes, are better for short season areas than indeterminate or vine type tomatoes. They will also produce a large crop in a shorter time, which makes them ideal for freezing, even in long season areas. Determinates are described by such words as "compact, bushy, extra early, short season type, free-standing, and small fruited," whereas indeterminates are described as "large, vigorous, continuously bearing, late or main crop, staking or pruning type, and extra large or jumbo fruited." Indeterminate tomatoes can be allowed to sprawl over the ground, where they will ripen sooner, or their growth can be confined upwards along a stake or in a space-saving cage.

### *Days to maturity and climate*

Perhaps one of the most confusing information items in seed catalogues is "days to maturity" for vegetables. The time from germination to harvest can easily be confused with the time between transplanting and harvest. In addition, days to maturity will be greater in the autumn than in the spring for the same seeds because of shorter days, cooler temperatures and lower light levels. Fortunately, maturity time does not vary within each vegetable group, so that beans, for example, can be compared with beans, but not necessarily with tomatoes.

Ordering from local seed suppliers ensures that any variety chosen is suited to the climate and length of growing season. If orders are made from out-of-area catalogues, choose early varieties if the gardening season is short. This is especially important for long season plants such as tomatoes, peppers and eggplants. Choose those with the fewest days to maturity. There are even sweet potato varieties, such as 'Carter' and 'Georgia Jet' that will mature in seasons as short as one hundred frost free days.

Catalogues for coastal areas offer varieties of vegetables that mature early and produce well under variable weather conditions. Varieties that will set fruit at temperatures several degrees cooler than other kinds are needed where summers are cool, breezy and foggy. Phrases such as "reliable under adverse conditions" are a good clue that the variety will perform well.

Short carrots are better than long varieties for short season areas, and they do better in soil which is heavy, lumpy, rocky or shallow. The long, elegant carrots are fine if the soil is deep and loose. Short carrots and round beets are also better for early crops as they mature faster than their long versions, but the long, late-maturing roots store better.

Spinach prefers cool conditions and thus grows well as an early spring crop or as a fall crop. If spinach is wanted in the summer, choose a long standing, bolt-resistant variety as it bolts (goes to flower before it can be harvested) when days are long. Another possibility is to grow New Zealand spinach, which is not a true spinach. It is not prone to bolting and it also grows better in poorer, drier soil. It has a spinach-like taste when cooked but is not comparable raw.

### *Habit of growth and space requirements*

How a plant grows can affect how much space is required. Members of the cucurbit family (cucumber, melon, squash, pumpkin) usually grow as vines that trail along the ground. Bush types that take up much less space are available, however, or cucumber and melon vines can be trained upwards to save space. Burlap or mesh slings on each fruit are required to support heavy melons.

Bush versions of winter squashes mature sooner in short season areas by as much as two to three weeks. How winter squashes will be used and stored should help determine which kind to choose. Hubbard squash is huge and keeps in storage for up to six months; it is fine for stuffing and for pies. Buttercup is smaller, keeps well and can be cooked in a variety of ways. Butternut stores well and is great for soups and pie, but it has a smaller cavity than buttercup so is not good for stuffing. Acorn squash is ideal for stuffing and baking; it will store for two to three months. Sweet Potato is a cream coloured squash that is sweet, tender and ideal for stuffing; it stores well for three or four months. Spaghetti squash is used quite differently from other squashes; it is boiled whole and eaten for its spaghetti-like pulp. Gourds are for looking at, not for eating. For pumpkin pies, order the varieties recommended in the catalogues; not all pumpkins make good pie.

Cucumber varieties abound. They may be long and smooth, requiring a cold frame or row cover to grow well in cool regions; short and prickly, coping just fine outdoors; or small gherkin types, ideal for pickling. If cucumbers are gynoecious (have separate male and female plants), the seeds of the male plants are the coloured ones in the seed packet. The required ratio of male to female plants for good pollination is provided in the packet.

Bush beans and dwarf peas are good short season crops, which makes them ideal for freezing. Climbing beans and peas can be planted as well to extend the crop over a longer period, if space is available. Use bush lima beans rather than pole lima beans in short season areas. Climbing types of peas, beans and anything else requiring support will mean extra fuss and bother setting up the supports, but the trouble may be worth it if space is limited. When ordering netting for climbing plants, remember that many plants find it easier to twine around or cling to nylon than to plastic.

Potatoes take up a great deal of space, unless only a few plants are grown for fresh eating. You might want to avoid corn unless there is adequate space and the soil can be replenished afterwards as corn is a heavy feeder. It needs to be planted in a block rather than a row to ensure good pollination. Because of the risk of cross-pollination, certain vegetables have to be grown separate from each other. Supersweet corn, popcorn and regular corn cannot be grown together, and sweet peppers have to be separated from hot peppers.

Radishes and turnips are good for interplanting (growing among other

### Focus on Plants

Turnips are different from rutabagas, or swede turnips as they are also called. Turnips can be used for their leaves or their roots, they mature in thirty to sixty days and they make a good spring crop. Their flesh is yellow or white, the roots are about 1 inch (2.5 cm) in diameter, and they have no crown as the leaves sprout directly from the root.

Turnip Rutabaga

Rutabagas mature in about ninety days and are grown as a fall crop. Their leaves are inedible, their flesh is usually yellow with a purplish colour on the outside, they taste milder and a bit sweeter than turnips, the 4 inch (10 cm) diameter roots store well, and they have a neck or crown about 1 inch (2.5 cm) long from which the leaves sprout. Both turnips and rutabagas turn tough and woody in hot weather.

## *Focus on Plants*

There is more choice in the onion family if plants are grown from seed rather than from sets alone. It is easy to obtain sets of storage onions, but not of large, sweet salad onions, boiling and pickling onions, bunching onions or leeks. Sets are more likely to bolt than onions grown from seed because they are a year older, but they will mature earlier than seeds and will produce reasonable crops in poor soil.

Scallions are grown for their greens and bunching onions for their white shanks. Scallions are easy to grow from seed, or use ordinary onion sets, and harvest while the onions are small. Bunching onions can also be used as scallions, or can be allowed to mature and used for their white shank. Sets or cloves are required for garlic and shallots. Garlic is best planted in the autumn unless winters are very severe, but if ordered now and planted in the spring, allow enough time to chill the garlic at 35 to 40°F (2 to 4°C) for eight weeks before planting it out as soon as the soil can be worked. If it does not have this period of chilling, the new garlic bulb that grows in the summer will not divide into cloves. Garlic is separated into cloves just before planting. It is a good idea to try several varieties of garlic because they require specific soil types.

plants). They grow quickly in a small space and can then be removed as the other crop matures. Radishes are also a good marker crop for seeds which are slow to germinate such as carrot, parsnip, salsify and parsley. Just mix a few radish seeds in with them when you plant.

### *Cost savings and choice*

Many vegetables can be bought as transplants, but there are advantages to growing your own from seed—the lower cost is a major factor.

Growing asparagus from seed will provide many plants for the price of one purchased asparagus crown, but there will be an extra year to wait for the first harvest. Female asparagus plants will also be mixed in with the males, which have a slightly higher yield, but the difference is not significant.

By all means choose old favourites when ordering vegetables, but try something new as well. It is fun to try a completely new vegetable. Kohlrabi is lovely when it is young, providing just the right crunchiness for vegetable dips and stir-fries.

Endive, escarole, kale and corn salad (mache) are excellent crops for the cold days of autumn. Radicchio (red endive) is an expensive gourmet item when purchased, but it is easily grown in much the same way as lettuce. Witloof chicory can be forced indoors for a fresh winter vegetable.

Baking or shell beans require little care in the garden, and dry readily for long winter storage. Young fresh soybeans have a delightful nutty taste, so can be used as both a summer treat and a winter standby. Jacob's Cattle Bean, Soldier and Yellow Eye are other readily obtainable baking beans.

It is essential that heirloom varieties be kept alive because they often have characteristics that are lost in modern breeding programs. Some of them may be particularly disease resistant or cold tolerant. Try to order a few from specialty companies or find seasoned gardeners in the neighbourhood who save their own seeds.

### *Pest and disease resistance*

Another factor to consider when ordering seeds is how healthy the plants are likely to be, especially if there have been problems in previous years. More time will be absorbed fussing over problem plants, and the yields will be lower than from healthy plants.

If a particular variety of bean, for instance, is noted as being disease resistant, it is probably safe to assume that other types, not so described, are susceptible to disease. "N" after the name of a tomato variety indicates nematode resistance. Yellow and red onions are more resistant to onion maggots, for some reason, than are white onions. To help reduce corn borer problems, choose early varieties so that the corn is past the susceptible stage when the corn borer arrives.

Climate may play a role in the selection of varieties. Some cucumbers, for example, are susceptible to various mildews; checking for resistance or tolerance of cucumbers to fungal diseases is particularly important in foggy, damp areas. Peas, beans and corn seed can be purchased with a fungicide coating. This is very helpful in preventing the seed from rotting, which can be a problem where soils stay cold and wet for a long time in the spring.

**Green Thumb Tip**

Perhaps one way to "have it all" when ordering seeds is to compare notes with friends. One rarely uses an entire packet of seed; by splitting orders and sharing seeds you can have access to many more varieties. It might be fun to have a seed ordering party some dreary winter evening, but the frenzy of seed ordering could become contagious, and you may be worse off than ever!

## Herbs

Depending on the required growing conditions, and on whether they are annual or perennial (see Table FEB-1, page 40), herbs can be tucked into the vegetable garden, grown among flowers, planted in the rockery or other sunny, dryish place, or grown in containers. There is no need to have a separate herb garden if space is limited.

### *Hardiness*

Perennial herbs come up year after year and will require a permanent location; annual herbs are started fresh each year, so their location can be easily changed. The hardiness and zone in which perennial herbs can be grown varies (see Table FEB-1, page 40). A herb that is hardy to zone 5, for example, will more likely survive the winter in zone 6 than in zone 5, and it does not stand a chance in zone 4. Herbs that are grown at the extremes of their range will have to be wintered indoors or in some other sheltered place. If left in the ground over the winter, they will need excellent drainage and shelter from winter wind. Bay leaf and geraniums are tender in all regions, and marjoram, although a tender perennial, is usually seeded each year as an annual.

### *Obtaining plants*

Many herbs can be grown from seed, but several can be obtained from friends and neighbours as divisions or cuttings. One seed package of each kind is more than enough for the average family.

There is usually little variety to choose from within each type of herb, unless purchases are made from a herb specialist. Thyme can be grown from seed, but flavourful varieties are more often sold as plants because of the poor taste of some plants grown from seed. Alternatively, thyme can be propagated from cuttings from the best flavoured plants among those started from seed. The different types of mint, of which there are many, are very difficult to grow from seed and are usually sold as plants. French tarragon can be obtained only as plants; tarragon sold as seed is not the tasty French form. Chives can be grown from seed or started from the division of an established clump.

### *Flowers*

Some gardeners can do without flowers, but others feel that they are the heart and soul of gardening. They can be grown in their own beds, in containers, under trees or in the vegetable garden. It is important to distinguish between annual flowers that will last only a year, and perennial flowers that will require a permanent space.

The sensible way to choose flowers is to determine which ones suit the growing conditions available. Planning a flower garden can be simplified by focusing on a certain season of bloom, one or two colours and a variety of heights. Annuals and perennials can be combined successfully in the same bed to give a wider choice in height or colour. Certain choices will present themselves if fragrance is a consideration. Seed and nursery catalogues are gold mines of information once an over-all plan is in place.

### *Green Thumb Tip*

In some cases it is useful to know the Latin name for the particular variety of a herb you want to grow to avoid disappointment. For instance, English lavender (*L. spica, L. officinalis, L. angustifolia,* 'Hidcote' and 'Munstead') has the traditional lavender scent and is hardier and larger than French lavender (*L. stoechas*). Varieties of the upright species of thyme (*Thymus vulgaris*) are used for cooking; the creeping kinds (*T. serpyllum*) are favoured for landscape purposes.

The orris root used in potpourris (see page 259) is the rhizome of Florentine iris, *Iris florentina*. It is a pale blue-white form of *I. germinica*, more correctly listed as *I. germanica florentina*, and is sold as a rhizome.

Garlic chives are also known as Chinese chives and Chinese leeks, and go by the Latin name *Allium tuberosum*. They have white flowers and a flatter leaf than the purple-flowered regular chives.

Some gardeners are confused about fennel. The herb fennel, also called sweet fennel, is named *Foeniculum vulgare*, and its leaves and seeds are used for flavouring. Florence fennel, also called finocchio, forms a bulbous swelling at the base of the plant and is used as a vegetable. Its leaves can also be used for flavouring, and its Latin name is *F. vulgare azoricum*.

## *Table JAN-1 Propagation Methods for Herbs*

| Plant | Seed | Division | Stem Cutting | Layering or Root Cutting |
|---|---|---|---|---|
| Angelica | fresh | * | | |
| Anise | fresh | | | |
| Anise Hyssop | * | * | summer | |
| Artemisia | | * | summer | |
| Basil | * | | | |
| Bay Leaf | * | | autumn | |
| Beebalm (Monarda) | * | * | summer | |
| Borage | * | | | |
| Calendula | * | | | |
| Caraway | * | | | |
| Catnip | * | * | | |
| Chamomile, German | * | | | |
| Chervil | * | | | |
| Chives | fresh | * | | |
| Comfrey | | * | | |
| Coriander | * | | | |
| Dill | * | | | |
| Fennel | * | | | |
| Fenugreek | * | | | |
| French Sorrel | * | * | | |
| Horseradish | | | | root cutting |
| Hyssop | * | * | summer | |
| Iris, Florentine | | * | | |
| Lavender | * | | summer, autumn | layering |
| Lemon Balm | * | * | | root cutting |
| Lovage | fresh | * | | |
| Marjoram | * | | summer | |
| Mint | (*) | * | summer | |
| Nasturtium | * | | | |
| Oregano, Greek | (*) | * | summer | |
| Parsley | fresh | | | |
| Rosemary | * | | summer | layering |
| Saffron | | bulbs | | |
| Sage | * | | late spring | layering |
| Salad Burnet | * | | | |
| Scented Geraniums | * | | any time | |
| Summer Savory | * | | | |
| Sweet Cicely | fresh | | summer | |
| Sweet Flag, Calamus | | * | | |
| Sweet Woodruff | | * | late spring, summer | |
| Tarragon, French | | * | summer | |
| Thyme | (*) | | summer | layering |
| Valerian | fresh | * | | |
| Watercress | * | | | |

(*) = plants grown from seed may have little flavour; choose those with best flavour and propagate from division or cuttings

fresh = use only fresh seed

### *Perennials*

Herbaceous perennial flowers can be grown from seed, at a terrific cost saving. They come up by themselves each spring, so they need to be sown only once (unless, of course, there is a particularly bad winter, which can kill some perennials). Comparing the purchase price of one perennial plant to the many that can be grown for the price of one package of seed and a little potting soil, convinces many gardeners that this is the way to go, even taking the time and effort of raising perennials from seed into account. In addition, a grouping of five or more perennials is more attractive than one or two plants of each sort.

Perennials often take longer to grow than annuals, requiring an early start indoors. Many are also reluctant to germinate (see February, page 48) because they have other methods of propagation. If efforts can be coordinated with other gardeners—each raising two or three kinds—a collection of perennials will quickly build. Besides, it is just plain fun to grow perennials from seed, especially if the plants cannot be purchased locally. Several types of tender perennial "bulbs" can also be grown from seed (see Table JAN-4, page 29).

### *Annuals and Biennials*

Growing annuals from seed instead of buying them as transplants is a major cost saving and provides a much wider choice of varieties than is available through nurseries each spring. Many annuals can be sown directly outdoors, which makes growing them quite easy, but they have to be planted each year. They make up for this inconvenience by blooming for weeks and weeks at a time. Their seeds usually germinate quite readily since seed is their main method of propagation.

There are many annuals to choose from. Some tolerate sunny, dry spots, and others need shade or moist conditions. Remember, though, that it is inadequate moisture, not inadequate light, that makes growth in the shade difficult for most plants.

Generally speaking, the flowers in Table FEB-4 (page 56) that can be transplanted or seeded when the weather is cool do better early or late in the season, or in regions with moderate summers. Flowers that are transplanted or seeded when the weather is warm tend to do well where summers are hot. Most of them will tolerate dry conditions, but some need plenty of moisture.

After the choice has been whittled down according to the growing conditions, check the time of bloom, and the ability to keep blooming after frost (if that is important in your area). Within each type of annual, varieties and cultivars vary most in terms of the size of the plant, colour, scent and disease resistance. Make the final selection based on these criteria (and see February, page 42).

### Size and habit of growth

When choosing the size of a variety, its purpose and the growing conditions should be considered. Snapdragons, for example, come as dwarf, short, medium and tall cultivars. For containers, fronts of flower borders and edgings, use the dwarf or short cultivars. Medium and tall cultivars are better in the middle or back of a border, but should not be placed in windy locations unless they are staked. Similarly, marigolds come in short and tall forms. Flower arrangers prefer the branching types of annual asters; their long stems make better cut flowers (see June, page 231, for flowers suited to cutting and July, page 256, for flowers suited to drying). Standard globe amaranth has longer stems than the dwarf form, and is better suited to arrangements, and tall sweet pea plants usually have longer stemmed flowers than short sweet peas.

The flower size varies in some plants with the overall size of the plant. Dwarf zinnias have little flowers and tall types have large flowers. Zinnias are susceptible to leaf-spot diseases and mildew, so avoid them if there is little air movement in the garden. Salpiglossis also has a compact form with small flowers which can withstand windy situations. Violas have smaller flowers than pansies, but neither is troubled much by wind. Multiflora petunias stand up to windy or rainy weather better than the larger flowered grandifloras; cascading types of petunias suit boxes and baskets.

The habit of growth may vary between varieties of the same type of annual. Nasturtiums are available as mounding and "vine" types. The vines do not climb very well but can be tied in place; they also suit hanging baskets and containers. Lobelia's upright or mounding form is a good choice for edging a flower bed, but choose the trailing form for window boxes and hanging baskets. When selecting browallia, choose upright varieties such as 'Blue Troll' for boxes, pots and edgings, and choose lax or hanging varieties such as 'Jingle Bells' for baskets. Dwarf morning glories can be used in hanging baskets, but choose the standard form if a climbing vine is wanted. Dwarf forms of sweet peas require no staking and are suitable for large containers (see pages 223-225, for other flowers suited to containers and hanging baskets).

#### Focus on Plants

Be careful not to confuse the perennial black-eyed-Susan (*Rudbeckia*), also known as brown-eyed-Susan, with black-eyed-Susan vine (*Thunbergia*). The latter is an annual which is ideal for hanging baskets and boxes and can also be encouraged to twine its way upwards on a trellis. There are also annual and perennial forms of Iberis (candytuft), baby's breath and aster. Perennial baby's breath also has a standard height, *Gypsophila paniculata*, suitable for flower borders, and a creeping form, *G. repens*, suitable for rockeries. Some varieties of certain biennials, such as foxglove and hollyhock, will perform as annuals if planted early indoors.

Other factors

Look for disease, pest and weather resistance when deciding what to grow. Order rust-resistant varieties of snapdragons, if possible. Hollyhocks also suffer from rust disease. They are biennial, but some varieties, such as 'Summer Carnival,' will bloom the year they are seeded, which helps to reduce the incidence of rust. Annual or China asters are disease prone, so they should be planted in a different place each year. If you have had trouble with earwigs in previous years, choose single types of flowers rather than doubles as the latter provide many hiding places for the little darlings.

Some flowers do not do well in damp weather. In coastal regions choose a strain of petunia which does not close up when wet, and grow single bachelor buttons rather than doubles, which tend to droop when wet. Strawflowers also close up when the weather is wet or drizzly, but they soon open when the sun comes out. Sweet peas prefer cool, damp weather, but there are also heat resistant varieties suitable for regions with hot summers.

Not all flowers are equally fragrant. The coloured forms of flowering tobacco (*Nicotiana*) are almost scentless, but the white forms are very fragrant and are lovely for evening viewing. Some *Dianthus* species, which include pinks, carnations and sweet william, are not nearly as fragrant as others. Read the catalogue descriptions carefully if scent is an important consideration.

Seeds for some annuals do not have to be re-ordered each year. Calendula, Chinese forget-me-not, sweet allyssum, portulaca, lobelia, snapdragon, nasturtium and many poppies will often self-sow from one year to another. Biennials such as foxglove, sweet william and hollyhock will also self-sow, but they should be seeded two years in a row when they are first planted. Pansies self-sow, but the seedlings will differ from the parent type because many of the original plants are hybrids.

### *Trees and shrubs*

Growing trees and shrubs from seed may seem like a slow proposition, but it is only the first few years that seem slow. A tree grown from seed grows just as fast as a purchased tree of the same size, and it may even grow more quickly because it has not been allowed to become pot-bound the way that many purchased plants have.

Tree, shrub and vine seeds can be very slow to germinate and may need an artificial winter or dormancy period. This can be achieved by putting them in the refrigerator, for example. Some seeds have what is called double dormancy. After the first "winter," they will grow a root, but nothing shows above the soil line. After a second "winter," the shoot or leafy part will emerge.

Some seed catalogues offer a few tree and shrub seeds, or seeds can be collected by hand (see September/October, page 369). To purchase trees and shrubs, including fruiting plants, see February (page 46) for a discussion of nursery catalogues and bare root ordering.

## Getting Ready

### Supplies

The time to get the growing area ready is before your ordered seeds start arriving. In a greenhouse, sunroom, sun porch or enclosed verandah, use a killing frost to destroy overwintering pests. To do this, remove any frost-sensitive plants, turn off the auxiliary heat (or close off the room from the main house), and open doors and windows wide on a cold day. Scrub the growing benches, seed flats and pots using water with a little bleach added, or scalding water and a little detergent, and clean the windows inside and out. Even a little dirt on windows can reduce the amount of light transmitted and, during the short days of winter and early spring, every bit of light available is required.

Start saving margarine and yogurt tubs and other similar containers for starting seeds. Whatever is used must be at least 2 inches (5 cm) deep with drainage holes in the bottom. Newspapers can be shaped into pots using a wooden form; at planting time, pot and plant are put in the ground together, avoiding any root disturbance. The same can be done with peat pots. Some people buy plastic four, six and nine-cell paks designed for growing individual transplants from a single seeding; transplanting to larger quarters is thus avoided. Soil blocks can be used without any container at all except a large flat to hold them. Using a metal form and plunger designed for the purpose, they are made with a peat-based potting soil. Plants grown in soil blocks do not suffer from encircling roots because the roots stop growing when they reach the end of their soil. Plastic lids with the rims cut off can be cut into strips for labels—they work very well when marked with waterproof pens.

Purchase a sterile starting medium for the seeds such as vermiculite, a peat-based potting soil with perlite, or a mix of peat moss and perlite or vermiculite. Vermiculite can be used by itself if seedlings are to be

#### Green Thumb Tip

If grow lights or plain, 40 watt fluorescent lights are used, consider changing the tubes. If used throughout the year, they should be changed every ten to twelve months before they burn out because the amount and quality of light can diminish without being obvious to the eye. When tubes are used in groups of two or more, it is best to change them one at a time over several months so that light levels stay constant. Ordinary fluorescent lights are as effective as the more expensive kinds designed for plant growth. To provide light to a few plants, use a 60 or 75 watt spot light. The wattage for either tube or spot lights should increase as the distance from the plants increases. In a cool greenhouse, incandescent bulbs will provide extra heat (see page 32).

transplanted soon after germination. Using clean containers and a sterile starting medium reduces the incidence of damping off disease, which can destroy a whole crop of seedlings.

A mild fertilizer, such as fish fertilizer, is useful for supplying nutrients to young seedlings. If you plan to start cuttings, purchase fresh rooting hormone as last year's supply will have lost much of its potency. Rooting hormone is sold in three grades, depending on whether it is soft, green material that is being rooted (a softwood cutting), partly mature woody material (a semi-hardwood cutting), or mature woody plant material (a hardwood cutting).

### Preventive Measure

"Damping off" is a fungal disease that causes young plants to rot at the soil line and fall over. To avoid this, fill containers nearly to the top with a sterile starting medium to ensure good air circulation across the surface. Fungal diseases flourish in still air, and a container with a large space between the soil surface and the top of the container will provide ideal conditions for damping off disease. A sterile medium is unlikely to contain the spores that cause damping off disease.

Planting seeds sparsely or in individual containers also helps, as crowded seedlings are more likely to succumb due to poor air circulation and rapid spread of the disease.

## Providing Heat

Decide how to provide warmth to your seeds. Many germinate best at soil temperatures of 70°F (21°C). Soil temperature (which you can measure with a soil thermometer) is usually 4 to 5°F (2 to 3°C) cooler than air temperature due to evaporation. A box 30 by 24 by 12 inches (75 by 60 by 30 cm) with a 40 watt light bulb inside will raise soil to the right temperature. Alternatively, place seed flats on top of the refrigerator, or near the furnace, wood stove, radiator or any other source of warmth. Putting seed flats on upturned clay flower pots over the radiator or wood stove will prevent seedlings from getting too warm. A sophisticated method is to bury a heating cable in sand and place the seed flats on the sand. If a propagation unit is made to provide bottom heat (see pages 442-443), avoid using mist because this makes seedlings more susceptible to damping off disease. Keep the unit open after the seedlings have emerged to promote good air circulation.

## Early Growing

### Vegetables

It is too early to start most vegetables yet, but asparagus plants which will be transplanted outdoors can be started indoors a good four months before the last spring frost is expected. If they are sown very early, they will produce extra growth their first year. This way, a very light harvest can be taken a year earlier than if they are planted outdoors a few months from now.

To encourage germination, soak asparagus seeds in water at 88°F (31°C) for forty-eight hours before sowing. A vacuum flask will hold the temperature of the water long enough to require only occasional changes. When soaking any seeds a long time, change the water every twelve hours to keep up the oxygen level in the water. Sow the seeds and cover to a depth twice the diameter of the seed (see pages 47-51 for sowing details). Keep the starting mix warm, at about 70°F (21°C).

### Flowers

Fuchsia, geranium, impatiens, coleus, fibrous or wax begonia and other tender perennials held indoors over the winter should be checked for new growth. If none is visible, encourage the plants to grow by placing them in bright light, mist them once or twice a day, and water them sparingly until new growth starts. Cut back those that were not cut back last autumn. In short season areas, wait until late in January or early in February before encouraging them, otherwise they may be ready for transplanting before they can be set outdoors. When new growth is well established, you may want to take cuttings to start new plants as young plants often bloom better than those saved from year to year. Cuttings are easiest to start when taken from young, vigorous growth.

Some flowers can be started from seed either this month or next (see Table FEB-4, page 56). See Planting the Seeds in February (page 47) for a full discussion of sowing methods. Hardy perennial flowers can be seeded in either January or February; they require eighteeen to twenty weeks from seeding indoors to be ready for transplanting outdoors. Many will not bloom the first year but a full growing season outdoors ensures they are well established before winter. Use bottom heat of about 70°F (21°C) for tender perennial seeds and bulbs. Provide the seedlings with slightly cooler temperatures (60°F or 15°C) after germination and shade them with cheesecloth for the first few days. Fourteen to fifteen hours of light each day produces the best results. Fewer hours may result in poor bloom and additional hours may cause lanky, weak growth. Hardy perennial flowers and many annual flowers grow best in cool conditions and full sunshine.

## Indoor Gardening

### The Location

Many gardeners extend their green thumb season by taking up indoor gardening. Adding a greenhouse or sunroom, putting in window shelves or a window greenhouse, or setting up a bank of fluorescent lights will allow the cultivation of vegetables, herbs, flowers and even some fruits indoors in the winter. If plants are grown during the depths of winter, additional lighting will be a benefit, even in a greenhouse, to compensate for the short days. Sun porches and enclosed verandahs may be too cold in midwinter, but they can be used to stretch the growing season into early spring and late fall, particularly for plants that grow well in cool conditions. Some people

The angle of your greenhouse glass should be20°plus your latitude degree.

practice indoor growing year round in conjunction with their outdoor garden, either for starting seeds or to provide sheltered conditions for sensitive crops that would languish outdoors.

If building a greenhouse is an option, its design—free-standing or attached to the house—will depend in part on what time of year it will be used and the orientation available. Heating a greenhouse is expensive, so if it is to be used in the winter it is best to attach it to the house. It is also easier to shelter it from winter winds, although a backdrop of evergreens for a free-standing greenhouse can be effective. Plumbing and electricity are also easier to arrange in an attached greenhouse or sunroom, although electricity is not essential.

For maximum winter sunlight, a free-standing greenhouse should run east to west, whereas one for spring and summer use should run north to south so that plants receive equal light on both sides. In an attached greenhouse, eastern or southern exposure is best; one facing west can easily overheat in the afternoon. One that faces east will warm up quickly in the morning, which is when the greenhouse is coldest.

The angle of the glass is important for temperature control. The ideal slope is the latitude at which you live plus 20°. If sunny days are rare relative to foggy or overcast days, add less than 20°. The popular greenhouse design with the rounded clear roof is particularly prone to overheating, as are sunrooms with skylights. Frosted glass in skylights will help to reduce this problem. It diffuses light more uniformly in all directions than clear glass does, and reduces the problem of extreme (high or low) light levels. Within each greenhouse there are also various microclimates to consider (see page 425) which will affect the types of plants that can be grown.

The back wall should ideally have a slope of 60 to 75°, but this is not feasible if the greenhouse is attached to an existing building. It should be painted with glossy white paint to increase the amount of light reaching the back of the plants, unless the wall is used for heat storage. A shiny surface of aluminum foil or silver paint is not appropriate as it may cause hot spots to develop.

One must also consider heat storage methods to modulate the extreme temperature changes between day and night. Walls and other solid surfaces painted dark green will absorb heat more effectively than those painted black. Use outdoor paint or marine grade varnish for any surfaces that require it. Thick concrete floors or stone walls will help to store heat when air temperatures are high and will release it when the air is cold. A method of ventilating the space and circulating the air is also important for controlling the temperature and keeping plants healthier. Fungal diseases abound if air circulation is poor.

The final consideration is how the plants will be grown. Large containers or pots in various sizes can be set on the floor, on shelves or benches, or hung from the ceiling. Large flats set on the floor and on shelves are also very useful. Some greenhouses have large growing beds right on the floor, either built in as wooden containers or else dug right into the ground.

Retrofitting an existing sun porch or verandah to improve the heat storage and air circulation may be a feasible option, depending on its orientation. Adding skylights may help increase the light levels. Even without a sunroom or greenhouse, however, there is plenty that can be grown indoors on a windowsill or with the aid of fluorescent lighting.

## Supplies and Method

Many of the supplies needed for indoor gardening are the same as those required for starting seeds for the outdoor garden (see pages 20-21). In addition, large pots and containers, deep flats, boxes and other suitably sized containers will be required (see Table JAN-3, page 26; see Green Thumb Tip, page 440, for the minimum depth required by various crops). Seeds are started as described in February (pages 47-51), and then the seedlings are transplanted to increasingly larger pots (potted on), or else they can be seeded directly in growing beds and later thinned to the required distances.

Some indoor gardeners rely on purchased potting soil and others use a mix of one-third good garden soil, one-third leaf mould or peat moss, and one-third sand or perlite to fill the larger pots and containers (see Soil Solarization, page 299, and Soil Sterilization, page 402). A quart (1.1 l) of manure per bushel (8 gallons or 36 l) of this mix will supply a good basis of nutrients, but additional fertilizers may be required. Fish fertilizer, seaweed extract and manure tea (see page 163) will meet most needs, and a little 20-20-20, 10-52-70 and 10-30-10 fertilizers will fill any gaps (see page 164 for a discussion of what the numbers mean).

## Vegetables

### Seeding schedule

A hankering for fresh greens often develops in the dead of winter. There is a wide range of seeds to choose from (see Table JAN-2 below), including Chinese cabbage, butterhead, cos and leaf lettuces, radicchio, celery,

**Green Thumb Tip**

Temperature has a major effect on the rate of plant growth. Flowers (see pages 28, 31, 461-466), herbs and vegetables (see pages 24-27) grow best at warmer or cooler temperatures. Below the minimum, growth is halted. Above the minimum, photosynthesis increases 2 to 2.3 times for every 10°F (5°C) rise in temperature. Beyond 85° to 95°F (30 to 35°C) the rate may decrease.

The optimum temperature for a wide range of plants is 50° to 65°F (10° to 18°C).

## Table JAN-2 Seeding Schedule for Greenhouse Vegetables and Herbs

(to complement outdoor garden production)

| Plant | Jan | Feb | Mar | Apr | May | Jun | Jul | Aug | Sep | Oct | Nov | Dec |
|---|---|---|---|---|---|---|---|---|---|---|---|---|
| Beans (55) * | | s | | | | | | s | | | | |
| Beet Greens (40) | s | s | (s) | | | | | | s | s | | |
| Broccoli (80) | | s | | | | | | | (s) | (t) | | |
| Brussels Sprouts (120) | (s) | | | | | | | | (s) | (t) | | |
| Carrots (65) | | s | | | | | | (s) | | | | |
| Cauliflower (100) | | s | | | | | | | (s) | | | |
| Celeriac (150) | (s) | | | | | | | s | | | | |
| Celery (150) | (s) | | | | | | | s | (t) | | | |
| Chinese Cabbage (75) | s | s | (s) | | | | | s | s | | | |
| Collards (80) | s | s | | | | | | s | s | | | |
| Cress-Peppergrass (20) | s | s | s | s | s | s | s | s | s | s | s | s |
| Cucumber (60) * | | | s | | | | | s | | | | |
| Eggplant (130) * | | s | | | | (s) | | (t) | | | | |
| Endive, Escarole (85) | s | | s | | | | | s | | (t) | | |
| Florence Fennel (105) | | | s | | | | | s | | | | |
| Herbs - Basil * | | | s | | | | | s | | | | |
| - Chervil | s | s | s | | | | | s | s | s | | |
| - Coriander * | | | s | | | | | s | | | | |
| - Dill | | s | s | | | | | s | s | | | |
| - Marjoram * | | | s | | | | | s | | | | |
| - Oregano * | | | s | | | | | s | | | | |
| - Parsley | | s | | | | | | s | | | | |
| - Summer Savory * | | s | s | s | | | | s | s | s | | |
| Kale (60) | s | | | | | | | | (s) | (t) | | |
| Kohlrabi (60) | | s | s | | | | | | s | s | | |
| Lettuce | | | | | | | | | | | | |
| - Butterhead (60) | | s | s | s | | | | (s) | s | s | s | |
| - Cos (Romaine) (75) | | s | s | | | | | (s) | s | s | | |
| - Looseleaf (45) | | s | s | s | | | | (s) | s | s | s | |
| Melon, Cantaloupe (100) * | | | s | | | | | | | | | |
| Mustard Greens (50) | s | s | (s) | | | | | | s | s | | |
| Onion Family | | | | | | | | | | | | |
| - Bunching Onions (70) | s | s | (s) | | | | | s | s | | | |
| - Chives (70) | s | | | | | | | (s) | | (t) | | |
| - Leek (100) | (s) | | | | | | | (s) | | (t) | | |
| - Scallions (70) | s | s | | | | | | s | s | | | |

| Plant | Jan | Feb | Mar | Apr | May | Jun | Jul | Aug | Sep | Oct | Nov | Dec |
|---|---|---|---|---|---|---|---|---|---|---|---|---|
| Peas - edible podded(70) | | s | (s) | | | | | s | | | | |
| Pepper (140) * | | s | | | | (s) | | (t) | | | | |
| Radicchio (75) | s | | | | | | | s | | | | |
| Radish (30) | s | s | s | | | | | | s | s | s | |
| Spinach (48) | s | s | (s) | | | | | (s) | s | s | | |
| Summer Squash * | | | s | | | | | s | | | | |
| Swiss Chard (60) | s | | | | | | | | s | | | |
| Tomatoes (130) * | | | | | | | | | | | | |
| - indeterminate | (s) | s | | | | (s) | (c) | | | | | |
| - determinate | s | | s | | | | s | | | s | | |
| Turnip Greens (40) | s | s | (s) | | | | | | s | s | | |
| Watercress (50) | s | | s(c) | | | | s | | s | | s(c) | |
| Zucchini * | | | s | | | | | s | | | | |

( ) = approximate number of days from seeding to first harvest; add 25 to 50% for late summer and autumn seedings
(c) = optional rooted cutting
(s) = optional sowing
(t) = optional transplant from outdoor garden
* = requires warm growing conditions, 60 to 85°F (15 to 30°C)

celeriac, watercress, turnip greens, Swiss chard, spinach, mustard greens, beet greens, collards, kale, escarole and endive (see February, pages 47-51, for seeding details if more information is required). A temperature of 50°F (10°C) is sufficient for these cool weather crops to germinate and grow, and they will tolerate periodic temperatures close to freezing. They should receive twelve hours of light a day; longer hours cause bolting in some of the crops. Start them off in small containers and pot them on gradually to larger quarters. To add a little extra bite and flavour to all of these greens, sow cress (peppergrass) every couple of weeks and chervil and radish every month.

A variety of onion family members can be seeded as well. Leeks, bunching onions, scallions and chives will germinate readily if the seed is fresh. Sowing leeks, celery and celeriac is optional at this time because they will be started sometime in the next month or two for the outdoor garden. Brussels sprouts

## Table JAN-3 Suggested Pot Sizes/Bench Spacing for Vegetables and Herbs

| Plant | Number of Plants per Pot Size (in./mm) | Distance Apart in Rows x Distance Between Rows (in. x in./cm x cm) |
|---|---|---|
| Beans- Snap | 2-3 per 6/150 | 5 x 5/13 x 13 |
| | 4-5 per 8/200 | |
| | 5-6 per 10/250 | |
| - Pole | 4-6 per 12/300 | 6 x 18/15 x 45 |
| Beet Greens | | 2 x 4/5 x 10 |
| Beets | | 3 x 6/7 x 15 |
| Broccoli | 3 per 12/300 | 8 x 9/20 x 23 |
| Brussels Sprouts | 1 per 12/300 | 18 x 18/45 x 45 |
| Carrots | | 2 x 2/5 x 5 |
| Cauliflower | 1 per 10/250 | 15 x 15/38 x 38 |
| Celeriac | | 9 x 9/23 x 23 |
| Celery | | 6 x 6/15 x 15 |
| Chinese Cabbage | 1 per 8/200 | 10 x 10/25 x 25 |
| Collards | | 8 x 8/20 x 20 |
| Cress (Peppergrass) | | 1 x 1/2 x 2 |
| Cucumber | 1 per 8/200 | 18 x 18/45 x 45 |
| | 2 per 12/300 | |
| Eggplant | 1 per 10/250 | 12 x 12/30 x 30 |
| Endive | 1 per 8/200 | 10 x 10/25 x 25 |
| Escarole | 1 per 10/250 | 12 x 12/30 x 30 |
| Florence Fennel | 1 per 7/175 | 6 x 12/15 x 30 |
| | 3 per 12/300 | |
| Herbs - Angelica | 1-2 per 12/300 | |
| - Anise | 2 per 8/200 | |
| | 3 per 10/250 | |
| - Basil | 3 per 5/125 | 4 x 4/10 x 10 |
| - Borage | 2 per 12/300 | |
| - Caraway | 2 per 8/200 | |
| - Chervil | 1 per 4/100 | 4 x 4/10 x 10 |
| - Coriander | 5-6 per 6/150 | 3 x 3/8 x 8 |
| - Dill | | 2 x 2/5 x 5 |
| - Geranium | 1 per 5/125 | |
| - Marjoram | 3 per 4/100 | 3 x 3/8 x 8 |
| | 6 per 8/250 | |
| - Mint | 1 per 10/250 | 10 x 10/25 x 25 |
| - Oregano | 2 per 4/100 | 4 x 4/10 x 10 |
| | 5 per 10/250 | |
| - Parsley | 2-3 per 8/200 | 6 x 6/15 x 15 |
| - Rosemary | 1 per 6/150 | |
| - Sage | 1 per 6/150 | |
| - Summer Savory | 2-3 per 6/150 | 6 x 6/15 x 15 |
| - Sweet Cicely | 1 per 6/150 | |
| - Tarragon | 1 per 10/250 | |
| - Thyme | 3 per 6/150 | |
| Kale | 1 per 8/200 | 10 x 10/25 x 25 |
| Kohlrabi | | 6 x 6/15 x 15 |
| Lettuce - Butterhead | | 8 x 8/20 x 20 |
| - Cos (Romaine) | | 8 x 8/20 x 20 |
| | | or 1 x 5/3 x 12 |
| - Looseleaf | | 8 x 8/20 x 20 |
| | | or 1 x 5/3 x 12 |
| Melon, Cantaloupe | 1 per 12/300 | 18 x 18/45 x 45 |
| Mustard Greens | | 4 x 4/10 x 10 |
| Onion Family | | |
| - Bunching Onions | | 1 x 3/3 x 8 |
| - Chives | 1 clump per pot | 1/8 x 1/0.3 x 2 |
| - Leek | | 6 x 6/15 x 15 |
| - Scallions | | 1 x 3/3 x 8 |
| Peas | | |
| - edible podded | 4 per 12/300 | 4 x 4/10 x 10 |
| Pepper | 1 per 10/250 | 12 x 12/30 x 30 |
| Potatoes - new | 1 per 8/200 | 8 x 8/20 x 20 |
| | or 3 per 10/250 | |
| Radicchio | | 10 x 9/25 x 22 |
| Radish | | 2 x 3/5 x 8 |
| Spinach - fresh greens | | 4 x 4/10 x 10 |
| - for cooking | | 8 x 8/20 x 20 |
| Summer Squash | 1 per 12/300 | 18 x 18/45 x 45 |
| Swiss Chard | 1 per 8/200 | 8 x 8/20 x 20 |
| Tomatoes | | |
| - indeterminate | 1 per 10/250 | 12 x 12/30 x 30 |
| | 2 per 12/300 | |
| - determinate | 1 per 8/200 | 9 x 9/23 x 23 |
| Turnip Greens | | 4 x 4/10 x 10 |
| Watercress | 1 per 6/150 | 8 x 8/20 x 20 |
| Zucchini | 1 per 12/300 | 18 x 18/45 x 45 |

can also be seeded but mature plants take up so much space that some gardeners prefer to grow them outdoors only.

Cold-tolerant tomatoes are able to grow and set fruit at cooler temperatures than most tomatoes, but they benefit from additional light at the end of each day. If a minimum night temperature of 65°F (18°C) and a day temperature of 75°F (23°C) is possible, more varieties can be chosen from. Pixie II and other small determinate tomato plants are fine in 8 inch (200 mm) pots. Vine tomatoes need a 9 to 10 inch (225 to 250 mm) pot if they are grown as full plants. Two vine tomatoes will fit comfortably in a 12 inch (300 mm) pot if each is pruned to a single stem and trained up a 6 foot (1.8 m) trellis or piece of netting.

Determinate tomatoes are planted three or four times a year: early January plantings are ready for harvest in April; March plantings in July; mid-July plantings in October or November; and (optional) October plantings are ready in February if conditions are warm enough for growing them. Indeterminate tomatoes, on the other hand, continue growing and producing for several months and need to be planted only twice each year.

Sow some annual rye for pet cats, and beebalm and carrots for pet rabbits. Both cats and rabbits like to nibble on pea seedlings and alfalfa sprouts; these fresh greens are a special treat for pets in the winter, and may also keep pets from ravaging houseplants.

Witloof chicory roots, planted in pots and put in cold storage the previous autumn (see September/October, page 345), can be brought into warmer temperatures and forced. Start just a few chicory roots at a time in total darkness at a range of 50 to 65°F (10 to 18°C). Heads will be ready in three weeks at 65°F (18°C), but they will take longer at cooler temperatures.

The heads are ready when the tips are clearly visible above the sand. Cut them off with a sharp knife about an inch (2.5 cm) above the neck. Sometimes the roots will resprout a second, smaller head. Keep the harvested heads in a dark place until you are ready to use them because they turn green and bitter when exposed to light.

## Fruits

There are several fruits that can be grown indoors, or dug up from the garden in the autumn and stored over the winter. Large plants such as grape vines, passion fruit and peach trees will require large containers or planters to allow good root development. Except for passion fruit, all of the fruits require a period of cold in the winter in order to develop properly (and see February, page 64).

Grape vines and passion fruit should be pruned now, if this was not done last autumn (see November, page 428). The days get noticeably longer and the sun stronger at this time, so buds will soon be swelling. Top dress these and other permanent fruits by removing the top 1 to 2 inches (2.5 to 5 cm) of soil and adding the same amount of worm compost (see October-November, page 401) or dried manure.

Strawberries and rhubarb can be coaxed into growth this month. Bring the potted plants out of cold storage (see October/November, page 404) and gradually expose them to warm temperatures and bright light. To obtain very tender rhubarb, bring pots into a warm place but keep them in the dark. This will cause the stems to become etiolated (long and lanky) as they stretch up for light. Rhubarb grown this way has absolutely no signs of stringiness and is sweeter than usual.

Strawberries produce best when they are exposed to sixteen to eighteen hours of light each day, and production will be better if the flowers are pollinated. This can be achieved by passing a camel hair paint brush over the centre of each flower during the warmest part of each day. Humid conditions also help pollination. Keep the plants evenly moist all through the stages of fruit development, and fertilize once a week with a weak solution of general purpose fertilizer. A little 10-52-70 could be used early on.

### Flowers

Depending on what the minimum temperature is at night, either "warm" or "cool" flowers can be grown for indoor bloom. Good light is essential and a greenhouse or sunroom is ideal, but enclosed verandahs and fluorescent lighting can also be used effectively. By sowing seeds of a wide variety of annual flowers and starting various perennial plants and bulbs into growth at different times of the year (see Table DEC-2, page 461), it is possible to have a long and varied succession of bloom.

### Warm flowers

A minimum night temperature of 60°F (15°C) is required for "warm" flowers. Sow seeds of various begonias and geraniums. Any of the tender perennials seeded or started into growth for the outdoor garden (see above under Flowers, page 21) can be grown indoors. Bottom heat of 65 to 75°F (18 to 24°C) will encourage faster germination.

There is a wonderful variety of tropical and subtropical bulbs that can be grown in warm conditions, and some will tolerate moderate to cool

## *Table JAN-4 Some Tender Bulbs that can be Started from Seed*

| Plant | Suggested Conditions for Germination |
|---|---|
| Agapanthus (Lily-of-the-Nile) | 70-80ºF (21-27ºC) |
| Alstroemeria | 70-80ºF (21-27ºC) |
| Amaryllis | 70-80ºF (21-27ºC) |
| Anemone | 65-75ºF (18-24ºC) |
| Calla Lily (*Zantedeschia*) | 70-80ºF (21-27ºC) |
| Canna | scarify, 70-80ºF (21-27ºC) |
| Freesia | remove chafe, soak seed 24 hours before sowing, 60-70ºF (15-21ºC) |
| Galtonia (Summer Hyacinth) | 65-75ºF (18-24ºC) |
| Gloxinia | 70ºF (21ºC) |
| Zephyranthe (Fairy Lily) | 70-80ºF (21-27ºC) |

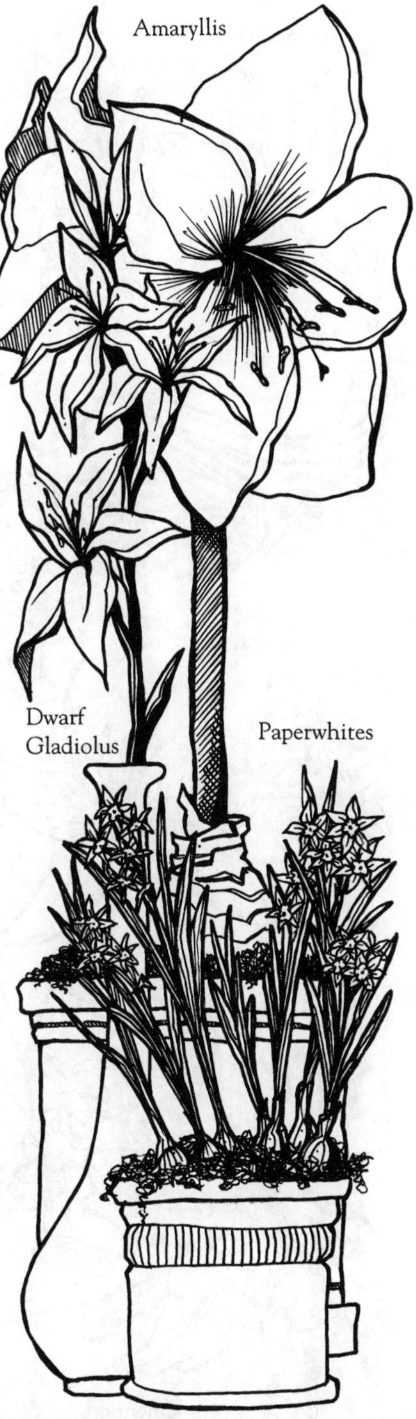


temperatures (see Table MAR/APR-3, page 88). Order a few, to be found in the pages of some of the larger seed catalogues, and try growing some from seed (see Table JAN-4). It takes several years for some of them to reach blooming size, but the very low cost is worth the wait for many gardeners.

Germination of most seeds in Table JAN-4 takes about twenty-five days at 65ºF (18ºC). The bulblets formed should be large enough, if growing plants are fertilized regularly, for potting up in the autumn to bloom the following spring.

Gloxinia seeds should be left uncovered because they need light to germinate, but more than fifteen hours of light each day after they have germinated will cause the little plants to form tubers prematurely and die. Dormant gloxinia tubers can be started in moist peat moss at warm temperatures out of direct sunlight and potted separately into 5 or 6 inch (125 or 150 mm) pots when the new growth is 1 to 2 inches (2.5 to 5 cm) high.

Corms of dwarf gladiolus (G. *byzantinus* and G. *nanus*) can be potted up; bottom heat will encourage bloom as early as April. They are winter-hardy in milder regions and can be planted outdoors in the spring after blooming is over. Any paperwhites not planted for December celebrations should be

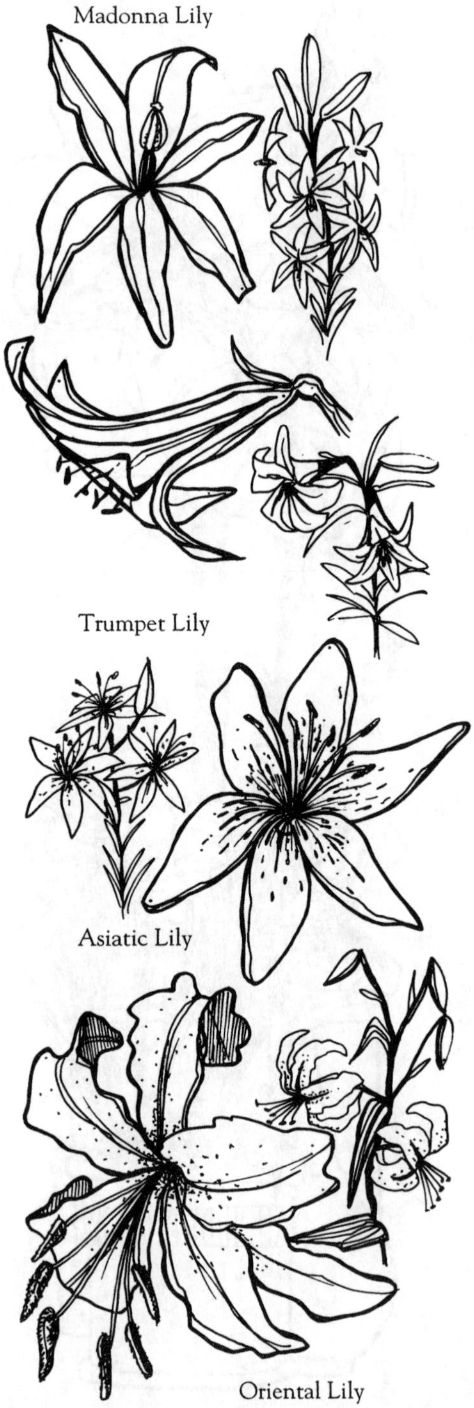


planted before they dry out. Repot crinum bulbs every three or four years, moving them gradually from a 7 inch (175 mm) to a 10 or 12 inch (250 or 300 mm) pot. Water all bulbs sparingly until new growth is visible.

The old flower stems of amaryllis, nerine, calla lily and other bulbs should be cut to about 2 inches (5 cm) above the bulb. Continue to water and fertilize them through to late summer or autumn and make sure they have bright light with some direct sunshine. When the foliage starts to fade, stop fertilizing and gradually reduce watering.

Amaryllis bulbs that have been dormant all winter can be started into growth in the next month or two. Top dress them with fresh soil after removing an inch (2.5 cm) or so of the old potting soil. Water them once lightly and supply additional heat if the ambient temperature is below 65°F (18°C). Use any of the methods described under Providing Heat (page 20). Water them regularly once new growth is evident and begin fertilizing. Amaryllis can be grown in cooler temperatures after growth is initiated, but it seems to need a boost of heat to get it started.

Fuchsias, hydrangeas and roses can be brought out of cold storage. Repot hydrangeas in an acid mix (plenty of peat moss), keep them in a warm place in bright, indirect light, and water them sparingly until new growth shows. Roses and fuchsias should be cut back fairly hard if this was not done in the autumn. Place the pots close together and mist them daily to encourage bud break, but be careful not to overwater plants that have been dormant. Try to keep them evenly damp and then increase watering once there are signs of new growth. The temperature should also be increased slowly, starting at 45 to 50°F (7 to 10°C) and increasing each month. Start fertilizing with one-third to one-half strength fertilizer only after new growth is visible. These plants also do well in a cool greenhouse, but will take longer to come into growth.

Madonna lily (*L. candidum*), Regal lily (*L. regale*), *L. speciosum rubrum* and Asiatic lilies can be brought out of cold storage (see page 407) one or more at a time over the next few months. Bring out crocuses, irises, daffodils, tulips and other spring blooming bulbs over the next two months in roughly the order that they bloom (see Table SEP/OCT-2, page 358). Start up hyacinths on January 1 and daffodils on January 15 to have them in bloom for Valentine's Day.

All of these bulbs, including lilies, will also do well in cool greenhouse conditions. Start early Asiatic lilies about eleven weeks before Easter; *L. speciosum rubrum* will take about six months to come into bloom, but a few hours of extra light each day will encourage it to bloom sooner. Lilies, like other bulbs (see page 29), can be grown from seed; *Let's Grow Lilies* by Virginia Howie (1978) gives more detailed instructions.

It is time to bring potted spring bulbs out of storage when there is about 1 inch (2 to 3 cm) of new growth showing above the soil line and roots are showing through the drainage holes in the pot—usually after about three months in cold storage. If these signs are not visible, carefully tip out the contents of the pot and check if the soil is too wet, causing the bulbs to rot. If the roots are brown and mushy instead of white or the bulbs are rotten, throw them out. Lilies may not show any top growth, but they can still be brought out into warmth and light.

Pots of spring bulbs should not be exposed to bright light for the first week, but need full sunlight and fairly cool temperatures afterwards to bloom within another five to six weeks. Temperatures above 70°F (21°C) will bring the bulbs into flower in as little as another three weeks, but the leaves will likely be weak and will tend to fall over. Some gardeners, to hasten bloom, grow the bulbs at fairly warm temperatures, and then keep them cool once the buds show colour.

If there are still some bulbs around that did not get planted outdoors last autumn, be sure to pot them up immediately and put them into cold storage (see page 405). Throw them out if they feel light and dry. Waiting until spring to plant them outdoors will only result in failure.

### *Cool flowers*

There are many annuals that can be sown for indoor bloom where indoor temperatures hover around 55°F (12°C) or cooler at night. Clarkia, nemesia, candytuft and godetia grow best in rather poor soil kept on the dry side. Iceland and Shirley poppies need a little warmth to germinate and are best planted where they are to grow because they resent transplanting.

Sweet peas grow best in a sandy mix in the winter, as it prevents rot. Add extra sand or perlite to whatever potting soil is used in the greenhouse. They can be sown monthly from June to February for continuous bloom and scent. When planted in the autumn and grown through the winter, they take five months to come into bloom, but when sown in June and grown through the longer days of summer, sweet peas bloom in three and a half months. Use winter-flowering sweet peas if most of the growth and the flowering period will occur in the winter. Winter-blooming snapdragon, African marigold, annual phlox, bachelor button, calendula, feverfew, larkspur, stock,

wallflower and annual scabiosa provide plenty of choice and are fairly easy to grow. Winter-flowering snapdragons and sweet peas are often not identified as such in seed catalogues, but rather as "greenhouse" or "forcing" types. Annual chrysanthemums can be grown from seed; do not cover the seeds with soil as they germinate better with light, and keep them at 65 to 70°F (18 to 21°C).

Oxalis tubers grow well in cool temperatures. An attractive way to grow them is in an 8 inch (20 cm) wire basket lined with sphagnum moss and filled with potting soil. Plant five to six tubers ½ inch (1.2 cm) deep and put them in full sunshine. Alternatively, plant three or four tubers in a 5 inch (125 mm) pan or shallow pot, or one in a 3 to 4 inch (75 to 100 mm) pan. They require a depth of only 2 to 3 inches (5 to 8 cm) of soil.

Bring perennial flowers out of cold storage (see page 415) and force them gradually by keeping them at 45°F (7°C) for several weeks, then at 50 to 55°F (10 to 12°C) for a month, and then at even warmer temperatures. This happens naturally in many greenhouses and sun porches as days get longer and the sun rises higher in late winter. Coreopsis and gaillardia require extra lighting until the flower buds have formed. Forcing is also used to propagate some perennials from cuttings or divisions, such as chrysanthemums, armeria, asters and delphiniums (see Table APR/MAY-3, page 138).

Most indoor plants should be watered sparingly, especially when days are cloudy or foggy. Ventilate the greenhouse or other growing areas on warm and sunny days to help reduce the incidence of fungal diseases. Of course, cold drafts must be avoided.

### Green Thumb Tip

Providing an extra four to six hours of light in the evening, or two hours around midnight (using a timer) will reduce the time it takes for certain flowers to come into bloom. The extra light will be needed for about forty days, or until buds form. It is actually short nights, not long days, that encourage some plants to initiate flowering. Ordinary 40 watt fluorescent lights can be used, or set up aluminum pie plate reflectors behind 60 watt incandescent bulbs set 2 feet (60 cm) above the plants, 4 feet (1.2 m) apart. Try it with aster, clarkia, centaurea, fever few, gypsophila, marigold, pansy, scabiosa, snapdragon, schizanthus, stock, violet and sweet pea. Some people give extra light to half the plants of each kind of flower to stretch out the season of bloom.

## Odd Jobs

It is a good idea to check tubers and corms that were stored away last autumn. Any that show signs of shrivelling need to be kept at a cooler temperature and perhaps surrounded by barely damp material, such as vermiculite or peat moss. A greater danger is rotting, caused by materials that are too moist. Throw out mouldy or rotting tubers, including the surrounding storage material. Dust the remaining tubers with sulphur and store them in clean, barely damp vermiculite or wood shavings.

Potatoes that have been stored at temperatures below 40°F (4°C) often develop a sweet taste because the starches have been turned to sugars. The sweetening process can be reversed by storing them at room temperature (50°F or 10°C) for about two weeks.

Inspect cabbages and gently roll off withered or diseased outer leaves. Onions that are sprouting should be kept colder but above freezing, or bring them into the warmth and light to encourage sprouting for use as green onions. They tend to have quite a bite but are very tasty.

Think "outdoors" to deal with the Christmas tree. The branches can be cut off and used to mulch roses, strawberries and perennials now that the ground is frozen. Mulch is important to keep the ground frozen in the spring to avoid the freeze-thaw cycle that kills many plants. Use some of the branches to decorate window boxes, and chop or shred some branches for mulch for acid loving plants. Nip off the branch tips for potpourris.

Shovel off salt-laden snow from over the roots of trees near the street. Use sand, wood ashes or kitty litter instead of salt to de-ice sidewalks and driveways—salt in the soil is just one more stress that urban trees can do without. Use calcium salts if that is the only choice; they are less detrimental to vegetation than sodium salts. As well, try to steer pets away from relieving themselves over tree roots because the salt content of urine is rather high.

Month-by-Month

# February

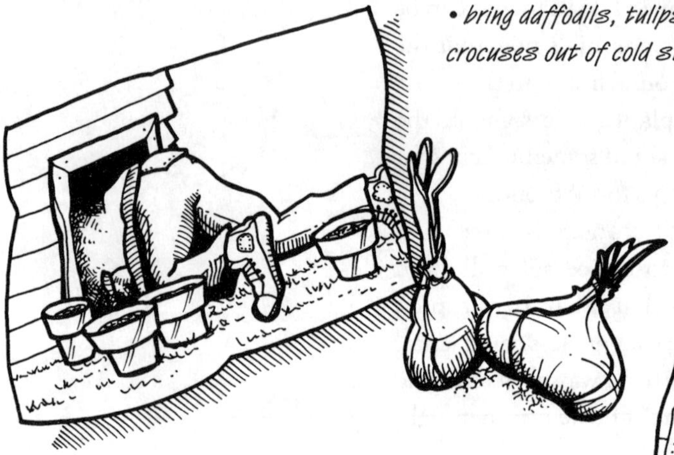

• bring daffodils, tulips and crocuses out of cold storage

• repair storm damage

• where do we put the herbs?
• rows or blocks for veggies?
• design flower border
• how many fruits to order?
• take cuttings of tender perennials (geraniums and fuchsias)
• force branches

• start seeds indoors for vegetables, herbs and flowers

Planning is one of the great pleasures of gardening. It slows us down and allows us to enjoy a sense of continuity with the seasons that is sometimes missing in the fragmented days of our lives.

There are seeds that can be started indoors this month for the outdoor garden, and a host of seedlings will already be in need of transplanting in the indoor garden. With luck, potted spring bulbs are in bloom and taking the edge off winter, and cut branches of flowering shrubs brought indoors to bloom require only a little gentle encouragement.

# February

**Seed**

*Costly, but highly nutritious form of bird food sold in handsome packets printed with colorful pictures of flowers and vegetables.*

*Beard and McKie*

## Armchair Planning

### Vegetables

#### Blocks versus rows

While waiting for seeds to arrive in the mail, it is a good idea to consider the various methods of growing vegetables. It is sometimes quite a challenge to fit all we would like into the space available.

In both raised and flat beds, vegetables can be planted in rows or blocks (see pages 381-382 for a discussion of raised growing beds). A combination of methods is probably best. Rows have the advantage of being easier to weed and mulch, particularly where children are concerned, and blocks give greater yields for the space available. Narrow beds planted in rows with no space used for paths have practically the same yield as blocks. The preferred method depends in part on the crop grown. As carrots form a good canopy of foliage, which keeps the weeds down, they suit block planting. Onions, on the other hand, do not form a thick canopy, so rows that can easily be weeded are better for this crop.

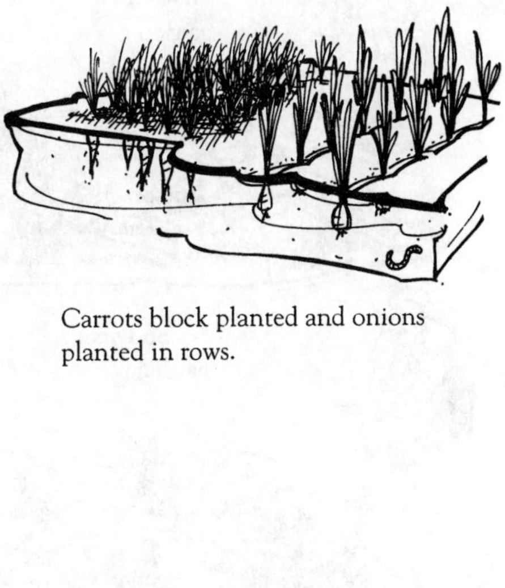

Carrots block planted and onions planted in rows.

A compromise for some crops is to use wide rows. Peas and beans are often planted in this manner as it keeps the weeds down and makes picking easy. Other techniques to consider when armchair planning the vegetable garden are crop rotation, interplanting and successional planting.

#### Crop rotation

Growing different crops, rather than the same vegetable or family of vegetables, in the same place each year is known as crop rotation. It seems to reduce disease problems and certainly reduces nutrient depletion caused by crops that are heavy feeders. It also aids weed control, increases soil nitrogen and bacterial activity, and improves the physical condition of the soil. In a small urban garden, however, crop rotation has a limited impact on reducing insect damage because the distances between areas are small and easily travelled by insects.

A three-year rotation cycle is the minimum requirement when tackling soil-dwelling nematodes, incorrectly called eelworms. Nematodes cause several plant diseases and poor growth—what some gardeners refer to as "soil sickness." The cysts can hibernate for many years. Marigolds depress nematode populations, but the effect is not felt until the following year. It is a good idea to plant marigolds in with the crop preceding tomatoes, which generally are susceptible to nematodes.

### *Four-year rotation*

If only a small garden area is available, divide it into four areas. In each of four years, there will be a different crop in each area, until the cycle starts all over again in year five. The four vegetable groups are the cucurbits (cucumber, pumpkin, summer and winter squash, melon and gourd); brassicas (broccoli, Brussels sprouts, cabbage, cauliflower, cress, kale, kohlrabi, mustard greens, radish, swedes or rutabaga, turnip and watercress); nightshades (tomato, pepper, eggplant and potato); and legumes (peas and beans). Cucurbits follow brassicas, brassicas follow nightshades, and so forth. Interspersed among these in odd corners are carrots, beets, radishes, onions, leeks, spinach and lettuces.

First year's garden.

Second year's garden.

### *Six-year rotation*

If the vegetable garden can be divided into six areas, plan six crop groups: cucurbits, brassicas, nightshades, legumes, root crops and leafy greens. If rotating flowers as well, perhaps for cutting purposes, it is probably easiest to think of them as a seventh group, even though many of them can be slotted into the groups mentioned above (such as nicotiana and petunia in the nightshades and sweet peas in the legumes). Annual herbs can also be added to a rotation scheme.

### *Eight-year rotation*

An eight-year rotation used by Eliot Coleman (1989) is, in this order: cucurbits, potatoes, corn, brassicas, peas, nightshades, beans and roots (carrot, beet, turnip, onion). Leafy crops could be interspersed among the root crops. Each year everything shifts over one space. In year two, cucurbits follow where the potatoes were grown, potatoes where the corn was, and so on.

In this rotation, weed susceptible root crops follow weed-suppressing crops of squash and potatoes. Corn, a heavy feeder, follows not far behind nitrogen-enriching peas and beans. Corn also follows brassicas because it is one of the few crops that does not show lower yields when planted in soil previously used for brassicas. Deep rooted crops help break up the soil. Potatoes, which belong to the nightshades, follow four years behind other nightshades—this is long enough to wait before repeating a crop. They also follow corn, which is one of the preceding crops that increases potato yields. Legumes have been shown to help control root maggots in a following crop of brassicas. Some people include the parsley family (carrot, parsnip, celery and celeriac) in their rotation.

To determine to which family a certain crop belongs , compare the shape of the seeds, the shape of the cotyledons (the first leaves that appear when the seed germinates), and the structure of the flower. Potato and tomato flowers, for example, have the same shape and structure, yet few people realize that these plants belong to the same family.

### ***Interplanting***

Interplanting means growing two crops in the same space. This can be done by alternating rows or blocks, or by alternating plants within a row or block. Usually a small, quick-maturing crop is interplanted with a large, slow-maturing crop. For example, beets can be interplanted with squash or

**Green Thumb Tip**

Some gardeners include green manures in their crop rotation. Each year half of the area is planted with such crops as clover, buckwheat or soybeans. The next year, vegetables are grown there and the green manure crop is grown where the vegetables were. Alternatively, green manures can be integrated into a four to eight-year rotation scheme. These manures depress beetle grub populations and add organic matter to the soil when turned under. The yield of tomatoes is greatly increased when they are planted where annual vetch was grown as a green manure crop, and then mulched with the vetch (not to be confused with perennial tufted vetch, which is a persistent weed). Spring oats or spring barley can be planted towards the end of the tomato crop, vetch after peas, and winter rye after potatoes.

zucchini, and early spinach or lettuce with broccoli, Brussels sprouts or cabbage. Good crops for interplanting are cress, radish, spinach, scallions, corn salad and root crops. Lettuce and other leafy crops benefit from the shade cast by tall crops such as peas, corn and pole beans. Broccoli is slower to bolt if it is grown in cool shade.

Interplanting is sometimes referred to as companion planting. Dedicated followers believe that some plants benefit certain others and that some may have a detrimental effect, but there is little scientific evidence to support most of the claims. It is true, however, that onions and garlic help to mask the smell of some crops that are host to certain insect pests; for example, when planted among carrots they confuse carrot rust flies. For more detail, refer to Louise Riotte's books *Carrots Love Tomatoes* (1975) and *Roses Love Garlic* (1983).

**Green Thumb Tip**

Another form of interplanting is undersowing. Eliot Coleman (1989) recommends that green manure crops be planted between the rows four to five weeks after the main crop is established. These green manures can be turned back into the soil or left in place over the winter to provide protection, increase nutrient levels and improve the physical structure of the soil. For example, soybeans can be grown among corn plants to increase nitrogen levels.

### Succession planting

Planting a crop in the space vacated by a crop harvested early in the season is known as succession planting. The same crop may be planted repeatedly in different places, or a succession of different crops, including green manures, can be planted in one part of the garden. For example, if lettuce is planted weekly from early in the spring until the end of May, and then weekly through the first weeks of August, a continuous supply of lettuce can be obtained by completely cutting back each plant once and letting it regrow. After peas are harvested in July, there is time to plant a different late season crop in the space just vacated.

A succession of different crops can be obtained by planting very early crops of turnip greens, Chinese cabbage, spinach, beet greens, early beets and early carrots. These are followed by heat loving summer crops, which are followed by late season plantings of Swiss chard, lettuce, kale, endive, corn salad and leeks. Later crops are sometimes seeded or transplanted among the first crop before it is harvested to gain more time. In short season areas, it is more realistic to aim for two successions of crops, and some gardeners are only too pleased to get one set of crops out of a season's growing.

Cold frames or row covers are a necessity if succession cropping is used to stretch the vegetable growing season into early spring and late autumn. Starting seeds indoors is also a big help. Transplants—which can be three or four weeks old before they are planted outdoors early in the spring or when a crop has been cleared and space becomes available—can make the difference between getting one or two crops.

## Herbs

### Growing conditions and location

Herbs can be grown in a bed of their own, mixed in with flowers, planted in blocks or rows in the vegetable garden, or settled into a rockery. Culinary herbs, however, are more likely to be used if grown close to the kitchen. Factors to consider when planning are the growing conditions required by certain herbs, whether they have attractive characteristics, and the amount of space available (see Table FEB-1, below).

Herbs which require soil rich in organic matter and regular watering during dry weather—such as summer savory, basil, chives, chervil, dill, cilantro (coriander), fenugreek and parsley—do well in the vegetable garden. Sorrel and French tarragon also grow well in moist, well-drained soil, but as they are perennial herbs it may be preferable to plant them where they will not be disturbed.

Herbs that do well in the sunny, drier conditions of a rock garden and prefer neutral or slightly alkaline soil include perennials such as thyme, oregano, lavender, sage and rosemary. Some annuals and biennials, including borage, anise and caraway, also prefer dry, light, sandy soil.

Angelica, horseradish and sweet cicely, among others, prefer moist, fertile, cool soil. Mint, beebalm, angelica and horseradish can be so invasive as perennials that you might want to restrict their growth by planting them in large pots plunged into the ground in areas of fairly dry soil or where they are isolated from other plants.

For colour and texture in the flower garden, include beebalm, calendula, sage, borage (a prolific self-seeder), dill, nasturtium, dark opal basil for its leaf colour, chives, fennel, geranium and lavender. For greenery, plant lemon balm, lovage, parsley, chervil and tarragon. Herbs that will tolerate dry shade include lemon balm, curly parsley, catnip (*Nepeta*), chamomile and sweet woodruff.

If only one area is available for growing herbs, work extra organic matter into the soil where moisture loving herbs will be grown, and raise the bed somewhat where herbs requiring drier conditions will be grown.

Herbs can also be grown in pots, although some perennials, such as French tarragon and lovage, do well in pots when they are young, but not when they get large and old. Herbs which tolerate relatively dry conditions are easier to manage in pots than those requiring a steady water supply.

## Table FEB-1 Herbs: Growing Conditions, Size and Spacing

| Life Cycle | Plant | Approximate Hardiness Zone | Sun | Soil | Height inches/cm | Spacing inches/cm |
|---|---|---|---|---|---|---|
| P | Angelica | 4 | * + | ! M | 60/150 | 40/100 |
| HA | Anise | | * | D | 18-24/45-60 | 6-9/15-23 |
| P | Anise Hyssop | 3 | * + | D | 40/100 | 18/45 |
| P | Artemisia | 3 | * | A,D | 12-24/30-60 | 12-24/30-60 |
| TA | Basil | | * | A | 12/30 | 8/20 |
| TP | Bay Leaf | | * + | A | 40/100 + | pot |
| P | Beebalm (Monarda) | 4 | * + | ! M,A | 24-40/60-100 | 12/30 |
| HA | Borage | | * + | D | 24-40/60-100 | 12/30 |
| HA | Calendula | | * + | A | 12/30 | 9/23 |
| B | Caraway | 4 | * | D | 24/60 | 6-9/15-23 |
| P | Catnip | 3 | * + | D | 15-24/38-60 | 12/30 |
| HA | Chamomile, German | | * + | D | 18/45 | 6/15 |
| HA | Chervil | | + - | M,A | 15/38 | 4/10 |
| P | Chives | 3 | * + | A | 8-12/20-30 | 6/15 |
| P | Comfrey | 3 | * + | M,A | 20-32/50-80 | 32/80 |
| TA | Coriander, Cilantro | | * + | M,A | 15/38 | 8/20 |
| HA | Dill | | * + | A | 24-36/60-90 | 4-8/10-20 |
| HA | Fennel | | * + | A | 40-47/100-120 | 8-12/20-30 |
| TA | Fenugreek | | * | A | 15/38 | 6/15 |
| P | French Sorrel | 4 | * + | A | 40/100 | 15/38 |
| P | Horseradish | 4 | * + | ! M,A | 24/60 | 12/30 |
| P | Hyssop | 3 | * + | D | 15-20/38-50 | 10-15/25-38 |
| P | Iris, Florentine | 3 | * | A | 20/50 | 12/30 |
| (P) | Lavender | 6 | * | D | 12-18/30-45 | 9-12/23-30 |
| P | Lemon Balm | 5 | + | M,A | 15/38 | 12/30 |
| P | Lovage | 4 | * + | M,A | 40/100 | 15/38 |
| TP(HA) | Marjoram | | * | D | 6-8/15-20 | 6/15 |
| P | Mint | 3 | * + - | ! M,A | 12-15/30-38 | 12/30 |
| TA | Nasturtium | | * | M, A | 12/30 | 8/20 |
| (P) | Oregano, Greek | 6 | * | D | 12/30 | 12/30 |
| B | Parsley | 4 | * + | A | 10/25 | 8/20 |

| Life Cycle | Plant | Approximate Hardiness Zone | Sun | Soil | Height inches/cm | Spacing inches/cm |
|---|---|---|---|---|---|---|
| (P) | Rosemary | 6 | * + | A,D | 12-24/30-60 | pot |
| P | Saffron | 4 | * + | A | 4/10 | 3-4/8-10 |
| (P) | Sage | 6 | * + | A,D | 18/45 | 12/30 |
| P | Salad Burnet | 3 | * | D | 18/45 | 12/30 |
| TP | Scented Geraniums | | * + | A | 18/45 | 15/38 |
| HA | Summer Savory | | * | A | 15/38 | 4-6/10-15 |
| P | Sweet Cicely | 4 | + - | M | 24/60 | 24/60 |
| P | Sweet Flag, Calamus | 3 | * + | M | 24/60 | 18/45 |
| P | Sweet Woodruff | 5 | + - | M | 6/15 | 10/25 |
| P | Tarragon, French | 5 | * + | A | 24/60 | 18/45 |
| (P) | Thyme | 6 | * | D | 8/20 | 8/20 |
| P | Valerian | 4 | * + | M,A | 40/100 | 12/30 |
| TA | Watercress | | + - | M | 15/38 | 10/25 |

**Life Cycle** = TA: tender annual, P: perennial, HA: hardy annual, B: biennial, TP: tender perennial, (P) borderline hardy

**Sun** = * 8 hrs. or more sun, + 4 hrs. or more, - tolerates less than 4 hrs.

**Soil** = M: moist, fertile, cool, A: average moist, well-drained, D: dry, light, sandy, non-acidic, !: even more invasive under moist, rich conditions

A mixture of textures.

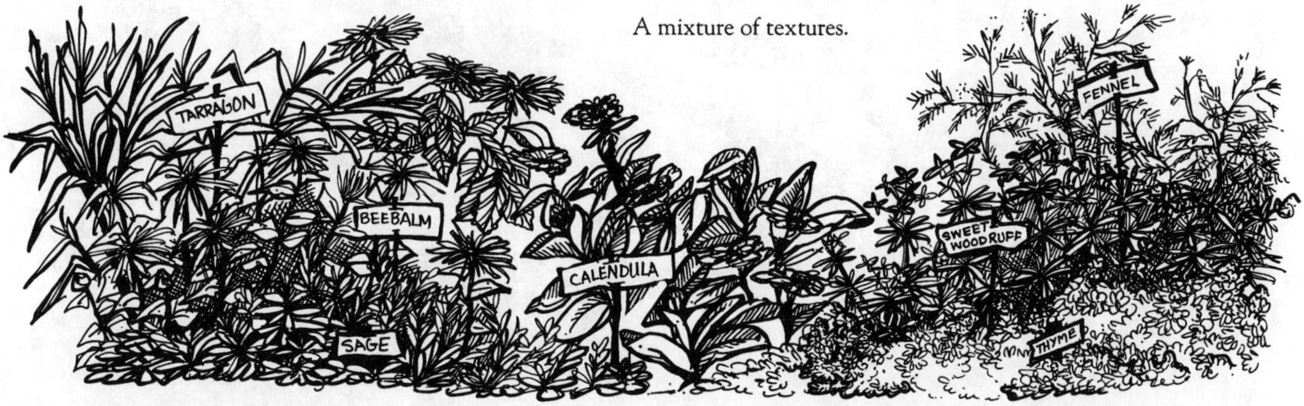

### Preventive Measure

If annual flowers are used extensively, it is a good idea to rotate their planting position, just as with vegetables. Certain flowers are more susceptible to diseases or pests than others, and growing them in the same place year after year can lead to problems.

## Flowers

### Location

Flowers can be grown in beds of their own, in front of trees and shrubs, or even in the vegetable garden. Growing flowers next to shrubs and trees extends the season of colour in that part of the garden. Spring bulbs planted under rhododendrons or near lilacs could start the season, followed by the rhododendrons or lilacs, and then perhaps a variety of lilies. A few chrysanthemums or asters would provide a splash of colour in the autumn.

### Design and colour

In flower beds, the traditional approach of putting tall flowers at the back, intermediate ones in the middle and short ones along the front creates a rather static effect. By all means have some of the taller ones drifting towards the middle of the bed and some of the intermediate ones infringing on the low ones along the front. Even the short ones can extend towards the middle of the bed to provide visual interest. This will necessitate beds of 5 feet (1.5 m) in width or more.

Plant drifts of plants rather than blocks to create a sense of movement. Think of tear drop shapes laid on the ground, all running in the same direction and each containing only one kind of plant, but several of them. The wide end of the tear drop gives the suggestion of movement in that direction, with the tail of the tear drop trailing behind. This arrangement can be used to draw the eye towards some feature or focal point, such as a gate or doorway.

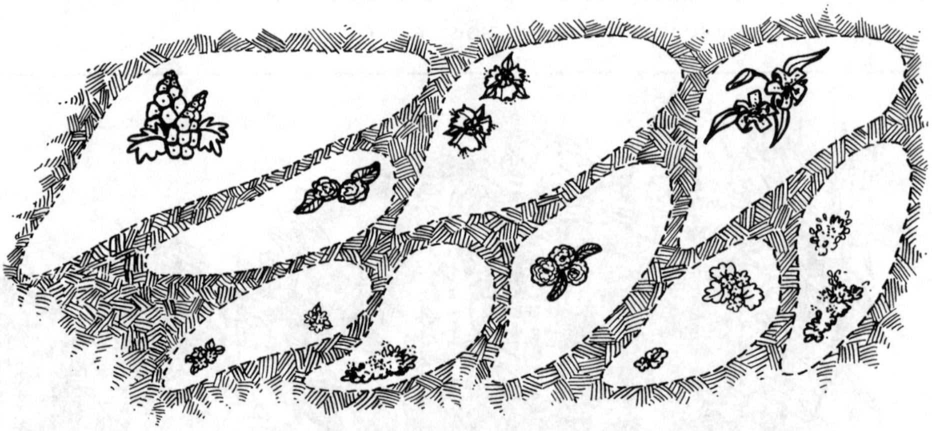

When selecting colour schemes, choose your personal favourites and use only two, or at the most three, colours. These can be related colours which appear together on a colour wheel, or they can be complementary, contrasting colours. A little bit of orange or red or yellow must be balanced with a lot of blue or green or purple when contrasting colours are used.

The warm colours of red, orange and yellow tend to give a feeling of action and movement and are often used in sunny areas. They also seem to come forward, so they enhance centres of activity, make distant parts of the garden seem closer, and make large areas feel smaller. Blue, purple and green are cool, soothing, receding colours, often used in the shade, where restful views are desired, or to make small spaces seem larger.

The intensity of the colours used also affects the mood created. A combination of red, blue and purple is quite different from a combination of soft bluish-pink, blue and mauve, yet they are just different intensities of the same related colours. Plants with grey or silver foliage complement soft, cool colours whereas plants with green foliage add strength and vibrancy to warm, strong colours.

## Fruits

### Soil and location

Most fruits require a slightly acidic soil of pH 6.0 to 6.5 that is rich in organic matter. A location sheltered from strong winds, both winter and summer, is essential. A multi-row tree and shrub shelterbelt, including a row of conifers, should be planted on the north and west sides, and a single-row shelter on the south and east sides. Plant fruits on a slight slope if soil drainage is a problem. A north-facing slope will provide the cooler conditions that are preferred by gooseberries and all the currants.

Avoid, if possible, planting fruit in a location that previously supported the same fruit. Apple replant disease, for example, is a complex disease that can be avoided by planting new trees in a new location. If new trees must be planted in an old orchard, put the new ones between the old trees, and back fill the new planting holes with fresh soil from another part of the garden.

### Size and pollination

Apples and some other fruit trees come in a wide range of varieties, and one variety may come in different sizes, depending on the rootstock it is grafted onto. Select the size on the basis of the amount of space available. Apple trees spread almost as wide as they are tall and are available in dwarf (6 feet

**Green Thumb Tip**

As some fruits bloom earlier than others, it is particularly important to ensure that plums, peaches, pears, red currants, white currants, black currants and elderberries are not planted in frost pockets. Although currants and gooseberries are exceptionally hardy, their flowers are sensitive to late spring frosts. Grapes require protection from early autumn frosts. A good flow of air as found on slopes reduces the problem with frosts at both ends of the growing season. Growing them against a sheltered wall provides some protection. Peaches are so sensitive to frosts, even after the fruit has set (the flower has been successfully pollinated and the fruit is beginning to grow), that getting a good crop one year out of four is not unusual. Growing them in fan form against a wall, where they can be covered on cold nights, may improve the odds for dedicated peach growers in zone 6 (see zone map).

or 2 m), semi-dwarf (10 to 13 feet or 3 to 4 m), semi-standard (16 to 23 feet or 5 to 7 m) and standard (23 to 32 feet or 7 to 10 m) heights. Dwarf and semi-dwarf varieties bear fruit sooner than the others, may be hardier, and are an easier size for home gardeners to manage. Sour cherries form smaller trees and are hardier than sweet cherries. Nanking cherry is shrub size.

Several single cordons (see March-April, page 98, for pruning espaliers) will fit into the same space as one tree with multiple arms, allowing more variety in a given space (see Tables APR/MAY-4, page 144, and APR/MAY-5, page 145). This might be important for pollination purposes. Try to grow cordons, fans and espaliers in the open against wire (see page 143) so that fruit production is more balanced. There are many shapes to choose from but make the decision after you have selected the growing space. Be sure to choose one-year-old trees on dwarfing rootstocks.

Pears, apples, many plums, and most cherries, elderberries and blueberries require two varieties for proper pollination. Most currants need a second variety of the same colour (two black currants, or two red) for good pollination and fruit set, with the exception of Consort black currant. One fruit tree may be sufficient if a neighbour has a different variety within 50 feet (15 m) of your tree. An apple tree with several cultivars grafted onto it is not a good idea. The cultivars usually vary in vigour, and maintaining a balanced tree becomes increasingly difficult as the years go by. Read the fine print in nursery catalogues to determine which varieties will pollinate which other varieties.

There are several groups of plums, including European and damson, Japanese, and American hybrids. Two plums from within one group are needed for pollination, such as two American hybrids, not one damson and one Japanese. Good nursery catalogues will specify compatible groupings.

Peaches and grapes are self-fertile, so only one tree or vine is required. Hardy kiwi fruit must have one male flowering plant for every one to nine female flowering plants for pollination. Sterility is sometimes a problem in blackberries, and is evident when flowering is prolific but no fruit develops. If all else fails, procure leaf buds, suckers or rooted tips from a neighbour's patch that fruits successfully (see page 274).

Nut trees carry separate male and female flowers on the same tree and are self-fertile. The blooming times may not always coincide, however, and the weather may be unfavourable at bloom time, so planting two varieties is a good idea. Nuts are pollinated by wind and cannot stand severe frost nor very wet and windy sites. They are best planted in the protection of large trees.

**Green Thumb Tip**

Training trees and shrubs flat against walls or along wires allows plants to be grown in two dimensional space and may provide more protection from harsh weather. Try to grow cordons, fans and espaliers in the open against wire unless extra shelter is required.

### *Quantities*

Aside from pollination requirements, one of each kind of fruit tree, unless they are grown as single cordons, is usually more than enough to meet the needs of the average sized family. Plant more if extensive preserving is planned.

See Tables APR/MAY-4, page 144, and APR/MAY-5, page 145, for the space requirements of the various fruits. Trees can be planted closer together in infertile soil than in fertile soil because they will not grow to their full potential. Tree roots spread so wide and deep that it is impossible to fully redress a soil fertility problem.

Raspberries are planted in wide rows rather than in individually prepared holes. The ground is dug in 12 inch (30 cm) wide strips in rows as long as desired. Shrubs that are to be grown in raised beds, such as blueberries, can be planted closer together. The beds should be in light shade, or in shade during the hottest part of the day, to reduce the amount of drying that occurs in raised beds. As well, work in extra organic matter to help retain moisture.

**Suggested Number of Soft Fruit* Shrubs or Vines Required Per Person**

| Name | Number of Plants | Name | Number of Plants | Name | Number of Plants |
|---|---|---|---|---|---|
| blackberries | 1 | grapes | 1 | rhubarb | 1 |
| black currants | 1 | kiwi fruit (hardy) | 1 | saskatoons (Indian pear, serviceberry, Amelanchier) | 1 |
| blueberries | 2 | mulberries | 1/2 | | |
| elderberries | 1/2 | raspberries | 10 | | |
| gooseberries | 1 | red currants | 1 | strawberries | 25 |

* a soft fruit is any fruit that is not a tree fruit

### *Disease resistance*

Check the fruit trees and soft fruits you purchase for disease resistance. Purchase certified strawberries and raspberries, rather than relying on friends and neighbours who may have diseased plants. Some apple varieties, such as 'Redfree,' 'Liberty' and 'Novamac,' are very resistant to scab disease, others are not and require spraying to control the disease. Nanking cherry seems more resistant to black knot than other cherries, and Consort black currant is immune to pine blister rust. 'Boyne' and 'Nova' raspberries are resistant to late yellow rust. A good catalogue or nursery will make clear which varieties are disease resistant and which are prone to certain diseases.

### Focus on Plants

Some strawberries bear several crops in a season, which may affect the number of plants required. The regular June bearing strawberries produce one crop of berries from flower buds initiated during the cool, short days of the previous autumn. In the summer the crop is followed by the growth of many runners from which new plants will grow. Choose one or more of the many June bearing varieties from those recommended in your area.

Everbearing strawberries have a major flush of berries in early summer from flower buds initiated the previous autumn. They are then able to produce another flush of fruit in the autumn. They produce fewer runners than June bearers so one might want to order more plants to establish a strawberry bed more quickly. Typical everbearers include 'Ogallala,' 'Fort Laramie,' 'Jubilee,' 'Ozark' (or 'Autumn') 'Beauty' and 'Quinalt.'

Dayneutral strawberries do not depend on any particular day length to initiate flower buds. They produce an autumn crop of berries the first year of planting and then, in later years, cycle through production peaks every six weeks from June or July until the first frost. Few runners grow because so much energy is put into flower and fruit production. 'Tristar,' 'Tribute' and 'Hecker' are dayneutrals.

### Green Thumb Tip

Apricots need hot, dry summers and cold, steady winters. Thaws in the winter can decrease their bud hardiness to such an extent that they may not bear fruit in milder zones. Dedicated fruit growers need to be inventive in light of the challenges facing fruiting plants. Peaches can be grown in tubs and moved under shelter for the winter. There are even varieties of grapes that are hardy to zone 3; depending on how they are trained (see March/April, pages 100-101), they can be given additional protection over the winter.

### Catalogues

Finding a reliable nursery from which to purchase trees, shrubs and perennial flowers is a challenge. Some nursery catalogues are misleading, and those from other regions may not offer plants suited to your area. Specialist nurseries distribute plants widely, but not all those available will flourish in your climate. In deciphering catalogues, remember that the presentation may misrepresent the actual quality of the plants. Shrub cuttings rooted at the wrong end are not unheard of. Good catalogues, however, are a wonderful source of plant and growing information.

### Hardiness

Too often the glowing descriptions in catalogues apply to plants that have been grown in a mild climate—they tend not to survive cold winters well. This is particularly true of fruit trees; the wood may survive the winter, but the flower buds which eventually form fruits may not be hardy. Even those plants that are supposed to be hardy in a particular zone will not survive as well as plants of the same species or variety that have actually been grown in nurseries in that zone. If in doubt about a plant, buy from local suppliers. Refer as well to Hall-Beyer and Richard's *Ecological Fruit Production in the North* (1983) for some varieties suited to different climatic zones. Keep in mind that plants hardy only to zone 5, for example, may not survive very well in zone 5. They should definitely be planted in sheltered positions. Plants that are hardy to zone 3 or 4 are much more likely to survive a winter in zone 5 or 6.

### Costs

It is a good idea to compare the cost of specific plants in various catalogues as there can be quite a difference in price, especially when shipping and handling costs are included. Sizes may vary, so take that into account. Buying as close to home as possible reduces shipping costs and the time plants spend in transit, and ensures that the plants will tolerate local winter conditions. Bare root plants sold by mail are less expensive than the same plants potted up at neighbourhood nurseries, but in both cases they may have been grown in milder zones. Bare root plants can be mailed only in the spring and autumn. Some gardeners prefer to buy two or three-year-old fruit trees, rather than small one year olds, even though they are more expensive. The older ones are already shaped by the nursery, making fruit growing a little less complicated.

## Starting Seeds

Starting seeds for transplanting outside is often a gardener's greatest pleasure in the winter. It never ceases to be a thrill to see a blank pot of soil come alive with green cotyledons reaching for the light.

### Why Grow Transplants

Using transplants instead of seeding directly outdoors has several advantages. Starting seeds indoors a month or two before outdoor planting is possible gives those plants which need a longer growing season (such as tomatoes, peppers, eggplants, some herbs and many annual flowers) the extra time required. Seeds which need warmth to germinate can be started in controlled conditions while the soil outdoors is still warming up. There is usually a higher rate of germination when seeds are started indoors because the required conditions can be more easily met. This is especially important when using either expensive seeds or those which are particularly difficult to germinate.

Cotyledons reaching for the light.

Some plants are adversely affected by very cool temperatures in the early stages of growth. For example, cauliflower will form only tiny heads, called buttons, if it is chilled too much when young. Lettuce will bolt early if it is exposed to temperatures below 50ºF (10ºC) during the three week period after sowing. Using transplants avoids these problems.

More crops can be grown in the same space when transplants are used. As soon as one vegetable has been harvested, transplants which are several weeks old can be planted in the same space and be ready for harvest by the time of the first autumn frost. There might not be enough time for a second crop started from seed outdoors to complete its growth.

Growing transplants instead of purchasing them also saves money and increases the selection of varieties available. Start with just a few different plants if you have never started seeds indoors before. If some do not work out, you can always buy transplants.

**Green Thumb Tip**

Preparing ground in the spring when the soil is cold and wet and plants are waiting to be settled in is an awful chore. Ideally, the ground should have been prepared in the autumn (see pages 375-382). If you did not get this done, be realistic when assessing how much digging and planting can be done to accommodate the plants when they arrive.

### Planting the Seeds

#### Individual containers or flats

Many seeds can be sown in a batch in one container and then thinned so that they are far enough apart to avoid root disturbance when they are finally separated and planted outdoors. Alternatively, the seedlings can be transplanted to individual pots or larger containers. Single plants can also

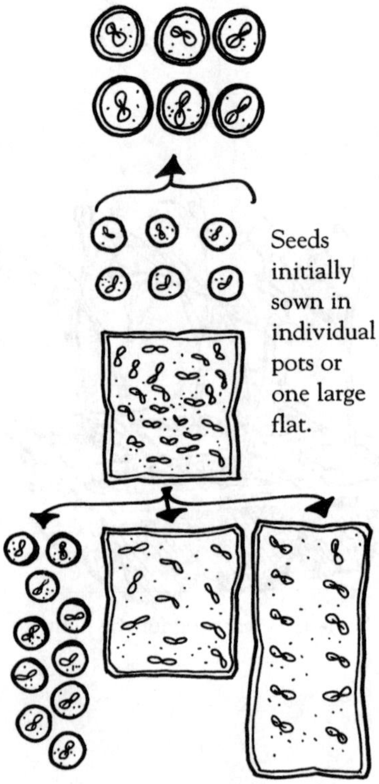


Seedlings can be transplanted, thinned or transplanted to larger flat.

### Green Thumb Tip

Whether seeds are started in batches or as singles, it is essential that plants not be checked in their growth because they have outgrown their quarters. Transplant seedlings to increasingly larger containers until they are ready to go outdoors. Two-litre milk cartons make good individual pots eventually for plants that need large quarters, such as tomatoes, peppers and eggplants.

be started in small individual containers and later transplanted to larger individual containers.

If sown in a batch, seedlings are transplanted once they have their first set of true leaves. Large flats which are 4 inches (10 cm) or more in depth are ideal for early greens for the vegetable garden. The entire flat can be moved as is to a cold frame as early as possible in the spring. If preferred, two or three seeds can be planted in a pot and later be thinned to one seedling per pot. This is a good strategy for certain annual flowers that resent root disturbance, and for brassicas. The latter are very susceptible to problems resulting from stress when they are transplanted, and are prone to root maggots. Individual containers or soil blocks ensure vigorous plants which tolerate transplanting well and which are better able to withstand insect attack. They also reduce the spread of damping off disease.

The variety of indoor sowing methods can be illustrated by looking at the requirements of sweet peas. These can be planted three seeds per 3 inch (75 mm) pot, and later thinned to two seedlings; planted six seeds per 5 inch (125 mm) pot and left as is until they are separated at transplanting time; planted 1½ inches (4 cm) apart in a 5 inch (12 cm) deep box and left as is until they are separated at transplanting time; or planted 1 inch (2.5 cm) apart and later potted on to larger quarters or individual pots. Play around each year with different combinations to see what suits you best.

For the most part, vegetables are best started in individual pots, soil blocks or plastic cell paks because of the reduced root disturbance at transplanting time and consequent reduction in transplanting shock. This is particularly important for continued, steady plant growth. Some vegetables, however, can be planted in multiples with three or four seeds in each container or soil block. This speeds things up at transplanting time because the entire block is planted without dividing up the seedlings. More plants are put in for the same amount of effort. Such vegetables should be started indoors a couple of weeks later than the normal starting date (see Table FEB-2, page 52) because multiple transplants are set outdoors at a younger age. They are also planted slightly further apart than normal. You might try this with corn, leeks, bulb onions, scallions, chives and peas.

### Breaking dormancy

Sometimes it is difficult to get seeds of perennial flowers, trees, vines and shrubs to germinate. Seed packages should have explicit instructions for the needs of each species but, failing this, there are several strategies to try.

An artificial winter (called stratification) helps some seeds break dormancy. Chilling may take the form of putting seeds in the freezer for twenty-four hours. This should be all delphiniums and pansies need. Columbine, cleome, allium, salvia, bergenia, some grasses and euphorbia require three to four weeks of chilling before planting. Rose seeds and many tree and shrub seeds require planting and then one to three months of temperatures around freezing. Alternatively, they can be stratified by mixing them with damp peat moss and sand in plastic bags and storing them for three to five months at 35 to 40° F (2 to 4° C) before they are planted. Primroses do well when planted in seed flats, covered with plastic and then put outside in a protected place in early spring to go through repeated freezings and thawings.

Scarifying is a physical breaking of the seed coat. It can be accomplished by nicking or removing a tiny sliver of the seed coat with a sharp knife. Sweet peas are nicked on the side opposite the "eye" of the seed. Fine seeds can be scarified by lining the inside of a jar with medium grade sandpaper and then shaking the seeds inside the jar. Seeds needing such treatment include campanula, poppy, hibiscus (mallow) and canna.

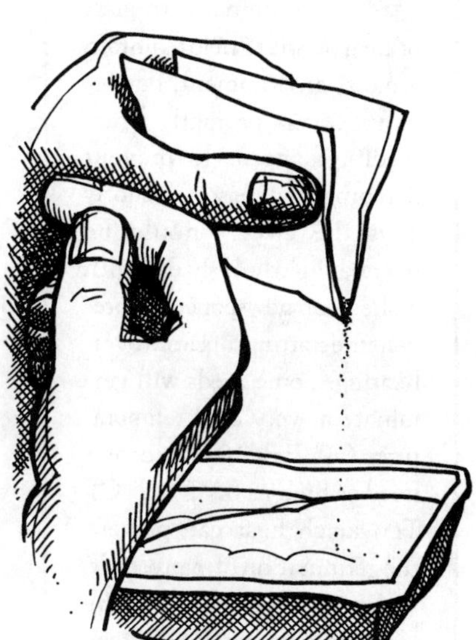

Planting fine seeds.

Soaking seeds is familiar to many gardeners. Putting the seeds in water for twenty-four to forty-eight hours to swell and soften the seed coat will hasten germination of such seeds as celery, asparagus, lavender, parsley, sweet pea, lupine, primrose and hibiscus (mallow). It is important to change the soaking water every twelve hours to keep up the oxygen levels.

Light or darkness may be required by some seeds. Generally speaking, very fine seeds need light to germinate and are not covered with soil or black plastic. If in doubt, try alternating a week of light with a week of darkness. Similarly, if unsure whether warm or cool conditions are required for germination, alternate warmth and coolness every two to three days. Sometimes the day-night temperature change is a sufficient stimulus for seeds to germinate. Generally, frost sensitive plants such as tomatoes, begonias, other tender perennials and some annuals seem to germinate better under warm conditions. Hardy annual and perennial flowers, trees, vines and shrubs often germinate well under cool conditions.

Despite all care and attention, some seeds fail to germinate. Celery can easily take three weeks to germinate, rosemary has a very low germination rate and lavender is erratic, so be patient—repeated attempts usually pay off.

### Preventive Measure

Cover each seeded container with glass or clear plastic to help maintain a moist environment, but remove covers promptly when seedlings appear to prevent damping off disease. On sunny days the cover should be opened slightly or shaded with a sheet of newspaper to prevent the starting mix from overheating. Some seeds will germinate at very cool temperatures (50° F or 10° C), others need as high as 80° F (27° C). Too much heat can prevent the germination of many seeds.

Provide warmth for the seeds, but be careful to keep the starting medium moist. Bottom heat will dry out containers of starting mix from the bottom up, leaving the surface looking moist. If new roots are allowed to dry out, seedlings can die. To keep the starting medium moist, set containers into water rather than applying it from the top.

Keeping the surface dryish also helps to prevent damping off disease. Another tip is to use No-Damp or an infusion of chamomile when watering. Steep 2 ounces (52 g) of the dried flowers in 1 pint (550 ml) of hot water. Let it cool to tepid and set the seed flats into it when watering.

### Sowing seeds

No magic is required to start seeds, but certain practices will increase the chances of success. Thoroughly moisten a sterile medium with warm water and fill the containers nearly to the top. Some seeds germinate faster if the medium is watered once with a high potassium fertilizer before they are planted. Let the medium drain for an hour and then scatter seeds thinly over the surface. This is made easier with very fine seeds if they are held on a piece of folded paper and sprinkled carefully by tapping the hand holding the paper. Lobelia has very fine seed and is prone to damping off disease; be particularly careful to sow these seeds thinly. Small seeds, such as those of marjoram and oregano, should be covered to a depth of only one to two times the diameter of the seed; some gardeners get even coverage by using a sieve to sprinkle the sterile medium over the seeds. A major cause of seed germination failure is planting to deep or covering to uneven depths.

Seeds that are very fine, such as those of petunias, usually require light to germinate. Sprinkle them on the surface of the starting medium and then mist lightly with water or press them gently onto the surface with a smooth board.

Label each container with the name of the plant and date of planting and make a note of the average number of days to germination if this information is on the seed packet. Plant only one kind of seed per container because different seeds germinate at different rates. Save seed packets for transplanting or spacing information later in the season when plants are put outdoors.

### After care

The first leaves that appear are cotyledons; the second leaves, which look quite different from the cotyledons, are the first true leaves. The seed coat may stick to the cotyledons (this is common with onions and peppers) and should be left in place as the seedling may still be drawing nutrients from it.

Once the seedlings have emerged, keep the temperature cooler than that required for germination. As soon as most of the seeds have germinated, remove the bottom heat or move the seedlings to a cooler position. Seedlings should be grown at about 15°F (9° C) cooler than the temperature at which they germinated. This would be approximately 60 to 65°F (15 to 18°C) for seeds that required warmth, and about 50°F (10°C) for seeds that required cool conditions to germinate.

Begin fertilizing after the first true leaves appear using one quarter strength fertilizer or a mild fish fertilizer. Repeat every ten to fourteen days thereafter, gradually increasing the fertilizer concentration to regular strength. Impatiens does not require fertilizer as often (see Cool Flowers, page 81).

Continue to keep the starting medium moist but not wet as some plants, such as gazania, will develop crown rot if they are overwatered. Once the true leaves have appeared and growth is steady, the surface may be allowed to dry out slightly between waterings. If it is on the dry side, water with clear water before fertilizing. Fertilizer salts can draw water out of the roots through osmosis if the surrounding medium is very dry, causing the plant to die.

Thin seedlings when the first true leaves have appeared or transplant them to larger quarters (see page 81). Maintain full light levels and good air circulation to prevent damping off disease. Provide additional lighting if seedlings lean towards the light. If fluorescent lights are used, they should be 2 to 3 inches (5 to 8 cm) above the tips of seedlings and 3 to 5 inches (8 to 12 cm) above the tips of taller plants. The distance can increase with the age of the plants because there is less tendency for older plants to stretch towards light. A less expensive alternative is to put a wall of aluminum foil behind and to the sides of seedlings to reflect light onto the backs of the plants.

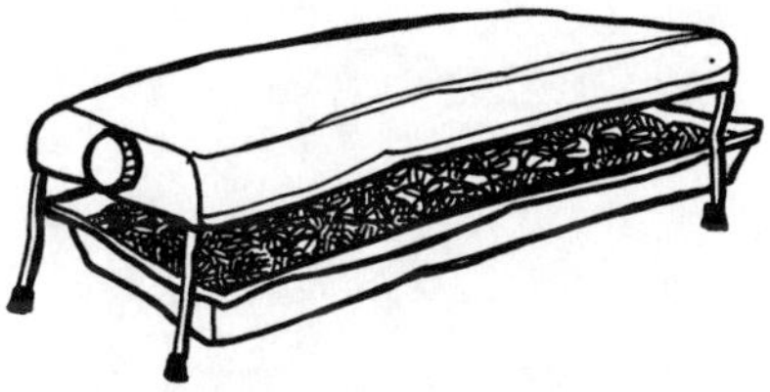

Lights should be 2"-3"above seedlings and 3"-5" above taller plants.

Try a wall of aluminum foil to increase natural light.

## Sowing Dates

Timing the indoor sowing of transplants so that they are ready for planting outdoors in the spring is always difficult. Last frost dates vary greatly, from late in April in some pockets of zone 6 to late May or sometime in June in zone 3. A garden in a frost pocket will have a different last frost date than one in a sheltered location on a slope even within the same neighbourhood. Furthermore, the last frost date for a particular location can vary from year to year by a month or more.

To be most accurate, keep track of the last frost date in your garden each year to determine the average (mean) or the expected (mode) date of the last frost. For the first year, refer to the wealth of such information that has been collected over many years and published in both Canada and the United States. Check in the reference section of the local library or with the district agriculturalist or extension specialist for this information and, at the same time, obtain the first expected frost date in the autumn to help guide activities in the fall.

**Green Thumb Tip**

Use tepid water generally when watering because it can take three to four hours for soil to become warm again if cold water is used; this may slow the germination process.

## Table FEB-2 Indoor Sowing Dates for Vegetables for Transplanting Outdoors

| No.Weeks to Last Frost | Vegetable | Range of Germination Temperature | Number of Weeks to Germinate | Transplant Age in Weeks |
|---|---|---|---|---|
| 16-12 | Asparagus | 65-75°F (18-24°C) | 4-5 | 8-10 |
| 12-10 | Early Leeks, Onions | 50-70°F (10-21°C) | 2-3 | 10 |
| | Tomatoes-early crop | 65-80°F (18-27°C) | 1-3 | 6-8 |
| 11-9 | Celery, Celeriac | 50-65°F (10-18°C) | 2-3 | 10-12 |
| 10-7 | Bunching Onions, Chives | 50-70°F (10-21°C) | 2-3 | 8-10 |
| | Peppers | 70-85°F (21-30°C) | 1-4 | 9-10 |
| | Chinese & Early Cabbage | 45-80°F (7-27°C) | 1-3 | 4-5 |
| 9-7 | Eggplant | 70-90°F (21-32°C) | 2-3 | 8-9 |
| | (Escarole) | 45-80°F ( 7-27°C) | 1-3 | 3-4 |
| | (Endive) | 45-80°F ( 7-27°C) | 1-3 | 3-4 |
| | (Kale) | 45-80°F ( 7-27°C) | 1-3 | 3-4 |
| | (Collards) | 45-80°F ( 7-27°C) | 1-3 | 3-4 |
| | (Mustard Greens) | 45-80°F ( 7-27°C) | 1-3 | 3-4 |
| | (Turnip) | 45-80°F ( 7-27°C) | 1-3 | 3-4 |
| 8-6 | Tomatoes-regular crop | 65-80°F (18-27°C) | 1-3 | 6-8 |
| | Early Cauliflower | 55-80°F (12-27°C) | 1-3 | 4-5 |
| 7-5 | Early Broccoli | 45-80°F (7-27°C) | 1-3 | 4-5 |
| | Early Cauliflower (2nd sowing) | | | |
| | Head Lettuce | 35-70°F (2-21°C) | 1 | 3-6 |
| | (Leaf Lettuce) | 35-70°F (2-21°C) | 1-2 | 3 |
| | (Peas) | 40-75°F (4-24°C) | 1-2 | 3 |
| | (Spinach) | 50-75°F (10-24°C) | 1-2 | 3-4 |
| | (Corn Salad - Mache) | 40-75°F (4-24°C) | 1-2 | 3 |
| 6-4 | Early Cauliflower (3rd sowing) | | | |
| | Summer Cabbage | 45-80°F (7-27°C) | 1-2 | 4-5 |
| | Sweet Potato | sprout roots to take cuttings | | |
| | (Potatoes) | sprout tubers for early planting | | |
| | (Beets) | 50-75°F (10-24°C) | 1-2 | 3-4 |
| | (Swiss Chard) | 35-70°F (2-21°C) | 1-2 | 3-4 |
| | (Kohlrabi) | 45-80°F (7-27°C) | 1-3 | 3-4 |

### Focus on Plants

The ideal temperature to germinate pepper seeds is 70 to 85°F (21 to 30°C). If the potting mix can be kept that warm and kept constantly moist, pepper seeds might well germinate in a week. Once the seeds have germinated, peppers should grow for eight to ten weeks before they are big enough to transplant outside. As a rough guide, peppers should be started somewhere between seven and ten weeks before the last frost date. This will result in transplants big enough to put outdoors a couple of weeks after the last frost date, when the weather is warm and settled. Thus, the total time from initial sowing to final transplanting may be as short as nine weeks or as long as fourteen weeks.

| No. Weeks to Last Frost | Vegetable | Range of Germination Temperature | Number of Weeks to Germinate | Transplant Age in Weeks |
|---|---|---|---|---|
| 4-3 | Melon, Watermelon | 75-85°F (24-30°C) | 1 | 4-6 |
| | Witloof Chicory | 60-70°F (15-21°C) | 1-2 | 4-6 |
| | (Beans) | 60-85°F (15-30°C) | 1-2 | 2-3 |
| | (Corn) | 60-95°F (15-35°C) | 1-2 | 2-3 |
| 3-2 | Cucumbers | 70-80°F (21-27°C) | 1 | 3-5 |
| | Squash, Pumpkin | 70-80°F (21-27°C) | 1 | 3-5 |
| | Zucchini, Summer Squash | 70-80°F (21-27°C) | 1 | 3-5 |
| | [Brussels Sprouts] | 45-80°F (7-27°C) | 1-3 | 4-5 |
| | [Winter Cabbage] | 45-80°F (7-27°C) | 1-3 | 4-5 |
| | [Late Leeks] | 50-70°F (10-21°C) | 2-3 | 4-5 |
| | [Late Broccoli] | 45-80°F (7-27°C) | 1-3 | 4-5 |
| | [Late Cauliflower] | 55-80°F (12-27°C) | 1-3 | 4-5 |

( ) = usually seeded directly outdoors but can be seeded indoors for an earlier crop

[ ] = transplanting recommended in short season areas for regular crop but can be seeded directly outdoors later if preferred

### *Vegetables*

Vegetable starts (seeding dates) depend on last frost dates and on how much gardening one wants to cram into a season. If cold frames, row covers and other crop protection devices are used (see page 73), seedlings can be started indoors as early as February in some locations (and see Green Thumb Tip, page 76).

Moderately close attention to seeding dates is required for transplants, particularly if the goals are high yields and a long season of harvest (see Table FEB-2). How soon seeding begins depends on what one wants to plant and on what germination temperatures can be provided. Peppers, for example, take anywhere from one to four weeks to germinate, depending on how warm the starting medium is.

Cabbage, which germinates within a couple of weeks even in very cool soil, can be planted out when it is four to five weeks old, even while there is a chance of frost. An early crop of cabbage can be started indoors at the same time as peppers, even though they are planted out at different times.

Celery, celeriac, leeks and onions are candidates for early starts indoors. Leeks, for instance, require a long growing season and are usually seeded ten to twelve weeks before the last expected frost date.

### Herbs

As a very crude guideline, most perennial herbs are started indoors three to four months before the last expected frost date, and annual herbs are started a little later (see Table FEB-3). Many herbs can be sown directly outdoors, some as soon as the soil can be worked and others after the last expected frost date.

Some gardeners prefer to start basil indoors, for example, five or six weeks before the last expected frost. It is rather sensitive to damping off disease, and starting it indoors means that one can give it the careful attention it requires. It is transplanted outdoors when the weather is warm and settled, about the same time as tomatoes. If seeding directly outdoors, start after the last frost date but a little before the tomatoes go in. Catnip can be started indoors or out, but seeding directly outdoors avoids the problem of scent release (and marauding cats) when young catnip plants are handled during transplanting.

### Table FEB-3 Indoor Sowing Dates for Herbs for Transplanting Outdoors

| No. Weeks to Last Frost | Herb | Comments |
|---|---|---|
| 16-12 | Angelica | sow, then cold stratify 6 weeks |
| | Bay Leaf | sow, then cold stratify 6 weeks |
| | Geraniums, Scented | erratic germination |
| | Lavender | erratic germination |
| | Rosemary | very low germination rate |
| | Sweet Cicely | sow, then freeze stratify; individual pots |
| 12-8 | Chives, Garlic Chives | |
| | Parsley | soak seeds 24 hours; individual pots |
| | Sage | |
| | Thyme | |
| 8-6 | Anise Hyssop | |
| | Catnip | can sow outdoors early spring |
| | French Sorrel | can sow outdoors early spring |
| | Hyssop | can sow outdoors early spring |
| | Lemon Balm | soak seeds 24 hours |
| 6-5 | Basil | can sow outdoors after frost |
| | Chamomile | |
| | Coriander (Cilantro) | individual pots; or sow outdoors after frost |
| | Marjoram | |
| | Greek Oregano | |
| 3 | Anise | individual pots; or sow outdoors after frost |

**Direct Seeding Outdoors**

Sow outdoors in early spring under protection or around the last frost date in the open:

| | |
|---|---|
| Beebalm (Bergamot, Monarda) | Dill - self sows |
| Borage - self sows | Fennel |
| Calendula - self sows | Lovage - self sows |
| Chervil - self sows; needs light to germinate | |
| Comfrey - self sows | |
| Summer Savory - successive sowings every 2 to 4 weeks | |

Sow outdoors after danger of frost has passed:

| | |
|---|---|
| Caraway | Nasturtium |
| Fenugreek | Watercress |

Herbs can be started in flats or individual containers. Germination may be erratic, particularly with perennial herbs, so do not be in a hurry to throw out seed flats. Some gardeners have luck germinating difficult seeds between layers of moist paper towels. Use a temperature of 55 to 70°F (12 to 21°C) for seeds of perennial herbs and 65 to 75°F (18 to 24°C) for seeds of annual and biennial herbs.

### *Flowers*

Dates for sowing flowers are less exacting than for vegetables. Perennial flowers are generally sown indoors ahead of annual flowers. Most perennials are slow to germinate, and it usually takes eighteeen to twenty weeks to reach transplant size. If preferred, they can be sown in June, transplanted to a sheltered position or cold frame in September, and then planted in their permanent position the following spring. This helps to cut down on the amount of sowing done indoors in the winter and spring, but there is a greater risk of losing plants over the winter.

Some annuals can be started indoors about three months before the last expected frost date (see Table FEB-4, below). The aim is to have plants that are neither pot-bound nor in flower when transplanted outdoors. Plants are less stressed and make better subsequent growth if they are not in flower at transplanting time. Whether or not the top growth of young seedlings is pinched also determines starting dates. If sweet peas and petunias are started in February, they will be too large at transplanting time unless they are pinched (as recommended in Table FEB-4) to increase bushiness. Unless specifically indicated in Table FEB-4, flowers can be planted in individual containers or in flats.

## Table FEB-4 Indoor Sowing Dates for Annual and Biennial Flowers

These flowers will be ready for transplanting outdoors after all danger of frost is past and the weather is warm and settled(w), or earlier while the weather is still cool(c). Alternatively, some can be seeded directly outdoors around the last frost date (c) or after the weather is warm and settled (w) (a blank indicates they are not suitable for direct seeding).

**16 to 18 weeks before the last expected frost**

| Direct Sow | Plant Name | Ideal Conditions for Germination | Transplant Conditions |
|---|---|---|---|
| | Dahlia | 80°F/65°F, 5-7 days; individual pots | w |
| | Eustoma - see Lisianthus | | |
| | Fuchsia | 70-75°F; individual pots | w |
| | Geranium | 72-76°F; individual pots | w |
| | Lisianthus | 70°F; individual pots; pinch | w |
| | Pansy | pre-chill seed 24 hours 2-4°F; 65-70°F after sowing; dark | c |
| | Tuberous Begonia | 70°F constant, seed barely covered | w |
| | Wax Begonia | 70°F constant, seed barely covered | w |
| | **N.B.** - most of these are tender perennials | | |

**12 to 14 weeks before the last expected frost**

| Direct Sow | Plant Name | Ideal Conditions for Germination | Transplant Conditions |
|---|---|---|---|
| | Ageratum (Flossflower) | 80°F; 7 days | w |
| | Busy Lizzie - see Impatiens | | |
| c | Carnation | freeze 1 week; 70°F/60°F; 7 days; individual pots | c |
| | Cobaea - see Cup and Saucer Vine | | |
| | Cup Flower - see Nierembergia | | |
| w | Cup and Saucer Vine (*Cobaea*) | 70°F; individual pots | w |
| c | *Dianthus*, Pinks | 70°F; 8-10 days; individual pots | c |
| | Dusty Miller (*Pyrethrum*, *Cineraria*) | 65°F | c |
| | Flossflower - see Ageratum | | |
| c | Foxglove | 70°F; 7 days; light | c |
| w | Gaillardia | 80°F; 21 days; dark | w |
| | Gazania | 60°F; 7 days; dark | c |

| Direct Sow | Plant Name | Ideal Conditions for Germination | Transplant Conditions |
|---|---|---|---|
| | Heliotrope | 70-80°F/60°F; 15 to 20 days | w |
| | Ice Plant (Mesembryanthemum) | 70°F; dark | w |
| | Impatiens (Busy Lizzie) | 70°F; 10-20 days; light | w |
| | Limonium - see Statice | | |
| | Lobelia | 70°F; 20 days; sow thinly | c |
| | Marigold, tall, African | 75-80°F; 3-7 days | w |
| | Mesembryanthemum - see Ice Plant | | |
| | Nierembergia (Cup Flower) | 65°F; individual pots | c |
| | Painted Tongue - see Salpiglossis | | |
| | Petunia | 80°F; light; pinch | w |
| | Rose Periwinkle - see Vinca | | |
| w | Salpiglossis (Painted Tongue) | 80°F; 20 days; dark, do not cover | w |
| w | Salvia | 70-75°F; 10-14 days; light | w |
| | Statice | 70°F; dark | w |
| c | Sweet Pea | soak, scarify; 55°F; 14 days; pinch | c |
| c | Sweet William | 70°F; 8-10 days; individual pots | c |
| | Vinca (Rose Periwinkle) | 80°F; 20 days; dark; pinch | w |
| | Viola | chill 24 hrs; 65-70°F; dark | c |
| c | Wallflower | 70°F; 7-10 days | c |

**8 to 10 weeks before the last expected frost**

| | | | |
|---|---|---|---|
| c | African Daisy (*Dimorphotheca*) | 55-60°F; 7 days; pinch | c |
| | Amaranthus | 70°F; 10 days | w |
| c | Ammi (Bishop's Flower) | 60-65°F | c |
| c | Anchusa (Bugloss) | 70°F | c |
| | Antirrhinum - see Snapdragon | | |
| w | Aster, China or Annual | 70°F | w |
| c | Baby's Breath | 70°F; repeat sowings outdoors every 2 weeks to mid-July | c |
| | Balsam Impatiens | 70°F; 8-10 days; light | w |
| c | Bells-of-Ireland | pre-chill 50°F; 5 days; alternate 50°F to 85°F; light; individual pots | c<br>c |
| | Bishop's Flower - see Ammi | | |
| w | Black-Eyed-Susan (*Thunbergia*) | 75-80°F; 15-20 days | w |

| Direct Sow | Plant Name | Ideal Conditions for Germination | Transplant Conditions |
|---|---|---|---|
| | Browallia | 80°F; pinch | w |
| | Bugloss - see Anchusa | | |
| | Burning Bush - see Kochia | | |
| c | Candytuft (annual Iberis) | 70°F | c |
| c | Catchfly (Silene) | 60-65°F; 10 days | c |
| | Chilean Glory Flower (*Eccremocarpus*) | 70-75°F; light; individual pots | w |
| c | Cleome (Spider Flower) | chill 40°F; 1 week; 85°F/65°F; do not pinch | c |
| | Coleus | 70-75°F; light; pinch | w |
| | Dimorphotheca - see African Daisy | | |
| | *Eccremocarpus* - see Chilean Glory Flower | | |
| | Flowering Tobacco - see *Nicotiana* | | |
| | Globe Amaranth | 80°F/70°F; 14 days; dark | w |
| c | Hollyhock | 60°F; 10 days; individual pots; do not pinch | c |
| w | Kochia (Burning Bush) | 65-75°F | w |
| c | Larkspur | 60-65°F; individual pots | c |
| w | Love-in-a-Mist (*Nigella*) | 65-75°F; individual pots | w |
| | Love-Lies-Bleeding - see Amaranthus | | |
| w | Marigold, dwarf, small | 75-80°F; 3-7 days | w |
| | Moss Rose - see Portulaca | | |
| c | Nemesia | 60-65°F; provide shade | c |
| w | *Nicotiana* (Flowering Tobacco) | 75°F; 14 days; light; individual pots | w |
| | Nigella - see Love-in-a-Mist | | |
| * | Ornamental Grasses | 70°F; 21 days | * |
| | Penstemon | 65-70°F; light | w |
| | Petunia | 80°F; light; do not pinch | w |
| | Pincushion (*Scabiosa*) | 75°F; 12 days | c |
| w | Portulaca (Moss Rose) | 70°F/60°F; 3-4 days; individual pots | w |
| | Purple Bell Vine (*Rhodochiton*) | 70-75°F; individual pots | w |
| | *Rodochiton* - see Purple Bell Vine | | |
| c | Saponaria | chill 10 days; 65°F | c |
| | Scabiosa - see Pincushion | | |
| c | Schizanthus | 60°F; 15 days; dark; pinch | w |
| | Silene - see Catchfly | | |
| c | Snapdragon | 70°F/60°F; 7 days; light; pinch | c |

| Direct Sow | Plant Name | Ideal Conditions for Germination | Transplant Conditions |
|---|---|---|---|
| | Spider Flower - see Cleome | | |
| c | Stock | 70°F; 7-10 days; light | c |
| | *Thunbergia* - see Black-Eyed-Susan Vine | | |
| w | Verbena | 70°F; dark | w |

**4 to 6 weeks before the last expected frost**

| Direct Sow | Plant Name | Ideal Conditions for Germination | Transplant Conditions |
|---|---|---|---|
| | Bachelor Button - see Centaurea | | |
| c | Calendula | 75°F/65°F; dark | c |
| w | Canary Creeper (*Tropaeolum*) | 70-75°F; individual pots | w |
| w | Castor Oil Plant | soak; 80°F; 10 days; individual pots (caution—seeds poisonous) | w |
| | Celosia (Cockscomb) | 70-80°F; 5 days | w |
| c | Centaurea | pre-chill 40°F; 5 days; 65-70°F; 7 days; dark | c |
| | Cockscomb - see Celosia | | |
| | Cornflower - see Centaurea | | |
| w | Cosmos | scarify; 75-80°F; light; pinch | w |
| w | Four O'Clock - see Mirabilis | | |
| | Helichrysum - see Strawflower | | |
| | Ipomaea - see Morning Glory | | |
| w | Mallow (Lavatera) | 70°F; 14-21 days; individual pots | w |
| | Marvel of Peru - see Mirabilis | | |
| w | Mexican Sunflower (*Tithonia*) | 70°F; individual pots | w |
| w | Mirabilis | soak 2 days; 70-75°F; individual pots | w |
| w | Morning Glory, Moonflower | scarify; soak 48 hours; 70°F; individual pots | w |
| c | Nolana | 70°F; 15 days; individual pots | c |
| c | Phlox, annual | 60-65°F; 10 days; dark; individual pots | c |
| w | Strawflower (Helichrysum) | 75°F; light | w |
| c | Sweet Alyssum | 75°F; 3 days | c |
| w | Sunflower | 65-70°F; individual pots | w |
| | *Tithonia* - see Mexican Sunflower | | |
| | *Tropaeolum* - see Canary Creeper | | |
| w | Zinnia | 80°F | w |

| Direct Sow | Plant Name | Ideal Conditions for Germination | Transplant Conditions |
|---|---|---|---|

**4 weeks before the last expected frost**

These flowers can be started indoors in individual pots at 65°F. Most perform better if seeded directly outdoors around the last frost date (c) or after all danger of frost is past (w).

| | |
|---|---|
| c | Baby Blue Eyes (*Nemophilla*) |
| c | Brown-Eyed-Susan (*Rudbeckia*) |
| w | California Poppy |
| c | California Bluebell (*Phacelia*) |
| w | Campanula |
| c | Chinese Forget-Me-Not (*Cynoglossum*) |
| c | Clarkia |
| c | Evening Scented Stock (*Myosotis*) |
| c | Flax (*Linum*)—make successive sowings every 3 weeks |
| c | Godetia |
| c | Immortelle (*Xeranthemum*) |
| w | Love-in-a-Mist (Nigella)—make successive sowings every 3 weeks |
| w | Mignonette - pinch |
| w | Morning Glory |
| w | Nasturtium |
| c | Poppies |
| c | Ten Week Stock |
| c | Virginia Stock |

| | |
|---|---|
| * | = seed or transplant under warm or cool conditions, depending on species of grass; use warm conditions for mixed seed packages |
| °F/°F | = day/night temperatures |
| days | = number of days to germination under specified conditions |
| individual pots | = sow seeds in individual pots or cell paks |

| | | |
|---|---|---|
| 55°F = 12°C | 65°F = 18°C | 75°F = 24°C |
| 60°F = 15°C | 70°F = 21°C | 80°F = 27°C |

Flowers can be thought of as "warm" or "cool" plants on the basis of the temperature at which they germinate and grow best (see Table FEB-4). Some of the flowers we call annuals are actually perennials but they are so frost sensitive, coming from warmer parts of the world, that they are treated as "warm" annuals in North America. "Warm" annuals are often frost sensitive and should not be transplanted nor seeded outdoors until all danger of frost is past.

"Cool" annuals will germinate quite well under very cool conditions, and actually flower better where summers are cool and moist, or during the autumn when conditions are cool. These flowers can often be transplanted (or seeded directly) outdoors while weather conditions are unsettled in the spring, about the time of the expected last frost date. Sweet peas can be sown outdoors just as soon as the ground is workable, or transplanted later while there is still a chance of frost.

Self-sowing biennials, such as foxglove, hollyhock and sweet william, will fill the niche of perennial flowers and come up year after year. By starting a new batch of biennials two years in a row, there should be a perpetual supply of seeds in all subsequent years. Biennials are sometimes started either indoors or outdoors in June or July to be enjoyed the following year, but if started indoors in late winter or early spring, some will bloom the first year.

## Propagating Perennials

### Cuttings

Tender perennials overwintered indoors and started into growth last month should soon be ready to yield cuttings. There is still time, however, to encourage new growth on dormant plants as cuttings can also be taken first thing next month, particularly in short season areas. If only the parent plants will be used and no cuttings made, early next month is soon enough to cut them back and start them into growth.

To root such plants as fuchsias, impatiens, wax or fibrous begonias, coleus and geraniums, take cuttings 3 to 4 inches (8 to 10 cm) long with three to four pairs of leaves. Remove the bottom one or two pairs of leaves, any flowers or flower buds, and trim off the cutting just below the last node using a razor blade or sharp knife. Dip the bottom end in rooting hormone, then tap off any excess powder. Use a starting mix made of equal parts of peat moss and perlite, or use a peat-based potting soil lightened with perlite. Make holes in the starting medium with a pencil, insert the cuttings, gently press the medium around each cutting and water well. Either mist the cuttings several times a day, place the pot and all in a closed plastic bag out of direct sunlight, or use a propagation unit (see page 442). Geraniums should not be enclosed in plastic bags as they are prone to rot at the soil level. A higher proportion of perlite should be used in the rooting mix prepared for geraniums and water the starting medium by placing the pot in water, rather than watering from the top. If many cuttings are taken, use a flat and cover it with clear plastic supported by metal hoops of coat hanger wire or plastic coated electrical wire. Placing the cuttings behind a screen of frosted glass will provide bright but indirect light. Alternatively, use 60 watt fluorescent lights.

Rooting occurs most easily when conditions are warm. A soil heating cable will provide bottom heat of 70°F (21°C) easily and efficiently, but this is not essential unless the air temperature is less than the 75 to 80°F (24 to 27°C) required to keep the soil at 70°F (21°C). Remember to use tepid water, not cold, when watering.

Another method that is used with fuchsias is to take tip cuttings. Cut just below a node very close to a growing tip, do not remove the lower leaves, dip in rooting hormone if desired, and rest each tip cutting in a slight depression in a pot of starting medium. A variation on this method is to set the cuttings on top of some starting medium inside a glass jar, water once and then screw on the lid of the jar. Again, keep the cuttings warm and well lit but out of direct sunlight.

After about three to five weeks, new growth will indicate that rooting has occurred. Transfer the cuttings into individual pots and gradually increase the intensity of the light they receive. Use only a mild fish fertilizer or one quarter strength 20-20-20 fertilizer until the new growth is vigorous. Seaweed fertilizer aids root development.

Cuttings of marguerite (Boston yellow daisy, *Chrysanthemum frutescens*) and chrysanthemums can be started indoors from overwintered plants either this month or early next month. Use 2 to 3 inch (5 to 8 cm) long, non-flowering side shoots and treat as for other cuttings. To take basal cuttings, cut off short lengths of the newly emerged basal growth at the base, or remove the plant from the pot and carefully remove the basal shoots by gently pulling the plant apart. Try to take a piece of root with each piece (this is not essential). Pieces less than 2 inches (5 cm) long are best; these are placed in a pot of starting medium, following the method described above (page 61). The same can be done with overwintered marguerites and delphiniums (see page 266 and Table APR/MAY-3, page 138). Cuttings can also be taken from plants in the garden once spring has arrived, except that several months worth of growth are then lost.

## *Indoor Gardening*

### *Vegetables and Herbs*

There are plenty of leafy greens to sow for indoor crops and some that were seeded last month can be seeded again (see Table JAN-2, page 24). Twelve hours of lighting each day is sufficient for radish, spinach and lettuce, but other crops can have up to sixteen hours each day if greater growth is desired. Spinach, however, can be kept from going to seed indefinitely if long days never arrive. Lettuce will go to seed eventually as it matures, but the process is speeded up by warm temperatures (see Preventive Measure, page 216). To avoid bitter lettuce and bolting spinach, grow them at cool temperatures with no more than twelve hours of light each day. Even street lights must be avoided!

Swiss chard planted last month and grown in benches can be thinned to 4 inches apart (10 cm); when the chard is 10 inches (25 cm) high, pull every other plant for a final spacing of 8 inches (20 cm) between plants. These thinnings can be eaten fresh or cooked. Alternatively, grow several plants in 8 inch (200 mm) pots and thin eventually to one plant per pot.

Some people prefer to grow peppers and eggplants indoors, particularly where summers are chilly. Germinate the seeds in warm conditions (see Table FEB-2, page 52). Plan on eventually putting peppers and eggplants into 10 inch (250 mm) pots, or else use bench space if it is available (see Table JAN-3, page 26, for spacing).

Broccoli, cauliflower and Brussels sprouts require a lot of space, so some people grow them outdoors in the summer only. The young leaves of these plants make a tasty cooked vegetable, however; you may want to sow a few seeds to increase the variety of greens, even if they are not grown to maturity. Cauliflower is not the easiest vegetable to grow outdoors, but success is easier under controlled conditions indoors. It needs to be grown in cool conditions after it germinates, but above 40°F (4°C). Too much time growing at lower temperatures, even as young plants, may result in button heads or other problems.

Carrots, beans and edible podded peas can be started. Add a little garden soil to the potting mix in order to provide the nitrogen fixing bacterium *Rhizobium* that is needed by legumes (including sweet peas). A purchased inoculant may work, but there is no certainty that it will contain the species required.

Tomatoes started in January will need potting on to larger containers, or start tomatoes this month. When tomatoes and other fruiting vegetables are transplanted, fertilize them with half strength 10-52-70 each week for three weeks, and then switch to 20-20-20. Other seeds that were started last month will need transplanting to larger containers or thinning if grown in bench space. Remember to fertilize all vegetables every couple of weeks with 20-20-20, but use only one-quarter strength fertilizer or a mild fish fertilizer for seedlings. Avoid watering on cloudy days, unless the soil is dry. Fungal diseases can be rampant in a cool, moist greenhouse, particularly if air circulation is poor.

Plant a few herbs for an early taste of summer. Refer to Table FEB-1 (page 40) for their preferred growing conditions. Dill, chervil, parsley and summer savory are all readily started and some young thinnings may have enough flavour to use in cooking. Use scissors to harvest them so that the roots of the remaining seedlings are not disturbed. Perennial culinary herbs (bay leaf, lemon balm, rosemary, sage, salad burnet and thyme) can all be started from seed this month or next. Basil, coriander, marjoram and oregano can be started this month if the growing conditions are warm. (For spacing, see Table JAN- 3, page 26.) Fertilize lightly with 10-10-10.

## Fruits

The variety of grape to choose for greenhouse growing depends on the temperature in the autumn. If a greenhouse drops below 55°F (12°C) at night in the autumn, choose early ripening varieties; if it stays at 60°F (15°C) or higher at night, then one of the fine, late ripening varieties can be grown. Passion fruits stay green all year if the temperature stays at around 60°F (15°C) or warmer; they will drop their leaves at cooler temperatures but will grow again in the spring. They are available as plants or can be grown from seed. Peach trees and other northern climate fruits must have a period of cold during the winter. If the greenhouse does not get cold, such fruits will have to be wintered in a cold but sheltered location.

## Flowers

### Repotting and dividing

As the days become brighter and noticeably longer, many plants start growing again. Gradually increase watering and begin fertilizing. Ferns and other plants may be pot-bound and in need of dividing and repotting. A plant is pot-bound if roots are growing through the drainage holes, the soil dries out very quickly and frequent watering is required, and growth is very slow even though the plant is watered and fertilized regularly in the spring and summer. To check, tip the plant out of its pot and examine the root ball. If there is a mass of matted roots on the outside and little soil visible the plant probably needs repotting. If it is not pot-bound, just pop the plant back into the pot.

Not all plants that are pot-bound should be repotted, however (see Table MAR/APR-3, page 88). Also, if you do not want a plant to get bigger, it should not be potted on into a larger container. Large plants in large pots need not be repotted, but can be top dressed by removing the top 1 to 2 inches (3 to 5 cm) of soil and replacing it with fresh potting mix or with a half and half mix of potting soil and worm compost (see page 401).

There is no need to purchase special potting mix for various kinds of plants. A regular potting soil or garden soil can be amended in various ways to suit the growing conditions required by various plants. Add extra sand or perlite for plants requiring excellent drainage, and add leaf mould or peat moss for plants requiring moist conditions and lots of organic matter (see Table MAR/APR-3, page 88).

To repot a plant, water it at least one hour before you tip it out of its pot. It may be necessary to run a knife around the inside of the pot or to tap the rim of the inverted pot on the edge of a table. Make sure the root ball is supported by spreading your fingers across the top of the pot before tapping it.

With your fingers or a dull stick, gently loosen some of the outer roots, and then cut off any damaged or mushy roots. Inspect bulbs for damage as well. Depending on the type of bulb, bad spots can sometimes be removed by peeling off an outer layer or two of the bulb. If the damage must be cut out, use a clean knife and sprinkle sulphur over the wound. Try to let it air dry for a day or two before repotting, but keep the roots moist.

Add some potting mix to the bottom of a pot one size larger than the original pot. There is no need to put gravel in the bottom for drainage if there are drainage holes in the pot. It is tempting to skip a few pot sizes and move a small plant to a large pot. Plants do not seem to perform any better when potted into considerably larger pots, and in some cases they do not bloom as well as those potted on in small increments. Make sure the larger pot has been well scrubbed and cleaned. Set in the plant and add or take away potting mix until the top of the original root ball is about 1 inch (2.5 cm) below the rim of the pot. Add and gently press additional potting mix along the sides of the root ball until the top of the root ball is reached. Do not plant it any deeper than the original level; this is particularly important for some bulbs (see Table MAR/APR-2, page 86). Gently tap the pot against the floor or table to settle the soil and then water the plant carefully. Keep it out of direct sunlight for a week and mist the leaves frequently.

Sometimes a plant that is being repotted can be divided to obtain more plants. Ferns, for example, usually need dividing as often as every spring. Ideally, one would pull the root ball apart with one's hands, but the reality is that some are so dense that a sharp knife is needed. Make vertical slices to divide the ball into two to four pieces. Put each piece with attached plant into a pot slightly larger than the size of the piece, and proceed as for any other repotting.

Bulbs are propagated by removing offsets. These are little bulbs growing near the base and around the outside of the bulb. Bulbs do not have to be divided when a new bulb is first observed growing beside the original one, but it can be done when conditions get crowded and the plant is ready for repotting.

Hymenocallis

Alstroemeria

### *Warm flowers*

Repot and water ismene and divide alstroemeria. The latter is actually a fleshy root, although it is usually listed in catalogues with bulbs. Tip the plant out of the pot and gently pull the root mass apart into three or four pieces. Put these divisions in 4 inch (100 mm) pots, and pot on as required to 8, 10 or 12 inch (200, 250 or 300 mm) pots as they grow.

Agapanthus can be forced this month by watering heavily with warm water and fertilizing, or it can be left alone and allowed to come more naturally into growth in the next month or two. It is best left pot-bound in 6 inch (150 mm) pots. Sow browallia and pot on December sown salpiglossis. In warm conditions, start up more corms of miniature gladiolus, if desired, and more gloxinias.

### *Cool flowers*

Sow stocks early this month to be in bloom for Mother's Day and sow sweet peas, French marigolds and annual asters. Annual aster seeds germinate irregularly and at a rate as low as 55%. January sowings can usually be potted on about six weeks after sowing, when the first set of true leaves is fully developed. French marigolds may be ready to transplant in just four weeks.

Use mild fish fertilizer at first, but graduate young plants eventually to 10-30-10 fertilizer. Give little if any fertilizer to nasturtiums, clarkia, candytuft, nemesia and godetia because they flower better on a poor diet. Geraniums also need very little fertilizer.

Continue to provide extra light as started for certain plants in January, and start lighting for stocks. Start the extra lighting for asters as soon as the seeds have germinated if early flowering is desired, or provide extra light for only half of the aster crop.

Gradually reduce watering and eliminate fertilizer for freesias, oxalis and other plants that start to fade after blooming is finished. Freesias are usually rested three months or more, but oxalis need only four to six weeks, either in their pots or in vermiculite inside paper bags (see Table OCT/NOV-1, page 390, for storage of bulbs).

### *Problems with forced bulbs*

Hopefully some of the potted spring flowering bulbs, such as daffodils and crocuses, are now in bloom indoors. Keep them watered and fertilized. Early blooming tulips will bloom in as little as four weeks if forced at this time. If they are forced in March and April they may bloom in three and a half or even three weeks. Bring ranunculus into growth by watering carefully. Start them off cool at 50°F (10°C) before exposing them to warmer temperatures. Early blooming Asiatic lilies, brought out of cold storage ten weeks before Mother's Day, should be in bloom or at least in heavy bud for the occasion.

Spring blooming bulbs sometimes do not perform as hoped. If there are no flowers at all, it could be that the bulbs were too small; that the pot was kept too warm or brought into bright sunlight too quickly; or that the soil was allowed to dry out. Deformed flowers indicate that the pot was not kept cool enough during storage. The storage temperature should be no more than 40°F (4°C). When flower buds form but fail to open, the usual cause is erratic watering. Overwatering will cause flowers to rot.

If bulbs of the same kind in the same pot flower at different times, either different sized bulbs were used at planting time, or one side of the pot received more light than the other. Turn pots occasionally to avoid the latter. Only one kind of bulb should be planted in each pot if simultaneous blooming is desired. Crocuses, daffodils and hyacinths planted in one pot will naturally bloom at different times.

Sometimes bulbs in cool storage send up long yellow shoots before we remember to bring them into the light. Do not despair! Often they can be salvaged by being grown at very cool temperatures after being brought into the light. This allows them to green up and become firm before they do much growing upwards. Next time, try to bring out pots when the shoots are 1 to 2 inches (2.5 to 5 cm) tall. Long, limp leaves may result if bulbs are grown at temperatures which are too warm or in insufficient light. Stunted leaves and flower shoots mean that the pot was not kept in storage long enough.

### *Forcing branches*

One of the pleasures of February is bringing in branches of flowering shrubs from outdoors and encouraging them to bloom early indoors. The proper term for this is "forcing," but that sounds rather harsh. The method is extraordinarily simple, taking two to four weeks, and is a pleasant, achievable project for children. Ideally, one would select branches from shrubs that would normally bloom in a month or two. It is quite feasible, though, to use shrubs that will not bloom for another three months or more. They will take an extra week or two to come into bloom, the flowers will not be as large, and there is a risk that the flower buds may shrivel up or fall off, but it is usually successful.

## Table FEB-5 Flowering Shrubs that can be Forced Indoors

| Plant | Best Times for Forcing | | | |
|---|---|---|---|---|
| | February | March | April | May |
| Apple | | x | x | |
| Azalea | | x | x | |
| Beautybush | | x | x | |
| Chinese Dogwood | x | x | | |
| Cornelian Cherry | x | x | | |
| Daphne | x | x | | |
| Deutzia | | | x | x |
| Flowering Cherry | x | x | | |
| Flowering Crabapple | | x | x | |
| Forsythia | x | x | x | |
| Hawthorn | | x | x | |
| Honeysuckle | | | x | x |
| Leucothoe | | | x | x |
| Lilac | | | x | x |
| Mock Orange | | | x | x |
| Mountain Laurel | | | x | x |
| Peach | | x | x | |
| Pear | | x | x | |
| Pieris | | x | x | |
| Plum | | x | x | |
| Pussy Willow | x | x | | |
| Quince, Flowering or Japanese | x | x | | |
| Rhododendrons | | | | |
| - early varieties | x | x | | |
| - later varieties | | x | x | |
| Saskatoon, Indian Pear, Serviceberry (*Amelanchier*) | x | x | | |
| Spirea - spring blooming types | | x | x | |
| Weigela | | | x | x |
| Witch Hazel | x | x | | |

Cut branches when there is a thaw or near noon on a mild day, taking pieces about 8 to 32 inches (20 to 80 cm) long. The length depends on the shrub—little pieces from short-stemmed shrubs, longer pieces from long-stemmed shrubs and trees. Scrape off the bark from the lower 3 inches (8 cm) of each branch, and cut several slits in the cut end. This step can be accomplished by hitting the end of the branch with a hammer, but do it gently without crushing the wood. Submerge the branches for twenty-four hours in a tub of water at 70°F (21°C). After the soaking, stand the stems upright in a container of cool water in a cool, semi-shaded place where the temperature is around 60°F (15°C).

In a few days, move the branches to a warmer, brighter place, but not into direct shunshine. Mist the branches once a day to help the buds swell, and change the water once a week. At each water change, cut 3/4 inch (2 cm) off the bottom of each stem. When the first flowers open, arrange the branches attractively and place in bright sunshine. To speed up the process, replace the water every day with warm water of 105°F (40°C) and mist the branches each day with warm water.

Some branches to try in the next month or two are Cornelian cherry, Chinese dogwood, flowering cherry, flowering or Japanese quince, forsythia, pussy willow, early rhododendrons, Indian pear (Saskatoon, serviceberry), daphne and witch hazel. There are other, later blooming shrubs that can be forced, but try them in March and April or even May. Shrubs that bloom after they leaf out, such as weigela, honeysuckle and deutzia, are harder to force than those that flower before they leaf out.

Forced branches require a daily mist.

Change water and cut stems weekly.

## *Outdoors*

### *Storm Damage*

Winter storms can be very hard on trees and shrubs. Ice and heavy snow often break branches and even trunks of trees. Sometimes it is possible to reduce the chance breakage by removing the weight of snow. This has to be done carefully, however, or more severe damage might result.

With evergreens, the trick is to lift the branches upwards. This is often all that is needed to shift the snow and relieve the pressure. It is all too easy to brush off the snow with a broom or shovel by stroking downwards, but this only increases the unnatural pressure already there, resulting in more breakage.

As soon as it becomes clear which branches are broken, cut them off without leaving a stub (see page 90). It is best to wait for a day when temperatures are above freezing to reduce the chance of the bark cracking. Regular pruning should be delayed until late February, March or April to prevent winter injury, but trees that ooze a lot of sap when pruned, such as maples, should be pruned in the autumn (see page 419).

Some damage is not as obvious as breakage and will not be visible until the buds begin to swell in the spring. Branches that have been encased in ice will sometimes die if the ice clings for a long time. Plants are pretty adaptable, though, and one can view winter damage as a case of natural pruning.

Month-by-Month

# March/April

- thin and transplant seedlings

- start compost pile

- set out cold frames and row covers
- remember to fertilize
- root hardwood cuttings
- check over fruit trees and soft fruits
- use dormant spray only if necessary

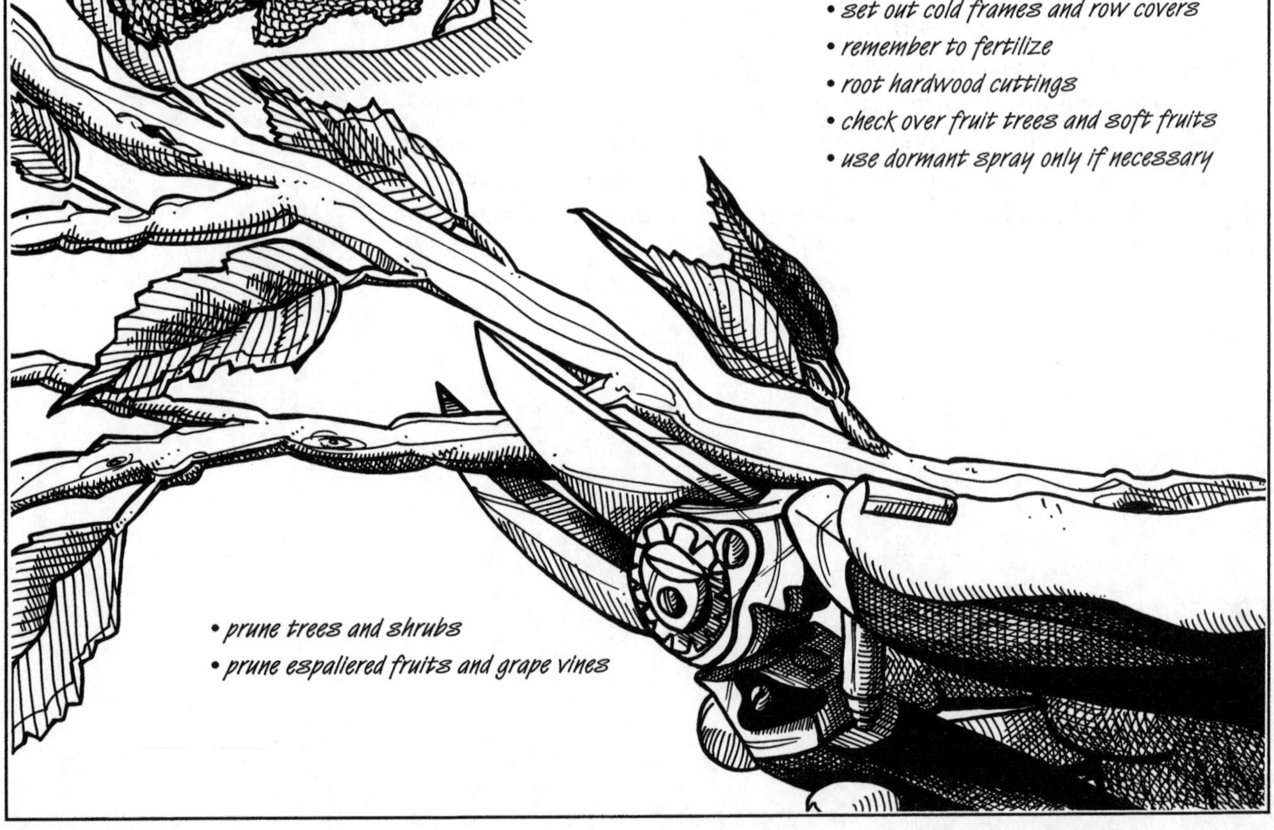

- prune trees and shrubs
- prune espaliered fruits and grape vines

# March/April

**Cold-Frame**
*Elaborate display case for showing off a gardener's collection of freeze-dried specimens.*

*Beard and McKie*

Many regions are still deep in snow in March and April, but on some days there is a hint of spring in the air. Gardeners start to look forward to planting the first seeds, although the risk of frost still has to be considered. Cold frames and other season extenders reduce some of the uncertainty. Watching outdoor plants for clues as to when to sow seeds and put out transplants will also lower the risk of losing flowers and vegetables to unseasonable weather. If the soil has warmed up enough for spring bulbs to come into bloom, for example, the soil is warm enough to do several things in the garden. At this point, various insects become active and woody plants start to come out of dormancy, indicating that pruning and insect management strategies can begin.

During mild spells, look around the lawn and garden to see where puddles of ice and water collect. These can be very hard on all kinds of plants. Clematis and chrysanthemums, for example, cannot tolerate water or ice over their roots, lilies and other bulbs will fail to show up in the spring, and lawn grasses can be killed. Such signs of poor drainage should be noted and remedied as soon as the soil is workable, either by improving the drainage or by raising the level of the soil in the problem areas.

This chapter suggests activities that can be carried out in March, April or even early May. Factors which influence timing include the location, how early or late spring occurs in a given year, the use of some form of crop protection, and how early you feel like doing certain things!

## Planting Schedule

### Season Extenders

Even though winter may still be hanging on, now is the time to decide which methods will be used to protect crops from cold weather if a longer gardening season is wanted. Cold frames, row covers, tunnels and other forms of protection are usually used in the vegetable garden, but they can also be used with flowers.

Cold frames are boxes usually made of wood with a glass or plastic lid (see pages 437-438). The top slopes upward and faces south or east-south-east so that sunlight can reach the plants and warm up the interior of the cold frame. At night, the temperature inside the cold frame remains a few degrees above the temperature outside. Some gardeners insulate cold frames or throw a blanket over the top at night to provide extra protection. Cold frames are best positioned out of the wind and against buildings, if possible. A variation on a cold frame that uses electricity to supply heat is the hot bed (see pages 348-349).

Cold frames can also be used in the summer to protect cuttings of shrubs and pieces of perennial flowers that are being propagated. They are placed in shade and help to keep the cuttings moist and protected from wind. In the winter they provide protection for young rooted cuttings, young perennials, or other vulnerable plants.

Row covers of plastic or agricultural fabric can serve the same function as cold frames in the spring and autumn. They can cover a large area more easily and more efficiently than cold frames, but do not offer as much protection from severe cold. If using clear plastic, a long length is laid along one or more rows in the garden, the sides are buried under soil, and the centre is supported by metal or plastic hoops to form a tunnel. For ventilation on sunny days, the sides of the tunnel can be lifted or the ends opened up, or small slits can be cut into the plastic on the leeward side for permanent ventilation.

Floating row covers of agricultural fabric allow light, moisture and air to pass through while raising the temperature inside. Generous quantities are laid over one or more rows and the sides held down with metal rods or soil. No supports are required because the fabric is so light that the plants simply lift it as they grow.

Protection for cuttings and tender transplants.

Putting protection around individual plants can also be beneficial. Tomatoes and other heat-loving plants are set out after the last expected frost, but there is always a chance of a late frost, or even just a run of chilly days and nights. Each plant can be covered with a clear plastic pop bottle or translucent vinegar jug with the bottom cut out. Originally such bell-shaped covers made of glass were called cloches. Gardeners who grow their tomatoes in cages sometimes wrap plastic around the sides, leaving the top open. A large metal can with the top and bottom cut out can also be put around each plant for the first few weeks of growth.

Specially designed plastic containers that hold water can also be put around each plant—the water helps to hold heat. They tend to be rather expensive for the area of coverage they provide. The same effect can be achieved using glass bottles filled with water and arranged in a circle around each plant. Some gardeners use season extenders in the autumn, rather than the spring, and are content to wait until the weather has warmed up before they even think about buying seeds and transplants.

### Vegetables

Many gardeners are surprised to discover how early vegetable planting can begin. Several leafy greens and members of the cabbage family actually grow better during cool weather than during the heat of summer. It is often possible to produce an early crop of these plants by starting seeds indoors about this time of year (see Table FEB-2, page 52), setting out the transplants under the protection of cold frames or row covers as soon as the ground is workable, and then seeding or transplanting the same crops later in the season to yield a late harvest in the autumn. This must be done with a certain amount of caution because a young plant's tolerance of cool temperatures and other shocks depends on its age.

Head lettuce grows best during cool weather and, as it takes about ninety days from sowing to form a head, it is often grown from transplants. It will bolt and send up a flower stalk before the plant can be harvested if it is started when the weather is warm. Other lettuces are ready for harvest much sooner and can be planted outside later than head lettuce, unless a very early crop is desired. Romaine or cos lettuce is ready in seventy to seventy-five days, butterhead types in fifty-five to seventy-five days, and looseleaf lettuces in forty to fifty days from sowing. The looseleaf types are best for early crops, or grow cos lettuce in close spacing and harvest it before it heads (see Table APR/MAY-1, page 124).

### Green Thumb Tip

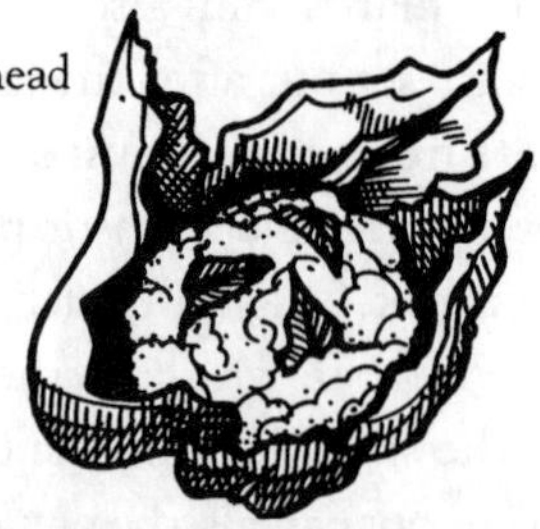
Bracteated head

Button head

All of the brassicas (such as cabbage, cauliflower, broccoli and Brussels sprouts) are sensitive to stress, particularly when they have five to eight leaves. At this stage they are more vulnerable to such stresses as sudden temperature fluctuations, root disturbance and drought. These situations occur readily at transplanting time—plants are said to suffer "transplant shock."

The results of stresses may not show up until weeks later. Cabbage, for example, will bolt instead of producing a proper head. Cauliflower may develop button heads (small and undeveloped heads), bracteated heads (where leaves grow out of the curds) or blindness (the death of the growing tip of the plant). This can best be avoided by planting out cauliflower when it is very young—otherwise wait until it has passed the eight leaf stage. Much depends on the weather! It also helps to start three batches of cauliflower, spaced a week or ten days apart, so that there is a variety of ages on hand when the right weather for transplanting arrives. Those transplants which are not used can be eaten as cooked greens.

Another way to avoid problems is to sow brassica seeds between the transplants when they are put outdoors, or rely entirely on direct seeding and not bother with transplants at all. Keep in mind, though, that brassicas do best during cool weather. If seeding directly outside in the spring, sow two to six weeks before the last expected frost date to allow enough time for plenty of growth before the warm weather arrives. Alternatively, or in addition, direct sow in the summer so that most of the growth occurs in the late summer and early autumn.

Some keen gardeners may start leaf lettuce, spinach, peas, mustard greens, collards, kale, endive, escarole, corn salad and turnips indoors this month to have young transplants ready for planting out in cold frames as soon as the crocuses are in bloom. Blooming could be as early as six weeks before the last expected frost date. Early greens planted in deep flats can be set out directly in cold frames without transplanting. Seeds can also be planted directly outdoors in cold frames at the same time that transplants are set out.

As the winter supply of potatoes starts to dwindle, select sets for the next crop. If there has been even a hint of disease problems in previous potato crops it is better to purchase potato sets certified free of disease.

Purchased potato sets are sometimes small, weighing 1.5 ounces (40 g) or less and having only one or two eyes per set. These are fine if they are planted fairly close together after the soil is warm (see Table APR/MAY-1, page 124). If using your own potatoes, select those weighing 2 to 3 ounces (50 to 80 g, peewee to large egg size). Whole potatoes, even on the small side, are preferable to cut sets as there will be more "eyes" per volume of potato and it is from the "eyes" that new plants arise. Too many plants will arise from each tuber if large sets are used and crowded tubers will result, forcing some to the surface—these will turn green without vigilant hilling. Small potatoes planted moderately close together, an even distance apart, will produce a high yield without any hilling required.

To prevent crowding cut potato sets before planting.

### Herbs

Many perennial herbs should have been started by now. They can still be started this month, the only concern is that they must have a good two or three months of growing outside in the summer before the ground freezes. Starting herbs early produces transplants that can be set outside earlier because they are larger—this gives them more time outside before their first winter. Chives and garlic chives can be seeded three or four to a cell or small pot. At transplanting time these are set out in clumps without dividing them. Parsley is slow to germinate and resents transplanting; individual pots are best for it. Table FEB-3 (page 54) gives suggested starting dates for annual and perennial herbs.

### Flowers

#### Seeding

There is a great deal of leeway in the starting time for flowers. Perennials should be seeded by now, although a later start is still all right, especially as some ordered seeds do not arrive by mail until this month! They will probably not flower during their first year anyway, so the main goal is to ensure they are big enough to survive their first winter. If worst comes to worst, small plants can be overwintered in cold frames.

If perennial seeds that were planted earlier still have not germinated, try putting them in the refrigerator for a week or two. Alternatively, cover the flats with plastic and put them outdoors, in a location protected from wind and direct sunshine, where they will freeze and thaw repeatedly. This will often encourage reluctant seeds to germinate and is particularly helpful with primroses.

If, on the other hand, seeds have been in cool conditions, try providing some extra heat for a couple of weeks and see if that helps. Ideally, each seed packet should give specific instructions for breaking dormancy (and see February, pages 48-49).

There are many annual flowers that can be started this month (see Table

#### Focus on Plants

Florence fennel has very particular starting dates—either indoors between March 15 and April 15 in long or short season areas, or outdoors after June 21 in long season areas. Florence fennel forms a bulbous swelling at the base of the plant which is very sensitive to day length. If planted between April 15 and June 21, fennel goes to flower in response to the long days and fails to form a "bulb."

FEB-4, page 56). Unless large quantities are needed, sow only part of each package and store the remainder under cool, dry conditions for next year.

Give slow seeds time to germinate before transplanting other seedlings in the same lot. Bells-of-Ireland, for example, will germinate irregularly over a period of five weeks. Others, such as globe amaranth, may have germination rates as low as 40%. Keep in mind that seeds that are sown too thickly are more prone to damping off, particularly those of coleus. Do not be daunted by problems the first time or two that a new kind of seed is tried. Much of the satisfaction in gardening is learning from experience.

### Green Thumb Tip

Large tubers of various plants can be divided. Cut through the tuber when the leaf buds are barely visible, before the roots form. Dust the fresh cuts with sulphur and let the cut surfaces air dry for two days, then place each half in damp peat moss and continue the growing and potting on process.

## Starting tender "bulbs"

Tender perennial flowers carried through the winter indoors as plants, such as geraniums and fuchsias, should have been started into growth and cuttings made in February or early March. Tender perennials carried over as tubers, corms, bulbs and rhizomes, however, can be started indoors later, usually in March or April or about six to eight weeks before the last expected frost date. This will give them an early start in the warmth they need and will lead to earlier flowering in the garden when they are finally planted outdoors. It is particularly important to start them early in short season areas where there is a chance that the first frosts of autumn will kill them before they have had a chance to bloom. It is also important where the soil stays cool all summer long; the bulbs may be better grown in pots rather than put in the ground in these conditions. In long season areas and where summers are really warm, tender bulbs can be planted directly in the garden after the danger of frost is past. They are good candidates for being encouraged with pre-warmed soil outdoors (see pages 117-118).

Plants usually grown in pots are started first. Caladium and tuberous begonia prefer soil temperatures of 70 to 80°F (21 to 27°C), although as low as 60°F (15°C) may suffice. They are best started in damp, but not wet, peat moss. Begonia tubers are planted with the hollow side up and covered with 1/2 inch (1 to 2 cm) of damp peat moss. It is usually clear which side of the tuber is up, but if in doubt, lift the tuber every few days to check for roots (or shoots!) on the underside. When new growth is well established, transplant the tubers to individual 4 inch (100 mm) pots. They can be planted directly in the ground, or transplanted to larger pots or tubs and moved outdoors, in early summer. Some gardeners use a peat-based potting soil and plant the tubers at their final depth right at the beginning to avoid later potting on. Care must be taken, however, that the tubers do not rot.

If growing pendulous types of "bulbs" for hanging baskets, the tip of the first shoot can be removed with a sharp knife while it is still very small to encourage branching. Pot on the tubers when the new leaves are growing well, planting one per 9 inch (225 mm) basket or three per 15 inch (375 mm) basket in a peat-based potting soil. Wire baskets can be used; line them with moist sphagnum moss packed with 1¼ inch (3 cm) thick, or with plastic that has slits cut into it, and fill them with potting soil.

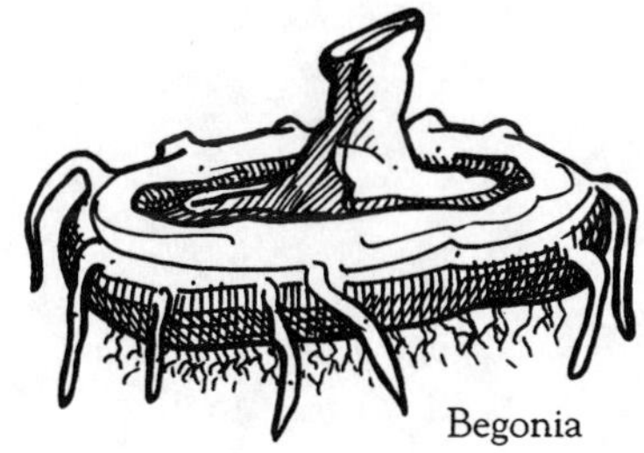

Begonia

Regular begonias for potting or planting directly in the garden should be potted on individually into a peat-based potting soil in 5 inch (125 mm) pots, or plant three per 8 to 10 inch (200 to 250 mm) pot. When arranging them, it may be useful to keep in mind that the flowers face in the same direction as the leaves point.

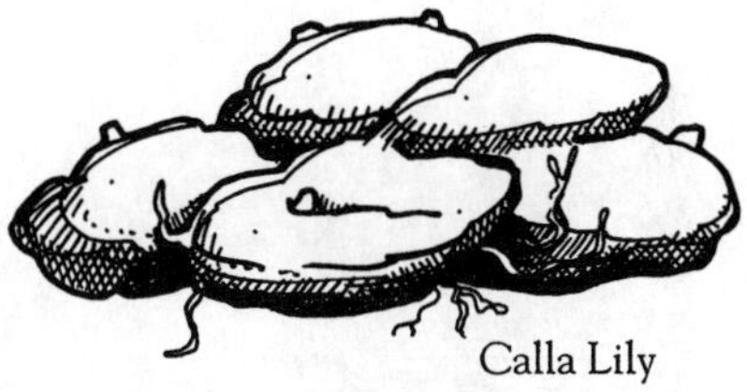

Calla Lily

Caladium is known for its beautifully mottled leaves of pink, red, cream and green. It is prone to rot when first started into growth, so warmth is absolutely essential. To reduce the risk of rot, simply lay the tubers, knobby side up, on top of the moist peat moss without covering them. Provide bottom heat if warm air temperatures cannot be maintained, and pot on as for regular begonias once leaf growth is well established.

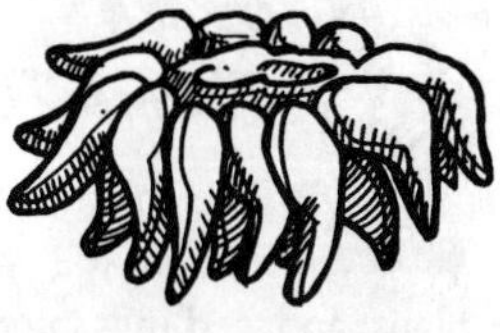

Ranunculus

Cannas can be started at the same time and in the same way as begonias, or they can be planted directly into pots of sandy loam. Divide the tubers so that each division has several good buds or "eyes." Achimenes are superb container plants, either in pots or hanging baskets. They can be planted indoors soon (see page 85 for starting instructions) and make lovely plants, indoors or out. Lily-of-the-Nile (Agapanthus) is also started six to eight weeks before the last expected frost, often directly in the pot it will be growing in outdoors. It can also be planted directly in the garden after an early start indoors, but not until all danger of frost is past. Treat calla lily (*Zantedeschia*) the same way. Table MAR/APR- 2, page 86, gives suggested pot sizes for various tender bulbs.

Anemone

On most corms and bulbs the place where the roots grow is moderately obvious; place that side downwards when planting. Ranunculus should be soaked for three or four hours before it is planted with the claws pointing downwards. Gloriosa is planted horizontally. Anemone tubers are so knobbly that it is often difficult to tell which way is up. There is usually a ring visible on the upper side from which the leaves emerge. If in doubt, plant them on their sides. It is also helpful to soak them overnight before planting. They swell up enormously and sometimes it is possible at this point to see where the leaves were located. After the initial soaking, put them in a bowl for about twenty minutes in water with a few drops of bleach. This seems to reduce the likelihood of their rotting.

Dahlias can be started into growth about one month before the last frost date (usually in May), but because they are so large they are usually planted directly outdoors once the soil has warmed up. This is a good time, however, to check over stored tubers for any signs of rotting or drying out. When dividing the clumps, make sure each tuber is attached to a piece of stem with a growing bud.

Freesias and gladioli can be started indoors eight weeks before the last expected frost date if they are grown in pots, but wait until four weeks before the last frost date if they are to be transplanted eventually to open ground. If they are started now they will be too big for transplanting. The same applies to acidanthera, tuberose, galtonia, amaryllis, montbretia (crocosmia), tigridia, zephyranthes, ranunculus, anemone, oxalis and other bulbs, corms, rhizomes and roots in Table MAR/APR-2 (page 86). In long season areas there will probably be enough time for these to grow and flower without an early start indoors. In short season areas, however, it is probably wise to give them a head start. Use containers at least 5 inches (12.5 cm) deep, filled with a potting soil that drains well or that has had extra perlite or vermiculite added to it. Alternatively, pre-warm the soil if planting directly outdoors (see page 117).

Some "bulbs" are also available as seeds; these should be started as soon as they are received in the mail (see Table JAN-4, page 29).

## Care of Seedlings and Young Plants

### Temperature and Light

Remember that tender bulbs start into growth best at 70 to 80°F (21 to 27°C). The temperature can be somewhat cooler after growth is established. Try to provide fourteen hours of light. When new growth is visible on various "bulbs," gradually increase the amount of moisture, but be careful not to overwater as this can cause bulbs to rot. Fertilization with 20-20-20 or 30-10-10 formulation can begin when new growth is well established.

When seedlings have emerged, keep them moist by placing the flats or pots in tepid water long enough for the medium to take up moisture, and then let them drain. Provide good ventilation, but avoid chilly blasts of air. Many seeds need warmth to germinate, but thereafter grow better under cool conditions. Asparagus, potted on into 3 inch (75 mm) pots, grows best at

> **Green Thumb Tip**
>
> Too much warmth can make young plants and seedlings spindly. A natural temperature regime for plants is warm days and cool nights, which is just fine as long as the difference is not extreme. Research has shown, however, that stockier seedlings result if nights are warmer than days (Bleasedale, Salter and others, 1991). This is often the situation where a wood stove is used only in the evenings. Plants are also more vigorous under these conditions and have better branching. Spindly plants may also be caused by insufficient light. Keep them in full light for twelve to fourteen hours a day.

60°F (15°C). Celery seedlings should be misted to maintain humidity and grown above 55°F (12°C) or they will bolt. Parsley, germinating best at 72°F (23°C), grows very well at quite cool temperatures, and sweet peas should be grown as cool as is possible without freezing them.

If a group of seedlings suddenly keels over at the soil line, the likely problem is damping off disease. Reread pages 20 and 50 to help figure out what went wrong. Seedlings that are still okay should be transplanted to individual containers to reduce the spread of the disease.

## Pinching, Transplanting and Fertilizing

When vegetable, herb and flower seedlings have one or two sets of true leaves they will need thinning or transplanting, unless they are already in spacious quarters. (The first leaves that appear on seedlings are the cotyledons; the true leaves, often quite different in appearance, form the next set of leaves). If the aim is to grow several seedlings in one pot—not for transplanting—take a pair of scissors and cut out any extras.

Cut out the weak and late emerging seedlings of vegetables and herbs, but leave some of the late emerging seedlings of mixed colour flowers. They may be a different colour from the others. Some flower seedlings can be pinched for bushiness when they are 3 to 4 inches (8 to 10 cm) tall, whereas others are best left alone (see Table FEB-4, page 56). Try to complete all pinching six weeks before the plants go outside, as each pinching delays flowering.

When transplanting, water the plants several hours ahead of time. Dig up a clump of seedlings and gently pull them apart. Handle them by their leaves, rather than their stems, to reduce the risk of damping off disease. Use a peat-based potting mix or other general purpose potting soil and moisten it thoroughly (but do not make it sopping wet). Poke a hole in the medium for each seedling, drop the seedling into place, and gently press the medium around it. Water it well with a weak mixture of tepid water and fish fertilizer.

Gradually increase the concentration of fertilizer given to seedlings until the regular strength is reached. After transplanting flowers and vegetables that produce fruits (tomatoes, eggplants, peppers, cucumbers, zucchini, melons, summer and winter squashes), fertilize them three times, a week apart, with 10-52-70 or another high phosphorous and potassium fertilizer (see Fertilizer Fever, page 163). Use an even balance formulation, such as 20-20-20 for vegetables and herbs and something like 10-30-10 for flowers, in further applications.

### Green Thumb Tip

Many plants with the growing point at the tip of the stem, such as tomatoes, brassicas and clarkia, can be buried up to their bottom leaves. This is a big help if the seedlings are spindly, but be sure not to bury any leaves when transplanting. Remove the lowest pair of leaves on tomatoes and plant them up to the base of the next pair of leaves so that rooting can occur along the stem.

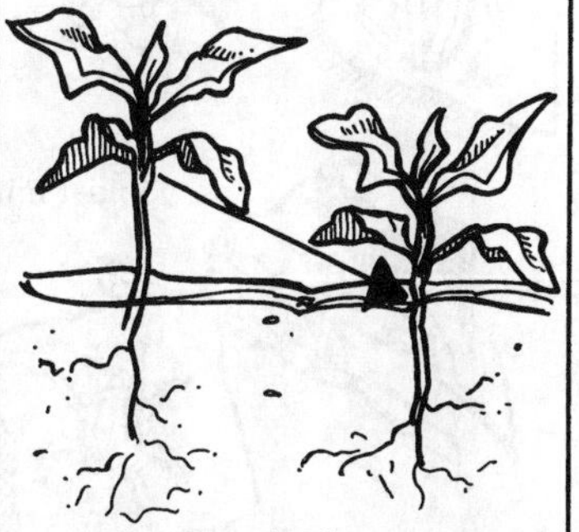

Plants with the growing point at the base of the plant in the centre of a rosette of leaves, such as lettuce, columbine and petunia, resent having the base of their leaves buried. Be particularly careful to replant them at the same level so that the growing point does not rot.

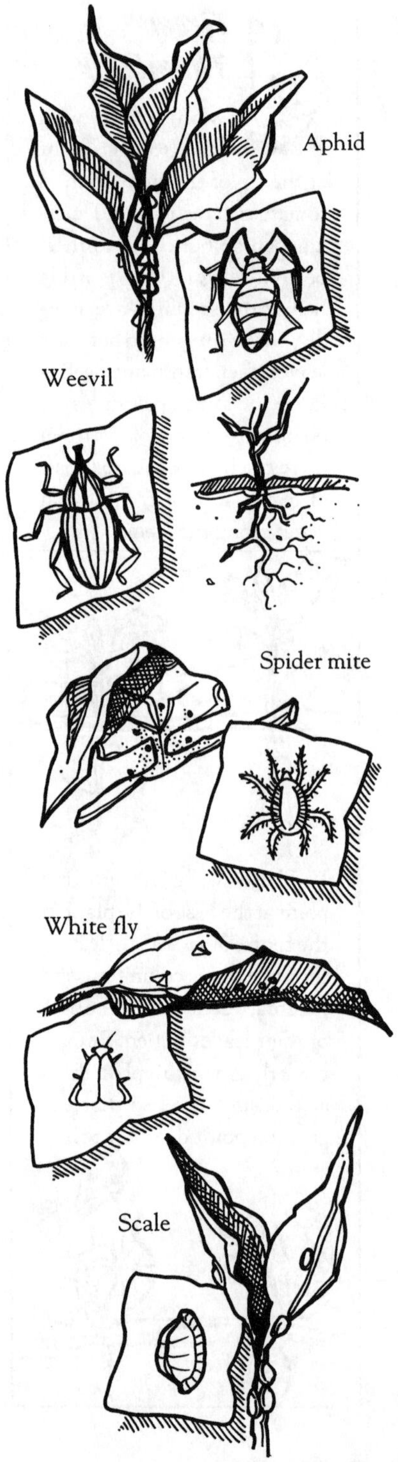


## *Indoor Gardening*

For those who want to grow vegetables, herbs and flowers indoors, there is plenty to do this month. Others will curtail their indoor gardening to focus on getting ready for spring outdoors.

As the days get longer, overheating can be a problem unless plants are grown under lights away from direct sunlight. Make sure ventilation is good and water more frequently as the soil dries out more quickly. Misting the entire greenhouse will also cool things off. Do not do this on cloudy days, however, because fungal problems may develop.

## *Indoor Plant Pests*

March seems to be the time when aphids get busy in the greenhouse. Since there are no ladybird beetles available yet to bring in from outdoors, it may be advisable to look into other biological methods of control—unless you have managed to establish an overwintering population of these beetles in the greenhouse or sunroom. Simply washing off aphids with a strong spray of water is often sufficient control, or use insecticidal soap if the problem has got out of hand. The trick is to keep a close eye on things, take action immediately, and keep plants healthy with good air circulation and regular fertilizing and watering.

Tiny black flies around plants are fungus gnats. These are rarely a problem, but sometimes their larvae will destroy the roots of young seedlings. Encouraging a resident population of spiders seems to provide good control. If the gnats are a severe problem, control them by pouring an insecticidal soap solution through the potting soil until it runs out the bottom. Rinse with clear water after half an hour or so.

Weevils can become a problem later in the season, the adults taking great notches out of leaves and the grubs devouring roots, bulbs and tubers. They are snout-nosed black creatures that play dead when disturbed and are hard to find during the day. When a ceiling light is turned on at dusk they will congregate on the ceiling—squash them with a long pole. They can also be found under pots in the morning and dealt with then. Clean up all debris.

Leaves will take on a stippled, yellow appearance when spider mites are present, and there may be fine webs in the crotches of branches. The aim is to keep conditions cool and moist as populations build up fastest under warm, dry conditions. They reproduce every eight days at a temperature of 86°F (30°C), every fourteen days at 70°F (21°C), and only once every forty

## Table MAR/APR-1 Management of Common Greenhouse Pests

| Insect | Description and Symptoms | Management |
|---|---|---|
| aphid | soft-bodied; leaves deformed, sticky | wipe off; soap once a week 4 times; ladybird beetles; yellow sticky traps |
| fungus gnat | tiny black flies | spiders; drench soil with soap, rinse |
| mealy bug | white fluff; leaves wilt, yellow and fall off | wipe off; alcohol or soap every 5 days for 1 month |
| scale | brown discs; leaves yellow and sticky | wipe off with damp cloth every week |
| spider mite | miniscule; leaves stippled yellow, white webbing, leaves fall | soap 3 to 4 times at 7 to 10 day intervals; keep air cool and moist |
| weevil | adults black snouted; bites out of leaves | hand pick, clean up debris |
| | larvae grub like; eat roots, bulbs | repot in clean soil |
| whitefly | tiny, moth-like; leaves turn yellow and drop | vacuum in evening; yellow sticky traps; pyrethrum, rotenone or soap once a week for 5 weeks |

alcohol = 70% rubbing alcohol (isopropyl); spray as mist; some plants react badly so do small trial first

soap = insecticidal soap

days at 55ºF (12ºC). If the situation is bad, spray plants on all surfaces, including the underside of leaves and in crotches, with insecticidal soap (see page 194). Spray three or four times at seven to ten day intervals. Rinse off the soap after an hour to avoid a buildup of soap on the leaves.

Whiteflies are a serious problem. These tiny, white, moth-like insects on the underside of leaves will fly up when disturbed. They suck sap out of leaves and deposit sticky honeydew. Leaves may turn yellow and drop off. Spray every three days with pyrethrum, insecticidal soap or 70% isopropyl (rubbing) alcohol. Some plants react badly to alcohol, so test a small area first. Alternate the sprays, spray in the evening when the insects are less active, and keep up the spraying for one month. Also try vacuuming up the insects every evening for one month, and hang yellow boards smeared with Tanglefoot nearby (see page 106 for a homemade version of Tanglefoot).

Small brown discs on the underside of leaves and veins and along the stems are scale and must be wiped off with a damp cloth. Badly infested plants turn yellow and sticky with honeydew; getting rid of the scale is nearly impossible at that stage. Be sure to wipe off the immobile adults regularly for a month or more (as egg stages continue to reach adulthood) until there are none left.

An insect that may be mistaken for a disease by the novice gardener is mealy bug. It is a small pest covered with white, cottony fluff; unlike a disease, it can be wiped off cleanly. Use a damp cloth to remove them, and spray with insecticidal soap every five days for a month. A severe attack can lead to wilting, yellowing and leaf drop, so be vigilant.

For long-term control of whiteflies, spider mites and other greenhouse pests, consider purchasing biological controls. When summer comes, collect a couple of dozen ladybird beetles to put in the greenhouse for aphid control. Rather than releasing all of them immediately, keep a dozen or more in a jar with their favourite leaves to encourage mating and egg-laying.

## Vegetables and Herbs

Greens and herbs that were not started in February can be sown this month. A repeat sowing of kohlrabi, radish, looseleaf and butterhead lettuce is a good idea to ensure a continuous, fresh supply. If spinach, edible-podded peas, mustard greens and other greens are not being started for the outdoor garden (see Table FEB-2, page 52), you may want to seed more for the indoor garden this month. Mustard greens are ready for a light cutting two to three weeks after sowing. Continue to sow a little cress every two weeks.

Late in March start melons, cucumbers and summer squashes (including zucchini). Melons and summer squashes need 12 inch (300 mm) pots, but cucumbers can get by in 8 to 10 inch (200 to 250 mm) pots. Vining plants can be grown in pairs in 12 inch (300 mm) pots. Tomatoes that were started last month will need potting on. As soon as growth is well established after transplanting, fertilize with 10-52-70 once a week for three weeks and then revert to 20-20-20. Do the same for other fruiting plants such as peppers, eggplants, melons and cucumbers. Continue to fertilize all other plants every two weeks with 20-20-20.

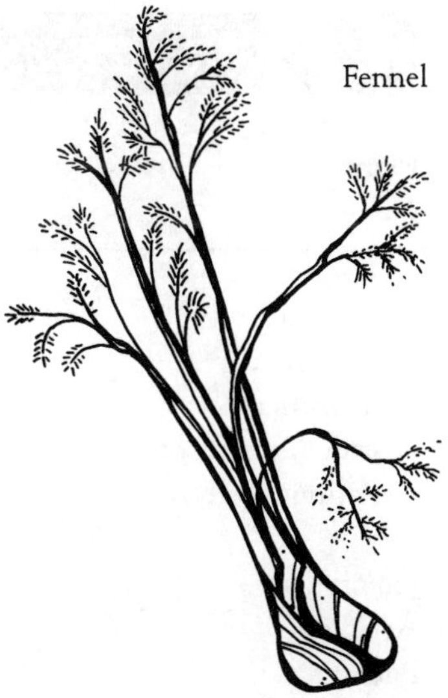

Fennel

Potatoes can be started from tubers for an early taste of "new" potatoes. Also, try Florence fennel (seeded between March 15 and April 15) for an exotic vegetable. Plant several seeds in a pot and then thin them because they tend to bolt if stressed by transplanting. Use deep pots and grow one plant per 6 inch (150 mm) pot or three per 12 inch (300 mm) pot. The bulbs will not be as large and succulent as the ones grown outdoors, but the leaves and stalks can be used (see Table AUG-3, page 302). Seed herbs thickly (except for basil which is prone to damping off disease) so that there are thinnings to use early on.

### *Warm Flowers*

Pot on begonias, gloxinias, geraniums and other seedlings into 2 ¼ inch (60 mm) pots. Geraniums and other plants started from cuttings can be potted in individual pots once rooting is clearly established. Pinch geraniums and fuchsias to encourage branching until six weeks before they will be set out.

Achimenes (Cupid's Bower or Magic Flower) is a relative of African violets but seems to be easier to grow under less than ideal conditions and comes in a wider range of colours. Place the rhizomes about 1 inch (2.5 cm) apart for a full look. The size of pot will depend on the number of rhizomes available; nine to sixteen rhizomes, for example, fit comfortably into a 5 to 7 inch (125 to 175 mm) pot. The plants have a lax shape and can be used either for regular pots or for hanging baskets. Cover the rhizomes with about 1 inch (2.5 cm) of a peat-based potting mix. Keep them moist at all times (but not wet) as drying out will induce dormancy. Place them in bright, indirect light in humid conditions, but avoid wetting the leaves. Pinch the new growth when 3 inches (8 cm) tall and watch for aphids.

Various tender bulbs can be planted as soon as purchased, either for indoor enjoyment or as potted plants outdoors in the summer. When ordered through the mail they often do not arrive until well into spring, but

## Table MAR/APR-2 Pot Sizes and Bench or Garden Spacing for Tender Bulbs

| Plant Name | In Garden or Bench: Planting Distance Depth x Apart inches(cm) | In Pots: Number of Plants per Pot Size inches (mm) |
|---|---|---|
| Achimenes | best in pots or hanging baskets | any size pot 1 inch (2.5 cm) apart |
| Acidanthera | 4-8 x 6(10-20 x 15) | 5-6 per 6(150) |
| Agapanthus* | | 1 per 6-12(150-300) |
| Alstroemeria (root) (Peruvian Lily) | 6-8 x 12(15-20 x 30) | 1 per 4-12(100-300) depending on size of root division |
| Amaryllis | ⅓ of bulb above soil x 12(30) | 1 per 5-6(125-150) |
| Anemone | 3-4 x 4(8-10 x 10) | 6 per 6(150) |
| Babiana | | 7-8 per 6(150) |
| Begonia, Tuberous | 1-2 x 8-16(2.5-5 x 20-40) | 1 per 5(125) or 3 per 8-10(200-250) in hanging baskets 1 per 9(225) or 3 per 15(375) |
| Caladium | 1-2 x 8-12(2.5-5 x 20-30) | 2-3 per 8(200) |
| Calla Lily (*Zantedeschia*) | 3-4 x 12-24(8-10 x 30-60) | 1 per 5-7(125-175) |
| Canna | 1-2 x 8-16(2.5-5 x 20-40) | 1 per 6(150) or 3 per 10-12(250-300) |
| Crinum | ½ of bulb above soil x 12(30) | 1 per pot slightly larger than bulb |
| Crocosmia | 2-3 x 3(5-8 x 8) | 5-6 per 6(150) |
| Dahlia | 6 x 12, 7 x 24, 8 x 36 (15 x 30, 18 x 60, 20 x 90) close spacing for small tubers | 1 per pot generously larger than tuber |
| Elephant's Ear | 4 x 60(10 x 150) | 1 per large tub |
| Eucharis (Amazon Lily) | | 1 per 5(125) or 3-4 per 8(200) |
| Eucomis(Pineapple Lily)* | 4-5(10-12) x nearly touching | 1 per 4-6(100-150) |
| Freesia | 2 x 2-4(5 x 5-10) | 6-8 per 5(125) |
| Galtonia (Cape or Summer Hyacinth) | 6-7 x 15(15-18 x 38) | |
| Gladiolus, Standard | 4-8 x 6-8(10-20 x 15-20) | 3 per 10(250) |
| Miniature | 3-6 x 3-4(8-15 x 8-10) | 5-6 per 6(150) |
| Gloriosa (Glory Lily) | 2-3 x 8-10(5-8 x 20-25) | 1 per 6(150) or 3 per 8(200) |
| Gloxinia | | 1 per pot 3 inches (80) wider than bulb |
| Haemanthus* | bulb slightly above soil x 12(30) | 1 per pot 2 inches (50) wider than bulb |
| Incarvillea (Hardy Gloxinia) | 3-5 x 12-15(8-12 x 30-38) | 1 per 6-7(150-175) |
| Iris, Dutch | 2 x 2(5 x 5) | 5-6 per 6(150) |

| Plant Name | In Garden or Bench: Planting Distance Depth x Apart inches(cm) | In Pots: Number of Plants per Pot Size inches(mm) |
|---|---|---|
| Ismene (*Hymenocallis*) | | |
| (Spider Lily) | 3-5 x 12-15(8-12 x 30-38) | 1 per 5-7(125-175)depending on bulb size |
| Ixia (Corn Lily) | 2-3 x 3-4(5-8 x 8-10) | 5-6 per 5(125) |
| Lachenalia (Cape Cowslip) | 1 inch(2.5 cm) apart, any size | |
| Lilies ** | | |
| - *candidum* | 1 x 12(2.5 x 30) | 1 per 4(100) |
| - small bulbs | 3-4 x 12(8-10 x 30) | 1 per 3 1/2(90) or 3 per 5(125) |
| (*canadense*, *cernuum*, *concolor*, *dauricum*, *pumilum*, Asiatics) | | |
| - medium bulbs | 4-6 x 15(10-15 x 38) | 1 per 4(100) or 3 per 6(150) |
| (*amabile*, *callosum*, *martagon*, *hansonii*, *regale*, *tsingtauense*, *davidii*, trumpets) | | |
| - large bulbs | 6-8 x 18(15-20 x 45) | 1 per 5(125) or 3 per 8(200) |
| (*auratum*, *speciosum*, *tigrinum*, *henryi*, orientals) | | |
| Lycoris (Japanese Spider Lily)* | bulb tip showing x 8(20) | 1 per 6-7(150-175) |
| Mirabilis | 18 x 18 (45 x 45) | 1 per 12(300) |
| Nerine (Guernsey Lily) | | 1 per 4(100) or 2-3 per 5-6(125-150) |
| Oxalis | 2-3 x 4-5(5-8 x 10-12) | 1 per 3-4(75-100) pot, 3-4 per 5(125) pot or 5-6 per 8(200) basket |
| Ranunculus (Persian Buttercup) | 2 x 4(5 x 10) | 3-4 per 6(150) |
| Sparaxis (Harlequin or Wandflower) | 4 x 4(10 x 10) | any size pot, 2-3 inches (5-8 cm) apart |
| Sprekelia | 3-4 x 8(8-10 x 20) | |
| Tigridia (Tiger Flower) | 4 x 4-8(10 x 10-20) | 3-4 per 8(200) |
| Tuberose (Polyanthes) | 3 x 6-8(8 x 15-20) | 3 per 6(150) |
| Vallota* (Scarborough Lily) | bulb tip showing x nearly touching | as small a pot as bulbs will fit in, 1 per 6-10(150-250) |
| Zephyranthes (Fairy Lilies) | 1-2 x 3(2.5-5 x 8) | 4-5 per 6(150) or 12-14 per 10(250) |

Planting Depth = top of bulb to soil surface (plant more shallowly in clay soils and deeper in sandy soils)
N.B. Plant bulbs more shallowly in pots than in the garden or bench to provide maximum space for root development.

* blooms best if pot-bound; do not repot unless absolutely necessary
** lilies vary in hardiness according to type (see page 242)

## Table MAR/APR-3 Growing Conditions for Tender Bulbs

### Key

c = grow at 40 to 55ºF (4 to 12ºC)
m = grow at 50 to 65ºF (10 to 18ºC)
w = grow at 60 to 75ºF (15 to 24ºC)
@ = blooms best if pot-bound
# = lilies vary in hardiness according to climatic zone
(*) = full sun with shade at midday
* = 8 hours or more sun (if grown indoors provide shade at midday)
+ = 4 hours or more sun
- = less than 4 hours sun
M = keep moist at all times but not wet
A = average moisture and good drainage
D = some dryness tolerated, otherwise moist

light, organic = soil, leaf mould and sand (or perlite)
light, rich = soil, manure and sand (or perlite)
rich, organic = soil, leaf mould and manure
non-acidic = add lime
acidic = use peat moss instead of leaf mould; or water with 1 teaspoon (15 ml) of vinegar per quart (1.1 l) of water once every two weeks during regular watering; or use fertilizer for acid-loving plants

| Growing Temp. | Plant | Sun | Moisture and Soil |
|---|---|---|---|
| w | Achimenes | + | M; light, organic |
| c | Acidanthera | * + | A; rich, organic |
| c | @ Agapanthus | * + | M; rich, organic |
| c,m | Alstroemeria (Peruvian Lily) | * + | M; light, rich |
| m | Amaryllis | * | A; light, organic |
| c | Anemone | * + | M; light, organic, non-acidic |
| c | Babiana | * | A; light |
| w | Begonia, Tuberous | + | M; light, organic |
| w | Caladium | + - | M; rich, organic |
| w | Calla Lily | (*)+ | M; rich, organic |
| m | Canna | * | M; light |
| m | Crinum | (*)+ | M; light, organic, acidic |
| c | Crocosmia | * + | A; light, organic |
| c | Dahlia | * + | A; light, rich |
| w | Elephant's Ear | (*)+ | M; rich, organic |
| w | Eucharis (Amazon Lily) | + | M; light, organic, non-acidic |
| c | @ Eucomis (Pineapple Lily) | * | A; light, organic |
| c | Freesia | (*) | A; light, organic |
| m | Galtonia (Cape or Summer Hyacinth) | * | A; light, organic, acidic |
| m | Gladiolus | * | A; light, organic |
| w | Gloriosa (Glory Lily) | * + | A; rich, organic |
| w | Gloxinia | + | M; light, organic |
| w | @ Haemanthus | (*)+ | A; light, organic |
| c | Incarvillea (Hardy Gloxinia) | * + | A; light, rich |
| c | Iris, Dutch | * | A; light |
| w | Ismene (*Hymenocallis*) (Spider Lily) | * + | M; rich, organic, acidic |
| c | Ixia | * | A; light |
| c | Lachenalia (Cape Cowslip) | * | M; light, rich |
| c,m | # Lily | * + | A; light, organic |
| m | @ Lycoris | * | A; light, organic, non-acidic |
| m | Mirabilis | * | A; light, rich |
| c | Nerine (Guernsey Lily) | * + | M; light, organic |
| c,m | Oxalis | * + | A; light, acidic |
| c | Ranunculus (Persian Buttercup) | * | A; light, organic |
| c | Sparaxis (Harlequin or WandFlower) | * | A; light |
| m | Sprekelia | * | D; light, organic |
| m | Tigridia (Tiger Flower) | (*) | M; light, organic |
| w | Tuberose (Polyanthes) | * | M; light, organic |
| m | @ Vallota (Scarborough Lily) | + | A; light, rich |
| m | Zephyranthes (Fairy Lilies) | * | D; light, organic |

in subsequent years they can be started into growth sooner for indoor use if temperatures are warm enough (see Table MAR/APR-3).

More lilies (such as *L. candidum*, *L. regale* and Asiatic) should be brought out of cold storage. Keep watering and fertilizing Easter and other lilies, place them in bright light but out of direct sunlight and mist them occasionally. Remove the anthers (which bear the yellow pollen) to prevent the flowers from setting seed. This measure, and keeping the plants cool, helps the flowers last longer. Remove individual blossoms as they fade to keep the plant looking trim. Lily-of-the-valley can be brought out of cold storage into warmth and light to bloom in time for Easter. They will bloom in three weeks if grown at 65 to 70°F (18 to 21°C), but will take up to six weeks if grown cooler.

*Primula sinensis*

Bring out any spring blooming bulbs that are still in storage. Continue watering and fertilizing those that are to be planted in the garden eventually, but throw out all tulips except the species tulips. Most hybrid tulips will not establish themselves in the garden after being forced in pots indoors, but the small species seem to thrive.

Roses should now be kept at a daytime temperature of 60°F (17°C). This increase in temperature occurs naturally in a greenhouse as the days get longer and warmer. On some days the greenhouse may even have to be ventilated to cool things off a bit; too much warmth will result in weak, sappy growth.

*Primula elatior*

The florists' hydrangea, *H. macrophylla*, can be grown outdoors in zone 6. The pink flowers will come out blue in future years when grown in acidic soils. Keep it watered and fertilized until outdoor shrubs are in leaf, then harden it off (gradually expose it to outdoor temperatures; see Preventive Measure, page 120) and plant it outside.

## *Cool Flowers*

In a cool greenhouse (around 60°F/15°C), sow primroses such as *Primula sinensis*, *P. elatior* and *P. obconica*. They will not germinate if the temperature is higher than 65°F (18°C). Sometimes a greater germination rate is achieved if the seeds are planted and then exposed to outdoor temperatures to break dormancy (see pages 48-49). Most primroses will not come into bloom until the autumn, so plant annual asters and snapdragons if summer blooms are wanted ahead of those in the outdoor garden.

*Primula obconica*

Pinch and pot up the seedlings that were sown a month or two ago. Use fish fertilizer or quarter strength fertilizer for a couple of weeks after the first true leaves have developed, then gradually increase to full strength. Use 10-30-10 every two to four weeks until the plants are in bud, and then use 20-20-20.

More cuttings can be started (see page 61 for the method) from such flowers as marguerite (Boston yellow daisy), and a variety of shrubs can have branches forced into bloom indoors (see Table FEB-5, page 69).

## Fruiting Plants and Woody Ornamentals

### Principles of Pruning

Pruning deciduous trees and shrubs is a pleasant activity to undertake between early March and bud break on days above freezing. If it is done in December, January or February, bud injury is more likely to result, and if the temperature is below freezing the bark is more likely to crack.

Pruning is done to improve the health of the plant, improve its shape, control the size, rejuvenate it, and increase flower and fruit production. Except to remove damaged and broken branches, pruning of coniferous and broad-leaved evergreens should be left until new growth is visible in a couple of months. Hybrid tea roses are traditionally pruned when forsythia is in bloom; pruning too early may encourage them into premature growth which will be killed by frost.

#### Six steps

There are several basic steps to pruning deciduous fruiting and ornamental plants. The first step is to remove all dead wood. As you gain experience, you will be able to tell which wood is alive just by looking at it—there will be buds and a fresh look to the wood. If in doubt, cut into the branch in question. Live wood is moist looking inside and is not brittle and fragile when cut. Keep cutting back until live wood is reached, and then cut back once more to an outward facing branch or bud.

The second step is to remove damaged or broken branches as these make plants vulnerable to attack by insects and disease. Cut them off so that there is no stub left. There is a ridge of bark, or a branch collar, around the base of larger branches. The cut should be made just above this so that the bark can grow in from the edges of the ridge and seal over the cut. Cut off large branches in three steps so that bark is not ripped off the main trunk. Broken branches should be cut back to a branch that grows outwards, rather than towards the middle of the shrub.

**Preventive Measure**

Before heading outdoors with the pruning shears, oil them. Put about three drops of all-purpose machine oil on the spring and two drops on the bolt holding the blades, then wipe the blades with an oily rag. Review the December notes on pruning equipment (pages 451-452) if pruning gear must be purchased.

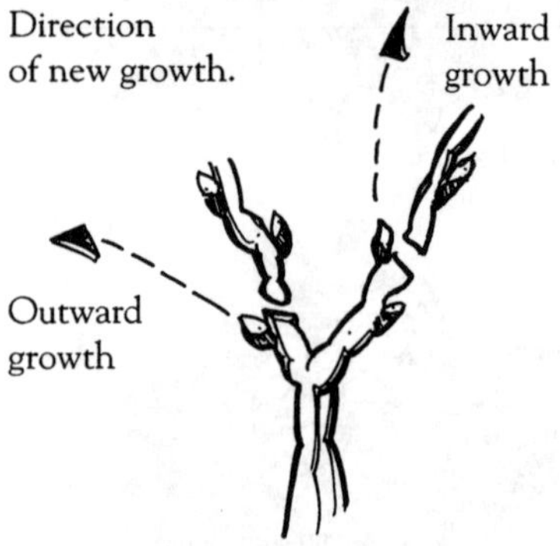


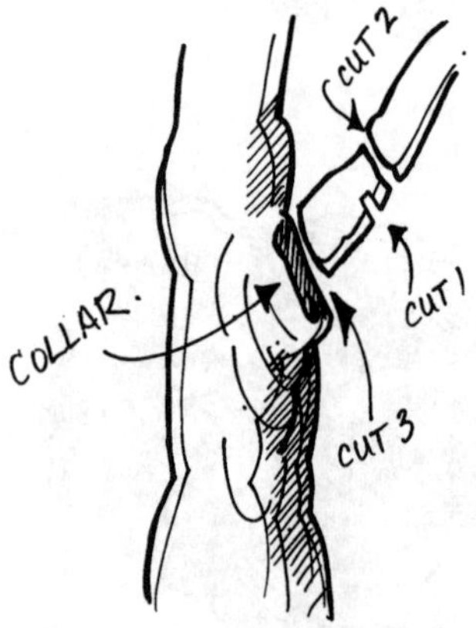

Three steps to cutting off a branch.

If bark has been damaged, cut off the ragged edges with a sharp knife and shape the wound (where the bark has been removed) so that it is pointed at each end. Remove loose, scaly bark by rubbing back and forth with a piece of chicken wire. Pear psylla adults hide under the edges of rough bark on pear and quince trees, and larvae of codling moth spin their cocoons under rough bark near ground level for the winter. Woodpeckers are natural predators of these insects and others and can be attracted to your area by hanging suet from tree branches (see page 423).

Split bark is caused by extreme temperatures in the winter, and by rapid growth in the summer. The latter results from high nitrogen levels in the soil or heavy rain after a dry spell. Loose bark should be cut away until only that which is firmly attached is left (for preventive measures see page 394).

The third step is to cut out diseased wood. Cut off branches at least 4 inches (10 cm) below the affected area. On the main stem or on large branches, use a sharp knife to cut away the bark until healthy tissue is reached. Dip pruning clippers or the knife used in a 1:40 solution of Lysol and water after each cut to prevent the spread of disease.

Black, knobby galls in the bark of cherries and plums indicate black knot disease. Purple blotches that become orange or brown sunken areas are signs of anthracnose. This disease affects apple, crabapple, pear, quince, raspberry, peach, *Amelanchier* species (Indian pear, serviceberry, saskatoon), apricot, cherry, flowering quince, hawthorn and mountain ash. Gummy twigs and bark, black or grey corky growths, and sunken areas in the bark on various trees indicate canker and should be cut off. Susceptible trees include apple, beech, birch, hawthorn, pear, and poplar. Cherries and peaches are affected by canker that oozes a gummy substance.

Dress those cuts made to remove diseased wood with latex paint or tree dressing, or spray with Bordeaux mixture or a copper fungicide. Spray the entire tree with a copper fungicide at bud burst in the spring. If a tree is severely infected it may have to be removed. Immediately burn, bury deeply or discard in the garbage all diseased trimmings.

Witch's broom on lilacs, firs, honeysuckles and other plants should be cut out well below the growth. It shows up as a proliferation of shoots, shortened internodes and stunted leaves and leads to reduced growth, impaired flower quality, dieback, and sometimes death. It is a twig's response to an irritation caused by fungi, insects or a virus, such as powdery mildew or gall mite. There is no remedy, but pruning out the affected twigs improves the appearance of the plant.

### Green Thumb Tip

If mice or lawn trimmers have removed the bark around the base of a tree in a complete circumference, the tree will die unless bridge grafting is done.

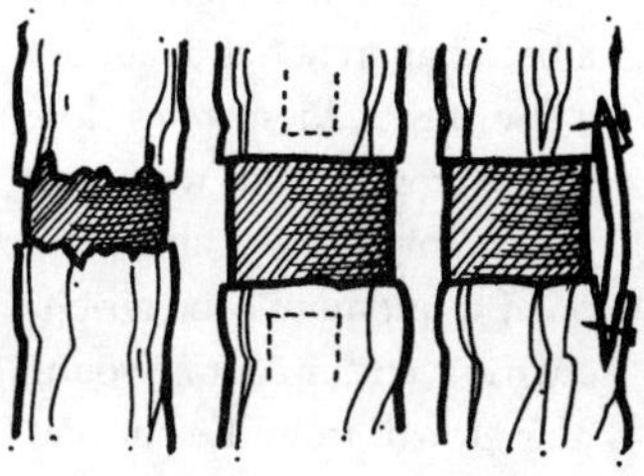

Cut one bridge for every 3/4 inch (2 cm) diameter of the trunk—use pencil thick pieces of twig from another part of the tree and make them 4 inches (10 cm) longer than the width of the wound. Clean up the ragged edges of the wound by trimming the bark with a sharp knife, and cut flaps of bark above and below the wound, one pair for every bridge. Cut the ends of the bridges to a slant and slip each end under a flap of bark. Finally, wrap the grafts above and below the wound with grafting tape.

## Green Thumb Tip

When pruning, many small cuts stimulate more new growth than a few major cuts. Rather than trimming all over the outside of a dense shrub and giving it a formal appearance, a better approach is to cut out a few of the oldest stems close to the ground. This will lower the height of the shrub, keep it open to promote good air circulation, and encourage young new growth from the bottom.

Heading cuts—those that remove the end of a branch—will induce more new shoot growth than thinning cuts that remove entire branches. Dense, crowded shrubs need thinning cuts, but heading cuts can be used to encourage more branching on sparsely branched shrubs and trees.

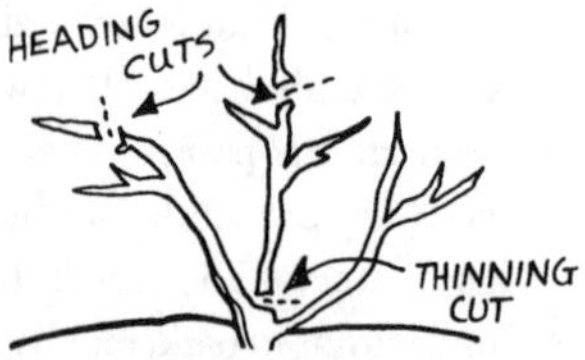


A branch that is too long can have a little removed from its tip, but cut off no more than one-quarter to one-third of its total length. Cutting back too hard will only make the branch grow even more vigorously in the coming season. In the case of a weak stem, you may want to cut it back hard to encourage it to grow more.

The fourth step is to cut out all crossed and rubbing branches to prevent bark damage. Cut out the branch that points towards the inside of the shrub, unless the other one is diseased or otherwise damaged.

The fifth step is to cut out spindly branches and those that grow towards the middle of the shrub. This will open up the centre of the shrub and improve air circulation; this is particularly important for trees and shrubs that are troubled by leaf spot and other fungal diseases.

The final step is to prune for size, shape and rejuvenation. When this is done—either when the plant is dormant or after it has flowered—depends on when the plant blooms (see Willison, 1989, page 128). Dormant pruning for size and shape stimulates growth, so you may want to use summer pruning instead if overly vigorous growth is a problem.

Formal hedges should be pruned so that the top is narrower than the bottom. This shape allows light to reach the lower branches which tend to

Bad hedge shape, large top shades bottom leaves.

Good hedge shape, allows sun to shine on most foliage.

lose their leaves and become bare. It also enables hedges to shed snow more readily, thus reducing the risk of breakage. Informal, naturally shaped hedges need to have only the oldest branches cut out just above ground level each year.

If excessive force is required to cut a branch, or if shears start to twist, use a larger pruning tool, such as long handled loppers instead of secateurs, or a pruning saw instead of long handled loppers. If blades are forced or twisted they will no longer close properly and will make jagged rather than clean cuts.

### Tree Decline

When trees start to decline and die back a little more each year the cause can often be traced back several years to some sort of root damage or change in soil level (see pages 320-321).Indications that a tree is nearing its end include, in increasing order of importance: smaller leaves than normal; late leafing out in the spring and premature discolouration in late summer; sparse foliage and excessive suckers and water sprouts; bracket fungi on the lower

## *Focus on Plants*

The different types of hydrangeas need to be pruned at different times and in different ways. Incorrect pruning may cause a lack of bloom, although other factors such as too much shade, overfertilization, poor soil and winter injury may also be to blame.

Climbing hydrangea requires no pruning except to control size; this should be done in the spring while the plant is dormant, if it is done at all. Peegee, paniculata or 'Grandiflora' hydrangea (*H. paniculata* 'Grandiflora') has large white panicles of flowers fading to pink and finally to brown. Cut it back hard each spring while it is dormant, cutting into the previous year's growth to two buds from where the last year's growth originated. If it is left unpruned it will grow to the size of a small tree.

'Annabelle,' 'Hills-of-Snow' or arborescens hydrangea, also known sometimes as 'Grandiflora' hydrangea (*H. arborescens* 'Grandiflora'), forms large, rounded, creamy white flower clusters that start out green. No pruning is required except to remove spindly branches in early spring. Allow the flower heads to drop off naturally as new flower buds for next year develop just behind the old ones.

Other hydrangeas are pruned only very lightly, if at all, after blooming in midsummer. Pruning any later would remove the flower buds that form in the autumn for the next season's bloom. Oakleaf hydrangea (*H. quercifolia*) and macrophylla type hydrangeas (*H. macrophylla*) that include the bigleaf or mophead types with big, round, blue or pink flower clusters, need no pruning at all. If shrubs get too dense, thin out one third of the weakest growth early in the spring. The lacecap macrophylla hydrangeas, such as 'Blue Wave,' are thinned ever so lightly, if at all, by removing the older, weaker wood in the spring. Do not cut them back hard as this stops the summer flowering. Remove dead and damaged wood each spring, however, regardless of the type.

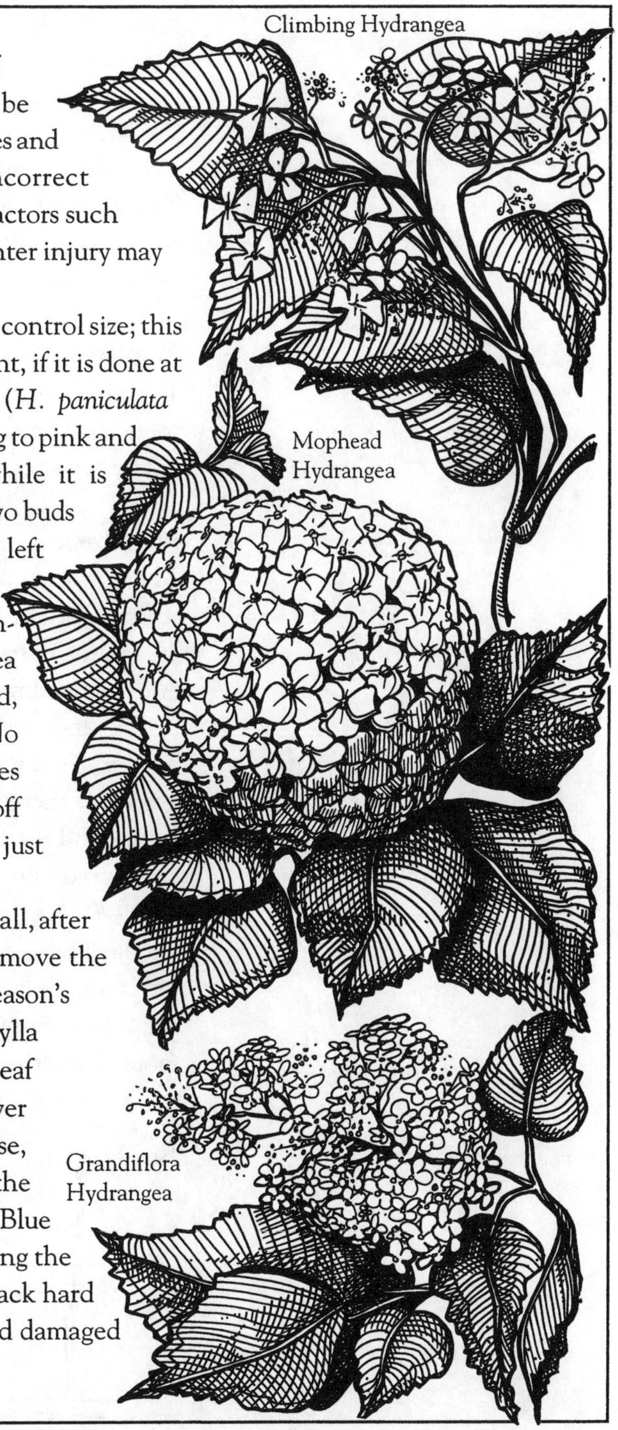

trunk; and dieback at the top of the tree and ends of branches. Eventually the entire tree may die. Lichens on bark do not harm trees or shrubs in any way and are an indication that the air is clean.

Call in an insured tree surgeon if a tree has to be removed. It is all too easy to hit wires, parked vehicles and roof tops if the tree is not felled properly. The stump should be cut as close to the ground as possible. Use a chain saw to form a cup shape in the stump to hold water, and make cross cuts or drill holes to open up the stump during freeze-thaw cycles.

## Pruning Fruits

The six pruning steps described above also apply to fruiting shrubs and trees. The final step of shaping, however, varies with fruit trees according to the type.

### Fruit trees

The aim with most trees, including apples, is to develop and maintain a strong, upright central leader. Many books on fruit tree pruning advocate an open centre, but a central leader is a better shape for the North American climate. Head back (cut) the leader by about one-quarter to one-third of its length each spring until the desired height is reached. This will encourage the development of lower lateral shoots with wider crotch angles. If there are two strong upright shoots at the top, select one as the leader and remove the other.

Cut back one-year-old whips (the central unbranched stem) to about 36 inches (90 cm) in height. Spindly whips less than 40 inches (1 m) should be cut back by one-third to one-half to develop a strong leader. On two-year-old trees, all lateral branches closer than 18 inches (45 cm) to the ground should be removed. Laterals should be left in place when there are three or more above the 18 inch (45 cm) level. If only one or two remain, cut them

Fruit Tree Pruning

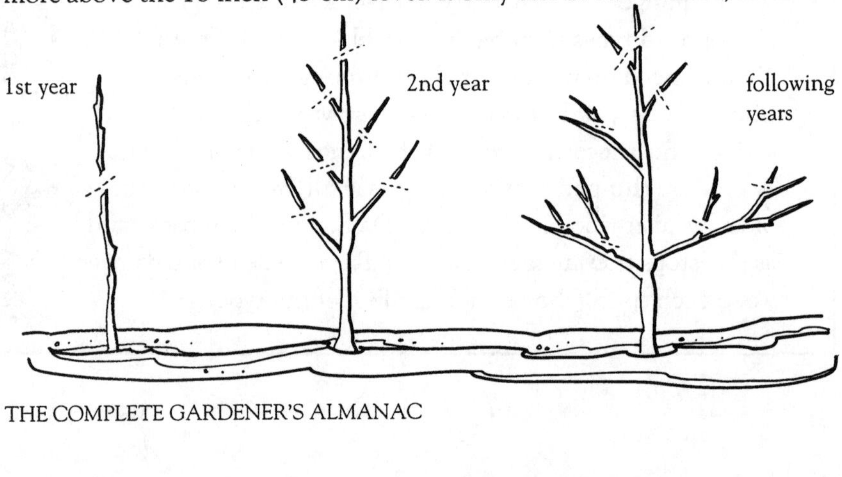

out because they will grow strongly and throw branch development out of balance.

Continue to allow three or four new laterals to develop each spring and cut out the others of the same age until the final height is reached. Cut back the leaders of the lateral branches by one-half to two-thirds their first year and by one-half or less in subsequent years. Cutting back stimulates growth—if less is cut off there will be less new growth, and less is required as the final shape is reached.

Cut out branches that are growing upright, even if they are growing more strongly than branches growing outwards and downwards. When the upright growth is removed, the lower, weaker branches will grow more strongly. Cut back lateral branches to downward and outward facing wood buds (wood buds are pointed, fruit buds are plump and rounded) to encourage growth outwards and downwards; this will make picking easier.

If a major rejuvenation on an old tree is required, no more than 25% of the wood should be removed. The same principles of cutting out strong, upright growth and preserving weaker, downward growth applies. Water sprouts are best removed in the summer (see pages 270-271), when there is less chance of triggering more sprouts. A superior reference for pruning and rejuvenating apple and other fruit trees is *Ecological Fruit Production in the North* by Bart Hall-Beyer and Jean Richard (1983).

Continue to tie the central stem of weeping trees to the supporting stake, but cut out all other vertical branches. Semi-upright branches usually become weeping and should be left.

In zones where nut trees are borderline hardy, it is best to leave a lot of stems coming from the soil, although this takes up a lot of space and makes them difficult to prune. In milder zones they can be pruned to a single stem that is clear of branches for 12 to 18 inches (30 to 45 cm) above the ground and a head of eight to twelve main branches.

Prune fruit trees to downward growing branches so as to make fruit more accessible for picking.

## *Soft fruits*

Pruning soft fruits is easier than trees due to their smaller size. Remove all of the two-year-old raspberry and blackberry canes that fruited last summer, if this was not done right after the last of the fruits were picked last year . Cut to ground level any canes with blotches or pock marks. These prunings are diseased and should be burned or deeply buried, not composted.

Black Currant bush has dark old canes and lighter young canes .

Raspberry canes can also be tipped (cut back) to 5 feet (1.5 m) tall to remove those tips killed over the winter and to encourage the growth of lateral branches—this is supposed to increase fruit production somewhat. Good fruit production, however, is far more dependent on weed and grass control and on sufficient moisture and nutrients in the form of compost and well rotted manure. All of the canes of autumn bearing raspberries are cut to ground level each spring (for a discussion of management methods, see page 315).

Cut back black currant canes to 1 inch (2.5 cm) above ground level if they are three years old or more, are particularly weak and spindly, or have withered tips. Old canes will be nearly black and very woody. One-year-old rooted cuttings should be cut back the same amount, and neglected black currants can have all of their canes cut back in the same manner. A well-spaced black currant bush should have about ten or twelve thick, healthy looking, light brown or golden coloured branches containing a mix of one-year-olds and well branched two-year-olds.

If cutting of any sort reveals black wood inside, keep cutting back until healthy clean wood is reached, and then cut off another 2 to 4 inches (5 to 10 cm). Any old or dead wood with coral pink spots on it should be cut out well below the affected wood and burned, buried or discarded.

Red currants and white currants are treated differently from black currants. They fruit best on older wood, so remove only those stems that are at least four years old. There should be eight to ten main stems remaining. Cut out suckers coming from the ground, and any branches on the central stem that are less than 4 inches (10 cm) from the ground.

On two and three-year-old bushes, cut back each remaining stem by half to an outside bud (one that points towards the outside of the shrub). On older bushes, cut back last year's growth by one-third. Established currants will need only 1 inch (2 to 3 cm) removed from the tips of last year's growth. All of the lateral branches growing from the main stems should be cut back to one bud from their base to encourage the production of fruit spurs. Do not be daunted by all of this. It will make sense when you are standing in front of a bush with clippers in hand—just go one step at a time.

Gooseberries are pruned in a manner similar to red currants and white currants. Cut out all weak shoots and those branches which are more than four or five years old. On two-year-old plants, cut back last year's growth by one-half. Some gooseberries are quite upright and should be pruned back to outward facing buds to help the plant spread out sideways. Other gooseberies are very lax and drooping. They should be cut back to upward facing buds to encourage upright growth. Remove any branches on the main stem that are closer than 4 inches (10 cm) to the ground.

In subsequent years, cut back each leader (the new growth from last year on the tip of each main stem) by one-half to a bud facing in the desired direction. Cut back lateral growths to 1 inch (2.5 cm) if growth is weak, and to 3 inches (7 cm) if growth is strong. (Remember that cutting back hard stimulates growth.)

Blueberries require little pruning. Remove all dead wood, any crossed and rubbing branches, and any branches that are broken. When the bush is four or five years old, remove about one-quarter of the stems by cutting out the oldest, least productive wood. Cut some branches back to the base and some back to a strong, young upright shoot. Mulberries bleed rather badly when pruned, so they should have only dead and crossed or rubbing branches removed. Saskatoons and elderberries are simply pruned for good health—cut out dead, diseased and damaged wood, and crossed and rubbing branches.

Pruning of
Red and White Currant Bushes

2-3 year old bushes,
prune to outside buds.

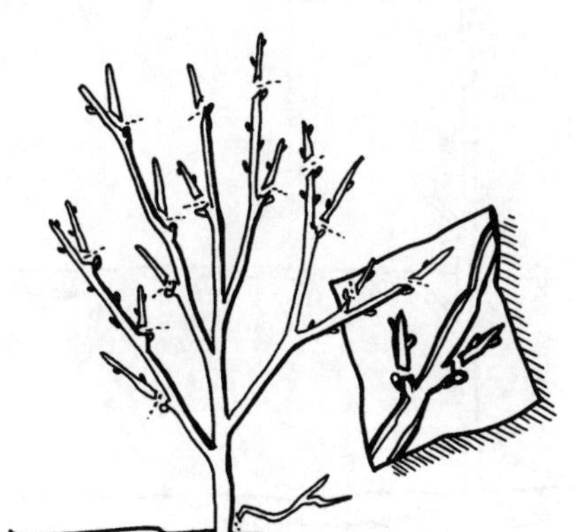

Older bushes, prune last year's growth by
1/3 and all lateral branches back to one bud.

***Espaliered fruits and grapes***

Each arm of an espaliered plant is called a cordon, although some people refer to single arm trees as cordons. The initial aim is to form a framework of branches. Bamboo canes are tied to wires (see pages 143 and 146) in the shape that the tree or shrub is to take. The cordons are tied to these canes to ensure straight branches in the desired shape. Pruning for shape is done during the growing season when the tree is in leaf (see page 272) rather than during dormancy as the latter stimulates branching.

The single cordon is used most often with apples, pears, gooseberries, and red and white currants, and is usually planted at an angle (see pages 143 and 146). On two and three-year-old cordons, all of the side shoots of the previous summer's growth that are more than 4 inches (10 cm) long are cut back so that three buds remain. If very few side shoots are being produced, the leader (central stem) can be cut back by up to one third of its length. Continue in this manner until the tree reaches its ultimate height, then cut back the leader each spring to leave 1/2 inch (1 cm) of the previous year's growth.

Notch to stimulate growth.

If there are not enough side shoots being produced in spite of pruning when the cordon is young, the wood immediately above a latent bud can be notched to stimulate it into growth. This involves removing a small portion of bark, usually in May. Nicking the bark below a bud has the opposite effect, causing the growth from that bud to be weaker.

An espalier form, with branches growing horizontally, is used most often

Training Horizontal Espaliers

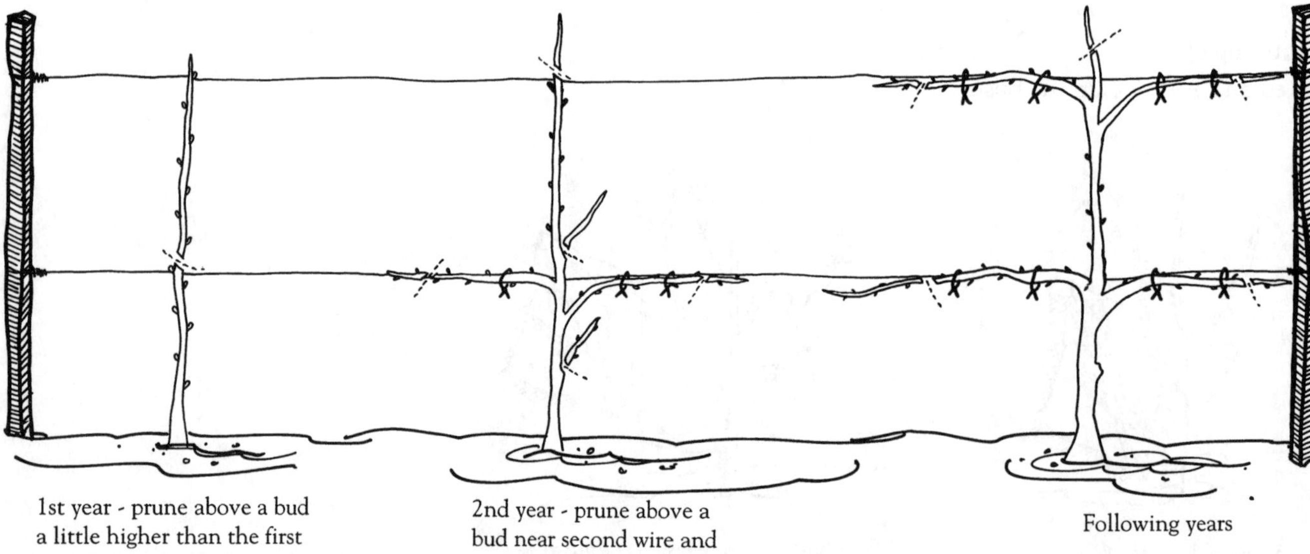

1st year - prune above a bud a little higher than the first support wire.

2nd year - prune above a bud near second wire and all laterals between wires.

Following years

with apples and pears. To achieve this, a one-year-old whip is cut above a bud a little higher than the first support wire (see page 146). There should be two buds below, not necessarily next to each other, with one facing right and one facing left. During the growing season, tie the shoot that grew from the uppermost bud to a cane to make it grow vertically, and tie the two lower shoots that grew from the right and left-facing buds to bamboo canes positioned at a 45° angle to the vertical. The growth of these lateral arms is slowed in subsequent years by lowering them further until they are horizontal; this also stimulates fruit buds. Additional shoots should be cut off, or the buds rubbed off before they grow.

The central stem of a two-year-old plant is cut above a bud just at or above the level of the second wire, again with two buds below, one facing right and one facing left. The branches that are stimulated to grow from this cut are then trained during the growing season to form the second tier. Lateral branches from the previous year's growth are not cut because pruning would stimulate unwanted vegetative growth. Instead, they are lowered further during the growing season. If for some reason vegetative growth gets out of hand, it can be controlled by summer pruning (see page 270). Continue each year in this manner until the third tier (usually the last) is formed at the topmost wire. Cut the leader 6 inches (15 cm) above it and prune each spring to leave 1/2 inch (1 cm) of the previous year's growth.

The fan form is used with many fruits, including plums, cherries, peaches, apricots, gooseberries and red and white currants. Fan-shaped fruits can be grown against a wall if extra warmth and shelter is needed. The following description applies to trees; shorten the lengths for smaller fruits.

During the first spring, cut back the little tree to a lateral shoot or bud about 2 feet (60 cm) above the ground. There should be two buds below, one facing left and one facing right. If the tree already has two laterals heading roughly left and right below this point, cut them back by two-thirds to an upward facing bud. Cut out any other lateral shoots. Those remaining are trained and tied during the growing season (see pages 272-273).

During the second spring, cut back the two main laterals (at this stage called main ribs) to a bud between 12 and 18 inches (30 and 45 cm) from the main stem. Several buds should remain on each rib. Three of the shoots that grow from these buds are tied in place during the growing season to form three new ribs on each of the two main ribs, creating a fan shape (see pages 272-273). The extra shoots are cut out or rubbed off early in the season.

In the third spring, cut back each of the eight ribs, leaving about 20 inches

(50 cm) of the previous year's growth. Cut them back to an upward facing bud, if possible. The size of the plant and the wall space available will determine whether this process may be continued for another year. Summer pruning is essential to continue the shaping of the fan. The central portion is filled in last because those branches which are nearly vertical will grow more vigorously than the more horizontal outer branches. For other shapes, refer to Brooklyn Botanic Garden Record *Trained and Sculptured Plants* (1982).

Grapes are often trained along wires, usually with a central trunk and two (the Geneva double curtain) or four (the four-arm Kniffin system) horizontal arms. Where winters are cold (-22°F or -30°C), grapes are better trained with a short central stem and either a fan shape or an oblique side-arm shape (see below). They can also be grown over arbours and other forms of support.

For the Kniffin system, train the most vigorous shoot to grow to the top wire (see page 146 for the arrangement of wires). Gently wrap it around a string stretched tautly between the wires to help it grow upright; it will form the central stem. If it has not reached the top wire at the end of the growing season, prune it back to just above the topmost good bud during dormancy the following spring. When the new shoot has reached the top wire, cut it off the following spring just above the wire and tie it securely to the top wire.

Once the central stem is established, retain four side shoots to form the main horizontal arms. These will grow during the summer and are tied into place during dormancy the following spring. Select two on each side, about 2 to 4 inches (5 to 10 cm) below a wire, and cut out all other side shoots. The four arms, spaced according to the distance between the horizontal wires, are cut back to four or five buds, or back to two buds if the vine is weak.

Each summer these arms will grow several side canes, on which the grapes

Kniffin System

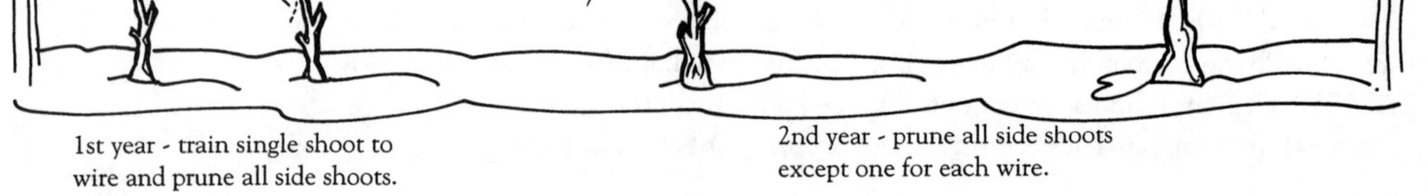

1st year - train single shoot to wire and prune all side shoots.

2nd year - prune all side shoots except one for each wire.

are produced. During spring pruning, cut back each main arm to one of the new canes close to the main trunk. Cut back each of these selected new canes to five to eight buds, depending on how vigorously the cane is growing. This way each of the four arms should yield five to eight new shoots on which the grapes are produced. Another cane should be left in place even closer to the main trunk; it is cut back to one or two buds and serves as the renewal spur. The following spring it will be cut back to five to eight buds to provide the fruiting canes for that growing season. Pruning in this manner is repeated each spring so that there is always plenty of vigorous, fruit-bearing growth.

Because there is always the risk of losing the central stem through winter injury or other damage, a variation of the method is to train two central stems together, with each one supporting two arms.

Many gardeners prefer to use the Geneva double curtain instead of the four-arm system. Grapes are planted in pairs so that the two central stems can be twined together as they grow to form a sturdy, self-supporting stem. Two horizontal wires are used, but the lower one merely supports the central stems. When the two central stems reach the top wire, they are trained to grow horizontally in opposite directions along the wire until each one is 6 to 8 feet (1.8 to 2.5 m) long. The two arms are tied to the wires at several points and tied tightly with a wire at the end of each arm. When they have reached their full length, the next step is to develop ten to twelve equally spaced, downward hanging, short vertical arms. The fruiting canes will grow from these each season.

The fan shape and the oblique side-arm shape are pruned much like the Kniffin system, except that the central stem is kept below the level of the lower wire. This makes it easier for the canes to be lowered to the ground in the late autumn and covered with soil for winter protection, as for climbing roses (see page 388). Once the vines are established, the fruiting canes that will grow each year can be spaced 15 to 18 inches (38 to 45 cm) apart. This is achieved by rubbing out the extra buds between the new growth just after it is established.

The easiest way to train grapes is casually over an arbour. Choose the hardiest varieties for this purpose, and do not expect fruit production to be as high as from other systems of training. A central stem is established to grow up and over the arbour, and side shoots are allowed to develop all along the stem spaced 15 to 18 inches (38 to 45 cm) apart. Cut out any extras. Each spring thereafter, cut each side shoot back so that a dozen or more buds remain; the aim is to provide good, leafy coverage for the arbour.

Grapevine Shapes

Geneva Double Curtain

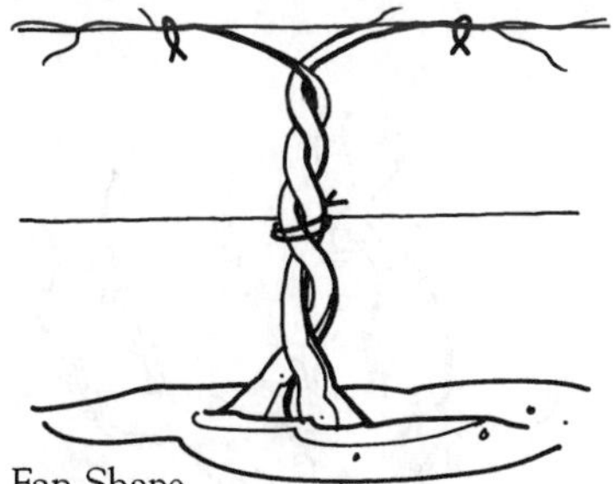

Fan Shape

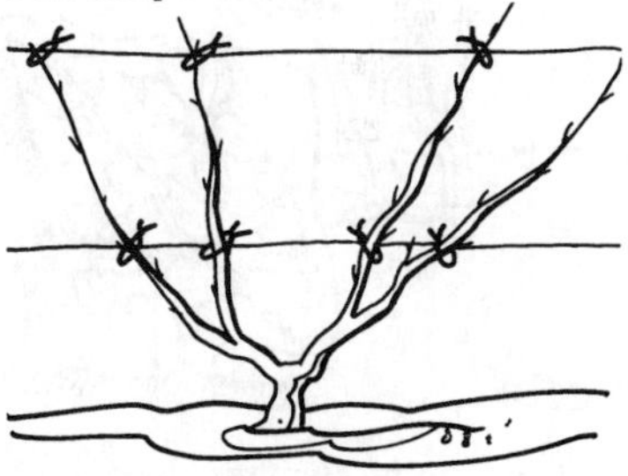

Oblique Side-arm Shape

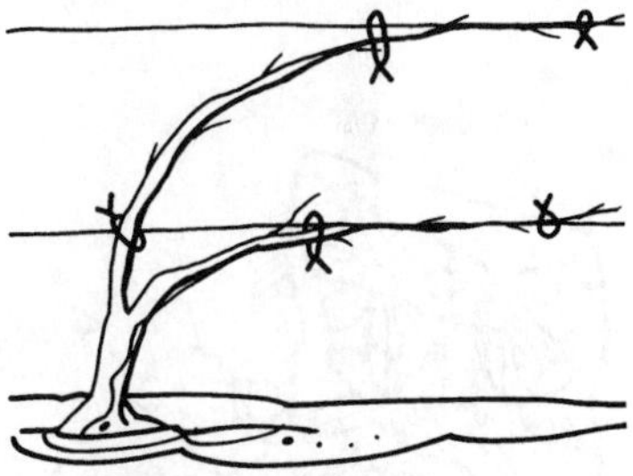

**Preventive Measure**

After all of the pruning is done, dry and oil the shears thoroughly before putting them away. Wrap them in an oily rag and store in a dry place with no hint of dampness.

Pruning Clematis

Early blooming clematis bloom on old growth and must be pruned early and to last pair of strong buds.

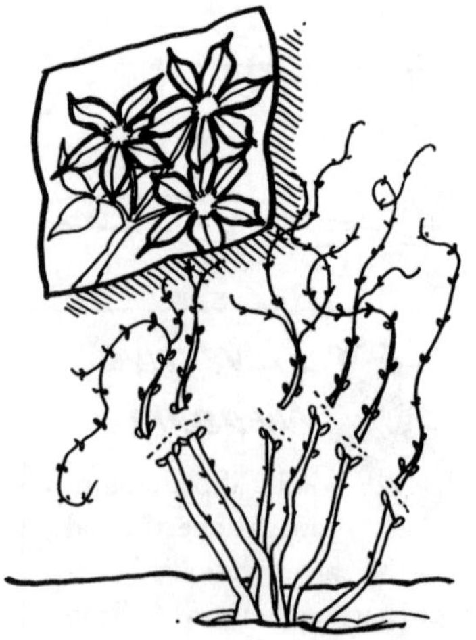

Late blooming clematis bloom on new growth and must be pruned early and just above lowest pair of strong buds.

For all grapes, there will come a time when the wood is very old and the vine needs renewal. Side arms are renewed by allowing new shoots close to the main trunk to develop. The central stem should be renewed less frequently (about every ten years) by allowing a shoot from close to the ground to grow and be trained as if it were a new plant. When the growth is well established, the old part of the plant is cut out during dormancy in the spring.

## Pruning Vines

Most vines are not cut back routinely each spring except to remove dead, damaged or diseased wood. It may be easier to wait until the buds are swelling before any pruning is done if it is not clear which parts of the plant are dead. Sometimes a vine gets rather crowded and can have several of the oldest stems removed to several inches above ground level. Much depends on how the vine has been trained and where it is growing.

Wisteria is encouraged to bloom by cutting back the previous year's growth to two or three buds above the base. Do this very early before there is much, if any, new growth. If wisteria is threatening to take over an area, refrain from any pruning until July and then cut back the current season's growth to five or six leaves. Less new growth is stimulated if pruned at this point instead of in the spring. Prune as usual the following spring.

Clematis is cut back severely or lightly or not at all, depending on the type. Varieties that bloom in the spring on old wood, such as 'Bee's Jubilee,' 'Duchess of Edinburgh,' 'Miss Bateman,' 'Nelly Moser,' 'The President' and 'Vyvyan Pennell,' will probably bloom early with a few double flowers after a severe winter, but put on a burst of growth and bloom in late summer or autumn with a mass of single flowers. Prune them back lightly to strong buds when it becomes clear which buds are alive. C. *alpina* and C. *montana* require only the removal of dead wood.

Summer and autumn blooming clematis, such as 'C. *tangutica*,' 'C. *texensis*,' 'C. *viticella*,' 'Comtesse de Bouchaud,' 'Ernest Markham,' 'Gipsy Queen,' 'Hagley Hybrid,' 'Huldine,' 'Jackmanii,' 'Lady Betty Balfour,' 'Perle d'Azur' and 'Ville de Lyon,' should be cut back hard each spring to 1 to 2 feet (30-60 cm) to encourage branching and more blooms.

Clematis suffers badly some winters, particularly if planted where drainage is poor. Either improve the drainage, or move the clematis. Do not despair if a clematis appears completely dead. New shoots will sometimes come up from live roots below ground.

## Propagation

### Hardwood cuttings

Many fruit and ornamental trees and shrubs can be propagated by taking cuttings (see Tables JUL-3, page 275, and JUL-4, page 282), either in the early spring or the autumn. Cut pencil thick pieces of last year's growth to 6 to 15 inches (15 to 38 cm) long, cutting the bottom end just below a leaf node. Some are cut with a heel (see Table JUL-4), leaving a 3/4 to 1 inch (18 to 25 mm) of last year's growth attached. At this stage, if it is more convenient, the cuttings can be stored in a plastic bag in the refrigerator for two to four weeks. The cuttings are rooted in pots, either indoors under plastic or in a cold frame, or in prepared ground outdoors (see page 369).

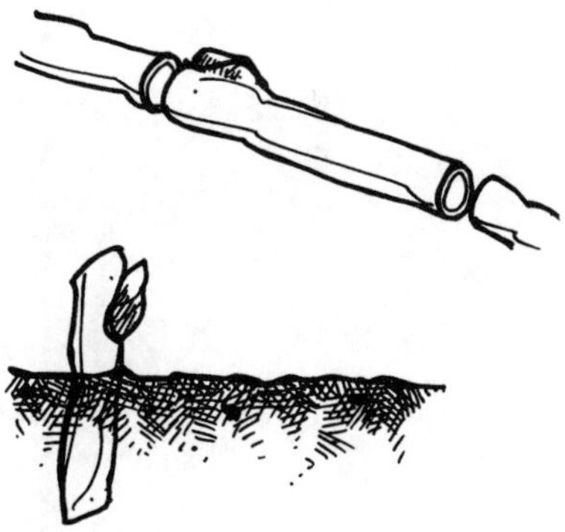

Bud cutting

Hardwood cuttings taken in the autumn (see pages 366-368) can be brought out of cold storage or dug up from their storage place in the ground as soon as the soil thaws . Dip the bases in rooting hormone and plant the cuttings in pots or in the ground outdoors. Those cuttings stored in pots since last autumn can also be brought into warmer temperatures and bright but indirect light.

Cuttings may have to be left in the same place for a year as rooting can take that long. The leaves on the cuttings will start to open during the spring. Rooting has occurred if they continue to expand to full size and if new growth occurs. Ventilate the plastic covering (or cold frames) as soon as new growth is visible and gradually expose the cuttings to drier air and full sunshine. Harden them off to outdoor conditions when other trees and shrubs have leafed out and the weather is stable, plunging the pots in a nursery bed under lattice-work or in a cold frame. Repot the cuttings in the autumn, store under protection for the winter, and plant out the following spring. Cuttings left in the ground over the winter should have their mulch removed gradually once spring arrives (see page 112).

### Eye cuttings

This method is often used with grapes. Cut 3/4 inch (18 mm) above and below a bud on a piece of last year's growth, remove a sliver of wood from the side opposite the bud, and bury the piece in a rooting mixture as for hardwood cuttings, leaving only the bud exposed.

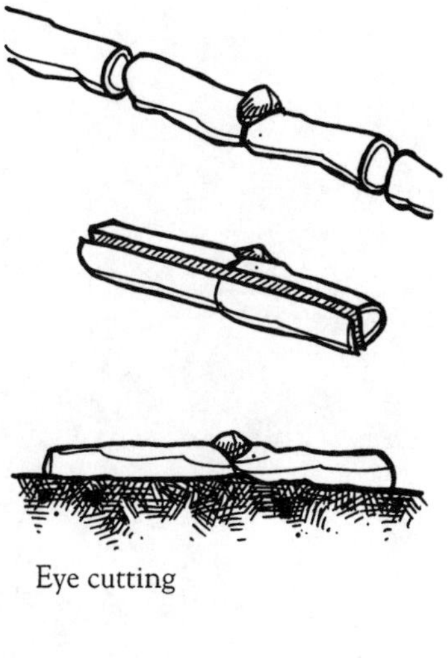

Eye cutting

Single bud cuttings of other plants can be used if there is not enough material available for full length hardwood cuttings. The cuts are made just above a bud and 1 to 1½ inches (2.5 to 4 cm) below the bud. The cuttings are then inserted vertically in a rooting mixture with the bud just showing above the soil line. They are treated in the same manner as hardwood cuttings, but are slower to root and get established. Leaf bud cuttings are taken during the summer when plants are in leaf (see page 274).

### Care of all cuttings

Any cuttings rooted last year, whether softwood, semi-hardwood or hardwood, can be potted on to wide but shallow 4 or 5 inch (100 or 125 mm) pots and encouraged to grow by gradually increasing temperatures and putting in brighter light. Fertilize them every month until they are planted out in nursery rows when the weather is warm and stable. If indoor growing space is a problem, they can be held back and not brought into growth until the buds on trees and shrubs outdoors are beginning to swell. They are then hardened off and planted out when their growth has advanced to the same degree as plants outdoors.

### Seeds

Seeds of trees and shrubs stratified (see page 369) over the winter can be sown in the same manner as any other garden seeds (see pages 47-50). Any that were planted last autumn and put in cold storage for the winter can be brought into warmth to encourage germination. When seeds finally sprout, they can be transplanted to individual 3 ½ inch (80 mm) pots or moved to larger flats when they have two to three true leaves. They can be planted outdoors in a nursery bed when the weather is stable. After another two or three years they will be large enough to plant in their permanent position.

## Living with Pests and Diseases

### Prevention

After pruning, some gardeners spray plants with lime sulphur or dormant oil if there have been severe problems in previous years. Mild damage can and should be tolerated.

Spraying willy-nilly as a preventive measure is not nearly as effective as good plant maintenance. Make sure that plants are pruned for good air circulation; that dead, diseased and damaged wood is removed; that old, loose bark is scraped off to reduce the number of places that insects can hide; that egg masses of unwanted insects are removed by scraping them off or pruning out the affected twigs; that disease or pest-infested fruits and leaves are regularly removed; that an area of cleared ground is left around the base of each plant to eliminate competition from grass and weeds; that there is sufficient moisture and nutrients during the growing season; and that excess nitrogen is not applied. In addition, pest and disease resistant plants should be chosen initially.

### *Dormant sprays*

Dormant oil is used to control scale insects, mites, apple scab spores, pear psylla, aphids, leafrollers, mealybugs, tent caterpillars and codling moths, but use it only if you had severe problems with these the previous year. Dormant oil either smothers the offending spores or eggs, or discourages egg laying, as with pear psylla, but it also smothers the eggs of beneficial insects, such as the predators of red spider mites. It can be used on coniferous and broad-leaved evergreens as well as deciduous trees and shrubs during dormancy, before the buds start to swell.

Ideally, there should be forty-eight hours of dry weather both before and after spraying. Spray in the morning on a dry, windless day when the temperature is 50°F (10°C) or more. It may be necessary to wait well into April or even early May where spring is late to get the right spraying conditions. As long as the spray goes on before the leaf buds swell and open and before the insects become active, it will be effective. There is some evidence that dormant oil delays peach blooming by a few days—this can be useful where early blossoms tend to be caught by late frosts.

Dormant oil can be purchased, or you can make your own by mixing 1 pint (550 ml) of Number 30 motor oil, 1/4 cup (65 ml) of liquid detergent, and 3 gallons (14 l) of water. Make sure that coverage is thorough.

Lime sulphur is used to help control black knot disease, leaf blight or leaf spot disease (which lilacs and some crabapples are prone to), peach leaf curl, plum pocket, and anthracnose and spur blights on cane fruits. When applied before bud burst, lime sulphur may decrease gall insects, although the galls the insects create are rarely a problem. Fungal infections often occur while leaf buds are swelling and opening, so the first application should be made on a mild, windless dry day before the buds begin to swell, usually sometime in April. Commercial preparations sometimes combine lime sulphur and dormant oil sprays so that only one application is needed. Later, as leaf buds are opening and regularly thereafter, a weaker, 10% solution of lime sulphur or other fungicide may be applied as required (see page 190).

### Barriers

A physical barrier helps some trees affected by various loopers and inchworms, such as spring cankerworms. The adult cankerworms emerge as moths in the spring right after the ground has thawed. Gray brown male moths flit around the trunk as the flightless females crawl up the trunk; each female will lay about four hundred eggs in cracks in the bark. The young cankerworms hatch in May, feed on the tree's leaves for several weeks, fall to the ground in June, and pupate in the soil until the following spring.

To break the life cycle, wrap a 6 to 8 inch (15 to 20 cm) wide strip of heavy paper or burlap around tree trunks at chest height. This should be done before the frost has come out of the ground, because insects become active soon after the soil has thawed. Fill in the bark crevices underneath the paper with cotton batting, and smear the outer surface of the paper with Tanglefoot to capture adults and larvae as they move up or down the trunk. A substitute can be made by mixing 1 ½ cups (375 ml) of rosin (available at athletic supply stores), 1 cup (250 ml) of linseed oil, and 1 tablespoon (15 ml) of melted paraffin. Renew as needed in June and again after the first hard frosts in September or October to help control codling moth, winter moth, bruce spanworm and fall cankerworm.

A different kind of barrier will prevent certain beetles, such as the apple tree borer, from laying eggs in the bark. When the beetles' eggs hatch into larvae, they bore into the wood and mine extensive tunnels. Loosely wrap the bottom 12 to 24 inches (30 to 60 cm) of trunk with wire screen, mosquito netting, hardware cloth or several layers of newspapers in early spring. Bury the bottom of the barrier under the soil, tie the top with a cord, and remove the barrier in late autumn.

Do not bother to apply sticky bands or barriers unless there have been problems in previous years (see also page 277).

## Composting

Pruned branches that are not diseased can be chopped up or shredded and applied as mulch. Alternatively, put the branches at the bottom of a new compost pile. They will form an open bottom to the pile that will help air circulation. It is too early to expect any action out of composting, but not too early to figure out where and how composting will be done in the coming season.

Composting can be done by making a free-form pile of organic matter, or by filling some sort of container that has a capacity of at least one cubic yard ($m^3$). It can be made of wood, plastic, concrete blocks, chicken wire stapled to a wooden frame, or even snow fence (made of wooden slats wired together and generally used to help control drifting snow). The tub part of an old washing machine, with all its holes, can be used as a small composter, and the shell of the washing machine can be used as a large composter, putting material in at the top and taking finished compost out at the back of the machine at the bottom. Try to leave gaps in constructed composters to enable air to circulate around the pile, although turning the pile is probably more effective. Line containers with 1/2 inch (1.25 cm) heavy guage wire mesh to prevent rats from getting into the pile.

If you are not in a hurry to get finished compost, one bin or pile is enough, but you may have to wait as long as a year. If a rapid turnover is wanted, set up two or three bins. This will make it easier to turn the compost pile to speed up the composting process. A free-form pile can be turned as well, as long as there is space available next to it.

It is best to locate the pile out of sight, but you are more likely to use it if it is handy to the kitchen and garden. All kinds of organic matter can be added to a compost pile, but avoid adding kitchen scraps in the winter as they attract rats, dogs and other animals. A worm compost bin indoors makes it possible to compost all year (see page 401).

**Green Thumb Tip**

Avoid spreading compost, manure and other fertilizers in the garden until the soil is workable. There are several times when it is best not to be too hasty especially in spreading manure. Nitrogen run-off into lakes and streams will occur if manure is spread on snow or frozen ground, before a heavy rain, or when the ground is very wet. To avoid burning young roots, do not spread it just before seeding or planting.

Month-by-Month

# April/May

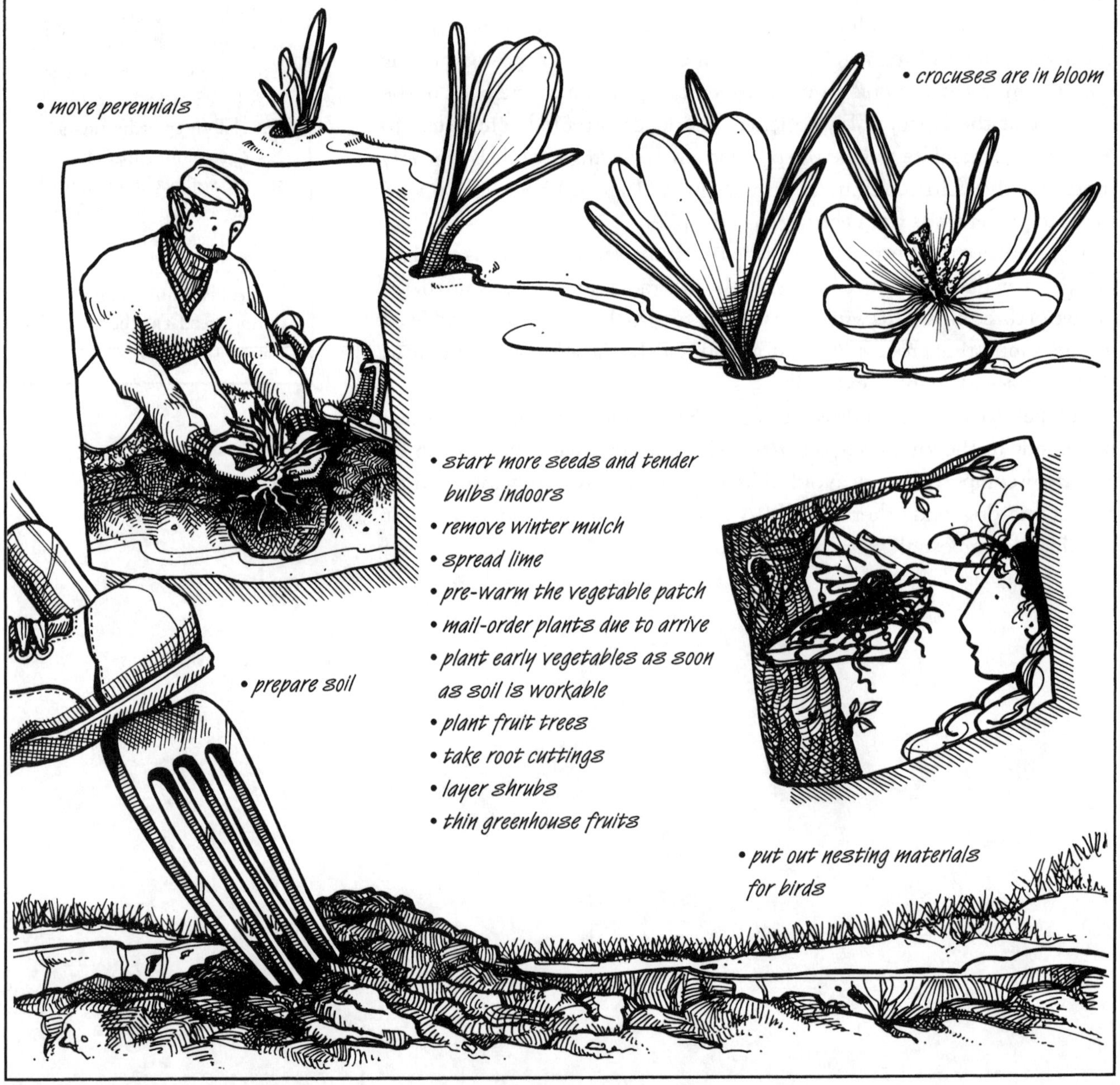

When crocuses are in bloom in exposed parts of the garden, the soil should be warm enough to begin various outdoor garden activities. The ground may be thawed enough to put certain transplants out in cold frames in the vegetable garden, divide and move perennial flowers and herbs, plant shrubs and trees, and start lawn rejuvenation. It all depends on the weather, how dry the soil is, and your inclinations.

Applying your energy in the right place at the right season can save a lot of work and frustration later on. When plants fail to thrive or succumb to insects and disease, the problem can almost always be traced to something lacking in the growing conditions. The maxim "treat the soil, not the plant" has particular relevance in the spring when so much of what we do in the garden involves digging the soil.

# April/May

**Hydrangea**
*Strange behavior observed in gardeners during periods of heavy rainfall. Symptoms include obsessive tool care, irrational mail order purchases, the neurotic sorting of seed packets, and buying alcoholic beverages by the case.*

*Beard and McKie*

## Gearing up Indoors

In some regions gardeners will have been out in the garden for some time now. But, if the weather is really lousy and it looks like there is no hope of getting out for days or weeks yet, spend some time playing with all those lovely seed packets. Arrange vegetables according to when they will be planted (see Table APR/MAY-2, page 130; MAY-1, page 167; MAY-3, page 172; JUN-1, page 213), or work out various planting arrangements and crop rotations. Sort herbs according to planting location (see Table FEB-1, page 40), or separate the ones that can be seeded directly outside around the last frost date from those that should not be planted until all danger of frost is past (see Table FEB-3, page 54). If you are running out of room indoors for starting annual flowers, do not start the ones that can be seeded directly outdoors (see Table FEB-4, page 56).

## More Transplants

More vegetables can be started indoors for transplanting outdoors (see Table FEB-2, page 52). Most cucurbits can be seeded directly outdoors when tomato transplants are put outdoors in May or June, but there is a better chance of obtaining ripe fruits in short season areas if they are started earlier indoors. Melons, canteloupes and watermelons need a long growing season so start them indoors four to five weeks before the last expected frost date. They grow rapidly once they get going and will need quite large containers before they finally go out in the garden.

Start cucumbers, winter squash, pumpkin, zucchini and summer squash

Pre-sprout potatoes in tray with rose end up.

Pre-sprout sweet potatoes in tray with soil.

two or three weeks before the last expected frost. They grow best when the air temperature is 65°F (18°C), with 70°F (21°C) bottom heat. Brussels sprouts, winter cabbage and late crops of leeks, broccoli and cauliflower can be started indoors as transplants about two weeks before the last expected frost date, or they can be seeded directly outdoors in June.

For a small crop of very early potatoes, pre-sprout some large sets by placing them in indirect light in a cool place. Stand them upright side by side in a shallow tray with the rose end up (the end that has most of the eyes). This is called "chitting" and is usually started four to six weeks before the last expected frost date. They can be planted out about a week before the last expected frost.

Sweet potato roots can be sprouted at the same time, but the method is slightly different. Place them in trays in a sunny place and barely cover them with soil. Carefully remove the sprouts when they are 6 to 10 inches (15 to 25 cm) long, plant them deeply in pots to form roots, then plant the rooted sprouts outdoors when the soil is thoroughly warmed. Treat the sprouts the same way as tender perennial cuttings (see page 61).

Herbs to start indoors include basil, chamomile, coriander, marjoram and Greek oregano (see Table FEB-3, page 54). If you plan to make pesto this summer, plant plenty of basil. Sow more basil directly outdoors when warm, settled weather arrives. Fluorescent lighting can be used to extend the growing space into poorly lit indoor areas. Keep lights close to young seedlings to prevent legginess (see page 51), and try to keep temperatures around 62°F (16°C) after seeds have germinated for the same reason.

More annual flowers can be started indoors (see Table FEB-4, page 56) or sow some of them directly outdoors sometime around the last frost date. Sowing outdoors is the safer route for those that do not transplant well, such as godetia and bachelor's button. Take precautions to prevent damping off disease in celosia, which is best started indoors (see pages 20 and 50).

Some of these later starts prefer cool conditions for germination. Annual phlox will not germinate at all if temperatures rise above 75°F (24°C). Its germination is erratic, but it helps to keep the seeds on the cool side.

Ten-week stock plants produce either single or double flowers. If they are grown at 55°F (12°C) after they have germinated, the plants that will produce double flowers can be distinguished by their lighter green, larger leaves.

Seedlings started last month should be potted on or thinned (see page 81).

Insert a small bamboo stake in each pot containing climbing vines (such as morning glory) so that seedlings do not become entangled.

Some annual flowers benefit from pinching when they have one or two sets of true leaves, or are 3 to 4 inches (8 to 10 cm) high (see Table FEB-4, page 56). Fuchsias, chrysanthemums and geraniums can also be pinched back to encourage branching. Do not pinch six weeks or less before blooms are wanted because each pinching delays flowering by several weeks.

Pinch annuals to encourage branching when they have one or two sets of true leaves.

With good care, seedlings will need regular repotting. Peppers, for example, are ready for 2 ½ or 3 inch (60 or 75 mm) pots when they reach the three leaf stage. Potting on promotes the growth of a large, healthy root system which will make transplants vigorous once they are put outdoors. Dahlia and perennial seedlings may also need potting on about this time, unless they were started off in large containers. To keep maintenance time down avoid unnecessary transplanting, but seedlings should not be allowed to get pot-bound.

Fertilize seedlings regularly, using only mild fish fertilizer or quarter strength fertilizer at first. Use 10-30-10 for flowers when they have graduated to full strength fertilizer, three regular doses of 10-52-70 just after transplanting for vegetables that fruit, and 20-20-20 for all vegetables and herbs once they are established. As planting time approaches, begin hardening off plants (see page 120) shortly before each kind is due to be planted out.

**Green Thumb Tip**

Pot-bound plants may flower prematurely before substantial leafy growth has taken place; consequently, the yield in size and number of flowers and fruits is considerably reduced. Some gardeners do this purposely to a few plants to get earlier blooms (and yields).

## More Tender Bulbs

Many tender perennial "bulbs" can be started into early growth indoors in a peat-based potting soil or regular potting soil with some extra perlite or vermiculite added. Start them a month or so before the last frost date, or wait until all danger of frost is past and plant them outside. Early planting indoors is helpful in short season areas, in regions where the soil stays cool all summer, and if an early flowering is wanted. See Table MAR/APR-2 (page 86) for the bulbs to start into growth. Agapanthus, begonia, caladium and others should have been started earlier (see March, page 78), but April or May is better than not at all. They can bloom indoors in the autumn if frost threatens.

To extend the period of bloom of acidanthera, freesia, gladiolus, montbretia, ranunculus or tigridia, start half of them indoors and save the other half for planting outdoors. Some gardeners space blooms by planting a few bulbs or corms every ten days. There are also early and late varieties of gladiolus to extend the season.

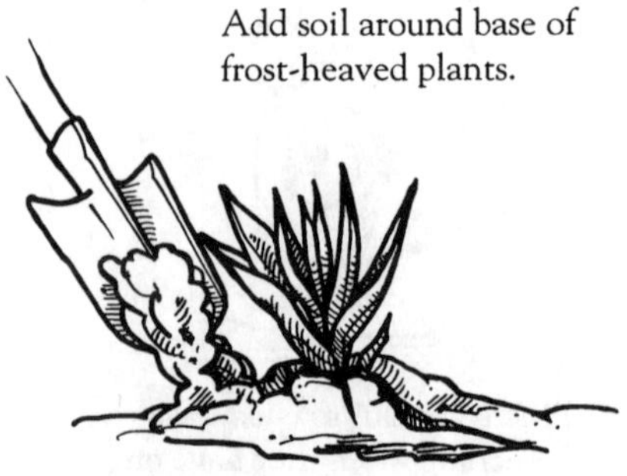

Add soil around base of frost-heaved plants.

## Gearing up Outdoors

It is time to prepare the outdoor garden for planting by removing mulch, tidying flower beds and shrub borders, adding soil amendments such as lime and compost, digging and warming the soil. Scrape your fingernails across a bar of soap before heading outside—they will be easier to clean afterwards.

### Removing Winter Mulch

Be careful not to remove winter mulches too early in anticipation of spring. The purpose of mulch is to keep the ground frozen until the hard frosts are over. Repeated freezings and thawings are hard on plants; if they start to come out of dormancy during a mild spell, they are less able to tolerate the freezing temperatures during the next cold spell than they were in the middle of winter. Many plants survive the winter quite nicely; it is spring that kills them off.

First loosen the mulch, then take away a little at a time from flowers, nurseries and strawberry beds once the ground has thawed (test by poking a stick into the ground). Too early removal from the strawberry bed will encourage early blossoms which may be damaged by late spring frosts. Damaged blossoms will either fail to set fruit, or the fruit will be misshapen. Remove part of the mulch when foliage starts to get light yellow and new leaf growth begins. Leave one-third to two-thirds of the mulch on the bed for the plants to grow through. Gradually remove mulch from tender roses. Leave the soil mound in place (see page 388) until the buds are bursting.

Repeated freeze-thaw cycles will heave some unmulched plants right out of the ground. If this is observed, do not try to push the plant back into the ground because that tears the roots. Rather, cover the roots with soil from another part of the garden, or dig up the plant and set it back in at the proper depth.

Cut back asparagus fronds, if this was not done last autumn (see page 383). Cut or pull out dried stalks from the flower bed. Instead of applying an autumn mulch, many gardeners leave old stalks in place to trap drifting leaves. This method is fine as long as there have been no disease problems. Leaves can either be gradually cleared out when the ground has thawed or left to form a natural summer mulch. Make sure they do not cover the crowns of plants because sodden masses of leaves can kill emerging perennial shoots.

### Green Thumb Tip

If extra early asparagus, rhubarb or strawberries are desired, remove the mulch in one part of each patch and put a cold frame or row cover in place. This will hasten warming and protect tender new growth from frost. For etiolated rhubarb, pile on a thick mulch of straw over the crown. This rhubarb will not be available sooner, but it will be extra long and tender when it does grow up through the straw. Try putting a large glass jar upside down over a clump of chives and put small cold frames over the larger herbs of French sorrel, lovage, mint, beebalm, salad burnet and French tarragon. If the vegetable garden was mulched last fall, the mulch can be pulled back in some areas and cold frames set in place to prepare for planting extra early crops of greens. Do this at least two weeks before planting.

### *Building the Compost Pile*

Winter mulches, old leaves and twigs from around the yard can be added to the compost pile, although not much decomposing will take place until temperatures are warm and settled. Mix in a variety of organic wastes as the compost pile is built up, aiming for approximately two parts of dryish material (such as wood shavings, sawdust, dry leaves, paper, hair, coffee filters, eggshells, straw, stems and nutshells) to one part wettish material (such as vegetable peelings, fruit skins, tea bags, seaweed, green manure crops, weeds, grass, animal bedding and manure). Include any other organic waste except meat, fat and milk products (which attract animals).

Decomposition will be faster and the finished compost available sooner if a variety of organic materials are used, materials are chopped fine and mixed together instead of adding them in layers, and the pile is mixed and turned once or twice a week. The soil clinging to roots of plants is enough to bring in the needed micro-organisms that do the breaking down; mixing in partially decomposed compost will accomplish the same thing. A sprinkling of lime will counteract acidity, but it is not essential. Avoid cat and dog faeces—bury these in soil where food will not be grown—but human urine is sterile and can be added to the pile to encourage faster decomposition. When the weather is more settled, introduce some worms from the indoor compost bin, if you started one (see page 401).

If rats invade the compost pile, make certain that rat poison cannot be reached by birds or other animals.

#### *Green Thumb Tip*

When all of the tidying up is done, it is tempting to add fresh mulch. It is probably wiser to wait until the soil has warmed up; plants will not grow much in cold soil and adding mulch too soon keeps the temperature down.

### *pH and Liming*

Liming need not be an annual spring chore for most gardeners. Garden lime is added to lighten the texture of clay soils and to neutralize acidic soils (see page 377). Soils are rarely alkaline enough to require the addition of sulphur to lower the pH. Once the correct pH is reached (see Green Thumb Tip, page 378, for application rates), lime needs to be applied only once every two to three years as it has a slow release time.

Except for ericaceous plants and a few other acid loving plants, most vegetables, flowers and lawn grasses grow best at a pH of around 6.5. It is essential that lime be spread several weeks before seeding and planting so that crops are not harmed—it is best to spread lime in the autumn, particularly on bare planting areas. It can be spread on the lawn in the spring, but not if the soil is still sodden as walking on it at this point will compact the soil. Repeat each spring and autumn until the pH is around 6.5 using small, regular doses rather than one heavy dose.

Spread lime or wood ashes (or sulphur if needed) in the flower garden as well. Lime should be scratched in or dug in once the soil is dry enough to work, but it can be left on the surface. Spread lime in the vegetable garden, but not where potatoes will be planted because there is a greater risk of scab in freshly limed soil. By following potatoes with lime in the crop rotation, and by liming only once every three or four years, it is not difficult to avoid freshly limed soil for potatoes. Most fruits grow well at pH 6.0 to 6.5, but blueberries prefer a more acidic soil (around pH 5.0 to 5.5). Only a few herbs prefer neutral or slightly alkaline soil (see Table FEB-1, page 40).

### Spreading Organic Matter

Organic matter in the soil serves several functions and can be supplied in several forms (see page 379). It should not be added too early, however. Give the lime at least two weeks to bind with the soil, and make sure the ground is thoroughly thawed before spreading manure and other fertilizers.

Spread a 1 to 2 inch (3 to 5 cm) layer of manure, garden compost, spoiled hay or straw, leaf mould, seaweed or mushroom compost (the horse manure and straw mixture from mushroom growing beds) on asparagus, rhubarb, strawberry and perennial flower beds. Avoid the crowns of plants and do not worry about working it into the soil. Digging it in only disturbs roots, whereas earthworms will do all the work without harming the roots. Compost or manure can be worked into the deeper levels when perennial flowers are lifted and divided every few years.

Spread a 2 inch (5 cm) layer of organic matter under fruiting canes, fruiting shrubs and fruit trees. Spread a little under ornamental shrubs and trees. Tired looking hedges and shrubs often burst into fresh growth after being pruned and top dressed with well rotted manure. Lawns can be top dressed in the spring with a mixture of screened manure or compost, good soil and sand, or this can be done in the autumn (see September/October, page 371).

There is some evidence that top dressing with manure and compost helps reduce soil borne diseases by reducing water splash and reduces the severity of anthracnose in plants, which shows up as irregular dark brown or black spotting. The number of lesions is reduced and defoliation is delayed if plants have sufficient nitrogen. Some gardeners find that used coffee grounds make a superb mulch for cedars (*Thuja*).

## *Preparing Bare Planting Areas*

### *Adding amendments*

Ideally, where really early vegetable crops are planned, manure should have been spread and the soil fully prepared and then covered with mulch in the autumn (see October/November, page 385). All that is then required in the spring is the early removal of the mulch to encourage faster thawing and warming of the soil, and perhaps a light raking to prepare the seed bed.

On established vegetable and annual flower beds, on ground broken and dug last autumn, and where top soil has been added, spread well rotted manure, spoiled hay or straw, mushroom compost, leaf mould, seaweed or garden compost. The thickness of the layer required varies according to the crop: 1 to 2 inches (3 to 5 cm) for new lawns, annuals and shallow rooted crops; 2 to 4 inches (5 to 10 cm) for deep rooted crops. Rotted manure, coarse compost and green manure crops should be dug in four weeks before sowing seeds and two weeks before setting out transplants. The soil must be dry enough to work, however, before any digging is done.

Manure should be incorporated in the autumn where root crops are to be grown, and where lilies and other bulbs are to be planted in the spring. Carrots, turnips, potatoes, beets, onions, leeks and other "root" crops are more prone to disease and cultural problems in freshly manured soil. It is all right, however, to use 1 or 2 inches (3 to 5 cm) of well rotted manure or purchased dried manure in the spring rather than doing without any at all.

Adding manure in the spring is ideal for leafy crops and heavy feeding crops such as corn. Fresh chicken manure can release ammonia in amounts harmful to young plants, so it should be applied at least one month before planting occurs and it must be incorporated thoroughly. Work fresh or rotted manure into the soil in the spring where bulbs are to be planted in the autumn, but avoid manure altogether if narcissus bulb fly has been a problem (see page 185).

### *Digging*

After organic matter has been spread fairly evenly over a bare planting area, either scratch it in when planting seeds and transplants, or simply loosen the soil with a garden fork or U-bar digger. Earthworms pull organic matter into the soil, so there is no need to dig it in, unless starting with very poor soils or growing root or tuber crops. By not mixing and turning the soil, the natural soil profile will be preserved, resulting in a quicker start for seeds and plants. To prevent clumps from forming, avoid working the soil when wet. A lumpy seed bed or one full of rocks can cause forked or misshapen roots in

### *Green Thumb Tip*

Peat moss has long been used to increase the organic content of soil, even though it is very low in nutrients. Because it is a natural resource that is being mined faster than it forms at each harvest site, more and more gardeners are refusing to use it, or are using it only in restricted situations indoors. Each time a bog is destroyed, rare and unusual plants are lost permanently from that site because it takes thousands of years for a bog to form. Compost, coconut fibre and leaf mould (see page 398) are good alternatives to peat moss and have the added advantage of supplying nutrients to the soil.

carrots and parsnips, and seed germination will be poorer. Winter frost heave helps bring rocks to the surface.

If the soil is poor, or if growing root or potato crops, work the organic matter into the soil throughout the rooting depth of the crop (see Green Thumb Tip, page 381). Organic matter mixed in well will help the soil retain moisture during the dry months of summer and thereby reduce knobbiness and hollow heart in potatoes, which are caused by an interruption in the water supply during tuber formation. Carrots and other root crops split if heavy moisture follows a dry spell, and cabbage heads may split if the soil moisture content varies widely.

Loosening the soil for deep-rooted crops will make it easier for them to expand in girth and to search for water during dry spells. If rapidly forming potato tubers have to expand and push against heavy soil, for example, they will be misshapen and have deformed eyes. In soggy soil low in oxygen, such as that without sufficient organic matter, potato pores will become very large, causing rough skin. Of course, they are still edible.

Expensive fertilizers such as bonemeal can be mixed with the soil for individual planting holes or spread over an entire area. The latter needs to be done only once every four years as bonemeal lasts a long time. Synthetic fertilizers can be incorporated but there are several disadvantages to using them (see page 163).

Turn green manure crops (see pages 178-180 and 298) into the soil as soon as the soil can be worked. Rye, for example, should be dug in when it is about 4 inches (10 cm) high, before the last spring frost. Do not let it set seed.

The fat, brown-headed C-shaped creatures found in the soil are the larvae of June beetles – they eat the roots of plants. The adults lay their eggs in sods or weeds, so the larvae are worst during the first year after sod has been turned. Their numbers diminish over the next two years (the larval stage lasts three years). It may be best to avoid root crops in freshly turned sod.

Wireworms are also most plentiful during the first two years after grass has been removed or dug in. Frequent cultivation before planting seems to reduce their numbers as it exposes them to predation by birds and discourages egg laying by the adults. Some gardeners report that sprinkling used coffee grounds along seeded rows or root crops seems to reduce the damage.

### *Final preparation of the seed bed*

How and when planting is done is directly tied to pest and disease control, including weed management. From preparing the planting area to sowing

### Green Thumb Tip

To test if the soil is dry enough to work, squeeze a handful or two into a ball, and poke a finger into it or drop it from shoulder height. If it shatters, the soil is dry enough to dig. The soil is also too wet if it sticks to your boots. If the soil is too dry to form into a ball, moisten it before digging.

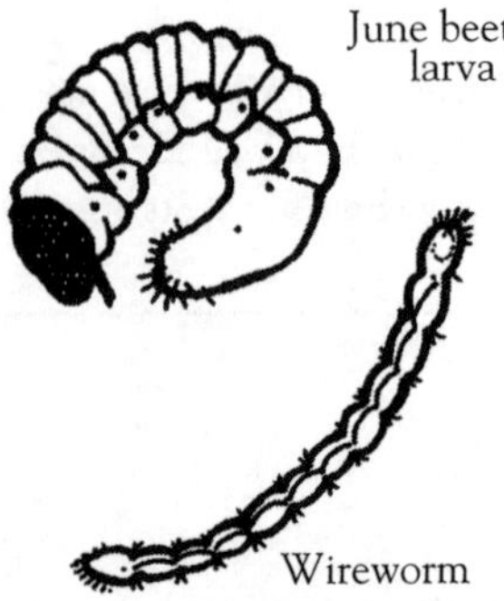

June beetle larva

Wireworm

One way to have the best of both worlds is to work the seedbed until the soil is fine, raking it with a metal rake to remove lumps and stones. Do not pulverize the soil to a fine dust with a cultivator, however, because that can lead to soil compaction. Try not to walk on the area after it is cultivated. If you cannot reach and area without stepping on the soil, put down boards to walk on so that the soil is not compacted as much.

Leave the cultivated area idle for about ten days to give the weeds time to germinate, then remove them with the least possible disturbance to the seedbed a day or two before sowing the crop. Preparing a seed bed ten to fourteen days in advance will also discourage some insect pests. The adult fly stage of onion maggots, for example, prefers to lay its eggs in freshly disturbed soil.

### Green Thumb Tip

Seed germination is dependent on water uptake, and the final soil preparations carried out in the spring can slow down or speed up the process. Lumpy soil will cause uneven germination because seeds will make poor contact with the soil and absorb water at different rates. A smooth, fine seedbed ensures that all seeds come into close contact with the soil and its moisture—this is particularly important for fine seeds. A smooth seedbed also helps weed seeds germinate, so if planting large seeds such as peas, beans or nasturtiums, you might want to stop cultivating the soil before it gets too fine.

### *Warming the soil*

Digging the soil and loosening it a couple of weeks before planting helps it warm up more quickly, and raised beds warm up before beds on the flat. Soil temperature determines as much or more than air temperature how quickly seeds germinate and transplants grow.

To warm the soil even more quickly, spread clear plastic over parts of vegetable, herb and flower gardens a couple of weeks before planting is to start. Eliminate as much air as possible from under the plastic. This can raise the soil temperature by as much as 16ºF (9ºC). Floating row covers and cold frames will also warm the soil, but less effectively. Depending on the weather, this can be done as early as six to eight weeks before the last expected frost date.

When you have decided where particular vegetables and flowers will be planted, other methods can be used to warm up the soil if you are in a very short season area, or want an extra early start. To be effective, the methods should be started two to six weeks before planting.

For crops planted in rows, mound the soil into wide rows running east-west, and later sow seeds on the south side. Where summers are dry, make a V-shaped trench, mound the soil on the north side, and use the warmed soil to fill in the trench after planting. A trench also works well for gladiolus corms and other tender bulbs needing warm soil, especially where summers are cool. Make small hills of soil for vegetables (such as corn) that are planted in small clusters. Make large mounds about 10 inches high (25 cm) by 3 feet wide (1 m) where melons, sweet potatoes, cucumbers and squashes will be planted. In dry regions, warm the soil for these crops by covering it with clear plastic; soil raised into mounds dries out faster than the surrounding soil. Dig holes 1 foot wide by at least 1 foot deep (30 cm by 30 cm) where tomatoes will be planted. Mound the dug out soil on the north side of the hole so more sun can reach into the hole. In short season areas, or if you are desperate to start planting, prepare a hot bed (see pages 348-349).

### New beds

Mark out positions of new beds or borders. A slow but strain-free way to prepare the soil for planting in the fall or next spring is to kill the grass by covering it with a mulch of newspaper (at least ten sheets thick), straw or hay bales, sheets of tar paper, black plastic, or any other light-eliminating substance. The ground will not look pretty, but three months later the sod will be exceptionally easy to turn and work into the soil. The area can be planted with late season vegetables or with annual rye or some other cover crop in August for winter protection and soil improvement.

## Planting Outdoors

Planting dates depend greatly on the weather and can easily vary by a month or more in any one location from year to year. There are several advantages to planting early, particularly in the vegetable garden. The main reason, of course, is to ease those aching green thumbs, but the amount of work is also spread out over a longer period, the first crops can be harvested sooner and a second crop planted, some crops grow better in cool weather, and insect damage is often less because the plants are well established before many insects have emerged. Crops planted in short season areas often catch up to those planted earlier in long season areas because they receive a greater amount of total warmth during the season.

### Pre-Planting Care of Mail Order Plants

Sometimes potted herbs and perennial flowers that were ordered from catalogues arrive before the ground is workable. Immediately remove the packaging, water them, and remove any dead or damaged parts. If planting can start in a week or so, simply keep them in a cool place (above freezing) out of wind and direct light for a couple of days, then put them in bright, indirect light when they have revived. Do not keep them in the house unless they are to be grown indoors in pots; the warm temperatures will stimulate growth that is much too tender for planting outside. They can be kept outdoors in a cold frame, or put in a sheltered position and covered if a hard frost threatens.

If planting will be delayed for a couple of weeks or more, put the plants in slightly larger pots in potting or garden soil. If the roots are in a tight ball, try to wash off some of the soil in water and gently loosen them. The roots will grow into the surrounding medium much more effectively after this treatment. If the root ball stays intact, the plant will grow as if it were still in a tight little pot, even after being planted outdoors. Bare root strawberries should be planted as soon as the soil is workable. If planting is delayed, pot them up into individual pots or in flats and keep them in a cool, bright location.

Loosen root ball in a pail of water.

The roots of bare root trees and shrubs need to be protected from freezing temperatures and from drying out, and the plants must be kept cool so that they are not stimulated into early growth. As soon as the plants arrive, unpack the roots and soak them in water for up to twelve hours, but no longer, then repack the roots in moistened packing material. The plants can be stored in a cold room or root cellar for two or, at the most, three days before they are planted out.

If planting is delayed more than two or three days, trees and shrubs should be heeled in. Dig a trench outside in a place sheltered from wind. It should be straight along one edge and sloped on the other so that the trees and shrubs can be "planted" close together at a $45^0$ angle to the ground. The roots are covered with soil but the tops are left open to the weather.

Heeling in trench for trees and shrubs that cannot be planted for two or three days.

Planting can be delayed almost indefinitely if plants are purchased in pots or in ball and burlap form, but it is best to settle the plants into their new quarters as soon as the soil is workable to give the roots plenty of time to become established before the autumn freeze-up. Keep them in a shaded position out of wind, and water them well before planting.

## Seeding and transplanting

With the soil prepared and warmed, the exciting day arrives when seeding and transplanting can begin.

If the soil has become dry, water the seedbed before you start planting. If watering is done after planting, the soil may form a crust that is difficult for fine seed cotyledons to push their way through. Spread a fine mulch of grass clippings to reduce crusting, especially over seeds that are slow to emerge.

If planting large seeds in dry soil, dig a shallow trench and water the

### Green Thumb Tip

The major causes of poor germination are planting too deeply and uneven planting depth. The appropriate planting depth is two times the seed's diameter. When seeding in rows, lay a rake handle or something similar down on the soil to make a shallow, uniform trench.

bottom of it. Plant the seeds and cover them with dry soil to a depth twice their diameter. The dry soil on the surface reduces the evaporation of the water in the trench—there is no wick effect as there would be if the soil were wet through to the surface. Remember to keep the soil moist until the seeds have germinated. Use a fine spray and water frequently, but be careful not to overwater if the ground is already moist.

Transplants need soil that is prepared almost as well as for seeding. Fine roots make better contact with fine soil than they do with soil full of lumps and stones. If preparing a large area for transplants is onerous, or if the soil is very poor, dig good big planting holes for each transplant and backfill with soil that has been enriched with organic matter such as compost.

Not all transplants are put out at the same time. Hardy annual flowers and some herbs can tolerate cooler temperatures and go out sooner than tender annuals (see Table FEB-3, page 54, and FEB-4, page 56). Some vegetables can tolerate near freezing temperatures, whereas others turn black and die. Celery will bolt if it is exposed to more than twelve hours of temperatures below 50°F (10°C), sending up tough flower stalks instead of tender stems. Lettuce will also bolt if it is exposed to cool temperatures before it is three weeks old, but seems relatively resistant after the one to three leaf stage. Three-week-old lettuce transplants grown indoors can be held for up to two weeks at 34°F (2°C) if they cannot be planted out as soon as they are ready. Peppers put out too soon will simply drop their flowers if the temperature falls too low. Brassicas are very susceptible to transplant shock and to stress due to drought and sudden temperature fluctuations during the five to eight leaf stage.

Transplant younger plants rather than older plants if you have a choice. If transplants are on the spindly side, those with the growing point at the top can be planted deeply (see Green Thumb Tip, page 81). Brassicas can have the stem buried up to the cotyledons or, if necessary, the cotyledons can be removed and the brassicas buried up to just beneath the first true leaf.

Transplants have not been hardened off properly if the leaves turn white, due to the sudden increase in sunshine, or if the leaves turn yellow, due to sudden exposure to cooler temperatures. Cold, wet soils can cause a temporary phosphorus deficiency, which shows up as a reddish-purple colouration of the leaves. This is corrected when the soil warms up and phosphorus becomes available, but try to warm the soil first next time, or plant later. Brown, dry leaf tips or edges indicate that the plant has dried out because the roots were not able to take up water as fast as it was lost due

### Preventive Measure

Harden off transplants for about ten days before setting them outside to get them used to cooler temperatures, drier air and wind. Start by putting the plants outdoors for an hour or two during the warmest part of the day, but keep them out of direct sunlight. Increase the length of time and intensity of sunlight daily over the next week to ten days. Start by putting them in weak morning sun and build up to full midday sunshine. Then leave them outside for a couple of nights, still in their pots, in addition to full days outdoors. Harden off transplants in a cold frame or row cover if that is where they will be grown early on.

To reduce the shock of being replanted, water the transplants well before planting outside; set them out on a cloudy, foggy or drizzly, windless day; water them immediately after transplanting; and water individual plants daily with a small cupful of water each until they are well established. If the daytime weather conditions are not suitable, transplant in the evening so that roots have overnight to adjust before the plant makes demands for more water. If it is windy, put a shingle in the ground on the windward side of the plant. Provide shade if transplanting must take place while it is sunny.

to wind, dry air and strong sun. Having well rooted transplants and protecting them from wind and sun helps reduce this.

Growing plants in individual containers rather than in flats helps to minimize root disturbance at planting time. If using peat pots, either remove the transplant before planting it in the ground, or tear off the rim of the pot. If the rim remains above the soil level, it will act as a wick and draw moisture away from the soil around the roots.

## Vegetables

### Protected crops

Cold frames, row covers, tunnels or other forms of protection are essential for really early planting. This can start when the first spring bulbs are in bloom, as soon as the soil is prepared. Set out transplants of head lettuce, Chinese cabbage and early head cabbage. Early greens growing in large, deep flats can be set directly into a cold frame without transplanting. Sets of onions, garlic and shallots should be planted as soon as the soil is workable and do not need to be protected by cold frames. Sow seeds or set out a few transplants of lettuce, bunching onions, spinach, mustard greens, peas, turnip greens, radish, arugula, corn salad, broad beans, Chinese cabbage, broccoli, cauliflower, escarole, endive, kale and collards under protection (see Table APR/MAY-2, page 130).

Extra early tomatoes can be transplanted into cold frames a week or two before the last expected frost, but use tomatoes that can tolerate cool temperatures. By this time, some of the greens in cold frames will already have been harvested to make room for the tomatoes, and many other vegetables can be seeded or transplanted without protection. If a hard frost threatens, the cold frames protecting the tomatoes will have to be covered with old blankets—tomatoes do not tolerate chilly temperatures as well as the green crops.

When the weather has warmed and is settled, sometime in May or June, move the cold frames to where there will be crops which need extra warmth and protection from wind. Heat loving crops such as canteloupes, watermelons and sweet potatoes will benefit from the extra shelter. Where chilly breezes blow all summer, eggplants, tomatoes and peppers will grow better and produce more fruit if grown in cold frames. You may want to leave protection around individual heat-loving plants, such as tomatoes, until there is no longer a chance of a late frost.

> **Preventive Measure**
>
> Be careful not to let covers such as cold frames, row tunnels or pop bottles overheat on sunny days. Provide ventilation so that plants do not cook!

### Preventive Measure

Sowing or transplanting with wider spacing than usual is a good idea if there is shortage of moisture or nutrients during some part of the growing season, or if the soil is very light and sandy. This gives each plant a larger volume from which to draw moisture and nutrients.

### Spacing

If seeding or transplanting beets very early in the season, space them 4 inches apart in rows 7 inches apart (10 by 18 cm). At planting time seeds are spaced closer together within the row, but later they are thinned to 4 inch spacing. At this distance there will be no restriction on moisture or nutrient uptake, and the beets can grow as quickly as is possible in cool soil without any competition. If planting in late May or early June when the soil is warm, beets can be spaced closer together at 1 inch by 12 inches (2.5 by 30 cm). This will give the greatest yield and the roots will be medium sized, good for fresh eating or pickling. When plants are close together in rows, the rows are spaced a bit further apart to increase the moisture and nutrients available.

Beets planted just for greens can be planted 2 inches apart in rows 4 inches apart (5 by 10 cm), and the first cut can be made when plants are 2 to 4 inches (5 to 10 cm) tall.

When planting beets at 1 inch spacing in rows, there is no need to plant more thickly and then thin later. Each beet "seed" is actually a capsule containing several seeds, so thinning may be required even when spaced at the outset. Swiss chard is the same, so seed thinly. Seeds sown later in the season will have a higher germination rate than seeds planted before the weather is warm and settled.

Sparse versus thick planting applies to early and late plantings of carrots and other vegetables, however you might want to wait a few weeks until the soil is warmer before planting parsnips, salsify, scorzonera and carrots. More of the seed will germinate, and faster, and weeds will have germinated and been cleared by then so the vegetables will meet less competition for moisture and nutrients. There is also less chance of damage by carrot rust fly larvae as the adults hopefully will have laid their eggs elsewhere before seeding occurred. These root crops should be planted in loose soil that you can easily poke a finger into.

If you do plant carrots early for an early harvest, use short, early varieties, pre-warm the soil (see pages 117-118), seed generously to compensate for lower germination rates (but thin later to wider spacing), or use fluid sowing (see page 132). Cover the crop with cheesecloth or agricultural fabric such as Reemay to protect it from carrot rust flies. If sowing carrots a few weeks hence, sow as thinly as possible to reduce the amount of thinning required. Bruising the foliage when thinning attracts carrot rust flies to the area.

In addition to beets and carrots, other seedlings that will probably require thinning to achieve the appropriate spacing include broccoli, Brussels sprouts, cabbage, cauliflower, lettuce, onion from seed, parsnip, radish, rutabaga, salsify scorzonera and turnip.

### *Pest and disease management*

Brassicas follow leguminous crops in the vegetable garden crop rotation. If root maggots have been a problem, work leaves into the soil the autumn prior to planting brassicas. It is not clear whether it is the leaves themselves that have an effect, or the digging that destroys the maggots. As well, work wood ashes into the top 2 inches (5 cm) of soil a couple of weeks before planting.

Putting a 5 inch (12 cm) circle of tar paper or cardboard on the ground underneath each brassica transplant will discourage the adult insects from laying eggs in the soil around the stems. It also helps to conserve moisture—so that the plants can better tolerate some root damage—and encourages beetles, which eat the maggots. There is less chance of egg-laying if planting is done during cool weather because fewer adults will be around. Transplants in individual containers are also better able to withstand damage than those grown together in a flat because they suffer less root damage at planting time.

Nematode damage shows up as cysts on brassica roots and the plants fail to thrive. Plant marigolds the year before brassicas if this has been a problem. Marigolds release root toxins that repel nematodes, but it takes a year or more for the results to show. Clubroot causes wilting and poor development of plants; club-shaped swellings on the roots develop and the roots function poorly. Affected plants should be dug up and destroyed, along with any weeds in the mustard family. Good drainage is required because the motile spores seem to spread more rapidly in wet soils.

Cutworm problems can be reduced by creating a barrier around each plant. Place a toilet paper roll or small tin can around each transplant. Sink 1 inch (2.5 cm) into the soil and leave 2 inches (5 cm) extending above the soil. Other barriers can be made by inserting a toothpick on each side of the stem, so that a cutworm cannot completely girdle it; spreading two handfuls of wood ashes and lime in a circle around each transplant, but not touching it; forming a ring of diatomaceous earth around each plant, but not if you have cats. Swallows and bats will eat the moth that is the adult form of cutworms, and many animals, including bluejays, sparrows, robins, chickens, snakes and toads, eat the worms.

Flea beetles, tiny insects that jump and disappear when disturbed, chew holes in brassica leaves. Early planting reduces the problem as plants are large and better able to withstand the damage by the time the insects emerge.

Clubroot

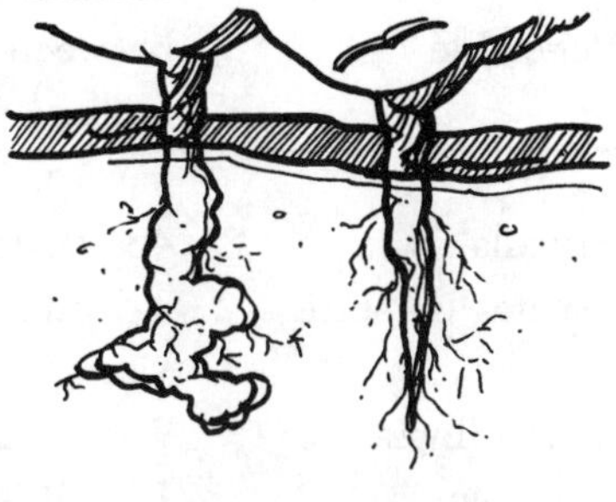

Cutworm Barriers

Wood ash and lime

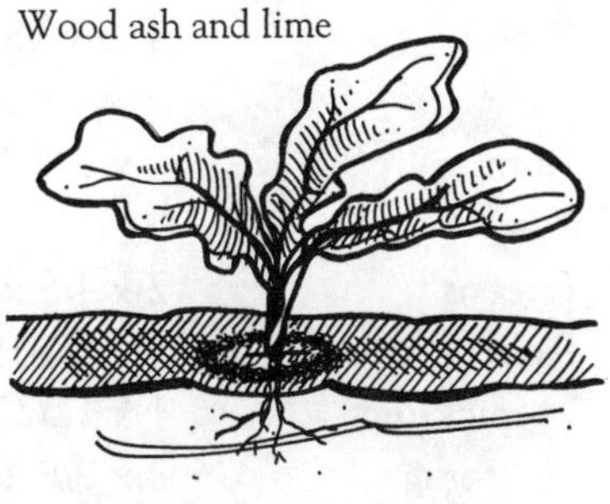

Toothpicks

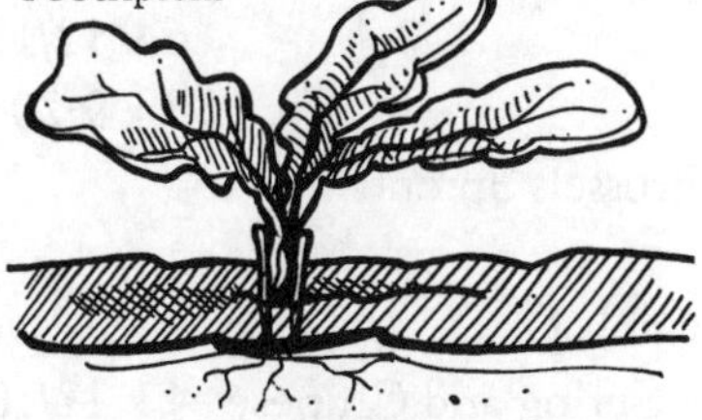

Paper roll or tin can

## Table APR/MAY-1 Final Spacing of Vegetables for Maximum Yield Outdoors

(use wider spacing if the growing season is very dry)

| Vegetable | Within row x between rows inches/cm | Grid or Block inches/cm | Comments |
|---|---|---|---|
| Arugula | 4 x 9/10 x 23 | 6 x 6/15x15 | space more widely if grown to flowering size |
| Asparagus - seeds | 3-5 x 12-18/8 -13 x 30-45 | | rows easier to weed and mulch than block plantings |
| - seedlings | 9-10 x 12-18/23-25 x 30-45 | | |
| - crowns | 18 x 36/45 x 90 | | |
| Beans | | | |
| Bush | 2-4 x 18/5-10x 45 | 6 x 6/15 x 15 | snap, wax, or shell beans |
| Lima | 3 x 18/8 x 45 | 7 x 7/18 x 18 | |
| Broad | 4 ½ x 18/11 x 45 | | tall plants |
| | | 9 x 9/23 x 23 | compact plants |
| Runner | 6 x 24/15 x 60 | | 36"/90cm between double rows |
| Beets | | | |
| Greens | 2 x 4/5 x 10 | | wider spacing in spring |
| Roots - spring | 4 x 7/10 x 18 | | soak seeds 1/2 hour |
| - pickling | 1 x 12/2.5 x 30 | | yields small to medium roots |
| - storage | 3 x 8/8 x 20 | | yields large roots |
| Broccoli | 4 x 18/10 x 45 | | early, small central head |
| | 6 x 12/15 x 30 | | central head and side spears |
| | 8 x 9/20 x 23 | | large central head |
| Brussels Sprouts | | 20 x 20/50 x 50 | one harvest, small sprouts |
| | | 36 x 36/90 x 90 | continuous picking |
| Cabbage | | | |
| Spring and Chinese | 4 x 12/10 x 30 | | thin later to 8 x 12/20 x 30 and finally to 12 x 12/30 x 30; can eat thinnings |
| Summer and Winter | | 14 x 14/36 x 36 | high yield, small heads |
| | | 18 x 18/45 x 45 | same yield, large heads |
| Canteloupe | | 36 x 36/90x 90 | bush type |
| | | 48 x 48/120 x 120 | trailing type |
| Carrots - spring | 4 x 6/10 x 15 | | |
| - main | 1 ½ x 6/4 x 15 | | |

| Vegetable | Within row x between rows inches/cm | Grid or Block inches/cm | Comments |
|---|---|---|---|
| Cauliflower | 4 x 9/10 x 23 | | mini heads |
| | | 17 x 17/43 x 43 | small heads |
| | | 21 x 21/53 x53 | large heads |
| Celeriac | | 12 x 12/30 x 30 | |
| Celery | | 6 x 6/15 x 15 | high yield, small stalks |
| | | 11 x 11/28 x 28 | good self blanching |
| Chives | | 9 x 9/23 x 23 | 2-3 seedlings per clump |
| Collards | | 10 x 10/25 x 25 | |
| Corn | 10 x 24/25 x 60 | 15 x 15/38 x 38 | sow thickly, then thin; separate different kinds |
| Corn Salad (Mache) | 2 x 8/5 x 20 | 4 x 4/10 x 10 | |
| Cucumber | | 36 x 36/90 x 90 | bush type |
| | | 48 x 48/120 x 120 | vine type, unless trained up |
| Eggplant | | 16 x 16/40 x 40 | closer if compact variety |
| Endive (Curly Endive) | | 12 x 12/30 x 30 | |
| Escarole | | 15 x 15/38 x 38 | |
| Florence Fennel | 8 x 15/20 x 38 | | |
| Garlic Cloves | 4 x 6/10 x 15 | | 1"/2.5 cm deep spring; 2"/5 cm autumn |
| Kale | | 12 x 12/30 x 30 | |
| Kohlrabi | 9 x 12/23 x 30 | | wide spacing helps prevent woodiness |
| Leeks - spring | 1 x 12/2.5 x 30 | | thin leeks, raw or cooked |
| - main | 6 x 12/15 x 30 | | maximum yield, normal size |
| | (4)6 x 12/15 x 30 | | groups of four for quick harvest of small leeks |
| Lettuce | | | |
| Head | 12.5 x 10/32 x 25 | 10 x 10/25 x 25 | |
| Butterhead | 9 x 8/23 x 20 | 9 x 9/23 x 23 | |
| Cos (Romaine) | 9 x 8/23 x 20 | 9 x 9/23 x 23 | |
| Leaf or early Cos | 1 x 5/2.5 x 13 | | |
| Melons | | 36 x 36/90 x 90 | bush type |
| | | 48 x 48/120 x 120 | trailing type |
| Mustard - spring | | 6 x 6/15 x 15 | |
| - fall | | 4 x 4/10 x 10 | |

| Vegetable | **Within row x between rows** inches/cm | **Grid or Block** inches/cm | **Comments** |
|---|---|---|---|
| Onions | | | |
| Bunching/Spring | 1 x 4/2.5 x 23 | | 12"/30 cm between band centres |
| | or ¼ x ¼/0.6 x 0.6 in | | 3"/8 cm wide bands |
| Pickling | 50 x 12/1.25 x 30 | | 12"/30 cm between band centres |
| | or ¼ x ¼/0.6 x 0.6 in | | 9"/23 cm wide bands |
| Storage | | | |
| - sets | 2 x 10/5 x 25 | | maximum yield, medium onions |
| | 3-4 x 10/80-10 x 25 | | large onions |
| - transplants | 1 ½ x 12/3.8 x 30 | | maximum yield, medium onions |
| | 3-4 x 12/8-10 x 30 | | large onions |
| Welsh/Evergreen | 1 x 9/2.5 x 23 | | thinned to 8 x 9/20 x 23 |
| Parsnip | | 5 x 5/13 x 13 | |
| | 3 x 8/8 x 20 | | 2 to 3 seeds every 3"/8 cm, thin to 1 every 3"/8 cm |
| Peas - dwarf | 4½ x 4½/11 x 11 | | 15"/38 cm between triple rows |
| -tall | 2 x 5/5 x 13 | | |
| Peppers - hot | | 15 x 15/38 x 38 | keep hot and sweet varieties separate |
| - sweet | | 18 x 18/45 x 45 | |
| Potatoes | | | |
| - very small sets | 8-10 x 30/20-25 x 76 | | for main crop |
| - small sets | 9-12 x 30/20-25 x 76 | | for main crop |
| - medium sets | 10-14 x 30/20-35 x 76 | | for early crops |
| - large sets | 11-16 x 30/28-40 x 76 | | for early crops |
| | | 15 x 15/38 x 38 | for very early crops or late summer crops |
| Pumpkin | 48 x 72/120 x 180 | 60 x 60/150 x 150 | |
| Radicchio | 12 ½ x 10/32 x 25 | | |
| Radish | 1 x 6/2.5 x 15 | | |
| Salsify | 4 x 6/10 x 15 | | |
| Scorzonera | 4 x 6/10 x 15 | | |
| Shallots | 1 x 1/2.5 x 2.5 | | early greens |
| | 6 x 8/15 x 20 | | sets 3/4"/2 cm diameter or less |
| | 6 x 12/15 x 30 | | sets larger than 3/4"/2 cm |
| Spinach - for cooking | 1 x 12/2.5 x 30 | | thinned to 4"/10 cm, then 8"/20 cm, then 12"/30 cm apart in row |

| Vegetable | Within row x between rows inches/cm | Grid or Block inches/cm | Comments |
|---|---|---|---|
| - for eating fresh | 1 x 12/2.5 x 30 | | thinned to 3"/8 cm, then 6"/15 cm |
| Squash - summer | | 3 x 3/8 x 8 | |
| - winter | 4 x 6/10 x 15 | 5 x 5/13 x 13 | |
| Sweet Potatoes | | 12 x 12/30 x 30 | numerous small roots |
| | | 24 x 24/60 x 60 | fewer large roots |
| Swiss Chard | 6 x 12/15 x 30 | | single cut harvest |
| | 12 x 18/30 x 45 | | cut and come again |
| Tomatoes - bush | | 12 x 12/30 x 30 | greater early yield |
| | | 19 x 19/48 x 48 | greater total yield, later |
| - vine | | 36 x 36/90 x 90 | 18"/45 cm diameter cage |
| | | 48 x 48/120 x 120 | 30"/76 cm diameter cage |
| Turnip | 4 x 9/10 x 23 | | add a little bonemeal to all root crops for good root development |
| Watercress | | 12 x 12/30 x 30 | |
| Watermelons | | 48 x 48/120 x 120 | |
| Witloof Chicory (French Endive, Belgian Endive) | 6 x 12/15 x 30 | | |
| Zucchini | | 36 x 36/90 x 90 | |

Based in part on information in *The Complete Know and Grow Vegetables* by Bleasdale, et al. (1991).

### *Early spring planting schedule*

Broccoli and cauliflower can be seeded directly in the garden at this time, or set transplants out in a couple of weeks. Direct seeding eliminates the problems of transplant shock. If possible, put broccoli where it will be shaded by other plants to slow the rate of bolting later in the season.

Plant radish seeds in rows or sow them between lettuce transplants. Make a small sowing every week or two so that fresh radishes are always available.

Broad beans or fava beans are the only beans that can be planted while the soil is still cool and wet. Pods will ripen while the days are still cool. Be sure to rotate them from year to year to avoid rot diseases. If grown as a green manure crop, turn them under before the beans are harvested—most of the nitrogen fixed by the plant ends up in the pods.

## Focus on Plants

When planting asparagus, the trench should be prepared the previous autumn (see October/November, pages 375-382, for the initial soil preparation), but many gardeners are not this organized. As soon as the soil is workable, dig a trench about 8 inches (20 cm) deep and 12 inches (30 cm) wide. Do not plant new asparagus where an old bed was. Space row centres 3 feet (1 m) apart. If there are to be several rows, run them in the direction of the prevailing winds to reduce the spread of insects and disease between rows. The spears will be larger and will emerge sooner if raised beds are used, but there is a greater risk of damage by late spring frosts. Work a 6 inch (15 cm) layer of well rotted manure and/or compost, a bit of bonemeal and some wood ashes into the soil that was removed from the trench.

Within a row, space crowns about 1 ½ feet (45 cm) apart. Closer spacing will give higher yields, wider spacing will give thicker spears. Select asparagus crowns with white, firm roots. One-year-old crowns will outproduce two-year-old crowns in the long run. Count on a dozen plants for a family of four for fresh eating, but quadruple that if some is for freezing.

Place mounds of the enriched soil in the bottom of the trench at the spacing you have decided on. Drape the roots of the asparagus crowns over the mounds and cover the crowns with more enriched soil until 2 to 3 inches (5 to 7 cm) covers the tips. As the plants grow, fill in the trench around the fronds.

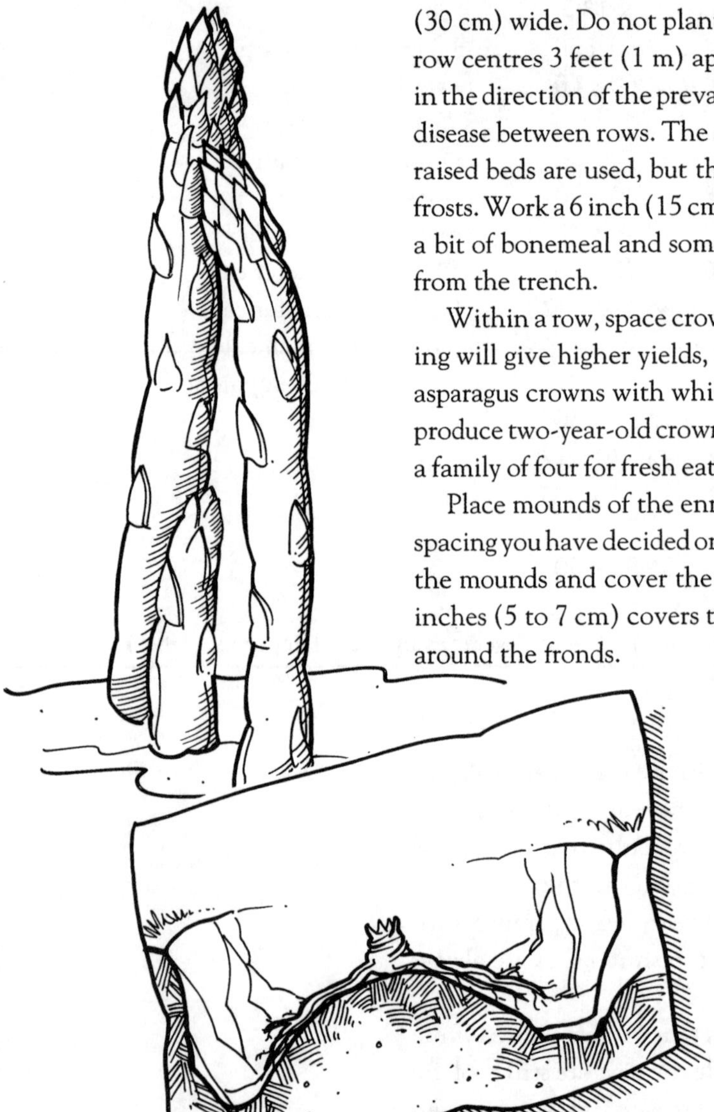

If growing asparagus from seed, plant soaked seeds directly in the trench that has been half backfilled with enriched soil, or start them in a nursery bed. Space them 3 to 5 inches (8 to 12 cm) apart in rows 12 to 18 inches (30 to 45 cm) apart. Thin them to half their final distance apart when they are well up and growing, and thin or transplant to the final spacing next spring. Seeds can be planted outdoors two weeks before the last expected frost, but wait until all danger of frost is past before setting out seedlings that were started indoors several months ago.

Peas can be planted as soon as the soil is workable, but will be ready to harvest only ten days sooner than those planted three or four weeks later. Ten days may be early enough, however, to avoid pea weevil larvae.

Dwarf pea varieties mature in eleven to twelve weeks, so plant them first for an early crop. Plant in bands of three rows, using 4 ½ by 4 ½ inch spacing (11 by 11 cm), with 15 inches (38 cm) between the bands. Tall peas that require staking are planted 2 inches apart (5 cm) in rows 5 to 6 inches apart (12 to 15 cm). They mature in thirteen to fourteen weeks but carry on producing for a longer period than dwarf peas and are good for the main summer crop. To stretch the harvest, plant peas every two to four weeks, starting and ending with dwarf varieties, and planting the last crop in early July, or plant early, mid and late season varieties on the same date.

The easiest spring crops to grow are greens of all sorts and sizes. Some, such as corn salad, escarole, endive, kale and collards, are grown in the autumn instead of the spring, or in addition to the spring. All of these tolerate very cool temperatures and actually seem to thrive when days and nights are chilly. They can be seeded or transplanted. Flats of well-spaced plants can be set directly in cold frames—they do not need to be transplanted.

Once established, lettuce will bolt in heat. You can reduce the incidence of this by planting the seed as early as possible; using heat-tolerant varieties, especially for head lettuce; and placing it in the shade of other crops. Some gardeners set up their tomato cages or stakes now and plant lettuce in between, or plant lettuce among the brassicas. Barely cover the seed as it germinates best with light.

Set out head lettuce and other lettuce transplants under protection as soon as the soil is workable and they are 3 to 4 inches (8 to 10 cm) tall. Bury the roots right up to the bottom leaves, but be sure not to bury any leaves (see page 81). Leave enough space between crisphead lettuce for a protective mulch to be added later on to keep the soil moist, the roots cool and the leaves clean. Cutworms commonly prey on young lettuce transplants, so take precautions. Butterhead and cos lettuce can be spaced 9 by 8 inches (23 by 20 cm) apart early in the season, or plant cos 1 inch (2.5 cm) apart in rows 5 inches (12 cm) apart and harvest it very young before it forms a head. It is less bitter than other lettuces when young .

A continuous crop of leaf lettuce can be obtained by planting every week once seeding starts, until mid to late May. Set aside various patches just for this and use 1 by 5 inch (2.5 by 12 cm) spacing rather than attempting to interplant lettuce with other crops. Each lettuce is harvested by cutting the

### Preventive Measure

Peas grow well during cool weather but germinate poorly in cold wet soils and sometimes rot. To reduce this problem, mound the soil in the row ahead of time (see page 117) and spread clear plastic over the area to pre-warm the soil; use pea seeds treated with a fungicide; or start the peas inside, where ideal germinating conditions can be provided. When the peas are two or three weeks old they can be planted outside; they will be quite tolerant of chilly spring conditions. Some gardeners only sprout the seeds indoors before planting them outside.

## *Table APR/MAY-2 Vegetables to Plant in Early Spring*

Planting can begin as soon as the ground can be worked when crocus, Siberian squill and glory-of-the-snow (*Chiondoxa*) are in bloom.

Crop protection is essential if planting is done in early spring. The same crops can be planted about two weeks before the last expected frost date without protection except from hard frosts.

| Plant | Transplant | Sow Seeds | Repeat Sow |
|---|---|---|---|
| Arugula | o | x | |
| Asparagus Crowns | x | | |
| Broad Beans (Fava) | | x | |
| Chinese Cabbage | x | o | |
| Collards | o | x | |
| Corn Salad | | x | |
| Early Broccoli | | o | |
| Early Cabbage | x | o | |
| Early Cauliflower | | o | |
| Endive | o | x | |
| Escarole | o | x | |
| Garlic Cloves | | x | |
| Kale | o | x | |
| Lettuce - Head | x | o | |
| - Looseleaf, Cos, | | | |
| - Butterhead | o | x | every week to May 31 |
| Mustard Greens | o | x | every 2-3 weeks to May 31 |
| Onion Sets | | x | |
| Peas | o | x | every 2-4 weeks to July |
| Radish | | x | every week to May 31 |
| Shallots | | x | |
| Spinach | o | x | every 2-3 weeks to May 31 |
| Spring Bunching Onions | | x | every 2 weeks to July |
| Turnips | o | x | |

x = common method
o = optional or additional method

entire plant off 1 inch (2.5 cm) above the ground; it is then fertilized and allowed to grow a second crop of leaves. After August 1, three more weekly sowings are made to carry on the harvest until frost, or later under protection.

Mustard greens can be planted as both a spring and fall crop. It matures in a matter of a few weeks. Sow it in blocks and thin to 4 to 6 inches (10 to 15 cm) apart (you can eat the thinnings). Harvest the remaining plants before they go to seed. Mustard greens can be planted successively two or three weeks apart or, as with lettuce, whole plants can be cut off and a second harvest made later of the new leaves.

Spinach is best suited to early planting as it bolts when the days are long. Choose bolt-resistant varieties if it will be planted late. Early planting reduces problems with leaf miners as the spinach is up and growing before the leaf miner adults are out and about laying eggs. It is a good idea to cover spinach with row covers or cheesecloth as soon as trees start leafing out to protect the crop from leaf miners.

Spinach is a heavy feeder and needs plenty of moisture, so work a little extra manure or compost into the top layer of soil (spinach is shallow rooted). Sow the seeds 1 inch (2.5 cm) apart in rows 1 foot (30 cm) apart, using the thinnings for an extra early treat, either raw or cooked.

The first spinach seeds or transplants can be interplanted with Brussels sprouts. For a continuous harvest, sow spinach every two to three weeks in various odd corners of the garden until mid to late May.

Do not sow onion seeds in the open yet, and wait a few weeks before setting out onion transplants grown from seed. Ideally, manure was applied last autumn because none of the onion family does well when over fertilized. Choose small onions and shallots over large ones because the small ones are less likely to bolt. Large shallots yield larger clumps of smaller shallots. Planting in rows makes cultivation and mulching easier. Cover tips if the soil is sandy, but otherwise leave the top one-quarter of each set showing.

Hungry birds often pull up sets by the tips. If no roots have formed yet, just push them back into the soil; if roots have started growing, dig them up and set them back in properly. If birds are a persistent problem, plant sets with the tips just buried, or try a deep light mulch such as salt hay from coastal marshes to foil them.

Onions stored over the winter do not keep past April, but the soft ones can be planted out for some early green onions. Be aware, though, that onion maggot flies are attracted to rotting onions.

### Green Thumb Tip

Onion sets, individual cloves of garlic and shallots should be planted as soon as the soil is workable. Early planting is desirable because the leafy top growth which nourishes the bulbs occurs during short days, before bulbing is initiated by long days. Late planting will mean a poorer crop of leaves and, consequently, smaller bulbs.

Garlic is often planted in the autumn in zones 4 or warmer, but an early spring planting of chilled garlic (see page 12) is also fine. In the autumn it is planted with 2 inches (5 cm) of soil over the tips of the cloves, but in the spring cover with 1 inch (2.5 cm) of soil. Pull each bulb of garlic apart and space the individual cloves 4 inches (10 cm) apart in rows 6 inches (15 cm) apart. Large cloves will yield larger bulbs than small cloves. If the soil is very heavy, put some sand in the bottom of the trench.

Garlic and other members of the onion family need plenty of water for the first three weeks to get them off to a good start. See June (pages 210-211) for the specific watering needs of various vegetables if spring happens to be dry.

### *Fluid sowing*

Fluid sowing can be used to plant the first crops of the season (see Table APR/MAY-2, above) or those usually planted later (see Table MAY-1, page 167). It is used indoors to speed up the germination of certain seeds that are to be planted outdoors. Research in Britain has been carried out on this form of early planting of vegetables, particularly of those that are slow to emerge such as carrots, parsnips, parsley and salsify. The method is as follows:

1) Spread paper towels 1/10 inch (2 mm) thick on the bottom of any plastic or glass container, moisten thoroughly and pour off excess water.

2) Spread seeds thinly over the surface—avoid leaving clumps. Put the lid on the container and keep at 70°F (21°C). Very fine seeds will need to be kept in the light, with the lid on, to trigger germination. Seeding instructions on individual packages should indicate if light is required.

3) When roots are 1/10 to 1/5 inch (2 to 5 mm) long, seeds may be sown immediately (explained below) or held one or two days in a refrigerator. Cold sensitive plants should be held at a slightly warmer temperature of 42°F (6°C).

4) Wash seeds with running water into a fine mesh plastic sieve and mix with a carrier jelly, such as cellulose wallpaper paste free of fungicides, or unflavoured gelatin, mixed at half strength. After mixing the seeds evenly throughout the jelly, they should stay suspended. If they sink the jelly is not thick enough. If just a few seeds will be planted, there is no need for the jelly.

5) Put the jelly in a plastic bag with a small hole cut in the corner. Sow seeds in a well moistened and prepared seedbed outdoors by squeezing the bag along the row (or place them individually by hand if no jelly is used). Cover with soil to the depth required by the particular seed.

## Herbs

### Early planting and division

It is too early to set out herb transplants that have been growing indoors, but seeds of beebalm, borage, catnip, calendula, chervil, comfrey, fennel, French sorrel, hyssop, lovage, salad burnet and summer savory can be sown in cold frames as soon as the soil is workable; a couple of weeks before the last frost date under protection; or around the last frost date out in the open (see Table FEB-3, page 54). Some of these will self sow. Put a cold frame where they grew last year to hasten the germination of seed already present in the soil.

Perennial herbs in the garden showing early signs of growth can be tidied up and divided if need be. Cut off old, dead growth but do not do any other pruning. Some herbs, such as salad burnet and horseradish, do not divide readily; Table JAN-1 (page 15) lists those that can be safely dug up and divided once the soil is dry enough to work. Dig up lovage for division when the cone-shaped buds first emerge, and divide French tarragon while the new growth is less than 1 inch (2.5 cm) high.

Division is carried out to rejuvenate clumps that are dying in the middle, or simply to create more plants. Beebalm grows so rapidly that it is best to replant the outer portions every year or two, and discard the central part. Division also helps keep rampant growers such as mint under some sort of control. Other herbs rarely need it, and some are killed over the winter before they ever become large enough to divide.

When dividing a clump, pull it apart by hand or use a knife or spade to cut it up. Remove every grass and weed root, both in the clump and in the bed. Work a good spadeful of compost or well rotted manure into the soil if the herb requires moist, fertile soil, and a little less if it requires moist, well drained soil (see Table FEB-1, page 40). Herbs growing in drier soils, such as hyssop and lavender, will need only a little compost. If they are grown on moist, rich soils, their fragrance and flavour are reduced.

Put central portions of clumps onto the compost heap if they do not look as vigorous as the outer portions. Set new pieces into the ground at the same level as they were before, and give each of them a good soaking with water, even those that prefer dry conditions at maturity. This will allow roots to make close contact with the soil and settle in to supplying the needs of the plants.

**Focus on Plants**

Lovage is a good celery substitute—its leaflets are useable all summer, and it makes a delightful addition to lettuce or potato salads and to chicken stock. Its only drawback in the garden is its considerable size, but that also makes it a centre of attention.

## Flowers

### Roses, annual transplants and seeds

Roses should be purchased as soon as they arrive in local stores and nurseries, and planted outdoors as soon as the soil is workable. If they cannot be planted out immediately, pot them up and store them in a cool place. This will prevent premature leafing out, but will give the roots a chance to start growing. If they come into leaf before being planted outdoors, water and fertilize them, but keep them as cool as possible. When planting roses, bury the bud union 3 or 4 inches (8 to 10 cm) below the soil line. This will encourage the scion (upper, budded portion) to root. Roses are grafted or budded as a speedy means of propagation, and the rootstock of many roses is less hardy than the upper grafted portion—it is best to buy roses on their own roots.

In mild regions a few hardy annual transplants (see Table FEB-4, page 56) can be set out in April, but May is soon enough in most areas (see page 180), or after daffodils and forsythia have bloomed. Some gardeners wait until June. Window boxes and hanging baskets are usually filled with transplants of annual flowers, many of which are sensitive to frost (see pages 223-225 for suggested flowers). Unless containers are easily moved indoors at night if frost threatens, or can be covered over in some way, it is best to plant them after all danger of frost is past and the weather is warm and stable.

A few annuals can be sown directly outdoors (see Table FEB-4, page 56) around the last frost date. Some gardeners plant window boxes and hanging baskets with annual seeds instead of using transplants.

### Focus on Plants

Sweet peas should be sown as soon as the soil is workable. Soak the seeds overnight, then plant them 2 inches (5 cm) apart in trenches 6 inches (15 cm) deep. Cover the seeds with 3/4 inch (2 cm) of soil and gradually fill in the trenches as they grow. Deep planting helps to keep the roots cool and moist during the heat of summer. Thin seedlings to 6 inches (15 cm) apart after the last one to emerge has one pair of true leaves. Save some of the smallest seedlings because their flowers will be different in colour from the others.

### Moving and dividing perennials

Clumps of perennial flowers can be dug up and divided the same way as perennial herbs, or simply moved when the ground is dry enough to dig. Fewer and smaller blooms, and dead or dying portions in the middle of the clump are signs that the plant needs to be divided and rejuvenated.

When replanting perennials the appropriate spacing is estimated by how tall the plants will be at maturity:

| Plant Height | Distance Apart |
|---|---|
| less than 1 foot (30 cm) | 6 to 8 inches (15 to 20 cm) |
| 1 to 2 feet (30 to 60 cm) | 12 to 15 inches (30 to 40 cm) |
| 2 to 3 feet (60 to 90 cm) | 18 to 24 inches (45 to 60 cm) |
| 3 feet or more (over 90 cm) | 24 to 30 inches (60 to 75 cm) |

As a crude guideline, perennials that bloom in the summer or fall can be divided and/or moved in the spring; spring-blooming perennials are best divided after they have bloomed, in late spring or early summer (see Table APR/MAY-3, page 138). Primroses, for example, bloom very early and are divided straight after blooming, usually every two or three years if they have survived the winters!

Sometimes perennials need to be moved to different growing conditions. If a plant is doing poorly, review its air, sun, soil moisture and nutrient needs. Phlox, for example, is prone to mildew and requires deep, rich, moist soil. If mildew or poor bloom has been a problem, move phlox to a place where the air circulation is good, plant the clumps further apart than usual (to further improve air movement), and work in plenty of well rotted manure, leaf mould or compost to supply nutrients and maintain moisture.

Work some bonemeal or fish bonemeal into all perennial planting holes to encourage flowering, spread the roots out so they are not all in a bunch, and water well after filling in with soil enriched with compost or leaf mould. Ferns do not require bonemeal but they do appreciate plenty of organic matter. They should be divided while the young fronds are still tightly curled, and planted where they will receive plenty of moisture and light shade throughout the growing season.

Some perennials need to be divided and rejuvenated nearly every other year, while others require attention after three or four years. Those, listed below, which actively resent any disturbance or have very deep tap roots that make division impossible should be left alone:

baby's breath
balloon flower
baptisia (blue indigo)
bergenia
butterfly weed
columbine
delphinium
gasplant
oriental poppy
pasque flower
peony
purple coneflower

Monkshood can be divided in the spring, if necessary, as soon as the first bit of green is noticed, but water it well as soon as you have moved it.

Oriental poppies will cope with transplanting in August, and peonies are usually divided in the autumn perhaps once every ten years at the most. True lilies are usually divided in the autumn. It is all too easy to break off the growing tip if they are dug up in the spring—lilies cannot grow another one until the following year. Bearded irises are divided about every four

**Green Thumb Tip**

Most perennials should be planted with the crown at soil level. Plants that are prone to rot, however, and those with variegated leaves, should be planted in a mound slightly above soil level. Those that prefer moist conditions, such as hosta, and those with a tuberous root system, should be planted with 1 to 2 inches (2.5 to 5 cm) of soil over the top of the crowns.

years between six and ten weeks after they have finished blooming (see August, page 306).

Perennials which usually die down in the summer, and can be dug up and divided at that time, are:

| | |
|---|---|
| bleeding heart | Jacob's ladder |
| bluebells, Virginia | oriental poppy |
| doronicum (leopard's bane) | shooting star (*Dodecatheon*) |

Perennials which can be divided either in the spring or early autumn are:

| | |
|---|---|
| astilbe | phlox |
| beebalm | Siberian iris |
| daylilies | veronica |
| hosta | yarrow (*achillea*) |
| Japanese iris | |

If for some unavoidable reason plants have to be moved, do not worry about the best time. Water them well several hours ahead of transplanting; dig up the whole clump, disturbing the soil as little as possible; and water the plants well after transferring them to the new location. It helps to shade them and shelter them from wind, and to treat them as carefully as you would young vegetable and annual flower transplants. Even plants that are in bloom can be moved this way, if necessary, but cut off the flowers.

Some gardeners move their spring blooming bulbs immediately after they have finished blooming or, in desperate situations, while they are still in bloom, but eight weeks after flowering is the best time. Try to keep the root ball intact, and water the plants well once they are relocated. Bulbs that were forced in pots indoors can be planted out as soon as the soil is workable, or they can be kept indoors until the autumn. Deadhead (remove faded flowers) in either case and keep the plants watered and fertilized until the leaves die back.

Some perennials, such as balloon flowers and lilies, are late to make an appearance in the spring. It is a good idea to mark them with sticks in the fall so that they are not inadvertently destroyed when tidying and digging in the spring.

Perennials that were seeded indoors during the winter should be gradually hardened off for planting outdoors. Do not plant them out until the perennials outdoors have leafed out as fully as the ones indoors. The young transplants can take chilly temperatures after being hardened off properly, but they should not be exposed to more than 2 or 3°F (1 or 2°C) below freezing.

### *Other propagation methods*

Perennial flowers that resent transplanting or dividing, die out after three or four years, or are difficult to propagate any other way, can be started from seed regularly. Some self sow (marked with *) and the seedlings can be moved around as needed. The *Dianthus* species include carnations, pinks and sweet william.

* anchusa (bugloss)
* basket-of-gold alyssum
  candytuft (*Iberis*)
* columbine
* coreopsis
  delphinium
* *Dianthus* species
  erigeron (fleabane)
* feverfew
  gasplant
  helenium (sneezeweed)
* Iceland poppy
* Jacob's ladder
  meadow rue (Thalictrum)
  meadowsweet (Filipendula)
  monkshood
* pasque flower
  penstemon
* wallflower

Sedum rarely needs dividing, but new plants can be started from basal cuttings taken from the edge of the clump early in the spring. Similarly, the basal shoots of asters, chrysanthemums and delphiniums can be cut from the plant, severing them right at the base, and planted in a nursery until they grow big enough for the flower bed. Basal cuttings can be taken in the spring or summer. Cut the top off summer cuttings just above a leaf so that they are only 2 inches (5 cm) high, and keep them moist and out of direct sunlight until rooting is established. Baby's breath can be started from basal cuttings in the spring or from stem cuttings higher up on the plant in the summer.

Plants with fleshy roots, and those that produce suckers, will often grow from root cuttings. These should be taken during dormant periods, either in early spring or in the autumn. This can sometimes be done without lifting the plant at all by digging carefully at the edge of the root mass. Roots 1/4 to 1/2 inch (6 to 12 mm) in diameter are cut into 2 to 5 inch (5 to 12 cm) lengths. Cut the pieces horizontally at the top and with a sloping cut at the bottom as you remove it from the root mass. Dust each piece with a fungicide and insert into a mixture of equal parts of garden soil, sand and peat moss or leaf mould in pots or boxes, and position the pieces in the same direction as

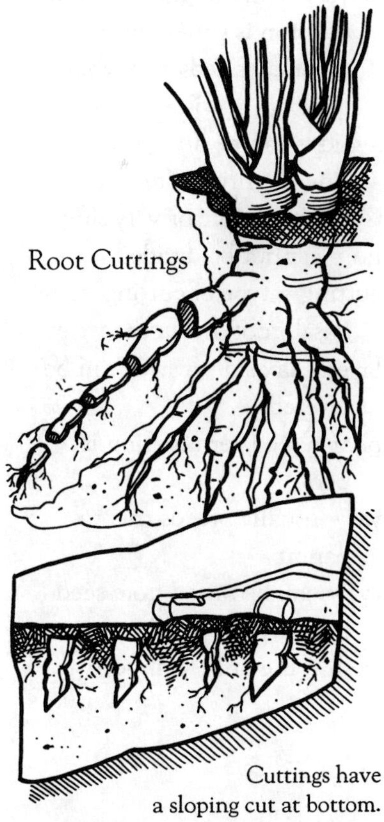

Cuttings have a sloping cut at bottom.

## Table APR/MAY-3 Height and Propagation of Perennial Flowers

**Key**

* = short lived perennial
> = greater than
< = less than
average height = average height under ordinary conditions; some plants may be considerably taller or shorter
division = appropriate time of year to divide root; autumn division is generally not recommended even when noted as possible
avoid = can be divided but is slow to thrive afterwards
@ = not feasible or very slow
no = cannot be divided
cutting = type of cutting: stem, basal, root, heel or rosette
layer = lax side growth can be layered
poor = seed germination is poor
yes = usually breeds true to parent
(y) = can be raised from seed but may not be like parent
fresh = use only fresh seed

| **Plant** | **Average Height** inches/cm | **Propagation Method:** division | cutting | seed |
|---|---|---|---|---|
| Achillea (see Yarrow) | | | | |
| Alumroot (see Coralbells) | | | | |
| Anchusa | varies | no | root | yes |
| Aquilegia (see Columbine) | | | | |
| Arabis | <12/30 | no | stem/root/layer | yes |
| Armeria | <12/30 | spring | basal | yes |
| Artemisia | <12/30 | spring | stem | @ |
| Aruncus (see Goatsbeard) | | | | |
| Aster | 18/45 | spring | stem | (y) |
| Astilbe | 18/45 | spring/fall | @ | @ |
| Aubrieta | <12/30 | spring | stem/layer | yes |
| Baby's Breath | 24/60 | avoid | stem/root | yes |
| Balloon Flower | 18/45 | avoid | @ | yes |
| Baptisia (see Blue Indigo) | | | | |
| Basket-of-Gold Alyssum | <12/30 | avoid | stem | yes |
| Beard Tongue (see Penstemon) | | | | |
| Beebalm | 36/90 | spring/fall | stem | yes |
| Bergenia | <12/30 | avoid | @ | yes |
| Bleeding Heart | varies | summer | root | @ |
| Blue Indigo | >36/90 | spring | @ | yes |
| Butterfly Weed | 24/60 | avoid | stem/root | poor |
| Campanula | varies | spring/fall | basal | yes |
| Candytuft (see Iberis) | | | | |
| Centaurea | 18/45 | spring | stem | yes |
| Centranthus | 36/90 | avoid | @ | yes |
| Chinese Lantern | 24/60 | spring | @ | yes |
| Chrysanthemum | varies | spring | stem/basal | @ |
| Columbine | 18/45 | avoid | @ | yes |
| Coralbells | 18/45 | spring | @ | yes |
| Coreopsis | 24/60 | spring/fall | @ | yes |
| Cranesbill | 18/45 | spring | root | yes |

| Plant | Average Height inches/cm | Propagation Method: division | cutting | seed |
|---|---|---|---|---|
| Daylily | 30/75 | spring/fall | @ | yes |
| Delphinium | >36/90 | avoid | basal | fresh |
| Dianthus | 12/30 | no | stem/layer | yes |
| Dictamnus (see Gas Plant) | | | | |
| Doronicum | 18/45 | summer/fall | @ | @ |
| Erigeron | 12/30 | spring/fall | @ | yes |
| Eupatorium (see Joe-PyeWeed) | | | | |
| Euphorbia (see Spurge) | | | | |
| Evening Primrose | 18/45 | spring | stem/root | yes |
| False Dragonhead (see Physostegia) | | | | |
| Feverfew * | 18/45 | no | stem | yes |
| Filipendula (see Meadowsweet) | | | | |
| Flax * | 12/30 | avoid | basal | yes |
| Fleabane (see Erigeron) | | | | |
| Foamflower | 18/45 | spring | @ | yes |
| Foxglove | 30/75 | no | @ | yes |
| Gaillardia | 24/60 | no | stem | yes |
| Gasplant | 24/60 | avoid | @ | fresh |
| Gayfeather (see Liatris) | | | | |
| Geranium, true (see Cranesbill) | | | | |
| Geum | 18/45 | spring | @ | yes |
| Globeflower | 24/60 | spring/sum. | root | yes |
| Globe Thistle | >36/90 | spring/fall | root | yes |
| Goatsbeard (Aruncus) | 36/90 | spring/fall | @ | @ |
| Goldenrod | 24/60 | spring | @ | @ |
| Helenium | 18/45 | spring | @ | yes |
| Helianthus (perennial sunflower) | >36/90 | spring | @ | yes |
| Heliopsis (orange sunflower or oxeye) | >36/90 | spring/fall | @ | @ |
| Heuchera (see Coralbells) | | | | |
| Hibiscus (see Rose Mallow) | | | | |
| Hosta | 24/60 | spring | @ | @ |
| Iberis | <12/30 | avoid | stem/layer | yes |
| Iris - Bearded | varies | summer | @ | (y) |

**Key**

* = short lived perennial
> = greater than
< = less than
average height = average height under ordinary conditions; some plants may be considerably taller or shorter
division = appropriate time of year to divide root; autumn division is generally not recommended even when noted as possible
avoid = can be divided but is slow to thrive afterwards
@ = not feasible or very slow
no = cannot be divided
cutting = type of cutting: stem, basal, root, heel or rosette
layer = lax side growth can be layered
poor = seed germination is poor
yes = usually breeds true to parent
(y) = can be raised from seed but may not be like parent
fresh = use only fresh seed

| Plant | Average Height inches/cm | Propagation Method: division | cutting | seed |
|---|---|---|---|---|
| - Japanese | 36/90 | spring | @ | yes |
| - Siberian | 24/60 | spring | @ | yes |
| Jacob's Ladder | 24/60 | spring/sum. | @ | yes |
| Joe-Pye Weed | 30/75 | spring | @ | @ |
| Lamb's Ear | <12/30 | spring | @ | @ |
| Liatris | 18/45 | spring | @ | yes |
| Lily-of-the-Valley | <12/30 | spring | @ | @ |
| Lupine | 36/90 | no | basal | yes |
| Lychnis * | 18/45 | spring | basal | yes |
| Maltese Cross (see Lychnis) | | | | |
| Matricaria (see Feverfew) | | | | |
| Meadow Rue | 36/90 | avoid | @ | yes |
| Meadowsweet | 18/45 | spring | @ | yes |
| Michaelmas Daisy (see Aster) | | | | |
| Monkshood | 36/90 | avoid | @ | yes |
| Mullein (see Verbascum) | | | | |
| Obedience Plant (see Physostegia) | | | | |
| Oenothera (see Evening Primrose) | | | | |
| Pasque Flower (Pulsatilla) | 12/30 | spring | @ | yes |
| Penstemon | 18/45 | no | stem | yes |
| Peony | 36/90 | avoid | @ | @ |
| Phlox | 24/60 | spring/fall | basal/root | @ |
| Physostegia | 24/60 | spring | basal | yes |
| Polemonium (see Jacob's Ladder) | | | | |
| Polygonatum (see Solomon's Seal) | | | | |
| Poppy - Iceland | 18/45 | avoid | @ | yes |
| - Oriental | 30/75 | avoid | root | yes |
| Potentilla | 12/30 | spring | @ | yes |
| Primrose | <12/30 | early spring /early summer | root | yes |
| Pulmonaria (see William and Mary) | | | | |
| Purple Coneflower | 30/75 | avoid | root | yes |
| Rock Cress (see Arabis) | | | | |
| Rose Mallow | 24/60 | spring | @ | yes |

| Plant | Average Height | Propagation Method: | | |
|---|---|---|---|---|
| | inches/cm | division | cutting | seed |
| Rudbeckia | 24/60 | spring | @ | yes |
| Salvia | 24/60 | no | heel | yes |
| Saponaria | <12/30 | spring | stem | yes |
| Saxifrage | <12/30 | spring | rosette/root | @ |
| Scabiose | 24/60 | spring | @ | yes |
| Sedum | varies | spring | basal/stem | yes |
| Shasta Daisy | 24/60 | spring | basal/stem | yes |
| Sneezeweed (see Helenium) | | | | |
| Soapwort (see Saponaria) | | | | |
| Solidago (see Goldenrod) | | | | |
| Solomon's Seal | 30/75 | spring | @ | fresh |
| Spiderwort (see Tradescantia) | | | | |
| Spurge (Euphorbia) | 12/30 | spring | basal | yes |
| Stokesia (Stoke's Aster) | 12/30 | spring | @ | (y) |
| Thalictrum (see Meadow Rue) | | | | |
| Tiarella (see Foamflower) | | | | |
| Tradescantia | 18/45 | spring | @ | yes |
| Trollius (see Globeflower) | | | | |
| Verbascum | 24/60 | avoid | root | yes |
| Veronica | varies | spring | stem | @ |
| Violet | <12/30 | early spring /early summer | basal | yes |
| Virginia Bluebell | 18/45 | summer | @ | fresh |
| William and Mary | <12/30 | spring/fall | @ | @ |
| Yarrow (Achillea) | 24/60 | spring | @ | yes |

they were growing. Cover the root cuttings with 1/2 inch (1 cm) of sand and keep them at 55 to 65ºF (12 to 18ºC).

Thin, fibrous roots, such as those of summer phlox, are cut into 3 or 4 inch (8 to 10 cm) lengths, laid horizontally on the soil-sand-peat mix, and covered with 1/2 inch (1 cm) of sand. After they have rooted, plant them in nursery rows outdoors. In the autumn, they should be potted up and wintered indoors, particularly in cold regions, or carefully mulch them before winter arrives (see October/November, pages 387-388). A shortcut method for taking root cuttings of phlox is to slice off the crown of the plant *in situ,* leaving only the roots. In early summer pot up the young plants that grow from the roots.

> **Green Thumb Tip**
>
> Plants grown in containers are sometimes very difficult to get established in the garden because the roots are so pot-bound. It is absolutely essential that the outer roots be loosened so that they stop circling the root ball and start to grow outwards into the soil. Sometimes it is necessary to use a sharp knife to make four or five vertical cuts through the outer inch (2.5 cm) of the root mass. Soaking the root mass in water and working at it with a hand cultivator sometimes helps.
>
> 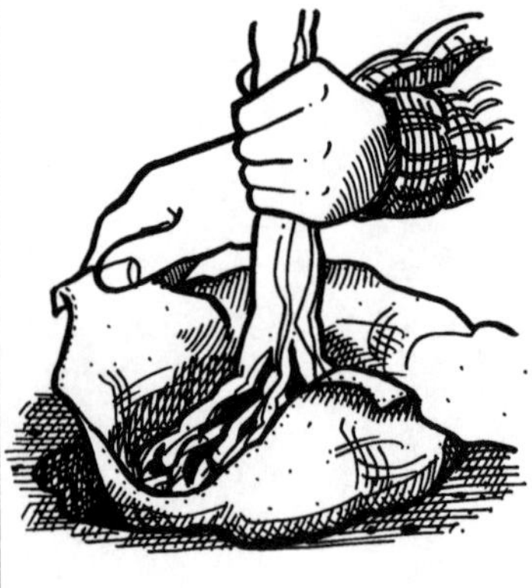

## Fruiting Plants and Woody Ornamentals

The ideal time to plant or transplant trees and shrubs is before they leaf out; this gives the roots time to settle in before leaves start demanding moisture and nutrients. Root growth is also more active in the spring than in the summer. Woody plants ordered through the mail or bought in nurseries come in a variety of containers, or without any at all, but the planting procedure is much the same for all of them.

### Bare root, burlap and basket

Bare root trees and shrubs ordered from nursery catalogues have a habit of arriving when the weather is miserable and the soil is sodden (see Pre-Planting Care of Mail Order Plants, page 118). They all, including cane fruits and strawberry plants, can be planted as soon as the soil is workable. Hopefully the planting areas were dug last autumn (see October/November, pages 375-382) or even the year before. Early planting enables strawberries to form runners in July; these early formed plants produce more fruit in their first season than those formed in the late summer and fall.

If the root mass is covered with burlap, untie the string holding it and lay it flat underneath the root ball when you position the plant in the hole. Plants in wooden baskets can be planted basket and all.

Other containers must be removed before planting. If it is difficult to remove a pot, try turning the plant upside down and whacking the rim of the container on some hard surface. Hold on to the plant throughout the procedure! Plants in peat containers or pressed cellulose can supposedly be planted pot and all. It is best to remove the pot, however, or at least to rip off as much as possible because roots do not grow easily through these materials.

### *Transplanting*

The best time to move most trees and shrubs from one area of the garden to another is after the ground has thawed but before the buds have swelled much. Rhododendrons are an exception and can be moved immediately after they bloom.

If it is more convenient to move a plant in the autumn, root prune it now. Take a spade and sever the roots in a broken circle around the tree or shrub. The radius of the circle is 12 inches (30 cm) for every 1 inch (2.5 cm) of trunk diameter. This pruning will encourage new roots to form within the circle and make replanting more successful. It will also help you realistically decide just how large a tree or shrub you can actually move.

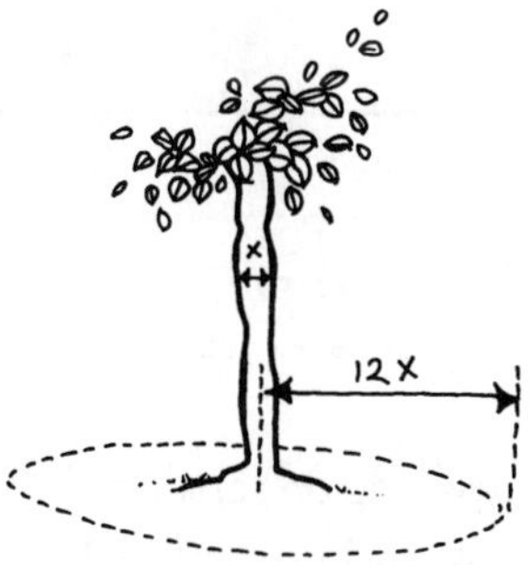


When transplanting small trees and shrubs, all the soil sometimes falls away from the roots, especially when there is only a thin layer of topsoil. If this is likely to happen, dig up the plant in the evening or on a cloudy, windless, misty or rainy day. Keep the roots moist and covered at all times by covering them with wet burlap or a plastic bag, and replant the tree or shrub immediately, planting it no deeper than it was before.

### *Planting distances and wire supports*

Large trees should be planted more than 6 feet (1.8 m) away from pavement and curbs so that their roots do not cause heaving and breakage. Concrete slabs are preferable to asphalt as surfacing near trees; they are less easily damaged by roots and moisture and air can more readily reach the roots.

The roots of vines should be planted away from buildings.

The distance required between trees or shrubs and a house depends on the ultimate height and spread of the plant. Trees less than 20 feet (6 m) tall at maturity should be planted 10 to 20 feet (3 to 6 m) away from the house; medium-sized trees need a distance of 20 to 30 feet (6 to 9 m); and large trees that will tower over the roof of the house at maturity should be planted no closer than 30 to 50 feet (9 to 15 m). Plant shrubs far enough away from the foundation of a house to allow for walking space between the shrub and the house after the plant has reached maturity.

If planting trees for espaliering or vines next to a wall, position the stem 6 to 12 inches (15 to 30 cm) away from the wall, and fan the roots outwards away from the wall. This will direct the roots towards the soil that gets wet when it rains (see page 146 for wire supports).

Fruit spurs on espaliered plants will form on the sunny side of the plants. If using posts and wires, run the rows north to south so that fruit spurs form on both sides of the row. One-year-old cordons are planted at a 45$^{\circ}$ angle,

## Table APR/MAY-4 Spacing Guide for Fruit Trees in Home Gardens

| Plant | Spacing | Comments |
|---|---|---|
| | In Row x Between Rows | |
| inches/cm | inches/cm | |
| Apples | | |
| - dwarf (6/2 tall) | 5-6 x 6/1.5-2 x 2 m | or espalier, cordon |
| - semi-dwarf (10-12 ½/3-4 ) | 10 x 10 or 13 x 13/3x3 or 4x4 | use wide spacing on fertile soil |
| | - semi-standard (16-23/5-7 ) | 16 x 16 or 23 x 23/5x5 or 7x7use |
| wide spacing on fertile soil | | |
| - standard (23-32/7-10) | 23 x 23 or 32 x 32/7x7 or 10x10 | use wide spacing on fertile soil |
| Apricots | | |
| - standard | 20 x 20/6 x 6 | or fan shape on sheltered wall |
| - semi or dwarf | 14 1/2 x 14 1/2/4.5 x 4.5 | or fan shape on sheltered wall |
| Cherries | | |
| - sweet | 20 x 20/6 x 6 | barely hardy in zone 6 |
| - sour standard | 20 x 20/6 x 6 | |
| - sour semi-standard | 13 x 13/4 x 4 | also suitable for fan shape |
| - sour dwarf or bush | 10 x 10/3 x 3 | also suitable for fan shape |
| Elderberries | 6 x 10/2 x 3 | some wetness okay |
| Mulberry, Red Weeping | 6 x 6/2 x 2 | stake first few years to establish central stem |
| Peach | | |
| - standard | 16 x 16/5 x 5 | or fan shape on sheltered wall |
| - semi or dwarf | 13 x 13/4 x 4 | or fan shape on sheltered wall |
| Pear | 20 x 20 or 20 x 26/6 x 6 or 6 x 8 | use wide spacing on fertile soil; or espalier, cordon |
| Plum | | |
| - Japanese x American | 16 x 16/5 x5 | hardiest |
| - European standard | 16 x 23/5 x 7 or 20 x 20/6 x 6 | or fan shape |
| - European semi-dwarf | 13 x 20 or 16 x 16/4 x 6 or 5 x 5 | or fan shape |
| Quince (Cydonia oblonga) | 10 x 10/3 x 3 | or espalier, cordon |
| Saskatoon (Indian Pear) | 4-6 x 10/1.2-2 x 3 | close spacing for windbreak |

N.B. Space fans and espaliered trees the same distances apart within rows, but space the rows only 6½ to 10 feet (2 to 3 m) apart. One row should not shade another. Cordons are spaced 2½ feet (0.8 m) apart within each row.

## Table APR/MAY-5 Spacing Guide for Soft Fruits in Home Gardens

| Plant | Spacing<br>In Row x Between Rows<br>inches/cm | Comments |
|---|---|---|
| Blackberries | 78 x 78/200 x 200 | 3 inches (7.5 cm) of soil over roots; cut back to bud 8 inches (20 cm) above soil |
| Blueberries | | |
| - highbush | 60-96 x 78/150-250 x 200 | use close spacing in raised beds and plant highbush |
| - lowbush | 20 x 39/50 x 100 | 1 inch (2.5 cm) deeper than in nursery |
| Currants | | |
| - black | 60 x 60-120/150 x 150-300 | plant 1 inch (2.5 cm) deeper than at nursery; prune to 1 bud above soil |
| - red or white | 60 x 60-120/150 x 150-300 | plant same depth as at nursery; prune leaders back half way; fan or cordon also suitable |
| Gooseberries | 60 x 60-120/150 x 150-300 | plant same depth as at nursery; prune leaders back half way; fan or cordon also suitable |
| Grapes | 48/120 | on arbours, fences; plant 1 inch (2.5 cm) deeper than at nursery |
| | 60-96 x 120/150-250 x 300 | horizontal arms on wires, wide spacing for vigorous varieties |
| | 39 x 120/100 x 300 | fan, oblique side-arm |
| Kiwifruit (hardy) | | plant one male for every one to nine females |
| - *A. arguta* | 96 x 120/250 x 300 | |
| - *A. kolomikta* | 60 x 120/150 x 300 | |
| Raspberries | 18-24 x 48 x 12/<br>45-60 x 120 x 30 cm wide row | 3 inches (7.5 cm) of soil over roots; cut back to bud 8 inches (20 cm) above soil surface |
| Rhubarb | 39 x 39/100 x 100 | buds 2 to 3 inches (5 to 7 cm) below soil surface |
| Strawberries | | soil level at junction between highest roots and lowest leaves |
| - June bearing | 15-18 x 30-36/38-45 x 75-90 cm | bed system |
| | 18-24 x 48-60/45-60 x 120-150 cm | row system |
| - everbearing | 12 x 24/30 x 60 cm | sends out fewer runners than June bearing |
| - dayneutral | 6 x 12/15 x 30 cm | sends out very few runners |

N.B. Space fan forms the same distance apart within rows but space the rows only 1 to 2 yards (1 to 2 m) apart. One row should not shade another. Cordons are spaced 2 ½ feet (0.8 m) apart within each row.

with the tops pointing north, if possible. Rows that run east to west will have most fruit spurs on the south side.

Set wooden or metal posts 3 feet (1 m) deep; their height depends on the crop grown. Space them at 30 foot (9 m) intervals along the row for grapes (use wooden posts which are 5 to 6 inches or 13 to 15 cm in diameter); and at 12 to 15 foot (3.6 to 4.6 m) intervals for cordons, fans and espaliered fruits (use 4 inch or 10 cm wooden posts). Wires should be at least 6 inches (15 cm) away from walls to allow for good air circulation and to get the roots out into moist soil.

Attach number 10 (3.15 mm) galvanized wires 2 ½ feet (75 cm) and 5 feet (150 cm) above the ground for grapes; and 1 ½ feet (45 cm), 3 feet (90 cm), 4 ½ feet (140 cm) and 6 feet (180 cm) for cordons and espaliered fruit trees. Space number 12 or 14 (2.5 or 1.2 mm) wire at 3 feet (90 cm), 4 feet (120 cm) and 5 feet (150 cm) for blackberries; and at 1 ½ feet (45 cm) and 3 feet (90 cm) for other soft fruits trained in cordons. The wires for fans should be 6 inches (15 cm) apart and start 15 inches (38 cm) above the ground. The top wire for any form should be 6 inches (15 cm) below the top of the posts. Make sure that all wires are tight by using tightening bolts. Run strut wires outward from each post or position wooden supports facing inward on each post. Contain cane fruits with strong string, twine or light wire strung at 2 feet (60 cm) and 4 feet (120 cm) above the ground.

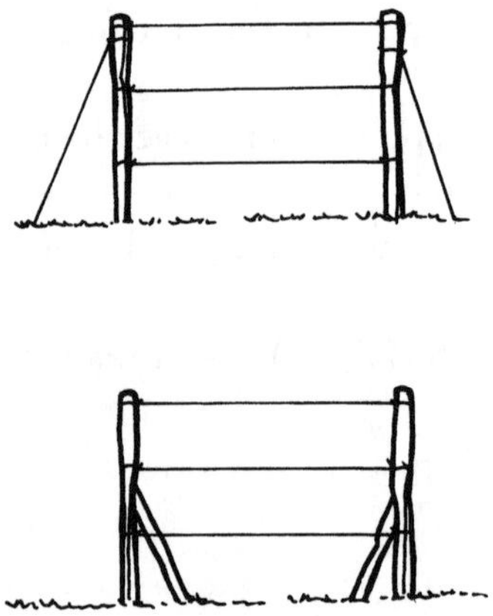

Grape posts can be supported either from the outside with wire or from the inside with wooden supports.

Suggested planting distances for fruits are listed in Tables APR/MAY-4 and APR/MAY-5. Choose the wider spacing suggested for between rows if mechanical cultivation will be practiced. All soft fruits can be dug up from established clumps and started in new beds, provided the plants are healthy and free of disease, but move them before they leaf out.

### *Planting holes and tree stakes*

Dig planting holes to suit the size of the root system of each plant. For woody plants, dig holes wider than they are deep: approximately 39 inches (100 cm) wide by 28 inches (70 cm) deep for standard fruit trees and large ornamental trees; 31 by 20 inches (80 by 50 cm) for small trees and large shrubs; and 20 by 12 inches (50 by 30 cm) for small to medium shrubs. Deep rooted trees can produce twice the fruit of trees whose root growth is restricted to shallower levels by hard pan, compact wet subsoil or ploghpans (the soil has been compacted just below the level of ploughing), so deep preparation is essential.

If the soil is a heavy wet clay, if it drains poorly, or if there is a layer of hardpan discovered when the hole is dug, plant the tree or shrub on a raised mound. If the soil is very sandy and dry in the summer, sink the planting area a couple of inches (5 cm) below the surrounding grade to help collect rain water.

To dig holes, first remove the sod, shake out as much soil as possible, and set it to one side. (If it is a really wet, late spring, use a fork instead of a spade.) Dig out the topsoil and pile it on a piece of plastic or tarpaulin. Remove the subsoil down to the suggested depth and cart off in a wheelbarrow—it will not be returned to the planting hole. Chop up the sod and lay it upside down in the bottom of the planting hole. If it is heavily infested with quack grass, however, it may be wiser to compost the sod instead.

Mix some well rotted manure, leaf mould or compost into the pile of topsoil, as well as a cupful each of bonemeal, fishmeal, and lime if required. Do not put manure, bonemeal or lime in the planting holes for blueberries, but compost, leaf mould or peat moss is fine. It will probably be necessary to add some extra topsoil to make up for the subsoil you removed.

Put a mound of this mixture in the bottom of the planting hole. Prior to planting, keep the roots moist in a bucket of water or, as Hall-Beyer and Richard (1983) recommend, dip the roots in a solution of liquid seaweed to stimulate root growth. Plants will have suffered enough from shippping, so do not prune the branches or roots except to remove damaged parts. Position the tree so that the trunk is 2 to 3 inches (5 to 7.5 cm) away from the stake, and fan the roots out over the mound of soil.

### Depth of planting

When replanting, most plants will suffer if they are not planted at the same depth as they were in their previous location (unless otherwise noted in Table APR/MAY-5, page 145). The soil line is usually visible. If planted too deeply, the roots are slowly smothered to death over the next few years (see Causes and Prevention of Tree Decline, page 320).

With fruit trees, be especially careful not to bury the union between the rootstock and the scion—a knobbly bit on the trunk about 4 inches (10 cm) above the soil line. If the scion is buried it may root, and the dwarfing, hardiness and early fruiting effects of the rootstock will be lost. Gradually fill in the planting hole with enriched soil, firming it as you go, and water when you are halfway through and at the end of planting. Tie the tree to the stake with old nylons in a loose figure eight.

### Green Thumb Tip

Drive in supporting stakes for trees after digging the holes but before planting the trees. Most trees require a stake only 12 to 18 inches (30 to 45 cm) tall initially. This will keep the tree upright yet allow the top to move naturally and develop fibre strength. Trees supported by tall stakes will grow upward more quickly but will have thinner, weaker trunks.

Dwarf fruit trees and weeping trees require longer stakes. Drive stakes about 18 inches (45 cm) into the soil, or deeper in sandy soils. For weeping trees, the stake should be the height you want the tree to be before it starts "weeping." Dwarf fruit trees require stakes which extend about 5 feet (1.5 m) above the soil line as their root systems may not be well enough anchored to provide adequate support.

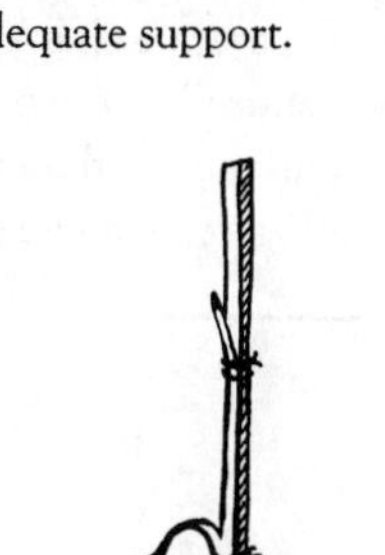

## Focus on Plants

It is best to plant rhubarb in the spring, although it can be planted in the autumn in mild areas. Rhubarb that had crowded, thin stalks last year probably needs to be divided. Dig up the whole crown in the spring before there is much top growth and divide it into two or three pieces, each with several eyes. Dig 2 foot wide (60 cm) planting holes, 3 feet (1 m) apart centre to centre. Enrich the soil from each hole with a couple of spadefuls of manure or compost, and replant the pieces with the eyes 2 inches (5 cm) below the surface of the soil.

If you want just a piece of rhubarb crown to give to a friend, drive a spade into the clump, without digging up the clump, before the leaves have unfurled. Separate a chunk of the crown and fill in the hole with soil enriched with compost or well rotted manure.

### After care and mulching

After planting and each June thereafter, fertilize and mulch fruiting plants and woody ornamentals. It is best to mulch once the ground has warmed up as trees and shrubs will not grow as much each season nor reach their full potential in size if the soil they grow in is always cold. Spread 2 inches (5 cm) or so of well rotted manure o compost over the soil, cover with heavy paper, cardboard or ten or more sheets of wet newspaper to discourage weeds and conserve moisture, and cover that with a 4 inch (10 cm) thick mulch of shredded bark, straw, old hay, rotted sawdust, seaweed, leaf mould or leaf mats (see page 398). The mulch should be spread around trees and shrubs in a 4 foot (1.2 m) diameter circle, or at least as far out as the drip line.

Landscape fabrics do not work very well as mulch; these woven, felt-like, or knitted synthetics have been shown to be ineffective in reducing or eliminating the growth of perennial weeds. The mulching system described above is friendlier to the environment and a lot less expensive. The occasional weed or sprout of grass that grows through the mulch is easily removed because the soil beneath is moist and soft.

The best care to give plants after planting is a thorough watering twice a week for the first month, once a week for the second month, and then once every week or two for the rest of the growing season.

### Propagation

#### Root division, rooted suckers and root cuttings

Some shrubs can be propagated by digging up the plant and dividing the roots just before the leaves appear in the spring (see Table JUL-4, page 282). This works best on shrubs that have many stems growing out of the ground. A more common method is to divide the plant *in situ* by driving a spade in and digging out a chunk of roots and connected stems. Water the plant well the day before and do the digging the following evening or during the day if it is moist or drizzly.

Some plants grown on their own roots (not as grafts) will produce suckers (see Table JUL-3, page 275, and JUL-4, page 282). These shoots usually arise from the roots and will eventually form their own root system. Often a multitude of suckers will grow from the roots of trees that are stressed in some way or that are nearing the end of their life naturally. Once rooted, the suckers can be dug up and replanted as new plants. Dig carefully, keep as much of the soil as possible around the roots, and replant the shoot at the same depth as it was growing initially.

> **Preventive Measure**
>
> In orchards and fruit patches grow a mixture of native grasses and flowers to attract a greater diversity of insect predators and parasites that will help to control harmful insects. This will benefit the whole garden, not just the fruiting plants. Between rows of mulched plants grow such things as clover, wild carrot (Queen Anne's lace), dill, caraway, catnip, mustard, brown-eyed Susan (*Rudbeckia*), goldenrod, buckwheat, nasturtiums, a bit of alphalpha and yarrow (and see Flowers, page 307).

Some lilacs, many roses, a few viburnums and other plants which are budded onto different rootstocks will produce suckers which are not necessarily the same as the budded portion above ground. Occasionally suckers from the root stock can be identified because their leaves are a slightly different shape or colour than on the budded part of the plant.

Not all suckers that are dug up and replanted will thrive. The usual reason is that the root system was not sufficiently formed at the time of digging. It may help to sever the underground root that supports the sucker, leave the sucker in the ground for a full growing season to encourage root formation, then dig it up and move it to a new location.

Some woody plants can be propagated from root cuttings (see Table JUL-3, page 275, and Table JUL-4, page 282). This is done in the same way as for perennial flowers (see page 137) in either the spring or autumn when the plant is dormant.

### *Layering, mounding and dropping*

The lower branches of some plants will root where they touch the ground. This can be encouraged by covering the bases of the branches with soil in one of three ways and will often succeed in cases where hardwood cuttings failed.

The easiest method is to layer healthy, one or two-year-old branches—this is particularly successful with vines. Spring and autumn—when root growth is most active—are the best times to do this, but it can be done any time during the growing season. Bend the selected branch or branches to the ground, then improve the soil where they touch by adding leaf mould and sand or perlite. On the underside of the branch where it bends upwards, encourage rooting by either cutting off a sliver of bark, or making an upward, diagonal cut one-quarter of the way through the branch, so that a tongue opens up when it is bent. Dust the wound or cut with a little rooting hormone. Remove all but the top three or four buds or leaves at the tip of the branch, then bury the lower portion of the branch under 4 to 6 inches (10 to 15 cm) of soil and anchor it firmly with a heavy rock. Insert a small stake beside it and tie the above-ground portion of the branch to it so that the branch tip is pointing roughly upwards. Use nylons in a loose figure eight as a tie. Layering a vine stem in several places is called serpentine layering.

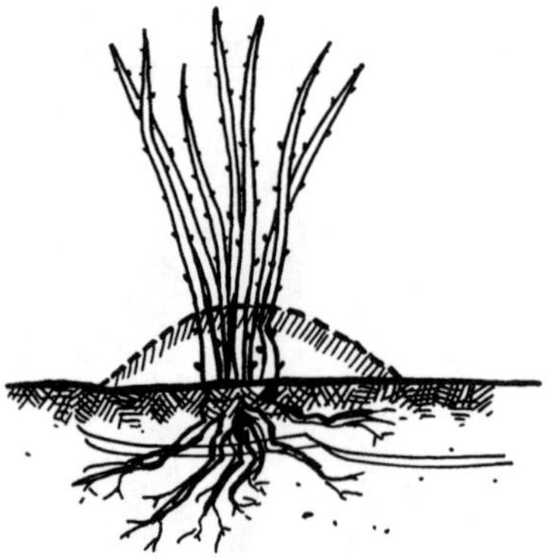

Mounding soil around the base of a plant will encourage rooting on the buried portion of each branch.

The second method is a modification of layering and involves mounding soil all around the base of the plant. This will hopefully encourage rooting on the buried portion of the stems. It is used on young plants or on older plants that have been cut back to just above ground level. Again, buried portions can be wounded and rooting hormone applied, but this is not essential. Make the mound 2 to 4 inches (5 to 10 cm) high when the new growth is 8 to 10 inches (20 to 25 cm) high, then add more soil in the summer to make it 10 to 12 inches (25 to 30 cm) high, or 6 to 8 inches (15 to 20 cm) below the upper end of the branches. Be sure to keep the mound of soil moist at all times. When the new growth is well hardened (firm and woody), remove the rooted pieces and pot them up, placing them in cold storage for their first winter (see October/November, pages 397-398).

The third method—called dropping—is more work but quite effective, especially in regions that are dry during the growing season or that have harsh winters. The idea is the same as mounding except that the entire plant is dug up and replanted at a greater depth.

Rooting can take anywhere from one to three years with any of these methods. The rooted branches are best dug up in the spring when they are finally severed from the parent plant. This will give them a whole growing season to become established in their new location.

### *Air layering*

If branches are too stiff to bend to the ground in traditional layering, then air layering may be the answer. Remove the buds, or leaves if this is done later in the season, on a section of healthy, one or two-year-old wood about 6 to 12 inches (15 to 30 cm) from the tip of the branch. Make an upward cut on the underside of the branch, as described above, to make a tongue and dust the opening with rooting hormone. Put a little sphagnum moss in the cut to hold it open.

Use string to tie a piece of plastic around the branch about 3 inches (8 cm) below the tongue. Form this into a tube larger than the branch and fill it loosely with a well moistened mixture of 1 part peat moss, 1 part sand or perlite and 2 parts sphagnum moss. Finish tying the plastic in place about 3 inches (8 cm) above the cut, forming an airtight package.

After one or more months, when roots can be seen, cut the branch from the parent plant and pot it up in regular potting soil. The potted cutting should be kept in a sheltered location over the winter (see pages 397-398).

Air Layering

### Other care

Make sure that all dormant spraying of woody plants is completed before buds start to swell and before any green tips show. If buds are visibly swelling, it may be time for the next round of spraying, if more is required (see page 190).

Trees and other woody plants exposed to winter salt should have the soil around their roots flushed with 10 to 20 gallons (45to 90 l) of water as soon as the ground has thawed. Dog urine is also high in salts that can be damaging to plants, so flush the soil used as dog latrines.

When the soil is workable, dig up hardwood cuttings that were buried to protect them over the winter, and plant them upright buried to two thirds their depth in pots or in a nursery bed. Rooted cuttings and other pieces of propagated plant material that were placed in cold storage over the winter can be brought outdoors when the leaf buds on plants outside begin to swell. Keep them in a sheltered location, such as in a cold frame. The pots can be plunged into the soil to help reduce watering requirements.

#### Green Thumb Tip

After working outdoors, it is a good idea to clean all minor cuts with soapy water and peroxide. Even a deep prick from a rose thorn can sometimes lead to severe infections. Soil that gets into just such a wound has been known to cause tetanus.

To get mud stains out of clothes, let the mud dry and then brush it off. Work in a heavy concentration of laundry or dish detergent, let it stand 15 to 30 minutes, then launder as usual.

## Odd Jobs

### Lawn Care

If starting a new lawn, prepare the soil with plenty of organic matter when the soil is workable (see page 324). Take as much care preparing a lawn for sodding as for seeding.

Check established lawns for low spots where water collects and high spots where the mower scalps the soil. These areas should be repaired as soon as there are signs of new growth in the lawn (see page 325). Fertilizing should be delayed until new growth is established.

Snow mould shows up as matted grass covered with a grayish white or pink fungus. It occurs in patches up to 1 to 2 feet (30 to 60 cm) in diameter. If you find it intolerable, sprinkle the area with sulphur every three to five days until the signs disappear. To reduce the chance of mould occurring next spring, aerate the soil and do not apply nitrogen fertilizer in the autumn, improve the drainage, and remove any excessive build-up of dead grass (see page 325). Thatch should not be a problem if the soil pH is around 6.5 and if there is plenty of organic matter in the soil. These conditions suit earthworms, which are energetic thatch-eaters.

Edging of flower beds can be done with a v-shaped ditch or a brick insert.

Trim lawn edges where they meet flower borders, vegetable beds, or any other border. Use a sharp spade to cut down vertically on the lawn an inch (2.5 cm) in from the edge. Shake out the soil onto the bed and add the leftover bit of sod to the compost heap. The edge of beds should slope 45° and meet the lawn in a V-shaped ditch. If preferred, a permanent edging, such as wood, bricks, stone, concrete or plastic, can be inserted to make mowing easy and trimming unnecessary. Bricks are best set in vertically, with the narrow side facing the lawn, on a bed of sand or crusher dust. The height should be the same as or just above the soil level so that the mower wheels ride along at the right height.

Neat edgings make beds look tidy, and will make weeds and other irregularities less noticeable. On the other hand, neat edges would be antithetical to the look of a natural garden of native plants.

### Attracting Birds

Birds are a great benefit in the garden as they eat many harmful insects. Plant cover, nesting sites and a reliable source of water and food are sure to attract birds. Not all gardens can meet these needs, but offering just one will encourage them to at least drop by (see pages 187 and 274, for suggestions on how to protect crops from birds).

The size and arrangement of plants and open spaces affects the composition of the visiting bird population, and certain trees and shrubs will provide food and/or cover and nesting sites. There is much that can be done without a major planting effort, however, to make the garden an inviting place.

### *Flowers and food*

Birds eat the flowers and seeds of many annual and perennial flowers, including:

| | | |
|---|---|---|
| amaranthus | coreopsis | pinks |
| aster | globe thistle | portulaca |
| brown-eyed-Susan | gloriosa daisy | purple coneflower |
| butterfly weed | goldenrod | sedum |
| calendula | grasses | statice |
| California poppy | marigold | sunflower |
| centaurea | nigella | zinnia |
| columbine | | |

Other foods such as seeds and nuts can be set out for birds, particularly in the early spring and through the winter (see page 423).

A variety of flowers will attract hummingbirds—which eat flower nectar and tiny insects and spiders—but they are particularly attracted to pink, orange and red tubular flowers. Some of their favourites are beebalm, balloon flower, butterfly weed, cleome, columbine, flowering tobacco, fuchsia, larkspur, lily, lupine, lychnis, mirabilis, trumpet honeysuckle, nasturtium, petunia, phlox, pulmonaria, scarlet sage, snapdragon, trumpet creeper and yucca. Fuchsias hung close to windows will make the birds clearly visible to people indoors. The tiny birds are also drawn to hummingbird feeders, but these must be thoughtfully managed. Use one part white sugar to four parts boiled water, stir it until the sugar is dissolved, and store it in the refrigerator. Do not add red food colouring to the water; instead, wrap the feeding tube with something red, such as ribbon, to make it more attractive to the birds. Do not use honey because it can result in fungal infections on hummingbird tongues. Feeders should be toppped up daily and scrubbed clean every few days, then rinsed with vinegar followed by clear water. Smear the hanger with vasoline if ants become a problem.

### *Nesting materials*

Birds also require nesting materials and nesting sites. Even without trees, nesting sites can be provided (see pages 443-445 for the construction of bird houses, and pages 322-323 for their placement). Many birds will visit to collect nest building materials even if they do not nest in the garden. An untidy or natural garden with its bits of twigs and other debris has an advantage in this regard, but even tidy gardeners can provide nesting materials. Bits of string, yarn and thread less than 8 inches (20 cm) long can be left in piles in visible places, or drape them in clusters over clotheslines. Birds also appreciate piles of small twigs, hair from people and pets, shredded fabric, narrow strips of cloth, loose cotton batting, and fine feathers and down. A big glob of wet clay soil will also be appreciated by some birds, such as phoebes, barn swallows and cliff swallows.

### *Water*

Water acts like a magnet for many birds. No matter how it is supplied, it must be fresh, clean and free from chemical contamination. *How to Attract Birds* (Ortho Books, 1983) specifies the best shape for bird baths. They should be 24 to 36 inches (60 to 90 cm) in diameter, be shallow at the edge and slope gradually to no more than 3 inches (7.5 cm) deep in the middle, have a lip to serve as a perch, and have a flat area so that birds can approach the water gradually. A bird bath placed in a pocket of shrubbery, as some birds prefer, should be 3 feet (90 cm) above the ground to protect the birds from predators. Make sure there are no overhanging

Birds require baths 24 to 36 inches in diameter and no deeper than 3 inches.

branches from which a cat can pounce. Bird baths out in the open can be at ground level, if preferred, but they should be about 15 feet (4.5 m) from dense cover so that birds can easily scan for predators in the area before they land for a bath.

To avoid it getting muddy under a bird bath, spread a 4 inch (10 cm) thick layer of pea gravel under it. First dig out the soil in a 4 foot (1.2 m) diameter circle to a depth of 4 inches (10 cm).

Birds particularly appreciate open water in the winter. To achieve this, bury an electrical line running from the house to the bird bath when it is put in place so that an immersion water heater can be used in the winter to keep the water from freezing. Choose a model that is suited to shallow water because it will be under less than 3 inches (7.5 cm).

Water can also be supplied in a shallow, 12 inch (30 cm) wide pan on a windowsill or windowbox, from a hose or bucket dripping into a wide, shallow basin, or as a fine spray from a nozzle or soaker hose. If the spray is turned on at regular times each day, birds will readily learn to come at the appropriate times. A series of pools with small waterfalls or dripping water also appeal as birds seem to like the sound of running water. Land birds are timid about deep water—they will not use garden pools or natural ponds unless the edge is very shallow or there are wide, flat rocks at the edge for them to land on.

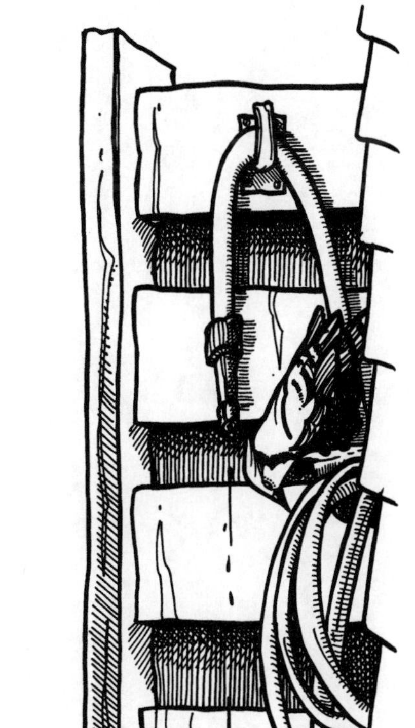

A simple solution to give your feathered friends some water.

## Odds and Ends

On those days when temperatures are 50°F (10°C) or higher, put paint or stain on window boxes, fences, trellises and any other surfaces where plants will grow. This will allow enough time for a bit of weathering, so that plants will not be harmed by the toxic substances. It is also a good time to paint or stain garden furniture, decks and other outdoor areas in the garden. Pressure treated wood can be used for planters and containers, but give it a chance to weather and do not put plants close to the boards the first season. Environmentally concerned gardeners are shying away from using pressure treated wood because of the long life of the toxic chemicals used. Instead, they are using paint to protect wood, or are replacing the wood more frequently.

If the lawn mower and other equipment was not serviced last fall, do it now. Sharpen the blade yourself, or have it done by a professional if you do not know how to balance it.

## Indoor Gardening

### Vegetables and Herbs

It is satisfying to keep fresh greens coming along, especially if planting outdoors is delayed. Many of the greens started in February or March will continue to produce leaves for cutting. Greens are heavy feeders and it is important to fertilize every two weeks with 20-20-20, manure tea or fish fertilizer. Herbs started last month will need thinning or potting on.

### Fruits

Rhubarb that was forced indoors over the winter will now be spent and should be composted. Grapes and other fruits may need to have their flowers thinned or removed (see page 187). Pollinating peach and other blossoms with a camel hair paint brush at midday will help to increase the yield, and keep the air humid to improve pollination. Be sure to keep all fruits evenly moist throughout the season as they are filling out.

### Warm Flowers

If you want indoor flowers for the coming summer, sow zinnia seeds about the first and fifteenth of the month and sow gypsophila once. Pot up more achimenes, if desired, and plenty of lilies. Some of the lilies can be held in cold storage, either before or after potting (see page 407), so that they will bloom in the autumn. Early Asiatic lilies potted up now and started into growth will bloom in about nine weeks.

### *Cool Flowers*

For fall and winter flowers, sow seeds of annual chrysanthemums, annual asters and wallflowers. Pot up stocks started in February and any other seedlings in need of attention. Continue to fertilize plants with 10-30-10 until the flower buds show. Iceland and Shirley poppies grown indoors for cut flowers should be cut early in the morning while they are still in the bud stage, and their ends seared immediately (see Green Thumb Tip, page 233).

Cut branches from deutzia, honeysuckle, leucothoe, weigela, lilac, mock orange and mountain laurel to force into bloom indoors (see Table FEB-5, page 69). These are difficult to force, but will bring a sense of spring into the house.

*Month-by-Month*

# May

- *prune evergreens*

- *plant a few more veggies*
- *weed and mulch*
- *sow green manure crops*
- *deadhead spring bulbs*
- *spray fruits?*
- *fertilize lawn*
- *start up mower*
- *pot up lilies in greenhouse*
- *sow primroses*

- *rhubarb!*

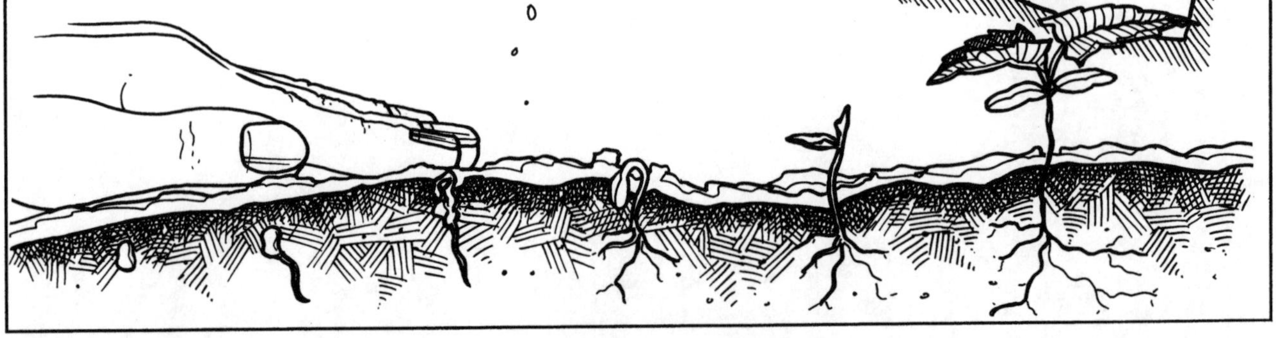

May is a busy month in the garden, full of promise and excitement as plants burst forth. Once the daffodils are in bloom and the first lilac leaves are peeking out—usually a couple of weeks before the last expected frost—many seeds can be planted directly outside. Insects are as busy as gardeners at this time, and 95% of them are either neutral or actively beneficial to plants. There are many little tricks which can be used to outwit the 5% that compete with us, and we can learn to get along with those we cannot outsmart.

Trees and shrubs are rich with flowers this month, unless they have failed to bloom yet again, and the first of the rhubarb is up. Asparagus and thinnings from the vegetable garden, including some tender young weeds, provide exquisite fresh nibbles. Spring flowering bulbs flaunt their colours, although some planted last fall may be shy about making an appearance. Hybrid tea roses are ready to be pruned once their leaf buds begin to swell, or when forsythia is in bloom, and many other roses benefit from a little judicious cutting at this point.

The fresh green of lawn grass sets off the whole scene. It may have more weeds and brown patches than grass, but can be brought to a thriving state of health with very little effort.

# May

**Scab**
*Disorder in plants caused by fungi.*

**Scald**
*Disorder in plants caused by excessive sunlight.*

**Scale**
*Disorder in plants caused by sucking insects.*

**Scorch**
*Disorder in plants caused by drought.*

**Screaming Meemies**
*Disorder in gardeners caused by observing the effects of scab, scald, scale, and scorch.*

Beard and McKie

## The Excitement of Planting

Whether you are working with vegetables, herbs or flowers as seeds or as transplants, there are several common themes to keep in mind when planting and caring for these little bundles of life.

### Planting Dates and Techniques

The timing of planting is important in the vegetable garden if a long season of continuous harvest is the goal. Unexpected frosts harm some plants but not others, some crops grow better in cool weather, and some can be planted more than once. Furthermore, early or late plantings of certain vegetables may be used to foil some troublesome insects. If extending the growing season and increasing the harvest by planting as early as possible is not a priority, however, then all vegetables can be planted in one fell swoop late this month or next month.

It is not usual to grow several crops of flowers and herbs in succession, so sowing dates are not as critical for these plants, except to avoid frost. Early planting may be needed if late bloomers are to have enough time to flower before the first frost strikes in the autumn. Anticipation of that first taste of fresh herbs may spur some gardeners to try planting early. If only part of the seed package is used, there will be a backup supply if inclement weather spoils the first sowing. Gardeners can also learn to predict when a frost is likely to strike in their garden on any particular night so that precautions can be taken to protect plants (see pages 331-334).

Any transplants that show signs of drying out rapidly between waterings probably need bigger pots. Those that are being put outdoors each day to harden off will dry out more quickly. Flowers and vegetables that are starved for water and nutrients will often flower prematurely; try to avoid this by potting on (planting in bigger pots) before plants reach the starved stage. Peppers, tomatoes and eggplants are often quite large before they are planted out, especially where the growing season is short and late frosts are a problem. They do quite well when transplanted eventually into 2 liter milk cartons.

## Thinning and Harvesting

Once seedlings are up, they may need thinning. The soil should be moist so that seedlings pull our easily, or use scissors to cut them off. Wait until they are 2 to 3 inches (5 to 8 cm) high or until they have their first one to two pairs of true leaves. Remove all of the excess seedlings at one time, or do it in two stages. Remove the excess seedlings to one-half the recommended spacing and then thin again about two weeks later to obtain the final spacing (see tables FEB-1, page 40, and APR/MAY-1, page 124). In soils low in nutrients or in areas subject to drought, use wider spacing than suggested in the tables. Refer to the seed packets for spacing of annual flowers.

It is often agonizing for novice gardeners to remove excess seedlings, but the remaining plants will be much healthier and will grow more vigorously as a result of an early thinning. Crowded, cramped seedlings are also more likely than well spaced seedlings to succumb to attack by insects and disease.

## Weeding Wizardry

Many gardeners do a fine job of getting the soil ready and planting their flowers, herbs and vegetables. When it comes to weeding, however, their enthusiasm wanes a little—or a lot. In the right frame of mind, weeding can be a very comforting, soothing activity, and there are little tricks to reduce the time it takes. If weeds are controlled during the first few weeks, much less weeding is required later in the season.

### Green Thumb Tip

Weeds between rows of crop plants compete much more for nutrients and moisture than weeds within a row. Use a hoe designed for weeding and cultivating (see page 451), and use a light sweeping motion to cut off weeds just below the soil surface between rows of plants.

Shallow cultivation is important for three reasons: 1) shallow roots of crop plants are not harmed; 2) moist soil from deeper levels is not brought to the surface, where it rapidly loses its moisture; and 3) fewer weed seeds from deeper levels are brought to the surface where they can germinate.

After hoeing, gently pull out weeds within rows of plants by hand, or use scissors to snip off annual weeds if pulling them disturbs the crop plants too much. (Seedling weeds are usually annual weeds since reproduction by seed is common among annual plants.)

It will probably be necessary to cultivate with a hoe about three times before the desired plants are tall enough to either shade the weeds, or to tolerate mulch between the rows. The need to weed within rows gradually tapers off.

Where flowers, herbs and vegetables are planted in blocks, weeding will have to be done by hand or with a hand trowel or claw. A little weeding done frequently is more effective than a lot of weeding done infrequently for several reasons: small weeds are much easier to pull than large ones; crop plants are not disturbed as much; and weeds will have taken fewer nutrients and less moisture.

To make hand weeding easier, water the soil if it is very dry. Kneel on a kneeling pad, squat on your haunches, or sit on a low stool; standing and bending from the waist is a killer on sensitive backs. Add weeds to the compost pile, or leave them lying on the surface of the soil to act as a mulch. If the soil is very moist, however, some weeds may reroot with this method.

A pleasant way to deal with weeds is to eat them (consult Szczawinski and Turner's *Edible Garden Weeds of Canada*, 1978). Young leaves of sheep sorrel, pigweed, lamb's quarters and dandelion can be eaten raw or cooked. Clover flowers can be pulled apart and used in salads. Even the dreaded Japanese knotweed can be cut when the new shoots are about 8 inches (20 cm) high, before the leaves unfurl, then cooked and served much as asparagus.

### Focus on Plants

Japanese knotweed and other persistent, invasive weeds can be controlled in several ways. Dig out as much as possible with a garden fork, aiming to remove every shred of root. Weeds may never be eliminated completely, but can probably be kept under control. Black plastic, tar paper or other light-eliminating materials can be spread over large areas after as much of the plant as possible has been dug out. If all else fails, paint the young growing tips with any herbicide containing the active ingredient glyphosate, which interacts with plants' growth hormones. Wait until the weather is warm, when the weeds are actively growing and have several sets of leaves (see page 229).

## Adding Fresh Mulch

Once plants are at least 4 inches (10 cm) tall, they can be mulched with various materials to prevent the germination and growth of weeds. Mulching also slows the evaporation of moisture from the soil. As a result of both of these outcomes less watering is needed and roots are better able to extract nutrients because the upper, nutrient-rich layers of soil are kept moist.

Some mulches add nutrients to the soil, and it has been shown that rotting matter such as mulch has a marked effect in reducing clubroot and helps to control some nematodes. Mulching also helps to improve soil structure by encouraging earthworm activity, and it reduces soil erosion from rain and wind. Vegetables and fruits are kept cleaner and drier, and there is less spread of disease because rain splash, which carries disease organisms and keeps plants wet, is reduced or eliminated with mulching.

Mulch is applied after weeding and while the soil is moist, rather than when wet or dry. It is important to wait until the soil is warm before mulching as a layer of mulch keeps the soil cool and plant growth is slow as a result. The soil may not be warm enough until June or early July in some areas. Plants that prefer cool soils, such as sweet peas and vegetables planted early in the season, can be mulched earlier. Woody plants can be mulched immediately after they have been planted, but it is also fine to mulch them this month or next, especially in short season areas, as this gives the soil time to warm up first.

Mulching materials include such things as grass clippings, old hay, straw, eel grass, salt marsh hay, seaweed, rotted sawdust, pine needles, loose oak leaves, leaf mats (see page 398) and shredded bark. The thickness of a mulch depends on the material used and the crop being grown; the denser the mulch and the lower the height of the crop, the thinner the layer required. If spreading shredded bark in perennial flower beds, for example, a thickness of 2 inches (5 cm) is sufficient, particularly if spring flowering bulbs will have to push their way through each spring, regardless of when the mulch is applied. Under trees and shrubs a 4 inch (10 cm) layer is a good depth to aim for. In paths, put down a thick layer of newspaper or cardboard and cover that with 2 inches (5 cm) of sand or gravel, or 4 inches (10 cm) of shredded bark or leaf mats.

> **Focus on Plants**
>
> 
>
> Do not be alarmed when weeding under rhododendrons to find many of their old leaves. Each leaf lasts approximately two years before falling off the plant and can be left in place as a mulch. As long as it is the older leaves toward the middle of the plant that are falling off, there is no need for concern. After weeding, apply a mulch of oak leaves, pine needles or other organic material.

Around most vegetables and annual flowers and herbs, short-term mulches consisting of materials other than wood products are usually used. Thin mulches of grass clippings can be used around small plants and chopped hay or straw can gradually be added as the plants get taller. Some gardeners, before applying mulch, spread a 1 to 2 inch (2.5 to 5 cm) layer of manure or compost to supply nutrients, or use compost itself as a mulch.

Some of the disadvantages of using mulch are that the number of slugs among the plants may increase, weed seeds may be introduced, stems may rot if mulch is applied too close to plant stems, and nitrogen may be temporarily removed from the soil. Mulches of wood derivatives, such as sawdust and shredded bark, are broken down by bacteria that require nitrogen to carry out the process. If there is little nitrogen in the mulch it will be taken from the soil, but the nitrogen is eventually returned as the mulch becomes part of the soil at the end of the process. If leaves look pale and growth seems slowed when a mulch of shredded bark is used, it may be necessary to mix in a little nitrogen fertilizer with the bark, mix in grass clippings or other green plant material, or water with manure tea (see below) in order to compensate for the temporary loss of nitrogen from the soil caused by the breakdown of the shredded bark.

Avoid mulching if slugs are a particular problem, or try a mixture of old sawdust and wood ashes as mulch, being careful not to let it touch the plants. The slugs will not like the dry environment, but you may have to water more often and perhaps use fish emulsion or manure tea occasionally to supply a little extra nitrogen.

Contrary to popular opinion, the acidifying or neutralizing effect of various mulches is so small that it is almost insignificant. Furthermore, it has been suggested that ericaceous plants, such as rhododendrons, are able to acidify the soil in the immediate vicinity of their roots to the pH they need, so there is no need to worry about using the "wrong" mulch or a little accidental lime.

### *Fertilizer Fever*

Extra fertilizing, or top dressing with compost or manure, is usually not essential if the soil was properly prepared before planting with organic matter rich in nutrients. In fact, too much nitrogen can cause problems. It makes trees, some annual flowers such as nasturtiums, and fruiting vegetable plants such as tomatoes, grow in size too much when they should be producing flowers and fruit. It also may promote fire blight in apple and pear trees, cause forking and malformations in root crops such as carrots, and cause the splitting of stems and growth of loose heads in brassica crops (cabbage and its relatives).

On the other hand, any plants that seem to be growing slowly may benefit from a little extra nitrogen. The soil may just be too cold for rapid growth. Until the soil warms up, the natural processes that release nutrients from organic matter present in the soil will be sluggish. A dose of readily available nitrogen may help promote growth at this time. Leafy green vegetables and herbs such as basil that will be picked heavily and repeatedly also benefit from additional nitrogen.

One problem with non-organic fertilizers is that gardeners tend to forget about adding organic matter to the soil. If there is nothing to hold the manufactured additives, fertilizer run-off will result. The amount added to a single garden may seem insignificant, but the total run-off from many home gardens adds up to nitrate and phosphorous overload in our lakes and waterways. Additionally, there is some evidence that chemical fertilizers tend to reduce earthworm populations, and they certainly acidify the soil, making repeated lime applications necessary.

Organic fertilizers, which are slowly broken down by bacteria and thus slow to release their nutrients, are easiest to use because repeated applications are unnecessary and there is little need to fuss over whether a high nitrogen or high phosphorous fertilizer is being added. Run-off is also less of a problem because nutrients are held in the soil for longer periods, partly due to the slow-release nature of the fertilizer and partly because of the greater amount of organic matter added to the soil at the time of application.

#### *Green Thumb Tip*

Fish emulsion, seaweed extract and manure tea supply nutrients in forms that are readily available to plants. To make manure tea, soak a cupful of fresh or dried manure in a gallon of water overnight, then water the plants with the solution. Alternatively, soak one part manure in three parts water and then dilute it to the colour of weak tea. This can be applied before or after a mulch is put on. Repeated infusions can be made with the same manure, although the nutrient content will be less each time. Worm compost runoff (see page 401) and used water from an aquarium also make good "manure" tea.

NPK: the plant parts affected

Nitrogen: part of chlorophyll and is needed for plant growth.

Phosphorus: necessary for early growth and development of roots and stems. It stimulates flower, fruit and seed production.

Potassium: essential for strong roots and stems and deep flower colour.

**Green Thumb Tip**

Good sources of nitrogen include manure, manure tea in all its forms, fish emulsion, green plant residues and dried bloodmeal. For phosphorous use bonemeal, fish bonemeal, phosphate rock and fishmeal. Potassium needs can be met with granite dust, liquid seaweed, chopped seaweed, kelpmeal, green plant residues and wood ashes.

Both organic and non-organic fertilizers purchased in packages are labelled with three numbers which identify their components. The first number refers to the proportion of the total volume that is nitrogen, which promotes leaf growth on all plants. The second number refers to the proportion of phosphorous, which strengthens stems, improves pest and disease resistance, and promotes flowering, fruiting and root branching. The third number refers to potassium, a mineral necessary for the development of root systems. The numbers do not add up to 100% because part of the total volume is filler material. Compost, leaf mould and manure also have a great deal of filler material, all of it organic matter!

Some fertilizers have more than the three major elements. In addition to NPK (nitrogen, phosphorous and potassium) they have calcium, magnesium and sulphur. Six minor elements that are needed by plants that may or may not be present in fertilizers are iron, manganese, boron, zinc, copper and molybdenum. Read the labels carefully. Compost, leaf mould and manure contain many of the minor elements.

## Vegetables

### Indoor Transplants

Start hardening off transplants of heat loving crops such as tomatoes, peppers and eggplants about ten days before outdoor planting time, or when the first of the dandelions out in the open are in bloom. The weather is usually stable enough for planting these crops outdoors when strawberries, lilacs and apple trees are in bloom.

Cucurbit seeds will rot if they are started in cold soil outdoors, but they do very well outdoors if the soil is warmed to 65 to 70°F (18 to 21°C) either naturally or with your help (see page 117). Planting seeds vertically rather than horizontally also helps to reduce their tendency to rot.

### About Two Weeks Before Last Expected Frost

There are several indicator plants that tell gardeners when it is time to carry out various tasks in the vegetable garden at this time of year. When forsythia and flowering quince are in bloom, or daffodils are flowering, or the first lilac leaves are showing, the soil has warmed up enough to do several things. In long season areas these events may occur over a period of several weeks—the forsythia may bloom before the flowering quince—but in short season areas or when spring is late arriving, these indicator plants may bloom in close succession or even at the same time. They do, however, provide a rough guideline.

Row covers put out in April or early May to protect plants can be gradually removed, only during the day at first and then at night, to slowly harden off the plants. In some cases, however, they might be better left in place to protect certain crops from insects, such as cucurbits from beetles, spinach and Swiss chard from leaf miners, brassicas from flea beetles and carrots from carrot rust fly.

Some of the earliest crops, such as spinach and mustard greens, might be ready to have a few of the outer leaves harvested. Collards might be ready, but endive and escarole take a little longer to reach full size. They might be ready for blanching (see Green Thumb Tip, page 217), however, and a few outer leaves can always be harvested for an early treat.

In all but the mildest areas, it is too early to put out tomato transplants, but some gardeners dig the holes to warm up the soil, and set the stakes or cages in place at 3 to 4 feet (1 to 1.2 m) apart, centre to centre (see page 214). In long season areas, or if spring is early and the weather is mild and settled, tomatoes, peppers and eggplants can be transplanted outdoors this month (see page 211). If there is still a risk of frost, a few plants could be put outside under protection, perhaps among the lettuces already growing in cold frames or in cages enclosed in plastic. In short season areas or if spring is late, plant lettuce or other early maturing crops between the cages or stakes.

Sweet potatoes also require warm soil. If rooted cuttings arrive in the mail before planting time, pot the cuttings in individual pots to encourage more root and leaf growth. They may look tired and yellow when they first arrive, but will revive quite nicely. If you are sprouting your own cuttings, remove the shoots with a twisting, pulling motion when they are 6 to 10 inches (15 to 25 cm) long. Strip off the lower leaves and pot the cuttings with several nodes below the soil surface—this will encourage more rooting.

Lettuce, spinach, pea, mustard green, corn salad, radish and turnip seeds can go into the ground as soon as the soil is workable. Some gardeners in mild regions will have planted these last month, and will be making a second sowing of them now. Lettuce can be seeded once a week, or make each sowing of lettuce when the previous sowing has just emerged. Spinach and lettuce planted past the end of May will have to be harvested young because they are prone to bolting (flowering before harvest), but they can be planted again in the summer for a fall harvest. Transplants of cabbages can also go in as soon as the soil is workable. Planting them when the soil is starting to warm up is also all right, as long as the weather is still cool. It partly depends on whether you want a continuous supply of fresh cabbage and some for storage, using two or more plantings, or want to grow just one main crop for autumn use and winter storage.

This is about the right time to put out transplants of cauliflower and broccoli. Try to put out all brassica transplants preferably before they have five leaves, or when they have eight or more leaves. Some gardeners sow seeds of cabbage, broccoli and cauliflower for a later harvest at the same time as setting out transplants for an early harvest. The seeds can be sown between the transplants. Chinese cabbage planted late in May will probably bolt, but more can be planted later in the summer for a fall harvest.

Early potatoes can also go in, if the soil is not too wet. Use the largest sets, which have more eyes and greater reserves, so that there is a back-up supply of sprouts and nutrients in case the first ones get hit by frost. Plant them in rows or blocks 15 by 15 inches (38 by 38 cm), and cover them with only 1 to 2 inches (2.5 to 5 cm) of soil if it is still cool and wet. If the soil is mounded slightly when covering the tubers at planting time, the young sprouts will be

## *Table MAY-1 Vegetables to Plant in Mid Spring*

About two weeks before last expected frost; daffodils, forsythia and flowering quince in bloom; first lilac leaves showing.
Plant anything from Table APR/MAY-2 (page 130) not yet planted.

| Plant | Transplant | Sow Seeds | Repeat Sow |
|---|---|---|---|
| Asparagus | | x | |
| Beets | o | x | |
| Beets, Bunching | | x | every 2 weeks to 8 weeks b.f. |
| Broccoli, early (main crop short season) | x | o | |
| Carrot, early | | fluid | |
| Cauliflower, early (main crop short season) | x | o | |
| Kohlrabi, Green | o | x | every 3 weeks to 4 weeks b.f. |
| More Lettuce | | x | every week to May 31 |
| More Mustard Greens | | x | every 2-3 weeks to May 31 |
| Parsnip, early | | fluid | |
| More Peas | | x | every 2-4 weeks to 11 weeks b.f. |
| Potato, early (sets) | | x | |
| More Radish | | x | every week to May 31 |
| Salsify, early | | fluid | |
| Scorzonera, early | | fluid | |
| More Spinach | | x | every 2-3 weeks to May 31 |
| Swiss Chard | o | x | |
| More Turnip | | x | every 3-4 weeks to 8 weeks b.f |

x = common method
o = optional or additional method
b.f = before the first expected frost in the autumn
fluid = use fluid sowing technique, or delay planting

protected from a late frost. Mound (hill) the plants with soil or mulch as they grow to ensure that developing tubers are well covered. If this is not done, potatoes will turn green and poisonous.

Sow beet, Swiss chard and green kohlrabi seeds, or set out transplants if you have them. Radishes can be sown wherever there is an odd corner. Asparagus seeds should be soaked before they are planted out. Plant them 3 to 5 inches (8 to 13 cm) apart and 1 ½ inches (4 cm) deep in rows 18 to 24 inches (45 to 60 cm) apart in a nursery or temporary location; next spring they can be transplanted to their permanent position and final spacing (see Table APR/MAY-1, page 124). Beets and kohlrabi can be planted every two to three weeks for a continuous harvest of tender young plants. Kohlrabi is definitely best when it is no bigger than an egg and can even be eaten as small as a golf ball, although some people grow them to tennis ball size. Beyond that, they tend to be woody. Ensuring that they never lack moisture will help prevent woodiness.

## Pests

As a preventative measure in efforts to reduce pest problems, remember to rotate and interplant vegetables (see pages 35-38). Planting onions among carrots sometimes helps to reduce carrot and onion pests because the foliage of each masks the attractive smell of the other.

Swiss chard and spinach are favourite foods of leaf miners. As soon as the trees start to leaf out, cover susceptible crops with cheesecloth or agricultural fabric to prevent the adult flies from laying eggs on young vegetables. These eggs turn into the larvae that mine or tunnel into the inner layer of the leaves. Alternatively, the damaged bits of each leaf can be torn out when preparing the crops for eating. Chickadees, robins and purple finches help to control leaf miners.

Flea beetles can be a problem for brassicas, but chickadees, purple finches, warblers, toads and spiders help to control them. They are shiny black beetles the size of a pin-head and jump like fleas if disturbed. The adults feed on leaves, and the larvae attack roots. Healthy, sturdy transplants can withstand and grow past moderate flea beetle damage, but young transplants may need to be protected with cheesecloth or floating row covers. A repellent can be made by steeping catnip in water, straining off the leaves and spraying the plants with the liquid.

If root maggots have been a problem (see page 123), try mixing lime with wood ashes and sprinkle the mixture around transplants after they have been

### Preventive Measure

Beets and turnips that grow very slowly, show leaf distortion or dieback or death of terminal buds, or have black heart (internal browning), are possibly suffering from boron deficiency. Cauliflower turns brown when lacking in boron. It is excess nitrogen, however, not boron deficiency as has traditionally been thought, that causes hollow and split stems in plants of the brassica family.

Boron deficiency is not likely in acidic soils, but if too much lime has been added, remedy the boron deficiency by adding pelletized Borax to the soil, or by watering through the season with 1 ounce of Borax per gallon of water (6 g/l).

Flea beetle

## Table MAY-2 Common Spring Pests

| Pest | Target | Management; Predators |
|---|---|---|
| Asparagus Beetle | Asparagus | handpick; chalcid wasps, ladybird beetle larvae, poultry |
| Bird | seeds, young plants | mulch, chicken wire, black thread |
| Cabbage Worm and Cabbage Looper | Brassicas | cover plants, Bt, tansy spray, butterfly net to capture adults, remove eggs; swallows |
| Cat | bare soil | chicken wire, twiggy brush, seaweed mulch, cayenne-pepper mix, ammonia, water; dogs |
| Clubroot | Brassicas | destroy weeds in mustard family, improve drainage, organic matter in soil, mulch |
| Corn Maggot | Corn | avoid early planting |
| Cutworm | young plants | collar, toothpicks, wood ashes and lime; swallows, bluejays, bats, sparrows, robins, bluebirds, chickens, snakes, toads |
| Flea Beetle | Brassicas | cover plants, catnip spray; chickadees, purple finches, warblers, toads, spiders |
| Gopher | many plants | wire mesh fence—half buried |
| Leaf Miner | Swiss Chard, Spinach, other leafy crops | cover plants; robins, chickadees, purple finches |
| Mole | dig soil | used cat litter in holes; cat, dog |
| Mosquito | humans | fly catchers, swallows, king birds, dragon flies, wasps |
| Nematode | many plants | organic matter in soil, mulch, marigolds |
| Onion Maggot | Onion family | avoid bruising, delay planting, interplant |
| Potato Beetle | Potato | deep mulch; tachnid fly |
| Rabbit | many plants | chicken wire fence, electric fence |
| Racoon | Corn | outer row late variety, plastic or wire or electric fence |
| Root Aphid | Lettuce | ashes in planting holes |
| Root Maggot | Brassicas, some roots | lime and wood ashes, barriers, transplants in individual containers, rotation, interplanting |
| Slug | anything green | crushed eggshell, sand, wood ash, dry mulch or no mulch; some snakes |

set out, or along rows of onions, turnips, radishes, cabbages, broccoli, cauliflower and Brussels sprouts. Planting susceptible crops in a different place each year is a big help, and interplanting onions among other crops will make it harder for adult onion maggots to find onions on which to lay their eggs. The adult looks like a hairy brown housefly with a rounded back. Rodale's *Color Handbook of Garden Insects* (Carr, 1979) should help to identify insects.

Cabbage white butterflies are often seen flitting around brassicas. Each time they alight they are depositing an egg which later hatches into a cabbage worm. This worm eats holes in brassica leaves and lurks in broccoli heads and other crevices. A medium-sized grey moth lays the eggs that develop into cabbage loopers. To avoid cabbage worms and loopers, cover plants with Reemay or cheesecloth to prevent egg laying, or pick off eggs, most of which will be on the underside of leaves. Putting up bird boxes to attract swallows seems to be very effective as well. As a last resort, spray with Bt as soon as the first larvae appear, and again every five days until they disappear. Bt stands for *Bacillis thuringiensis*, which is a bacterium that causes caterpillars to sicken and die.

Spraying with tansy extract is not as effective as Bt, but it will reduce the feeding of cabbage worms. Prepare it by chopping 2 ounces (52 g) of fresh tansy leaves in a blender with 32 ounces (1 l) of water. Mix in a drop of detergent to help the solution adhere to the plant and spray every five days.

After any seeds are sown, cats seem to be inexorably drawn to the area to dig. Spread chicken wire over the area, crisscross thread over the area, or poke twiggy brush into the ground between the rows. Once plants are up and well established, spread seaweed between the rows. Cats dislike walking on it when it is dry and crunchy and when it is wet and slippery. At least one gardener has had great success keeping cats at bay by sprinkling a mixture of two parts cayenne pepper, three parts dry mustard, and five parts flour around the garden. Straight cayenne can also be used in this way. Film canisters with a hole punched in the lid and filled with household ammonia will also discourage cats.

Slugs can get very active once plants are up, in both flower and vegetable gardens. Holes in leaves and a slimy trail are telltales of their nocturnal visits. They like moist, cool conditions, so do not spread any mulch until plants are well up and growing. Spread a ring of finely crushed eggshell, sand or wood ashes around transplants that are bothered by slugs, and hunt for them early in the morning, or in the evening with a flashlight. Your best ally is a slug-loving snake, such as the friendly little Eastern Smooth Green Snake.

Use collars or toothpicks (see page 123) against cutworms, if necessary, but be comforted that most plants are at risk only while they are young.

### About One Week Before Last Expected Frost

When the first leaves are beginning to show on trees, or when lilac leaves are about 1 ½ inches (3.5 cm) long, set out transplants of leeks, onions, spring bunching onions and chives. Drop leek transplants into 5 inch (12 cm) deep holes, and water them well. If soil is very shallow or heavy, plant them on the flat. Their fibrous root system helps improve soil structure. Leeks which are transplanted in blocks of four can be harvested early while they are still small.

Chives, pickling onions (pearl, white boiling) and bunching onions can also be seeded directly outside, every two to three weeks until July. Thinning is not required because of the moderate germination rate. A few leeks can be seeded thickly, separate from the main crop, for some tender ones that can be harvested when only 3/4 inch (2 cm) thick.

Adult flies of onion maggots are attracted to damaged or rotting onions so handle transplants carefully to avoid bruising or damaging them. If maggots have been a severe problem in previous years, delay putting out onion family transplants or seeds for another couple of weeks, until after the last expected frost, when the worst of the maggot season will hopefully be past.

Potatoes that were pre-sprouted indoors can be planted out for an extra early taste of new potatoes, or plant out unsprouted tubers for an early crop. Some gardeners plant a few early, short season potatoes, and then a main crop later on. Others plant one variety all at once, but harvest a few plants early, or just grub around underneath the plant to mine a tuber or two from several plants. The main planting of potatoes for winter storage is usually carried out when apple trees are in bloom, but any time the soil is dry enough and there is little chance of frost is all right.

Space potatoes in rows 30 inches (75 cm) apart. Within the row, spacing depends on the size of sets you have (see Table APR/MAY-1, page 124). Remember to leave potatoes whole, rather than cutting them up (see pages 76-77). Large sets have so many sprouts that an overcrowded clump of stems is produced, so largest is not best. Potato varieties that tend to form large tubers are spaced further apart within each size class than those varieties that tend to form small tubers. The total yield will be the same for any one variety,

## Table MAY-3 Vegetables to Plant in Mid Spring

About one week before the last expected frost. Plant anything from previous schedules not yet planted (see tables APR/MAY-2, page 30 and MAY-1, page 167).

| Plant | Transplant | Sow Seeds | Repeat Sow |
|---|---|---|---|
| Beans, Runner (Climbing) | | x | |
| Beans, Shell | | x | |
| Beans, Snap, Wax (Bush) | o ! | x | every 2 weeks to 8 weeks b.f. |
| Beets, Leaf | | x | every 2-4 weeks to 8 weeks b.f. |
| Cabbages, Summer (main crop short season) | x | | |
| Chives | x | o | |
| Corn | o ! | x | every week to 11 weeks b.f. |
| Cucumbers | o ! | | |
| Leeks, Early (main crop short season) | x | o | |
| More Lettuce | | x | every week to May 31 |
| Onions | x | | |
| Onions, Pickling | | x | every 3 weeks to 10 weeks b.f. |
| Onions, Spring Bunching | x | o | every 3 weeks to end June |
| Potatoes, Early (sets) | | o | |
| Potatoes, Sprouted | o | | |
| More Radishes | | x | every week to May 31 |
| Summer Squashes, Zucchini | o ! | | |
| Tomatoes, Early | o ! | | |
| Witloof Chicory | | x | |

x = common method
o = optional or additional method
b.f. = before the first expected frost in the autumn
! = must provide protection, or plant later in season

regardless of wh … are used. Spacing too widely can cause hollow b … at are forced to the surface because of overabun…

Plant set … cm), with the rose end up, and cover with 1 inch (2.5 c… ardeners lay seaweed in the bottom of the hole first to provide ex… nts. Gradually add more soil and hill up the potatoes as they grow, or mulch with seaweed or straw. If small sets are used and they are spaced correctly, there should be no need to hill.

If there has been trouble in the past with potato beetles, try laying a thick (1 foot or 30 cm) layer of straw, seaweed or oak leaves over the area after the potatoes have been planted. They will grow up through the mulch just fine, and for some reason the potato beetles are reduced in number. Potatoes do not even need to be planted in soil; simply lay them on the surface, or on top of the winter mulch, before piling on new mulch.

Witloof chicory—the kind that is dug up in the autumn and forced indoors for winter use—can be seeded directly in loose, deep soil in the same manner as carrots. Its final spacing should be 6 by 12 inches (15 by 30 cm). It is also called Belgian endive or French endive, but is not a true endive.

### Green Thumb Tip

A support system that makes picking easy and provides the space required by climbing beans can be erected as follows: space pairs of 8 foot (2.4 m) canes 2 feet (60 cm) apart from each other at intervals along each row, so that their tops can be crossed and tied together tee-pee style. Run a horizontal string under tension between the paired crossed canes, and peg it into the ground at the end of each row. Run another horizontal string along the bottom of the canes, and then run vertical strings at 6 inch (15 cm) intervals between the top and bottom horizontal strings. Or, set and tie the canes in place as described, but spread wide-spaced netting instead of strings between them.

Alternatively, set long poles 1 foot (30 cm) into the ground 3 feet (1 m) apart in a circle, and tie the tops together tee-pee style. Plant 6 beans around each pole, 6 inches (15 cm) from the pole. Once up, thin to 3 plants per pole. Bean tee-pees are great fun for children to play in, and they may even eat some young raw beans. An old metal frame swing set is also an excellent set up for climbing plants when strung with string or nylon netting (plants seem to have trouble grabbing plastic netting).

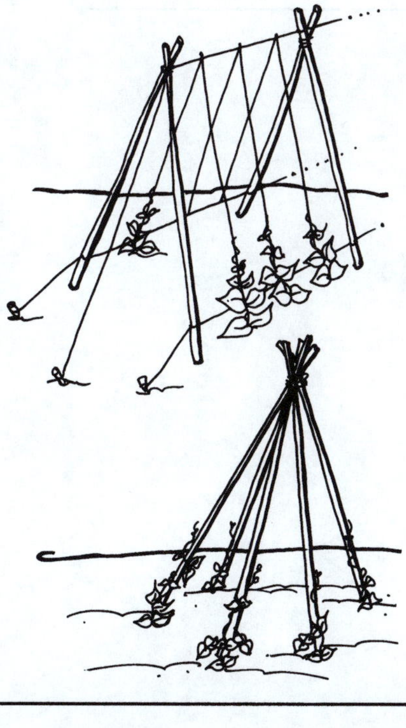

Beans, including green (snap), yellow (wax), runner and shell (baking), can be planted now. The soil has to be warm enough to ensure rapid germination, or the seeds will simply rot. Some gardeners plant a few snap beans every two weeks until the middle of July to get a long continuous harvest of fresh beans. Continuous picking of the crop from one sowing will also extend the harvest. Other gardeners make one large sowing and harvest over a short period if they are freezing, canning or pickling the crop.

**Green Thumb Tip**

To speed up and encourage more uniform corn germination in cool soils, pre-soak corn in distilled water at 77°F (25°C) for sixteen hours, then dry at room temperature for eight hours before planting. Do not do this if using seed treated with fungicide.

Runner beans are planted only once and can yield three times the harvest of bush beans in the same space. They continue to grow and flower until stopped by cold weather and frost. Continuous picking of this variety also encourages the production of more pods.

Delay planting lima beans until several weeks after the average last frost date—wait until the weather is truly warm and settled, about the time apple trees and strawberries are blooming. Corn is planted a little sooner, traditionally when lilac leaves are $1\frac{1}{2}$ inches (4 cm) long. The soil is warm by this time, ensuring rapid seed germination and little chance of decaying seeds which attract corn maggots. It may be possible to plant earlier in porous or sandy soils as these warm up quickly. Some gardeners make repeat sowings of corn to extend the harvest, whereas others plant early, mid and late season varieties at one time.

Birds will often peck at corn seeds; try a light mulch of straw or eel grass, plant extra seed to compensate, cover the area with chicken wire or plastic netting (to be removed when corn is 6 inches or 15 cm high) or crisscross the area with fine black thread.

If using corn transplants for an early start, wait until all danger of frost is past, or be prepared to protect the young plants from frost. Plant corn in large blocks rather than a long, narrow row, and plant sweet and regular varieties separately (25 feet or 8 m apart) so that they do not cross-pollinate. Isolate popcorn, white corn and Indian corn from other kinds of corn, including that of the neighbours.

Work in plenty of well rotted manure beforehand, sow corn generously in multiple rows or blocks, and thin later to the desired spacing. Plant seed 1 inch (2.5 cm) deep if the soil is on the wet side, or up to 2 inches (5 cm) deep if crows are a problem and the soil is drier.

To discourage racoons, plant the outer two rows in a block of corn with a late maturing variety. Hopefully you can harvest the inner corn before the racoons realize it is ripe. Another trick is to put stakes 10 feet (3 m) apart around the plot and wrap thick black plastic sheeting or 1 inch (2.5 cm) mesh wire around the outside. Make it 30 to 36 inches (75 to 90 cm) high, with the bottom 6 inches (15 cm) resting on the ground outside.

Do not interplant corn with other crops in short season areas. Squashes and cucumbers can be planted around the outside of a block of corn, however, and may help to discourage racoons.

The only way to keep rabbits out of the vegetable garden is by putting chicken wire around the perimeter. Three feet (1 m) is tall enough, with the bottom 6 inches (15 cm) turned outward and buried. Staple the wire to 2 by 4 inch posts, and roll it up in the winter so that it will last for several years. To ensure complete success at keeping out rabbits and racoons, use two strands of electric wire around the garden—one at 6 inches (15 cm) above the ground and the other at 12 inches (30 cm). Attach the wire to plastic posts, which racoons cannot climb. Keep gophers out with a 4 foot (1.2 m) wire mesh fence, with the lower 2 feet (60 cm) buried vertically under the soil.

## After Planting

### Thinning and harvesting

It is a pleasure to thin seedlings in the vegetable garden because so many of the thinnings can be eaten. Any of the brassicas, and of course young plants normally eaten for their leaves, can be devoured on the spot or cooked lightly first.

Beets and Swiss chard may need particular attention. Where seedlings are very crowded, cut the extras out with scissors to avoid disturbing the roots of the remaining ones. Thin kohlrabi when it is just 2 inches (5 cm) high so that development is not slowed down. Wide spacing for a vegetable harvested while small ensures that there is no competition for moisture (such competition results in woodiness). Sow more kohlrabi every three weeks, using a purple variety in June and July.

Thin spinach when it has two true leaves or more, using wider spacing for plants intended for cooking. Make repeated thinnings and use the thinnings for fresh salads. After the final thinning, start picking the spinach regularly when each plant has 8 to 10 leaves, taking the outer leaves, or cut plants off entirely about 1 inch (2.5 cm) above the ground when they have 4 or 5 leaves, and let the plants regrow.

Lettuce can also be harvested a few leaves at a time, taking the outside leaves, or cut plants off entirely about 1 inch (2.5 cm) above the ground. These plants will regrow and can be harvested for a second time in about

### Preventive Measure

Thin carrots in the evening, preferably on a windless, misty day, so that there is less chance of attracting carrot rust flies. As soon as you are finished, bury the carrot thinnings in the middle of the compost pile. Some people put crushed artemisia cut from the herb garden along the rows to mask the scent of carrots, or cover the patch with cheesecloth or floating row covers to protect the crop against these flies.

The delicious, edible, ostrich fern.

The unfurled frond of the bracken fern is not edible.

seven weeks. Early crops of arugula and other greens may also be ready to use. (See page 216 for methods of harvesting them.) Fertilize lettuce, spinach and other leafy crops by watering with manure tea or fish emulsion.

Thin radishes early on and keep them moist and weedless. This treatment enables them to grow quickly so that they have a mild flavour and are tender and crisp. Harvest them as soon as they mature, before they get woody.

Onions can be thinned and harvested as scallions when the tops are 6 to 8 inches (15 to 20 cm) tall. Leeks can be eaten raw if picked at scallion size. The stalks of Swiss chard can be cooked and served like asparagus, and the leafy part cooked as a green. Thin pairs of Chinese cabbage to a final 12 by 12 inch (30 by 30 cm) spacing, and use the thinnings as raw or cooked greens. Turnip greens can sometimes be harvested as early as one month after planting if growth has been rapid.

Snap off leaves of mustard greens just before they mature, or cut back the whole plant to delay flowering. When plants start to flower, the leaves become tough and bitter. Use the leaves immediately as cooked greens or in salads.

A delectable spring vegetable is fiddleheads from the ostrich fern (*Matteuccia struthiopteris*). Bracken fern (*Pteridium aquilinum*), which is not recommended, can be distinguished from ostrich fern by the shape of the unfurling frond. Fiddleheads are gathered while the fronds are still tightly curled and no more than 6 inches (15 cm) high. The thin, brown papery covering is easily rubbed off and the fiddlehead can be nibbled raw or cooked like asparagus. Be sure to leave plenty of fiddleheads in each clump to ensure harvests in future years.

### *Weeding, mulching and fertilizing*

After the asparagus harvest, spread another thin layer of well rotted manure along the rows, be vigilant in maintaining a weed-free bed so that harvests are not reduced in subsequent years, and provide a steady supply of moisture. A mulch of compost or other organic material will help with weed control and moisture.

Some gardeners plant annual ryegrass as a cover crop instead of spreading mulch over asparagus beds. It keeps weeds down and dies back over the winter, so it does not interfere in the spring when the new asparagus emerges. After planting asparagus crowns, try planting bush beans (snap or wax) among the plants during the first year, and lettuce in subsequent years both for cover and if short of growing space.

## Focus on Plants

The first delicious, delightful, delectable spears of asparagus push through the ground this month. If plants were started from seed three years ago, or from crowns two years ago, the first spears may be harvested. Within a two week period, harvest all spears that emerge by snapping them off when they are 6 to 8 inches (15 to 20 cm) high. Leave those which emerge after the two week period so that there are enough photosynthesizing leaves remaining to allow the crowns to grow and develop and hence produce a bigger crop next year. By snapping rather than cutting, spears break at the point where tenderness ends and tough, woodiness begins. Cutting spears below ground level reduces the overall yield. Thin spears are usually due to the close planting of crowns, but the total yield will be higher than wide spacing, which produces thick spears.

If the bed is younger than two or three years it is best to restrain yourself and harvest nothing. If the agony is too great, take one spear from each crown for one glorious, mouth watering, self-indulgence. In the second year of harvest, snap off all spears that emerge for three to four weeks, and in subsequent years harvest everything for a full five to six weeks. Asparagus will keep for over two weeks in the refrigerator if the cut ends are placed on wet tissue paper. Spears can also be stood with their cut ends in a container of water in the refrigerator, but the water should be changed every few days.

If misshapen spears are found, suspect the asparagus beetle (1/4 inch long, slender, black with four white spots) and its larvae (1/3 inch long, plump, grayish green, black head and legs). Keep an eye out for their black, shiny eggs laid individually on young spears. Chalcid wasps and the larvae of lady bird beetles will help to keep them in check, as will poultry if you have any stray chickens or ducks around. Pick the beetles off by hand in the morning when they are sluggish and wet with dew if they are plentiful enough to threaten to defoliate the asparagus by the time summer comes.

Beware the asparagus beetle.

Other vegetables will also need careful weeding. Onions, leeks, garlic and other members of the onion family need particular attention for the first six weeks as they are more readily set back in their growth from weed competition than other plants.

Mulch carefully after weeding. Carrots will form a canopy with their foliage, eliminating the need for mulching unless they are planted in rows, but the onion family will benefit from a mulch of chopped leaves applied when they are a foot tall (30 cm).

If beans are mulched so that the need for watering is reduced, there is less opportunity for their leaves to get wet. This reduces the spread of fungal diseases, which beans are prone to. Bush tomatoes, cucumbers, zucchini and summer squash are less likely to develop rot if they are mulched with a dryish mulch, particularly under developing fruits. Use straw rather than moist grass clippings, for example.

For other crops, use a thin layer of grass clippings while plants are small; use straw, chopped hay, salt marsh hay, chopped leaves, seaweed, pea vines or clover when plants are 8 inches (20 cm) tall or more. Spinach and Swiss chard need 3 to 4 inches (8 to 10 cm) of mulch, but wait until the plants are at least twice that height, or build up the thickness gradually.

Use a coarser mulch of small twigs, coniferous branches or coarse straw under lettuce. These will keep the lettuce clean from soil splash when it rains; fine mulches could cause the lower leaves of lettuce to rot. Lettuce that is mulched and kept evenly moist will be less bitter than lettuce stressed due to lack of moisture.

Any plants that seem to be off to a slow start can be given a little boost with liquid seaweed, fish emulsion or manure tea. Give leaf crops a little extra help also. Some gardeners apply fine, finished compost along the rows half way through the season, but before the middle of July, to give plants an extra boost. Finished compost is no longer actively decomposing, so there is no risk that nitrogen will be removed from the soil to aid decomposition. Spread it only if you have compost to spare. Otherwise, work it into new planting areas.

## Green Manures

Green manures can be planted either between rows of plants instead of applying mulch or, if they are low growing, as are the clovers (although sweet clover is taller than most clovers), underneath tall crops (see page

## Table MAY-4 Spring or Summer Planted Cover Crops

| Plant | Seeding Rate (lbs/acre; lbs/1000 sq ft. or kg/hectare; g/100 sq. m) | | | When to Turn Under |
|---|---|---|---|---|
| * Alphalpha | 15-20; 1/2-1 | or | 17-22; 244-488 | the following spring |
| * Beans, Broad | 110-160; 10-16 | or | 123-179; 4880-7808 | before harvest of beans+ |
| * Beans, Snap or Wax | 85; 8-10 | or | 95; 3904-4880 | before harvest of beans |
| * Beans, Shell | 80; 5-8 | or | 90; 2440-3904 | before or after harvest |
| Buckwheat | 60-75; 2-3 | or | 67-84; 976-1464 | when 1/2 crop in flower |
| * Clover, Alsike | 10; 1/4 | or | 11; 122 | the following spring |
| * Clover, Red | 15-20; 1/2-3/4 | or | 17-22; 244-366 | the following spring |
| * Clover, Sweet | 15; 1/2 | or | 17; 244 | the following spring |
| * Clover, White | 5-10; 1/4 | or | 6-11; 122 | the following spring |
| * Peas | 120; 12 | or | 134; 5856 | before harvest of peas |
| Spring Wheat | 120-140; 4-6 | or | 134-157; 1952-2928 | before seed sets |

+ peas and beans will add more nitrogen to the soil if turned under without first having harvested the pods

* leguminous crop

250). They contribute to the soil in several ways and should go in after four weeks but before five weeks after each vegetable has been planted, according to Eliot Coleman (1989). Green manures can also be cut early and used as a mulch. Red clover and pea vines both make good mulches.

Areas of ground newly opened last fall or this spring can be planted with a green manure crop. Such crops will help to reduce the number of weeds and unwanted grasses by suppressing their growth; add organic matter to the soil, both through their roots and when the tops are dug in; break up deeper levels of soil and bring minerals to the surface; and, in the case of leguminous crops, add nitrogen to the soil by fixing nitrogen from the air.

Cultivate the area every ten days or so for a month, then work in some organic matter throughout the rooting depth—18 to 20 inches (45 to 50 cm) deep if possible. This works well for fruiting shrubs, perennial beds and vegetable gardens. If only shallow rooted crops will be planted, such as lawns or annual flowers, then work in the organic matter to a depth 8 to 10 inches (20 to 25 cm).

Planting time for beans depends on the type: broad beans should be planted as soon as the soil is workable, shell and snap beans around the last frost date, or anytime after.

Buckwheat is one of the best crops for smothering weeds and grass. Plant it three weeks after the last frost date, and then cut it down before it goes to seed, about the time that half the crop is in bloom. If it is left too long there will be unwelcome buckwheat plants next year! In long season areas a second crop can be planted and then, in all areas, a winter cover crop such as annual ryegrass can be planted a few weeks before the first expected frost in the autumn.

### Preventive Measure

Remember to plant annuals and tender bulbs in different places each year to avoid pests such as thrips and nematodes, and to avoid a build up of diseases such as wilt and clubroot. Not all plants are equally susceptible to all pests and diseases, which makes life easier for the gardener. As well, use organic matter in the soil to keep plants healthy and thus better able to resist attack. Organic matter also benefits fungi and bacteria that feed on certain soil pests, such as nematodes.

Clover can be planted very early in the spring or later in the season. It is turned under the following spring when a few inches tall. If clover cover crops are turned under in the autumn, dormant buds dug into the soil throughout the area may survive the winter to sprout in mass profusion in the spring. Clovers are usually not totally winter hardy, but some plants will likely survive. Most of the clover "weeds" found growing in the garden are there through self-seeding. Clovers grow best in soils with a pH of 6.0 or higher, and Alsike clover will tolerate wetter soils than most clovers.

## Annual Flowers and Herbs

Hardy annual flowers such as bachelor's button (see Table FEB-4, page 56) and herbs such as fennel and chervil (see Table FEB-3, page 54) can be sown outdoors in cold frames where they are to grow, a couple of weeks before the last expected frost, or they can be sown in the open around the last frost date. This saves considerable time and energy as it avoids the transplanting stage. Cold frames can also be used if there is no space left in the house for starting transplants, and early bloom is desired. These transplants will be extra sturdy and stocky. Indoor transplants of flowers that tolerate cool growing conditions can be hardened off gradually (see Preventive Measure, page 120) and planted outdoors around the last frost date. Plant tender annuals after apple trees bloom.

One sowing of each type of annual flower is usually sufficient. Many can be cut back in the summer when they start to flag for a burst of fresh growth and more blooms in the autumn. To stretch the blooming season, some gardeners save a few seeds when sowing indoors and scatter these among the transplants when they are set outdoors, or make a second sowing in June or even late July or early August in long season areas.

Prepare a fine seed bed as for vegetables, and outline areas on the ground where each type of seed or transplant is to grow. Use lime or flour to mark the outlines, and arrange the shapes in drifts, with low and mid height flowers intermingling towards the front, and mid height and tall flowers weaving between each other at the back. Annuals also make good fillers in perennial flower beds and the taller ones, such as larkspur and clarkia, can be seeded among tulips and other spring bulbs when they are in bloom to hide the bulbs' foliage when it starts to die.

One sowing of herbs is also usually enough as most of them can be lightly harvested almost continuously, or be cut back fairly hard to regrow again. Exceptions to this are summer savory, which is harvested by cutting the entire plant, and chervil, which is short-lived, so is usually sown every two to four weeks for a continuous harvest. Chervil grows best in cool weather; plant it a couple of times in the spring, and again in the summer for fall use.

French sorrel is very invasive and will never, ever have to be planted again, as anyone knows who has the weed sheep sorrel. Both are edible, but the leaves of French sorrel are broader and tastier. Cut off the flower heads as soon as you notice them to encourage a steady supply of new leaves.

Fennel is often planted away from other plants because of its reputation for adversely affecting the growth of other plants. It is nonsense to suggest, however, that dill and fennel will cross-pollinate and produce badtasting seeds. They are not only different species but different genera as well.

Novice gardeners often find it difficult to distinguish between weed seedlings and desirable plants. Although one does not usually plant herbs and flowers in rows, it may be helpful to do so the first time to determine which are weeds. Another method is to compare suspects with weed seedlings coming up between the rows of vegetables (see also Mulligan's *Common Weeds of Canada*, 1987).

Be particularly careful to mulch moisture loving flowers and herbs. Annual herbs and flowers, which are usually shallow rooted, may benefit from extra fertilizer, but be careful not to overfertilize or vegetative growth may occur at the expense of flowers.

Perennial herbs may be ready to have a few leaves picked for an early taste (see Table AUG-3, page 302), although the new growth is sometimes not as flavourful as more mature growth. Sweet woodruff is made into Maywine when the new growth is well established but still young. This may be in June in some regions. To make Maywine, fill a glass jar full of fresh leaves and fill it with Rhine wine until the leaves are covered. Cover the jar and let it steep in the refrigerator for four weeks.

**Green Thumb Tip**

Remember after sowing to store all remaining seeds in a cool, dry, airtight place (see page 8). Seeds will stay viable for possibly years longer, depending on the type, but may deteriorate in a few weeks if left at room temperature in moist conditions, making them useless for summer or subsequent sowings.

## Perennial Flowers

### General Care and Planting

Adding fertilizer and mulch in the form of well rotted manure or compost will encourage healthy, young growth even in old flower beds. There are a few things to watch out for and some extra chores in the flower bed that can be carried out this month.

Weeding in the flower bed is best done with a hand trowel or claw since there really is not enough room to swing a hoe. Be sure to watch out for perennials that are slow to emerge. Balloon flower is particularly slow to make an appearance in the spring. It is also discouraging to break off a lily shoot as the bulb will not grow another one until the next year. Lilies should be marked with a stake in the fall, or leave the old flower stalks in place until the new shoots emerge in the spring. As well, lily bulbs that were planted the previous autumn are much slower to appear in the spring than established lilies. Ferns should be hand weeded since it is easy to break off the young fiddleheads.

Sometimes weeds will invade a clump of plants, such as grass in "blue-eyed grass," the little wild iris. The only solution may be to dig up the clump, sit comfortably with a newspaper spread out, pull apart the clump, and quietly pick through to remove all the foreign roots. Sprinkle the roots with water occasionally to keep them moist.

Watch for sawfly larvae on columbine leaves. Scrape off their eggs which adhere to the underside of leaves. As soon as you see a nibble taken or a hole chewed in a leaf, start squashing them. They are tiny and hide under the leaves, but in the space of a week they seem to increase a thousand-fold in size and number and there will not be a leaf left on your columbines.

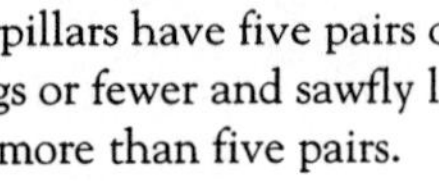

Caterpillar



Sawfly

Caterpillars have five pairs of prolegs or fewer and sawfly larvae have more than five pairs.

Unlike caterpillars, sawfly larvae have more than five pairs of false legs, or prolegs, at the back end of their body. Because they are sawfly larvae and not caterpillars, Bt has no effect on them. Keep the soil around columbines cultivated all summer long as there can easily be three generations of sawfly larvae. Disturbing the soil and keeping it turned might help to reduce their numbers as they spend part of their life cycle in the soil, but avoid damaging the columbine roots. Keep the plants well fertilized to enable them to grow without interruption.

Dahlia tubers can be planted about a week before the last expected frost, but if they were sprouted indoors, wait until all danger of frost is past. The same guidelines apply to other tender bulbs such as gladioli and begonias. If planting begonia tubers directly outside in open ground or containers, remember to plant them with the concave, rough side facing up, and the convex, smooth side where the roots will emerge facing down. The smaller-flowered tuberous begonias tolerate drier conditions than some of the others—a boon to gardeners who have trouble keeping up with watering. Dwarf dahlias and cannas grow well in containers.

Tradition has it that roses should be pruned when forsythia is in bloom, or a couple of weeks before the last frost date. This is not a hard and fast rule, but it is easier to see the swelling buds at this time, making pruning decisions a little easier.

### Focus on Plants

Whether pruning hybrid tea roses, floribundas or bush type roses, the first three steps are the same. First, cut back dead and diseased stems to where they join healthy stems, or to just above outward-facing buds. Second, cut out thin or weak stems to where they join a vigorous stem or to ground level. Undersized shoots are where diseases often begin. Third, cut out stems that cross or rub. Remove the stem that points towards the middle of the bush, or cut out the weaker stem if they both point outwards.

Roses that bloom repeatedly through the summer, such as hybrid teas, floribundas and hybrid perpetuals, should be pruned back fairly hard. Cut hybrid tea stems back to outward-facing buds that are 4 inches (10 cm) above the ground, and floribundas to 6 inches (15 cm) above the ground. Hybrid musks should be tidied somewhat, and the main canes perhaps shortened by up to one-third their length.

Many old garden roses that bloom only once, such as the gallicas, damasks, albas and centifolias, should be pruned only after blooming, except to remove dead wood. The same goes for climbers and ramblers. When an old stem of a climbing rose stops growing new shoots, cut it out at the base. With rambler roses, prune after flowering by removing entire stems that have just flowered. Bourbons and moss shrub roses, which are a mixed bag of repeat bloomers and one-time only bloomers, should be pruned in the spring if repeaters, but after flowering if summer-only bloomers.

Species and rugosa roses rarely need any pruning, except to occasionally remove some of the oldest wood to ground level in well established shrubs.

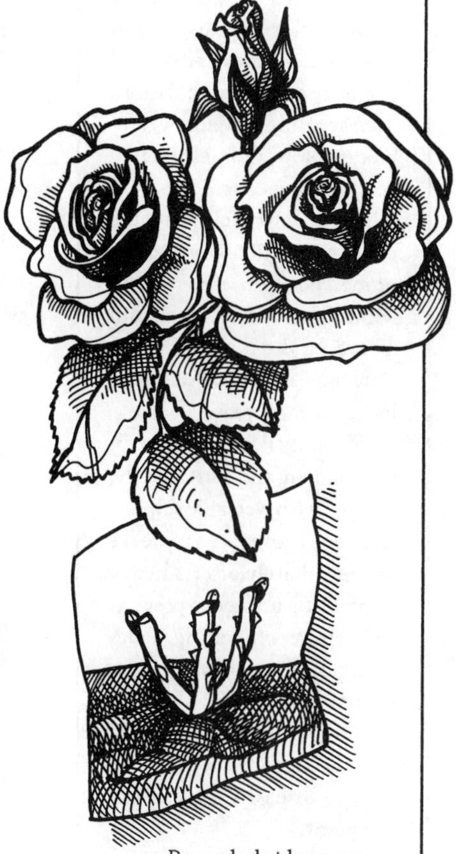

Prune hybrid tea roses to outward-facing bud.

### Preventive Measure

To reduce disease problems among flowers, such as hollyhocks affected by rust, phlox afflicted with mildew and roses suffering from blackspot, put susceptible plants in full sunshine, or at least where they get sun in the morning, so that their leaves dry off quickly after rain or dew, and avoid watering from overhead. Space plants further apart than usual, and keep roses thinned and pruned to ensure good air circulation.

As well, put plants where breezes blow, rather than in a dead air space, again to help foliage dry off quickly. If some plants are particularly disease-prone, position them down wind from others to avoid spreading the disease. If possible, put plants in a different location each year.

Plants that have been troubled in the past can be sprayed with wettable sulphur (see page 190) every two weeks or immediately after a heavy rainfall, or a weekly preventive spray of baking soda, mineral oil and water (see page 190) may help. Through the summer, pick up and destroy any fallen leaves, and remove diseased leaves from the plant.

Gladioli can be made more stable without staking if the corms are planted deeper than the usual 5 inches (12 cm) deep, and in blocks rather than rows. Plant them 6 inches (15 cm) apart in the bottom of a 10 inch (25 cm) deep trench, preferably pre-warmed or at least pre-dug to warm up the soil. Half fill the trench with soil enriched with bonemeal or other phosphorous rich fertilizer, and gradually fill in the rest as the glads grow. This method will produce big corms for next year's planting. Plant glads in a different place each year to combat thrips and various diseases.

Carry on dividing and transplanting perennials as described in April/May (pages 134-137), being careful to water in thoroughly. If days are sunny and warm, move established perennials in the evening, or wait for a cool, foggy, windless day, particularly if there is a lot of leafy growth established. They should be treated with the same care and consideration as delicate transplants.

If you stake tall perennials such as dahlias and delphiniums, and floppy ones such as peonies, drive the stakes in early or at planting time, about 4 inches (10 cm) from the shoots. Try to make them as unobtrusive as possible, using twigs or green bamboo and neutral coloured ties.

To propagate roses, dig up suckers coming out of the ground. Most hybrid teas and floribundas will be on root stocks other than their own, so suckers would not be like the parent shrub. In fact, if you see suckers coming out of the ground with leaves that look different, or if your rose suddenly blooms with a different coloured or shaped rose, suspect that the root stock is sending up suckers. If this happens, dig up the plant, remove all the suckers by tearing them off rather than cutting, and replant deeper with at least 4 inches (10 cm) of soil above the graft. If left unattended, the root stock will probably grow more vigorously than the desired rose, eventually eliminating it.

Hardy shrub roses on their own roots can be propagated by digging up their suckers. Choose small ones, and keep the roots moist at all times. This is best done before they come into leaf. Roses can also be layered using branches above ground to increase the stock (see pages 149-150).

## Disease Control and Management

Proper cultural management can go a long way towards preventing disease in flowering plants. Roses have a reputation for being difficult because of their susceptibility to diseases, but this is not the case with many of the hardy shrub roses. If you are purchasing shrub roses, look for those that are resistant to black spot, rust and mildew (Osborne, 1991).

Peonies that have shown signs of botrytis in previous years (young shoots rot at base, buds turn dark, flowers fail to develop properly) can be sprayed with Bordeaux mixture as soon as the leaves begin to emerge, and every two weeks thereafter. Bordeaux mixture may cause discolouration of leaves and flowers, but hopefully in subsequent years spraying will not be needed. Alternatively, try baking soda solution and spray weekly as a preventive measure.

In addition to spraying, remove all mulch and wait until the soil is thoroughly warm before adding fresh mulch so that plants grow quickly and vigorously. Do not let any of it touch the stems. For severe cases, the top 2 inches (5 cm) of soil can be removed and replaced with fresh soil. In the autumn, be sure to remove all faded foliage from the plant.

## Spring Bulbs

Spring flowering bulbs such as daffodils and tulips should be blooming this month, or be about to bloom. Bulbs planted new last fall are sometimes slower to appear in the spring than established bulbs. If they never make an appearance, dig them up to see if they are rotten. Planting too late in the autumn so that roots do not have time to form, planting in soil that drains poorly, and planting in a shaded place where soil is slow to warm up in the spring, will all cause rot. If daffodils have been infested with narcissus bulb fly larvae, there will be grubs inside the rotting bulbs when you dig them up. Manure may make bulbs more susceptible to narcissus bulb fly as the flies will use either the manure or bulbs to lay their eggs. Put all rotting bulbs in the garbage, or bury them deeply, rather than putting them in the compost.

Failure to bloom can be caused by planting too deeply or by overcrowding. Bulbs that were forced indoors the previous year and then planted out will also fail to bloom initially, but will gradually fatten up and bloom again in subsequent years. Flowers at soil level indicate the bulb was planted too deeply. If buds form but fail to open, the usual cause is soil which is too dry. Hybrid tulips often fail to bloom well after the first year; they should be discarded and new bulbs planted each year or two. Species tulips, in contrast, seem to thrive year after year.

Siberian Squill
can be moved while in bloom.

If moving or dividing bulbs, it is best to leave them in place for at least six weeks after they have bloomed, but eight weeks or more is even better. This will give the bulbs time to build up reserves so that they can bloom well next year. The tiny bulbs such as snowdrops and Siberian squill can be moved while in bloom, or immediately after, but be sure to take a good clump of soil around the roots. Divide up clumps of bulbs before replanting if they are crowded, but leave daffodils as twin or triple noses. If preferred, bulbs can be dug up six weeks after blooming and stored in a cool cellar until planting time in the autumn.

Top dress bulbs with compost or very well rotted manure, but do not mix manure into the soil just before planting bulbs. Bonemeal can also be scratched into the soil; its phosphorous will encourage flowering. If fish bonemeal is used instead of regular bonemeal, bulb leaves will grow better because of the higher nitrogen content. Adding bonemeal once every four or five years is frequent enough because its nutrients become available slowly.

The most important thing to do for bulbs that are healthy and blooming well each year is to leave them alone. Let the foliage die back naturally so that the bulb can store enough nutrient reserves for the next year. If there are bulbs in the lawn, do not mow them until six weeks after they have finished blooming. This is easy to do for small bulbs, such as crocuses, but daffodils are later blooming and take a long time to die back. They are best planted in flower beds or meadows rather than lawns.

When bulbs have finished blooming, remove the faded blossoms. This is called "deadheading" and ensures that nutrients are channeled into the bulb instead of into seed pods. If tulips have been live-headed, suspect deer. Tulip petals are also a tasty treat for humans (see Creasy, 1988). Deer can sometimes be deterred by movement-sensing outdoor lights. A less attractive method is to put a human sized wooden cross in the ground and put a T-shirt, worn that day, on the cross each night. Still, this is less obtrusive and considerably less expensive than the only really sure solution for keeping deer out of gardens—electric or double fences. A double fence is 2 rows of 4 foot (1.2 m) high fences placed 5 feet (1.5 m) apart. For electrical fencing use two rows of wire—one placed 12 inches (30 cm) above the ground and the other at 36 inches (90 cm).

## Cut Flowers

If bringing tulips indoors, cut them when the colour is clearly visible but the buds have not opened. They will open quickly once cut. The same guideline applies when purchasing tulips. Stand cut tulips in water for several hours, with the upper part of their stems above the waterline wrapped in newspaper. With this treatment they are less likely to flop over when arranged in a vase. Violets from the garden can be totally immersed in cold water for an hour to crispen them.

Cut and sear (see Green Thumb Tip, page 233) the stems of daffodils, and then stand them in water with a few drops of household bleach added, but keep them separate from other flowers because of daffodils' unfriendly exudate. After several hours of soaking, they can be arranged with other flowers but do not recut their ends.

Avoid picking wildflowers, but if you want some for cut flowers, grow them in your garden. Dig plants only in areas that are threatened by construction, but do take cuttings from wildflowers such as the Mayflower, or else mark plants and collect seed later in the season (see Table AUG-4, page 308).

## Fruiting Plants and Woody Ornamentals

If you are still planting bare root trees and shrubs this month, do it early, and be cautious about so-called bargains. Bare root plants that have already leafed out in the store will probably die, in spite of every type of care you give them. If you receive such plants in a mail order, reject them and ask for your money back. Maintain deep, weekly waterings of plants put in last month, and weed and mulch them if you have not done so already.

### Flowers and Pollination

One does not usually think of flower care for fruiting plants, but blossoms are essential for a good harvest. Fruits that flower early, especially espaliered plants or fans against a warm wall, may need to be hand pollinated if the weather is cool and bees are not active. Use a soft, natural bristle paint brush to dust the flower centres. Plants at all stages of flowering should be covered at night if a frost is predicted. Some birds will eat flower buds and blossoms on fruit and nut trees to such an extent that fruit and nut protection is lowered. If this is happening, cover susceptible plants with bird netting, available at many garden centres.

First year fruit trees and blueberries must have all the flower blossoms removed. Flower buds are usually rounded and plump. It is tempting to try to obtain fruit early on, but even limited fruit production will almost certainly stunt the vegetative growth of the plants. In the second year, you can leave twenty to thirty flower buds on blueberries to produce fruit. All of the flowers on young grape vines, espaliers, cordons and fans still being trained should be removed. On mature grapes, remove all but one, or perhaps two, of the flower clusters on each fruiting cane. This will maximize the chances of the grapes maturing fully in the autumn.

**Green Thumb Tip**

To assess bee activity, scan all your fruit trees—to a maximum of ten trees—for one minute each and count the number of bumble, honey and solitary bees attending the flowers. Add up the number of bees and divide by the number of trees to determine the number of bees/tree/minute. For best pollination this should be 10 to 35 bees/tree/minute.

Young apple trees with a heavy crop of flowers can have extra blossoms thinned out just as they are opening, if they are of fruit bearing age. You may prefer to thin the fruit on young trees one or two weeks after blossoming when the fruit has set, in case a late frost destroys some of the blossoms (see page 238 for the correct way to thin various fruits).

First year strawberries should have the flowers removed so that plants can channel their energy into vegetative growth and runner production for a good crop next year. On the other hand, if strawberries are planted close together so that fewer runners are required, or if a few blossoms are left in place accidently on purpose, they will not suffer a major setback should some fruit form. Any mature plants that are to be used for runner production (see page 269) should have all of the flower buds removed as well. That way, runners will be produced sooner and young plantlets will be bigger and better established before winter arrives. Strawberry plants that wilt or fail to grow were probably planted too deep or else the drainage is not good (also, see red stele disease, page 268).

Srawberry Weevil

If frost threatens, it is worth while covering the strawberries because frost can damage the blossoms, resulting in absent or misshapen fruit. Frost damage causes blackened pistils and stamens in the middle of the flowers. The first flowers are the most likely ones to be damaged—this is unfortunate as they produce the largest berries!

Strawberry weevils are about 1/8 inch (2 to 3 mm) long and chew holes in petals and cut through stems of blossoms. Keep plant debris picked up and cultivate the soil. Tarnished plant bugs chew holes in petals of strawberries and other plants close to the ground. Put out white boards 8 by 12 inches (20 by 30 cm), smeared with Tanglefoot, but recognize that some beneficial insects will be trapped as well.

When black currants are in bloom, be sensitive to cool temperatures. Gardeners often complain that their currants bloom but fail to fruit. There are several possible reasons, including chilly temperatures at bloom time, particularly where winds blow off the water. Either the bees are not active, or pollen tubes fail to grow because of the cold. Black currants also need two varieties (both black) for proper pollination, except for 'Consort' plants. A third possible reason for failure to fruit is currant fruit fly. There will be spots on the berries, and the fruit falls off at a very immature stage. Larvae then burrow into the soil. Dispose of all dropped fruits, and lightly cultivate the soil to destroy the insect. Bantem hens caged under currant bushes are said to be an excellent control.

What is most upsetting is the lack of bloom altogether in fruiting trees and shrubs, but there are several possible explanations that may give gardeners hope (see pages 237-239).

## Rhubarb

For many people, the gardening year starts with the first taste of rhubarb. If rhubarb stalks are very thin, the plant is either starved or crowded. If starvation is suspected, try top dressing with a good 3 to 4 inch (7 to 10 cm) layer of rotted manure around each plant every spring, and see if that makes a difference. If the stems are crowded, or if the rhubarb has been in the same spot for many years, the clump should be dug up and divided in early spring, or in the autumn in mild areas (see Focus on Plants, page 148).

Red stalked varieties of rhubarb seem to be tenderer and tastier. Growing rhubarb in the sun will bring out the redness. If stalks rot at the bottom, dig up the whole plant and burn it. To avoid the problem, plant rhubarb in soil that drains well, stop mulching, and plant in a sunnier place (in at least six hours of sun per day) with better air circulation.

Rhubarb that was forced over the winter can be replanted, but it probably will not grow much until the following year. If there is plenty of rhubarb in the garden, simply compost the forced crown.

An excellent book to tempt your taste buds is Jo Ann Gardner's *The Old-Fashioned Fruit Garden* (1989). It is full of growing tips as well as recipes for soft fruits.

### Focus on Plants

In the first year of planting rhubarb do not harvest any of the leaf stalks, but do cut off the flower stalks as soon as they are visible. In the second year, pick off those stalks that are 1 inch (2.5 cm) thick, and the flower stalks, but leave most stalks on the plant. In the third year, pick the thick stalks for about 1 month, and continue to remove the flower stalks. In the fourth year and after, pick as many thick ones as desired until midsummer, or until the stalks grow in thin. Flower stalks may be either removed or left at this age. Flowering is associated with wet summers and too much nitrogen, but some gardeners like the look of rhubarb flowers.

When harvesting rhubarb, pull and twist each stalk, rather than using a knife. Excess quantities can be frozen (see pages 316-317). The leaves can be cut off and used as mulch, either around the rhubarb or between rows of vegetables. It is quite all right to mix rhubarb leaves throughout the compost pile; they are poisonous to eat but are perfectly harmless used as mulch or in compost.

## Preventive Measure

Ideally and in practice, healthy plants that have been properly thinned to ensure good air circulation should be able to tolerate some disease without the gardener having to resort to sprays. If plants do succumb, healthy ones are better able to recover. Repeated attacks may mean that the plant should be got rid of altogether and another species or variety tried. Another preventive approach is to select a resistant variety next time a tree or shrub is planted. There are some newer apple varieties, for example, that are quite resistant to scab.

Also, practice garden hygiene by immediately removing any affected leaves and burning or burying them. This may mean cutting out entire branches in the case of lilac blight or fireblight in order to remove a lot of affected leaves. Clean up all dropped leaves throughout the summer and again before winter sets in. This will help to reduce the overwintering disease populations.

## Fungicides and Insecticides

### Diseases

Spraying dormant oil or lime sulphur (see page 105) to control specific insects and diseases should be finished before buds swell, but spraying is not necessary if trees have been relatively trouble-free. For example, the spores of peach leaf curl remain on the tree through the summer, fall and winter and are then washed into the opening buds in the spring. Lime sulphur sprayed during dormancy will destroy many of the overwintering spores, but if peach leaves did not develop large reddish blisters and then turn brown and fall prematurely last year, there is no need to spray this year.

If there was a problem, and green tissue is showing in the buds, it is too late to spray dormant oil or dormant strength lime sulphur. As soon as the buds show a 1/4 to 1/2 inch (1 cm) green tip, however, it is time to spray 2% lime sulphur or other fungicides to prevent infection. Some leaf blights can cause complete defoliation of trees and shrubs, rusts can be hard on plants, and scab and powdery mildew are both unsightly and unhealthy if extensive.

If you decide to spray, there are three periods when spraying should be carried out, and four suggested fungicidal sprays to choose from. The first spraying time is during dormancy (see March/April, page 105). The second period is during the growing season, with repeated sprays needed more or less frequently, depending on the type of fungicide used. The last period is just before leaf fall in the autumn (see pages 365-366). Good control early in the season will lessen disease pressure because there will be fewer spores around.

Baking soda spray is the mildest of all the fungicides and is effective only as a preventative measure. It can be used alone but research is showing that it is more effective when mixed with a light oil. Mix 4 teaspoons (20 ml) each of baking soda and mineral oil or light horticultural oil (not dormant oil) in 1 gallon (4.5 l) of water and spray weekly. It helps to prevent powdery mildew, leaf blight, leaf spot and possibly other fungal diseases and anthracnose.

Sulphur can be sprinkled on as a dry powder, but usually a wettable form is mixed with water and sprayed on. It should be applied at weekly intervals from the time of bud break—when the first bit of green shows—until late in the summer, or starting immediately with the first observation of disease to prevent any further new activity. Do not spray when blossoms are open. Every two weeks may be often enough where humidity is low, but spraying should be repeated immediately after heavy rainfalls which may wash off a previous sulphur application. Spraying this often puts a lot of fungicide into the environment, so do not spray unless there is a real need.

## Table MAY-5 Fungicidal Sprays*

| Spray | Effectiveness | Precautions | Problems |
|---|---|---|---|
| Baking Soda Mixture | preventative | avoid dribbling on soil | |
| Sulphur | preventative | not in bright sun; below 80°F (27°C); not before frost; 30 days or more after dormant spray; avoid dribbling on soil | skin reaction |
| Bordeaux Mixture | preventative | avoid dribbling on soil | discolours flowers and foliage; toxic to earthworms |
| Dilute Lime Sulphur | preventative/ kickback | apply when leaves are dry immediately after rain; avoid dribbling on soil | can burn foliage |

* DO NOT SPRAY FUNGICIDES WHEN BLOSSOMS ARE OPEN

Bordeaux mixture can be bought ready made, or it can be made by adding 4 ounces (100 g) of copper sulphate mixed with 1 gallon (4.5 l) of water to a solution of 8 ounces (200 g) of lime mixed with 9 gallons (40 l) of water and 3 cups (750 ml) of superior oil. It can cause discolouration or even burning of foliage and russeting of apples so is best used early in the season before leaves have expanded much, or in situations where sulphur is not effective. A sub-class of Bordeaux mixture is copper sulphate, which is sprayed when the flower buds show pink, and then is repeated five or six times every seven to ten days, but not when the blossoms are open. It may discolour foliage and flowers, but it is less likely to burn foliage.

Full strength lime sulphur is used during dormancy, but a dilution to 2% can be used when plants are in leaf. It can burn fruit and foliage even at this strength, and is a stronger fungicide than Bordeaux mixture. It has some post-infection activity or kickback, which means that it can prevent fungal infections from developing further, so it can be applied less frequently than sulphur. Spray lime sulphur when blossoms are still in the pink bud stage, but not during blossom time. Spray again two weeks later, and after an extended period of rain or high humidity as soon as the leaves have dried off somewhat.

Deciding what spray to use depends on how frequently one is willing to

## *Table MAY-6 Conditions Conducive to Scab Infections*

Below is a modified version of Mill's Periods, which give the relationship between temperature and length of a wet period required for primary and secondary apple scab infections.

Taken from *Organic Apple Production Guide for Nova Scotia*, Nova Scotia Department of Agriculture and Marketing.

| Mean Temperature During Leaf Wetness Period (°F/°C) | Hours of Leaf Wetness Required for Infection | Mean Temperature During Leaf Wetness Period (°F/°C) | Hours of Leaf Wetness Required for Infection |
|---|---|---|---|
| 39.2/4 | 36.7 | 59.0/15 | 6.7 |
| 41.0/5 | 23.8 | 60.8/16 | 6.5 |
| 42.8/6 | 19.1 | 62.6/17 | 6.2 |
| 44.6/7 | 15.6 | 64.4/18 | 5.9 |
| 46.4/8 | 12.9 | 66.2/19 | 5.7 |
| 48.2/9 | 11.0 | 68.0/20 | 5.5 |
| 50.0/10 | 9.6 | 69.8/21 | 5.4 |
| 51.8/11 | 8.6 | 71.6/22 | 5.5 |
| 53.6/12 | 8.0 | 73.4/23 | 5.9 |
| 55.4/13 | 7.4 | 75.2/24 | 6.6 |
| 57.2/14 | 7.1 | 77.0/25 | 8.0 |

spray, and on the performance of a particular fungicide. If, for example, sulphur has been used to control lilac blight and is found ineffective, try a stronger fungicide. During the growing season, affected lilac leaves blacken and die, and whole branches may die. It is worse in white lilacs than coloured.

Repeated sprays of baking soda or sulphur may be more effective in controlling powdery mildew than less frequent sprays of stronger fungicides. There is also a relationship between temperature during the time that leaves are wet, and the length of time that they are wet. A scab infection can occur after only five and a half hours of wetness at a mean temperature of 68°F (20°C), but will not occur until thirty-six and three-quarter hours of wetness have passed at a mean temperature of 39°F (4°C).

### *Green Thumb Tip*

Organic gardeners usually select from four fungicides: baking soda, sulphur, Bordeaux mixture and lime sulphur. They are less toxic to animals and the environment than many other fungicides, but it is erroneous to believe that "organic" sprays can be used casually or that they are a safe and simple cure-all. For example, sulphur does not cure fungal diseases once they get started. Rather, it prevents the spores from gaining a foothold. It must be used with care because some people develop allergic skin reactions to it. It should not be applied in bright sunlight; not above 80°F (27°C); not in high humidity; not before a night frost; and not within thirty days of a dormant spray.

Leaf blights on crabapples and other plants start out as spots on the leaves. These grow and coalesce until the whole leaf is coloured, turns brown and drops off. If there has been trouble in previous years, begin spraying with the baking soda mixture (see page 190) or sulphur as soon as green tissue is visible, at pink bud stage, at petal fall, and then weekly or every other week as required, or spray with copper sulphate immediately after flowering.

For brown rot in cherries, spray with wettable sulphur or copper sulphate when the flower buds show white just before they open, again at petal fall, and five or six more times at seven to ten day intervals. For leaf blister on birch and oak, peach leaf curl and plum pocket, spray with Bordeaux mixture or 2% lime sulphur when there is less than 1/2 inch (1 cm) of green tissue showing at the tip of the buds, again two weeks later with 2% lime sulphur, and finally just before leaf fall in the autumn. Do the same for canker in pear, apple, beech, birch and poplar. Black knot in plums and cherries is controlled by spraying with 2% lime sulphur when the buds first show pink, again just as the flower buds show white, and for a third time after the petals fall. For anthrochose infections, spray with 2% lime sulphur when the buds show a 1/2 inch (1 cm) green tip; spray copper sulphate just before bloom and again immediately after harvest. Regular sulphur sprays help to control some rusts.

Various fungi cause blights on evergreens which cause needles to become reddish and distorted, usually in the *current* season's growth. Needle cast makes the trees appear scorched, and needles may drop prematurely, but do not confuse this with winter dieback of the previous season's growth. Tip blight turns needles brown, and terminal buds exude a lot of resin. For all of these, spray with Bordeaux mixture or copper sulphate when the new needles are half grown, again ten days to two weeks later, and a third time if the weather is wet.

If none of the fungicides work for a disease, it may be that a bacterial or viral infection is at work, which is much more difficult to deal with. The principles of cutting out affected parts and careful hygiene still apply, however, and can be effective in preventing further spread of the disease.

**Preventive Measure**

For all spraying, make sure coverage is complete, but be careful not to let fungicides dribble onto the soil. They will destroy beneficial fungi, some of which are essential to plant growth and the break down of organic matter. This will result in unhealthy plants that are less able to fight off and tolerate disease. Also, the copper in Bordeaux mixture is toxic to earthworms.

### Insects

Some insect problems (and see pages 235-236) are worse than leaf blight diseases. Currant sawfly larvae on gooseberry and red currant bushes can strip entire plants of their leaves, leaving only leaf skeletons. A deep mulch seems to reduce their numbers if applied before the leaves come out. Shallow

### Preventive Measure

At all costs avoid spraying insecticides during the day when bees are active. Avoid spraying at all while trees and shrubs are in full bloom. Dead bees mean no pollination, and no pollination means no fruit. Rotenone is touted as a "safe" organic pesticide, but it is nonselective and kills bees and all other insects.

cultivation in the autumn under affected plants also seems to help, or add more mulch in midsummer. Just as soon as the leaves emerge on these bushes in the spring, check the undersides of leaves on the lower part of the bush for oblong, white eggs laid in rows along the main rib and veins of the leaves. Scrape them off gently, and then keep a close eye on plants in the coming weeks for the first tell-tale holes in the leaves. What you may see first is black frass (excrement) on the lower leaves. Immediately squash the newly emerged larvae, and scrape off any remaining eggs that you missed. Continue your vigilance through the summer as there can be several generations. Sawfly larvae on evergreens devour young needles; they are best controlled by handpicking as soon as the infestation begins.

Most leaf miner damage is quite tolerable and should be ignored. If it has been particularly severe, spray insecticidal soap once a week for three weeks as soon as the leaves start to emerge. This will help to reduce the number of adults that are flying around and laying eggs. Insecticidal soap can be purchased in concentrated form and mixed with water, or it can be made at home. Use 1/2 cup (125 ml) of soap, not detergent, in 1 gallon (4.5 l) of water.

Spray quince or pear trees at the same stage if they have shown leaf yellowing in the past and a general decline in vigour; they are probably suffering from pear psylla. Cool temperatures prevent the adults from laying many eggs, but in most years the eggs are laid before flower buds open, and are hatched by the time petals fall. Alternatively, they can be left to chalcid wasps which will prey on them, provided there is a varied population of native flowering plants and grasses in your garden.

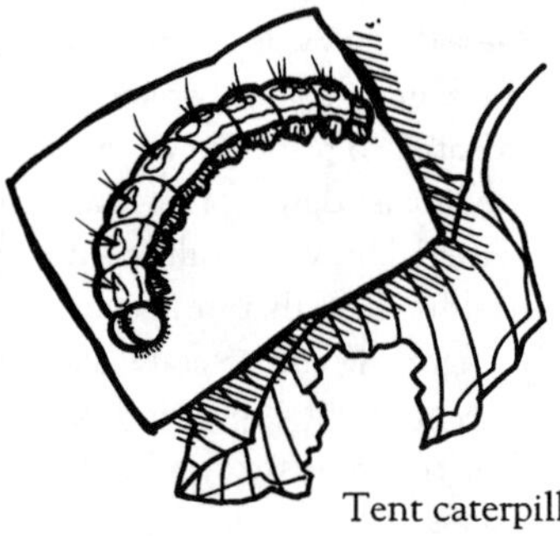
Tent caterpillar

Tent caterpillars usually hatch when the first leaves are opening. They and their tents can easily be removed with a broom in the evening, and the survivors can be crushed. Only if there are too many to handle this way, use Bt mixed with skim milk powder and spray every five days during daylight—when they are out of the nest feeding—until they are gone. Ground beetles and wasps are gardeners' friends in controlling tent caterpillars.

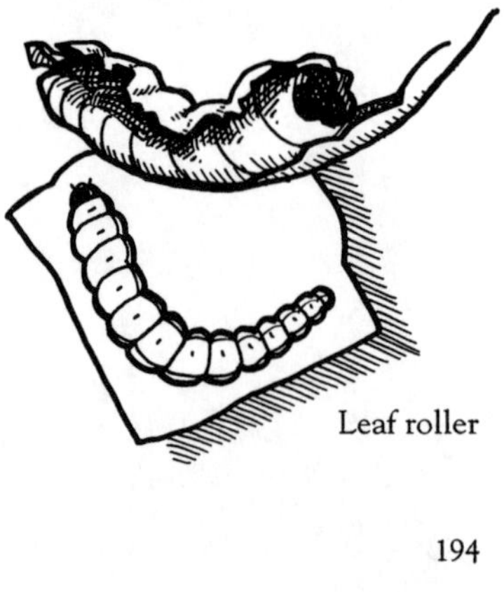
Leaf roller

Leaf rollers hatch at about the same time as tent caterpillars but rarely do enough harm to warrant spraying. You may want to remove them by hand from the branch tips of young trees, which are particularly sensitive to foliage feeding that causes stunted terminal growth. If Bt is used it must be applied before the larvae roll up inside the leaves. Mix it with skim milk powder to increase the larval feeding, and begin spraying when there is 1/4 inch (6 mm) of green tip showing every five days for a total of five sprays. Do the same if winter moth has been a problem in previous years.

## Table MAY-7 Management Suggestions for Common Insects

| Insect | Symptoms | Management; Natural Control |
|---|---|---|
| Apple Maggot | larvae in fruit | hang sticky red balls in apple, pear, plum, cherry, hawthorn in early July |
| Beetles | tunnels in bark, shoots wilt, die-back, conifer needles yellowish | insert wire in tunnel, keep plants fertilized and watered, remove and burn affected branches, apply barrier to trunk in early spring |
| Canker Worm, Inchworm | leaves eaten | band trees in autumn, tolerate damage |
| Currant Sawfly | leaves chewed | apply deep mulch, remove eggs, squash larvae |
| Gypsy Moth | leaves eaten | trichogramma wasp |
| Leaf Miner | tunnels in leaves | insecticidal soap 3 times when leaves emerging, tolerate damage |
| Leaf Roller | leaves rolled, insects inside | apply Bt early, squash affected leaves |
| Pear Psylla | leaf yellowing, decline in vigour | insecticidal soap 3 times when leaves emerging; chalcid wasp |
| Pine Shoot Moth | caterpillars feed inside buds, shoot tips deform and die | handpick, Bt every 5 days from budburst until caterpillars are gone, remove and burn infested shoots |
| Plum Curculio or Weevil | crescent-shaped marks on fruit, grubs inside apple, cherry, plum, pear | shake tree after petal fall with sheet on ground, pick up fruit drops 3 times per week minimum |
| Spruce Budworm | caterpillars feed on new needles | Bt every 5 days when new needles separate and flare |
| Tent Caterpillar | tents formed, leaves eaten | Bt every 5 days, remove by hand; ground beetle, wasp |
| Winter Moth | "inch worms" feed on leaves, buds | Bt every 5 days, band trees in autumn |

> ### Preventive Measure
>
> It is worth repeating that the best defence against insects and diseases are healthy, well-maintained plants and garden hygiene. Keep trees and shrubs top dressed with manure or compost in the spring, mulched through the growing season, and well weeded and free of grass in a ring 4 feet (1.2 m) in diameter. Clean up dropped fruits and litter under the plants, pick off and rake up diseased leaves, and grow a diversity of wildflowers and grasses to attract beneficial insects (see Preventive Measure, pages 149 and 307-309).
>
> Increasingly, gardeners are finding that insects are not a problem, are coming to appreciate beneficial insects, and are learning to live with and tolerate more insect damage than they used to.

Canker worms, or inchworms, are best controlled by banding trunks with Tanglefoot in March and September. Bt will work against canker worms and the grayish brown, hairy larvae of gypsy moths, but the larvae blow in from other areas when they are in the thread-hanging stage, so they are probably not worth bothering with. Populations rise and fall, and spraying seems to interfere with and delay the population crashes. Trichogramma wasps eat gypsy moth eggs.

Apple maggots are dealt with later in the season, but American hawthorn is a host to the insect. Hawthorns bloom this month, which makes them easier to find and mark on a large property, so that they can be cut down or preventive measures can be taken in July, along with treating apple trees, cherries, plums and pears. English hawthorn is not a host and is recognized by its smaller leaves and shorter thorns (less than 1 inch or 2.5 cm).

Plum curculios, or weevils, leave crescent-shaped marks on plums as well as apples, blueberries, peaches, cherries, pears and quince, and the grubs feed within fruits, causing them to drop and decay. The snout-nosed adults appear just before trees are in bloom and hang around until a few weeks after. To reduce the number of adults, spread a sheet or tarpaulin on the ground when the tiny fruits are first visible after the petals fall. Shake and hit the tree early in the morning so that the weevils drop onto the sheet. Interrupt their life cycle by picking up dropped fruits, daily if possible or three times a week at least. This prevents larvae from going into the soil to pupate. Either bury the fruit drops, put them in a plastic bag in the sun for two weeks, or feed them to livestock.

Tunnels in the bark of trees and yellowish needles on evergreens indicate beetles. Infestations are worse after dry periods, when trees are in a weakened state, so keep trees watered and fed. Insert a thin wire to kill borers; they cause shoots to wilt and die back. Remove and burn dying, unhealthy branches in the spring before the adults emerge (and see page 106 for more prevention). Pine shoot moth caterpillars feed inside young buds, causing the tips of young shoots to become deformed and die; budworm caterpillars cause new growth and terminals to become wilted and deformed in the spring. Caterpillars can be controlled by handpicking, or by spraying with Bt every five days as the new needles separate and flare until caterpillars are gone if infestations are severe. Pine shoot moth is most troublesome on trees less than 5 feet (1.5 m) high but rarely causes serious injury on trees over 20 feet (6 m) high. *Landscape Problem Solver*, by Jeff and Liz Ball (1989), gives detailed descriptions and solutions to conifer problems.

## *Care and Pruning of Evergreens*

Coniferous evergreens can be pruned when the new growth shows, but only if their size needs to be restricted or if a fuller, thicker look is desired. Much of the beauty of evergreens lies in their natural shape, which is also a perfect design for shedding snow loads. It is tempting to wait until evergreens reach the desired height before pruning them, but this will result in trees and hedges with a lopped-off look. Windbreak evergreens pruned regularly from a young age will be denser and provide better cover close to the ground.

There are two ways to prune conifers, depending on the tree's pattern of growth. Those that grow in whorls, such as spruce, pine, fir and hemlock, have their branch tips cut back about one-third of the way into the new, bright green growth. Pines have long "candles" that can be cut back by one-third to one-half while they are still tightly closed so that new buds will be initiated. If pruning is done after the growth has started to harden it is unlikely that new buds will grow. If pruning cuts are made into last year's wood, ugly stumps will remain as no new growth will sprout behind the cut.

Avoid cutting the central leader, or the conifer will probably develop two or more stems. If the leader has been damaged or broken, a new one can be developed in one of two ways. If the damage is recent and there are several young branches at the top, select one that is more upright than the others and lightly tip the remaining branches. The uncut branch will gradually head upwards and form a new central leader. If the damage is a year old or more, select a supple side branch from near the top of the tree and ease it into an upright position by tying it to a long wooden stick that is also tied to the main stem of the tree. Use nylon stockings or other soft material between the plant and the stick and as a tie, so that the plant is not damaged by rubbing against the stick.

Conifers with an all-over pattern of growth, such as cedar (*Thuja* or arborvitae), juniper and false cypress (*Chamaecyparis*), can be pruned all-over by trimming the new, bright green growth with a pair of hedge clippers. These trees can be shortened and trimmed on the sides by cutting back as much as one-third of the total green material, but do not cut into old wood without any greenery on it. The only exception is yew, which can be cut back quite severely if a drastic rejuvenation is required. It will look dreadful for several years but will gradually fill in and look healthy and vigorous. If other conifers have outgrown or are threatening to outgrow their allotted space, junipers and others with an all-over pattern of growth can have their side branches shortened by cutting back the leaders on each branch to a strong side shoot.

Growth Patterns

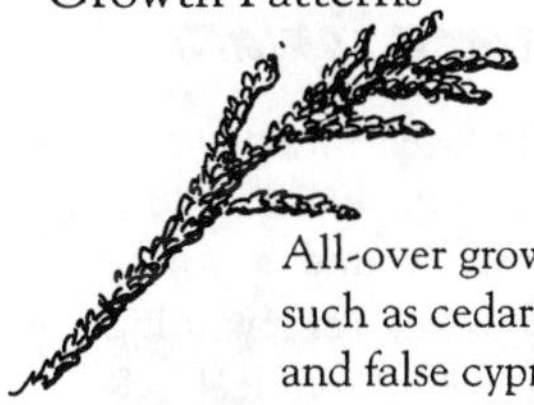

All-over growth pattern, such as cedar, juniper and false cypress.

Whorl pattern of growth, such as spruce, pine and fir.

Prune "candles" back by one-third.

Repairing a Broken Leader

Select a branch to be the new leader and prune the tips of remaining branches.

For older breaks tie a stick to the branch and carefully train the leader.

## Evergreen Topiary

To create topiary (sculptured plants), build a strong framework around a young plant of boxwood or yew, using 1/4 inch (6 mm) soft steel rods or wooden stakes to create the desired shape. Plants trained into rounded shapes are easier to form and maintain. Train stems while they are young and pliable by tying them onto the frame with natural fibre twine, which will eventually rot. Clip the young plant a couple of times during the season to keep it within the frame, but make the last cut well before autumn so that any new shoots have time to harden off before winter arrives.

Fertilize the plant well each spring while the shape is being developed, using a 2 inch (5 cm) layer of rotted manure or compost, and mulch and water well throughout the growing season. When the plant has grown and has filled the frame, clip it all around the outside once a year (clip boxwood in the spring before new growth has started, clip yew in late July). Use the framework to guide the cuts. The plant at maturity will form a dense cover over the framework—an annual clip should be all that is needed to maintain the shape.

Do not be hasty in cutting out what seem to be dead branches on conifers and broad-leaved evergreens, such as rhododendrons; wait until after the time when new spring growth occurs. Amazing recoveries sometimes occur, and evergreen needles and leaves naturally drop off after two years of life—their loss is usually not noticed because of the new growth produced each year.

Browning caused by winter injury is usually restricted to the windy side of evergreens. Cut off branches that show no signs of new growth. In the autumn, to help prevent this, water trees well and mulch before the ground freezes (see pages 396-397).

Rhododendrons, boxwood, hollies, Oregon grape (*Mahonia*), pieris and other broad-leaved evergreens rarely need pruning, except to remove dead or damaged branches. It is natural for the oldest leaves, toward the bottom of branches and the middle of the shrub, to turn brown and fall off. If leaves at the tips of branches are turning brown and falling off, they probably suffered from too much winter wind and drying. Either move them to a sheltered position early this month or after blooming, or take steps in the autumn to protect them over the winter (see pages 396-397).

Occasionally rhododendrons will become diseased with fungal dieback. It seems to attack older, established plants and those stressed from being grown in full sun or dry conditions. The leaves are dull, rolled up and pale olive or brown. Affected branches should be cut out completely before the fungus moves down into the main trunk. Dip pruning clippers in Lysol after each cut (see page 91).

If other pruning is required, say to shorten branches that have grown too long, cut them back after the spring bloom to an outward facing branch lower down on the stem. To encourage new growth in a bare place, cut a branch or branches back to buds that are facing in the direction where new growth is required. Boxwood and holly can be clipped during the growing season if they are used as hedges, but they are usually so slow growing that a single light trim each spring is generally all that is required, unless trimming is done to obtain decorations (see December, pages 454-455). If not grown as hedges, only dead, damaged or diseased branches need be pruned. Any broad-leaved evergreens that need rejuvenation should have only a few of the oldest branches cut out several inches above ground level each spring over a period of several years. Boxwood and holly can be cut back all at once, but do not remove more than one-third of the total green material, and do this early before much, if any, new growth is visible.

Evergreens can be fertilized when new growth is visible. A 1 to 2 inch (2.5 to 5 cm) layer of well rotted manure or compost spread under each plant out to the drip line is quite sufficient to meet the nutrient needs of evergreens. Skipping a year once in a while or every other year is not a problem, unless the soil is very poor.

### *Care of Newly Propagated Plants*

Seedlings of trees, shrubs and vines, various rooted cuttings taken last year, and pieces of root that have grown shoots can all be planted outdoors in a sheltered location when the weather is warm and stable. They will require another two or three years of growing before they are ready to be transplanted to their permanent location.

Many of these will have been growing indoors since early spring and will need hardening off. Seedlings in flats and root cuttings with shoots can be transplanted into nursery rows. Keep them under the shade of cheesecloth or a lath for the first season. Rooted cuttings in pots with healthy, vigorous growth can be transplanted to nursery rows and given the same care. Hardwood cuttings that have barely rooted or are still in the process of forming roots are best left in their pots to avoid any disturbance. They, too, should be shaded somewhat and sheltered from wind. The pots can be buried in the ground up to their rims to reduce the amount of watering required.

## *Lawns*

More and more gardeners are doing their best to reduce their total lawn area and mowing time, and to eliminate perfectionist lawn care routines. Along with a growing sensitivity to the health of the environment is a growing realization that a weed-free lawn with every blade of grass in place is neither practical nor natural. It is also unnecessary to hire lawn care professionals on a regular basis, unless of course you want to. The excessive care required by Kentucky bluegrass lawns in the form of repeated fertilizer applications and pesticide and fungicide sprays may have warranted professional care in the past, but environmentally conscious gardeners are moving toward lawns of mixed grasses which are much healthier and easier to care for.

### *General Care*

Seeding lawns in the spring should take place immediately after the last frost; if seeding is left until the time when lilacs bloom in the spring it is too late

**Preventive Measure**

The trick to a healthy lawn is to provide the growing conditions that grass prefers so that weed, moss, disease and insect problems are reduced—they may not be eliminated, but will be adequately diminished. The right pH (see pages 113-114), proper drainage (see page 371 and 377), adequate moisture (see page 208), high organic content in the soil (see page 371), the right nutrients and regular mowing (see below) will do more for your lawn than a regime of herbicides and insecticidal sprays.

for grasses to establish before the heat and drought of summer. Six weeks or so before the first fall frost in expected, or when nights first start to cool off, is a better time to do major lawn repairs and planting of new lawns (see pages 324-326 for details).

It is a good idea, however, to take time in the spring and summer to improve the soil on which the lawn will be planted. One method, which has been used by several generations of gardeners, is to plant one or two crops of buckwheat where a lawn is to be located. Even if so-called topsoil is ordered, work in manure, compost, old hay, spoiled straw, leaf mould or any other organic matter before you seed the buckwheat. Cut the buckwheat down and plough it into the soil just as it comes into flower, in time for seeding or sodding in late summer. Incorporating organic matter in this way will improve the soil, ensure better drought resistance and fewer weeds in future years, and keep people from swimming in mud in the meantime. Clover and annual rye can also be used as cover crops. The aim before seeding or sodding is to have at least 6 inches (15 cm) of soil rich in organic matter.

For routine spring care, give the lawn a light raking to remove debris. A hard raking is best reserved for August, when grass is growing roots and sending out side shoots. As weeds are dug out in the spring, sprinkle grass seed onto the resulting bare spots. There must be a maxim somewhere to the effect that bare spots in lawns never, ever fill in with grass, only weeds.

### Little Horrors

Most weed problems can be traced to incorrect mowing, low fertility, compacted soil and low pH. Excessive dandelions are a sign of compacted soil low in fertility. It pays to dig them out while they are young; the fresh leaves are tasty in salads, and nutrient reserves in the roots are low so that regrowth from any remaining roots is weak. Digging them out, instead of zapping with a herbicide, helps to aerate the soil, which improves the growing conditions for grass. On the other hand, a few dandelions in the lawn look bright and cheery. To keep neighbours happy, mow the lawn before the dandelions go to seed. Each gardener has to decide what his or her weed tolerance level is.

Brown patches in the lawn may be caused by disease, insects, too much fertilizer or poor drainage. Patches of grass killed by dog urine can be identified by the ring of lush growth—where the concentration of nitrogen was just right for grass growth—around the dead area. Where sod seems to have been lifted, or small, dead-end holes dug, the likely culprits are racoons.

They are a mixed blessing because they eat grubs that feed on the roots of lawn grasses and their digging helps aerate the soil. Table MAY-8 summarizes some of the common lawn problems (and see page 152). For a more detailed discussion, refer to *The Encyclopedia of Natural Insect & Disease Control* (Yepsen, 1984).

Moss is viewed by many as a problem, but it is a luxurious ground cover in shady areas, provided there is little foot traffic. To get rid of moss, it is essential to correct the growing conditions that caused it. If the growing conditions are ideal for grass, it will win out over moss. Throwing on moss killer (which is nothing more than ferrous sulphate) is only a temporary solution.

Moss grows well if there is one or more of the following conditions: less than six hours of sunshine per day; acidic soil; compacted soil that does not drain well; low fertility. To correct these conditions, use grass seed that is tolerant of shade, such as tall fescues; apply lime (see Green Thumb Tip, page 378); aerate the soil (see page 371); and apply fertilizer as required. Where moss has been removed, be sure to sprinkle in grass seed.

If there is considerable shade, it might be better to grow some other ground cover, such as periwinkle (*Vinca minor*), Japanese spurge, ferns, astilbe, William and Mary (pulmonaria), fringed bleeding heart, bugleweed (Ajuga), hosta, wild ginger or Solomon's seal.

### Fertilizing

Depending on how you mow your lawn, the kinds of grasses in it and the mix of clover present, you may or may not have to fertilize. Seedmixers used to purposely add 20% clover to their lawn seed mixes. Clover is a nitrogen fixer, and it is mainly nitrogen that makes the grass grow and keeps it green. Adding extra nitrogen—as is required for bluegrass lawns to keep them looking green—means you have to mow more often, the grass is less tolerant of drought, the lush growth is more vulnerable to disease and insect pests, and thatch buildup is a problem. So, do not dig out the clover in your lawn. Besides, clover stays green even when some lawn grasses are turning brown from drought, it adds an interesting textural detail, and it is ideal on heavily trodden areas and next to sidewalks where soil is easily compacted.

Additionally, if nitrogen is never removed from the lawn, it will not have to be replaced. By mowing regularly so that 1 inch (2.5 cm) or less of grass is cut off, the clippings can be left in place to return their nitrogen to the soil. (Clippings on new lawns should be raked up.) Clippings will also increase

Clover is good for grass. Seedmixers used to purposely add 20% clover to their lawn seed mixes.

**Green Thumb Tip**

The type of grasses in a lawn can affect how much fertilizer is needed. Kentucky bluegrass needs a lot of nitrogen to look good, but this leads to problems. A better mix is one that contains only some Kentucky bluegrass, with the rest made up of chewing, hard and creeping red fescues and perennial ryegrass. Avoid tall fescues except in shady areas. Some grass mixes also contain annual ryegrass as a nurse crop. This germinates quickly and prevents weeds from becoming established, giving the permanent grasses time to start growing and sending out runners. Clover seed could be added, but there is plenty of it floating around in the air to do the job.

## Table MAY-8 Lawn Problems and Management Suggestions

| Symptom | Cause | Management |
|---|---|---|
| Grass poor and thin | lack of fertilizer, lack of water<br>soil compaction<br>nematodes (galls on roots of grass) | cultural*<br>aeration<br>spread compost in autumn, fertilize with fish emulsion in spring |
| Small dead spots with green edges | dog urine | soak with water, reseed |
| Overtaken by weeds | incorrect growing conditions | cultural, dig out and reseed |
| Moss | soil compaction, low fertility, shade, poor drainage, low pH | cultural, improve drainage, reseed |
| Bare areas (appear in summer) | armyworm (1 ½ inches or 4 cm long, brown body, 3 lines, black head; found under sod) | apply Bt every 10 -14 days and after it rains |
| Small dead areas (appear in summer) | cutworms (plump, dull grey or brown, soft 1-2 inches or 2.5-5 cm long) | hunt at night, sprinkle bran or cornmeal around areas |
| Small dead areas that grow large (appear in summer) | sod webworms (3/4-1 inch or 2- 2.5 cm) long, tan with dark spots on back and sides, stiff hairs) | apply Bt every 3-5 days for 2 weeks, plant more varied grasses |
| Large yellow areas that turn brown and die (appear in heat of summer) | chinch bugs (1/5 inch or 0.5 cm long, white wings, black or red triangle behind head) | cultural, insecticidal soap (see page 194 for full details) |
| Dead areas, sod lifts easily (appear in summer) | white grubs (fat bodies, cream colour, 3/4-1 ½ inches or 2-4 cm long, larval form of several beetles) | peel back sod and crush grubs |

| Symptom | Cause | Management |
|---|---|---|
| Fairy Ring: circle of toadstools, ring of dead grass | fungus growing in soil that prevents water from reaching grass roots | aerate deeply from 2 feet (.6 m) outside the circle towards the middle of ring and water deeply; dig out if necessary and replace with fresh soil |
| Diseased areas: spots on grass; mildew; red or pink areas; snow mould; rust; water-soaked areas | various diseases caused by improper lawn care, damp weather, excess fertilizer | cultural, apply sulphur every 3-5 days but only if damage is intolerable |

* cultural refers to deep, rich, loose soil; good drainage; correct watering, mowing and fertilizing; appropriate pH

the organic content of soil, which aids in moisture and nutrient retention. Thatch buildup, from leaving grass clippings on the lawn, is not a problem if there is a healthy earthworm population, which in turn is promoted and encouraged by organic matter in the soil. A little thatch is beneficial and acts as a mulch, keeping the soil cool and moist. If you do not like the look of short clippings left on the lawn, investigate mulch mowers. They chop up the grass clippings very finely before returning them to the lawn.

Some fertilizing is not amiss. Lawns mainly need nitrogen and some phosphorous and potassium during the growing season when leaf growth is active, but less nitrogen and more phosphorous and potassium in the late summer and autumn when root growth becomes more important. The nutrients in organic fertilizers are more evenly available throughout the growing season so that grasses can draw on what they need at any given time.

Fish meal (7-9-4) applied in the spring, and again in the autumn, and perhaps some wood ashes (0-0-1 to 0-0-10) each spring, is sufficient. There are other organic fertilizers that have nitrogen, phosphorous and potassium in equal quantities (7-7-7); price may be a determining factor in deciding what to use. Research in progress in Nova Scotia is investigating fish waste fertilizer and unprocessed brewery wastes for their potential as fertilizers.

Some gardeners use finished compost screened through a 1/2 inch (12 mm) or smaller mesh, but this is usually applied in the fall as part of top dressing (see page 371). Seaweed extract or fish emulsion—high in nitrogen that is readily available—can be applied as a quick perk-up as soon as the grass starts to green in the spring, again in late June or early July, and once more in late August. It is not essential, but may ease the transition from chemical to organic management. It can take a while for nutrients to become available when organic matter is first added to a lawn; a little extra nitrogen in the form of seaweed extract or fish emulsion will help to tide things over until natural processes are rė-established.

**Green Thumb Tip**

The right mowing height for a lawn of mixed grasses is about 2 inches (5 cm) high in the spring and fall, 3 inches (7.5 cm) or more during the heat of summer, and about 1 ½ inches (nearly 4 cm) high at the last cut before winter. Grass needs cutting about twice a month in the spring and fall and as often as every five days during periods of rapid growth. No more than one-third of the total height of the grass should be removed at any one cutting, and preferably no more than 1 inch (2.5 cm). Each time, mow the lawn at right angles to the direction it was cut previously.

### Mowing

Correct mowing will help a lawn tolerate drought better and keep down weeds and coarse grasses. Most people mow their lawns too short; coarse grasses win out over fine lawn grasses as a result. Roots grow as deep as the top growth is long, thus long grass with deep roots is better able to withstand drought. Tall grass also helps to shade the soil, keeping it cool and reducing evaporation, and has a better chance of shading out broad-leaved weeds.

Keep the blades of your mower sharp. If grass is torn rather than cut it is more vulnerable to disease. Avoid cutting the grass when it is wet because mowing will be uneven and clippings will form heavy clumps.

Before starting up your gasoline mower in the spring, clean out the oil in the cylinder. To do this, remove the spark plug and then pull the starter cord several times. Put the spark plug back in, fill the fuel tank, check the oil level and then start it up. Do not worry if it smokes for two or three minutes; this is normal and you can safely start mowing.

## Indoor Gardening

### Vegetables and Herbs

By the time that spring has properly sprung, you may want to stop any further seeding of indoor crops until late in the summer, and simply keep the last crops that were planted in previous months going. Where summers are cool, however, indoor growers may choose to seed green pepper, eggplant, tomato, melon, cucumber, zucchini and summer squash. It is a lot easier to provide the heat that these crops need if grown under glass, and there is plenty of time for fruits to ripen in the autumn without fear of frost.

Some of the greens planted in previous months will be ready for harvest and can be kept going until the first greens are ready outdoors. After that, it may be easier to discard the plants and focus attention on the outdoor garden.

## *Fruits*

Depending on how advanced the growth is in the greenhouse, grapes and espaliered plants may be ready for summer pruning and training (see pages 270-274). Passion fruit flowers must be hand pollinated; remove the anthers and brush them against the stigmas of other flowers

## *Warm Flowers*

Sow seeds of asparagus fern in soil which is 60°F (16°C) and debud zinnias to a single stem if wanted as cut flowers. Pot on gerbera when about four to six weeks old, or when the second true leaves appear. Keep the crown above the soil when transplanting, until eventually a 4 inch (100 mm) pot size is reached.

Pot up lilies: *L. speciosum rubrum* will bloom in September or October, *L. auratum* will bloom in August, and *L. regale* will flower at about the same time. Pot on gloxinia to 4, 5 or 6 inch (100, 125 or 150 mm) pots, depending on the size of the tuber. Continue to fertilize and water hydrangea, and amaryllis and other bulbs that are still green. Dry off white calla and store the bulb warm, and dry off ixia and other bulbs whose foliage is fading and turning yellow.

## *Cool Flowers*

The greenhouse needs to be kept well ventilated at this time of year to keep temperatures down. Established primroses can be kept cool by setting them outdoors in a cold frame in light shade, if this was not done last month. Primroses sown in March will be ready for transplanting to 2 ½ inch (60 mm) pots. Aster and gypsophila potted on now should be in bloom for June and July (and see Table DEC-2, page 461). Keep Christmas cactus out of direct sunshine and fertilize it monthly until August with a high potassium fertilizer, such as 10-10-27. Continue to fertilize other plants regularly with a fertilizer for flowering houseplants.

Sow primroses, such as *Primula obconica*, *P. veris*, *P. sinensis*, *P. kewensis*, *P. elatior* and *P. malacoides*. Cineraria sown now will bloom in November, and calceolaria planted now or next month should be in bloom for December. Sow *Anemone coronaria* and wallflower, or start anemone from root cuttings (see page 137).

Month-by-Month

# June

- plant containers and hanging baskets with veggies, herbs and flowers
- tackle lawn pests
- cut a bouquet for Auntie's birthday (and one for yourself)
- take softwood cuttings

- check on bird houses and clean them out
- water wisely

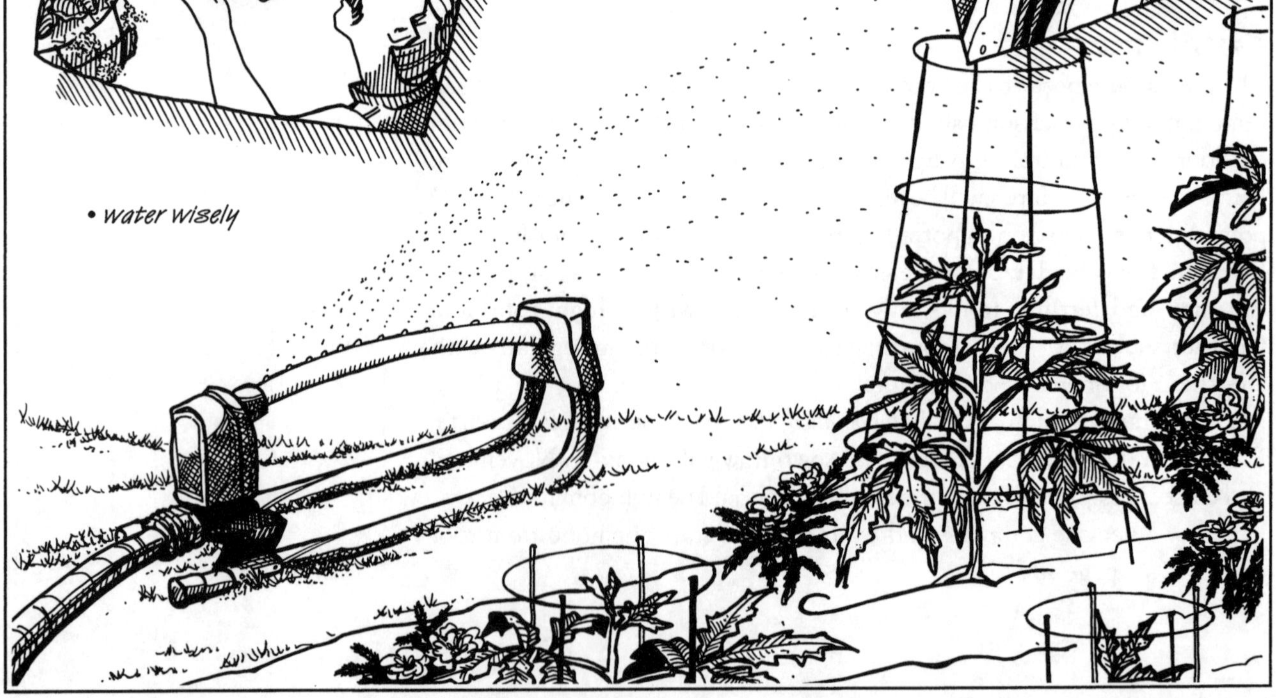

June brings long days and enough jobs to keep ardent gardeners working full time. Doing little parts of big chores throughout the week, instead of trying to do everything in one day, will help to make the tasks more manageable. Gardening only at weekends, on the other hand, means finding ways to water the garden and meet the needs of plants without exhausting oneself for two days.

The modern passion to excell and the need for perfection have no place in our gardens. There ought to be room for a less than perfect rose that still smells sweet, and a patch of fresh, tasty lettuce that has been shared with a slug or two. Instead of trying to rigidly manage insects and diseases, it is wiser to build up the soil to produce healthy plants that are better able to resist and grow past various attacks. It is better to work out long-term strategies and tolerate some damage by insects and disease than to reach for a spray at the first sign of trouble.

# June

**Hose**

*Crude, but effective and totally safe type of scythe towed through gardens to flatten flower beds and level vegetable plantings.*

*Beard and McKie*

## Lawns

### Low Key Pest and Disease Control

Many gardeners unwittingly create a chinch bug problem. There is no need, however, to spray chemicals on the lawn to get rid of the bugs. As they multiply rapidly during hot, dry spells, regular watering of lawns may be used more for insect control than to meet the growing needs of grasses which become dormant during drought. Chinch bugs can be a serious problem on Kentucky bluegrass lawns which are managed intensively with chemicals and fertilized heavily with nitrogen.

Heavy nitrogen use encourages fungal growth on grass, and fungicides used to manage the problem kill a fungus that is parasitic on chinch bugs. Heavy nitrogen use also makes grass more susceptible to drought, which encourages chinch bugs, but watering and nitrogen combined tend to encourage fungal problems. In addition, pesticides used to kill chinch bugs kill one of its natural enemies. Chinch bugs will also multiply and spread on lawns that have too little nitrogen, have excess thatch (which is common on intensively managed bluegrass lawns), or grow on compacted soils.

Chinch bugs first exhibit their damage next to sidewalks and driveways, where the heat is greatest. The lawn becomes off-coloured and yellow in an irregular pattern. To determine their presence, spread the grass apart in various places and look for small, 1/5 inch (5 mm) long, black or red insects with white markings. Another way to check is to push a large, open-ended can 2 inches (5 cm) into the soil and fill it with water. Chinch bugs will float to the surface in five minutes (this is a good way to check for other insects as well), and can be identified by their offensive odour when crushed. A lawn in good condition can tolerate ten to fifteen chinch bugs per square foot.

Chinch Bug

If worse comes to worst, let chinch bugs run their course to the end of the summer, then build up and aerate the soil by thoroughly working in organic matter. Reseed it with a variety of grasses that include perennial ryegrass, chewing and hard fescues, creeping red fescue and a little Kentucky bluegrass.

As an emergency measure, saturate affected areas with insecticidal soap (see page 194), adding 1/4 cup (65 ml) of isopropyl alcohol to each gallon (4.5 l) of solution. Repeat this every three to five days for two weeks.

When lawns are attacked by insects, the grass is usually easy to pull out, but when it is attacked by most diseases, it remains firmly attached to the soil. Proper growing conditions reduce the vulnerability of grass to disease as well as to insect attack.

For more details on low key lawn management and troubleshooting, see *How to Get Your Lawn & Garden Off Drugs*, by Carole Rubin (1989), and *Landscape Problem Solver* by Jeff and Liz Ball (1989).

### Preventive Measure

For long-term management of chinch bugs, plant trees and shrubs where they will shade the lawn and help keep it cool in future years. For the present, apply seaweed extract or fish emulsion if the lawn is pale green or yellowish from lack of nitrogen. Chinch bugs and other insects live longer and lay more eggs when deprived of nutrient rich grass, but they are also attracted to the rich, succulent growth of overfertilized grasses. Dethatch and aerate lawns well in the autumn—chinch bugs overwinter in thatch and the upper layer of soil—and keep lawns moist. Moisture is most effectively retained when the soil under the lawn is at least 6 inches (15 cm) thick and rich in organic matter (see page 371 to remedy this).

## Watering

The first indication that a lawn is lacking water is its loss of springiness; footprints, for example, stay in place after the grass has been walked on. Do not wait until the grass turns brown to remedy the problem. Water deeply and regularly once every two to three weeks if there is less than an average of 1 inch (2.5 cm) of rain per week. Water less often on clay soils and slightly more often on sandy soils. A light sprinkling every day is actually harmful to the lawn because it keeps roots short and close to the surface instead of encouraging deep growth into cooler, moist soil.

Set up a sprinkler or spray hose in the morning or evening and let it run on each area of lawn for three to four hours or until a can fills with 2 to 3 inches (5 to 8 cm) of water, depending on whether the lawn is watered once every two or three weeks. If the entire lawn cannot be watered this way in one day, do a small area each day until the whole area is watered. Grass dries off more quickly if watered in the morning, reducing the chance of fungal diseases developing, although wetness for more than fourteen to sixteen hours is needed for spores to become active.

If converting a grassy bank to ground cover shrubs, water erosion may be a problem, particularly when watering the new shrubs. Dig wide, generous planting holes, mulch well after the shrub is planted and leave stretches of grass between shrubs to reduce erosion from rain. Alternatively, remove a long strip of grass at the top of the bank, plant shrubs and spread mulch, and then repeat the process lower down next year. This ensures there is both grass in place to hold the soil and prevent erosion, and a good mulch cover on recently planted ground. Once the shrubs are well established, the last of the grass can be removed.

### Green Thumb Tip

If water is in short supply, reduce the amount of lawn by planting drought tolerant ground covers, and use drought resistant grasses rather than Kentucky bluegrass in the remaining lawn. Mow less frequently as longer grass provides more shade and thus reduces evaporation. Tall grass also grows deep root systems. Gradually increase the organic content of the soil (see page 371). If water supplies are severely limited, forget about watering the lawn unless it was recently planted, and focus on new trees and shrubs instead.

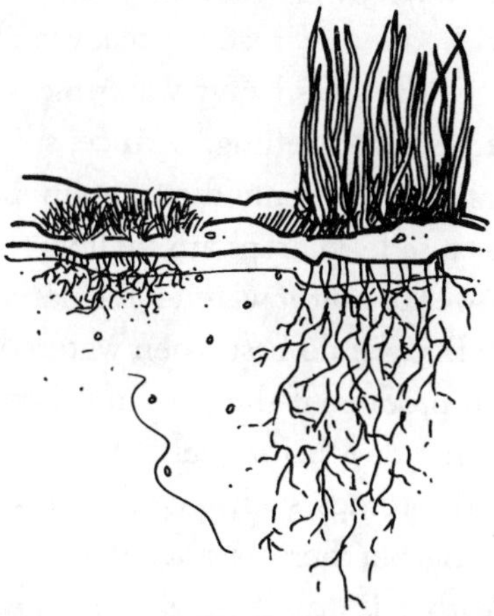

### Preventive Measure

There are several cultural activities that can reduce the risk of disease. Dethatch in the autumn, aerate the soil, and improve soil drainage. Trees and shrubs casting heavy shade or causing poor air circulation should be removed or thinned in late winter or early spring. Do not over fertilize with nitrogen during the summer, as this encourages lush, susceptible growth, and water only in the mornings. Cut the lawn often at the recommended height and remove the clippings from the lawn. It is the tender leaf growth which is vulnerable to fungus attack; mowing regularly continually removes any diseased tips. If the attack is intolerably severe, apply sulphur to affected areas every three to five days until the symptoms are gone.

## Vegetables

### Watering Strategies

When the weather is dry and water is limited, it is difficult to know how to distribute one's watering efforts. After newly planted trees and shrubs, most gardeners focus on the vegetable garden. Ideally, vegetables should be kept evenly moist throughout the growing season. This is easiest when the soil is weed-free, well mulched and rich in organic matter. There are several ways to get the most out of very little when water is severely limited, according to the research of J.K.A. Bleasdale et al. (1991).

All transplants should be watered every day until they are well established. Pour a small cupful around each plant rather than watering the entire area, and give priority to tomatoes, peppers, eggplants, melons, zucchini, cucumbers and squashes. Water these vegetables regularly when flowering starts and thereafter to enable fruits to fill out. Unlike transplants, deep watering a couple of times a week is better than a little every day. Zucchini in particular needs plenty of water when it is fruiting, and cucumbers are less likely to be bitter if they have an even supply of moisture and temperatures do not fluctuate too much. Be careful not to get water on cucurbit flowers or pollination may be adversely affected.

Legumes, such as peas and beans, do not need watering until they begin flowering, unless they are actually wilting. Too much water can actually lead to lush growth and lack of flowering. Water twice a week at flowering time or, if water is very limited, water deeply as the first flowers open, and then again as the pods are swelling. The development of stringiness in beans is delayed if they receive steady, sufficient moisture.

Corn needs heavy watering at the tasselling stage and again when the kernels are swelling. Lettuce, spinach and other leafy crops need frequent watering, but only the top 6 inches (15 cm) of soil needs to be moistened because leafy crops are shallow rooted. Lettuce is less bitter and spinach is slower to bolt if watered regularly. Brussels sprouts, cabbages, broccoli and cauliflower do best when watered regularly, but all except cauliflower will still produce if they are mulched well, then given a good soaking ten to twenty days before harvest.

Rootcrops, such as carrots and turnips, should receive a little water when young, but thereafter need watering only once every two to three weeks if the weather is dry. If the soil is allowed to get too dry, roots may split when watered and turnip centres may brown.

### Green Thumb Tip

Tomatoes grown under somewhat dry conditions (watered twice a week) have better flavour than those grown under wet conditions (daily watering), although the yield will be lower. Tomatoes grown under very dry conditions will be small and may develop blossom end rot. This is a brown, water-soaked area at the bottom of the fruit that gradually turns black and leathery. It is caused by insufficient or irregular moisture and by insufficient calcium reaching the fruits, either because the soil lacked calcium, or because there was insufficient water to carry the required calcium to the fruit. Green shoulder in tomatoes is also caused partly by an uneven supply of moisture.

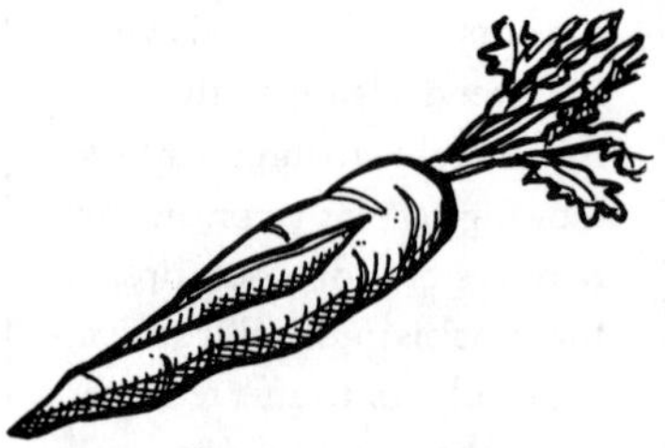

Carrot with a split root due to watering after a drought.

Members of the onion family need frequent watering during the early stages of growth to promote good leaf development, but they need very little once the bulbs start forming after mid July. For less pungent onions, keep them moderately moist. Mulch them with chopped leaves, loose straw or other dryish material once the leaves are about 6 inches (15 cm) high.

Potatoes can get by with very little water until they start to develop tubers. When tubers are marble-sized—usually when the plants are in flower—give potatoes a thorough, deep soaking, and mulch the plants well, if you have not done so already, to conserve moisture. It is not necessary for potatoes to flower in order to produce tubers; the two events merely coincide.

## Planting Warm Season Vegetables

When transplanting heat loving crops this month, get them off to a good start by properly preparing planting holes (or hills). Cucurbits (cucumbers, zucchini, various squashes and melons) are traditionally planted in hills because the soil stays warmer (see Warming the Soil, page 117). Space hills widely (see Table APR/MAY-1, page 124), especially for pumpkins and winter squashes which grow vines 10 to 12 feet (3 to 3.6 m) long. Provide 6 inch (15 cm) mesh netting to a height of 6 feet (1.8 m) if growing any cucurbits vertically. Do not plant on compost or manure piles as they dry out quickly and are so rich that leafy growth develops at the expense of fruit.

Mound soil in advance so it is warm by planting time, usually two weeks after the last expected frost. Work a spadeful or two of compost or well rotted manure into each hill to supply nutrients and help hold moisture. Mounds dry out more quickly than level soil, so if drought is a problem, plant on the flat and use clear plastic to warm the soil.

Cucurbit seeds can be sown outdoors at the same time that transplants are set out. In each hill, plant six seeds 1 inch (2.5 cm) deep and on their edge to reduce the risk of rotting. Thin them to three per hill once they have germinated, and finally to one per hill. If cold frames are available, put them over canteloupes, melons and watermelons, but be sure to provide ventilation on bright or sunny days.

A warm, sheltered, sunny place is needed for sweet potatoes, and the ground will have to be covered with plastic unless summers are very warm. Cut holes in the plastic to set in plants and leave it in place for the growing season. Plastic used over extended periods as a mulch gradually reduces the supply of oxygen in the soil, but this is not a problem when used for a couple

### Green Thumb Tip

To further conserve water, use a drip or soaker hose rather than a spray or sprinkler system and water in the morning rather than at midday to reduce loss through evaporation; put a rain barrel under the downspout from roof gutters and cover it to reduce evaporation; and reuse household water—if it does not contain bleach or borax—at the base of plants.

Weeds compete with seedlings for moisture, particularly during the three weeks after a crop germinates, so start weeding as soon as the crop row can be seen. If there is very little time for weeding, at least run a cultivating hoe just under the surface of the soil between rows of plants (see pages 160-161). In block plantings and within rows weeds must be pulled by hand.

Sweet potatoes keep warmer if planted in ground covered with plastic.

### Preventive Measure

Protect summer squash and other cucurbits from cucumber beetles while plants are young by covering the plants with

agricultural fabric or a cheesecloth covered frame. The beetles lay eggs in crevices in the plants and larvae hatch in ten days. They then move to the roots and stems below the soil line where they feed and weaken the plant. They can infect plants with bacterial wilt—stem after stem just wilts and dies. Remember to remove the covering when plants have female blossoms (see page 248), so that they can be pollinated by visiting bees.

of months and in different places each year. Add a little bonemeal and wood ashes to the soil to supply phosphorous and potassium, but hold back on nitrogen as too much will result in plenty of vine and not much tuber. Make sure the soil is free of lumps and rocks.

For tomatoes, peppers and eggplants, the soil can be prewarmed by digging holes in advance, using clear plastic (see page 117), preparing raised beds, or planting these crops against warm walls or in sunny places sheltered from wind. Enrich planting holes with a spadeful of compost or well rotted manure, and a handful of powdered bonemeal for phosphorus to aid flower and fruit development. Working in wood ashes or finely crushed eggshells, crustacean or mollusc shells (crabs, lobsters, mussels, chicken grade oyster grit) will help meet calcium and magnesium needs. Chopped seaweed, liquid seaweed, kelp meal, chopped banana peel and green plant residues such as grass clippings will also add potassium to the soil. Tomatoes need plenty of this mineral, but high potassium fertilizers reduce magnesium uptake, and magnesium deficiency (see Green Thumb Tip, page 248) shows up as delayed maturity of fruits, green shoulder in tomatoes and blossom drop in peppers, eggplants and tomatoes. This does not seem to be a problem with slow acting organic fertilizers. Huge amounts of nitrogen are not required; tomatoes in particular will grow beautiful, bountiful leaves but no fruits.

Peppers are ready to be transplanted outside when plants are 4 to 5 inches (10 to 12 cm) tall, or transplant peppers, eggplants and tomatoes when flowers are showing provided they are in big pots and have good root systems. After plants flower they do not send out roots as readily. Nights should be consistently above 55°F (12°C), otherwise the blossoms will drop off. Separate hot and sweet peppers in the garden so that they do not cross pollinate, and separate peppers, tomatoes, eggplants and potatoes. Plant them in areas of the garden where none has been planted for at least three years as this reduces the risk of nematodes and other problems.

Hold off mulching all of these heat loving crops until July, when the soil is truly warm, unless mulching with clear plastic. Tomatoes sprawling on the ground should have a mulch of coarse straw or another material that will keep the fruits dry.

Water with fish emulsion or manure tea (see Green Thumb Tip, page 163) every couple of weeks until mid July. Both will supply boosts of nitrogen while the plants are getting established; stop adding nitrogen when flower and fruit development are desired. Alternatively, spread fine, finished compost around the plants late this month or early next month. If the growth of peppers seems weak, remove the first terminal flower to encourage leafy growth.

## *Table JUN-1 Early Summer Vegetable Planting Schedule*

Soil is warm, air temperatures are warm and steady, apples, cherries and strawberries are in bloom or just past and dandelions are in peak numbers or just past.

Plant anything not yet planted from spring schedules (Tables APR/MAY-2, page 130; MAY-1, page 167; MAY-3, page 172) plus:

| Plant | Transplant | Sow Seeds | Repeat Sow |
|---|---|---|---|
| Asparagus | x | | |
| Beans, lima | | x | |
| Beans, snap, shell | | x | every 2 weeks to 8 weeks b.f. |
| Beets | | x | every 2-3 weeks to 8 weeks b.f. |
| Broccoli, late | o | x | to 12 weeks b.f. |
| Brussels Sprouts | x | | |
| Cabbage, winter | x | x | |
| Carrots, main crop | | x | every 2 weeks to 10 weeks b.f. |
| Cauliflower, late | o | x | to 12 weeks b.f. |
| Celery, Celeriac | x | | |
| Cucumber | x | x | every 3 weeks to 9 weeks b.f. |
| Eggplant | x | | |
| Florence Fennel | o | x | after June 21 |
| Kohlrabi | o | x | every 3 weeks to 4 weeks b.f. |
| Leeks, late | x | o | to 12 weeks b.f. |
| Melon, Watermelon | x | | |
| New Zealand Spinach | | x | |
| Onions, Summer Bunching | | x | every 3 weeks to 9 weeks b.f. |
| Parsnip | | x | |
| Peas | | x | every 2-4 weeks to 11 weeks b.f. |
| Pepper | x | | |
| Potatoes, winter, sets | | x | |
| Pumpkin | x | x | |
| Salsify | | x | |
| Scorzonera | | x | |
| Squash, summer | x | x | |
| Squash, winter | x | x | |
| Sweet Potato | x | | |
| Tomato | x | | |
| Witloof Chicory | x | | |

o = optional method
x = usual method

b.f. = before expected first fall frost

## Focus on Plants

Tomato plants can be larger than peppers before planting out. Remove the lowest leaves and bury the lower part of the stem when planting. In order to keep the root ball in warm soil, plant it and the stem semi-horizontally in the soil. The tops can be gently eased into an upright position if they are to be staked or caged, or allowed to sprawl on the ground, where their fruits will ripen faster in cool locations.

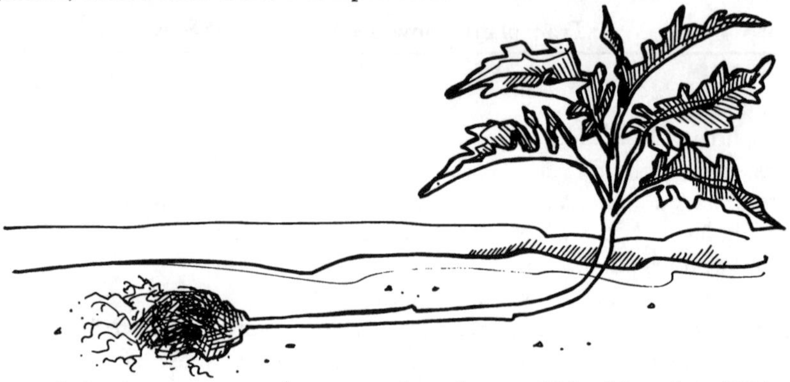

Early bush tomatoes can be spaced as close as 12 by 12 inches (30 by 30 cm), but the overall yield will be somewhat less than those spaced at 19 by 19 inches (48 by 48 cm). Caged vine tomatoes can be spaced 3 to 4 feet (1 to 1.2 m) apart, with corresponding cage diameters of 18 to 30 inches (45 to 75 cm), each 5 feet tall (1.5 m). Such wide diameters are needed only where summers are warm and growth is lush and vigorous. Use 4 by 6 inch (10 by 15 cm) metal mesh, and a 6 to 7 foot (1.8 to 2.1 m) stake driven into the ground to hold the cage in place in windy locations. The cages can be wrapped in plastic while the plants are young to hold extra heat, but leave the tops open. There is no need to prune caged tomatoes.

Pinch out all suckers on tomatoes.

Stakes, placed on the windward side of tomato plants, can be used instead of cages to fit twice as many plants in the same space. Fruits will be more uniform in size, but there will be a decrease in total yields and more losses to cracking and sunscald. There will be no significant effect on the rate of ripening. Staked tomatoes also require more attention as all the suckers (side shoots in the axils of plants) have to be removed. One or two main stems can be allowed to develop; if three or four develop tomato cages might as well be used. The big advantage to single stems is that they give giant tomatoes, even if few in number.

## More Planting

Sow Florence fennel after June 21 in long season areas so that it will not bolt in response to long days. In short season areas, transplants of Florence fennel that were started inside in March or April can be set out as soon as the weather is stable. It will also bolt if growth is checked by sudden temperature fluctuations, drafts and wind, or a shortage of water. It prefers fertile, light, sandy, well-drained soil.

Sow kohlrabi every few weeks from June onward. Set out asparagus seedlings in a nursery bed after all danger of frost has past, and then transplant them to their permanent position next spring (see Table APR/MAY-1, page 124, for spacing).

Plant out celery and celeriac into very moist soil rich with organic matter. The soil can be so moist that it is mucky—this will help prevent toughness in these crops—but keep a sharp eye open for slugs. Plant celery crowns a bit below soil level when plants are 3 to 5 inches (7.5 to 12.5 cm) tall. Celeriac is hardier than celery, less prone to pests and easier to grow.

Sow radicchio and culture it in much the same way as lettuce. It forms round heads that are usually ready to harvest before the first frosts in the fall. About half of the plants will form heads, another one fifth will form loose heads, and the rest will not form heads at all, but the leaves can still be used.

More snap beans can be sown, but lima beans need warm, rich soil and should be planted a little later. If limas do not germinate in five or six days, the soil was either too cool or they have rotted. Wait a couple of weeks and try again, or else pre-sprout them indoors before planting outside .

Find odd corners for sowings of scallions, pickling onions, shallots and summer bunching onions. If onions bolt, remove the flower stalk; try more nitrogen and smaller sets next time to reduce the chance of flowering.

Sow the main carrot crop, then sow more every couple of weeks, if desired, until ten weeks before the first expected autumn frost. Short, round varieties can be planted later. Sow parsnip, salsify and scorzonera in loose, deep, and lump-free soil. If the soil is really poor, enrich a 10 to 12 inch (25 to 30 cm) deep, V-shaped trench and plant the seeds in that. Be sure to use fresh parsnip seeds, soak them overnight in warm water, and sow them thickly due to their low germination rate. Plant more beets, perhaps among squashes. Pickling beets need to be planted close together (see Table APR/MAY-1, page 124).

For fall crops, sow seeds of broccoli, cauliflower, winter cabbage and leeks. This will be the second sowing for some gardeners. Alternatively, they can be started indoors four or five weeks earlier, especially in short

Radicchio

### Focus on Plants

There are two basic types of garlic—hard neck and soft neck. The hard neck kinds produce a solid flowering stalk, also called a scape. Soft neck strains do not develop a scape and usually have a larger number of smaller cloves per bulb than hard neck strains.

For bigger yields in the hard neck strains, remove the scape as soon as you notice it. If it is not removed, the tiny bulbils that form can be used for cooking, or else planted and grown for two years to produce bulbs large enough for planting.

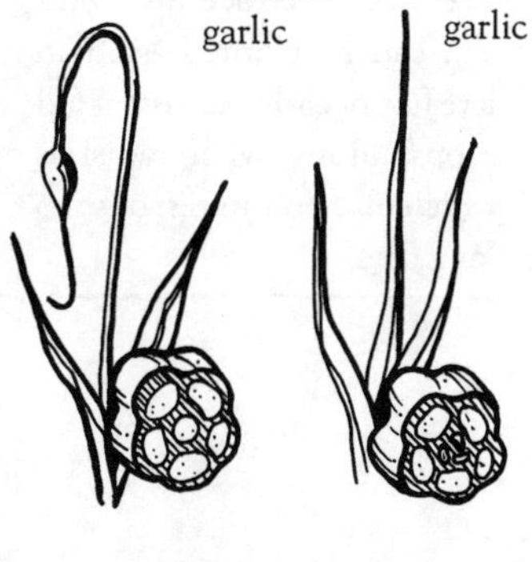

season areas, and set out as transplants. Plant broccoli and cauliflower in a bit of shade to help keep them cool. Consider undersowing vegetables with green manure crops when the vegetables are between four and five weeks old (see July, page 250).

Brussels sprouts can be sown directly outside or set out as transplants. Add compost instead of extra manure as the latter can cause loose heads (leaves arranged loosely instead of tightly). If you wish to harvest gradually, set transplants 1 yard by 1 yard (1 m by 1 m) apart. For a one-time harvest of small sprouts for freezing, set transplants 20 by 20 inches (50 by 50 cm) apart. Make the soil around the transplants moderately firm with your feet, so that a leaf pulls off rather than the plant coming out when a leaf is tugged. Brussels sprouts get very large and need a firm footing in the soil so that they will not topple over.

Plant potatoes for winter storage in a 4 to 5 inch (10 to 12 cm) deep trench with the rose end facing up (the end that has most of the eyes), and then fill in the trench with soil. If the soil is poor, dig a slightly deeper trench, put seaweed in the bottom before the tubers go in, and then fill it in with soil mixed with compost. Annual vetch sowed between the rows of potatoes four to five weeks after they are established will also help to improve the soil.

Hill potatoes when they are 4 to 6 inches (10 to 15 cm) tall, if they are not under thick mulch. Keep hilling them until the plants are 1 foot (30 cm) tall and flowering starts. Alternatively, hill them once when they are 9 inches (23 cm) high, mounding the soil 4 to 5 inches (10 to 12 cm) high around the plants. Hilling is usually not required if small tubers are planted (see pages 76-77).

Hill tall varieties of corn when the plants are 12 to 18 inches (30 to 45 cm) high. Remove puny stalks, but leave side shoots. All corn should be planted by the end of June. Even short season varieties need a good eleven weeks from the time of sowing to ripen and corn does not ripen well in cool weather.

## Care and Harvest of Other Crops

Fertilize spinach, lettuce and other leafy greens with manure tea. Lettuce picked in the morning is sweeter than that picked later in the day. Arugula is best harvested when it is less than 5 inches (13 cm) tall. The entire plant can be cut back three or four times as long as it is given adequate moisture. Unlike lettuce and spinach, it is a pleasure to see arugula go to flower and make seeds. The flower buds and flowers are edible and tasty and the seeds add crunch and texture to salads. The seeds can be dried and stored for later

### Preventive Measure

Spinach and lettuce will bolt in response to longer days. As Patent and Bilderback (1982) explain, although bolting is speeded up by warm weather, it is long days not the warm weather that causes it. Avoid planting these crops near street lights or house night lights, and do not give extended lighting to seedlings indoors in the early spring. As well, pick off the oldest leaves as this reduces the amount of florigen, a plant hormone that causes flower buds to form in the apical tip. This technique is very effective with spinach, but it slows down the bolting process in lettuce for only a week to ten days.

If spinach is looking old and tired, cut the entire plant back to an inch tall to stimulate young, tasty growth. If it is already showing signs of bolting, harvest the whole crop—it freezes well (see page 294). Both lettuce and spinach can be planted again in late July or early August for fall crops, along with radishes which also bolt in response to long days.

Arugula

eating or for planting in the late summer. Corn salad can also be harvested by cutting the whole plant, or just remove the outer leaves.

When beets are half grown, top dress them with fine compost. Pick up to one-third of the leaves on each plant when harvesting the greens, or pull the entire plant when the roots are 1 to 1½ inches (2.5 to 4 cm) wide. Start picking collards when the first six or eight leaves reach full size. Cut young, tender leaves that are about the size of your hand, but avoid cutting the central growing point if a continuous harvest is wanted. Harvest the bright green and crisp leaves of kale—the dark green, heavy leaves are overmature. The outer leaves of Swiss chard are ready to harvest when the plants are about eight weeks old. Harvest the outer leaves of endive, or the whole plant.

Continue to harvest mature asparagus plantings until the middle of June. Apply another 1 inch (2.5 cm) of rotted manure or compost along the rows after the harvest is completed and keep the patch well weeded, mulched and moist to ensure a good harvest next year.

Dust peas with sulphur if they have been troubled in previous years with mildew; usually this treatment is not essential because peas are generally harvested before mildew becomes a problem. Refrain from weeding or

### Green Thumb Tip

All greens are slower to wilt after picking and when preparing them for eating if the leaves are torn rather than cut. Tearing separates the leaves between the cells rather than through the cells, resulting in less loss of moisture.

### Green Thumb Tip

Some plants are blanched before they are harvested. Blanch endive and escarole during the last two or three weeks of growth if you wish to reduce the bitterness—some people prefer the sharp taste. There are several methods of blanching: either tie the outer leaves together (make sure they are perfectly dry); cover the plant by resting a plate on top of it; put a pot over the plant; or cover the top of the plants with a board supported at each end with bricks. Blanch only a few plants at a time—it takes about ten days—and use them as soon as they are ready because they quickly become green and bitter on re-exposure to light.

When cauliflower has a head the size of a walnut or egg, blanch it by pulling the leaves over it (make sure it is perfectly dry) and holding the leaves in place with string or a clothes peg. It should be ready two to three weeks later. Self-blanching varieties do not usually need this treatment.

Blanch celery by mulching deeply with straw in late summer, or by wrapping the stems below the leaves with 3 to 4 inch (8 to 10 cm) wide strips of brown paper or black plastic, adding more strips as the plant grows.

working among beans when they are wet to avoid the spread of various bacterial and fungal diseases.

## Container Vegetables

Vegetables grown in containers require much the same treatment as those in the garden, except that they will have to be watered more frequently and fertilized regularly. Table JAN-3 (page 26) gives suggestions for container sizes and spacing. Use garden soil or any regular potting soil; these can be enriched with leaf mould, compost or well rotted manure if desired. Suspended planters and window boxes should have the soil mix lightened with perlite (see Preventive Measure, page 224 for other methods of reducing weight).

The amount of watering required can be reduced by using several techniques. One is to group containers together so that the soil and the containers are shaded by neighbouring plants. Soil in containers often overheats, increasing the amount of water lost and stressing the plants. Mulching is an effective way to reduce evaporation and it can keep soil up to 10% cooler. Light coloured containers are less likely to overheat, but you may prefer to use dark colours for heat loving crops. Use large, insulated containers (see page 439) to reduce temperature fluctuations and to provide a larger reserve of moisture and nutrients. A wick system (see pages 223-224) can also be used to reduce the need for watering, or simply drape strips of terry towel between a bucket of water and the surface of the potting soil.

To avoid fertilizing every two weeks, mix a slow release fertilizer into the potting soil at the time of planting. Manure or compost alone may be enough, but there is little room in containers for reserves.

## Pests and Other Nuisances

When working in the vegetable patch, keep an eye open for insect activity. Much of it is benign or actively beneficial. In assessing insect damage and deciding whether or not to take action, consider three levels of damage:

- if insects might kill the plant before harvest, take action;
- if they are damaging edible parts of the plant, remove the affected bits instead of trying to fight the insects;
- if insects are damaging other, non-edible parts of the plant, but not threatening its life, there is probably no need to take any action at all.

The best defence against insects is fertile, well-drained soil with plenty of organic matter and adequate moisture; healthy plants are less likely to attract insects and are better able to continue growing and developing if harmful insects do attack. One could view insect damage early in the season as a sort of pruning as healthy plants respond with more, healthy growth.

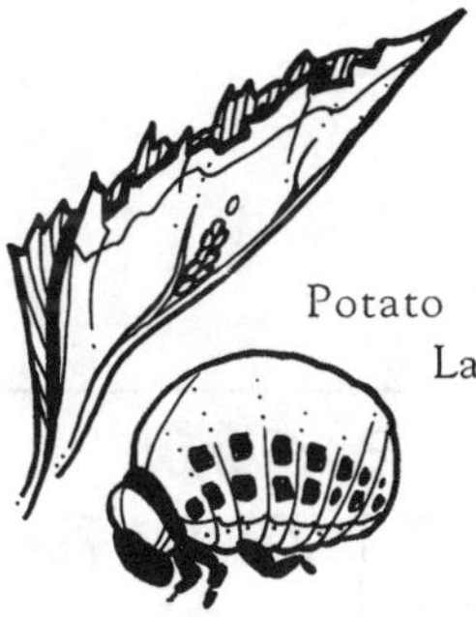

Potato Beetle Larva

Some pests are exceptionally harmful. Potato beetles emerge when potatoes are growing vigorously. They are 1/3 inch (8 mm) long striped beetles and their larvae are voracious eaters. Crush the reddish-orange egg masses on the underside of leaves and knock adults and larvae into a container. Normal larvae look rather like fat pink ladybird beetles. If there are any lumpy looking larvae, leave them alone because they are infected with tachnid flies and will die. Chickadees, purple finches and robins eat the adult potato beetles.

It is easiest to pick up grasshoppers early in the morning while they are still sluggish. Their numbers can be reduced further by encouraging toads. A half buried dish of water and an overturned flowerpot, or piles of twigs and debris, will provide welcome shelter for toads. The welcome visitors also devour aphids, slugs, ants and cutworms.

Root aphids may be a problem in the lettuce crop. Work wood ashes into the transplanting holes or seeding rows to discourage them and drench the soil with insecticidal soap if their numbers threaten to get out of hand. They are nurtured by ants, which will even carry aphid eggs to plant roots.

Brassicas will continue to be visited by cabbage white butterflies, which have a very long season. Keep plants covered with floating row covers or cheesecloth, or spray with Bt every five to seven days as soon as you notice the first larvae. They have to ingest the bacterium in order for the spray to work so immediate action is essential.

If possible, keep brassicas well watered until the flea beetle season is past. The holes they chew in foliage are not troublesome to the final crop but severe attacks can weaken young seedlings. They do the greatest damage in the first month of the growing season and flourish in wet, cold years.

Several generations of cutworms are produced each year, but they are usually less of a problem in the summer than the spring, except for very young plants. A soaking rain at the right time can drown young cutworms, and bluejays, robins, sparrows, blackbirds, wrens and chickens will happily eat the pests (also see page 123).

If brassicas develop discoloured and wilting leaves and have solid swollen galls on their roots, they have club root. Next time you plant them, choose a location that has not had a brassica crop for at least three years, and make sure the soil has a pH of 7.0 and excellent drainage.

## Herbs

### General Care

Hopefully some of the herbs that were planted early are up by now and in need of thinning, weeding and mulching. Weeding is a pleasure among herbs as the smell and feel of the different leaves delight the senses. Gerald A. Mulligan's *Common Weeds of Canada* (1987) will help to distinguish weeds from desirable plants. Mulch with any organic material as for vegetables. Leaf mould is particularly good among sweet woodruff and other herbs in woodsy settings.

Herbs are less troubled by insects than vegetables and flowers, so they demand less attention. In short growing season areas plant or thin herbs closer than recommended (see Table FEB-1, page 40) to compensate for less growth; space them more widely if conditions are very dry. Fennel thinnings and others grown for their foliage can be used immediately (see page 300, and Table AUG-3, page 302, for culinary uses of herbs). A superb book on uses of fresh herbs is Noel Richardson's *Summer Delights* (1991).

There is still time to plant herbs, particularly the tender annual ones. Make repeat sowings of summer savory every two to three weeks to maintain a fresh supply. Even perennial herbs could be sown now, grown in pots indoors over the winter, and planted out permanently next spring. Perennial herbs that were started indoors this winter should be planted outside now so that they have time to become well established before the next winter sets in. Small perennials can be grown on for a year in a nursery bed, which may be no more than a row in the vegetable garden, whereas larger ones might be ready for planting in their permanent location. Plants in a nursery can be spaced closer together than their recommended final planting distance.

### Green Thumb Tip

Flower removal increases leaf growth and, therefore, the herb crop. Herbs that are harvested continuously, such as basil, should be cut back regularly before they flower to keep young growth coming along. Basil can be pinched when it is 4 inches (8 cm) high to encourage bushy growth. Pinch angelica when it is 1 foot (30 cm) high to keep it bushy, and keep cutting out the flower stalks as soon as they appear. Angelica is a biennial and a prolific self-seeder, but it can be kept going for years as a perennial, without a horde of seedlings, if it is never allowed to flower. French sorrel will also continue to grow fresh leaves for longer if its flowers are removed. Removing the flowers on comfrey, chervil, borage and salad burnet will reduce the amount of self-sowing.

### Watering

Herb transplants and freshly seeded herb beds should be watered daily until growth is well established. Give each transplant a cupful of water, and gently spray seedlings. When they are established, water according to the general growing conditions they require (see Table FEB-1, page 40). There are three general groupings, although some herbs are tolerant of a range of conditions.

Herbs requiring moist, cool soil should be watered deeply about once a week unless there is heavy rain, and should be mulched before the soil gets really warm. Soil rich in organic matter is essential. Angelica, beebalm, horseradish and mint will grow more vigorously and invasively if kept very moist but not waterlogged. Water them less frequently to control their growth, but do not allow them to get really dry. To control mint, plant it inside a bottomless pot or bucket sunk into the soil with the rim above soil level.

Herbs without specific moisture requirements growing in well-drained soil should be watered every seven to fourteen days—water less often if there is plenty of rain and more often if you want the plants to grow quickly. Lemon balm, for example, will grow more lushly if it is kept evenly moist. Mulching will keep down weeds that compete for moisture and nutrients and will help to preserve moisture in the soil. Water every two weeks with fish fertilizer or manure tea, as part of the regular waterings, to encourage leafy growth in those plants that are being heavily harvested, such as basil, parsley, chives and sorrel. Parsley can have the outer leaves repeatedly picked or the entire plant cut off an inch (2.5 cm) above ground. Encourage it to regrow by watering and fertilizing regularly. Chives can be cut back completely the same way just before they go to flower, unless you want the flowers to add to salads or to make pretty chive vinegar (see pages 255-256).

Some herbs tolerate quite dry conditions, and will have a higher content of the oils that give herbs their particular flavour or fragrance than the same plants grown under moist conditions. This does not mean that herbs should be grown so dry that they wilt. Soak established plants every two to three weeks and mulch to keep down the weeds. Drought tolerant perennial herbs, such as lavender, should be watered more often during their first year to allow them to become well established.

Most herbs, even the large perennial ones while they are young, can be grown in containers (see page 26). Group herbs according to their watering needs, either together in large containers or in smaller, individual containers. They will need to be watered more frequently than those in the ground and most will need fertilizing every two to four weeks, depending on how heavily they are cut. They require more care in the summer but they are easier to move indoors for the winter. Some gardeners plunge the pots into the ground to reduce the amount of watering required.

### Harvest

Perennial and biennial herbs can be harvested this month, but most annuals will not have grown enough except perhaps to have a few leaves picked, unless they were started in cold frames. Beebalm grows so rapidly that it can be cut back to an inch (2.5 cm) above ground before it goes to flower and/ or immediately after it flowers.

French tarragon is usually up early and a few leaves can be taken now to use in sauces, salads, eggs, fish, poultry and tomato dishes. When the plants are well established, in July or August, they can be cut back to 1 or 2 inches (2.5 to 5 cm) above the ground. In long season areas, tarragon can be cut back hard a second time, as long as it receives plenty of moisture and fertilizer.

Parsley is best picked early in the morning when most turgid with moisture; it will keep for up to a month if kept cool and humid. Chervil grows best in cool weather and should be picked just before use as it wilts readily.

Some herbs are delightful fresh, very pleasant frozen and quite disappointing when dried. Others develop their best scent when dried. Refer to July, pages 251-256, and Table JUL-2, page 252, for storage methods, and see Table AUG-3, (page 302) for some of the culinary uses of herbs.

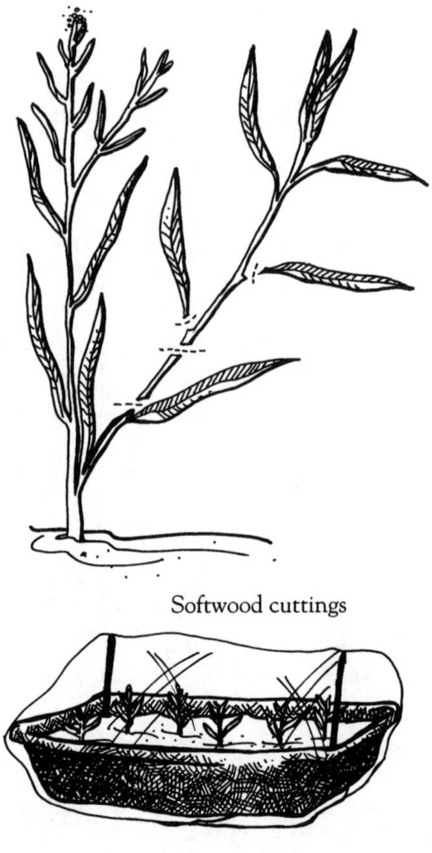

Softwood cuttings

## Propagation

A few herbs can be propagated this month from softwood cuttings (see Table JAN-1, page 15). This is a useful method for French tarragon, which is sometimes bothered by nematodes. The new growth used for cuttings should be flexible but firm enough to snap when bent. In the morning, when plants are most turgid, cut growing tips off just above a leaf node, trim off the bottom of the cuttings just below a leaf node with a sharp knife or razor blade, and remove the lowest leaves. The finished cuttings should be 2 to 3 inches (5 to 8 cm) long.

For each kind of herb cutting, prepare a pot or box containing equal amounts of moist peat moss and perlite, erring on the side of more perlite. Poke several 3/4 to 1 inch (2 to 2.5 cm) deep holes in the medium with a pencil, dip the cut ends of the cuttings into mild rooting hormone and tap off the excess, drop each cutting into a hole, lightly press the soil around the cuttings, and water gently. Put the entire pot in a plastic bag or cover the box with plastic—provide supports so that the plastic does not touch the cuttings—and place in a bright place out of direct sunlight. If possible, provide bottom heat of around 70°F (21°C). This is easiest if you are using a propagation unit (see pages 442-443). The cuttings should root in ten to forty days and show new growth. Ventilate the cuttings once they have rooted and gradually harden them off to drier, cooler conditions before planting them in individual pots or a lightly shaded cold frame.

## Flowers

### General Activities

There is a host of planting and maintenance tasks to take care of this month. Pinch out the side buds of roses if extra big flowers are wanted as this will direct more of the plant's energies toward the central flowers. Pinch out the central growing point of chrysanthemums to make the plants bushier and hence more floriferous. Each new piece of growth can be pinched when it is 3 to 4 inches (8 to 10 cm) long. Continue pinching to the middle of July. It is probably not worth while to plant out florists' chrysanthemums because they are not as hardy as garden mums. In addition, they need a longer period of long nights and short days to initiate flower buds, so they will not bloom before killing frosts come in the autumn.

Take stem cuttings of perennial candytuft (*Iberis*), aubrieta, arabis, baby's breath, armeria and beebalm (and see Table APR/MAY-3, page 138), and treat them in the same manner as herb cuttings (above). Cuttings from hardy shrub roses should be taken just as flower buds begin to appear. *Dianthus* species seem to deteriorate after a few years, but pips (short segments of stems) for starting new plants can be obtained by pulling off the ends of leafy stems when flowering is over, and rooting these.

Seeds of biennial flowers should be sown this month so that they will grow enough in a nursery bed to survive the winter. Next spring they can be planted in their permanent location. Seeds can also be sprinkled among existing biennials to keep the cycle of bloom going. Fertilize plants with manure tea or fish fertilizer to give them a boost. Plant out Easter lilies in soil that drains well. They may bloom again before frost hits and in zone 6 they sometimes survive the winter, particularly if they are well mulched in the autumn. Keep planting gladioli every ten days to the end of June.

Cut off faded flower stalks unless they are being saved for birds, for their seeds, or for dried arrangements (see pages 386-387). Perennials being grown for winter forcing (see pages 415-416) which should have their flower buds removed include: coreopsis, gaillardia, delphinium, butterfly weed, wallflower, shasta daisy and yarrow (achillea).

### Window Boxes and Container Plantings

To reduce the watering required, set up a wick system before the window boxes are planted. Use nylons cut into long strips and thread them part way through the drainage holes. Add potting mix or garden soil to one-quarter

Dianthus can be easily propagated by pulling off a pip.

**Green Thumb Tip**

Cut back vigorous rockery plants that have finished blooming, including basket-of-gold alyssum, iberis and arabis. Alternatively, put some rich soil on top of the middle of the plants, such as creeping phlox, and work it down around the stems. This will encourage rooting and fresh growth from which new plants can be started. Creeping phlox can be ripped out by the handful if it is getting too big and the pieces can be rooted in moist soil out of direct sunlight. What is left behind will respond with fresh, new growth; a little fertilizer will help but is not critical.

Wick watering is a plant saver during vacation times.

> ### Preventive Measure
>
> If large containers are to be used on rooftops or balconies, the weight should be minimized and spread out as much as possible. Lighten the garden soil or potting mix with up to one-third perlite by volume, and use compressed cellulose or plastic instead of clay or wooden containers. Set containers on rooftops close to the edge to ease the burden on the roof. It also helps to put heavy containers on wooden platforms to spread the weight over a larger area. Several small pots inside a container will lighten the overall load and will allow you to change the plants throughout the season.

the depth of the window box. Lay one end of each strip of nylons across this and then finish filling and planting the window box. The ends of the nylons dangling out of the drainage holes should drop into a large tray (such as those used for wetting wallpaper) affixed to the house just below the window box. If you water the potting soil in the window box and fill the tray beneath with water at the same time you should only have to water once every few weeks—this is ideal if boxes are hard to reach. Flowers in pots and other containers should be grouped and managed the same as vegetables in containers (see page 218) to conserve moisture and prevent overheating.

When selecting window boxes and hanging baskets, choose generous sizes (see Green Thumb Tip, page 440 for suggested sizes).

For the middle of containers, choose erect plants such as:

| | | | |
|---|---|---|---|
| annual aster | celosia | dwarf snapdragon | zinnia |
| calendula | dianthus | geranium | |
| carnation | dusty miller | salvia | |

Good trailing plants for the edges include:

| | | |
|---|---|---|
| browallia | morning glory, dwarf | petunia, trailing |
| campanula | nasturtium | portulaca |
| English ivy | nierembergia | sweet alyssum |
| geranium, ivy-leaved | periwinkle (*Vinca minor*) | thunbergia |
| lobelia, trailing | | |

Other good candidates for containers, although many of them prefer moist conditions, are:

| | | |
|---|---|---|
| asparagus fern | coleus | schizanthus |
| baby's breath, annual | nolana | sweet pea, dwarf |
| begonia, fibrous | phacelia | verbena |
| begonia, tuberous | phlox, annual | |

Coleus and caladium have such striking foliage colours that they are better used with plain green foliage plants or with plants that have white or pink flowers. Lobelia, nemesia, ivy, fibrous and tuberous begonia are particularly good for shady places. In light shade or where sun is available for only a few hours each day, plants to consider are:

| | | |
|---|---|---|
| achimenes | flowering tobacco (*Nicotiana*) | nemophila |
| ageratum | fuchsia | nierembergia |
| browallia | impatiens | pansy |
| caladium | Italian bellflower (*Campanula isophylla*) | vinca, annual (*Vinca rosea*) |
| candytuft, annual | | |
| ferns | | |

Water hanging baskets and window boxes twice a week or daily as required if you are not using a wick system. Fertilize every two weeks with a soluble houseplant fertilizer for flowering plants (except nasturtiums, candytuft, geraniums and impatiens as these grow all leaves instead of flowers when fed a rich diet). Alternatively, mix slow release fertilizer into the potting mix at planting time.

Geraniums grow well in 5 inch (125 mm) pots. These can be sunk into the ground to reduce watering requirements and to make lifting easier in the fall. If growing them for indoor fall and winter flowers, remove all buds as soon as they appear this month. Plant out other tender perennials as well.

Removing faded flowers—also called deadheading—will encourage a longer season of bloom, improve the appearance of the plant and reduce self-seeding. Annuals flower to produce seed—if the faded flowers are removed, the plants will keep flowering in successive efforts to produce seed.

## Watering Stategies

If working with a very limited water supply, forget about watering annual flowers and focus on permanent plantings. Drought resistant annuals will survive a dry summer if they are given sufficient moisture during the first three weeks after planting. A small cupful of water a day poured around each annual or perennial transplant is enough to get them established and is more effective than a light sprinkling over the whole area.

Established perennial flowers can survive a dry summer if they are watered deeply every ten to fourteen days, although they may not flower very well. Thorough weeding and mulching will also help to conserve nutrients and moisture. If possible, water perennials in the weeks before flowering and

### Preventive Measure

A long-term approach to dealing with water shortages is to select drought-resistant plants. These will have either greyish or silvery foliage; waxy leaves; thick, fleshy leaves; or very narrow leaves. Avoid flowering plants with thin, yellow-green foliage because they tend to require large quantities of water, or group them together along with other moisture loving plants (see pages 355-356) to make watering more efficient. Try to plant moisture lovers in moist soil and shade, and aim for a complete plant canopy to reduce evaporation from exposed soil.

during flowering, then limit the quantity of water. Irises thrive under this regime and seem to prefer hot, dry summers. Other perennials, such as delphiniums, will sometimes die out completely if water is limited.

Some plants cope with a summer drought by going dormant. Bleeding heart goes dormant only in dry years whereas some plants, such as Jacob's ladder, shooting star, Oriental poppy and bluebells, do so nearly every year.

## Diseases and Pests

Crop rotation and cultural management will prevent most plant diseases. Water the ground, not the plants, to reduce the incidence of various leaf diseases. Wet foliage increases the incidence of mildew, rust and anthracnose, particularly among plants grown in crowded conditions with little air circulation and poor soil drainage. Remember to thin annuals (check seed packages for final spacing distances). Moulds and mildews usually start at the bottom of the plant and move upwards. William and Mary (pulmonaria), hollyhocks, phlox, snapdragons and begonias, among others, are quite susceptible.

Immediately remove and destroy affected leaves; remove entire plants and the surrounding soil if the disease is severe. When replanting in the autumn or next spring, improve fertility and drainage by incorporating organic matter and perhaps creating a raised bed. Spacing plants further apart and moving them to sunnier areas sometimes helps, particularly if they can be placed where the morning sun will dry off their leaves. Dusting with wettable sulphur every week before an attack occurs, especially after a period of rain, will help to reduce the incidence. Spraying with baking powder solution (see page 190) also works as a preventive measure in some situations. Avoid Bordeaux mixture and other copper fungicides because they may discolour flowers and foliage.

Suspect bacterial or fungal crown rot if no new shoots appear in the spring. Roots will be black, rotten, and possibly covered with white fungal threads. If poor drainage is the cause, dig in organic matter and raise the level of the soil. Avoid damaging the crowns when working among plants because wounds act as entry points for disease organisms, and plant perennials at the correct depth (see Green Thumb Tip, page 135).

Many of the insects that trouble vegetables also trouble flowers, and the methods of managing them are much the same. Nematodes leave plants stunted with small, yellowed or bronzed leaves and cysts on poorly developed, partially decayed roots. Preventive measures include: working organic matter into the soil; locating flowers in different positions each year; and destroying weeds belonging to the mustard family, such as shepherd's purse.

It is probably unreasonable to put cutworm collars around every transplant or to sprinkle wood ashes and lime (see page 123 and Table MAY-2, page 169), but a thorough tilling of the soil before planting will turn up many of the pests which can then be destroyed by hand or by birds. Cutworms produce more than one generation per year; the adults emerge as night flying moths sometime in July or August to produce another round of the damaging larval stage a few weeks later. Fortunately, plants are most at risk only during their first week or two, which for most plants is in the spring.

Beetles that chew holes in leaves are usually not severe and can be managed by handpicking. Leafrollers do little damage, but the rolled leaves that contain them can be removed to keep their numbers down.

Leaves attacked by aphids are puckered and curled.

Aphids suck out plant juices and may cause puckering or distortion in young shoots. You may not notice them until you see ants on the plant. Ants do not harm the plant directly but they do nurture the aphids for their honeydew. Hover flies, lady bird beetles and their larvae, wasps, lacewings and many other insects are effective predators, given a chance. Chickadees, purple finches and warblers also eat aphids. If waiting for nature to take its course is intolerable, remove aphids from very young plants (which are less able to withstand damage) by wiping them off, washing them off with strong blasts of water every other morning for a week (but be careful not to knock over plants such as delphiniums); or spraying with insecticidal soap (see page 194) every two or three days until the aphids are gone. Unfortunately, reducing aphid numbers will limit the buildup of predator populations, so the problem will probably be worse next year.

Ants are actually beneficial in the garden as they aerate the soil—they do not harm peonies or other flowers. They tend to be more numerous in dry soil which is low in organic matter. If the population size becomes distressing and threatens to take over the house, a mixture of borax and icing sugar, placed away from where other creatures can reach it, will reduce their numbers. A gentler method is to scatter freshly cut citrus peels where ants tend to enter the house. Do not use diatomaceous earth because if cats get any on their paws it may get in their eyes and damage the surface of their eyes. A strong dose of manure tea (see page 163) or tansy extract (see page 170) poured on the ant hill may persuade them to move. For next year, put up nest boxes for flickers, which love to eat ants (see Setting Up Bird Houses, pages 322-323).

Slugs find quackgrass unnerving.

Hot, dry weather encourages red spider mites, which turn leaves a stippled yellow. Mist plants to keep the leaves damp and cool and mulch to keep the soil moist. Wash off webs carefully every week.

Quackgrass is one of the world's ten worst weeds. Take heart, though, because dead quackgrass releases a chemical that acts as a nerve poison for slugs. Dig up the weeds, cut the roots away from the tops and put them in the garbage rather than the compost, and use the tops as mulch for slug infested areas. Hunting for slugs at night with a flashlight in the spring is also an effective way to reduce their numbers before they become a devouring horde—robins will eat their share as well. Other methods include putting barriers of sand, crushed eggshells, ashes or lime around plants, and setting out traps of boards, or lettuce or brassica leaves. Check underneath each morning for hidden slugs. Next year, try putting vulnerable plants into hanging baskets or window boxes to thwart the slugs.

## Weeds and Mulch

Perennial weeds such as quackgrass need to be dug out and every scrap of root removed, but annual weeds can be pulled by hand when the soil is moist. Leave them lying in the flower bed unless they have gone to seed. Some may reroot in damp soil, but most will quickly break down—this is a direct way to add compost.

Be sure to pull weeds before they go to seed. There are thousands of annual weed seeds in soil, some of which remain viable for decades. Regular cultivation will reduce them by about 50% each year. After seven years, only 1% of the original reserve is left, which accounts for the old saying, "one year's seeding is seven year's weeding."

Velvet leaf is a widespread weed in central North America, and it is making an appearance along the east coast. The plant is an annual and has large, velvety, valentine-shaped leaves as large as 6 inches (15 cm) across. It has small yellow to yellow-orange flowers about the size of a dime and green seed pods that turn black on maturity. As with most annual weeds, the best control is faithful pulling or hoing before any seeds are set.

Persistence is needed when digging out invasive weeds. To deal with severe infestations of perennial weeds such as goutweed, Japanese knotweed and poison ivy, smother the area using tar paper, black plastic, cardboard or other light eliminating substances.

Poison ivy rarely spreads to the point of becoming a problem in the garden as it usually restricts itself to open woods and damp roadsides. Do not burn poison ivy; the oils that irritate the skin can also irritate the eyes, nose and throat when released into the air.

If weeds are very deep rooted or, despite much digging, the battle is being lost, chemical control may be necessary. When weeds have well developed shoots and are actively growing with plenty of foliage, brush them with a herbicide containing the active ingredient glyphosate. Glyphosate is less toxic than other herbicides and is less likely to cause environmental problems. The leaves should be dry, with no rain predicted for at least six hours. Glyphosate is non-selective and will kill any plant it touches, so brushing it onto the growing tips of plants is better than spraying. When it touches the soil, it breaks down and becomes inactive. Allow at least a week for the glyphosate to be translocated to the roots and rhizomes. The chemical acts slowly by interfering with the plant's hormone system, so it may take several weeks before some weeds finally die.

After weeding, mulch flower beds with organic matter as in the vegetable garden. Mulch itself helps to reduce insect problems because of the predatory spiders that thrive and multiply in it.

As the compost pile builds up with weeds and kitchen debris, it should be working away. Bags of dry leaves saved from last autumn can be sprinkled into the pile. Turn it regularly with a pitch fork to mix and chop the ingredients and add air; finished compost will be ready by midsummer for top-dressing flowers and vegetables. If you leave the pile alone, you will have finished compost next spring, but crude, unfinished compost will be available by the autumn for working into the soil in new or renewed planting beds. Composting is one of the healthiest things to do for a garden, and it has the added advantage of reducing the amount of garbage destined for landfill sites.

### Failure to Bloom

The pleasure that flowers bring is what spurs many gardeners to take painstaking care of their flowering plants. Failure to bloom is perhaps the most frustrating problem a gardener can face because there are so many possible causes to consider.

Suspect thrips if flower buds die without opening, if petals are distorted, or if there are irregular whitish streaks on petals. This can happen to daylilies, hollyhocks, gladiolus, irises, peonies, tuberous begonias, dahlias and peonies. Take action four weeks after the last frost by hanging boards painted yellow and smeared with Tanglefoot near the affected plants. These

#### Preventive Measure

One "weed" that should be removed is purple loosestrife, or lythrum. It is planted by some gardeners as an ornamental flower, but it escapes readily to neighbouring waterways and makes them unsuitable for muskrats, beavers, ducks and other shorebirds by choking out bullrushes,

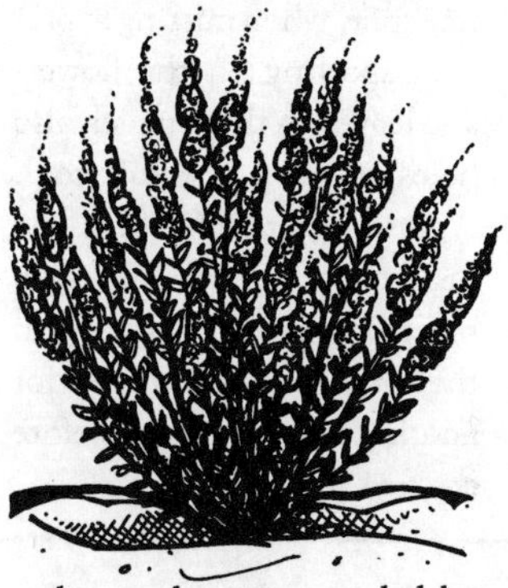

sedges and grasses needed by the animals. Only one little seed from your garden is needed to establish lythrum in a local pond. Even the supposedly sterile forms are harmful. Dig out plants before they go to seed as the seed may well survive in compost piles and garbage bins. Consider tall forms of veronica or gayfeather (liatris) as substitutes.

will trap thrips, which are only 1/25 inch (1 mm) long. As soon as you see the insects, spray susceptible flowers with insecticidal soap (see page 194) every three days for two weeks. Cut out any affected flowers and dip them in the soap to destroy the thrips.

Thrips may be worse in years when plants are water stressed, but lack of water can also cause buds to drop without opening, as happens with begonias. Too much water can cause the same thing, as can sudden temperature fluctuations from hot to cold or vice versa. Sometimes the first flowers to open on begonias are single, with only one row of petals. Removing them may encourage more flowers to appear, most of which will be double (with several rows of petals).

Roses that ball up and fail to open completely are reacting to cool nights or damp, cloudy days. In foggy areas, choose roses with fewer petals. If conditions are really dry, rose buds will dry up and turn brown without opening at all. Bud blast, a similar condition in peonies, is caused by drought, low temperatures in early spring when buds are forming, insufficient light, and a shortage of potassium in the soil. Insufficient potassium also causes weak stems. Rectify deficiencies by adding liquid or chopped seaweed, kelp meal, chopped banana peels, green plant residues or wood ashes two weeks before planting time. Fishmeal and bonemeal will also help flowering as they add phosphorous to the soil.

There are other conditions under which plants fail to bloom. Crowded plants with dying centres need to be divided and replanted in the appropriate season, and peonies more than ten to fifteen years old need dividing if the stems are very crowded and bloom is reduced. Peonies, roses, and others grown in too much shade will fail to bloom; many need a minimum of five to six hours of direct sunlight each day. Peony crowns planted more than 1 to 2 inches (2.5 to 5 cm) below the soil surface, or with fewer than five "eyes," will fail to bloom. Buds that turn brown and become covered with a gray mold have a flower blight and should be promptly removed. You may want to spray the remaining buds with a copper fungicide every ten days starting when the buds are formed.

Geraniums, strawflowers, clarkia, candytuft, nemesia, godetia and nasturtiums may fail to bloom if they are allowed to grow too vigourously, or if they are given too much nitrogen. Avoid planting these next to lawns, which are often over fertilized, and keep geraniums slightly pot-bound.

Annuals that were planted too late may not have enough time to flower before the first frost. All annual flowers should be seeded or transplanted by

### Green Thumb Tip

Hot, dry summers are particularly hard on some annuals. As a rough guideline, those annuals that are seeded or transplanted during cool weather are the least tolerant of hot summers (see Table FEB-4, page 56). Sensitive plants should be planted where they are shaded during the hottest part of the day, or mist and water them with cool water around noon hour. Use a fine spray when misting to prevent spotting on the flowers and leaves. A thick mulch also helps to keep the soil cool. Annuals that suffer from the heat or get leggy and stop blooming can be cut back in the summer and fertilized for another flush of bloom before the first frost.

the time strawberries, cherries, apple trees and dandelions have finished blooming (see Table FEB-4, page 56). A late spring frost after this date is rare (see Frost Prediction, pages 331-334). Transplants that are in flower when set outside suffer significant transplant shock and may take some time to start flowering again. Double zinnias show their stress by producing single flowers. Bullheaded flowers, where one flower grows out of another, is caused by cold temperatures and a genetic predisposition—it is not uncommon in cultivated roses.

Some diseases will cause bloom failure. Aster yellows occurs in more than asters and shows up as greenish yellow leaves and flowers, no matter what the true flower colour is. Stems proliferate and the plants take on a twiggy appearance. Immediately remove and destroy affected plants. Spray susceptible plants with insecticidal soap (see page 194) mixed with a tablespoon (15 ml) of isopropyl alcohol per quart (1.1 l) of solution to control the leafhoppers that spread the disease. An easier solution is to grow different flowers!

Roses will sometimes grow a different coloured flower. This is usually due to suckers from the rootstock taking over from the budded stock. There is no set rule regarding the number of leaflets which indicate a sucker, but the leaves of a sucker are usually different from those of the upper, budded stock. Cut out the suckers and, in the autumn or spring, dig up the plant and replant it so that at least 4 inches (10 cm) of soil cover the crown. Roses may also mutate in colour, particularly those with a complex breeding history.

A sharp knife is a must for cut flowers.

## *Cut Flowers*

Cutting flowers and bringing them into the house or giving them away is a delight and is quite easy to do. As a general rule, cut flowers in the morning when plants are most turgid, or else in late evening. Aim for long stems and cut them with a sharp knife at an angle, then immediately set them almost up to their heads in tepid water in a deep jug or pail (do not worry about leaves below the water line). This helps to reduce the shock of a sudden temperature change when flowers are brought indoors. Flowers should be conditioned all day or overnight in a cool, dark place.

Cut some single flowers which are still in bud, some which are partly open, and others which are fully open. Flowers with several buds per stem may be cut when just one or two are open, or when the first half are open. Many of the flowers in the following list will not be in bloom for another month or two, but the groupings may help you decide at what stage to cut certain kinds of flowers.

**Single flowers**

Loose, coloured bud, or just as flower opens:

| | |
|---|---|
| bulbous and rhizomatous iris | daffodil |
| calla | poppy |

Flower three-quarters open:

| | | |
|---|---|---|
| aster | centaurea | petunia |
| calendula | globeflower | salpiglossis |
| carnation | marigold | scabiosa |

Flower fully open:

| | | |
|---|---|---|
| dahlia | marguerite | sunflower |
| daisy | pansy | violet |
| gerbera | rudbeckia | zinnia |

Cut daisies and others that have a central disc when the petals are fully spread but the central flowers are still tightly closed.

**Clusters**

ageratum - when some buds are half open
azalea - several in cluster open
geranium - half of the flowers in a cluster open
heliotrope - half of the cluster open
mignonette - one-quarter of the flowers open
primrose - more than half the cluster open
verbena - outside two or three rows open
wallflower - nearly all open; does not last well

**Spikes**

bleeding heart - half the flowers open
campanula - half the flowers open
canna - first few flowers open
clarkia - three to four flowers open
gladiolus - first flower open
larkspur - one-quarter of flowers open
lily-of-the-valley - one-quarter of flowers open
lupine - half of flowers open
salvia - half of flowers open
ten-week-stock - one-quarter of flowers open

### Preventive Measure

Be sure to use clean vases, scrubbed well and rinsed with a bleach solution, and new florists' foam. Bacteria from used foams may shorten the life of cut flowers, but used, dried foams are fine for dried flower arrangements. After conditioning, keep the arrangement of flowers and leaves away from drafts and out of strong sunlight to reduce dehydration.

**Multiple flowers or sprays**

One half of flowers on one stem open.

baby's breath
candytuft *(Iberis)*
Chinese forget-me-not *(Cynoglossum)*
columbine
feverfew
forget-me-not (*Gypsophila)*

**Other flowers good for cutting**

| | | |
|---|---|---|
| amaranthus | gaillardia | nicotiana |
| bells-of-Ireland | gazania | schizanthus |
| celosia | globe amaranth | snapdragon |
| cleome | godetia | strawflower |
| cosmos | hollyhock | sweet pea |
| dimorphotheca | lisianthus | sweet william |
| doronicum | marvel-of-Peru | vinca *(V. rosea)* |

Cut flowers that also have a sweet perfume include mignonette, nicotiana, stocks and sweet peas.

Check the blossoms for hidden insects; immersing the flower heads in water for a few minutes will often dislodge hard to reach insects. Some flowers, such as roses, violets, rhododendrons, peonies and lilies, can be totally immersed in water for several hours to crispen the blossoms.

Tip hollow stemmed flowers such as lupines upside down, fill the stems with water, then plug the ends with cotton batting before conditioning them in deep water.

Cut off, rather than tear off, leaves that will be below the water line in the final arrangement, and do not dethorn roses. Each wound provides opportunities for the growth of micro-organisms that cause vascular blockage and, consequently, wilting.

Recut the ends, except for those that have been seared, when arranging the flowers and add cut flower food to the water. Cut flower food is better than adding bleach and colourless pop to the water, although a few drops of bleach help some flowers last a few days longer. Two ounces (65 ml) of Listerine per gallon (4.5 l) of water used for roses will help prevent the drooping caused by bacterial growth that blocks the water conducting columns. If roses do develop drooping heads, cut off 1 inch (2.5 cm) of each

### Green Thumb Tip

Stems that secrete a milky substance should have their ends seared with boiling water or an open flame. Cut 1 inch (2.5 cm) off the end of a stem, and put the end in an open flame for ten seconds. Some people carry a candle to the garden to do this immediately after the stems are cut. Alternatively, cut a hole in a piece of cardboard and insert the freshly cut stem through it; place the bottom inch (2.5 cm) of the stem in boiling water for thirty to sixty seconds. The cardboard shield prevents steam from reaching the leaves and flowers. Resear the stems if the ends are recut.

stem and sear the ends in boiling water for one minute. There is some evidence that fluoridated water shortens the life of cut flowers, so some arrangers prefer to stand them in distilled or rain water.

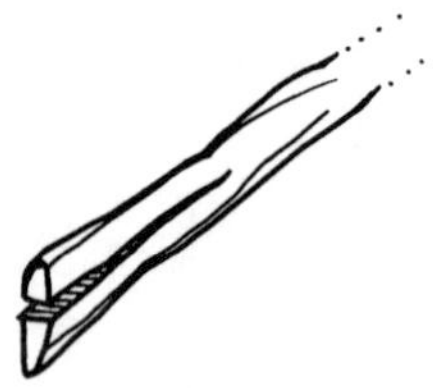

Cut diagonally and split the ends of woody stems to increase water intake for cut flowers.

Foliage alone can be very attractive, or include some with flowers. Woody stems are often cut diagonally to increase the surface area available for taking up water. This can be achieved by splitting the ends of the stems for 2 or 3 inches (5 to 8 cm), either by slicing upwards with a sharp knife or by pounding lightly with a hammer. The aim is to separate the fibres somewhat, not mash the wood.

## Fruiting Plants and Woody Ornamentals

### Watering and Symptoms of Drought

It is important to water newly planted trees and shrubs. They will not immediately show water stress—particularly evergreens—and so are easily forgotten. A deep soaking once a week for the first month, and once every week or two thereafter, is essential. Giving plants a sprinkling every day is useless. Instead, lay the end of a hose on a wooden shingle or board and let it run until the water around the tree puddles. Keep a 4 foot (1.2 m) diameter circle around each tree and shrub, or at least a circle a little larger than the diameter of the drip line, clear of grass and weeds and mulch well to keep the soil moist.

**Green Thumb Tip**

Trees near the street may benefit from having annuals rather than a mulch at their base. The flowers will remind you to water the tree, which needs 10 to 14 gallons (44 to 62 l) per week; discourage foot traffic that results in soil compaction; and remind dog owners to keep their pets from relieving themselves over the tree roots.

A steady, even supply of moisture is crucial for fruiting trees and shrubs to produce a good yield of fruit and to prevent fruits from aborting (dropping off). Apple trees and other large fruits go through a natural thinning process about this time, but excessive dryness may cause too many fruits to drop. If water is limited, water from the time plants flower until fruiting is finished.

If trees do not seem to be benefitting from watering and show dry leaf edges and wilting, the roots might not be growing out properly from the original root ball. Container grown plants are prone to root circling, and may have to be dug up. Sever the compacted root ball on the outside with several vertical cuts, or use a cultivating claw to loosen pot-bound roots. This removes the circling roots and stimulates new roots that will grow into the surrounding soil.

Trees and shrubs may exhibit signs of water shortage if the roots have been damaged in any way, such as if they have been cut during construction or driveway installation, suffocated by being covered with more than 4 inches (10 cm) of soil, or had construction materials piled on them (see pages 320-

321). It may take several years for plants to show that they have been damaged. The first sign of root problems is premature fall colouration and dieback in the uppermost branches; this progresses down the tree in successive years.

Excessive dryness can damage root systems and weaken many trees and shrubs, making them more susceptible to insect attack. The real danger, however, is that a severe winter could completely kill the plant. Sometimes branches start to leaf out normally, then suddenly stop growing. This is almost certainly a sign of some form of root damage which may have been caused by drought, waterlogged soils, winter kill, or soil being added over the root system or compacted in some way.

Bark damage, such as that caused by grass trimmers, clotheslines, guy wires or boring insects, can also cause signs of drought if the tree is so damaged that adequate amounts of water do not move upwards. Less severe damage is exhibited by changes in leaf colour, heavy seed set and smaller leaf size than normal.

## Pest Resistance and Remedies

There is no doubt that healthy plants are better able to withstand pests than unhealthy plants. Drought, soil compaction, defoliation, insufficient nutrients, and other stresses cause low levels of root starch to be stored in the tree over the winter; this results in reduced vigour in the spring and early summer and makes plants more susceptible to attack by borers—the most difficult tree pests to deal with—and other insects. Most of our garden tree and shrub pests are opportunists that exploit trees already weakened by their environment (and the lack of care we give them). Non-native plants are further stressed by our climate, so choosing native plants makes sense from a pest management point of view.

Failure to grow and overall poor health can often be attributed to competition from weeds and grass, and to lack of top dressing with manure or compost in the spring. Some plants, such as magnolias and ashes, will grow very little for the first year or two while their roots are getting established.

To keep trees and shrubs healthier, mulch generously with compost, pine needles, seaweed, straw, hay, shredded bark or other organic material (except peat moss). Mulching helps to maintain an even moisture level, and dryish mulches such as straw help to keep the fruits of strawberries clean and free of mould.

Insect pests fall into several categories. Sucking insects, such as scales and aphids, can be wiped or washed off. For severe scale infestations, spray with

### Preventive Measure

It is a good idea to have a wildflower meadow or a collection of native plants to broaden the variety of insects in the garden, particularly near fruiting plants. A wide variety of insects reduces the possibility of one becoming a pest—they keep each other in check. Start by collecting seeds through the summer from plants in neighbouring fields (see page 307). Sow them while they are still fresh in a prepared seedbed outdoors, or store them in a cool, dry place and plant them indoors in the winter (see Table AUG-4, page 308).

## Green Thumb Tip

There is some evidence that plants respond to insect attacks with chemical changes that discourage the insects; however, there is often no need to respond at all to insect attacks as established trees and shrubs can readily tolerate 10 to 15% damage to their canopies, provided they have good growing conditions. It is usually gardeners who are distressed by insect damage, not healthy trees and shrubs.

Any trees or shrubs that have been hit by diseases or insects can be helped to recover in several ways. During dry periods, water woody plants with 1 gallon (4.5 l) of water for every square foot (900 cm$^2$) of soil under the leaf canopy. Continue watering every two weeks until the plant's new leaves are fully expanded.

During the growing season, fertilize trees and shrubs with a readily available source of nitrogen, such as manure tea, seaweed extract or fish fertilizer. Spraying a foliar fertilizer on the young leaves also helps. Spray the first time when the leaves are about half their mature size, and once or twice more. In the spring, spread a 1 to 2 inch (2.5 to 5 cm) layer of rotted manure or compost over the root zone and apply a mulch of leaves or shredded bark.

a mixture of 1/2 cup (125 ml) of isopropyl alcohol to every quart (1.1 litre) of insecticidal soap every three days for two weeks. Chewing insects, most of which are caterpillars, can be controlled by spraying with Bt (*Bacillus thuringiensis*) as soon as they are noticed, and every five to seven days until they are gone. A better method for some caterpillars is to renew Tanglefoot on banded trees late this month or early next month (see March/April page 106). Rasping insects, such as spider mites and gall mites, rarely cause severe problems. Severe cases of leaf and needle miners can be controlled by spraying with insecticidal soap when trees first leaf out. This will reduce the adult population before many eggs are laid.

Borers can be killed by inserting wires into their holes, or more easily by woodpeckers. Woodpeckers, except for sapsuckers, are helpful rather than harmful to trees as they only pay attention to those trees that already host insects. Keep the bases of trees free of weeds and grass so that other birds can help control the beetles (adult borers). Some borers are controlled by pruning (see page 196) and others can be prevented from laying eggs by applying a physical barrier in the spring (see page 106). Examine raspberries for cane borer and remove them by cutting off the affected tips. The damage caused by leafrolling caterpillars is quite harmless and merely makes the tree a little unsightly.

Eliminating the insects that devastate a plant can be quite a challenge for home gardeners. Currant sawfly larvae begin their attack on gooseberry and red currant bushes usually early in June. The first signs are not obvious, but a close inspection of the leaves towards the bottom of the bush will reveal holes and perhaps some black frass. Since these are sawfly larvae, not caterpillars (see May, page 182), they are not susceptible to the disease bacterium in Bt sprays and must be handpicked.

There are two approaches to take with the black vine weevils which eat rhododendron leaves. One is to spread Tanglefoot on the stems near the ground to capture the weevils as they climb the stems each night. They spend the day in litter under the plant. The other is to spread a drop sheet on the ground and gently beat the bush; take into account that many species of weevil play dead when disturbed.

## Pruning

Many shrubs are not pruned until after they have bloomed because they produce flowers on wood that grew last year. If they were pruned during dormancy, flower buds would be cut off and it would be too late for new ones to grow. It is not necessary to cut off the faded blooms of lilacs and rhododendrons. Leaving them on does not reduce flowering the following year, and cutting them off may cause unnecessary damage to buds and new young growth.

Newly planted fruit trees should have good shoot growth by now. Select one strong terminal shoot as the central leader and remove those (usually only one) that are competing with it. Shoots in the top portion of young trees can have the tips pinched out to slow them down and allow the lower shoots to catch up. Young shoots left on to form the lateral branches should have narrow crotch angles corrected; use clothespins or toothpicks to increase the angle to between 45 and 60°. With espaliers, fans and cordons, remove only the unwanted shoots and tie the remaining ones into the desired positions (and see July, pages 272-274).

Narrow crotch angles can be corrected with the help of a clothespin.

Rhododendrons and azaleas can be pruned after they have bloomed, if a little reshaping is necessary. To encourage sideways growth, cut back stems to branches that are growing outwards in the direction desired. Formal hedges can be given their second pruning in mid June.

Peaches and apricots produce most of their fruit on the previous summer's growth, so it is important to encourage a steady supply of new shoots each year on established, fully grown trees. Soon after new growth begins, look at the base of last year's shoots. There are usually two or more new shoots just beginning to grow. Allow one to continue growing and pinch the other one back to one leaf. About half way up the shoot, allow another new shoot to continue growing. This acts as a replacement shoot if the first one dies or fails to grow well. All other new shoots are pinched or cut back to one leaf. In the autumn, immediately after the fruits have been picked, cut back the shoot that just fruited to the replacement branch that grew during the current season.

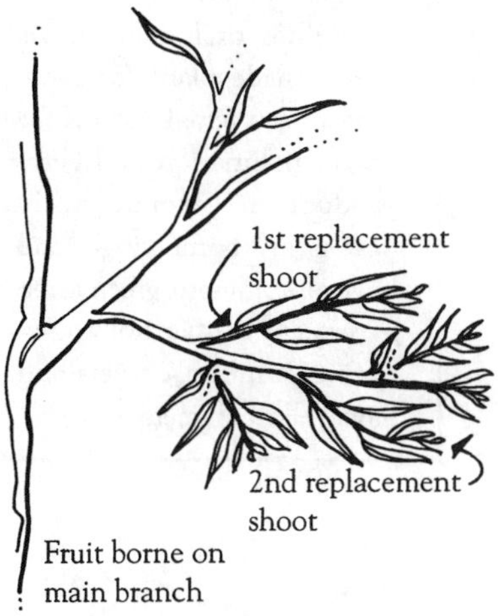


All other shoots pinched back to one leaf.

## Encouraging Flowers and Fruit

It is discouraging when trees and shrubs fail to bloom, but often time is all that is needed. Some flowering trees and shrubs, including fruit trees, may just be too young—they need time to mature before they attempt to bloom and set fruit. You can assist this process by not adding too much nitrogen fertilizer to the soil.

Very often, newly purchased plants will bloom the same year but fail in subsequent years. The reason is that many woody plants form buds the year before flowering. When first planted in a garden, they bloom from buds already formed at purchase time, but then put all their energies into growing roots and getting established. After one or more years, when plants are growing well, they will again put energy into forming flower buds. Woody plants may also fail to bloom if the previous summer was dry and few if any buds were inititated.

Too much shade also reduces the amount of bloom. Sometimes a flowering shrub does well initially but in time is shaded by neighbouring trees. In this case, move the shrub to a sunnier position or prune the trees. Either remove the lower limbs or have the crowns of the trees thinned, or both.

The wrong pH, poor drainage, root damage, planting too deeply and piling extra soil over a plant's root system can cause failure to bloom. Often a plant's flower buds are its least hardy part. If a winter has been very severe, or if cold temperatures have developed after flower buds start to swell, blooming may not occur that year.

Young trees may be bearing their first crop this year. If there is little fruit, the trees may have not yet reached the level of maturity needed to bear plentiful fruit. If a bountiful crop is produced, there is often a natural dropping of fruits about this time, but a little more thinning may be required. It is important to balance vegetative growth with fruit production. If the leader or major branches are bent over from a heavy crop, vegetative growth is reduced. On young trees, all of the fruit on the outer third of the canopy should be removed.

Fruit clusters on apple trees should be thinned a couple of weeks after blooming is over, when fruits are about 1/2 inch (1.2 cm) in diameter. Remove small, deformed, damaged, blemished and insect-injured apples. Excess apples on established trees are then thinned for a final spacing of one or two per cluster spaced 4 to 6 inches (10 to 15 cm) apart on a branch, or closer on spur types. If clusters are widely spaced, leave two or three fruits per cluster. Pears are thinned to one fruit per cluster, or two fruits per cluster if there is good leaf cover, and plums are thinned to 2 to 3 inches (5 to 8 cm) apart along the branches. Apricots are best thinned in two stages. When they are about 1/2 inch (1.2 cm) in diameter, thin them to one per inch (2.5 cm), removing small, misshapen and badly spaced fruits. When the apricots are almost an inch (2.5 cm) in diameter, thin them to one every 2 to 3 inches (5 to 8 cm) along the branch. Peaches, too, are thinned in two stages; once when they are 3/4 inch (2 cm) in diameter, to 4 ½ inches (11 cm) apart, and again when they are 1 ½ inches (4 cm) in diameter, to 9 inches (23 cm) apart.

### Green Thumb Tip

If plenty of flowers bloomed but none were pollinated, the causes could be chilly temperatures during blossom time, a late frost, a low bee population (see page 187), birds that eat flower buds and blossoms, rain, strong winds or the absence of a nearby pollinating tree. Many fruits, including blueberries, need a good bee population for proper pollination. Avoid using insecticides during flowering, including "organic" ones, as they may kill bees. If there is no choice but to spray for a specific insect problem, do it in the evening after the bees have settled for the night. Even with a large bee population, inclement weather may keep them at home during the critical blossom time.

Hollies and hardy kiwis need a male plant for every nine to ten female plants for proper pollination and berry production. Female holly flowers are borne singly and have a prominent green knob in the centre. Male holly flowers are borne in clusters and have yellow stamens.

Remember to pick up dropped fruits. They may harbour fruit insect pests which will soon leave the fruit and burrow into the soil, thereby continuing their life cycle. Fruits so affected may have pin holes in the skin, where the egg was deposited.

Thinning grapes will help to hasten their maturation in the autumn. This is particularly important in short season areas. Whole clusters should also have been thinned before blooming, as soon as the flower clusters appeared (see May, page 187). Within each cluster, remove abnormally small, misshapen, diseased and blemished berries. In long season areas, where grapes have adequate time to ripen, this sort of thinning is not required, particularly for grapes destined for juice and jelly. You may want to thin those to be eaten fresh, however, to improve their size and appearance.

## Other Care

Fireblight is a bacterial disease in apples, pears and hawthorns that causes branch tips to wilt and then progresses downwards. It shows up several weeks after the plant comes into bloom and it may be July before the disease is evident. The bark becomes soft and brown, then turns dry and black, and the branch hardens in a hook shape. A bacterial ooze develops on branches, petioles, leaves or fruits which first looks like a milky droplet, then turns brown and hard. Leaves turn black and hang down, looking as if they have been scorched by fire. The disease is exacerbated by succulent growth caused by too much nitrogen or too heavy pruning and often shows up in watersprouts, suckers and twigs. The disease can spread quickly in warm, humid weather.

Control fireblight by immediately pruning out affected branches 12 inches (30 cm) below the diseased area, when the weather is dry, and dip pruning clippers after each cut in 1 part Lysol to 40 parts water. Burn or bury the prunings or dispose of them in the garbage, but do not compost them. If the infestation is severe, remove the entire plant.

If there has been severe trouble in previous years with such diseases as leaf blight, scab, rust, black spot and powdery mildew, continue spraying once a week with baking soda spray (see page 190) or every week or two with sulphur, depending on how often it rains. Continue the spray program until the terminal buds are set. A total of three sprayings is usually sufficient if using lime sulphur (when trees first leaf out, immediately after flowering, and again a couple of weeks later). In warm, wet summers additional sprayings may be needed. Leaf blights on willows are particularly difficult to control, and the wisest course of action may be to remove the plant entirely.

Mock orange, forsythia and other shrubs sometimes show dieback of one or more branches for no apparent reason. It is usually caused by fungal infections, controlled by cutting out and destroying the affected branches and by spraying with Bordeaux mixture.

## Propagation

### Softwood cuttings and seeds

As with flowers and herbs, many trees and shrubs can be propagated from softwood cuttings (see Table JUL-4, page 282). The procedure is similar and the need for warmth and a moist environment is just as essential. Blueberries, and anything that seems to rot rather than root, is better started in a mixture of one part peat moss to three parts sand or perlite. Short side shoots that are not flowering make the best cuttings. Cut off pieces 3 to 5 inches (8 to 12 cm) long and then use a sharp razor blade to make a clean cut just below the lowest leaf node. Finished cuttings, with the lowest leaves removed, should be 2 to 4 inches (5 to 10 cm) long. On clematis cuttings, remove the stem that is twining. Hollow stemmed plants seem to root better if a piece of heel (a sliver of old wood) is included at the base of the cutting.

Dip the base in rooting hormone immediately after the cut is made and place the cutting carefully in a hole made in the rooting medium. Two-thirds of each cutting should be buried. A propagation unit is ideal for providing bottom heat and mist (see pages 442-443). A cold frame outdoors in a shady location or on the north side of a building will sometimes work, provided the soil is warm, but it is not as effective. Other methods of maintaining humidity over cuttings indoors are an upturned glass jar, a plastic bag tied over each pot, or a box covered in clear polythene supported by wire coat hangers. The coat hangers should be bent so that the top is flat rather than curved, if curved, condensation drips down onto the surface of the rooting medium rather than running down the sides of the polythene.

Cuttings usually root within ten to thirty days, but may take considerably longer. As soon as the cuttings have rooted, whether started indoors or out, gradually expose them to drier air and outside temperatures, and then transplant them to a nursery bed or individual pots. A lath structure over the young cuttings will keep them semi-shaded and reduce their demand for water. Keep a close eye on them until they are well established by watering and weeding as necessary, and protect them over the winter (see pages 397-398). Plants started from cuttings last year should be planted out early so that they have all summer to establish good root growth (see page 199).

Pieris and other ericaceous plants will soon produce fresh seeds. Break the seed pods open when they have turned brown and dryish. Plant them as you would any seeds (see page 50), using a fine dusting of peat moss to cover them. Continue to collect the seeds of other woody plants through the summer as they become ripe, either planting them immediately, storing them in cool, dry conditions, or stratifying them.

## Care of Bird Houses

As soon as young birds have left their bird house nests, the houses should be cleaned out completely. There is always a chance that it will be used again, either by the same pair of birds or by another pair, but not if it has a dirty, used nest in it. It is also important to get rid of parasites. Assuming that the side of the bird house is hinged (see page 444), undo the latch and clean out all of the nesting materials and any other debris. You may want to scrub out the interior and spray or fumigate it against parasites.

If there are any dead chicks or unhatched eggs, it is better to immediately close up the box again. There is a strong chance that the parents will try again in the same bird house and they will do the cleaning up themselves. Do not, under any circumstances, open or peek into the house while there are incubating eggs or young birds inside. The parents are almost certain to abandon them if that happens.

## Indoor Gardening

Ventilation to prevent overheating and almost constant watering are needed in the summer greenhouse. Provide light shading from June 1 to September 15 with either a cheesecloth or gauze curtain or by painting shading compound on the exterior. Mist the whole greenhouse a couple of times during the warmest part of the day, if possible, to keep down the population of red spider mites and to keep plants cool.

### Vegetables and Herbs

Most gardeners prefer to put all their energy into the outdoor garden at this time, but some vegetables can be started indoors this month for autumn and winter harvests. Eggplants, peppers and tomatoes can be seeded now, or you can dig up the eggplant and pepper plants growing in the garden in late summer and bring them indoors. This is easiest if they have been grown as pot plants. Most tomato plants are too big to dig up successfully, but they can be started from cuttings next month to avoid seeding them now.

Herbs and cool season crops such as leeks and celery can be dug quite late in the autumn and brought indoors to continue the harvest. Again, this avoids starting them from seed and nursing them during the summer when there is so much else to do.

Herbs can be brought indoors for continued harvest in the winter months. They make attractive as well as practical centerpieces.

### *Warm Flowers*

Lilies that have finished blooming can be planted outdoors. Easter lilies and Madonna lilies are marginally hardy in zone 6, and Asiatic lilies are hardy to zone 3. Trumpets and orientals are a little less hardy—to zone 4, perhaps—and they sometimes die over the winter even in milder zones, particularly where snow cover is unreliable, if the drainage is poor or if they have not been well mulched. All lilies, however, can be kept growing in pots indoors for a number of years, provided they are regularly watered and fertilized and given a three month rest period at some point each year.

Pot up more lilies if desired, such as *L. speciosum,* and tiger lily for Thanksgiving. Divide established gerbera and grow it outdoors through the summer.

Some greenhouse and indoor plants, except those with fuzzy leaves, can be put outdoors in a lightly shaded place for the summer. Amaryllis and other bulbs sometimes seem to bloom better after a few months of fresh air. Expose them to outdoor temperatures gradually, as when hardening off transplants, but do not expose them to full sunshine at midday.

Plants that like moist and humid conditions may be better off indoors, but it depends on what your summers are like. Bulbous plants such as haemanthus, caladium and achimenes should certainly be provided with a little shade during the hottest part of the summer, at least at midday.

### Cool Flowers

There is little sowing to do this month. Pehaps some sweet peas and forget-me-nots could be sown early in the month. Take softwood cuttings of marguerite the same way as for herbs and other softwood cuttings.

Many flowers can be put outdoors. Put primroses into 4 inch (100 mm) pots and use a high potassium fertilizer when the pots are full of roots. Except for marguerite and wallflower, keep plants in light shade, particularly at midday. Be sure to regularly water and fertilize all of the potted plants you move outdoors for the summer.

Month-by-Month

# July

- train espaliers

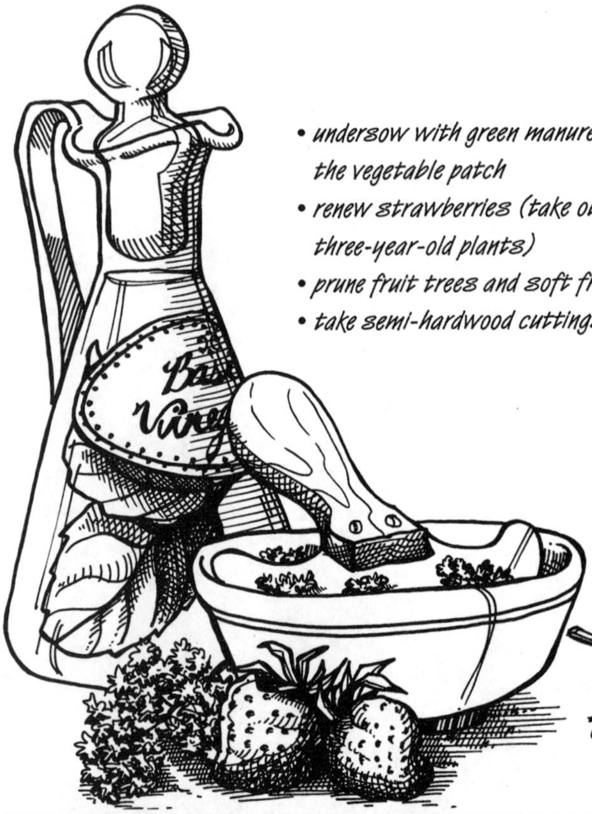

- undersow with green manures in the vegetable patch
- renew strawberries (take out three-year-old plants)
- prune fruit trees and soft fruits
- take semi-hardwood cuttings

- dry/freeze herbs
- make herbal vinegars/butters
- dry flowers
- make potpourri

Much of the heavy work of the gardening season is over and the pleasures of eating ripe strawberries and fresh vegetables, preserving herbs in various ways, and drying flowers for winter bouquets or potpourris take precedence this month. A little summer pruning may be in order among the fruits, but there should be plenty of time left over to enjoy the sights, scents and sounds in the garden.

# July

### *Border*

*Strip of ground that divides the area where the shrubs were from the place where the lawn will be with a neat row of white plastic markers indicating where the flowers would have been.*

*Beard and McKie*

## Vegetables

Remember to keep vegetables watered regularly when they are flowering and the fruits are filling out, but do not water onions after the bulbs start filling out. Mulch heat loving crops well after fruits start appearing (by this time the soil is warm enough), but keep mulch 3 to 4 inches (8 to 10 cm) away from the stems. Plants that run along the ground, such as melons, should have dry mulch placed under the developing fruits to avoid rot.

Heavy feeders, such as corn and Swiss chard, can be mulched with fine compost or watered with manure tea (see Green Thumb Tip, page 163). Swiss chard does not bolt like spinach in the summer and will continue to produce if it is cut off an inch (2.5 cm) above the ground and kept watered and fertilized.

### Summer Harvest and General Care

Early planting, a warm and moist growing season, and regular weeding can result in vegetables in some gardens being ready for picking a month or two earlier than in other gardens. Gardens in the north, where there are more hours of daylight and heat, will often catch up to those planted earlier in the south. But the state of the vegetable itself, rather than the calender, should determine when you start picking.

Garlic, for example, can be harvested when the leaf tops begin to dry and turn a yellowish green (but this is not always a clear indicator during a dry summer). The sheath leaves surrounding the bulb also become thinner when it is time to harvest. Garlic planted last autumn should be ready sometime this month, whereas garlic planted in the spring will probably not be ready until next month. Softneck garlic (see Focus on Plants, page 215) is sometimes ready for harvest two or three weeks before hardneck.

It is important to pick garlic as soon as it is ready so that the new cloves do not have time to grow roots. Leave the tops on, do not wash or separate the cloves, and dry the bulbs in a warm, shady place until the covering is papery.

Garlic braid

To make a garlic braid, start braiding with three plants, then add in more as they can be fitted in and as the original leaves get too short to braid. Overlap the new leaves, starting just above the garlic, with a couple of inches of the old leaves before they run out. Some people start with a piece of twine, make a sliding loop in one end, thread in two garlic plants, and then proceed as above, using the twine as one of the three strands. This strengthens the braid and makes it easy to hang when it is finished.

Alternatively, remove the tops and store the garlic in mesh bags. Whether braided or bagged, garlic keeps best—for up to eight months—when stored at 32°F (0°C) and 70% humidity.

Constant picking is the key to extending the harvest of many vegetables as it prevents plants from setting seed. Pick snap beans every two days before the seeds start swelling. Wait until the morning dew has dried—working among wet plants increases the spread of disease—and use two hands (one to hold the plant and one to pull the beans) to avoid pulling up the whole plant or breaking off branches. If pods are shrivelled at the end, the plants have not been receiving enough moisture. Scarlet runners and other climbing beans will continue to flower and produce beans until cold weather slows them down, but bush beans will stop producing flowers if ripe beans are not being picked.

Wax beans are ready when they are butter yellow. Lima beans are ready when the pods first start to swell and are still green. Few beans in the pod indicates that the plant lacked moisture. Shell young limas before cooking or freezing them, or allow them to grow longer and dry the mature beans for winter use. Immature soy beans, shelled, have a delightful nutty taste when cooked briefly. If they and other shell beans are to be shelled and dried for winter storage, harvest the pods when they start to become dry and brown, late in August or September.

Too much heat will cause blossom drop on beans. If this is a perennial problem, try planting them where they get a bit of shade during the hottest part of the day. Bean plants that rot at the soil line need drier soil; make sure that mulch does not actually touch the stem. If aphids are a severe problem on broad beans, the easiest solution is to cut off the affected tips—this has the added advantage of hastening bean development.

Pick peas every day, using two hands. Failing to hold the plant when pulling on the pods may result in the entire plant coming out of the ground because they are shallow rooted. Cut rather than pull large weeds that are growing amongst the pea vines.

### Preventive Measure

It is very disconcerting to break open lovely pea pods, only to discover worms inside. Try planting earlier in the spring to reduce this problem next year, and pull up and destroy this year's pea vines as soon as the last pod is picked. This will prevent the worms from overwintering in the soil. Burning the vines or putting them in the garbage is better than composting, unless the compost pile gets very hot. Similarly, pull up and destroy mildewed pea plants and those with other fungal diseases as soon as you notice the problem. Mildew does not usually occur until towards the end of the pea season, and the peas are usually harvested before the disease takes hold. Healthy, post-harvest pea vines make an excellent mulch for other crops.

Cut off the central broccoli head below the second pair of leaves beneath the head. Cutting higher slows the development of side shoots, and cutting lower reduces the number of potential side shoots. Immediately cut out any flowering stalks. Only one central head can form, but many side shoots will continue to form until late in the autumn if the plant is not allowed to flower and set seed. Broccoli plants that go to flower very quickly were probably exposed to temperatures that were too cool when they were young.

To get rid of cabbage loopers and worms, soak broccoli in 4 teaspoons (20 ml) of salt per gallon (4.5 l) of cold water for twenty minutes, tap the head against the sink to dislodge the loopers, and then rinse it with clear water. If there are any dark coloured loopers that look unhealthy, leave them alone because they are infested with the larvae of a parasitic wasp.

If there is a heavy rain after a period of dryness and cabbages show signs of splitting, try disrupting the roots so that less water is taken up. This can be done by giving each cabbage plant a slight twist to tear some of the roots; pulling up gently on the plant; or pushing a spade into the ground to sever some roots. After summer cabbages are harvested, cut a cross in the top of the stalk; four small heads may develop.

Use kohlrabi while it is golf ball to tennis ball size. It gets woody and fibrous if allowed to grow too large, or if the soil is dry. Pull beets within ten days after they reach full size as they deteriorate in quality if left in the ground. Sow more beets to extend the harvest.

Harvest cauliflower while the curds are still compact, usually two or three weeks after blanching is started. Check daily as maturity approaches, and harvest immediately if the head begins to feel loose on the stem. Ripe heads left on rot quickly. Rather than cutting off the head, pull up the whole plant and put it, roots and all, in a cool, dark place such as a refrigerator or cold room. Kept this way the heads will last up to two weeks longer.

If the curds look fuzzy and separate, the growing temperature is too high, there is too much nitrogen, or the humidity is too high. Buttoning or premature flowering is caused by the growing temperature being below 40°F (4°C), poor soil, insufficient nitrogen, drought, or slow growth caused by weed competition.

New Zealand spinach must be picked regularly, otherwise the leaves become tough. Pick the oldest leaves even if you are not going to use them, but do not pick the growing tip. Lettuce leaves can be crispened by immersing them in water for an hour or two.

It may be possible to harvest a few new "baby" potatoes, either by pulling

### Green Thumb Tip

Tomatoes that fail to flower have probably been given too much nitrogen; tomatoes, peppers or eggplants should not be fertilized past the middle of the month. Flowering without fruiting, however, is due to pollination failure. Because tomatoes (and probably peppers) originated in the mountains, they do best when days are warm and nights are cool. As long as night temperatures drop below 74ºF (23ºC), there should be no difficulty. If temperatures drop below 55ºF (12ºC), or if day temperatures skyrocket, the flowers may drop off without setting fruit. Remove individual plant protectors when the soil is warm and the weather settled, so that plants do not overheat and watering and other care is easier.

Inadequate moisture and light, and magnesium deficiency may also cause blossom drop. For the latter, spray the foliage with 1 teaspoon (5 ml) of epsom salts per pint (550 ml) of lukewarm water. Magnesium deficiency causes leaf edges to turn yellow, then brown, and whole leaves to eventually become brittle, curl upwards, and die. High temperatures, drought, pro-longed wetness and a heavy fruit load are sometimes associated with upward curling leaves.

up a plant or two, or by feeling under the mulch and picking a few from several plants. If there are any diseased plants, dig them out immediately; the potatoes may safely be used.

## Flowering and Fruiting in Cucurbits and Tomatoes

Cucumbers should be picked four or five times a week. Roll the vines over gently to find the fruits, rather than lifting the plants off the ground. Cucumbers which are 2 to 3 inches (5 to 8 cm) long are ideal for sweet pickles, 5 to 6 inches (12 to 15 cm) for dills, and 6 to 8 inches (15 to 20 cm) for eating fresh. If some cucumbers get too huge and yellow, try peeling them, cutting 1/2 inch (1 cm) slices, dipping the slices in batter, and frying.

Pick zucchinis when they are about 4 inches (10 cm) long, and pick daily; a 6 inch (15 cm) zucchini can double in length in twenty-four hours. Scallop squashes are ready when they are 3 to 4 inches (8 to 10 cm) in diameter.

If fruits wither, starting at the blossom end (opposite the stem end), two probable causes are lack of pollination or faulty root action. Check for foot rot at the base of the stem (brown and soft areas) or root rot (roots are mushy), and remove the plant entirely if either is found. If neither is found, remove the affected fruit, water the plant, and give it some manure tea or fish emulsion if the leaves are a poor colour. Fruits resting on moist ground may also rot, so mulch with something dryish such as straw, dry leaves or salt marsh hay. Once the plant canopy is well developed, cut weeds instead of pulling them as root disturbance can cause cucurbits to wilt.

For a truly giant pumpkin, fertilize every week or two prior to fruit development with fish emulsion or manure tea. Remove all of the flowers and all but one fruit when it is clear that the fruit will develop and grow. Water frequently and copiously. For fun, scratch a child's name or some design 1/4 inch (6 mm) deep into the rind of any pumpkin when it is half formed; the name and design will grow with the pumpkin.

## Mid Summer Sowing

After crops are harvested, other vegetables can be sown in the ground that has been cleared (see Table JUL-1, below, and AUG-1, page 297). In regions where first sowings are just nicely getting underway, or if planting is just beginning, second plantings are not an option.

Root crops grown for winter storage can be planted in July or early August, and crops such as corn salad and kale that survive frosty autumns quite well can be planted at various times late in the growing season. The planting of

## Table JUL-1 Mid Summer Vegetable Planting Schedule

(from late June or early July)

Where summers are short and the first fall frost is expected in late August or September, see the Late Summer Vegetable Planting Schedule (page 297) for additional crops that can be planted in July.

| Plant | Transplant | Sow Seeds | Comments |
|---|---|---|---|
| Beans, snap, wax | | x | rr to 8 weeks b.f. |
| Beets | o | x | rr to 8 weeks b.f. |
| Carrots | | x | rr to 8 weeks b.f. |
| Collards | o | x | to 8-10 weeks b.f. |
| Corn, early varieties | | x | to 10 weeks b.f. |
| Escarole, Endive | o | x | to 10-12 weeks b.f. |
| Kohlrabi | o | x | rr to 4 weeks b.f. |
| Onions, Summer Bunching | | x | rr to 9 weeks b.f. |
| Peas, dwarf | o | x | rr to 9 weeks b.f. |
| Potatoes (planted close for "new" potatoes) | o | x | to 10 weeks b.f. |
| Radicchio (Red Endive) | | x | to 10 weeks b.f. |
| Rutabaga (Swede) | | x | to 8 weeks b.f. |

x = usual method
o = optional method; transplants will shorten the time from planting to harvest, allowing later planting than from seed. Transplanting in summer heat is hard on young plants unless special care is taken.
rr = repeat sowings every two to three weeks
b.f. = before the first fall frost is expected

other crops, however, needs to be timed more carefully. If hardy bunching onions are sown early, for example, they will become too large and will bolt the following spring after their winter in the ground; if sown too late, they may be too small to surive the winter. Experiment to find the right timing in your area for each crop.

Seeding and transplanting ten weeks before the first expected frost will give quite a number of vegetables enough time to mature; others can be

### Green Thumb Tip

If your cucumber plants are producing flowers but no fruit, be patient. Unless separate male and female plants were planted, cucumbers bear male flowers a week or so before they produce female flowers. The flowers are easy to distinguish as the females have a fruit-shaped swelling underneath the petals.

During flowering, remember to remove the cheesecloth or agricultural fabric covering the plants so that pollination can occur. If the weather is cool and wet, pollination will not occur. If there are no flowers at all, the plants are either too young or over fertilized with nitrogen. If they seem to be growing poorly or very slowly, water with manure tea (see Green Thumb Tip, page 163) or fish emulsion.

Male flowers also bloom first on zucchinis and summer and winter squashes. Until the female flowers start emerging, the male flowers might as well be eaten—either stuff them or dip them in batter and fry.

### Green Thumb Tip

The heat and dryness of summer can make good seed germinating conditions hard to arrange, but there are several ways to cool things down: mulch the planting area ahead of time with a light coloured material such as white cloth or brown paper; plant summer crops in light shade provided by taller crops, cheesecloth, a lath structure, or eastern exposure; water the soil the day before sowing with cold water; plant the seed slightly deeper than when planting in the spring, or make a deeper trench and only partially fill it in after the seeds are planted; water the trench before planting, and cover seeds with dry soil to reduce evaporation from the moistened soil; and mulch the soil lightly with grass clippings after planting. Spreading kitty litter or vermiculite over the soil after the seeds are planted will also help keep the soil cool, but avoid kitty litter if rain is expected. If seeds are started in shade and then transplanted, take every precaution to shade the transplants and reduce transplant shock (see Preventive Measure, page 120).

planted even later and protected with cold frames. Chinese cabbage, for example, can either be sown indoors early in July for transplants to set out as soon as ground becomes available, or it can be seeded directly outside in August in long season areas (see Table AUG-1, page 297). Seeding in August may be more successful as summer heat can be very hard on transplants.

If the first expected frost is at least nine weeks away, it may be possible to squeeze in one last planting of dwarf peas, but do not put them in the just cleared pea patch and remember that peas cope well with cold temperatures early in life, not at the end. Peas can be followed by a green manure crop of annual vetch or a clover mix. A few potatoes can be planted close together for an autumn harvest of "new" potatoes.

### Undersowing with Green Manures

Eliot Coleman (1989) recommends undersowing certain vegetables with green manure crops. Plant them at least four weeks, but not more than five weeks, after the main crop is established. Soybeans or red or sweet clover can be planted between rows of corn. Annual vetch can be planted with beans and potatoes, or wait until the potatoes have been harvested and sow winter rye. Plant spring oats or spring barley with tomatoes in September when the tomatoes are almost over. He recommends using white or sweet clover between rows of brassicas, white clover between root crops and sweet clover between squash plants. Use alsike clover alone or under tall crops. The thought of introducing clover into your vegetable patch may be worrisome, but it does not tend to persist as a "weed" if turned into the soil in the spring.

## Herbs

### General Care and Propagation

In the garden, keep herbs watered and fertilized, particularly those in containers. Herbs in containers should be protected from the full force of the midday sun, if possible, or be prepared to water them twice a day if need be (see page 218 for water saving strategies). Chervil may start to look miserable in the heat; a fresh batch can be sown next month when nights start to cool off.

Rosemary, sage, lavender and thyme can be propagated by layering this month. Choose a branch of this year's growth that can be lowered to the ground. Make a diagonal slice upward one-quarter of the way through the stem where it touches the ground, 5 inches (12 cm) or more from the tip, then prop open the slit with a bit of toothpick and dust with some rooting hormone. Alternatively, scrape a 1 to 2 inch (2.5 to 5 cm) area off the underside of the branch where it touches the ground and dust with rooting hormone. Bury the cut or scraped section of the stem in a trench under 2 to 3 inches (5 to 8 cm) of soil, making sure that the growing tip is not covered. Lay a rock on top, or use a bent wire to hold the stem in place. The rooted stem can probably be cut from the parent plant in a couple of months and potted up to overwinter indoors, or it can be left attached over the winter and separated in the spring.

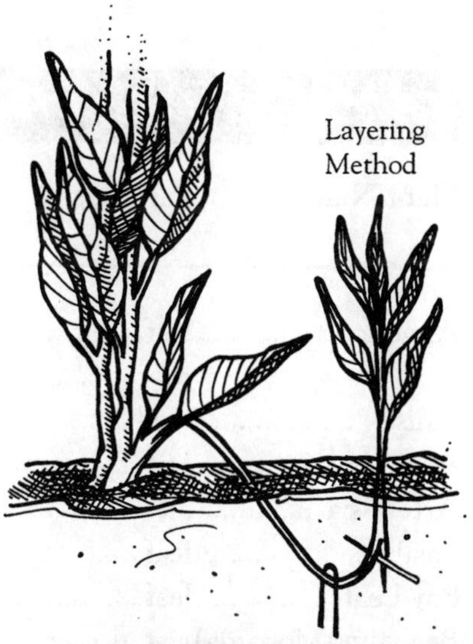

Layering Method

Thyme, oregano and mint plants grown from seed can be tested for flavour and the best ones propagated by layering. Many herbs can also be started from stem cuttings (see Table JAN-1, page 15) in the same way that semi-hardwood cuttings are started (see pages 280-281).

## Harvesting and Preserving

When picking herbs to use fresh, take the central growing tips and flowers of stemmed plants such as basil, mint, chervil, thyme, oregano and sweet marjoram to encourage branching. Pick the outside leaves and stalks of plants that grow from crowns, such as lovage and parsley.

For a major harvest, cut back woody perennials such as sage by approximately one-third. Branches should be cut back only once, although individual leaves can be harvested indefinitely. If they are cut back after mid July, new growth may not have time to harden off before temperatures fall below freezing in the autumn. Lavender flower spikes should be removed the first year as soon as you notice them to encourage branching. The flowers on older plants are harvested just as the lowest flowers on the spike begin to open; plants can be pruned if needed immediately afterwards.

Cut back annuals and soft stemmed perennials such as French tarragon to within 3 inches (8 cm) of the ground, making not more than three cuts over the whole growing season. Fertilize and water regularly if heavy cuts are made.

> **Green Thumb Tip**
>
> Dill and coriander stop growing leaves and go to seed quickly in hot weather. To slow this down, grow them in partial shade or where the soil is cool and moist, and cut off any flowers as soon as you notice them. It is also best to directly seed these herbs because the stress of transplanting seems to hurry them towards seed production.

### Drying

Drying is used mostly for fragrance herbs. It is not usually the method of choice for the best flavour in culinary herbs, but it will produce acceptable results. For drying, most herbs (see Table JUL-2) are harvested when the flower buds are fully developed but not open as this is when plants have the highest content of the oils which give herbs their flavour or scent.

Cut herbs after the dew has dried off, but before noon if possible. If plants

## *Table JUL-2 Harvest Time and Storage Methods for Fragrant and Culinary Herbs*

| **Plant Name** | **Parts Used** | **Main Harvest** | **Storage Method** | | | |
|---|---|---|---|---|---|---|
| | | | Freeze | Dry | Vinegar | Butter or Oil |
| Angelica | leaf, stem | e.s. | x | | | |
| | root | autumn | | x | | |
| Anise | seed | l.s. | | x | | |
| Anise Hyssop | leaf, top | m.s. | | x | | |
| Artemisia | all | autumn | | x | | |
| Basil | leaf | m.s. | x | - | x | b,o |
| Bay Leaf | leaf | m.s. | | x | x | |
| Beebalm (Monarda) | leaf, flower | m.s. | | x | | |
| Borage | leaf, flower | m.s. | | x | | |
| Calendula | flower petals | m.s. | | x | | |
| Caraway | seed | l.s. | | x | | |
| Catnip | leaf and stem | m.s. | | x | | |
| Chamomile | flower | m.s. | | x | | |
| Chervil | leaf | spring, autumn | bl | - | x | b |
| Chives | leaf | e.s. | x | - | | b |
| | flower | m.s. | | | x | |
| Comfrey | leaf | m.s. | | x | | |
| Coriander | leaf (fresh) | e.s. | bl | x | x | o |
| | seed | autumn | | x | | |
| Dill | leaf | e.s. | x | - | | o |
| | seed | autumn | | x | x,p | |
| Fennel | leaf | e.s. | bl | - | x | o |
| | stalk | e.s. | | | p | |
| | seed | autumn | | x | | |
| Fenugreek | seed | autumn | | x | p | |
| French Sorrel | leaf (fresh) | spring | bl | - | | |
| Horseradish | root * | autumn | | | p | |
| Hyssop | leaf, flower | m.s. | | x | | |
| Iris Florentine | rhizome | l.s. | | x | | |
| Lavender | flowers | l.s. | | x | | |
| Lemon Balm | leaf | e.s. | | x | | |

| Plant Name | Parts Used | Main Harvest | Storage Method: Freeze | Dry | Vinegar | Butter or Oil |
|---|---|---|---|---|---|---|
| Lovage | leaf (fresh) | e.s. | | | x | |
| | seed | autumn | | x | | |
| Marjoram | leaf, top | m.s. | | x | x | o |
| Mint | leaf | m.s. | | x | x | b |
| Nasturtium | leaf (fresh) | e.s. | | | | |
| | flower | m.s. | | | x | b |
| | seed | m.s. | | | x | |
| Oregano, Greek | leaf, top | m.s. | | x | x | o |
| Parsley | leaf | e.s. | bl | - | | b |
| Rosemary | leaf | m.s. | | x | x | o |
| Saffron | stigma | autumn | | x | | |
| Sage | leaf | m.s. | | x | | o |
| Salad Burnet | leaf (fresh) | spring | bl | - | x | b |
| Scented Geranium | leaf | m.s. | | x | | |
| Summer Savory | leaf | m.s. | | x | | b,o |
| Sweet Cicely | leaf | e.s. | x | - | | b |
| | seed | l.s. | | x | | |
| Sweet Flag | leaf | m.s. | | x | | |
| | rhizome | autumn | | x | | |
| Sweet Woodruff | leaf (fresh) | spring | | | | |
| | leaf and stem | m.s. | | x | | |
| Tarragon, French | leaf | e.s. | bl | - | x | b,o |
| Thyme | leaf | m.s. | | x | x | o |
| Valerian | root | autumn | | x | | |
| Watercress | leaf (fresh) | e.s. | | | | b |

e.s. = early summer
m.s. = mid summer
l.s. = late summer
x = recommended method but not exclusive
- = not recommended
bl = blanch one minute before freezing

b = chop fine and mix with butter
o = chop fine and marinate in oil
p = used to flavour pickles or is itself pickled
* = roots may be stored fresh in damp sand
(fresh) = usually used fresh

A traditional *bouquet garni*.

> ### *Pesto...presto!*
> Use two cups (480 ml) of packed basil leaves for pesto, or include some parsley, and process in a blender with two to four cloves of crushed garlic and 1/2 cup (120 ml) of olive or vegetable oil until smooth. Use a good quality olive oil that is green in colour. Add a little water or more oil if it clumps up, and freeze the mixture at this stage. To use it, thaw it and stir in 3 tablespoons (45 ml) of crushed pine nuts, walnuts, almonds, pecans or sunflower seeds, and 1/2 to 1 cup (120 to 240 ml) of grated parmesan cheese. Use it immediately after the last traces of ice crystals have disappeared. For fresh pesto, process and stir in all of the ingredients as described, then store it in sterilized jars. Cover the pesto with a skim of oil and cover the jar with plastic wrap or a screw-on lid. It should keep several weeks in the refrigerator.

are dirty enough to need washing, dry them off in a salad spinner or wrap them in a tea towel. Stems can be held together with an elastic band, which accommodates the shrinking of stems as they dry. Hang them upside down in a warm, dry, dark, airy place. Dry thyme and marjoram tied into bundles for soups and stews, or to make a bed on which to roast meat, poultry or fish. A traditional *bouquet garni* is two sprigs each of thyme and marjoram and one bay leaf. A dry fennel stalk is added for fish dishes and a bunch of fresh parsley or a sprig of fresh tarragon is usually added later because neither dries well (but both can be frozen).

Herbs will dry faster if large leaves are stripped off the stems and laid in a single layer on a screen, a sheet of newspaper, or a piece of cheesecloth draped over a cake rack placed in a warm, dry place. For much quicker drying, put herbs in a 140°F (60°C) oven with the door ajar, or in a homemade drier (see page 295). They can also be dried in a microwave oven: place leaves in a single layer between two paper towels, and set the microwave at low power for two minutes, or for three minutes for thick leaves. Repeat at thirty second intervals until the leaves are brittle.

Small leaves, such as those of oregano, can be left on their stems, dried in any of the ways mentioned above, and then rubbed off gently between the palms of the hands. Try not to crumble any dried herbs until you are ready to use them as this releases their aroma and flavour. Detach marigold petals but dry chamomile flowers whole, and handle them gently to avoid bruising.

When herbs are dry to the point of being somewhat crisp but not powdery dry, store them in airtight containers, such as glass jars with screw-on lids, pottery jars with tight corks, or plastic bags. Keep all containers in a dark place and away from heat. When using dried herbs, use only one-third the amount of fresh herbs called for (see pages 300-304, for culinary uses).

Combine some herbs with flowers and roots to make scented potpourris (see pages 259-260), and throw out last year's herbs. They can be spread around the garden to mask the smell of those vegetables and flowers that attract insect pests, added as a mulch to container plants or put on the compost pile.

### *Freezing*

Chervil, parsley, chives, French tarragon, fennel, sweet cicely and dill leaves seem to retain their flavour better when frozen, rather than dried, and can be stored up to six months this way. To freeze any herb, wash the leaves, blanch one minute if required (see Table JUL-2, above), cool in ice water and dry the leaves in a salad spinner or tea towel. Roll the leaves into a cigar-shape, wrap the roll in plastic, and place it in the freezer. Shave off thin slices with a sharp knife as required. Individual basil leaves or any other large-leaved herb can be coated in olive or vegetable oil and frozen between sheets of waxed paper.

Another way to freeze herbs is to combine two lightly packed cups of a herb or mixture of herbs with one cup of water in a blender, and then freeze the slush in ice cube trays. Simply add a cube or two to your cooking as required. The same can be done using oil instead of water, and even pesto can be frozen.

### *Herbal butters*

Herbal butters can be frozen and thus are another form in which herbs can be preserved—either in rolls, blocks or individual patties. Combine approximately 1/4 cup (65 ml) of fresh, finely chopped herbs with 1/2 cup (125 ml) of butter or margarine. One-quarter cup (65 ml) of olive oil or canola oil can be substituted for the butter to make a healthier spread. Experiment with different quantities of various herbs to get the flavour concentration you like. Try adding a little lemon juice to mint, chive or chervil butter, a couple of cloves of crushed garlic or finely chopped shallots to basil butter, or fresh ground black pepper to tarragon butter. Try a combination, such as parsley, chives, tarragon and dill with touches of pepper and garlic. Chopped nuts add a delightful texture to butters that will be used fresh, but should not be added to those that will be frozen.

To make herbal butters with dried herbs, soak about 2 tablespoons. (30 ml) of dried herbs in a tiny amount of hot water for a few minutes before combining with the butter. Similar proportions of fresh or dried herbs can also be combined with 1/2 cup (125 ml) of sour cream, cream cheese, mayonnaise or cottage cheese for a variety of dips and spreads. These should be made to be eaten fresh rather than for freezing.

Herbal vinegars and oils

### *Oils, vinegars and jellies*

Herbal flavours can also be transferred to and stored in vinegar. Pack a jar lightly with sprigs of herbs and fill it with cider, malt, rice, red wine or white wine vinegar. Regular white vinegar captures the purest herbal flavour. Use roughly 2 cups (500 ml) of loosely packed herb to 4 cups (1 l) of vinegar. After two or three weeks, strain the vinegar, pour it into clean bottles, cover with a non-metal cap, and store in a cool, dark place. Add a fresh sprig of the herb to each bottle for a finishing touch. Use French tarragon, basil, purple

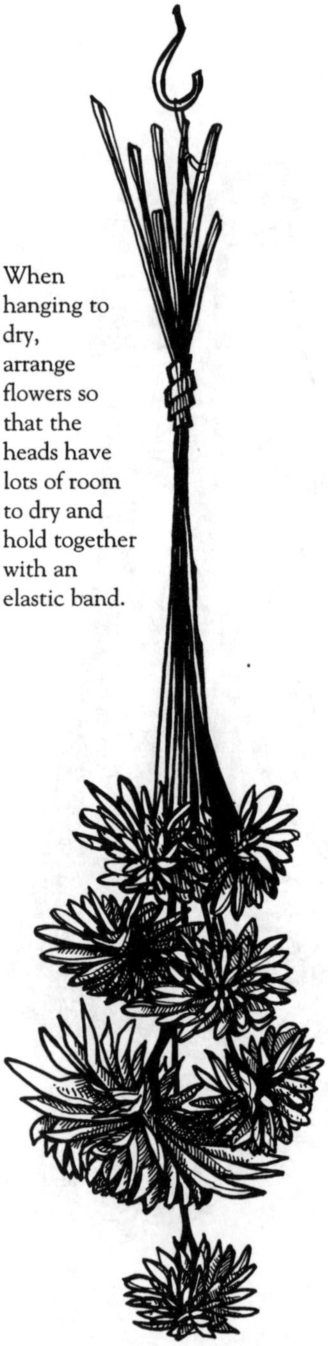

When hanging to dry, arrange flowers so that the heads have lots of room to dry and hold together with an elastic band.

basil, thyme, rosemary, lovage, marjoram, chive flowers, unripe seed heads of dill, chervil, salad burnet, shredded horseradish, chopped shallots, bruised garlic, mint or savory, or try combinations such as fennel and bay leaf; tarragon and dill; tarragon and shallots; basil, thyme, oregano and chives; or cilantro and garlic.

A pretty nasturtium vinegar can be made by simmering 4 cups (1 l) of vinegar and 4 cups (1 l) of packed nasturtium flowers (stems removed) for ten minutes, then adding chopped chives, green onions, shallots, garlic, cayenne pepper and salt to taste. Two cups (500 ml) of half-ripe nasturtium seeds (with some stem attached) can be pickled in 1 cup (250 ml) of sugar and 1/4 cup (65 ml) of salt dissolved in 1 cup (250 ml) of freshly boiled cider vinegar. Let them stand for one month before using.

For herbal oils, loosely fill a jar with washed, lightly bruised leaves. Fill the jar with olive oil so that no leaf surfaces are exposed to the air, and leave the jar in a sunny window for a month, covered with muslin. The best flavoured olive oils are light green in colour. After a month, strain off the oil and check its flavour. If a stronger flavour is required, the process can be repeated two or three times by adding fresh leaves to the same batch of oil each time. Use thyme, fennel, tarragon, marjoram, savory, basil, purple basil or rosemary, or combine several herbs, such as chives, marjoram and a bit of sage, to create a unique flavour (see page 304 for uses of herbal oils and vinegars). Store the oil in a sterilized jar with a tight lid to reduce the possibility of spoilage.

Herbs can also be used in jellies; try lemon balm, rosemary, sage or basil jelly in addition to the usual mint. See Noel Richardson's *Summer Delights* (1991) and Rosalind Creasy's *Cooking from the Garden* (1988) for jelly recipes.

## Flowers

Most flowers are cut for fresh bouquets, but some are dried and used in winter bouquets or potpourris. Some are even candied and eaten, or eaten without candying!

### Drying

The appropriate method for drying flowers depends on the kind of flower. Use flowers which are in good condition and at different stages of development. Pick globe amaranth before the flowers look loose but after the buds on side shoots look full. Cut strawflowers just before they open, when the central disc is still covered, but cut bells-of-Ireland as soon as the calyxes (bells) are fully open. Statice is cut when two-thirds of the flowers on a spike are open, and xeranthemum can be cut at any stage (and see pages 231-234).

Cut flowers for drying near midday when they are perfectly dry, preferably after a couple of days of dry weather. Strip off all of the leaves and gather the stems into small bunches with an elastic band. Arrange the stems so that the heads are at varying levels and do not crush each other. Hang the bunches upside down in a warm, dry, dark, well ventilated place, as for herbs. When dried this way, most flowers do not need wiring. Flowers can also be dried in the oven or in a food drier, particularly if they have not air dried sufficiently within two to three weeks. Light must be avoided at all costs because it causes the colours to fade. Grasses can be stood upright to dry for a more natural look. Drying works well for:

| | | |
|---|---|---|
| ageratum | delphinium | larkspur |
| annual statice | dusty miller | liatris |
| artemisia | gaillardia | peony |
| astilbe | globe amaranth | physostegia |
| bells-of-Ireland | goldenrod | salvia, blue |
| broom | grasses | scabiosa |
| celosia | heather | strawflower |
| centaurea | honesty | xeranthemum |
| Chinese lantern | hosta | yarrow |
| chrysanthemum | hydrangea | zinnia |
| crocosmia | lady's mantle | |

Individual lavender flowers can be stripped from the stalks after they have dried and used to stuff sachets or added to potpourris. The seed heads of many flowers are also attractive when dried (for suggested types, see pages 386-387).

Flowers dried using silica gel, which comes in granular form, keep their colours very well, except for dark red. Gather flowers as when air drying, but leave only 1 inch (2.5 cm) of stem attached to each flower. Put 1 or 2 inches (2.5 to 5 cm) of silica gel in the bottom of a metal container. Place the flowers face up on the gel if they are cup shaped, saucer shaped or have multiple petals, and position other flowers face down. Be careful that they do not touch each other and carefully sprinkle in more silica gel to cover the flowers. Those in spikes, such as snapdragons, can be laid horizontally, supported underneath on folded pieces of cardboard. Put the lid on tightly and leave for two to six days in a dry, dark place. Drying time depends on the

### Safety Tip

Silica gel is a very fine powder that can cause harm if improperly used. Avoid breathing in the dust. Avoid getting it anywhere near your eyes and mouth.

Helpful strategies include the following:

- use silica gel outdoors, so that no dust remains in the house;
- cover nose and mouth to prevent breathing in the dust;
- avoid touching yourself, especially the face, to avoid transference from hands;
- use gloves, and wash your hands thoroughly after using silica gel.

Drying Flowers in Silica

Cup shaped flowers are placed facing up while others face down.

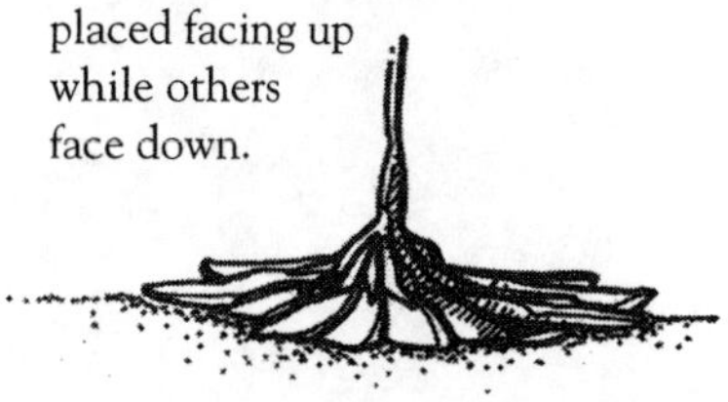

Spiked flowers may need a stand.

flower size and the thickness of the petals. They should feel like tissue paper when they are dry, and not feel brittle.

Slowly pour off the silica, holding the flowers back with your hand. Shake excess silica gel off each flower, and remove stray particles with a soft brush. Position flowers for storage in dry floral foam, and store in airtight boxes with several tablespoons of silica gel sprinkled in the bottom. Reuse silica gel by drying it for half an hour in a 25°F (120°C) oven. Silica gel works well for the flowers listed below, but experiment with others as well.

- anemone
- aster
- azalea
- bleeding heart
- buttercup
- calendula
- clematis
- columbine
- coralbells
- coreopsis
- crocus
- dahlia
- daisy
- delphinium
- feverfew
- forget-me-not
- foxglove
- freesia
- geranium
- gladiolus
- hollyhock
- hydrangea
- larkspur
- lilac
- lily
- marigold
- nigella
- pansy
- peony
- phlox
- pinks
- poppy
- primrose
- rhododendron
- rose
- rose mallow
- rudbeckia
- scabiose
- snapdragon
- tulip
- verbena
- violet
- zinnia

Ordinary household borax can be used in place of silica gel, but place the flowers face down and leave the lid off during the drying process. Borax is less expensive, but it takes longer and does not preserve flower colour as well as silica gel.

Many flowers can be dried with a flower press (see page 449) or by pressing them between two layers of face tissue inside a phone book. Leave an inch (2.5 cm) of pages between each layer of plant material, weigh down the book with bricks or more books, and store for three or four weeks in a dry place. Try this with ferns, other attractive foliage, and with open flowers rather than buds from the list of flowers suitable for air drying.

Foliage can be dried using glycerin, which results in a more supple, less brittle product. Gather the leaves while they are still tender, and scrape or lightly hammer the ends of the stems or branches. Make a solution of one part glycerin and one to two parts boiling water in a jar, to a depth of 2 inches

(5 cm). Stand the branches in the solution for one to four weeks until the leaves stop changing colour. They will look spotty at first but will gradually assume even tones of dark green, rust or soft brown. Individual leaves can be immersed in the solution. Store dried leaves in loose tissue paper in open boxes without any silica gel. Glycerin is reusable and should be stored in tightly covered jars.

A fine book that covers all aspects of preserving flowers, including ways of using them and methods of wiring, is *Flowers that Last Forever* by Betty E.M. Jacobs (1988).

### Potpourri

To dry flowers for potpourris, gather them on a dry day in the morning, after the sun is high (but before noon, when the release of volatile oils is the highest), just as the blossoms open. It is tempting to leave roses on the stem for a couple of days to enjoy their colour and fragrance, but the essential oils that give them their fragrance diminish rapidly once they open. Roses are the best flowers for potpourris, but also try:

| | | |
|---|---|---|
| carnation | magnolia | stocks |
| heliotrope | mignonette | tuberose |
| honeysuckle | peony | violet |
| lavender | pinks | wallflower |
| lilac | | |

After picking, gently pull the petals off larger flowers and discard the rest of the flower. Small, simple flowers can be left whole. Lay the petals on a screen in a dry, dark place where there is good air circulation. Stir and turn them every few days until they are dry and crisp, or dry them in the oven or microwave as for herbs. Flowers with little scent but good colour include borage, calendula petals, pansy, bachelor button and feverfew.

Use the flowers or leaves of the following herbs for potpourris:

| | | |
|---|---|---|
| angelica | hyssop | scented geranium |
| anise hyssop | lavender | sweet marjoram |
| artemisia | lemon balm | sweet woodruff |
| basil | mint | tarragon |
| bay leaf | rosemary | thyme |
| beebalm | sage | |

The tips of fir and spruce trees, juniper berries and dried strips of citrus peel can also be used.

After the ingredients are dry, store them separately in airtight containers until you have enough to mix various combinations with spices and a fixative. Spices to use include ground cinnamon, allspice, nutmeg, aniseed, caraway, coriander, vanilla pod, ginger and cloves.

Fixatives help to preserve leaves and petals and retain their natural scents. Four that can be grown in the home garden are the roots of sweet flag (calamus), valerian and angelica (see page 350 for their preparation), and the rhizome of Florentine iris (also called orris root—see page 306 for its preparation). Orris root, once called "violet powder," is the best and is also available commercially. Other fixatives which are less well known but can be grown at home include holy basil, clary sage, sweet woodruff and hyssop.

Use your imagination and be willing to experiment when combining various plant materials. As a crude guide, for every 2 cups or 4 ounces (500 ml or 100 g) of dried flowers and leaves, use 1 teaspoon (5 ml) of mixed spices and 1 tablespoon or 1 ounce (45 ml or 26 g) of powdered orris root.

To make a moist potpourri—which reputedly keeps its scent for up to fifty years—partially dry flowers and leaves until they feel leathery. The following instructions are a "distillation" of the method and of the vast quantities of materials used by Gertrude Jekyl, the great flower garden designer, at the turn of the century.

Layer 14 cups (3.5 l) of partially dry rose petals in a crock with salt (the petals of clove carnations and peonies could be mixed in to partially substitute the roses). Use two handfuls of petals and a sprinkling of coarse, non-iodized salt for each layer and weigh down the lot for several months. Do the same with 7 cups (1.75 l) of a mixture of dryish scented geranium leaves and lavender flowers mixed with salt, and half the amount of a combination of dryish bay leaves, rosemary and other herbs layered with salt and weighed down.

After several months (but several weeks will do), mix all of the leaves and flowers together thoroughly. Just mix in any froth that has developed, and crumble and mix in any hard cake that forms. At the same time, mix in 2 tablespoons (30 ml) each of ground allspice, cinnamon and nutmeg; 1 tablespoon (15 ml) of whole cloves; and 3/4 cup (180 ml) of powdered orris root. Mix everything thoroughly, perhaps giving it a good stir every day for a week or so, then pack the mixture tightly into jars with lids and store them in a cool, dry place for several months before using. To release the scent, remove the lid and place the jar near heat.

A useful little book for more ideas is *Potpourri, Incense, and other Fragrant Concoctions* by Ann Tucker Fettner (1977).

## Edible (and Inedible) Flowers

Another way to preserve flowers is to crystallize them for use on cakes and desserts. Pull apart geranium and lilac clusters to obtain the individual flowers; use whole flowers of violet, pea (garden pea, not sweet pea), miniature roses and borage (remove the sepals first); and use individual petals of pansies, roses, Johnny-jump-ups, apple and plum blossoms. Pick them when they have just opened and are in perfect shape, leaving some stem attached. Wash them carefully several hours ahead of candying time, stand the stems in water, and let the flowers dry thoroughly.

Use a fine camel hair brush to paint slightly beaten egg white over all surfaces of each flower or petal, then sprinkle finely ground sugar over all the surfaces until every part is covered. Arrange them so they do not touch each other on a cake rack in a warm, dry place or in an oven or drier (see page 295), and move each one around after an hour or so to prevent them from sticking to the cake rack. After several days of drying, or after several hours if using an oven or drier, store them in a tin with a tight fitting lid. They are best when used within a few days, but can be kept for up to one year.

Many flowers can be eaten fresh, either in salads and desserts or as a garnish for soups and beverages. Rosalind Creasy, in *Cooking from the Garden* (1988), gives several delightful recipes using flowers, including such things as Tulip, Crab, and Asparagus Appetizers and Lavender Ice Cream. Not all flowers are edible, but in addition to the ones listed for crystallizing, the following flowers are both safe and tasty:

anise hyssop
arugula
beebalm petals
calendula petals
chive petals
culinary herbs
daylily petals or buds
elderberry
honeysuckle
lavender
mustard
nasturtium
pinks
radish
runner bean
squash
tulip petals

It is also possible to make flower flavoured vodka. Rosalind Creasy suggests that edible flowers (just one kind for each batch of vodka) be steeped for several days at room temperature in good quality vodka. Try roses, dianthus or lavender, or use herbs such as mint, rosemary or sweet woodruff. After steeping, remove the plant material and store the vodka in a freezer.

**Preventive Measure**

## Injurious or Poisonous Plants

Be careful that curious children do *not* eat flowers and other plant parts without supervision as the berries, flowers, leaves, bark, seeds, roots and/or bulbs of several familiar plants are injurious or poisonous. Children have even been poisoned by using pieces of pithy elderberry stems for blowguns.

| Plant | Injurious or poisonous part |
|---|---|
| Anemone | all parts |
| Azalea | all parts |
| Black Locust | bark, seeds, sprouts, foliage |
| Bittersweet (*Celastris scandens*) | berries |
| Bleeding Heart (Dutchman's Breeches) | foliage, roots |
| Buttercup | all parts |
| Caladium | tuber |
| Cardinal Flower | all parts |
| Castor Bean | seeds |
| Cherry, wild and cultivated | twigs, foliage, pits |
| Christmas Rose (*Helleborus*) | leaves, roots |
| Crocus | bulbs |
| Daffodil | bulbs |
| Daphne | berries |
| Delphinium | seeds, young plants |
| Elderberry | leaves, shoots, bark, unripe berries |
| English Ivy | berries |
| Flowering Tobacco (*Nicotiana*) | leaves |
| Foxglove | leaves |
| Golden Chain Tree (Laburnum) | seeds, seed capsules |
| Holly | berries |
| Honeysuckle | berries |
| Hyacinth | bulbs |
| Hydrangea | leaves, buds |
| Iris | rhizomes |
| Jack-in-the-Pulpit | all parts, especially roots |
| Larkspur | seeds, young plants |
| Lily-of-the-Valley | leaves, flowers |
| Lupine | seeds |
| Monkshood | roots |
| Mountain Laurel | all parts |
| Mulberry | unripe berries |
| Narcissus | bulbs |
| Nightshade | all parts, especially berries |
| Oak | foliage, acorns |
| Peach | leaves |
| Peony | roots |
| Privet | berries |
| Queen Anne's Lace | roots |
| Rhododendron | all parts |
| Rhubarb | leaves |
| Sheep Laurel | all parts |
| Snakeberry | berries, roots |
| Snowdrop | bulbs, flowers |
| Star-of-Bethlehem | bulbs |
| Sweet Pea | seeds |
| Wisteria | seeds, pods |
| Yew | berries, foliage |

Based in part on information in Hardin and Arena's *Human Poisoning from Native and Cultivated Plants* (1974).

If you suspect that someone has ingested parts of any of these plants, call your physician or poison control centre immediately. Tell them the name of the plant, what parts were eaten, how much, when, the age of the person and any symptoms noticed.

## *General Care and Disease Prevention*

If planning to preserve and eat flowers, you will likely find it frustrating if plants fail to bloom (see pages 229-231), or buds drop off prematurely. The latter is usually caused by not enough water or, less often, by too much water. Excessive heat will also cause buds to drop; this can sometimes be counteracted by putting plants in shade and watering them with cool, not cold, water. Container plants such as fuchsia and begonia seem most prone to flower and bud drop.

Regular deadheading helps plants to bloom longer—individual flowers will not last longer, but new flowers will continue to be produced. Deadhead cosmos and poppies regularly to prevent prolific self-seeding, but let a few set seed late in the season. Some annuals, such as marigold, blanket flower (gaillardia), verbena and pansies, need deadheading almost weekly to keep them looking trim. Other annuals such as *Nicotiana* (flowering tobacco) and impatiens do not need deadheading because the spent flowers drop off cleanly. Deadhead repeat blooming shrub roses to prevent hips from forming and to keep flowers coming. Hybrid teas and floribundas can be fertilized and cut back lightly after blooming until mid July to encourage more flowers. To encourage bigger blossoms in dahlias, pinch out the side buds as soon as they are visible.

With delphiniums, cutting out the flower stems as soon as they have finished blooming seems to help plants last a few years longer, and may result in a second, smaller crop of flowers if the autumn is long and mild. Cut back catnip and other early blooming flowers—there may be a second burst of bloom in late summer or early fall. Fading annuals can also be rejuvenated by cutting them back by half and fertilizing, but do this at least six weeks before the first autumn frost is expected.

Cutting fresh flowers helps keep more coming, but avoid taking more leaves than necessary. At least two full sets of leaves should remain on each stem when cutting roses (and see pages 233-234). Lilies should be cut only once every second or third year as yearly cutting can reduce the size of the bulb. Cut them just as the first bud on a stem opens; buds higher up will open after being cut. Some people remove the anthers because of their staining pollen. If any does get on clothes, brush it off with a dry brush before laundering with soap and water. Stubborn stains will disappear if put in direct sunlight. Both lilies and roses can be entirely submerged in water for a few hours after cutting to crispen them.

Keep watering flowers to extend the season of bloom and fertilize annual flowers and vines every two weeks with manure tea (see Green Thumb Tip, page 163), fish emulsion or liquid seaweed. Flowers are shorter lived on drought stricken plants. Avoid wetting flowers when watering or fertilizing because water adds extra weight and causes them to droop or bend, and can cause spotting on the petals. Soaker hoses and drip irrigation water only the soil and leave foliage dry, helping to reduce the chance of various diseases.

As soon as diseases are noticed, remove and burn the affected leaves. If the condition is severe, you can resort to spraying with sulphur every one to two weeks, or spraying weekly with baking soda spray (see page 190), but these will only prevent further problems from developing, not cure them after the fact. Bordeaux mixture works well but may discolour leaves and flowers. Try to prevent fungicides from dribbling or spilling onto the soil.

Rust can be a problem on hollyhocks, geraniums and snapdragons. As soon as pustules appear on leaves, stems and flowers, remove and destroy the affected parts—do not compost—and spray with wettable sulpher. This may stop the disease from spreading, although it will not cure it. Badly affected plants will wilt and die.

Irises affected by borers are disfigured with irregular tunnels in the lower part of the leaves, and areas may appear water soaked. The larvae are pink with brown heads and in midsummer they begin to eat out the centre of the rhizomes. In late spring, pinch the larvae as they mine the leaves. Dig up the plants after flowering, cut out the affected leaves and rhizomes, kill the larvae, and discard or burn all of the affected parts (see page 306 for planting details). In the autumn, cut out iris stalks and leaves at the base and burn or discard them to remove overwintering eggs.

A wet summer will cause roses and other flowers to turn brown. Geraniums sometimes get blossom blight, which causes the petals to turn dark and wilt prematurely. Not a lot can be done to prevent this as it is usually caused by high humidity and low temperatures, but a baking soda spray may help. Make sure that the plants are in a sunny position, and water carefully to ensure that the flowers and foliage are dry at night.

Botrytis on lilies shows up as brown spots on the leaves and flowers. The spots look damp around the edges and eventually coalesce to turn the leaves entirely brown or black. Remove affected stalks and mark the location of lilies with stakes. Again, a baking soda spray may help prevent it, as with mildew on phlox, william and mary (pulmonaria) and other flowers with fungal problems. Often, such disease troubles occur only occasionally, and some years are trouble free.

### Preventive Measure

Downy mildew and powdery mildew regularly make a summer appearance whether conditions are wet or dry. The two types are often lumped together, but they are quite distinct from each other and grow under different conditions.

Downy mildew grows from within plant leaves and emerges on their underside, creating pale patches. It thrives in damp, overcrowded conditions and is associated with bachelor's button, forget-me-nots, poppies and asters. Powdery mildew lives on leaf surfaces, appearing as a white fuzz, and is associated with light soils and hot, dry, crowded conditions. It is found on asters, balloon flowers, coralbells, dahlias, delphiniums, larkspur, phlox, pulmonaria, roses, begonias and zinnias.

To control the diseases, thin out plants through pruning, or space them further apart so that air circulates better. Lighten the soil in damp areas by working in organic matter, or choose moisture-loving plants. Raised beds will improve drainage and air circulation, and foliage will stay dry if plants are watered with a soaker hose. Locate susceptible plants where they will receive morning sunshine, so that leaves wetted from rain or dew will be dried off more quickly. Keep dry soils more moist by watering regularly and deeply and mulching, or choose drought tolerant plants.

Wet soil will cause some plants, such as geraniums, to rot at the soil line. Try to improve drainage, add sand or perlite next time if there is already plenty of organic matter in the soil, and allow the soil surface to become dry between waterings.

## Moving and Propagation

Perhaps the best cure for some plants suffering from diseases is to move them to a better position. Plants that are doing poorly for other reasons may also benefit from being moved to a new location, but do not move them around willy-nilly. For good results, look into the ideal growing conditions for a particular plant, talk to neighbours and fellow gardeners who are having success with the same plant, or try growing a different variety.

### *Division*

July is a good time to move or divide spring blooming perennials that have finished flowering (see Table APR/MAY-3, page 138). Bearded irises, however, are best moved six to ten weeks after they have finished blooming because this is when they have a fresh burst of root growth. In most regions this is sometime in August (see page 306).

Primroses which were not divided last month can still be lifted and moved. They will need plenty of moisture, so water them well several hours before digging them up, and again after replanting.

Sometimes perennials need to be moved around because they are crowding each other. All things being equal, try to move the plant that least minds disturbance. If beebalm, for example, is crowding a balloon flower plant, dig out and move the beebalm because it is nearly impossible to kill, whereas the balloon flower transplants poorly.

### *Seeds and cuttings*

Most perennials, except for hybrids, breed fairly true to the parent, so you may want to gather ripe seeds to try propagating more plants (see Table APR/MAY-3, page 138, for appropriate plants). Particular needs vary, but there are basically two methods to use: plant the fresh seeds outdoors in a protected location or in a cold frame as soon as they are harvested (many will not germinate until next spring); or store the dried seeds in cool, dry conditions (see page 8) over the winter, stratify the seeds for one to three months (see page 49), and plant them indoors in January. Not all perennial seeds need stratification, but if you are missing specific instructions, stratifiction will not hurt and it may help. See February (pages 48-49) for other methods of breaking dormancy.

Basal shoots on delphiniums

Sow delphinium seeds indoors this month if you are going to force them indoors this winter. If flower stalks of delphiniums are bent over at soil level, either accidentally or on purpose, they will often send up young basal shoots. These can be cut off right at the base and rooted in moist soil with good drainage, either in a cold frame or indoors where they can be kept misted and moist. When established, these seedlings or rooted cuttings are transplanted to a cold frame—if not already planted there—usually in August. They are kept there until just before the ground freezes, potted up and then stored in a cold room until forced in January.

Baby's breath and marguerite (see also Table APR/MAY-3, page 138) can be started from stem cuttings in the summer. Use 2 to 3 inch (5 to 8 cm) cuttings, strip off the lower leaves, remove any flower buds, dip the bottom ends in rooting hormone, and insert in pots of moist perlite and peat moss. Keep them enclosed in plastic and in bright light but out of direct sunlight, or put them in a propagation unit (see pages 442-443). The cuttings can be potted up once they have rooted and can be grown as winter flowers indoors.

## Fruits

### Management of Strawberries

If your strawberry crop is so abundant that it is impossible to eat all the fruit fresh, try freezing them (see page 316) or making them into jams, alone or combined with other fruits. Use a mix of ripe and slightly underripe fruits for jams and jellies, but use fully ripe fruit for freezing. If combining strawberries with other fruits that ripen later, pre-measure and freeze them without sugar. They can also be made into fruit vinegars and cordials (see page 318).

Leave the hulls in when picking, and refrigerate the berries as soon as possible if they are not eaten fresh. Choose only the ripe fruits because they do not ripen further after picking. Pick them early in the morning or on cloudy days if they will be stored for a few days (see Table SEP/OCT-3, page 364, for storage conditions). Spread them on a tray or in a shallow bowl and cover them loosely with perforated plastic, or not at all. Do not wash the berries until you are ready to use them, and then only rinse them.

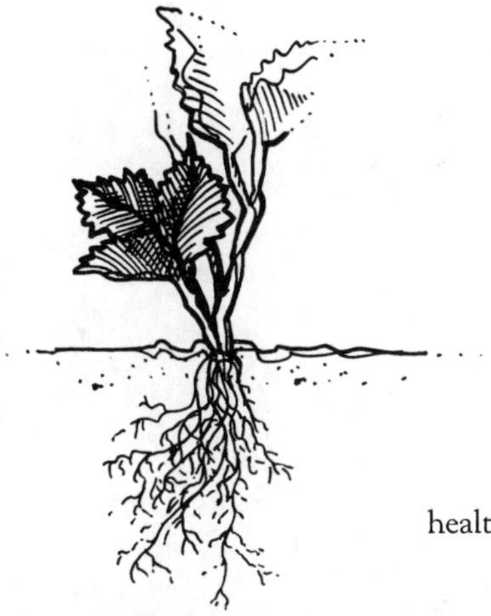

healthy

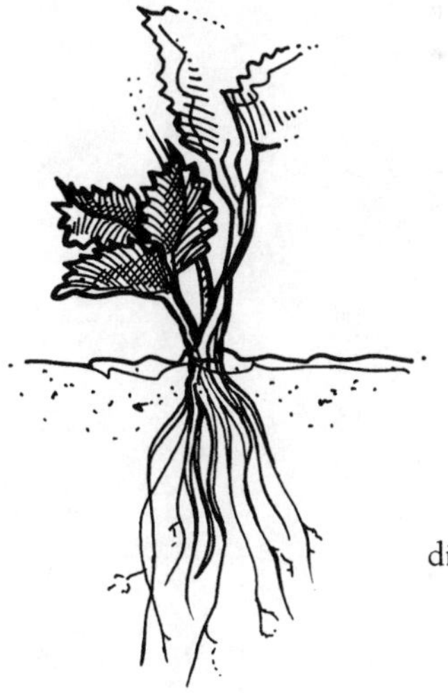

diseased

The result of red stele in strawberries can be seen in the plant's roots.

### General care

Dayneutral strawberries are different from everbearing and the old June bearing plants. They flower and fruit continuously from June on, as long as tempertures are moderate. They do not respond to day length, which is what initiates flowers in other strawberries (see Focus on Plants, page 45).

Unlike everbearers, which produce a large spring crop and a smaller fall crop, dayneutrals have production peaks every six weeks throughout the growing season. They must be watered and fertilized regularly right through to the end of the growing season. Either side dress with manure, or water monthly with manure tea or fish emulsion. During their first year, remove all blossoms for the first six to eight weeks, but then allow flowers to develop. Remove all runners the first year as well.

When picking strawberries of any kind, remove all mouldy and overripe fruit from the patch. This, a dry mulch of straw or salt marsh hay, raised beds, and well-spaced planting in full sun will help to reduce the spread of fruit rot.

These measures help to improve air circulation and faster drying of the fruit and leaves each morning.

Plants that appear wilted, dwarfed and dull may have red stele disease. The red core or stele of the roots can be seen by stripping off the outer layer of the root. It may show either only at the tip of the root or throughout the root. Some strawberry varieties tolerate the disease well enough to produce a crop, but affected plants are best removed to restrict the spread of the disease. The only control is to buy certified plants and to avoid planting in poorly drained soil or in soil previously infected (the fungus can live ten years or more in soil).

Verticillium wilt also causes plants to droop. To eliminate it, use a very long rotation system and do not include plants such as eggplant, pepper, tomato or potato.

Slug damage can be very frustrating. There are several preventive measures to try: remove mulch from around plants if the problem is severe; let the soil surface dry out between waterings, if possible; sprinkle barriers of sand, crushed eggshells, ashes or lime around plants; and set out traps of raised boards, lettuce or cabbage leaves. Cedar shingles placed under ripening fruits will deter slugs and help to keep fruits dry and free of mould.

If overall production is low, strawberry weevils may have cut through some flower stems. The holes they chew in strawberry petals are more obvious but less harmful to overall production. The usual causes of lowered fruit production, however, are plant age and insufficient moisture at bud initiation. Bud initiation in most strawberries occurs during the cool, short days of autumn. Peak production is at two and three years of age.

### *Maximum production*

There are several ways to arrange an ongoing supply of two and three-year-old plants. The traditional method, where plenty of space is available, is to have three patches—one, two, and three years old—and to start a new patch and rip out the oldest one every year. If pests or diseases have been a problem, it is better to start an entirely new bed instead of replanting the bed just ripped out. Otherwise, do a thorough job of pulling out weeds and grass and add more organic matter, and lime if necessary, to the soil. It is wise to start again if a bed of young plants is badly infested with weeds and grass.

Either transplant healthy, vigorous and disease free runners in the summer from existing beds, or prepare the bed this season and purchase new plants as early as possible next spring. August plantings will produce bigger

Peg down runners of strawberry plant, either in a pot or directly into the ground but no more than five runners per plant.

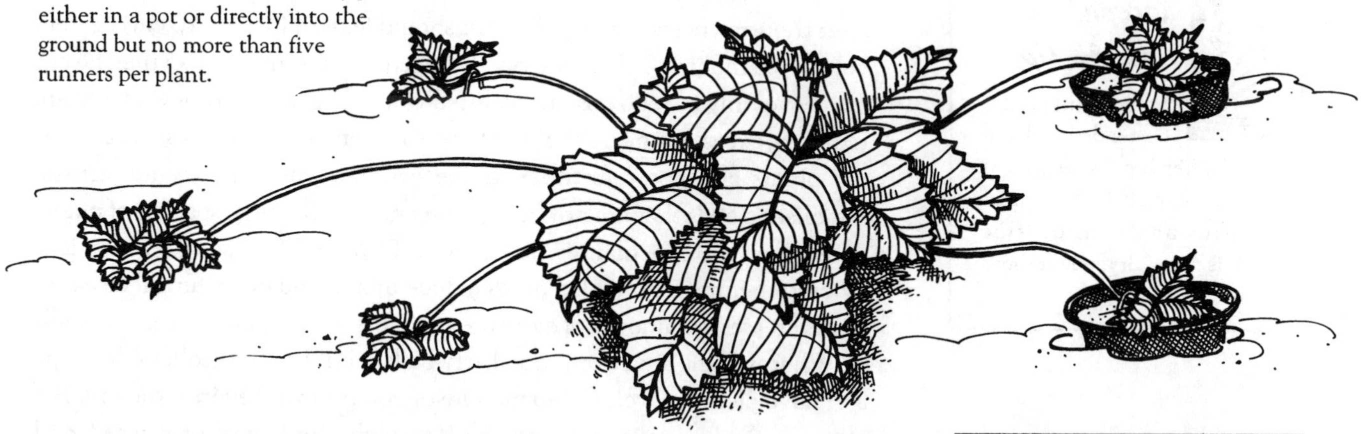

plants next year, but some may not survive the winter, particularly if runners are transplanted late in the summer or have small root systems.

To encourage rooting of new plantlets on runners, peg down the runners with a wire staple or a rock close to the plantlet as soon as the plantlets have formed. Make sure that the soil underneath is light and loose. All flowers should have been removed from the main plant to encourage earlier runners and hence larger plantlets. If plantlets are to be moved to another position this August rather than next spring, a better method is to root them in 3 ½ inch (90 mm) pots filled with a peat-based potting mix or soil lightened with organic matter. This produces well rooted plants and minimizes root disturbance at planting time. Sink the pots into the ground to reduce the watering required. Whether plantlets are pegged or potted, cut off excess runners if there are more than five runners from each main plant, and cut off each runner beyond the first plantlet.

A population of young plants can also be maintained in one patch if the oldest plants are removed each year after fruiting. The gaps are then filled in with young plantlets formed on runners, pegged down to encourage earlier rooting. If plants are in rows, the oldest rows can be removed with a cultivator, the organic material can be worked into the soil, and new plants or runners set in. The oldest plants in a solid, matted system must be removed individually and can be identified by their large crowns. Work organic matter into the gaps before replanting, and avoid putting new plants exactly where the old plants were.

A minor variation on this method is to set the lawn mower on its highest

### Green Thumb Tip

Several factors cause misshapen strawberries. Late spring frosts during flowering can damage the pistil or cause it to die and turn black. Cool weather during flowering may cause poorly formed stamens, and without these pollen bearers, there is poor fertilization and fruit set. Protect crops at night next year during cool or frosty weather. If the weather is cool, wet or windy during flowering, bee visits will be reduced, again resulting in poor pollination. The nymphs of tarnished plant bugs will suck on developing fruits and cause hardened, nubbin areas, so clean up all trash and plant debris in the autumn to reduce their hiding places. Insufficient water when the fruits are filling out will result in smaller, seedier strawberries.

### Green Thumb Tip

Strawberries need to be tended and watered after harvest as that is when the fruit buds for next year's crop are initiated. If the soil is very dry, fewer buds develop.

setting and run it over the entire patch to remove old foliage immediately after the strawberry harvest. The cut should leave 4 inches (10 cm) of stem behind, so that the crowns are not damaged. Excess runners can then be cut off; leave only as many as are required to fill in gaps. If no new plants are required, excess runners should be cut off as soon as they are noticed. Dig out old plants and apply fertilizer. Some gardeners even mow and fertilize established beds that are not being rejuvenated. The final spacing of plants depends on the type planted (see Table APR/MAY-5, page 145), but wider spacing than recommended helps reduce mould and other fungal diseases, and increases the amount of moisture available to each plant in very dry soils.

Whatever the situation, strawberry beds should have excellent drainage and have plenty of well rotted manure or compost worked into the soil. For all methods of management, remove old mulches and get rid of all weeds and grass. Water deeply if the soil is dryish, and apply fine compost, chopped seaweed, rotted manure, fish meal or liquid seaweed and a dusting of wood ashes over the soil. Bonemeal is alright, but it supplies mainly phosphorous, whereas fishmeal and the others mentioned supply phosphorous, potassium and nitrogen.

## Summer Pruning and Training of Fruits

### General principles

Fruit trees, bushes and espaliered forms may need pruning in the summer to limit their size and reduce unwanted growth, and to stimulate the production of fruit buds. This should not be a routine each year, however, as unlike winter pruning, which stimulates growth, summer pruning removes leaves. This reduces the amount of carbohydrates directed towards the roots for root growth and storage, which results in reduced growth the following spring. It is used to shape plants, to adjust the balance between excessive vegetative growth and poor cropping, and to reduce the number of fruit drops. Weak plants should never be pruned in the summer.

Summer pruning also lets more light and air into the centre of the tree, which results in well-coloured fruits, and in well-ripened wood and buds better able to withstand the rigours of winter. The improved air circulation reduces leaf spot and other fungal diseases.

### Fruit trees

In general, when pruning fruit trees start by pulling or cutting the water sprouts and suckers (thin, vigorous, upright twigs arising from main branches and the central trunk, stimulated by hard pruning in the spring), then cut out all upright growth and any branches that are crossed or rubbing. Other summer pruning of apple and other pryamid shaped fruit trees takes the form of thinning cuts (see March/April, page 92), rather than heading cuts that leave three or four leaf nodes. Thinning cuts are made in the upper two-thirds of the tree by cutting the current season's leafy shoots back to a fruit cluster, a weak side lateral, or a main limb. The aim is to allow more light to reach the middle of the tree. You may need to make a few cuts into two-year-old wood, and perhaps one or two cuts into three-year-old wood.

Examine all trees for disease, such as the oozing of fireblight and the olive coloured swellings of black knot disease, and cut these out 12 inches (30 cm) below the affected area. The amount of wood removed now is greater than during dormancy. Immediately burn or discard diseased material and remember to dip pruning shears in disinfectant and water between cuts.

Young trees should have crotch angles corrected, if this has not been done already. Use clothespins or toothpicks to increase the angle. The ideal angle between the branch and the trunk is 45 to 60$^{0}$. Branches that grow vertically will have mostly vegetative growth and few fruit, whereas branches that grow horizontally will have poor vegetative growth but good fruit production. Horizontal branches, however, are prone to breakage. Heavily laden limbs of apple, plum and other fruit trees should be supported. This should not be necessary if the crotch angles are within the right range.

Check ties on fruit and other trees that are staked. Ties in a loose figure eight will protect the bark from rubbing against the stake. If ties are getting tight, either loosen or replace them.

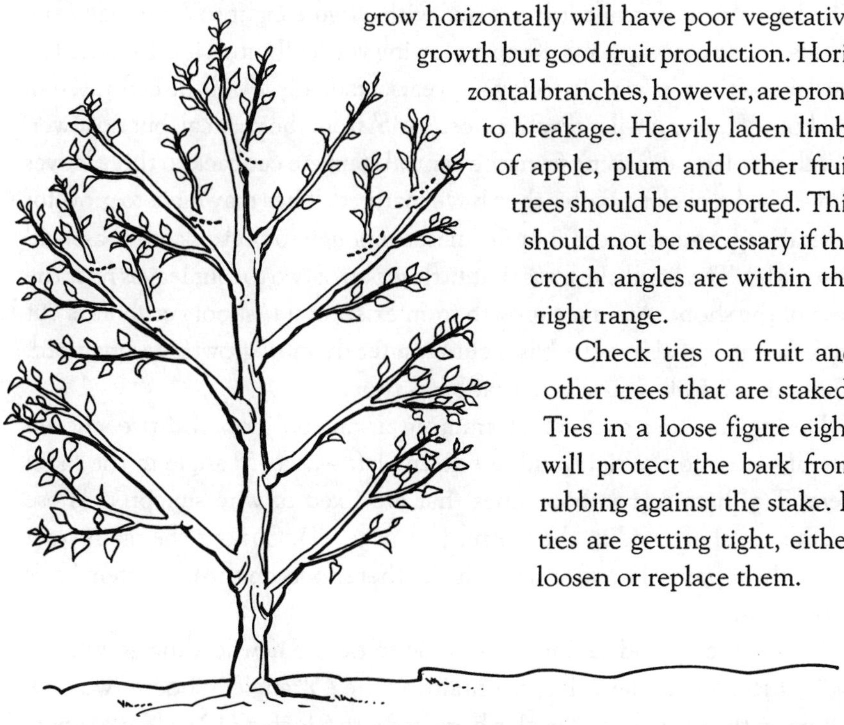

Pyramid Tree Pruning
Make thinning cuts back to down facing branches or to main stem. Remove current season's vertical growth.

## Green Thumb Tip

Summer pruning has to be done after the current season's growth has stopped and the terminal bud is set (no new leaves are emerging from the tip) to avoid summer regrowth—a result contrary to the intent of summer pruning. Where the soil is dry and poor, growth is slowed and pruning can usually be done in late July. In warmer zones or where there is plenty of moisture and soil nutrient levels are high, growth will continue later in the season and summer pruning should not be done until growth stops sometime in August, or even later in some years.

Cut back laterals to 3-5 leaves.

### *Soft fruits and grapes*

On fruiting shrubs, summer pruning consists of heading cuts. Cutting back the young lateral growth encourages the formation of fruit buds. With red currants and gooseberries, for example, the laterals are cut back to three to five leaves, just above a leaf joint.

Raspberry and blackberry canes planted earlier this year should be cut out once the new canes are produced. Removing them makes more moisture and nutrients available to the young canes that will bear next year's crop, and thereby will increase the yield. Keep watered any canes and other fruits that are filling out. Black currants and blackberries are also cut out once the crop is finished, either immediately after fruiting is finished or first thing next spring.

Thin grapes within each cluster if larger grapes are wanted, but do not bother if you are using them only for jellies or juice. For self-supporting grapes, twine two young stems around each other to a height of 2 ½ feet (75 cm), then train the stems horizontally in opposite directions (see page 101).

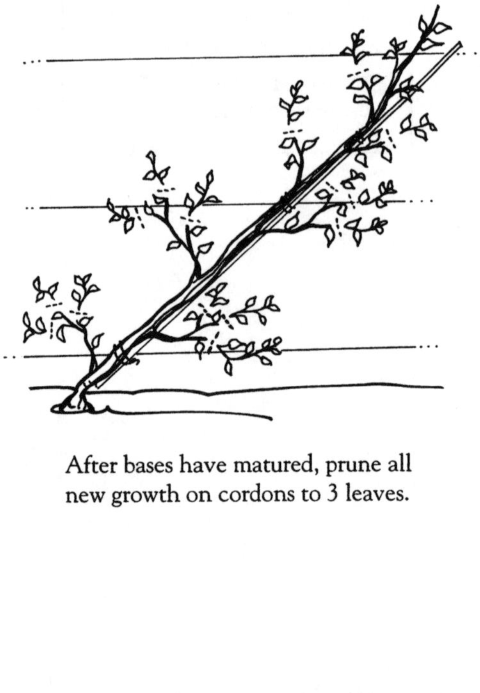

After bases have matured, prune all new growth on cordons to 3 leaves.

### *Cordons, fans and espaliers*

The leader of a central cordon is tied with a figure eight to a bamboo cane that is tied to wire supports. Keep it growing vertically until it is 6 inches (15 cm) above the top wire. In following years, gradually lower the central stem by about 5° a year until it reaches close to 35° from the vertical, but no lower.

All new laterals arising from the central stem are cut back to three leaves above the basal cluster after they have matured. They may have to grow for several weeks more before they are mature enough to cut back (the base will be woody). The basal cluster is that little group of two to four leaves near the base of the shoot. Any new growth from existing side shoots or spurs is cut back to one leaf above the basal cluster after the new growth has matured. The spur is a stubby structure that bears fruit.

During the first summer of training a fan, position the two chosen laterals—one to the right and one to the left—at a 45° angle to the main stem. Tie them to bamboo canes that are fixed to wire supports. These laterals are shortened in the winter (see page 99). Cut out the main stem above the topmost lateral and pinch all other shoots on the main stem back to one leaf.

During the second summer, continue to tie the new leading growth on each of these two main ribs, maintaining the 45° angle. Choose two new shoots on the upper side of each rib, spaced 4 to 6 inches (10 to 15 cm) apart

Fan Training

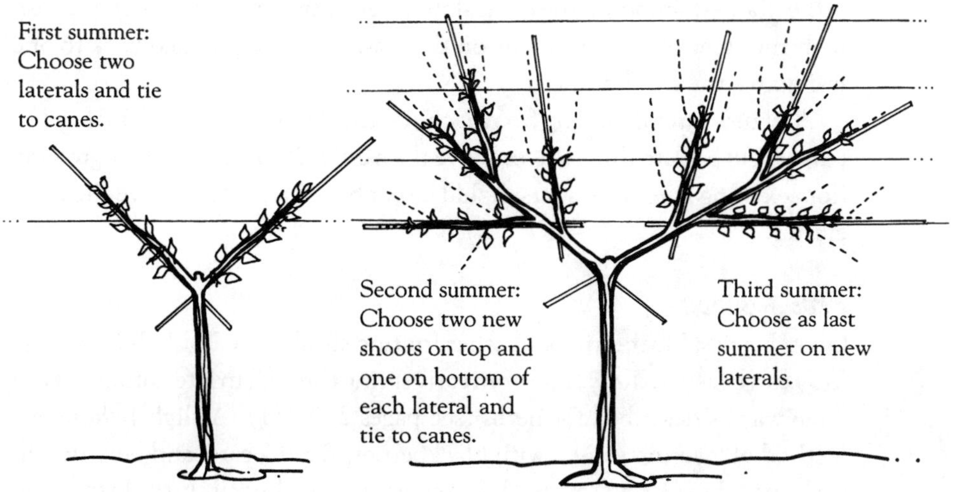


and choose one new shoot on the underside of each rib. Tie them all into a fan position, using bamboo canes attached to the wires. There are now the two main ribs plus six new ribs radiating outwards in a fan shape. These will all be shortened next spring.

Early in each growing season, rub off or cut out any laterals growing towards the wall. Laterals that are growing away from the wall and excess laterals not required for ribs are pinched back to one leaf at the midsummer pruning.

The following summer, tie the leading growth of each of the eight ribs in place, maintaining the direction and the pattern that has been set. Depending on the size of the space available, this training can be continued next year with more new ribs.

The espalier form with horizontal arms (tiers) is tied in place with figure eight ties to bamboo canes. These have been attached to supporting wires in the position that the espalier is to take during training. The topmost shoot is tied vertically and two new laterals below it are tied at 45° angles, one to the right and one to the left. If one of the laterals is growing faster than the other, lower it more than 45°, or do not lower the weaker lateral as far. The more vertical a branch is, the faster it will grow, but fewer fruit buds will form. In October, the two branches of the new tier are lowered further to horizontal positions. This is repeated each year until the top wire is reached

Espalier Training

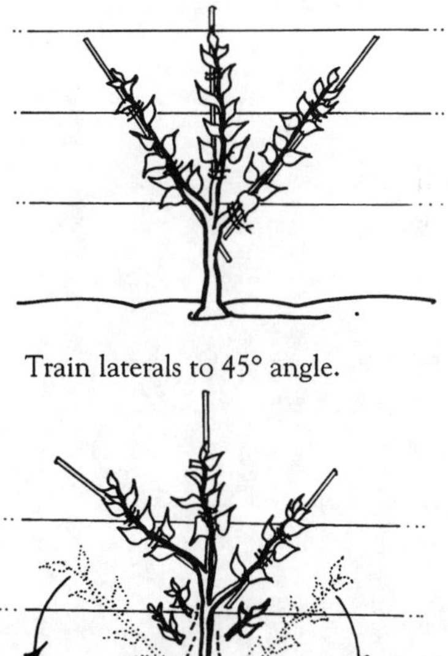

Train laterals to 45° angle.

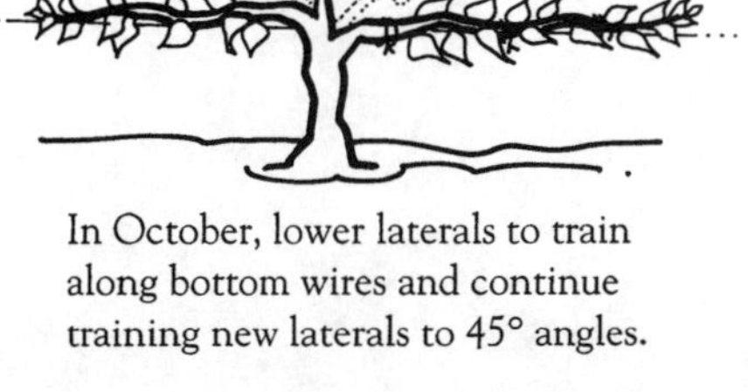

In October, lower laterals to train along bottom wires and continue training new laterals to 45° angles.

and the final tier is formed. At that point, the central leader is cut out in the spring (see page 99).

Unwanted shoots on the central stem below the first tier are cut out flush with the stem. All other shoots on the main stem are pinched back to one leaf above the basal cluster.

Any new laterals arising from each tier that are longer than 9 inches (22 cm) are cut back to three leaves above the basal cluster. Any that are growing from existing laterals or spurs should be cut back to one leaf above the basal cluster.

## Propagation

Gooseberries, blueberries and other fruiting shrubs (see Table JUL-3, page 275) can be layered any time from early spring through to late autumn in the same way as described for herbs (see pages 250-251). A slightly different method of layering is used with blackberries. Bend a cane and bury the tip under 6 inches (15 cm) of soil. Tread gently to firm the soil and hold the cane in place. Next spring, cut off the rooted tip leaving approximately 12 inches (30 cm) of the old cane attached.

Blackberries can also be propagated with leaf bud cuttings. The cane must still be growing actively for this method to be effective. Obtain several short pieces of stem by cutting just above a leaf and 3/4 inch (2 cm) below, or scoop half-moon pieces out of the stem, including a leaf with each piece. Remove a 1/4 inch (6 mm) sliver of bark at the base of the cutting and dust it with rooting hormone. Insert the pieces firmly in a pot of moist peat moss and sand or perlite, allowing only the leaves to protrude. From this point they are treated the same way as semi-hardwood cuttings (see page 281).

Blueberries can be propagated from cuttings, but they are difficult to start no matter which method is chosen. A successful modification, originating in Québec, is to pinch young growth ten days before taking a 6 inch (15 cm) long cutting with a 3/4 inch (2 cm) heel of last year's growth attached at the base. Proceed as on page 281, and provide the planted cuttings with plenty of humidity.

## Pests and Diseases

Birds that are eating fruit can be discouraged by spreading bird netting over trees and shrubs. Throw it over affected trees, but put stakes in the ground to support netting over fruiting shrubs to make picking easier. Under all fruiting plants, keep weeds and grass under control, water deeply and

### Table JUL-3 Propagation of Fruits

| Plant | Types of cuttings | | | | |
|---|---|---|---|---|---|
| | Soft | Semi- | Hardwood | Layering | Other |
| Blackberry | | | | | rooted tip, leaf bud, suckers |
| Blueberry | d | d,h | | (slow) | root cutting |
| Currant - Black | | | x | x | |
| - Red/White | | | x | x | |
| Elderberry | | h | x | x | |
| Gooseberry | | | x | x | |
| Grape | | h | x | x | eye cutting |
| Hardy Kiwi | | x | | | |
| Mulberry | | | h | | |
| Quince | | | h | x | |
| Raspberry | | | | | suckers |
| Saskatoon (Indian Pear) | | | | x | root division |
| Strawberry | | | | | runners |

d = difficult method
x = useful method
h = take heel of old wood at base of cutting
N.B. Tree fruits are propagated by grafting.

regularly if required, and keep the ground mulched. Also pick up all dropped fruits. Any which are mouldy or diseased, whether still on the plant or fallen to the ground, should be removed daily to keep diseases in check.

Insect larvae will leave the dropped fruits and enter the soil, so removing the fruit also prevents insects from overwintering and completing their life cycle. Apple sawfly larvae, for example, leave fallen fruits to burrow into the ground, where they overwinter. Plum curculios (weevils) have a grub stage that feeds inside the fruits of plum, apple, blueberry, cherry, peach, pear and quince, and they also leave fallen fruits to pupate in the soil.

There is a natural thinning process that causes fruits to drop, but those which are insect infested have holes in the skin. Even currant fruit fly larvae can be detected by tiny holes in the small fruits. Lay a sheet on the ground

Life cycle of an Apple Maggot

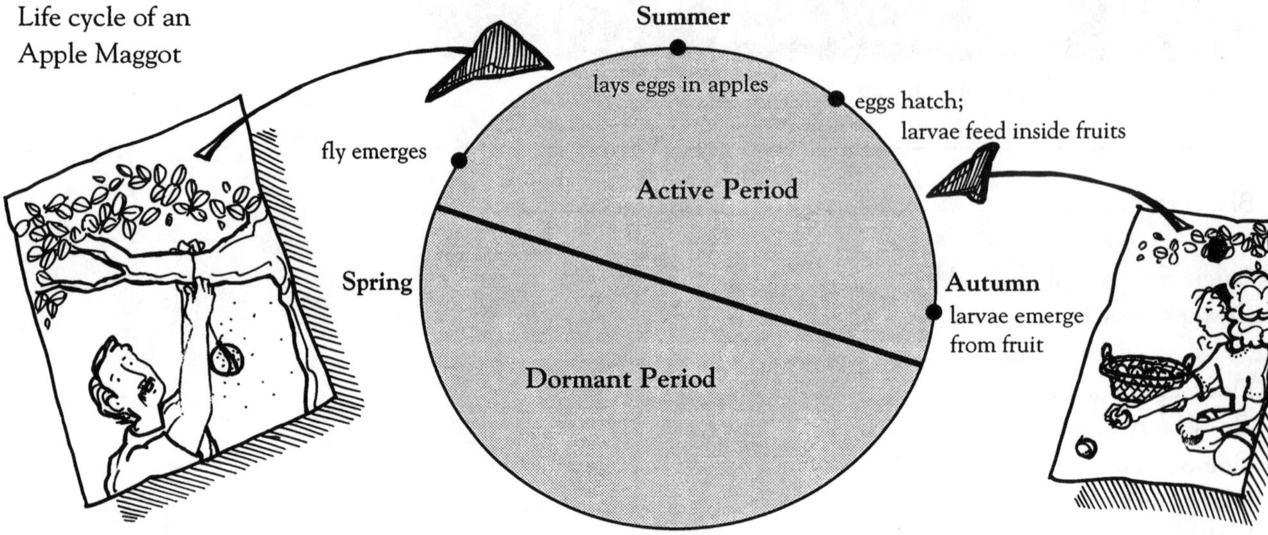


Intervention: hang sticky balls in fruit trees

Intervention: pick up fruit drops

under fruit bushes each morning, and shake the plants vigorously to dislodge the affected fruits with their resident insects. Rake up all fruits that reach the ground this way or naturally, and cultivate the top layer of soil in the autumn. Bantam hens are reputed to be a tremendous help, as they forage for fruits and insects on the ground. Unless the compost pile gets hot enough to kill larvae and disease organisms, it is best to bury affected fruit deeply somewhere in the garden, put it in the garbage, or solarize it in a plastic bag for two weeks (see page 299).

Some insects require a different approach. Apple maggots emerge when fruits are reaching a good size later in the season, and then pupate in the soil. Their life cycle can be interrupted this month, however, by hanging traps in apple, pear, plum, hawthorn and cherry trees. Use dark red or black 3 inch (8 cm) balls (such as croquet balls) covered in Tanglefoot on branches about 5 feet (1.5 m) above the ground. Hang two traps per dwarf tree and four to six per large tree. Adults will attempt to lay their eggs on the traps instead of on fruits. Continue to pick up all dropped fruit at least twice a week.

Codling moths emerge when petals are falling on apple trees, and lay their eggs on leaves shortly afterwards. The pink-bodied, brown-headed larvae that hatch tunnel into fruits—where they make a mess—and stay there until sometime in August. On leaving the fruits, they crawl down the trunk and go under loose bark where they spin cocoons and spend the winter.

Spraying Bt mixed with skim milk powder every five days for a total of five sprays throughout July may help to reduce their numbers. To interrupt their life cycle, wrap several thicknesses of 6 inch (15 cm) wide strips of wide-wale corrugated cardboard, rough side inward, near the ground around the trunks of apple, pear, quince and apricot trees this month. Remove and destroy these bands in the autumn, along with the pupae inside that thought they had found a secure place for the winter. Scrape off rough, loose bark this month if it was not done in the spring (see March-April, page 91).

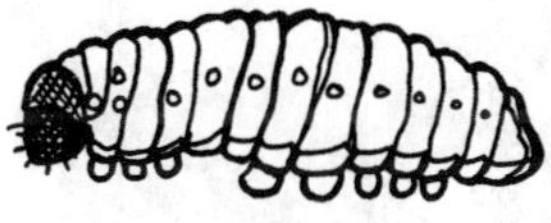

Codling moth

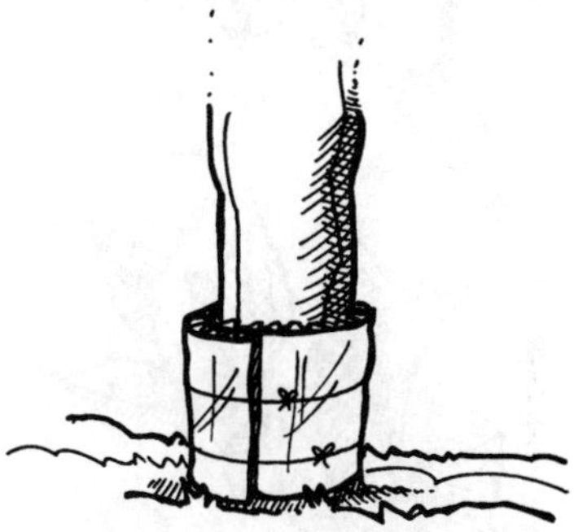

Cardboard around tree bases will give a place for the codling moth to spend the winter. Destroy the cardboard in the autumn along with the pupae inside.

Canker worms or "loopers" defoliate many fruit and other trees during June or July. They tend to appear in cycles of two to three years, so the easiest course of action is to wait out the cycles, but some steps can be taken to manage them.

The larvae drop down on threads from the trees where they are feeding, and then climb up to start feeding again if they are not blown onto another tree. There is little that can be done to control them at this feeding stage, but you can wash them off with a strong spray of water.

When they drop off or are knocked off the trees onto the ground, the mature larvae burrow into the soil and then pupate. Shallow cultivation of the soil under affected plants will control them to some degree—pupae will be destroyed, and fewer adults will emerge to lay eggs.

Another measure which reduces their numbers requires wrapping each tree trunk with a strip of heavy brown paper or burlap, and then smearing on Tanglefoot to trap adults as they crawl along the trunk. For spring cankerworm, which overwinters in the egg stage, apply the Tanglefoot in March or early April before the ground thaws; for fall cankerworm, which hibernates in the soil, apply it in September, when the adults are laying eggs.

Blistering on currant leaves is due to aphids and is usually not severe enough to warrant attention. Aphids are often attended by ants, which collect the honeydew exuded by the aphids. The honeydew can turn black with sooty mould, but this is more unsightly than harmful unless coverage is extensive. Aphids that cause tender shoots on young fruit trees to become deformed, however, are a more serious matter because they can ruin the shape of the tree. They can be removed every three days by hand, with a strong spray of water, or with insecticidal soap (see page 194). In other situations, allow natural predators such as lacewings, hoverflies, wasps, ladybird beetles and their larvae to control the aphids. Chickadees, purple finches and warblers also eat aphids.

If leaves are dropping prematurely and are spotted, the tree is probably suffering from leaf blight. Remove the affected leaves from the plant, pick

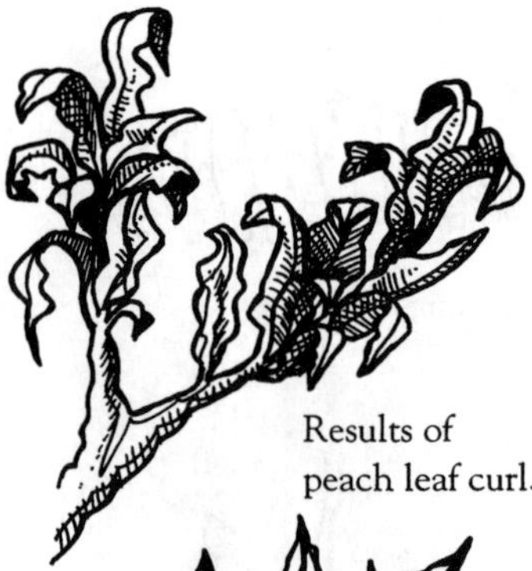

Results of peach leaf curl.

up all dropped leaves and bury them or put them in the garbage but not in the compost. Do a thorough raking up job in the autumn as well to reduce the number of overwintering spores. Summer pruning to improve air circulation may help, and faithfully applying sulphur or other fungicide every week or two, especially after rain, will help to prevent further infections of leaf blight and scab on apples.

Peach leaf curl, which shows up as reddish blisters and premature leaf fall, should be tackled in the spring. If there are signs of it now, remove all affected and fallen leaves, and make a note to spray peach trees with lime sulphur in early spring (see March/April, page 105) just before the buds swell, again at green tip stage (see May, page 193), and finally just before leaf fall (see September/October, pages 365-366).

Cherries that turn brown and fall off are suffering from brown rot (disease names are always so descriptive!). Immediately remove all affected fruits. Spraying with sulphur as soon as you notice spots on the fruit, and every seven to fourteen days thereafter, may help a little. Remember that sulphur only prevents spores from becoming active and does not cure fungal diseases once they are established. Next spring apply preventative sprays (see May, page 193).

## Woody Ornamentals

### General Care and Insects

Much of what fruits need in terms of general care applies to other shrubs and trees. Continue to provide deep, regular waterings. Flower buds for next year are forming on many kinds of plants and lack of water could reduce next year's bloom. After July, however, it is all right to reduce watering. Plants must stop growing so that wood can firm up and harden off for the winter.

A 1 to 2 inch (2.5 to 5 cm) layer of compost can be spread on the ground as far out as the drip line (the ends of the branches). If the supply of compost is limited, however, it is best applied beside vegetables, flowers and soft fruits. Use coarser compost for large plants and fine compost for small, shallow rooted plants. One application of compost in the spring is usually sufficient for most plants except those that are growing vigorously, but a little extra in July will give an additional boost. A wisteria that grows vigorously but refuses to flower should have no nitrogenous fertilizer applied. It can be further encouraged to bloom by summer pruning. Cut back this year's shoots to five or six leaves.

Do not fertilize after mid July as new growth after this time will not have time to harden off before winter. Excessive watering after the end of July can also cause growth to continue too long and not harden off properly for the winter. You can pinch out the growing tips of lanky shrubs, such as azaleas, up to the middle of July, but not any later because each pinching stimulates new growth.

If plants are showing signs of nitrogen deficiency, take steps early in the month to correct the situation. Deficiency shows up as slow growth, stunting, and smaller leaves than normal. Leaves are pale in colour, the tips become yellow, and then the whole leaf turns yellow and may drop off. Older leaves are affected first.

Immediately spray the leaves with diluted fish emulsion or liquid seaweed, and apply it weekly until the plant looks healthy again. As well, add about an inch (2.5 cm) of well rotted manure or compost before the middle of July, again in the spring, and every spring thereafter.

Leaves also turn yellow and drop off if plants receive too much water. This can occur if trees or shrubs have been planted in soil that drains poorly. A generous planting hole dug out of an area that drains poorly acts as a catchment for excess water in the area, so plant on a slight mound instead.

Spittlebug, which fits its name, appears on shrubs, flowers and all kinds of plants, but it is not a problem. Scale, which appears as hard, brown discs on stems and leaf veins, can be destructive. Its waxy coating protects it from sprays, but it can be wiped off with a damp cloth. Leaves of badly infested plants turn yellow and sticky with honeydew. If conditions are intolerable take preventive steps next spring by spraying with dormant oil (see March/April, page 105). As well, make certain that plants have all their requirements met so that they can grow vigorously and tolerate scale and other insects.

Gall insects lay eggs inside leaves; the affected leaves respond by growing more leaf tissue. These odd, upright growths are no cause for concern and should be viewed as an interesting curiosity. Over time, they will become rounded, brown in colour and firm. Since less than 10 to 15% of the entire leaf area of a plant is usually affected, plants continue to thrive and grow, provided all their needs are met.

Black, green and other coloured aphids are quite common and usually nothing to be bothered about. On mock orange plants—which tend to be rather upright and lanky—the affected tips can be cut out, which will encourage branching.

Summer pruing may be in order, too, for overly vigorous plants. Maple trees, for example, can be pruned once the leaves have fully matured and the terminal bud is set (see Green Thumb Tip, page 271). It pays to keep trees healthy, not only for our own enjoyment but for the environment as well. One 40 foot (31 m) maple is the same as an air-conditioner for an eight room house—it can filter up to 60 pounds (27 kg) of pollutants each year.

## Summer Planting

Many problems arising from too much growth can be avoided by purchasing trees and shrubs whose ultimate height and spread will fit the space available. Nurseries often have sales at this time of year, and good bargains can be obtained, but know what final size you want before purchasing any plant. As well, leave plenty of space between plants, and between plants and houses (see page 143).

When planting, take the same care as discussed in April/May (pages 146-147). The sooner plants are put in the ground, the longer they will have to get their roots established before the ground freezes solid and autumn and winter winds start knocking the plants around. Wind rock can easily prevent roots from becoming established—plants will die as a result.

If transplanting trees or shrubs, wait until after the new growth has firmed up and the terminal buds are set. The leaves of deciduous plants and the needles of evergreens require less moisture and will make fewer demands of the roots at this point. Root growth is usually out of phase with top growth—roots start growing again after top growth has slowed or stopped for the summer.

Shallow rooted plants, such as rhododendrons, are easier to move than deep rooted plants, but with any plant be careful to keep the roots moist and cool while they are out of the ground. Water well a day or two before moving, cover the root ball with wet burlap after lifting the plant, mist the leaves frequently, and give the roots another good soaking after replanting. Make sure that broad leaved evergreens are planted in sheltered locations to prevent winter damage and are on a slight mound with plenty of organic material worked into the soil.

## Propagation

### Semi-hardwood cuttings

As growth on shrubs starts to firm up, take semi-hardwood cuttings of those to be propagated (refer to Table JUL-4). This is done through July and August, depending on each plant type's stage of growth. Take cuttings from this year's growth. The base should be getting firm and woody, but the tips will still be growing. They are a little easier to manage than softwood cuttings because they are not quite so prone to wilting, but they still need plenty of attention.

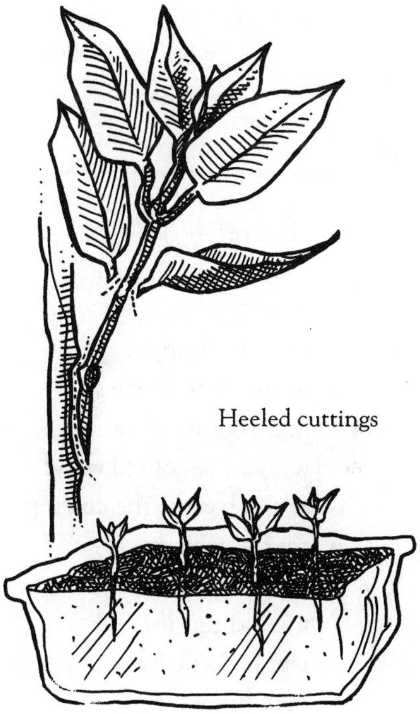

Heeled cuttings

Cut 6 to 8 inch (15 to 20 cm) side shoots close to the main stem. Make a clean cut just below the lowest leaf and strip the leaves from the bottom end of the shoot. Cut off the soft tip just above a leaf, so that a 4 to 6 inch (10 to 15 cm) long cutting remains. Some gardeners have better luck if the tips are pinched seven to ten days before the cuttings are taken. Some plants do better with heeled cuttings (refer to Table JUL-4). Using a sharp knife, cut a piece of the bark and a bit of the underlying wood of the main stem (last year's growth) at the base of the cutting. This will yield a cutting that is mainly this year's growth, with about 3/4 to 1 inch (2 to 2.5 cm) of last year's growth attached to the base. Take more cuttings than required because some will not root.

Fill a pot nearly to the brim with a moist rooting medium as for softwood cuttings (see page 61). Four or five cuttings will fit in a 3 inch (75 mm) pot, or as many as ten in a 5 inch (125 mm) pot. Dip the bases of the cuttings in rooting hormone and proceed as for softwood cuttings. Bottom heat is not essential, but it does hasten rooting. Keep the cuttings out of direct sunlight. A cold frame in the shade is ideal, or use lattice-work, a shaded greenhouse or a propagation unit (see pages 442-443).

After two to four weeks, if rooting has occurred (the cuttings stay inserted in the soil when gently pulled), gradually expose the cuttings to drier, cooler conditions. After two weeks more, they should need no cover at all, but leave them in their pots for one more week before potting them into individual pots. Softwood cuttings that have taken root should also be moved on to individual 4 inch (100 mm) pots. Use low profile containers which have a diameter that is twice the container's height. It has been shown that trees grown in such pots transplant better because they have a more natural root formation and no circling roots. This becomes increasingly important as the pot size increases. Keep the cuttings evenly moist, still in the cold frame, greenhouse or under a lath structure. In the autumn, pot them on into larger pots and keep them indoors over the winter in cold storage (see November, page 418).

If cuttings do not root successfully, try layering plants (see pages 149-151) anytime between spring and when the ground freezes. This works well for hardy shrub roses, for example, which are sometimes difficult to start from cuttings.

## Key

- al = air layer
- c = root cutting
- d = root division
- dr = layer by dropping plant deeper into ground
- h = may root more easily with a heel of old wood at the base of the cutting
- k = rooted suckers
- l = layering, and see mounding (m)
- lb = leaf bud cutting
- l# = bury branch tips
- m = layer by building up mound of soil at base of plant with new growth; works well for plants that can be layered
- sk = soak seed before sowing
- st = stratify three to five months at 2 to 4°C before sowing
- st-d = stratify five months at room temperature and another three months at 2 to 4°C before sowing
- x = fairly reliable method
- * = not suitable with grafted plants

## Table JUL-4 Propagation Methods for Woody Ornamentals

| Plant Name | Seed | Root | Suckers or Layering | Softwood Cutting | Semi-Hard Cutting | Hardwood Cutting |
|---|---|---|---|---|---|---|
| Amelanchier | x | c | k | | | |
| Aralia | sk | c | k | | x | |
| Arctostaphylos | st | | l | | h | x |
| Ash (*Fraxinus* spp.) | st | | | | | |
| Azalea | x | | l | | x | |
| Bayberry | sk,st | | | | | |
| Beautybush | | | | | h | |
| Beech-species | st | | | | | |
| Berberis (banned in many areas) | st | d | k | | h | x |
| Birch-species | x | | | | | |
| Bittersweet (Celastrus) | st | c | l | | x | x |
| Boston Ivy | st | | l | | x | |
| Boxwood | st | | | | x | x |
| Broom | sk | | | | h | |
| Buckeye (Bottlebrush) | st | | m | | | |
| Buffaloberry | x | | | | | |
| Butterfly Bush | x | | | | h | x |
| Caragana-N.B | x | c | | x | x | |
| Caryopteris | | | | | x | x |
| Catalpa | | | | | h | |
| Cedar-N.B. (*Thuja* spp.) | x | | | | | x |
| Clematis-N.B. | st | | l,al | lb | x | |
| Cotoneaster | x | | l | | h | x |
| Currant, Flowering | | | c | l | | x |
| Daphne | st | c | | | h | x |
| Deutzia | x | d | | | x | x |
| Dogwood | st | | | | h | x |
| Dutchman's Pipe | x | | l | x | | |

| Plant Name | Seed | Root | Suckers or Layering | Softwood Cutting | Semi-Hard Cutting | Hardwood Cutting |
|---|---|---|---|---|---|---|
| Elder | x | | | | h | x |
| Elm | | c | l,al | x | | |
| Enkianthus | x | | l | | h | |
| Euonymus | | | l | | h | x |
| False Spirea (*Sorbaria sorbifolia*) | x | d | k | | h | x |
| Fir-N.B. | x | | | | | |
| Firethorn | st | | | | x | |
| Forsythia | | d | l | | x | x |
| Ginkgo | x | | | | | |
| Hawthorn-N.B. | st | c | | | | |
| Hazelnut | st | | k,l | | x | |
| Heather | x | | dr | | h | x |
| Hibiscus | x | | l | x | x | x |
| Holly | | | | | | |
| - evergreen | st-d | | l | | x | |
| - deciduous | st-d | | | x | | x |
| Honey Locust-N.B | x | | | | | |
| Honeysuckle | | | | | | |
| -shrub | | c,d | | | x | x |
| -vine | st | c | l | | | |
| Horse Chestnut | st | c | | | | |
| Hydrangea | | | | | | |
| -shrub | x | | | | x | x |
| -climbing | | | l | x | | |
| Japanese Tree Lilac | x | | | | h | |
| Juniper | st-d | | l | | | h |
| Kerria | | d | | x | x | x |
| Kiwi | x | | | | x | x |
| Koelreuteria (Golden Rain) | x | | | | | |
| Laburnum-N.B (Golden Chain) | x | | | | | |

## Key

- al = air layer
- c = root cutting
- d = root division
- dr = layer by dropping plant deeper into ground
- h = may root more easily with a heel of old wood at the base of the cutting
- k = rooted suckers
- l = layering, and see mounding (m)
- lb = leaf bud cutting
- l# = bury branch tips
- m = layer by building up mound of soil at base of plant with new growth; works well for plants that can be layered
- sk = soak seed before sowing
- st = stratify three to five months at 2 to 4°C before sowing
- st-d = stratify five months at room temperature and another three months at 2 to 4°C before sowing
- x = fairly reliable method
- * = not suitable with grafted plants

| Plant Name | Seed | Root | Suckers or Layering | Softwood Cutting | Semi-Hard Cutting | Hardwood Cutting |
|---|---|---|---|---|---|---|
| Lavender | x | | dr | | x | x |
| Leucothoe | x | d | l | | x | x |
| Lilac | st | | k*,l | x | h | |
| Magnolia | st | | l,al | | h | |
| Mahonia | st | | k | x | x,lb | x |
| Maple-N.B. | x | | | | | |
| Mock Orange | x | d | l | x | x | x |
| Mountain Ash (*Sorbus* spp.) | x | | | | | |
| Mountain Laurel | st | | l | | | |
| Mulberry | | | | | | x |
| Ninebark | x | d | | | x | x |
| Oak | st | | | | | |
| Pachistima | | | l,m | | x | |
| Pearlbush | x | d | l | x | | |
| Pieris | x | | l,al | | x | x |
| Pine-N.B. | x | | | | | |
| Poplar | | | k | | | x |
| Potentilla (Cinquefoil) | x | d | | | h | x |
| Privet | st | c | | x | | x |
| Prunus-N.B. | st | c | | | h | |
| -Flowering Almond | | | | | | |
| -Nanking Cherry | | | | | | |
| -Purpleleaf Sandcherry | | | | | | |
| Quince (*Chaenomeles* spp.) | | | d | l | h | x |
| Redbud (*Cercis canadensis*) | x | c | | | | |
| Rhododendron | x | | l | | h | x |
| Robinia (Rose Acacia) | x | c | k | | | |
| Rose | st | | l,k* | x | h | x |
| Russian Olive | st | c | l,k | | x | x |
| Sea Buckthorn | x | | l | | | |

| Plant Name | Seed | Root | Suckers or Layering | Softwood Cutting | Semi-Hard Cutting | Hardwood Cutting |
|---|---|---|---|---|---|---|
| Silver Lace Vine | | | | | h | x |
| Smoke Tree | st | | l | | h | |
| Snowberry | | d,c | k,l | | | x |
| Spirea | | d | k | | x | x |
| Spruce | x | | | | | |
| Stephanandra | x | d | k,l# | | x | x |
| Sumac | st-d | c | k | | | |
| Summer Sweet (*Clethra alnifolia*) | | | d | k,l | h | |
| Tamarix | x | | | | x | x |
| Trumpet Creeper (*Campsis radicans*) | x | c | l | x | | x |
| Tulip Tree | st | | al | | | |
| Viburnum | st-d | c,d* | l | x | h | x |
| Virginia Creeper | st | | l | | x | |
| Weigela | x | c | | | h | x |
| Willow | | | | | x | x |
| Wisteria | | | l | | h | |
| Witch Hazel | st-d | | l | | h | |
| Yew-N.B. | st-d | | | | h | |
| Yucca | x | d,c | | | | |
| Zelkova | x | | al | | | |

N.B. Many woody ornamentals are propagated using grafts; seeds of varieties do not come true (are not like the parent plants).

## Lawns

### General Summer Maintenance

Mowing is about the only necessary lawn chore in the summer, and may have to be done as often as twice a week if the soil is moist. If it gets too long, mow the lawn in several stages, removing no more than one-third of the total length with each cut. This stresses the grass less than taking off a huge amount in one fell swoop. Mow the lawn higher than in the spring and fall if the soil is very dry as long grass helps to shade the soil and keep it cool and moist. Clippings can and should be left on the lawn as long as they are no longer than 1 inch (2.5 cm). Longer ones should be raked off, but do not throw them out. They make wonderful mulch for vegetables, flowers and herbs, but be careful that they do not touch the stems of plants as the stems may rot.

If nutrient levels are low—evidenced by a paler shade of green— consider applying more seaweed extract or fish emulsion early in the month. Unfinished compost used as a fertilizer may cause a temporary shortage of nitrogen. Clover in the lawn helps supply nitrogen needs, but it may end up forming a higher proportion of the total cover in lawns that are short of nitrogen. If it seems to be taking over, supply more nitrogen, try mowing the lawn higher than usual, and aerate the soil in the autumn—clover seems to predominate on compacted soils. It is lovely and green, though, even during dry spells, so try to keep about 20% clover throughout the lawn.

Water deeply every two to three weeks if conditions are very dry, but water new lawns and those on sandy soils more often. Lawn problems tend to show up during dry spells (see Table MAY-8, page 202). To avoid problems, make sure sufficient water is supplied (see pages 208-209), and increase the amount of organic matter in the soil (see page 371).

One of the prettiest sights to see on a summer morning is hundreds of spider webs on the lawn, glistening with dew. And never mind the weeds; mowing keeps them from going to seed!

**Green Thumb Tip**

Newly seeded lawns should not be cut until the grass remains firmly anchored when tugged on. If it comes out by the roots, wait a little longer. When it is ready for cutting, make sure the mower blade is really sharp, so that grass is cut cleanly without being pulled. Try to cut it before it goes to seed so that roots are encouraged to run and form a tighter sod. Sodded lawns should not be mowed until the joins have knit together with new root growth.

## Indoor Gardening

The summer is a good time to put all your plants outside so you can clean the greenhouse. If indoor growing is to continue, however, the main challenge is keeping glassed in areas from overheating. Regular misting and good ventilation will be sufficient for most situations (and see page 241). Remember to fertilize regularly, and pot on seedlings as required.

Pay particular attention to watering, and move plants that seem to dry out too quickly into larger containers. Keeping plants watered can be a real challenge if you go away. Try wick systems and automatic watering, or hire someone, but be sure to take the time to show him or her what needs to be done. It is a good idea to have the person water once before you leave, so that any problems or misunderstandings can be cleared up before you go.

### Vegetables

There is little to plant indoors this time of year. Peppers and eggplants started last month will need potting on and regular fertilizing. If tomatoes were not started from seed last month, take cuttings from plants in the garden or from greenhouse plants nearing the end of production (see pages 291-292).

### Warm Flowers

*Lilium speciosum rubrum*, if brought out of cold storage early this month, should be in bloom by Christmas. Grow it cool at first, if possible, perhaps by putting it outdoors against the north side of the house for a few weeks. Begonias potted now should also be in bloom for Christmas.

### Cool Flowers

Several flowers can be seeded for indoor autumn and winter bloom, but next month is soon enough, too. Planting in consecutive months, however, will extend the season of bloom.

Some flowers seem prone to damping off, so pay particular attention to how they are watered (refer to Preventive Measure, page 50). Try early varieties of stock, calendula, feverfew, winter-flowering sweet pea and pansy (with extra hours of lighting from November onwards to encourage earlier blooming). Winter-flowering snapdragons can be planted both early and late in the month to extend the season of bloom. Avoid peat based potting soils for snapdragons; potting soils can be lightened with extra perlite, sand or finely chopped straw.

Provide extra light for snapdragons and nasturtiums, and for feverfew if desired (see page 32). Place chrysanthemums in darkness from 5 p.m. to 7 a.m. by covering them with black sateen over a frame or by putting them in a dark closet. Start this on July 1 for one or two plants and continue until buds form, usually around September 1. Each week, begin this dark treatment for another plant or two until September, when nights become naturally long enough.

Month-by-Month
August
• pick up fruit drops
• try cooking with herbs
take root cuttings of perennial flowers
• freeze veggies, dry some
• start winter cover crops
• collect and dry herb seeds
• build tree well
• mount new bird houses
• seed lawn
• start winter veggies indoors
CINNAMO

August can be both satisfying and overwhelming as you enjoy the results of your labour in the vegetable garden, but wonder what on earth to do with all the food. It is a good time to review the successes and failures in the flower garden, and to make notes and plans for next year. Cast a mildly critical eye over the lawn to note areas that need attention, and review any plans you have to bring in topsoil to expand the lawn or gardening area, considering the impact on trees. Sowing more seed outdoors is a bit of a gamble, but more seeds and bulbs can safely be started indoors for winter food and flowers.

# August

**Bluegrass**

*Rare lawn condition in which normally brown, crisp lawns develop odd patches of a sort of hazy green growth. Don't be alarmed! These strangely colored areas usually disappear within a few weeks.*

*Beard and McKie*

## Vegetables

### Development and Pest Management

There are several factors that affect the development and ripening of vegetables. Some are beyond our control, whereas others can be modified, enhanced or diminished.

Cabbage worms are still around this month. Use Bt as soon as you see them or the spray will not be effective. Continue every five days for as long as required (see page 170 for other methods of control). A warm, soapy, garlic water spray helps to bring the worms out of the plant, making handpicking easier.

Potatoes will sometimes develop various wilts and blights. To prevent the spread of disease, cut off any plants that look unhealthy and do not compost them. The potatoes may be safely eaten. Dig them up right away if it is early in the season, or leave them in the ground until the rest of the potatoes are harvested if a late blight strikes. They will not keep well if they have not developed thick skins, and should not be saved for planting next year because they could continue the disease cycle. Any potatoes that have not been hilled or mulched should be attended to now. If swelling tubers are forced to the surface they will turn green and poisonous if they are not protected from the sun.

Potato beetles and their larvae can be devastating. Handpicking them and crushing the reddish-orange egg masses are about the only measures that can be taken. Next year, however, plant potatoes under a 12 inch (30 cm) thick mulch to reduce beetle numbers.

Thin radicchio when it is about 4 inches (10 cm) tall, and do the same with any other crops planted several weeks ago. Continue to keep weeds pulled or hoed, but leave them to work as a mulch, unless they have gone to seed. Some weeds will form seed when pulled at the flowering stage, and

## *Focus on Plants*

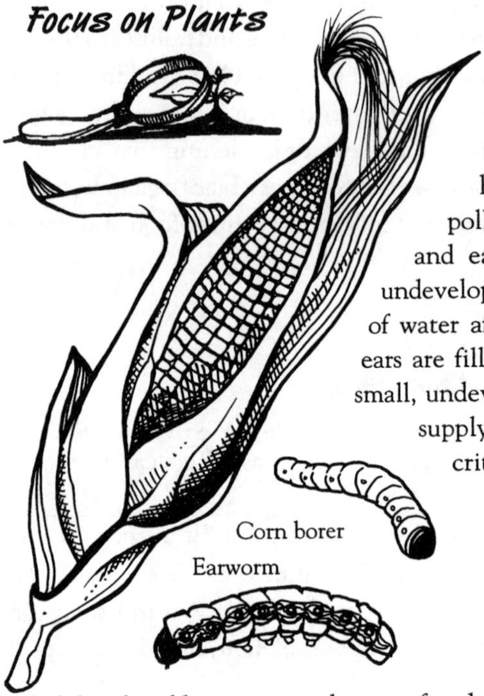


The weather during corn pollination—a period of about one week for any one variety—affects how well the ears fill out. If it is very hot and dry or wet and rainy, pollination may be incomplete, and ears of corn with areas of undeveloped kernels will result. Lack of water after pollination, when the ears are filling out, will also result in small, undeveloped kernels; be sure to supply water during these two critical times.

What is more frustrating than the weather is corn borer and corn earworm damage. The mature corn borer is about 1 inch (2.5 cm) long, grayish-pink with a dark head and has spots on the top of each segment. The mature corn earworm is slightly longer, white, greenish or reddish and has four pairs of prolegs. It invades from the south each summer and is worse some years than others, depending on what storms and winds come to pass. Corn borer overwinters in the soil. It can be controlled by removing all corn stalks and leaves immediately after harvest, and by fall ploughing.

Some gardeners have successfully discouraged both pests by cutting back the corn silks and 1 inch (2.5 cm) of the husk once pollination is complete, when the silks begin to dry. Alternatively, apply three to four drops of mineral oil to the silks and husk tip as soon as the silks begin to dry, and twice more at five to six day intervals. Both of these measures presumably discourage the pests which lay eggs that turn into kernel-eating larvae. Bt is not effective because the spray cannot reach those areas the larvae will ingest.

Corn with some borer or earworm damage is preferable to a patch devastated by racoons. Some gardeners put a paper bag over each ear when they start to fill out to puzzle and foil racoons. Early corn will have one ear per stalk, while late corn has two per stalk (see pages 174-175 for effective fencing against racoons).

purslane can even set seed without the flowers ever opening.

Do not water onions or root crops such as parsnip and salsify any more, unless the soil is very dry. If the tops of parsnip roots turn black and crack, and eventually rot, they have canker. This can be a problem in garden soils that have been cultivated for many years and is managed by a combination of crop rotation, later sowing than usual, establishing a pH of 7.0 and eliminating manure applications.

Sweet potatoes are quite drought tolerant, but they do most of their filling out over the next few weeks, so water regularly to obtain good sized roots. Giant pumpkins require as much as 200 buckets of water per week to fill out properly. Turn each pumpkin a little occassionally to prevent a flat side from developing. (See pages 210-211 for the water requirements of other vegetables.)

Green shoulder in tomatoes is caused by several factors, including uneven moisture in the soil and inadequate potassium and magnesium levels. Some varieties seem more prone, so try different varieties each season. Shading the plants in hot weather helps to reduce the incidence slightly, and spraying or watering with an epsom salts solution will raise the magnesium level (see page 248).

## Ripening and Development

If it appears that some vegetables will not ripen before the first frost hits, several steps can be taken to promote or hasten development and ripening. Excessive heat and overwatering reduce the sweetness of tomatoes, cantaloupes and melons, but cold, cloudy weather slows ripening and also makes fruits less sweet. About six weeks before the first expected frost, remove the growing tips of tomato plants, melons, winter squashes and pumpkins. This will channel the plants' energies into fruit development instead of foliage growth.

If growing indeterminate tomatoes, pinch out the tip of the vine at one or two leaves above the top truss of tomato flowers, and pinch out the tips of branches as well. Some gardeners even remove any flowers that have not yet set fruit, but leave them in place if green tomatoes are wanted. Lowering tomato vines to the ground also hastens ripening. Removing leaves does not help and is likely to result in sunscald. Tomatoes can ripen in the dark after they have been picked, if necessary, but while developing, and for the best flavour, they need nutrients photosynthesized by the leaves.

Tomato cuttings about 6 inches (15 cm) long can be taken at the same

### Green Thumb Tip

Brussels sprouts will continue to develop well after cool weather arrives. The harvest period can be shortened, if desired, by removing the tip of the plant once the lowest sprouts are 3/4 inch (2 cm) in diameter, four to eight weeks before the crop is wanted. A hormone in the top of the plant suppresses the development of sprouts; those at the bottom, however, are far enough away to no longer be affected. By removing the plant tip, all of the sprouts can begin to develop. This results in many sprouts becoming ready at once, which is ideal for freezing quantities.

Brussels sprouts will tolerate light frosts, so there is no hurry to tip or harvest them—next month is soon enough in many regions, or even as late as October in mild regions. Of course, if a gradual, extended harvest is preferred, leave the tip in place. Mound up the soil and firm it around the base of the plants to help them stand upright. Remove yellowing leaves as the crop matures to avoid the spread of fungal disease.

time as pinching, using either vine tips or suckers. Remove any flowers and the lowest leaves, and insert the cuttings in pots of moist rooting medium or potting soil as for any softwood cutting (see page 61). Grow them warm and with extra light each day to produce tomatoes indoors in December.

To promote the growth and ripening of peppers, remove the central, topmost pepper on each plant, even if it is still unripe. This can increase the total yield by up to 25%. Hot peppers should be allowed to ripen fully on the plant to develop their full "hotness," but young mild ones can also be eaten.

Remove the flowers on pumpkin and winter squash plants, and cut about 8 inches (20 cm) off the growing tips of the vines. These tender bits can be cut up into 1 inch (2.5 cm) chunks and stir-fried. Very small fruits can also be removed, as they probably will not have time to grow and ripen properly. Cut out the flower stalk of chicory to increase the size of the root and subsequent forced top growth when potted up for indoor growth (see September/October, page 345).

Additional heat may help fruits ripen, particularly as days start to cool off and nights get chilly. Putting cold frames over melons, peppers, eggplants and tomatoes will provide the extra heat that these plants need, especially in cool regions. Row covers may be used to cover large areas, but they do not hold the heat as well at night. Remember to lift the covers on hot or bright days.

Sometimes it is hard to know when fruits are ripe. Pick eggplants while they are still shiny, and summer squash before the rind hardens. A ripe watermelon sounds hollow when thumped, and gives a "thunk" sound. It will be yellowish, not white, where it touches the ground, and the tendrils on the stem near the fruit will be brown. Stop watering watermelons when they start to ripen to increase their sweetness. When fully ripe, the skin cannot be pierced with a fingernail.

Muskmelons and canteloupes should not be given the fingernail test. Instead, look for a more pronounced netting effect on the skin. The area between the netting lines will change from green to tan as the fruit ripens. There should also be small cracks where the stem joins the fruit. To be fully certain, do the slip test: press lightly on the fruit at the stem-fruit junction using your thumb; if the stem separates from the fruit with a small pull, the fruit is ready. Melons do not ripen further after they are picked, so leave them on the vine until fully ripe. Honeydew melon will be creamy yellow and have a sweet odour when it is ripe.

Bulbing in onions is not hastened by bending the tops over, although it does seem to help the necks dry out. Bulbing is initiated by long days. Bend the tops only after three-quarters of the tops are already drying and falling over, if the soil is very wet, or if frosts are imminent. Brush the soil away from the tops of onion and shallot bulbs to make it easier for them to fill out, particularly if the soil is heavy.

## Harvest

Different vegetables require different methods of handling and storage (refer to Table SEP/OCT-1, page 336). For successful storage, harvest them when they are at their peak of perfection. Before you get very busy harvesting, however, clean out and prepare the cold room for winter storage (see December, pages 449-450, for how to build one). Wash down the ceiling, walls and shelves with a water and bleach solution, and scrub out the nooks and crannies. If necessary, apply a new coat of outdoor paint. Make sure the vent door or other ventilation system is clean and working, then give the room a good airing. Ventilate it on cool nights to help lower the temperature.

When melons are finally ready to harvest, cut them off the vine, leaving 1 inch (2.5 cm) of stem attached. They will keep for one to two weeks, depending on the storage conditions. Honeydew melons should be stored at slightly warmer temperatures than muskmelons and canteloupes (see Table SEP/OCT-1, page 336). Also cut eggplants and peppers off the plant with a bit of stem attached.

Regular picking is the key to continued production for many plants. Beans should be picked every day or two, and the outer leaves of lettuce, spinach and other greens removed, even if they are not used. Pick the outer stalks of celery as they become ready, and keep plants mulched to help the blanching process (see page 217).

Continue to harvest kohlrabi while it is small and tender. Quality is lost in storage, but it can be stored for two to four weeks in a plastic bag in the refrigerator. Trim off the outer leaves, but leave the central tuft in place.

Dig up carrots as soon as they are ready instead of waiting until September to (hopefully) avoid the second generation of carrot rust fly larvae that mine tunnels and holes in carrot roots. Small, tender carrots can be frozen; large carrots are best stored under cool, moist conditions, such as in a cold room (see September/October, pages 341-342). Twist off the greens, leaving a small stub, and put carrots in plastic bags with holes, or store them in damp sand or vermiculite.

Fennel leaves can be used as seasoning, but it will be some time before plants "bulb" up. Those that have flowered never will form bulbs but the leaves and stalks can be used (see Table AUG-3, page 302). Dig leeks rather than pulling them when they are about 1 inch (2.5 cm) across. They can be stored for several months in moist sand in a cool place, or kept in the refrigerator if they are going to be used within a couple of weeks.

Summer squashes, zucchini and cucumbers should be cut as soon as they are ready; they will last up to two weeks in a cool, humid room. Refrigerators are colder than the ideal temperature range of 45 to 50°F (7 to 10°C); a cold room might be cool enough by now.

## Preserving Vegetables

Freezing, canning and drying, probably in that order, are the most reliable ways to preserve vegetables. Cold storage is used to keep vegetables in their fresh state for varying lengths of time (see Table SEP/OCT-1, page 336), and pickling has been a popular method for many years.

### Freezing

Immediately after blanching (see Preventive Measure), place the vegetables under cold running water or in ice water. Cool them only as long as necessary and then drain them well. Roll them gently in a clean tea towel to remove excess moisture, or dry them in a salad spinner. Do not let cooled pieces sit at room temperature. They should be packed immediately in freezer bags, or individually quick frozen in a single layer on cookie sheets. Leave the individual items in the freezer for only an hour and then pack them in freezer bags. With either method, draw out as much air as possible from the bag by sucking on a straw tucked inside the neck of the bag.

Green peppers do not seem to require blanching, although it does not hurt, but remove the stem and seeds first. Tomatoes only need to be skinned or can be frozen as they are, whole or cut into pieces. To skin tomatoes, dip them in boiling water for thirty seconds and then plunge them into cold water. The skins will slip off easily. Tepid water works if tomatoes are frozen with the skin on and are skinned just before they are used. Do not bother to blanch shredded zucchini, but squeeze it to remove excess moisture before bagging it in two cup (480 ml) quantities for winter use in cakes, cookies, muffins and pancakes. Eggplant, summer squash, zucchini and tomatoes can be combined in ratatouille and frozen; some people include sweet peppers as well.

### Preventive Measure

Most vegetables must be heated (blanched) and then immediately chilled before they are frozen to reduce enzyme action and preserve appearance and flavour. Use high quality vegetables and prepare them as for cooking and eating. They will last for up to one year in the freezer.

Use a large pot of boiling water, or a pot of boiling water with a steamer on top. Blanching time depends on the size and thickness of the pieces, and only small quantities should be steamed or boiled at a time. Small or thin items, such as peas and spinach, require two minutes; small pieces of green beans, broccoli, asparagus, carrots, cauliflower, 1/3 inch (8 mm) thick slices of eggplant and small Brussels sprouts require three minutes; whole or large pieces of the same items require four minutes. Corn on the cob requires seven, nine or eleven minutes, depending on the cob size.

Start timing when the water returns to boiling after the vegetables have been added, or immediately after vegetables are added if a steamer is used. Lift and shake the steamer once or twice throughout the steaming time so that the heat reaches all of the vegetables evenly.

### *Canning*

If canning is not done correctly the food may spoil and become toxic. The details of the process to follow to can food safely are beyond the scope of this book, but the process is not difficult. Vegetables stored this way are usually not as tasty as when frozen, but it is a useful way to store tomatoes and should be investigated if you have a glut of tomatoes to deal with.

### *Drying*

Drying vegetables is becoming increasingly popular, particularly with the advent of dried tomatoes in avant-garde cooking. Other vegetables can also be dried and are a special treat when camping or hiking. It is best to use a commercial or homemade drier or a slow oven, unless there is plenty of hot sunshine for ten to fourteen days and the drying food can be protected from insects and pests.

A solar drier is easily made, can dry foods up to three times faster than drying in the open air, and keeps food free of insects and pests. To make one model, designed in Russia, stretch clear plastic over hoops to form a tunnel that runs east to west. Gaps in the plastic at ground level along the sides of the tunnel provide ventilation. Spread black plastic inside on a south-facing angle. This absorbs heat and provides a surface on which to spread the food for drying.

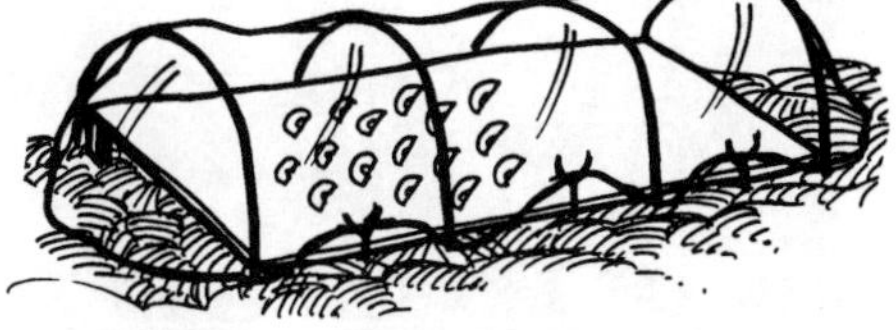

Russian solar drier

Another simple drier can be made for indoor use. It is made of wood, masonite and half a dozen cake racks which serve as drying shelves when set into the upper half of the box. A 100-watt or 150-watt light bulb at the bottom of the box will dry food in a few days in a box 28 to 30 inches (70 to 75 cm) tall with interior dimensions to match the cake racks. Be sure to leave gaps in the wood at the top and bottom of each side so that air can circulate. The kitchen oven, set at 140°F (60°C) with the door propped open a crack, will dry food in six to eight hours.

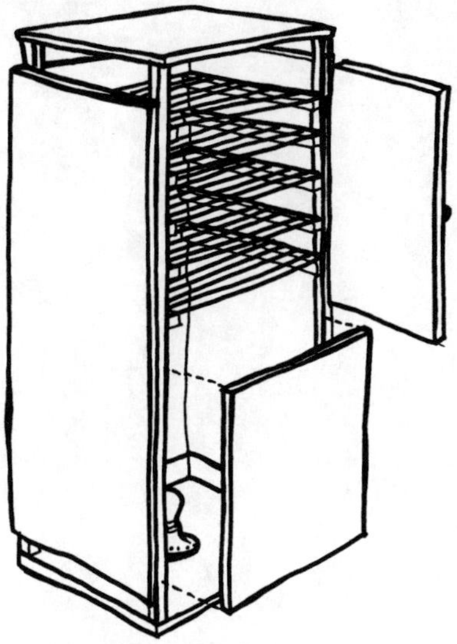

Simple light bulb drier

Most vegetables only need to be scrubbed, peeled and sliced thinly before drying. Some people like to blanch the pieces for one minute to help preserve their colour. The vegetables can be sliced in many different ways; carrots, for example, can be julienned, sliced lengthwise, cut into thin coins, or grated and chopped to make colourful bits to add to soups and stews; spread cheesecloth over the drying racks to keep the small pieces from falling through. Red chillies can be dried whole; if preferred, string them together first with a needle and strong thread.

A few vegetables need a little extra preparation. Cook peas and green beans cut small for seven minutes before drying; cook corn for two minutes before cutting the kernels off the cobs; cut tomatoes in horizontal slices and spread with olive oil; dip potato slices in water with a little lemon juice before drying to keep them from turning dark; blanch slices of winter squash and pumpkin for six to eight minutes, or cook and mash them and then spread the puree in a thin layer on a cookie sheet lined with a heavy plastic wrap or sprayed with a nonstick coating; cook paste tomatoes until a thick sauce forms and dry as for pureed squash. Sliced vegetables are dry when they take on a leathery texture; peas and other small vegetables become hard like little pebbles; purees are leathery, pull easily from the pan and are best stored in the refrigerator, rolled in fresh plastic.

## Late Summer Planting

It is difficult to think of sowing more seeds while the harvest is going on, but there are several vegetables that can be planted to extend the harvest well into the autumn. Extending the gardening season makes a lot of sense because soil holds heat for a long time in the fall (and seems to take forever to warm up in the spring!). Some of the early crops, such as lettuce and peas, will be finished and can be cleared away to make way for second crops of other vegetables, or perhaps an early crop failed, leaving a gap in the garden. Putting out transplants instead of starting from seed is equivalent to adding a good month to the growing season. Some transplants may suffer badly in summer heat, however, if they are not kept shaded and cool.

For fall crops, select vegetables that tolerate or thrive in cool temperatures, and those that mature quickly. Small, round varieties of beets and short varieties of carrots will mature sooner than regular large types. Mustard greens and radishes will be ready in a few weeks, and spinach and leaf beets can be harvested at a young age and grow well in cool weather. Winter radishes take longer to mature but grow well in the autumn.

Three weekly sowings of leaf lettuce from August 1 onwards will ensure a continued supply in the autumn, particularly if the plants are cut back entirely at harvest and allowed to regrow under the protection of a cold frame. Head lettuce may not have enough time to head up, but it can still be used as a crunchy leaf lettuce. Instead of using cold frames or row covers, plant lettuce in a wheelbarrow so that it can be rolled under shelter when hard freezes are predicted.

Lettuce seed is very reluctant to germinate at temperatures over 77°F (25°C), but research has shown that success is higher if the seed is sown between 2 and 4 p.m. The temperature sensitive phase of germination then

## Table AUG-1 Late Summer Vegetable Planting Schedule

Crop protection as harvest time nears is essential for many crops; others are moderately (*) to very (**) frost tolerant. The harvest can be extended well past the expected last frost date if all crops are protected.

| Plant | Transplant | Sow Seeds | Seeding Comments |
|---|---|---|---|
| ** Arugula | | x | to 4 weeks b.f. |
| * Beets (small, round) | o | x | to 7 weeks b.f. |
| * Leaf Beets | o | x | to 5 weeks b.f. |
| ** Bunching Onions (fall/winter variety) | | x | to 9 weeks b.f. |
| * Carrots (short) | | x | to 8 weeks b.f. |
| Chinese Cabbage | o | x | to 10 weeks b.f. |
| * Collards | o | x | to 8 weeks b.f. |
| ** Corn Salad (Mache) | | x | to 4 weeks b.f. |
| * Escarole, Endive | o | x | to 10 weeks b.f. |
| ** Kale | o | x | to 5 weeks b.f. |
| * Kohlrabi | | x | rr to 4 weeks b.f. |
| * Lettuce - Leaf | | x | rr to 7 weeks b.f. |
| - Butterhead | | x | to 9 weeks b.f. |
| - Cos, Romaine | o | x | to 10 weeks b.f. |
| - Head (fall variety) | | x | to 11 weeks b.f. |
| * Mustard Greens | o | x | rr to 7 weeks b.f. |
| * Radish | | x | r to 4 weeks b.f |
| * Winter Radish | | x | rr to 8 weeks b.f. |
| * Spinach | o | x | rr to 7 weeks b.f. |
| ** Swiss Chard | o | x | to 9 weeks b.f. |
| * Turnip | o | x | to 8 weeks b.f. |

x = usual method
o = optional method; transplants will shorten the time from planting to harvest, allowing later planting than from seed
r = repeat sowings every week
rr = repeat sowings every two to three weeks
b.f. = before the first expected fall frost

occurs at night when it is cooler. Shade and cool the soil if possible a couple of weeks before lettuce and other seeds are sown (see Green Thumb Tip, page 250).

Swiss chard and kale will continue to produce long after days turn cold, and Chinese cabbage grows quickly and vigorously in cool weather. Sow more seeds of leaf beets, mustard greens and spinach for a continuous supply. Whether these late plantings will need cold frame protection will depend on how long the mild weather continues in the autumn. Fall and winter bunching onions and corn salad (mache) can also be planted. Corn salad will do quite well without protection, but it will continue to produce for a longer period if it is grown under a row tunnel or other protection. It has a low germination rate, so plant generously and then thin to 2 inches (5 cm) apart in the row or 4 inches (10 cm) apart in a block planting.

## *Cover Crops*

Cover crops, or green manures, use up the nutrients from crop plant residues left in the soil, help prevent erosion, protect soil from compaction over the winter, help to keep the soil slightly drier, add organic matter to the soil, and improve the texture of the soil when they are dug in next spring. They can be planted four weeks or more before the first fall frost, after digging over the soil as described in October/November (pages 384-385). In short season areas and where vegetables are grown as late as possible into the autumn, plant cover crops between the rows or in ground just cleared of crops. If crops are planted close together and grown intensively, there may be no room for undersowing.

Annual ryegrass, annual vetch, winter rye, winter wheat, spring oats and spring barley make good winter cover crops. The grains do not do well in acidic soils, but vegetable gardens should be at pH 6.5 which is fine for grains. Kale is a good cover crop with an added advantage; the thinnings can be eaten (and see page 250 for undersowing with green manures).

Buckwheat planted in the spring as a green manure, whether for a new vegetable garden, lawn, flower bed or patch of fruit bushes, should be cut when half of it is flowering. Two days after cutting it or any other cover crop, till it into the ground. Spread lime if required, cultivate the soil two or three times ten days apart if weeds or grass are a problem, dig in plenty of organic matter to the appropriate depth (see Green Thumb Tip, page 381), and then sow a winter cover crop (refer to Table AUG-2). This is also a good time of year to break new ground for a new or expanded garden next year because the soil is dry enough to work (see pages 375-382).

## Table AUG-2 Late Summer and Autumn Planted Cover Crops

Sow at least four weeks before the first expected fall frost.

| Plant | Seeding Rate (lbs/acre; lbs/1000 sq. ft or kg/ha; g/m²) | | | When to turn under |
|---|---|---|---|---|
| Annual Vetch | 40-60; 1 ½-2 | or | 45-67; 732-975 | the following spring |
| Annual Ryegrass | 35-40; 1-1 ½; | or | 39-45; 488-732 | does not regrow in spring |
| Barley | 90-100; 2 ½-3 | or | 101-112; 1220-1464 | the following spring |
| Kale | 15; 1/2 | or | 17; 244 | the following spring |
| Oats | 90-100; 2 ½-3 | or | 101-112;1220-1464 | does not regrow in spring |
| Winter Rye | 120-140; 4-6 | or | 134-157;1952-2928 | the following spring |
| Winter Wheat | 120-140; 4-6 | or | 134-157;1952-2928 | the following spring |

### Soil Solarization

To "clean" soil for indoor potting, try soil solarization during the warmest time of the year (or see Soil Sterilization, page 402). Saturate the soil with water and cover it with clear plastic so that there is very little air space between the plastic and the soil. Leave the plastic in place for four to six weeks. Small quantities of soil can be treated in a clear plastic bag—draw most of the air out and turn the bag over weekly. Solarization will destroy most plant pathogenic fungi and bacteria, weeds and weed seeds, and will reduce harmful nematode populations, but it will also destroy beneficial fungi and bacteria.

## Herbs

### Drying Seeds

The seeds produced by dill, fennel, anise, coriander and other herbs will be reaching maturity over the next few weeks. The biennial herbs—parsley, angelica and caraway—will not produce seeds until their second year. Seeds should be harvested when they are dry, but before they drop to the ground. As soon as the first seeds turn black or a darker brown, shake the seed head into a paper bag each day or two to loosen the ripe seeds. Alternatively, tie a paper bag over the seed head and let the seeds drop off at their own pace. The stems can also be cut as the first seeds turn brown. Either hang them

A paper bag over the seed head can catch seeds for you while you are absent.

Dill seed head

upside down over paper, or lay them on top of a piece of clean paper in a warm, dry place with good ventilation. Dry ripened seeds for another one to two weeks by spreading them in a thin layer on a piece of paper in a dark, warm, airy place. Mature dill seeds are dried in this manner, but if you are using dill for making pickles, cut it when there are both flowers and unripe seed heads on the same stalk. The head and a few inches (several cm) of the stalk are cut and the entire piece is laid out to dry.

Since few herbs are hybrids, seeds can be saved for planting next spring. Do not use heat or microwave, however, to dry seeds destined for planting. Store them carefully in cool, dry conditions (see page 8). Some seeds that germinate best when fresh (see Table JAN-1, page 15) can be sown immediately. The young plants can be kept indoors for their first winter.

## Culinary Uses of Herbs

Perhaps more gardeners would grow herbs if they were comfortable using them. One of the easiest ways to be imaginative and creative in the kitchen is to use herbs in baking and cooking. Basil, for example, is delightful in more than just tomato based dishes and pesto. Try it with vegetables, in soup, on fish, included with poultry and meat dishes, in sauces and in souffles and other cheese concoctions. An added bonus when preparing a romantic meal is that basil is reputed to be an aphrodisiac.

Basil has an added bonus for a romantic meal.

Beebalm (also known as bergamot or monarda) can be used fresh or dried. Fresh young leaves and individual flower petals can be added to salads, and the dried leaves can be made into tea. The tea is lovely served cold with a slice of lemon, or steep a few leaves, fresh or dried, with weak orange pekoe to make a blend reminiscent of Earl Grey tea.

The lemon-flavoured, minty leaves of lemon balm can be added to sauces, omelettes, salads, stuffings and fruits. The leaves are often used in herb teas, and a couple of bruised leaves can be added to fruit juice or wine.

It is useful to remember that cilantro (Spanish), Chinese parsley and dhania (Indian) are the same as coriander leaves. Some people prefer using dried leaves for cooking because the flavour is more mellow (it has a strong odour just before it goes to seed), but others cannot imagine using anything but fresh cilantro. Try it fresh, dried and frozen.

Herbs release the most flavour if they are chopped before they are added to various dishes. Bay leaf is an exception. It is used only to flavour foods and is not actually eaten; leaving it whole makes it easier to remove. Dried seeds are used whole or ground, while dried herb leaves are crumbled before they are added to dishes. When adding dried herbs, use only one-third of the amount of fresh used to obtain the same flavour. Frozen herbs are used in equal quantities to fresh.

There are various points at which herbs can be added when cooking. They can be mixed in with the dry ingredients when baking. Add 1/2 cup (120 ml) of finely chopped fresh or frozen herbs (one-third the quantity if dried) to every 2 cups (480 ml) of flour for biscuits and bread, for example. Some herbs to try are chervil, chives, parsley and dill. Use smaller quantities if adding stronger flavoured herbs such as rosemary and sage. Dried seeds can also be added to the dry ingredients.

Herbs can be added to the liquid ingredients when preparing such dishes as omelettes, quiches and souffles. Add them to the eggs at the beaten stage. Herbs can be added at any stage to soups and sauces; some herbs, such as basil (and see Table AUG-3, below), are best added during the last few minutes of cooking so that their delicate flavour is not destroyed, whereas the flavour imparted by thyme and oregano seems to improve the longer they are cooked. Some herbs and seeds are added to hot liquids and allowed to steep to make an infusion. The flavoured liquid is then used in various ways; aniseed flavoured milk can be used in custard, for example.

To make herb tea, use 1 tablespoon (15 ml) of fresh herb or 1 teaspoon (5 ml) of dried herb for each serving. Steep it for ten minutes and strain before serving. Try blends of two or more herbs from Table AUG-3, such as lemon balm with a trace of mint, or add a little anise hyssop or sweet cicely to various herbs. For an attractive finish, float a small violet, rose, calendula, borage, lavender or rosemary flower or petal or two in each cup.

Herbs are sometimes used to wrap food or are placed underneath the food item for flavouring. Basil leaves wrapped around morsels of cheese or flavoured couscous make delightful hors d'oeuvres; sorrel can be wrapped around fish as it is being baked; dried bunches of thyme and marjoram can be placed under roasting meat.

Sometimes the flavour of herbs is best captured in marinades. A marinade for chicken based on yogourt or white wine could include one or more of the herbs suggested for poultry or marinades in Table AUG-3. One for fish based on lemon juice might include cilantro, fennel, oregano or parsley. A marinade for beef based on red wine could be flavoured with oregano, rosemary, bay leaf, lovage or thyme. Crushed garlic or finely chopped shallots can also be added to various marinades.

As a tablespoon or two (15 to 30 ml) of oil is sometimes added to

### A cool break... Iced Mint Tea

To make iced mint tea, mash together 1 cup (240 ml) of fresh mint leaves and 2 tablespoons (30 ml) of sugar. Let this stand while preparing a light syrup of 4 tablespoons. (60 ml) of sugar in 2 ½ cups (600 ml) of water. Boil it for five minutes, allow it to cool, then add the juice from three lemons and the mint pulp prepared earlier. Stir and let it steep for several hours. Serve chilled with a sprig of mint.

## Table AUG-3 Culinary Herbs

| Plant | Part Used | Culinary Uses |
|---|---|---|
| Angelica | leaf (fresh) | fish, stewed fruit |
| | leaf (dried) | tea |
| | seeds | tea, flavour alcoholic beverages |
| | stem (fresh) | peeled and chopped to flavour jam, marmalade, candied |
| Anise | leaf (fresh) | salad, vegetables, butter |
| | seed | poultry, fish, baked goods, tea, steeped in liquid to make sweet sauces and cream soup, hot milk |
| Anise Hyssop | leaf | tea |
| Basil | leaf | * soup, salads of cucumber, seafood, tomatoes or potatoes, tomato dishes, beef, stews, fish, poultry, pesto, vegetables, sauces, marinades, cheese dishes, butter, food wrapping |
| Bay Leaf | leaf (dried) | + to flavour tomato dishes, stew, fish, marinades, steep in warm milk for sauces |
| Beebalm | leaf (young) | salad, cold beverages, tea |
| (Monarda) | leaf (dried) | tea |
| Borage | leaf (young) | salad |
| | flower (fresh) | salad, fruit salad, candied, in beer, cider or wine |
| Calendula | dried petals | cheese, soup, salad, stew, saffron substitute for colour |
| Caraway | seed | vegetables, especially cabbage, beets and potatoes, baked goods, cake, biscuits, rye and other breads, cheese, apple dishes |
| Chervil | leaf | * egg dishes, salad, vegetables, butter, light cheeses, soup, sauces, garnish |
| Chives | leaf | salads, garnish, sandwiches, butter |
| | flower | salads |
| Coriander | seed | curry, soups, chili, stew, marinades |
| (Cilantro) | leaf | * curry, fish, soup |
| Dill | leaf | * sour cream, cucumbers and other vegetables, poached salmon and other fish, potato salad, egg dishes, light cream cheeses, garnish, sandwiches |
| | seed | pickles, fish, vegetable soups |
| Fennel | leaf | * chicken, lamb, fish, ham, pork, dahl, yogurt, cream sauce, salad, vegetables, soups |
| | stalk (fresh) | peeled for salads |
| | (dried) | in bottom of roasting pan for chicken, fish, red meat |
| | seed | tea, Italian sausage |
| Fenugreek | seed | curry, pickles |
| French Sorrel | leaf (fresh) | sautés, soups, salads, fish and other sauces |
| Horseradish | root | grated in tomato cocktail sauces, relish, mustards |

| Plant | Part Used | Culinary Uses |
|---|---|---|
| Hyssop | leaf (fresh) | stewed fruit, fruit pies, salads, sausages, stuffing, tea |
| | leaf (dried) | tea |
| Lavender | flower | candied |
| | leaf | stews, marinades, wild game |
| Lemon Balm | leaf | milk desserts, fruit salad, salads, omelette, sweet sauces, garnish, tea, to flavour wine and cold fruit drinks |
| Lovage | leaf (fresh) | soups, stew, rice, vegetables, salads |
| | seed | cheese dishes, potato soup, cabbage, bread, biscuits, sandwich spreads |
| Marjoram | leaf and plant tops | vegetables, chicken, egg dishes, cream sauce, salad, light soups, butter, mushroom dishes |
| Mint | leaf | yogurt, dahl, chutney, tea, new vegetables, duck, lamb, salads |
| Nasturtium | leaf (fresh) | salad |
| | flower, bud | salad, vinegar, butter, sandwich, garnish |
| | seed | pickled when half ripe |
| Oregano, Greek | leaf, plant tops | stews, stuffing, winter vegetables, tomato dishes, beans, hearty soups, meat pie, stews, in bottom of roasting pan for fish or beef |
| Parsley | leaf | stuffing, tabouli and other salads, soups, stews, beef, fish, vegetables, butter, chick peas |
| Rosemary | leaf | stew, wild game, lamb, pork, fish, marinades, dumplings, biscuits, poultry stuffing, infuse milk for puddings and custards, a little with citrus fruits |
| Saffron | stigma | infuse milk, water or cooking liquid and use to flavour rice and paella, use in fish stew |
| Sage | leaf | cheese, pork, wild game, lamb, poultry, veal, tea |
| Salad Burnet | leaf (young) | cheese, butter, salads, soups, cordials |
| Scented Geraniums | leaf | jelly, tea |
| Summer Savory | leaf | meat pie, pea and other soups, beans, lentils, peas, sausage, salads, butter, cheese dishes, cabbage, turnip and other vegetables |
| Sweet Cicely | leaf (fresh) | butter, salads, stewed fruit, tea |
| | seed | apple pie |
| Sweet Woodruff | leaf (fresh) | Maywine, tea |
| Tarragon, French | leaf | chicken, fish, tomato dishes, vinegar salad dressings, tartar and béarnaise sauces, egg dishes, butter |
| Thyme | leaf | beef, wild game, lamb, soups, winter vegetables, stuffing, stews, strong cheese, marinades, pickles, sausage |
| Watercress | leaf (fresh) | soup, butter, sandwiches, salads |

**Key:** * = add at the end of cooking + = used only to flavour, not itself eaten marinades, a herbal flavoured oil could be used instead of herbs (see pages 255-256 regarding flavouring oils). Flavoured oils can also be added to soups, used in salad dressings and applied as basting to barbecued and roasted meats. Herbs can be incorporated into cheeses, butter, mayonnaise and other similar spreads (see page 255 regarding herbal butters). They enliven sandwiches and crackers or can be used in dips for fruits and vegetables. Herbal butters can be spread on cooked vegetables or used to make sauces.

Herbal vinegars can be used in marinades, salad dressings and mayonnaise, soups, stews and gravies. Use them in traditional combinations, such as dill vinegar with cabbage dishes and tarragon vinegar with chicken salad or gravy, or experiment with some of the many possibilities. Noel Richardson's books *Summer Delights* (1991) and *Winter Pleasures* (1990) are devoted entirely to cooking with herbs. Also take a look through the Brooklyn Botanic Garden Record *Herbs & Cooking*, (1990), and Sarah Garland's *The Herb and Spice Book* (1979).

### *Other Uses*

There are many uses of herbs which are less well known than those mentioned in the above sections. Dried mint, for example, can be scattered in animal bedding to discourage pests, amongst clothing to repel moths or on food shelves to discourage ants. Dried mint stems add a delightful fragrance to a room when burnt on a fire in the winter. Dried chamomile flowers can be saved and used next winter in a solution which helps reduce damping off disease in young seedlings (see February, page 50). An extra strong tea of lemon balm leaves added to the bath water is supposed to aid relaxation.

A herbal wreath can be made by starting with a base of 'Silver King' artemisia.

A pleasant activity is making herbal wreaths. For a base, the stems of 'Silver King' artemisia can be tied with string or wired together to form a circle, or use Virginia creeper or grape vines. For tiny wreaths use small pieces of artemisia. Insert dried whole herbs and flowers between the stems or vines, or wire or glue them in place. Some inserted pieces may need their stems strengthened by wrapping the stem and a piece of florists' wire together with florists' tape.

Kitchen wreaths of all sizes can be made using culinary herbs, but they should be used fairly soon if they are meant for more than decoration. The heat, moisture and light in a kitchen will cause dried herbs to lose their flavour more quickly than those stored in closed containers kept in a cool, dark, dry place. Fragrance wreaths can also be made for hanging in clothes closets or linen cupboards. Use any of the herbs used in potpourris (see page 259). *Country Wreaths from Caprilands* by Adelma Grenier Simmons (1988) is full of ideas for dried herbal wreaths and ways to emphasize various themes or holidays. The folklore and history behind many plants is also included.

Dried herbs, including ground coriander seeds, are lovely in potpourris. Use these to fill sachets or pillows. Ann Tucker Fettner, in *Potpourri, Incense, and other Fragrant Concoctions* (1977), describes how to make bath potpourris by mixing equal parts of household borax and dry potpourri, letting the mixture blend in a tightly covered jar for a couple of weeks, and then tying small amounts in silk to hang under the hot water tap in the bath.

Preserving herbs this month will ensure that you have plenty of material to experiment with in the winter, when there is time to browse through a variety of herb books.

## Dividing and Transplanting

It is best to wait until spring, if possible, to lift and divide perennial herbs that are crowded or need moving. Unless this is done now or early in September, with as little disturbance as possible to the roots, there may be some losses over the winter. Still, doing it now does get the job done while the changes required are still fresh in your mind.

Water plants well a day or two before digging them up, water them well after replanting, and provide some shade if the sun beats down on them. Cloudy, foggy or drizzly days are best for moving plants. Wait until woody plants such as sage have firmed up their new growth before moving them.

When dividing plants, small, healthy pieces of each herb clump can be potted up with regular potting soil and brought indoors for the winter. Annual herbs, however, are best started from seed each autumn. Add extra perlite or sand to the potting soil for herbs that prefer dryish conditions (see Table FEB-1, page 40). Borderline hardy perennials can be left in the ground until well into September, or even October or November in long season areas (see September/October, pages 349-350, if they will be left outdoors over the winter). Tender perennials must be brought in before the first frost. Sow a little chervil outdoors, and even some summer savory this month. Saffron bulbs should be planted as soon as they are available in the stores (see page 312).

## Flowers

### Dividing

It is best to dig up and divide perennial flowers this month, rather than waiting much longer. Most plants enter a period of active root growth as top growth slows and nights become cool. September is usually all right in long season areas, but moving things around in October is pushing one's luck, and waiting until November is inviting disaster. Roots need a good six to eight weeks to settle in before the ground freezes. Even when moving is done carefully, plenty of time is allowed and a good mulch is used, as many as one-third of the plants may be lost, particularly if winter arrives early or spring brings poor snow cover and irregular thawing.

As a general rule, divide spring blooming plants and summer bloomers that have finished flowering this month. Gardeners tend to think of moving things when they see them blooming, but sedum, for example, is best moved in the spring.

The rhizomes of florentine iris (*Iris x germanica florentina*, *I. florentina*, or *I. germanica*, better known as orris root) can be used as a fixative in moist or dry potpourris. To prepare them for drying, trim off the roots and peel off the outer layer of the rhizome. It is impossible to cut or grind the rhizome once

### Focus on Plants

Siberian irises rarely need dividing, but bearded irises are usually divided in August every three or four years, or when the number of blooms diminishes. They prefer full sunshine, although some seem to thrive with half a day of sunshine, and require excellent drainage; resort to a raised bed if necessary.

Cut off young rhizomes growing around the outside of each clump, making sure there are one or two fans of leaves with each piece. Pull away old leaves, and trim the remaining healthy leaves so that they are six inches (15 cm) tall and in a fan shape. This will help reduce wind rock—thereby reducing root distrubance while plants are getting established—and will hopefully remove thrips if plants are infested.

Discard any rhizomes that are mushy or show signs of rot, cut off any damaged roots on the remaining rhizomes, and dip these rhizomes in a 10% solution of bleach to reduce rot (see page 264 for control of iris borer). Work some bonemeal and a little wood ash into the soil, and dig an upside-down

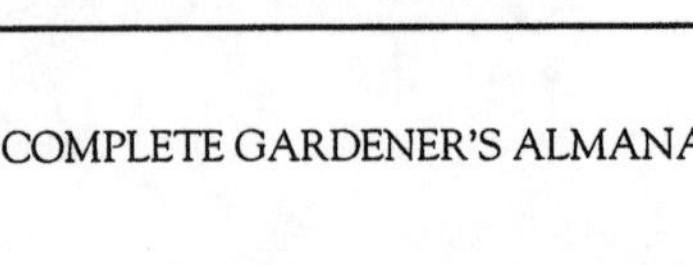

V-shaped trench for each rhizome. The rhizome rests on top of the mound of soil in the middle, and the roots are spread down into the trench on each side and covered with soil. The rhizome itself can be buried 2 inches (5 cm) deep in light, sandy soil, but the upper surface should be exposed in heavy clay soils. To increase the amount of sun the rhizome receives, position it so that the leaves are on the north end. Rhizomes are usually planted all facing the same direction. Space tall bearded irises 10 to 14 inches (25 to 35 cm) apart, and the dwarf varieties as close as 6 to 8 inches (15 to 20 cm). The dwarfs make a lovely show several weeks before the tall beardeds.

it has dried, so slice, chop, or grind it soon after digging it. It takes two years or more for the violet scent to emerge after drying, so do not be discouraged by the initial scent. Valerian root and others used as fixatives are dug in the autumn (see page 350) after the roots have become plump.

## Seeds, Spores and Root Cuttings

Biennial flowers, such as sweet william, foxglove and honesty, will have set seed by now. If your garden is casual, just leave the plants in place and let them self sow. For a more orderly garden, collect biennial seeds and sow them in a corner of the garden; they can be moved next spring to their blooming position. Biennials that were sown a couple of months ago can be transplanted to their flowering positions now or left in the nursery and planted in flower beds next spring.

Perennials such as gasplant, columbine and coreopsis can be propagated from seed (see Table APR/MAY-3, page 138), although seed from hybrids will not be true to the parent plant. Gasplant may not survive if it is divided—it is better to increase the stock by starting new plants from fresh seed. Rudbeckia, anchusa, feverfew, some campanulas, dianthus, basket-of-gold alyssum and Jacob's ladder often self sow without any help.

Fruit growers and wildflower gardeners may want to increase their supply of native flowering plants, both for beauty and to diversify the insect life in the garden. Collecting seed from the wild has less of an impact on the environment than digging up plants.

Collect the seed as described under Herbs (pages 299-300). Seeds are nearly ripe when the seed capsule splits. Those that are not fully ripe will sometimes ripen further if the entire flower stalk is cut and hung to dry, but it is essential that a portion of the seeds be left behind if harvesting wildflower seeds. Collect grass seed when the inflorescence has fluffed up.

Sow them immediately outdoors in a protected, shaded location such as in a cold frame or in pots in a greenhouse, or save the seeds for planting indoors in late winter (refer to Table AUG-4, below). Some seeds will germinate well in the warm soil once nights are cool, but many perennials and wildflowers germinate better if exposed first to winter temperatures. Phlox germinates best if frozen in an ice cube for six weeks before being planted (see pages 48-49 for other ways of breaking dormancy). Seeds sown outdoors in pots can be stored in a cold room or similar location for the winter after they have been exposed to autumn frosts. Any seeds that are to be stored over the winter should be thoroughly dried before being put away in cool, dry conditions.

### Green Thumb Tip

There are basically three methods for starting a meadow. On bare ground, prepare the planting area as for seeding a lawn (see page 324) and spread seeds of wildflowers. Packaged mixes often have a lot of annual flowers, which look very good the first year, but it takes several years for the perennials to become established.

If grass already exists, the second method is to stop mowing except for a single cut each year. This will allow local native plants to gradually become established. If mowing is desired, wait until late in the season after the plants have had a chance to set seed. Such an area could also be overseeded with wildflowers, as for lawns (see page 325).

The third method is an enhancement of the second. Start wildflowers in bare ground or in pots and transplant them to the grassy area. Dig holes in the sod, plant the flowers, and mulch around them with wooden shingles to prevent competition from the grass until the wildflowers are well established.

## Table AUG-4 Wildflower Propagation from Seeds and Cuttings

| Plant | When to Sow Seeds | Special Treatment | Season for Stem Cuttings |
|---|---|---|---|
| Aster | late winter | | summer |
| Beebalm (*Monarda*) | late winter | | summer |
| Bleeding Heart (*Dicentra*) | immediately | | |
| Bloodroot (*Sanguinaria*) | immediately | | |
| Blue-Eyed Grass (*Sisyrinchium*) | immediately | | |
| Blue Star (*Amsonia*) | late winter | scarify, soak | spring |
| Brown-Eyed-Susan (*Rudbeckia*) | late winter | | |
| Butterfly Weed (*Asclepias*) | late winter | | spring, root |
| Catchfly (*Silene*) | late winter | stratify three weeks | summer |
| Columbine (*Aquilegia*) | late winter | stratify four weeks | |
| Coralbells (Alumroot) | late winter | | |
| Coreopsis | late winter | | |
| Cranesbill (Wild Geranium) | immediately | | |
| Erigeron | immediately | | |
| Evening Primrose (*Oenothera*) | late winter | | summer |
| Foamflower (*Tiarella*) | late winter | | |
| Gaillardia | late winter | | summer |
| Goldenrod (*Solidago*) | late winter | | summer |
| Iris | immediately | | |
| Jack-in-the-Pulpit (*Arisaema*) | immediately | | |
| Joe-Pye Weed (*Eupatorium*) | late winter | | |
| Liatris (Blazing Star) | late winter | | |
| Lobelia | late winter | | summer |
| Mayflower (*Epigaea*) | immediately | | spring, layer |
| Meadow rue (*Thalictrum*) | immediately | | spring |
| Meadowsweet (*Filipendula*) | immediately | | |
| Moneywort (*Lysimachia*) | immediately | | spring to fall |
| Nodding Onion (*Allium*) | immediately | | |
| Ox-Eye Daisy (*Chrysanthemum*) | late winter | | spring, summer |
| Partridgeberry (*Mitchella*) | immediately | | spring |
| Penstemon (Beard Tongue) | immediately | | summer |
| Phacelia | late winter | | |
| Phlox, Blue | late winter | stratify six weeks | spring, layer |

| Plant | When to Sow Seeds | Special Treatment | Season for Stem Cuttings |
|---|---|---|---|
| Potentilla (Cinquefoil ) | late winter | stratify six weeks | spring to fall |
| Purple Coneflower (*Echinacea*) | late winter | stratify four weeks | |
| Queen Anne's Lace (*Daucus*) | immediately | | |
| Rose Mallow (*Hibiscus*) | late winter | | summer |
| Sedum | late winter | | spring to fall |
| Shooting Star (*Dodecatheon*) | immediately | | root |
| Skunk Cabbage (*Symplocarpus*) | immediately | | |
| Toothwort (*Dentaria*) | immediately | | |
| Trillium | immediately | | |
| Trout Lily (*Erythronium*) | immediately | | |
| Trumpet Vine (*Campsis*) | immediately | | summer |
| Turtlehead (*Chelone*) | late winter | stratify six weeks | summer |
| Twin Leaf (*Jeffersonia*) | immediately | | |
| Verbascum (Mullein ) | late winter | | |
| Violet (*Viola*) | immediately | | spring |
| Virginia Bluebells (*Mertensia*) | immediately | | |
| Virgin's Bower (*Clematis*) | late winter | | spring |
| Wild Ginger (*Asarum*) | immediately | | summer |
| Yarrow (*Achillea*) | late winter | | |

late winter = seeds may be stored cool and dry after collecting, and sown indoors in late winter

immediately = germination is best if seeds are sown fresh immediately after collection, which may be spring through autumn, depending on when the plant flowers and sets seed

root = may be propagated from root cuttings

layer = may be propagated by layering

Oriental poppies should be moved this month if they need to be, but for propagation purposes take root cuttings rather than dividing the plant. Dig around at the edge of the clump to find some roots, sever a few, and proceed as described on page 137. If an Oriental poppy seems not to be thriving, the soil may be too moist. Improve the drainage when replanting and do not mulch around the base of the plant.

Species roses that are to be grown from seed must be allowed to form hips. This will also encourage tender roses to think about slowing down their growth and getting ready for winter. Stop deadheading spent roses six weeks before the first expected frost. Hybrid teas and other tender hybrids grown from seed will not form plants true to the parent and it is a waste of time to try, but allowing them to develop hips with seeds will tell them that autumn is coming. It also helps to cut back on watering, as dryness encourages the wood to stop growing and harden off. To grow other roses from seed, remove the seeds from the pulp of the hip and stratify them for three months (see page 369).

### Focus on Plants

Fern spores can be collected and sown immediately or stored in cool, dry conditions for several months (see page 431 for the sowing method). Sometime between the early summer and early autumn ferns develop sporangia (spore cases) on the underside of the fronds. The size, shape and pattern of distribution varies with the species. They are narrow cases under the outer edges of the fronds in maidenhair ferns, for example, and round cases arranged between the veins on the underside of crested fern fronds. If collecting spores to grow fiddleheads, be sure to identify Ostrich Fern (*Matteuccia struthiopteris*) correctly and do not confuse it with Bracken Fern. Ostrich Fern is very large and grows in clumps, often on its own. It is usually found in rich soil near stream beds and sometimes over limestone or gypsum outcrops.

When the sporangia begin to turn a darker colour, they are getting ready to open. A magnifying glass will make it easy to determine when the first ones have opened. Cut off a frond and lay it on a piece of clean, white paper. Fold the paper in half with the frond inside, and keep it out of drafts. Within a week the spores will have been released from the sporangia, if they were ready, and will show up as a fine dust on the paper. If you are not going to sow them immediately, fold them inside the paper and tuck it into an envelope.

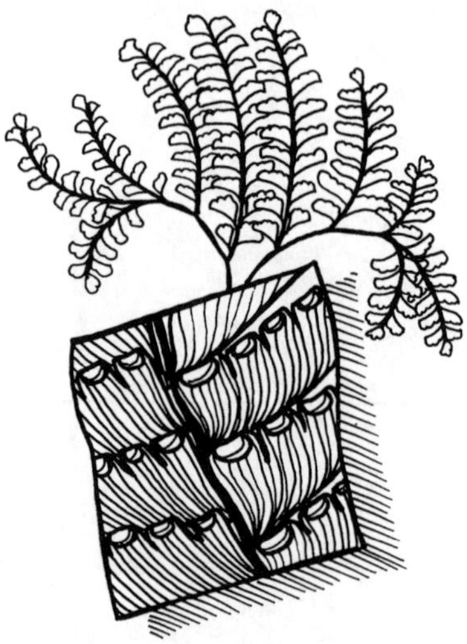

Sporangia on ferns

### *Colour and Bulbs*

This is a good time of year to wander, note book in hand, through the flower garden. Even if plants are not moved now, make a note of the changes to make next spring. They will serve to remind you that the yellow daylilies would look attractive in front of the purple monkshood, the red asiatic lilies near the evening primrose, and orange geum with the yellow globeflower. Try less usual colour combinations, such as soft orange daylilies or asiatic lilies with blue delphiniums, or blue lobelias with orange begonias, for example (and see pages 42-43). Red and purple is very striking; try deep red lilies or burgundy flowering tobacco with purple monkshood. A softer, more restful version of that combination is pink and mauve, such as pink Shirley poppies and Ramona clematis, pink roses and various campanulas, or pink petunias and liatris. A smashing combination is deep blue and purple, as captured in the spring with Siberian squill and purple crocus or purple aubrieta. To experiment with new combinations, wander around, flower in hand, looking for another plant that blooms at the same time.

It is also a good time to look for blank spots that need some autumn colour. Annual flowers that start looking tired and miserable can often be perked up and encouraged to bloom again if they are cut back by half about six weeks before the first fall frost is expected. Water and fertilize them well. Annuals, such as impatiens, that are cut back now will yield a flush of new growth suitable for cuttings in the autumn. Continue to deadhead spent flowers, both annual and perennial. Veronica, for example, may rebloom, though not with as many flowers nor as spectacularly as the first time.

Other bulbs to plant this month or next are bulbous iris, glory of the snow (*Chiondoxa*), the little yellow winter aconite (*Eranthis hyemalis*) and snowdrops. All of these are among the first flowers to bloom in the spring, so they should be planted where they can be readily appreciated in March or April, and look best growing up through low growing ground cover plants. All bulbs require excellent drainage (see pages 356-360 for more on spring bulbs).

Lily bulbs can be ordered for fall planting, although there may be poor survival rates if they are planted late. Some gardeners prefer to plant lilies in the spring to ensure a greater survival rate, particularly in regions where snow cover is unreliable and winters are not consistently cold. Provide excellent drainage and plant early enough to give roots time to grow and get established before the ground freezes. Lily bulbs are never truly dormant the way that crocuses and spring blooming bulbs are, so they must be planted as soon as they arrive if ordered through the mail.

## *Focus on Plants*

Colchicum

Crocus

This month, or as soon as possible in September, plant autumn crocus and colchicum for rich colour under shrubs or in various nooks and crannies in the autumn. Autumn crocus belongs to the iris family, the same as the spring blooming crocus, and has three stamens in each flower. *Crocus sativus* is one of the autumn blooming crocuses and is the source of the saffron used in cooking. It takes a vast number of crocus stigmas to get a bit of saffron, so plant them generously. They will multiply rapidly in the right growing conditions; provide well drained soil in full sun or partial shade and plant them 3 inches (8 cm) deep and 2 to 3 inches (5 to 8 cm) apart.

Colchicum, also called autumn crocus or meadow saffron, is a member of the lily family, has six stamens, is not a source of saffron, and is larger and considerably more expensive than the true autumn crocus. Its large, strap-like leaves, which appear in the spring, make it better suited to growing under shrubs than in the flower border. As both colchicum and autumn crocus bloom before developing leaves, they look best among low ground cover plants. Try them with such spring bloomers as aubrieta, creeping thyme, periwinkle (*Vinca minor*), Irish moss (*Arenaria verna*), pearlwort (*Sagina glabra*) or soapwort (*Saponaria caespitosa*).

## *Cut Flowers*

Many of the summer blooming tender bulbs should be flowering now, or very soon. Acidanthera or peacock orchid (*Gladiolus callianthus*), summer hyacinth (*Galtonia candicans*), freesia and tuberose are particularly fragrant. Crocosmia, formerly montbretia, makes a good cut flower. Canna as a cut flower can be immersed for an hour in cool water to help crispen the flowers. Annual bells-of-Ireland should have the leaves pinched off to better show off the bells, and it can also be immersed in water for an hour, unless it is to be dried for winter arrangements. Dahlias make superb cut flowers as they last for a long time, but check for earwigs. Immersing cut flowers in water for a few minutes will often dislodge these and other critters. Wet or misty weather can cause dahlia buds to turn soft and fail to bloom; just cut off the spoiled buds and wait for drier weather.

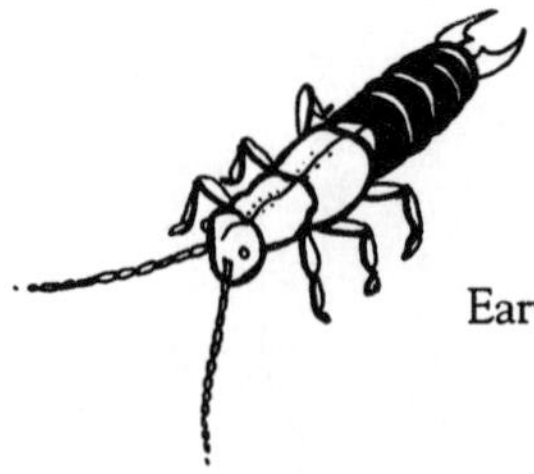

Earwig

Earwigs are often numerous and distressing as they feed on valued flowers and foliage; however, they also consume decaying plant material, insect larvae and aphids. They are nocturnal feeders and can be trapped by setting rolled newspapers or corrugated cardboard on the ground and emptying any visitors into a bucket of soapy water in the morning. Very strong insecticidal soap will also reduce their numbers if a direct hit is made, and chickens consider them a gourmet treat. The persistence of earwigs is causing more gardeners to become somewhat tolerant of the pests and to develop a "let live" attitude. After all, they cannot eat the entire garden!

Pinch out the side buds of chrysanthemums for extra large, but fewer, flowers. Continue to deadhead all spent flowers and cut out large, unsightly flower stalks unless the seeds are being saved.

## Fruits

### Harvesting Soft Fruits

Many of the soft fruits do not last long in cold storage (see Table SEP/OCT-3, page 364), but there are a few little tricks which help make them last a day or two longer while they are held before being eaten or processed for long-term storage. Fruit should be picked regularly and at their peak of perfection. Some of those destined for jams and jellies can be slightly underripe so that the jams set better.

The easiest way to harvest mulberries is to spread a cloth on the ground and give the plant several good shakes. Repeat this every few days until the harvest is complete. The berries do not last long in cold storage (see Table SEP/OCT-3). Pick raspberries daily; they should pull off easily leaving the stem and pith behind.

It is easy to pick highbush blueberries too early. Harvest only those blueberries that have no hint of pink anymore, and even those that have turned completely blue need another three to six days to develop their full sweetness. The ripe ones should come off the plant easily when rolled gently between your thumb and finger. Cover the plants with netting if birds are a problem.

Leave the stems in individual fruits until just before they are used (except for raspberries); removing them early provides an entry point for organisms that cause spoilage. Black currants and similar fruits are best picked in whole clusters and the fruits removed just before use.

Remove any spoiled or rotting fruits from the patch. Dropped fruits should also be removed because they may harbour fruit worms or weevil larvae.

Do not wash the fruits until you are ready to use them, and put them into the refrigerator immediately after picking. If this is not possible, at least keep them in the shade. Loosely covering the fruit with perforated plastic in the refrigerator will help to keep them from drying out if they are to be stored for more than a day or two. Avoid storing blueberries in metal containers. Jo Ann Gardner (1989) suggests some delicious uses of soft fruits, including sauces and drinks. Excess supplies can be frozen or dried (see pages 316 and 317).

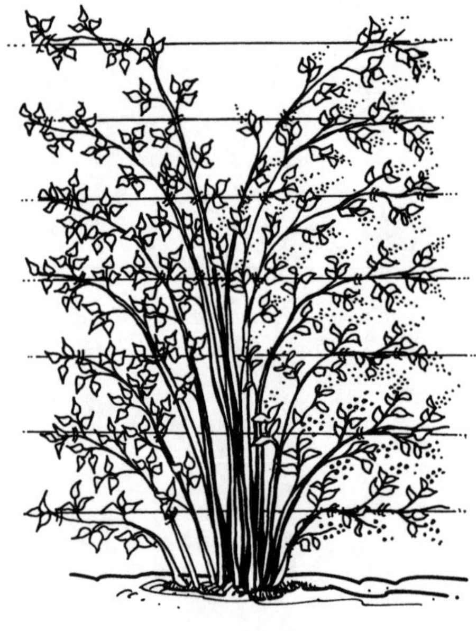

Training Blackberries
New growth is tied to one side and year old fruiting growth is tied to the other. After fruit is picked these canes are cut back, making room for new ones.

## Pruning and Disease Management

Trees that have finished growing for the summer can be pruned, if they need to be (see July, page 270). Certainly raspberries, blackberries and black currants can be pruned immediately after fruiting.

If the raspberry crop was less than expected, the cause could be insufficient moisture during flowering and fruit development, lack of top dressing in the spring with manure or compost, competition from weeds and grass, or overcrowding.

Overcrowding is a common problem in raspberry patches, and leads to disease as well as poor fruiting. There should be no more than seven or eight canes per clump, with clumps 18 to 24 inches (45 to 60 cm) apart. They can also be grown en masse, but individual canes should be at least 6 inches (15 cm) apart. Raspberries that are prone to mildew should be spaced further apart for good air circulation.

Pruning immediately after fruiting will make more light, air, nutrients and moisture available to the young growing canes. Leaving old canes in place until the spring, however, will help to protect young canes from severe winter winds.

The two-year-old regular summer fruiting raspberry canes that have just finished fruiting should be cut out to ground level. They are brown in colour, thicker than the other stems and will have side branches that bore the fruit. Any diseased canes with blotches or pock marks on them should be cut out to below ground level and burned, buried or discarded in the garbage. Do not compost them. The young canes that should be left in place will be green or light brown and will have no side branches. Cut out spindly young canes, and any extra canes that cause crowding until the desired spacing is reached. When properly spaced, a dog should be able to run through the patch.

Two-year-old blackberry canes that bore fruit this year should be removed immediately after fruiting, usually sometime next month. Some gardeners train all of the one-year-old canes to the right one year, and all of the one-year-old canes to the left the next year. That way, all of the canes of the same age are together, making picking and pruning easier.

After pruning the brambles, spray them with copper sulphate or another fungicide if anthracnose or spur blight has been a problem. Antracnose shows up as gray sunken areas and pock marks on new shoots. Spur blight shows up as brown or purplish areas, and leaves on fruiting canes may wilt and wither. Leaf spot first develops as spots on the leaves and leads eventually to defoliation. Good spacing will reduce the risk of leaf spot, and a regular spray program of fungicides may be needed (as for leaf spot and other leaf blights on crabapples and other trees and shrubs, see page 193).

Late yellow rust is not uncommon in raspberries and shows up as yellow dots on the leaves, which later erupt into powdery masses of spores. Infected plants should be dug up and destroyed. Lack of nutrients seems to encourage this disease. As well, avoid planting susceptible varieties near white spruce, the alternate host for rust. The varieties 'Carnival' and 'Festival' are susceptible, but 'Nova' and 'Boyne' are immune. 'Nova' seems to be immune to cane diseases as well. Tarnished plant bugs may feed on fruits, causing distortion, but they are not usually a serious problem.

Prune black currants by cutting out three-year-old branches at ground level after the fruit is harvested, or during dormancy next spring (see page 96 for more details). Do not prune red or white currants or gooseberries after fruiting.

Sometimes in a group of highbush blueberries, there will be a plant that remains stunted and just does not seem to grow well. If the leaves turn yellow and then red in August before those on other blueberry bushes, the affected plant probably has blueberry stunt. The only remedy is to dig out and destroy the infected plant.

Continue to remove the runners from dayneutral strawberries, and keep them well watered and fertilized to encourage more fruit production. Cut off excess runners from other strawberries once enough new plants have been produced to either fill in the gaps or populate a new bed (see pages 268-269). Rooted plantlets can be transplanted now or in the spring as soon as the soil is workable.

> ### Focus on Plants
>
> 
>
> There are two ways to manage autumn bearing raspberries. If there is a patch each of summer and autumn bearing raspberries, wait a few weeks until the autumn crop has been harvested, and then cut all of the autumn bearing raspberry canes down to ground level. The idea is to encourage young growth each year that will bear fruit on the tips of the canes late in the season.
>
> If there is only a patch of autumn bearing raspberries, cut out only the two-year-old canes this month that have finished fruiting on the lower part of the canes. They will look woody and have side branches. Leave the one-year-olds in place to bear their autumn crop on the tops of the canes next month, and next spring cut off these tops to encourage fruit production lower down. Of course, diseased, spindly and overcrowded canes should be removed.

## Fruit Drops and Insect Management

It is natural—although frustrating—for a little of the apple crop to drop as it nears maturity. There are several reasons, however, for excessive premature apple drop: magnesium or boron deficiency; too much nitrogen; moisture deficiency during the growing season; or insect infestation. Short-stem varieties also have a greater tendency to drop.

Any fruit drops in the garden should be picked up and disposed of immediately in case they are infested with insects or disease. Late in the season some of the fruits may be ripe enough to eat. If the compost pile heats up enough to destroy insects, the unusable fruits can be composted. Otherwise, it is best to bury the fruit deep in the soil or put it in a sealed clear plastic bag in the sun for two weeks before adding it to the compost pile. When picking up small fruits such as currants, it is easiest to enlist the help of chickens.

Cultivate the soil under brambles and all currants if insects have been a problem. Do not go at it too vigorously because they are all shallow rooted shrubs. Remove all weeds and grass that have invaded as well, as they can lower fruit production and restrict growth.

## Preserving Fruits

Fruits can be frozen, canned or dried for winter use, and fruit vinegars and cordials are a novel way of preserving their flavour.

### Freezing

Several fruits, including blueberries, currants, strawberries, gooseberries, chopped rhubarb, cranberries and Indian pears (Saskatoons), can be individually quick frozen (IQF) without any special treatment. This yields a high quality product and is very simple to do. Put whole or sliced berries in a single layer on cookie sheets in the freezer; bag them as soon as possible after they are frozen.

In general, other fruits retain better colour, flavour and firmness if they are frozen with sugar. Leave small fruits whole but cut up large fruits and remove pits or stones. For each 4 cups (1 l) of whole or sliced berries, gently stir in 1/4 to 1 cup (65 to 250 ml) of sugar, according to the tartness of the fruit and your sweet tooth. Freeze them in plastic bags, removing the air by sucking on a straw before sealing each bag with a twist-tie. When freezing apricots, apples or peaches you may want to use one of the commercial preparations composed largely of ascorbic acid to prevent discolouration.

If you prefer, use light to heavy syrups instead of sugar. Mix 1 cup (250 ml) of sugar with 2 cups (500 ml) of water for a thin syrup; 1 cup (250 ml) with 1 ½ cups (375 ml) of water for a moderately thin syrup; 1 cup (250 ml) with

1 cup (250 ml) of water for a medium syrup, and 1 cup with 3/4 cup (190 ml) of water for a heavy syrup. Stir until the sugar dissolves, then chill the syrup until you are ready to use it. Completely cover the fruit with syrup, and leave 1/2 inch (12 mm) of headspace in the plastic tub to allow for expansion. Use crumpled waxed paper in the headspace to hold peaches and other floating fruits under the syrup.

Melon slices and watermelon balls will last four months in the freezer; most berries last six months; and other fruits such as cherries will last up to twelve months. Canned peaches and plums have a better flavour than frozen ones, but be sure you fully understand the canning process before you start it.

### *Drying*

Fruits can be dried whole or sliced, or can be cooked and pureed to make fruit leather. Fruits to be dried must be in perfect condition and any of the drying methods described for vegetables (page 295) can be used. Slice large fruits such as apples, but leave small fruits whole. To prevent discolouration, dip apricot, peach, apple and pear slices in a commercial preparation or in 1/4 cup (65 ml) of lemon juice mixed with 1 quart (1.1 l) of water before drying, or simmer for eight minutes in a syrup of 1 cup (250 ml) of sugar to 3 cups (750 ml) of water. For a sweet treat, dip pieces in a medium syrup and drain well before drying.

Fruits are dry when pieces do not stick to each other, or when they spring apart after being squeezed in the hand and leave no traces of moisture on the skin. Store in airtight containers and check occasionally to make sure they are still dry. If they are not, reheat the fruit in a 140°F (60°C) oven for half an hour. Dried fruits last better at cooler temperatures. Dried peaches, for example, will keep for six months at 70°F (21°C), but will last for up to two years at 52°F (11°C).

To make fruit leather, cook cleaned and pitted fruit in a little water until it is soft but not mushy, as for making applesauce, then mash or puree the fruit. Spread it no deeper than 1/4 inch (6 mm) thick on a cookie sheet lined with heavy plastic wrap or sprayed with a nonstick coating. Various fruit purees can be combined before they are dried—you may want to mix apple with less abundant fruits—or the puree can be flavoured with cinnamon or other spices. When the leather is dry enough to pull easily off the pan, turn it and dry the other side. To store, roll it up in fresh plastic; it should keep for six months in a cool, dry place, and up to one year in the refrigerator.

### *Vinegars and cordials*

The flavour of summer fruits can also be stored in vinegars. Steep two parts clean, prepared fruit in one part good quality wine vinegar—or enough to cover the fruit—for several weeks. Choose red or white wine vinegar according to the colour of the fruit (red for strawberries, for example, and white for blueberries). Strain off the vinegar and store it in sterilized bottles in the refrigerator.

To make fruit cordials, combine four parts clean, fully ripe fruit with two parts alcohol (gin, vodka, alcool or brandy) in a glass container with a lid. Add two to four parts sugar—according to the sweetness of the fruit—or less if brandy is used. A good combination, for example, is four parts quartered crabapples, three parts sugar and two parts alcohol. Shake the container daily for one week, then weekly for four months. Strain the liquid and bottle it in clean glass bottles. The remaining fruit can be pureed, if it is free of seeds, for use as a topping on ice cream or cake.

Blackberries and elderberries are cooked in water (approximately three parts fruit to one part water), then the juice is strained and cooked with sugar (approximately three parts juice to one part sugar) until slightly thickened, before it is mixed with brandy or alcohol (approximately three parts fruit syrup to one part alcohol).

### *Jams and jellies*

Use a combination of ripe and slightly under ripe fruit when making jam or jelly, and follow directions exactly. Frozen jams store well and taste delicious but they may take up valuable space in the freezer. It is frustrating, however, when cooked jams and jellies do not seal properly with the traditional paraffin method. A more reliable technique is to use sealer jars filled to within 3/4 inch (2 cm) of the top and processed as for canned fruits or fruit juice.

## *Woody Ornamentals*

### *Summer Care*

Woody plants require little attention at this time of year, although a little pruning may be in order (see July, page 270, for summer pruning). Hardwood trees can also be pruned in November after leaf fall when the branches are lighter and it is easier to see what needs to be cut out. Summer pruning, however, reduces the growth of overly vigorous trees. Removing

## Focus on Plants

Most clematis plants should have bloomed by now, although some, such as 'Ramona,' bloom very late in the season. Sometimes clematis needs to be several years old before it blooms well. Young plants should be cut back to about 2-3 feet (60-90 cm) tall each spring to encourage branching near the base. After several years, the pruning pattern varies with the type of clematis (see page 102) and can affect the flowering. Clematis needs some sun to bloom well, although even those on a bright north facing wall will bloom successfully. Avoid hot, dry locations, or plant annual or perennial flowers at the base to help shade the soil and keep it cool. Working bonemeal and wood ashes into the soil will sometimes encourage clematis to bloom.

Young plants sometimes succumb to clematis wilt—the whole plant seems to wilt overnight. If the original planting was deep enough, new shoots may emerge next spring. Be very careful not to break or damage young vines when working around them because this provides an entry point for the organism that causes wilt. Sometimes part of a vine will wilt simply because the stem was broken, not because it is diseased. Make certain that there is no standing water over the roots in the winter as this may kill even the healthiest clematis plants, let alone those already weakened by wilt disease.

If a new clematis plant just does not grow, it probably needs lime and manure. It may also be that the original propagated cutting rooted well but for some reason failed to make any top growth. These plants never do start into growth and are best discarded. If purchasing clematis from a nursery instead of by mail order, check to see if there are new leaves sprouting from the vine before making the purchase.

leaves reduces the carbohydrates formed and then stored in the roots over the winter, so less new growth will develop next spring.

Shrubs should have damaged, broken and diseased branches removed, and any shrubs that are overly vigorous can be pruned. Established formal hedges can be pruned and tidied up at this time of year, but do not prune young hedges or those growing weakly—they are best done in the spring.

Horse chestnut trees get a blight each year that is of more concern to gardeners than it is to the trees. As long as the trees are well cared for and growing well, they do not seem to suffer from the blight. The same holds true for birches, honeysuckles and other woody ornamentals that seem prone to blights. Pruning to improve air circulation and thoroughly raking up the leaves in the autumn may help to reduce the incidence of disease.

Continue to take semi-hardwood cuttings for propagation purposes (see pages 280-281) and pot on other cuttings that have already rooted.

## Causes and Prevention of Tree Decline

If for some reason soil is being added over tree and shrub roots or the grade is being changed, proceed with caution. Roots for each species develop at the optimum depth for absorbing the nutrients, moisture and oxygen they need. Adding too much soil over the roots can disturb these processes, and cause the eventual death of the tree. Try to avoid adding more than 4 inches (10 cm) of extra soil, and make sure it is a porous or gritty soil. Just an inch or two (2.5 to 5 cm) of a clay soil can suffocate a tree.

Adding soil in the vicinity of the root zone may not harm the roots themselves, but it may change the water level or runoff pattern. Plants may then lack adequate water, or be exposed to too much water and suffer from root rot and eventual decline.

A related problem is planting too deep. Many healthy trees and shrubs fail to thrive and may actually die because overly enthusiastic gardeners planted them deeper than they grew in their original pot. If a plant seems to have this problem, remove the extra soil from over the roots this season and replant it next spring, or dig up the plant as soon as the leaves drop in the autumn and set it in at the appropriate level.

Other situations which can damage tree roots and cause gradual root death include compacting the soil over the root zone by driving heavy equipment over it, or stockpiling soil or construction materials over the root zone. If you are building a home or adding a driveway, pay particular attention to the trees before you start. Put temporary fencing up around the root zone of trees, not just around their trunks, so that heavy equipment keeps clear of the roots. If traffic is unavoidable, put down a 1 foot (30 cm) thick layer of coarse wood chips to minimize compaction.

After construction is completed, remove the coarse wood chips and apply a 4 inch (10 cm) layer of shredded bark as a mulch on the soil over the tree roots. This will encourage the growth of fine tree roots and thereby increase the absorption of water, nutrients and oxygen. As well, water deeply and regularly throughout the growing season, and apply well rotted manure or compost in the spring. This is the best care that can be given to all trees and shrubs.

## Preventive Measure

A tree well can be used to protect tree roots if the surrounding grade is either raised or lowered, but it only works if it is as large as the diameter of the root zone. It should extend out at least as far as the drip line. A small well or pit to keep added soil away from the trunk does nothing for the roots.

Before fill is added, set up a parallel or radiating system of drainage pipes or agricultural drainage tiles over the full zone of the tree's roots and extending at least as far out as the drip line. The pipes should slope slightly downwards away from the tree. Next, build a retaining wall around the tree trunk. Make it of porous construction, such as a dry stone wall. It should be 20 inches (50 cm) away from the trunk of mature trees, but even further away from young trees. The wall should straddle the ends of the drainage pipe spokes. Add a layer of broken rock between the spokes and then cover the rock and pipes with a layer of gravel. Next add soil to the depth required by the plants that will be grown underneath the tree (see page 381).

The removal of soil can be even harder on established trees. If the level must be lowered, preserve the original soil level at least as far out as the drip line of the tree. Contain the original soil and root mass by building a wooden, brick or stone retaining wall.

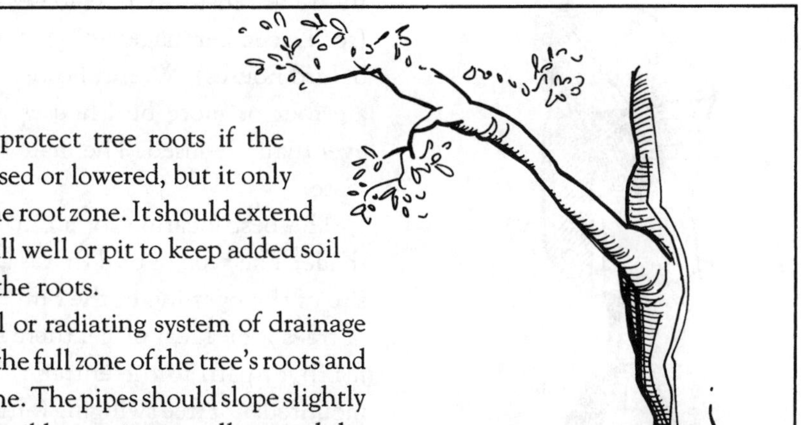

Tree Well
Fill between spokes with rock then cover with a layer of gravel.

## Setting up Bird Houses

People usually get the urge to set out bird houses or nest boxes in the spring, but sometime in the summer or early autumn is a better time. The amount of shade in any given position can be identified while the trees are in leaf, and the bird house will weather over the winter and thus be more appealing to birds. Aged trees with cavities are ideal nesting sites but very few gardens have any. If bird houses are set out in the spring, do it as close to the beginning of the year as possible.

Small gardens will usually support only one pair of nesting birds, and the usual density for bird houses is about ten different types per acre of land (see December, pages 443-445, for a discussion of types and construction of bird houses). Wrens, however, are more likely to be attracted if there are four or more bird houses in a garden, even though only one will eventually be used. The male bird builds several trial nests to attract a mate.

Squirrel guard

The best location for a bird house is an open, sunny area, not dense shade. The type of bird that is attracted will partly be determined by the size of the opening in the bird house. Near the edge of woods or a group of trees is an ideal place; there should be a clear, 5 to 15 foot (1.2 to 4.5 m) flight path to the entrance hole. The house or box should be firmly mounted, not free swinging (although house wrens will tolerate a hanging bird house). Mounting it on a pole or post is often better than mounting it on a tree; there is a clear view all around, and predators are less able to creep up unobserved. For owls and other birds that prefer high nests, a tree will more easily provide the necessary height; nuthatches and chickadees seem to prefer bird houses mounted on trees. The height of a bird house above the ground will determine the type of bird that is attracted (see Table AUG-5).

On poles or posts, use a metal cone to keep birds safer from predators, and wrap an 18 inch (45 cm) wide collar of metal around tree trunks. Position the collars about 5 feet (1.5 m) above the ground, and check twice a year to make sure they are not girdling the tree trunks.

The orientation of the bird house is also important. The opening should face away from summer prevailing winds, which in most cases means the hole would face south or southwest. The front should also tilt slightly downward so that there is no chance of rain getting in. When

## *Table AUG-5 Height of Bird Houses Above the Ground*

| Bird | Height Above Ground In Feet | In Metres |
|---|---|---|
| Barn Swallow * | 8 to 12 | 2.5 to 3.7 |
| Chickadee | 6 to 15 | 1.8 to 4.6 |
| Downy Woodpecker | 6 to 20 | 1.8 to 6.2 |
| Eastern Bluebird | 5 to 10 | 1.5 to 3.1 |
| Eastern Phoebe * | 8 to 12 | 2.5 to 3.7 |
| House Wren | 6 to 10 | 1.8 to 3.1 |
| Northern Flicker | 6 to 20 | 1.8 to 6.2 |
| Nuthatch | 12 to 20 | 3.7 to 6.2 |
| Red-headed Woodpecker | 12 to 20 | 3.7 to 6.2 |
| Robin * | 6 to 15 | 1.8 to 4.6 |
| Screech Owl | 10 to 30 | 3.1 to 9.2 |
| Song Sparrow * | 1 to 3 | 0.3 to 0.9 |
| Tree Swallow | 10 to 15 | 3.1 to 4.6 |
| Winter Wren | 6 to 10 | 1.8 to 3.1 |

* These birds will sometimes use nesting shelves
Based on information in *How to Attract Birds* (Ortho Books, 1983).

attaching it to a post or tree, put two small strips of wood on each side of the back so that a small air space is created and the back of the house does not collect or soak up water when conditions are wet.

Some birds prefer nesting shelves. They are best mounted under eaves against the house, shed or garage. Robins like a vine-covered arbour, while barn swallows prefer a more open shelf without a roof, but it must be attached under overhanging eaves. Barn and cliff swallows will both build nests on nothing more than a 2 by 4 mounted horizontally on the wall under the eaves. Put it on the side of the building that is sheltered from prevailing summer winds.

## Lawns

If established lawns are looking pale or tired, spead a little seaweed extract, manure tea (see Green Thumb Tip, page 163), fish emulsion or other quick acting nitrogen fertilize. If more than half of the lawn is weeds and bare areas, and if the soil is poor, it may be best to start all over with a new lawn. Overseeding, thatch removal and other repairs may be enough to rejuvenate an old lawn that still has some redeeming qualities.

> **Green Thumb Tip**
>
> The seed bed must never be allowed to dry out. Spread burlap, floating row covers or a thin covering of straw over the area to keep the seeds moist, or water as required with a gentle mist. Do not use hay as a cover because it is full of weed seeds. Remove the covering once the seedlings emerge, and water lightly and frequently at first, then deeply and regularly. Autumn rains may take care of most of the watering, but a light mulch will prevent erosion until the grass is an inch (2.5 cm) high. A covering made of wood fibres, made specifically for covering newly seeded lawns, acts as a thin mulch that does not have to be removed.

### Seeding a New Lawn

The best time to start a lawn from seed is when the worst of the summer heat is over and nights are getting cool—about six weeks before the first frost is expected. The soil is dry enough to be workable and warm enough to encourage the grass to germinate, there is less competition from weeds because they germinate less readily in the autumn, and the new grass will have a well developed root system by the time it faces its first summer next year. The only disadvantage to starting a lawn at this time is that leaf drop under trees can be a problem. A mulch, however, or some ground cover plant other than grass may be a better choice under trees (see page 201 for suggestions).

The best long-term insurance for a healthy, relatively weed-free, drought resistant lawn is at least 6 inches (15 cm) of topsoil which is rich in nutrients and organic matter. Four inches (10 cm) is acceptable, especially if you are adding soil over tree roots, but aim for more rather than less, except over roots (see page 320). The same holds if sod is being laid, as relatively little soil comes with the sod. Remove any buried tree stumps or roots as these can encourage the growth of toadstools and the sinking of soil as the wood decays. See page 379 for methods of removing old sod.

To improve the quality of the soil, work in organic matter such as compost, leaf mould or well rotted manure. Add garden lime if the pH is much below 6.5. Level the soil so that there are no bumps or hollows, raking back and forth across the area in different directions. Pulling a board across will also reveal unlevel areas. Leave it so weeds can germinate, then rake again.

Use fresh seed to ensure a high and even germination rate. Lawn seed comes as various mixtures—if the seed is old some types are more likely to germinate than others, so the final mix of grasses will be different. Seed which is a few months old should still be good, but avoid any that has been sitting around for several years, particularly if it has not been kept cool and dry. Avoid mixtures containing large amounts of Kentucky bluegrass seed as this grass requires extra care (see pages 207-208).

Spread one-quarter of the recommended amount of seed in one direction over the area, reverse and spread another quarter, and then spread the other half at right angles, again reversing the direction after each quarter. This will reduce the number of bare areas. Rake the ground lightly at right angles with the back of a rake to cover the seed. Do not roll it with a heavy roller because this compacts the soil unnecessarily.

Established lawns can be overseeded if they have bare spots or more weeds than can be tolerated. Overseeding works well if at least half of the lawn is in good condition. Begin by mowing the grass as low as possible—to 1/2 inch (12 mm) high or less. Dethatch the area, as described below, and pull or dig out all visible weeds. Rake the area thoroughly to clean up all debris and then top dress the lawn with compost as described on page 371. Spread one-half the usual amount of seed for new lawns, going in different directions to scatter the seed evenly. Keep the lawn moist until the seed germinates, then mulch it lightly.

## Thatch and Repairs

A lot can be done to improve lawns at this time of year, not only for appearance's sake but also for insect and disease control. Chinch bugs, for example, hibernate in thatch and in the upper level of soil, and fungal problems are reduced if thatch is removed.

Thatch is the layer of dead grass; a layer less than 1/2 inch (12 mm) thick is not a problem. Buildup usually only happens on lawns that have a low earthworm population. Earthworms will increase and multiply as the organic content in soil is increased and as the use of inorganic fertilizers is decreased. Keeping the pH around 6.5 also suits earthworms.

Dethatching can be done by raking vigorously with a metal rake or with a special cutting rake designed for the job. For severe problems or large areas, rent a good dethatching machine or hire a lawn care company to do the work. Rake off the thatch and compost it. It does not matter if roots and grass are torn in the process in the late summer or autumn because grass sends out side shoots and actively grows roots at this time of year. Dethatching must be done more carefully in the spring. Sprinkle bare areas with fresh grass seed and water well.

Bumps and hollows in lawns can also be repaired sometime in the coming weeks. Cut an H shape over the area needing repair and peel back the sod.

Repairing lawn bumps

Add top soil to hollows or remove excess subsoil, not topsoil, from bumps. Replace the sod, trimming off any excess or filling in gaps with topsoil and grass seed, and water the area deeply. Sod edges should knit well as the days get cooler and grasses start an active stage of root growth.

Soils that are compacted should be aerated, but September or October is soon enough for this and for adding organic matter to existing lawns (see page 371).

## Indoor Gardening

### Vegetables and Herbs

Many of the late season vegetables planted outdoors can also be started indoors, either this month or next. Several will take longer to grow to maturity now than they do in the spring, due to shorter days and cooler temperatures, but the reward is worth the extra wait.

Looseleaf lettuce will grow well indoors, or extend its season outdoors well into autumn using crop protection. Butterhead and cos or romaine lettuce need a slightly longer growing season, so they may be better planted indoors unless autumn frosts are late. Swiss chard, spinach, mustard greens and Chinese cabbage grow quickly indoors and round out the variety of greens. Collards, escarole and endive take longer to grow and require a little more space, so some gardeners rely entirely on their outdoor crop.

For a change in taste and texture, sow edible-podded peas, radicchio, carrots and beans. These are best started before the greenhouse gets too chilly, although planting in September is fine if the weather or the greenhouse stays warm. Outdoor carrots will last well into the autumn—

unless they are harvested early to avoid carrot rust fly—so their indoor seeding can be delayed for another month or two. Bunching onions and a variety of herbs will provide a welcome spark of taste and freshness in the winter. Many annual herbs can be started from seed (see Table JAN-2, page 24). Perennial herbs, however, are more easily dug from the outdoor garden than started fresh (see pages 349-350).

If cucumbers, summer squash and zucchini are started indoors this month, they will be available for harvest well into winter. They prefer warm conditions, however, and are not suited to greenhouses that get very cool in the autumn. Peppers and eggplants can be dug up from the garden and brought indoors before the first frost to continue producing (see page 372). Even without a greenhouse, a pot or two of lettuce, mustard greens, onions and parsley will perk up winter fare. Cats and pet rabbits will appreciate young pea plants and some alphalpha.

## Warm Flowers

August is a busy month for winter flower growers. Pot up Madonna lily and store it cool at 45 to 50°F (7 to 10°C). Bring *L. regale* and *L. speciosum album* and *rubrum* out of cold storage. The last two ought to bloom in January.

If daffodils and hyacinth bulbs can be obtained early, they can be potted up around August 1, given their cold treatment to mid November (see page 405), and be in bloom by Christmas. Large, healthy daffodil bulbs can be dug up from the garden if they cannot be obtained commercially this month. Start up white or pink calla lily in warmth, one per 5 to 7 inch (125 to 175 mm) pot, water generously once new growth has started, and fertilize with a high nitrogen fertilizer. Dry off yellow calla and caladium, and store them in their pots (refer to Table OCT/NOV-1, page 390).

Remove any faded leaves from amaryllis and stop fertilizing it sometime between August and November, depending on whether midwinter or early spring bloom is desired. Cut back on watering at the same time but do not dry it out completely. It is not necessary to force it into complete dormancy, but a three month rest from growing will encourage it to bloom when it is started into growth again. Unless the leaves die back, amaryllis can be kept in the light during the day as any foliage plant. Bulbs that lose all of their top growth can be stored out of sight until the three month rest is completed. Other bulbs that require an autumn or winter rest (see Table OCT/NOV-1, page 390) are treated the same way.

Sow browallia and lisianthus (see Table FEB-4, page 56, for germination temperatures) this month. Thin or transplant seedlings when the true leaves appear six to eight weeks later. Start seven or eight morning glory seeds in an 8 inch (200 mm) pot, and then thin them, leaving the three strongest seedlings, once they are up and growing.

Order roses for winter forcing; the best ones are climbers, hybrid teas, hybrid perpetuals and floribundas. Bring gerbera, tender bulbs in pots and other plants in from outdoors before there is a risk of frost.

### Cool Flowers

Many annual flowers can be started from seed this month or next. Some, such as schizanthus (butterfly flower or poor man's orchid), can be seeded monthly for a long succession of bloom. Forget-me-nots are started every six weeks. Sow winter flowering sweet peas around August 1 for bloom in December, and sow some winter flowering snapdragons. Nugget marigolds can be sown twelve seeds per 4 inch (100 mm) pot, and nasturtiums can also be planted directly in a pot.

Other flowers are best sown in small flats and then transplanted to pots after they develop their first true leaves. Try pansies, calendula, sweet alyssum, ageratum, nemesia, annual aster and wallflower. Fertilize with half strength 5-10-10 or with fish fertilizer when the true leaves appear, and pinch snapdragons, schizanthus and others (see Table FEB-4, page 56) when they are 4 inches (10 cm) tall.

Annuals that flower outdoors and are showing signs of flagging can be cut back, potted up, and fertilized for winter bloom indoors. Petunias in particular respond well to this treatment, perhaps because they are actually a perennial. This is usually done in late August, September, October or any time before the first autumn frost.

Freesias potted up this month, six to eight per 5 inch (125 mm) pot, or ten to twelve per 6 inch (150 mm) pot, may flower for Christmas. Starting a potfull or two each month from August to December will stretch out the season of bloom. Water sparingly until new growth shows, then fertilize every two to three weeks with 10-30-10 until flowers are in bud.

There is such a wide choice of flowers to grow that most indoor gardeners will not have room for everything. It is surprising how much can be grown under lights, however, and even a few pots of flowers can make a big difference on dark winter days.

Month-by-Month

# September/October

- start frost prediction graph
- store vegetables
- make a hot bed
- bring herbs and tender perennials indoors
- harvest roots and fixatives
- take hardwood cuttings
- plant tree seeds
- aerate and top dress lawn
- start more plants indoors
- save seeds
- plant spring bulbs

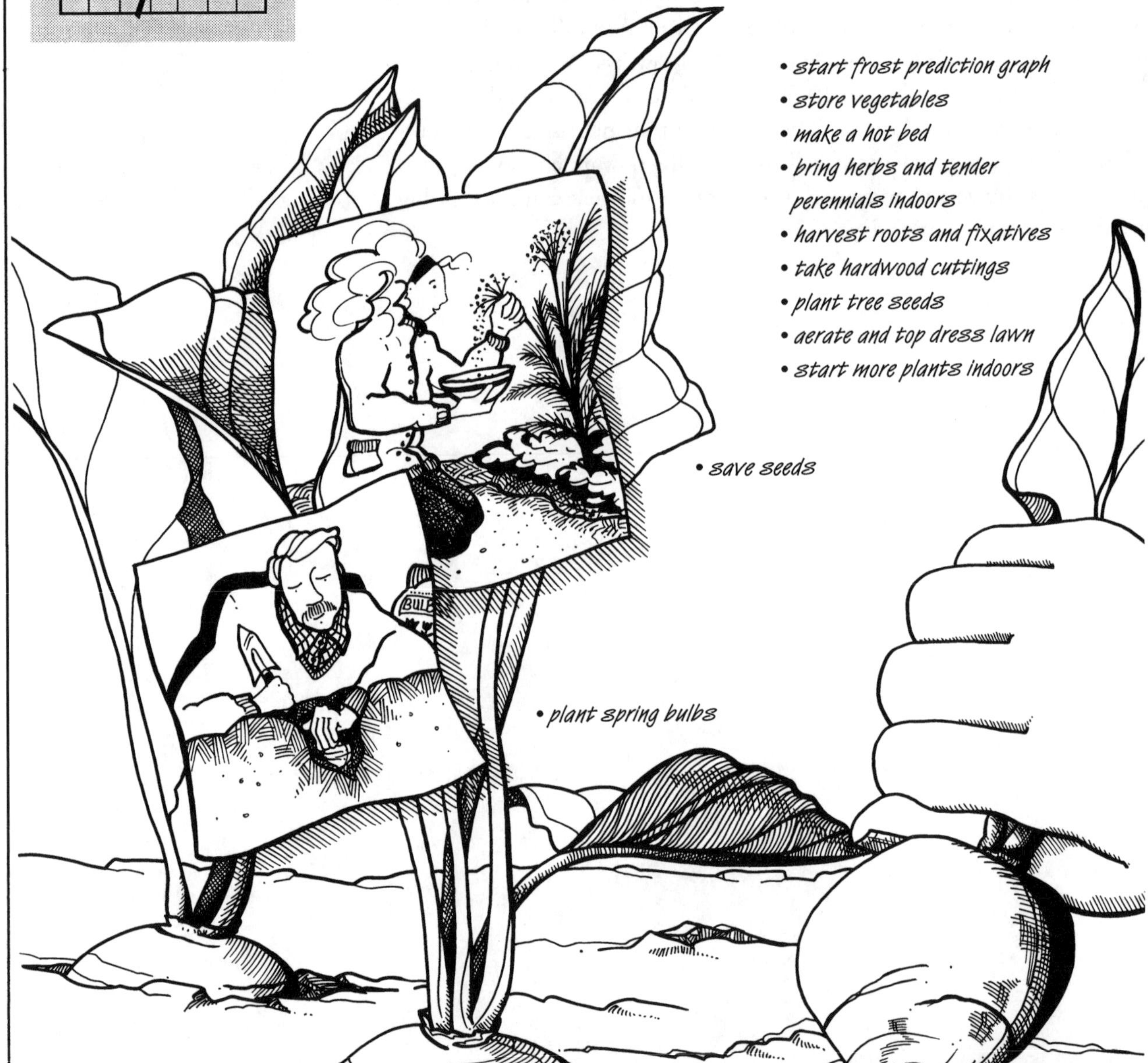

As the days grow shorter and frost threatens, much of your gardening energy will be absorbed by preparations for winter. Storing fruits and vegetables, bringing in herbs to grow on a sunny windowsill, potting up daffodils and other bulbs which will brighten winter days indoors, and sowing seeds for fresh winter greens and flowers, can occupy many hours. This time of year can be immensely satisfying: surveying nature's handiwork that we have helped nudge along instills a sense of completion, while contemplating winter pleasures heightens our anticipation.

Outdoor activities are mostly directed toward next spring and include taking soil samples, spreading compost, aerating the lawn, and propagating herbaceous plants and shrubs.

# September October

**Mushroom**
*Small room where vegetables are stored until they decompose into a pulpy mass suitable for the compost heap.*

*Beard and McKie*

## Frost Prediction

Frost records kept in both Canada and the United States are used to determine the date of the first expected frost date of autumn in different areas. This date is helpful when deciding how late in the season to plant certain crops (see Table AUG-1, page 297), but it is quite unreliable in terms of predicting on which night that first frost will actually come stealing through the garden. If plants can be protected from the first few frosts, they can benefit from the stretch of mild weather that often follows. The trick is knowing when to cover the plants, and how to do it.

The frost warnings issued with the weather predictions are a help, but they do not necessarily apply to your particular garden. On a frosty night, some gardens may be badly damaged while others are untouched within the same neighbourhood. According to Dr. James Rahn (1979), a past state climatologist for Pennsylvania, there are several ways of predicting frosts, including watching weather patterns, and keeping records of these patterns in your own garden.

The weather pattern most likely to bring frost begins with the passing of a cold front. The winds shift to westerly or northerly and there may be some showers. While the winds are brisk and there is some cloud cover, there is little risk of frost. Winds keep the air stirred up, so that the heat radiating from the earth is brought back down again, and clouds interfere with the radiation of heat into upper levels of the atmosphere. As a ridge of high pressure moves in from behind, the winds drop and the skies clear. It is at this stage, when heat radiates readily from the earth, that the likelihood of frost is greatest. As the high moves in, warmer, milder air flows in from the south or southwest and the risk of frost drops off.

Keeping weather records for a particular garden makes a good tool for predicting frost. If the temperature drops quickly between early in the evening and later the same night, there is a greater risk of frost than if the temperature remains constant or drops very little. It is very useful to keep track of the temperatures at two distinct times and over several seasons on potentially frosty nights, and to note whether or not a frost occurs that night.

It is essential that temperatures are taken at exactly the same times every night to make the results as reliable as possible. Take careful note of the temperature at, say, 7 p.m. and 10 p.m., then plot the difference in the temperature between these two times against the temperature at 7 p.m. What will emerge over several seasons is a graph from which to make predictions. Say, for example, that the temperature at 7 p.m. was 42°F (5.6°C); if it drops 4°F (2.2°C) or less by 10 p.m., frost is unlikely; if it drops 4 to 7°F (2.2 to 3.8°C), there is a chance that frost will occur, but it is not certain; if the temperature drops more than 7°F (3.8°C), frost will probably occur. The longer the records are kept, the more reliable the tool will be.

### Graph 1: Frost prediction based on the rate of change of temperature

F = Frost occurred
N = No frost occurred
(To make a graph in °C, use ordinates 0, 1, 2, 3, 4, 5...)

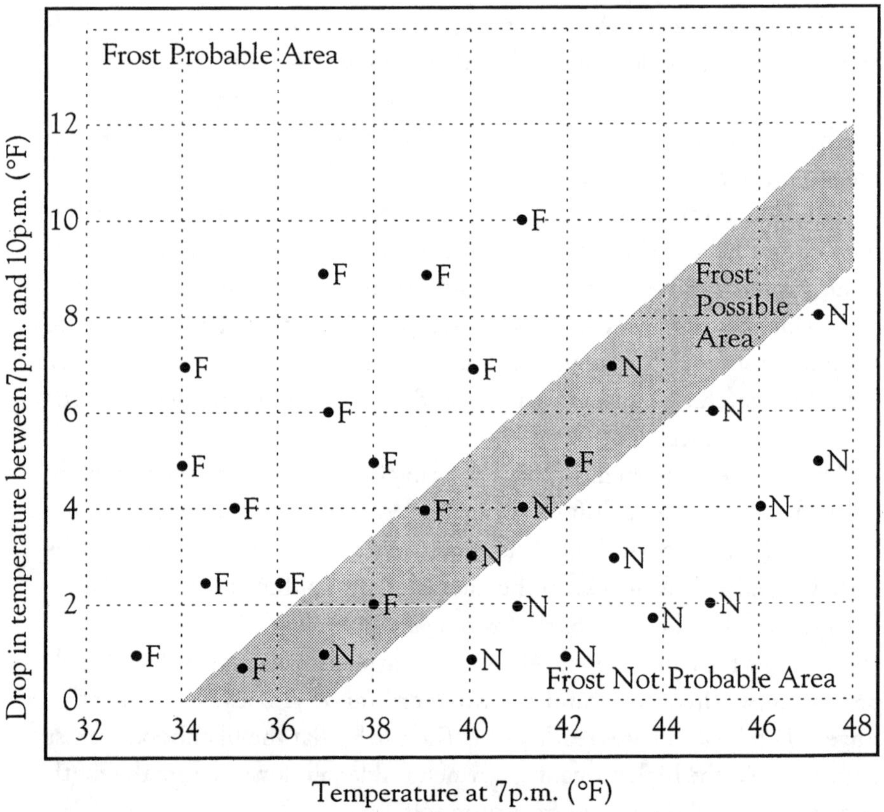


Revised from Rahn,1979

A third way of predicting frost is to observe the temperature at dewpoint, that is, when dew first begins to form on objects outdoors. Dew forms rapidly and in great quantities if the heat from the ground radiates rapidly into the air, but the amount of humidity in the air will also affect the rate. Generally speaking, the drop in temperature is greater the drier the air is. If there is lots of moisture in the air, the dewpoint temperature will be higher and there is less risk of frost. Because air temperature cannot fall lower than the dewpoint temperature, and is usually a few degrees higher, the latter is a better predictor of frost than relying on air temperature alone. This can be plotted on a graph, taking note of the temperature at dewpoint and whether or not a frost occurs. Alternatively, determine a cutoff point or critical temperature for the garden in question after keeping records for several seasons. If this critical temperature at the dewpoint you have determined is 40°F (4°C) or higher, there is little risk of frost, but the risk increases as the temperature at dewpoint decreases below 40°F (4°C).

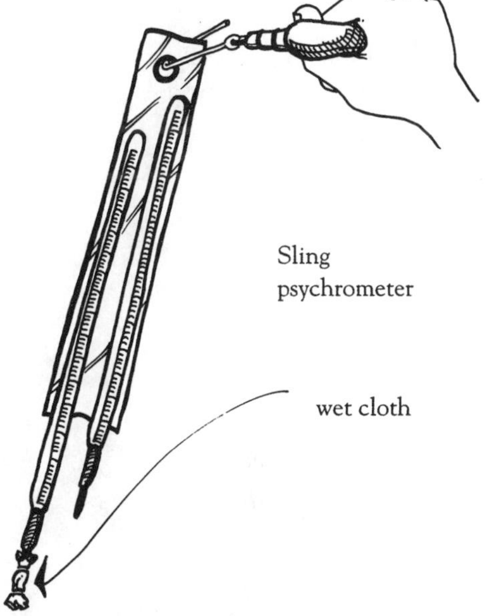


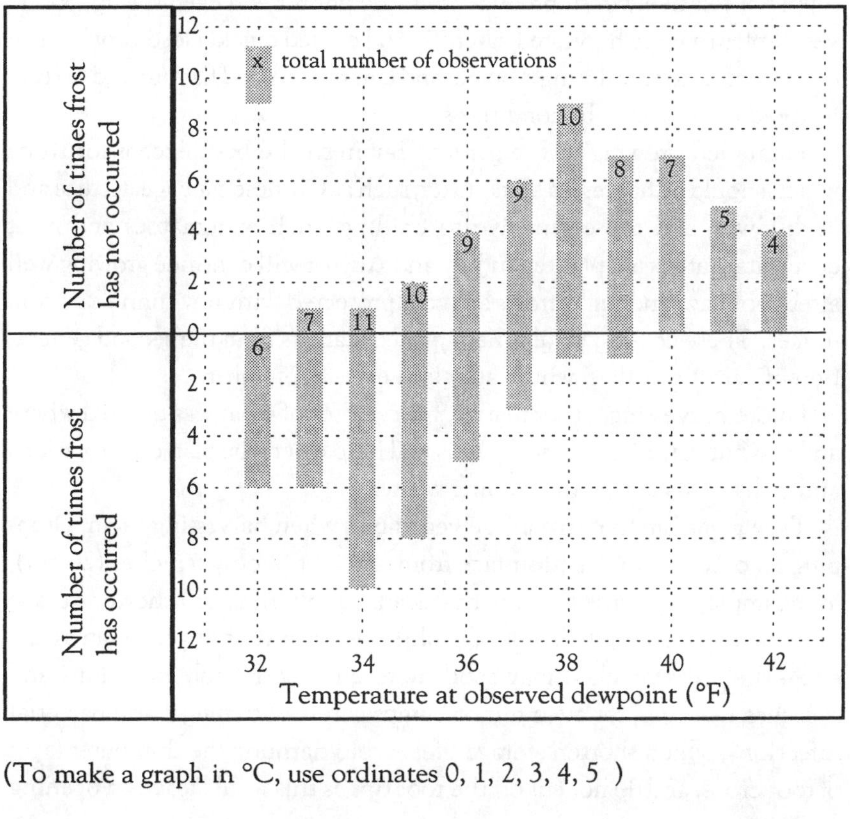


(To make a graph in °C, use ordinates 0, 1, 2, 3, 4, 5 )

### *Graph 2: Frost prediction based on temperature at observed dewpoint*

Dewpoint temperature can be measured more easily and exactly by taking a reading at 9 p.m. with a sling psychrometer. This simple instrument has a dry bulb thermometer and a wet bulb thermometer; these are swung through the air until the temperatures reach their equilibrium. If the dewpoint temperature is 36°F (2°C) or lower, frost will probably occur. These methods can also be used for predicting spring frosts, but keep separate records for each season.

To protect crops when frost is predicted, or even to protect heat loving crops such as tomatoes and peppers from chilly nights, use plastic, a canvas tarp, blankets or some other covering. Cover as large an area as possible and make sure the cover does not touch the plants anywhere. Water can be used instead if a mist system can be rigged up that will supply 1/10 inch (2.5 mm) of water per hour, starting when the temperature approaches 32°F (0°C). It also helps to remove any mulch from the garden; bare, untilled soil absorbs more heat during the day than mulched, sodded or tilled soil. The stored heat is released at night, warming the air next to the ground. Cold frames and row covers can be set in place to both protect plants from frost and extend the growing season considerably.

## Vegetables

### Harvest and Storage

Storing vegetables in cold rooms and cool basements ensures a continuous supply of relatively fresh produce well into winter and even spring. Sound vegetables that are harvested carefully and cooled quickly lose very little in the way of nutrients during storage, and can retain good flavour and texture if stored under the right conditions.

Plants left growing in the garden stay fresh the best, except for those which should be harvested at maturity, such as Chinese cabbage, lettuce and cauliflower, and those sensitive to chilling, such as tomatoes and most cucurbits. Late crops planted in July and August will continue growing well after cool days and night frosts arrive if protected with row tunnels or cold frames. These covers will also help protect carrots from the second generation of carrot rust flies, which attack in early September.

Before harvesting, or soon after, make notes of what was planted where and of what varieties grew well. This will help when you plan crop rotations and order seeds during the coming winter.

Take great care not to damage vegetables when harvesting them. Dropping an onion onto a hard surface from a height of only 8 inches (20 cm), for example, will cause bruising that leads to softening and shorter storage life. Avoid touching the curds of cauliflower with your fingers or anything else—the areas touched may spoil more quickly. Handle pumpkins and squashes like eggs, for even minor bumps can lead to fungal and bacterial infections, which shorten storage life. Avoid harming the thin outer layer of root crops, and do not cut off the root tips as this would leave an opening where spoilage could begin. Vegetables that are damaged in any way should be stored separately from unblemished produce and used first.

The major factors affecting how long sound produce will last in storage are temperature and humidity. Taking humidity and temperature together, there are three basic storage conditions suitable for vegetables, depending on the kind: warm and dry; cool and dry; and cool and moist. Freezing and canning provide longer term storage (see page 316), but with little preparation, many vegetables can be stored fresh for weeks or months (refer to Table SEP/OCT-1).

### *Warm and dry*

When storing vegetables in warm and dry conditions, "warm" is around 50°F (10°C) and suits those vegetables sensitive to chilling injury, including tomatoes, peppers, eggplants, beans (excluding shell beans), cucumbers, honeydew melons, zucchini and summer squash.

Refrigeration is not recommended for these vegetables. Chilling leads to pitting in the surface and subsequently to spoilage and loss of flavour and texture. Even the cool nights of August and September can cause damage if crops are not protected.

At this time of year it is difficult to determine whether frost sensitive crops in some regions will ripen before they are hit by frost. As long as the days are pleasantly warm and above 45°F (7°C)—but above 50°F (10°C) for tomatoes—it is worth leaving them in the garden and covering them at night. Use row tunnels or cold frames on chilly nights, or even during the day to keep sensitive crops going longer in the garden if there is a short run of chilly days. The sugars and vitamin C that give tomatoes their sweet but sharp taste are increased during the last stages of ripening on the vine. During ripening off the vine, sugars and vitamin C are actually destroyed. Vine tomatoes lowered to the ground and covered in this way will ripen sooner and be protected from frost. When there are more chilly days than warm, or if a hard freeze is predicted, pick tomatoes for ripening indoors, or pull up the entire vine and hang it in a warm, dry place.

Chili peppers ripen best on the vine, but sweet peppers will ripen after picking. Like tomatoes, the entire plant can be pulled up and hung in a room kept at a temperature of around 50°F (10°C). Sweet peppers left on the plant will keep fresh weeks longer than those cut off. Eggplants can be harvested and used at one third their mature size, or the whole plant can be hung up. They will keep only one to two weeks at 50°F (10°C) once they are cut from

## Table SEP/OCT-1 Storage Conditions for Fresh Vegetables

**Vegetables Requiring Warm and Dry Storage Conditions**
Temperature: 45 to 50°F (7 to 10°C) Relative Humidity: 70 to 90%

| Vegetable | Storage Life | Methods of Extended Preservation |
|---|---|---|
| Bean, green | 8-10 days | freeze, can, dry |
| Cucumber | 1-2 weeks | pickle |
| Eggplant | 1-2 weeks | freeze |
| Honeydew Melon | 2-3 weeks | freeze as for fruits |
| Pepper | 8-10 days | freeze, dry |
| Potatoes, new | 2-3 weeks | |
| Pumpkin | 2-3 months | freeze, can, dry |
| Squash | | |
| - summer | 2 weeks | freeze, can |
| - winter | 4-6 months | freeze, can, dry |
| Sweet Potatoes | 4-5 months | dry |
| Tomatoes | | |
| - ripe | 5-7 days | freeze, can, dry |
| - unripe | 1-2 months | pickle, chutney, mincemeat (store unripe tomatoes at 54 to 82°F/12 to 28°C to ripen them) |

**Vegetables Requiring Cool and Dry Storage Conditions**
Temperature: 32°F (0°C) Relative Humidity: 50 to 70%

| Vegetable | Storage Life | Methods of Extended Preservation |
|---|---|---|
| Bean, shell | 1-2 years | |
| Garlic | 6-8 months | dry |
| Nuts | 1 year | |
| Onion- bulbs | 5-7 months | dry |
| Peas - dried | 1-2 years | |
| Popcorn | 1-2 years | |
| Shallots | 5-6 months | |
| Sunflower Seeds | 1 year | |

**Vegetables Requiring Cool and Moist Storage Conditions**
Temperature: 32°F (0°C) Relative Humidity: 90 to 95%

| Vegetable | Storage Life | Methods of Extended Preservation |
|---|---|---|
| Arugula | 7-10 days | |
| Asparagus | 3 weeks | freeze, can, dry |
| Bean, Lima and Broad | | |
| - shelled | 2 weeks | freeze, can, dry |
| - unshelled | 2 weeks | |
| Beet | | |
| - greens | 10-14 days | freeze |
| - roots | 1-3 months | freeze, can, dry |
| Broccoli | 1 week | freeze, dry |
| Brussels Sprouts | 3-4 weeks | freeze |
| Cabbage | | |
| - early | 3-4 weeks | |
| - winter | 3-4 months | sauerkraut, dry |
| Carrots | 4-5 months | freeze, can, dry |
| Cauliflower | 2 weeks | pickle, freeze |
| Celeriac | 1 month | |
| Celery | 3 months | |
| Collards | 10-14 days | |
| Corn | 5 days | freeze, can, dry |
| Corn Salad | 7-10 days | |
| Endive, Escarole | 2-3 weeks | |
| Florence Fennel | 2 weeks | freeze |
| Horseradish | 10-12 months | relish |
| Kale | 2-3 weeks | |
| Kohlrabi | 2-4 weeks | freeze |
| Leeks | 1-3 months | dry |
| Lettuce | 2-3 weeks | |
| Melon, Cantaloupe | | |
| and Muskmellon | 2 weeks | freeze |
| Watermelon | 2-3 weeks | |
| Mustard Greens | 10-14 days | |
| Parsnip | 2-4 months | freeze, dry |

| Vegetable | Storage Life | Methods of Extended Preservation |
|---|---|---|
| Peas, green | | |
| - shelled | 1 day | freeze, can, dry |
| - unshelled | 3-5 days | |
| Potatoes N.B. | 4-9 months | dry |
| Radicchio | 3-4 weeks | |
| Radish | | |
| - spring | 2 weeks | |
| - winter | 2-4 months | dry |
| Rhubarb | 2-3 weeks | freeze, can, dry, jam |
| Rutabaga (Swede) | 6 months | dry |
| Salsify | 2-4 months | |
| Scorzonera | 2-4 months | |
| Spinach | 10-14 days | freeze, can |
| Swiss Chard | 10-14 days | freeze, can |
| Turnip | 2-3 months | |
| Witloof Chicory | 2-4 months | |

N.B. Store potatoes slightly warmer at 42 to 50°F (5 to 10°C).
Based in part on Agriculture Canada Publication 1478/E.

### Focus on Plants

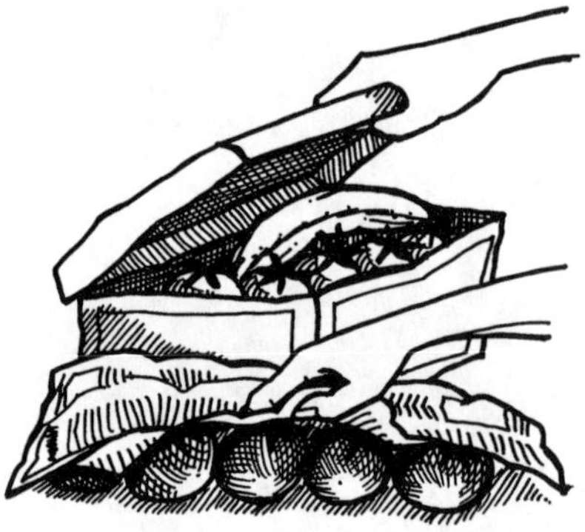

Green tomatoes that are small, hard and opaque will not ripen, and should be fried, pickled or made into chutney or mincemeat. Full grown green tomatoes that have started to whiten in the shoulder or have taken on a translucent quality will probably ripen, and pink tomatoes should ripen well if they have not been chilled, bruised or damaged.

Leave a short stem on tomatoes as removing it creates an entry point for organisms that cause spoilage. There is some evidence that fruits and vegetables last longer in storage if kept in their natural position, so stand tomatoes and other vegetables upright. Sort them according to stages of ripening so that they can be easily monitored as ripening progresses.

Manipulating the temperature can also speed up or slow down ripening: 64 to 82°F (17 to 28°C) gives the fastest results; 54 to 61°F (12 to 16°C) will extend the ripening time. The cold temperature of refrigerators—35 to 40°F (2 to 4°C)—is entirely unsuitable.

Wrap individual tomatoes in newspaper, or spread them stems up in a single layer and cover them with sheets of newspaper to help trap the ethylene gas that causes ripening. Plastic is not a good idea because it tends to encourage rot. Alternatively, put a few tomatoes and a ripe banana or apple in a closed box to trap the ethylene from the already ripe fruit.

the plant, but if left on the pulled plant they should be harvested before the skin loses its shininess. Peppers and eggplants can also be potted up from the garden and brought indoors (see page 372).

Beans, cucumbers, melons, zucchini and summer squash will keep for a week or two in the refrigerator, but will last up to three weeks at 45 to 50°F (7 to 10°C). They will not ripen or mature further once they are picked.

Cut ornamental gourds when the stems are brown, before the first frost. Wash them in a solution of one part bleach to ten parts water, dry them carefully, and cure them in a warm, dry place for several months until the seeds rattle. Coat them with paste wax or clear shellac when they are fully dry.

Pumpkins and winter squashes are best stored in warm, dry conditions, such as in a heated basement, but try to leave them on the vine as long as possible. They do not ripen properly once picked, and cool nights or a very light frost or two will increase their sugar content. Try to protect them from hard frost, but if a light frost kills the leaves or blackens the leaf tips, the fruit will still be all right. Their storage life is reduced if a hard freeze occurs, so bring them in before that happens. Pumpkins that have started to turn colour will continue the process once picked—which is fine for jack-o'-lanterns—but the flavour will not be as good as those ripened on the vine.

Squashes and pumpkins are ripe when the skin is so hard that it cannot be marked easily and the stem near the fruit looks dry and shriveled. Cut them from the plant leaving 4 to 6 inches (10 to 15 cm) of stem attached. Do not use this as a handle; fungi and bacteria that cause spoilage will enter more easily if the stem is loosened or torn off completely. Handle the fruits gently to avoid nicks and bruises, and either use damaged ones first, or steam and freeze or dry the flesh of any that will not store well.

Squashes and pumpkins are traditionally cured before they are put in storage by being kept for two weeks in a warm (80 to 85°F or 27 to 30°C) location with 80% humidity. This is not essential if they are fully mature and the skin is well hardened when they are harvested. In storage, position them so that they do not touch each other and check them regularly for signs of decay.

Sweet potatoes are ready for harvest when the vines turn yellow and die or are killed by frost. To start house plants, take 10 inch (25 cm) cuttings from the vine tips while they are still green. The plants will not continue to grow below 65°F (18°C), and roots have usually filled out as much as they can by mid September—or a little later in mild areas—so the roots might as well be harvested once chilly days set in. Unlike the tubers of regular potatoes, the roots of sweet potatoes grow wide and deep, so dig carefully in a large circle around each plant. The roots should not be exposed to temperatures below 50°F (10°C) because they will deteriorate rapidly—a day in the refrigerator is sure to cause early spoilage.

Cure sweet potatoes before you store them by keeping the roots at 90°F (32°C) and 90% humidity for four to six days. Either drape wet towels with their ends in water over open boxes of sweet potatoes in a hot porch or the upper level of a greenhouse; drape them with plastic in a warm room; or use an electric heater and vaporizer in a small room to create the appropriate conditions.

Sweet potatoes store best at 55 to 60°F (12 to 15°C), or can be kept at room temperature. They should be stored for several months before they are eaten because their sweetness develops as the starches turn to sugars. Baking sweet potatoes (as with winter squashes and pumpkins), rather than steaming, boiling or microwaving them, also enhances their sweetness.

Dried Beans
Jump on a bag of beans and then winnow. The kids will like this job.

### *Cool and dry*

Dried beans, peas and popcorn keep best in cool, dry locations, such as in attics, porches or garages that do not drop below freezing. It may well be October or November before they are dry enough for storage, but once they are, put them in plastic bags or glass jars with lids to maintain their dryness.

Let popcorn dry on the plant for one month until the husk is completely brown, then remove the husk and let the cob dry for another month or so after it is cut from the plant. Test the kernals two weeks after cutting the cobs from the plant, and regularly thereafter until they will pop. If they become too dry and no longer pop, mist them with water and try again after half an hour. Finally, remove the kernals from the cob—they should fall off without much pressure—and store them dry in sealed jars or bags.

Leave shell bean plants in the garden until the pods turn brown and show signs of drying. If the weather is very wet and plants are looking mouldy, pull the plants up and keep them in warm, dry conditions until the pods are thoroughly dry and cracking open. Throughout the autumn and even into November and December, shelling beans by hand makes a pleasant evening activity when eyes or ears are tuned to something else. Quicker methods include beating the plants, pods and all, inside a large box; or putting them in a cloth sack and walking and jumping on them, or beating the sack with a stick or flail. The rough bits left over can be winnowed out on a windy day by pouring the beans and chaff back and forth between two buckets several times. The beans fall into the bucket and the chaff is blown away.

Once shelled, dry the beans in warm, dry conditions in shallow containers until they can no longer be dented with a fingernail or tooth. Remove those which are immature, odd-shaped or discoloured, then store the good ones cool and dry in closed containers.

Harvest sunflower seeds when the back of the flower head is brown, thin and brittle like paper. Hang the head in a dry, warm, airy place until the seeds can be brushed off. Spread them out in a thin layer and air dry for one week after removing them before storing them in airtight containers.

Onions, garlic and shallots also require cool, dry storage conditions that remain above freezing. Garlic is usually ready to be harvested in late July or August, but the timing depends on the type and when it was planted (see page 245). Harvest shallots when the tops are yellow and shrivelled, and lift onions once the necks have thinned out and most of the leaves have fallen over. Knock over the few tops that are still standing and let the bulbs ripen for three or four more days before pulling them up. If most tops are still standing, wait a little longer before harvesting. They should not be bent over to hasten maturation unless the soil is very wet or a severe frost is coming. There are sprouting inhibitors in onion leaves that travel to the bulb to prevent the bulb from sprouting more leaves, so leave the tops in place until drying is complete.

Onions can be pulled and left in the garden to dry for a week if there is no rain, but finish drying them indoors, or in a sun porch or greenhouse below 80°F (27°C). Good air circulation is important. Shallots and onions are ready for storage when the roots are withered, the tops are dry and the skins are papery. Some onions will not dry properly, and the necks will stay moist and thick instead of turning dry and thin. These should be used first.

Store onions and shallots either two layers thick in slatted trays, in net bags, or braided as for garlic (see page 246), and keep them at 32 to 34°F (0 to 1°C). Onions grown from seed have a longer storage life than those grown from sets. It is essential that no water come near the bulbs because the roots will be stimulated and sprouting will occur, reducing the storage life.

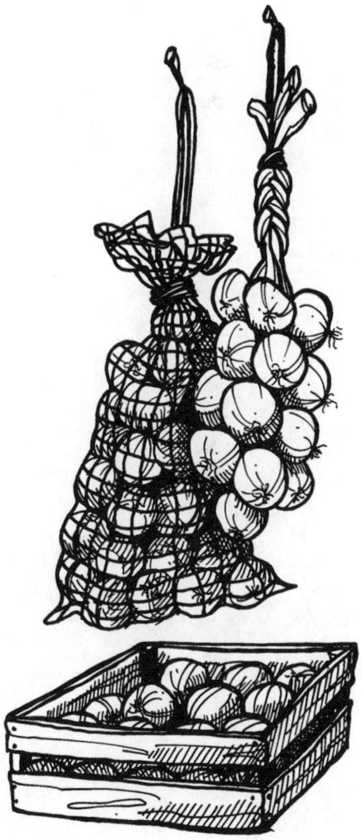

Storing onions

### *Cool and moist*

Root crops and brassicas require storage temperatures of 32 to 34°F (0 to 1°C) and humidity levels of 90 to 95%. A cold room, cellar, unheated garage (if it does not freeze), or against a cool basement wall are all possibilities.

Humidity levels can be kept up by setting open trays of water nearby and sprinkling the floor with water. Cool temperatures extend the storage life of brassicas and leafy greens considerably. Lettuce, for example, will keep for fourteen days at 32°F (0°C), for seven days at 40°F (4°C), for five days at 50°F (10°C), and for less than two days at 68°F (20°C).

Cool harvested produce as soon as possible. Cooling stops the growth of leafy crops and brassicas; slows the conversion of sugar to starch in peas and corn; and slows the rate of cellulose thickening, which leads to toughness in turnips, rutabagas and beets. Spray leafy crops with water to hasten cooling, place them in a refrigerator or cold room and, once they have cooled, wrap them loosely with plastic to preserve moisture.

Leave salsify, winter radishes, parsnips, carrots and other root crops in the ground until the tops are killed back by frosts. If carrot rust fly larvae are a problem each year, carrots should be harvested in late August or early September before the second generation of the fly attacks. Rutabagas, turnips and beets can also stay in the ground a little longer. They become sweeter after light frosts, but they must be dug before hard frosts arrive because part of their roots are above ground.

Twist off, do not cut, the leaves of root crops as soon as they are dug. Twisting severs the leaves along cell lines, leaving cells whole, whereas cutting destroys the cells and results in a greater loss of moisture. Removing the leaves will prevent moisture from being drawn out of the roots through respiration in the leaves. Wash off the roots only if they are caked with mud (try to dig them when the ground is dry). Store beets and other round roots in perforated polyethylene bags or in boxes of moist sand. To preserve moisture, some people dip turnips and rutabagas in paraffin—the kind used for sealing jams and jellies—after cutting off the long roots. Carrots and other slim roots can also be stored in bags, but they seem to last longer than when stored in slightly moistened sand. Layer them in slatted crates with enough sand between the layers to cover the roots completely.

Parsnips, carrots and other roots that are deep in the ground can be left outside all winter if other storage space is limited, provided the soil is light and well drained. It is often difficult to harvest them in the dead of winter, however, and they must be dug up and used as soon as spring comes, before they burst into growth. As soon as the tops die back, but before the ground freezes hard, add a deep layer of loose straw, oak leaves or any organic matter that does not pack down. One bale of straw covers about 3 square yards (3 $m^2$) to a depth of 12 inches (30 cm).

Kohlrabi, while not a root, can be stored in plastic bags or in sand, but it does not keep very long in storage. The lower, outer leaves should be removed, but leave the central tuft in place. Twist off the tops of celeriac, cut off and throw out the side roots, and place the main roots in boxes of moist sand. Delay harvest as long as possible as it keeps poorly once dug.

Cauliflower should be harvested as soon as it is ready because it does not store well once it has matured. To extend its storage life, dig up the entire plant instead of cutting off the head, cover it loosely in perforated plastic and store it whole in the cold room or refrigerator.

Other brassicas should be left in the ground until hard freezes are predicted. Except for Chinese cabbage, most brassicas are frost tolerant, and kale will even tolerate quite hard freezes. Harvest Chinese cabbage as soon as it is ready; it will keep for several weeks in the refrigerator or cold room.

Remove the tip of Brussels sprouts when the bottom sprout is 3/4 inch (18 mm) in diameter if you want all the sprouts to develop at the same time (see page 292). Do this four to eight weeks before you want to harvest the crop. The sprouts can tolerate light frosts and are ready for harvest when they are 1 to 1 ½ inch (25 to 37 mm) in diameter. Dig up entire plants before hard freezes arrive, remove the leaves, and hang the plants in the cold room. The sprouts will keep very well this way as long as the humidity level is high. Alternatively, twist off the sprouts—rather than cut—and store small amounts in perforated plastic bags. If the sprouts on a plant freeze solid outdoors, they can still be eaten if they are cooked immediately after harvesting. Sprouts cook more evenly if you cut a cross in the bottom of each one.

Savoy type cabbage

Cabbages that feel dense and heavy store better than those that are loose and light. Cut them from the plant leaving a long stock attached, chill them quickly, and store them on slatted shelves or in net bags. Handle them carefully as bruises may lead to rotting. Crinkly savoy type cabbages can be harvested last.

It is important that these leafy-type crops be cooled rapidly and stored where the humidity is high to delay the death of the outer leaves. They should not be stored with foods that release ethylene gas, such as apples, because the gas will hasten the death of the leaves. This is not a problem, however, if the cold room is well ventilated.

The flavour of kale is improved when plants are touched by frost. They are best left growing in the garden under a row tunnel once severe weather comes, or they can be buried under a deep mulch of loose straw or oak leaves just before the ground freezes. Continue to pick individual leaves or entire plants as needed. Kale grown as a green manure crop is left uncovered.

Other leafy greens, such as spinach, Swiss chard, mustard greens and collards, can also be kept growing under row tunnels, but they should be cut and blanched for the freezer (see Preventive Measure, page 294) before they are killed back by repeated hard frosts. Whenever possible, remove the leaves by tearing rather than cutting. A few fresh leaves can be kept in the cold room or refrigerator for up to two weeks. Pick them early or late in the day when they are cool, plunge them into cold water for several minutes, shake them dry, wrap them loosely in perforated plastic and then refrigerate.

Radicchio should either be harvested or mulched deeply with straw or oak leaves just before frosts arrive. Harvested heads should be cooled quickly with water or refrigeration and stored in perforated plastic bags in the refrigerator or cold room.

Endive and escarole tolerate frosts, but cover them with row tunnels or cold frames once frosty weather arrives to extend the season even further. Where winters are very harsh, entire plants can be dug up with a large ball of soil and planted close together either in coldframes outside, or in boxes in a bright, cool basement, chilly sun porch or cool greenhouse. Delay digging and moving plants for as long as possible. Other plants which can be replanted or "heeled in" in this way include broccoli, kale, Brussels sprouts, celery and leeks. Celery can be dug up once tight heads have formed and should be planted upright in the cold room with moist soil or sand around the roots. It will keep better this way than if the stalks are cut off and refrigerated. If the plants need more time in the garden to form heads, provide a deep mulch of straw before hard frosts come. Leeks tolerate light frosts quite readily but they should be dug up before the ground freezes. Plant them in boxes in soil which is deep enough to cover the white parts. All of these plants can be put in a dark cold room if lighted space is not available, but they will become blanched.

Potatoes require cool, moist storage conditions. They can be dug two or three weeks after the tops either die back or are killed by frost, but do not let the tubers freeze. Use a fork rather than a spade to dig so that fewer potatoes are injured, and try to dig when the soil is dryish.

There may be common scab on some potatoes. It is just that—common—and is started by a soil borne bacterium that seems to thrive under dry soil conditions. Use only well rotted manures, preferably dug into the soil the autumn before planting; do not let calcium levels in the soil rise high; and keep the soil pH on the acidic side (do not use lime). If scab does develop, avoid planting potatoes in that area for at least three years. Black bruises on the inside of potatoes occur as a result of less than gentle handling during harvest. Treat potatoes as carefully as you would tomatoes or peaches to avoid internal bruising.

Store potatoes at 50 to 60°F (10 to 5°C) for a few weeks to allow them to develop a corky layer and heal minor wounds. Those with deep gashes should be used right away. Afterwards, store them between 42 and 50°F (5 and 10°C), either in bins or packed loosely into double layer paper bags. When they are stored cooler, the starches turn into sugars; this makes them less tasty and causes French fries and roasted potatoes to turn dark. If storing them in a cold room, put some form of insulation under and over the bins, such as boards or thick layers of newspapers. The heat produced by respiration will help to keep the temperature above that in the rest of the cold room.

**Focus on Plants** Roots of Witloof chicory (alias French endive or Belgian endive) can be "forced" in damp soil. Dig them up carefully after the foliage dies down and before the ground freezes. Cut off the stems and leaves an inch or two (2.5 to 5 cm) above the root, cut off any side roots, and cut off the bottom of the main root so that the remainder is 8 or 9 inches (20 to 23 cm) long. Roots smaller than 3/4 inch (2 cm) in diameter will form insignificant heads and should be discarded; those larger than 2 inches (5 cm) will form only loose heads and should also be discarded.

Plant several roots upright in 14 inch (35 cm) deep containers. Bury the roots in 8 to 9 inches (20 to 23 cm) of soil and fill the rest of the container with 5 to 6 inches (12 to 15 cm) of sand or sawdust. Just a little soil is needed between the roots, so plant them fairly close together. Using several containers allows you to force a few at a time. If only 8 or 9 inch (20 or 23 cm) deep pots are available, cover the roots with soil, but instead of adding a layer of sand, cover with an inverted pot that has the drainage holes blocked to keep out the light. The heads produced will be looser, but they will taste fine.

Keep the potted roots in the cold room and water them occasionally by poking a stick into the soil and pouring water in the hole. When you are ready to force a few, bring a container into warmer temperatures (see January, page 27).

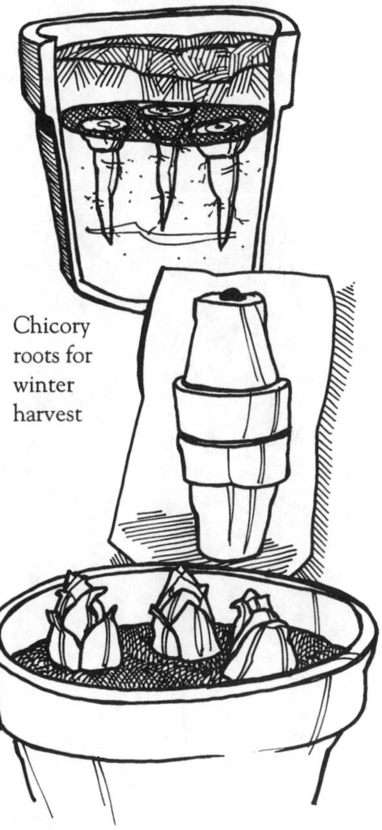

Chicory roots for winter harvest

If potatoes are exposed to temperatures below 40°F (4°C), they can be reconditioned by keeping them at room temperature for two weeks.

Several vegetables will keep for one to two weeks in the refrigerator or cold room (refer to Table SEP/OCT-1, page 336). Harvest lima beans, broccoli, Florence fennel, corn and peas as soon as they are ready as they will become overmature if left on the plant. If there is more than can be eaten in a week or two, blanch and freeze the excess (see page 294). Do not shell peas until just before you are going to eat them—shelled peas convert sucrose to starch faster than unshelled peas.

Florence fennel will bulb up late in the season, so it will need to be protected from frost. If it fails to bulb and goes to seed instead, it was probably planted at the wrong time (see Focus on Plants, page 77), was stressed in some way, or was the herbal kind (see page 14). The bulb, simmered until tender and served in a white sauce, traditionally accompanies fish. It can also be used in the same way as celery hearts, eaten raw in salads, served with a dip or used in stews.

Corn is ready when the ears are big and dark green, the tassels are brown, the tip is rounded not pointed, and a pricked kernal is milky. Cobs infested with corn earworms or corn borers (see page 290) can be made edible simply by cutting out the affected portions. Pull up and shred corn stalks, or bury them deeply immediately after harvest to help control corn borers. Fall ploughing or digging also helps (see Preventive Measure, page 384).

## Saving Seeds

Although most gardeners prefer to purchase vegetable seeds, many people find it satisfying and easy to collect and save seed from their own garden. Seeds can be saved from non-hybrid plants, but the process depends on the plant.

Shell beans such as Jacob's Cattle and Yellow Eye will cross pollinate unless separated by about 200 feet (60 m). Although the harvested seeds look like the seeds initially planted, they will produce plants and seeds that differ. The results are interesting, though, and certainly edible.

Allow non-hybrid peas to dry on the plants, but pull up the plants and let the seeds dry indoors if the weather is wet. Save corn seed, as described for popcorn (page 340), but only from open-pollinated varieties (refer to the catalogue description of the original seed).

Spinach and lettuce plants have to bolt and flower before they can produce seed. Spinach produces male and female plants, so only half of the plants will bear seed. Lettuce is self-pollinating; any plant that has flowered should produce seed. Shake the seed heads into a bag every couple of days for a week or more to collect seeds as they mature.

Seeds from any of the cucurbits can be saved as long as the parents were non-hybrids. Cucumbers will not cross pollinate with squashes, melons or any other species in the cucurbit family. Within the squashes—which are all varieties of the same species—cross pollination is common and flagrant, unless they are separated by 200 feet (60 m).

For seeds from melons, watermelons, winter squashes or pumpkins, simply collect and dry the seeds when you use the fruit. Cucumbers and summer squashes must be allowed to mature on the vine; ripe cucumbers are golden coloured, without a trace of green.

Peppers must also be allowed to ripen fully if the seeds are to be saved. Mature green ones must have turned red, either on or off the plant, and have started to soften before the seeds are scraped out and dried. For tomato seeds, use ripe fruits from a non-hybrid type. Put the seeds with their gel coating in water at room temperature for three days and stir daily. Strain the seeds, rinse them with clean water, and spread them out on waxed paper to dry for two days.

Always dry seeds at room temperature, not in an oven or microwave. After one to two weeks of drying, store them cool and dry (see page 8) until you are ready to use them.

## Fall Planting and Hot Beds

There are several ways to manage soil and prepare it for the winter, and several views on ploughing, cultivating and the use of winter mulches and cover crops.

To plant a cover crop, the soil should be dug over as described in October/November (pages 384-385), raked smooth, and sown about four weeks before the first fall frost is expected. Use annual ryegrass, winter wheat, winter rye, spring oats or spring barley as winter cover crops (see Table AUG-2, page 299). If less than four weeks remain, or if the first frost has already hit, it may still be worth your while to gamble and sow a cover crop anyway, otherwise apply a mulch (see page 385). Sow cover crops between the rows if vegetables are still growing, or sow where early crops have already been harvested. If heavy autumn rains are a yearly event and you have not sown a cover crop, dig the soil early before it gets too wet.

Garlic can be planted in open ground between late September and early

October in short season areas, and until late October in milder, long season areas. Some gardeners have better luck planting in the spring as soon as the soil can be worked.

Plant individual cloves in well drained soil, covering the tips with 3 inches (8 cm) of soil where winters are harsh, and with only 2 inches (5 cm) in mild areas. Space cloves 4 inches (10 cm) apart in rows 6 inches (15 cm) apart. Mulch the area just before or soon after the ground freezes—sometime in November or December—to protect the cloves and prevent frost heave.

Quick maturing crops such as corn salad (see Table AUG-1, page 297) can be planted late in the season, even after the first frost. If you have access to fresh manure you might want to try making a hot bed as the Victorians did in Britain. Fresh manure was mixed with leaves and aged for several days until the temperature was about right, fresh soil was added on top, and then the crop was planted. A glass frame—you might use a cold frame—was placed over the bed, and fresh manure was added around the outside as required to keep the temperature up. The Victorians planted cucumbers in October to harvest for Christmas, but in our climate it would be more realistic to plant quick maturing, cold tolerant vegetables such as lettuce, radish, corn salad, arugula, kohlrabi, kale, beet greens, mustard greens and spinach.

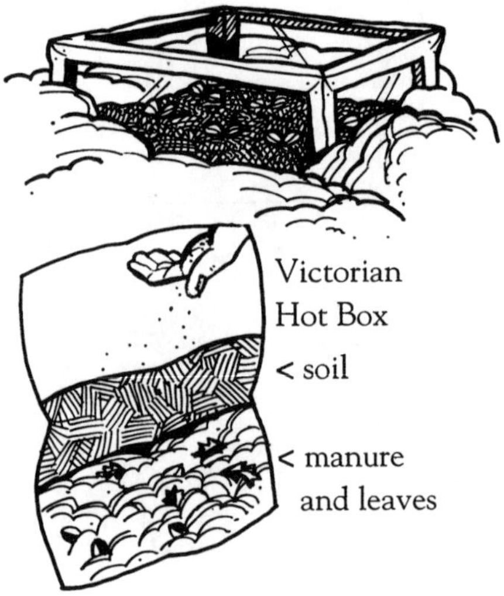


A more modern hot bed uses electricity to heat the soil and air in which the plants are growing. This method is particularly appealing if you have no indoor growing space. Use a cold frame that extends 1 foot (30 cm) into the soil and at least 8 inches (20 cm) above, and has typical cold frame heights on top of that (see page 437). Aim for a bed 3 feet by 6 feet (1 m by 2 m), and excavate the soil to a depth of 1 foot (30 cm). Fit the hot box into the cavity and spread 2 inches (5 cm) of vermiculite in the bottom to act as insulation. Spread 10 inches (25 cm) of subsoil on top of the vermiculite. Additional insulation in the form of below grade Styrofoam could be added all around the outside of the box. Either way, back fill the cavity and mound soil above the surrounding grade all around the box.

Heating cables form the next layer. These are mostly needed in the spring when the soil is cold and wet. Cables come in various lengths and wattages; one would need 66 feet (20 m) to cover the area inside the box with parallel cables spaced 4 to 4 ¾ inches (10 to 12 cm) apart. Cool weather crops need a soil temperature of 50ºF (10ºC) or above, but below 70ºF (21ºC). (Most heating cables with internal thermostats are set at 70ºF or 21ºC.) Cover the cable with 1 inch (2.5 cm) of soil and then spread a mesh screen to prevent

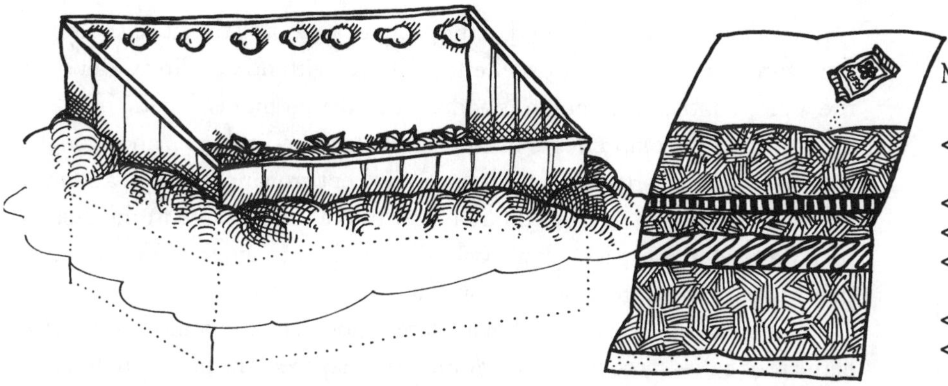


Modern Hot Box

roots from reaching the cable. On top of the screen, add 8 inches (20 cm) of enriched topsoil.

Some gardeners do not bother with heating cables in the autumn, partly because they tend to make the soil dry out more quickly. Instead of a heating cable, or in addition to one, use light bulbs. To provide about 200 watts of power, wire in and attach eight, 25-watt incandescent light bulbs along the back wall near the top. Make sure that the sloping lid of the box will close without touching the light bulbs. An interior car warmer can also be used to heat the box. Either its own thermostat can be used or one can be wired in. This mechanism has the advantage of a fan that circulates the air, keeping the temperature more uniform inside the box.

## Herbs

Many herbs have already been harvested and dried or frozen for winter use (refer to Table JUL-2, page 252). Some annuals, however, regrow enough for second and even third harvests to be taken right up until killing frosts hit. Woody perennials should not be cut back after July or early August as new growth needs time to harden off before winter comes, but individual leaves can still be harvested.

### Bringing Plants Indoors

To continue the harvest of fresh herbs into winter, pot up and bring indoors tender perennials such as rosemary. Sweet marjoram is actually a perennial but it is so tender that it is treated as an annual; bring it indoors, or start more plants from seed. Thyme plants which are more than three or four years old get straggly and are probably not worth bothering over. Borderline hardy perennials can be overwintered in the ground outdoors if the site is sheltered from winter winds; there is excellent drainage, with no standing water over the winter; and a deep mulch is added once the ground is frozen.

Annual herbs planted late in the season can also be dug up and brought indoors, or transplanted to a cold frame and kept growing well into autumn. Hardy annuals such as chervil fare better in cold frames late in the season than do tender annuals such as basil. Rather than trying to pot up annuals that have grown large, start new ones from seed indoors.

When potting up, use pots that are large enough to accommodate the size of the root ball—if roots are only minimally disturbed, the plants should not suffer any setback. When adjusting plants to indoor conditions, bring the potted plants into the house at night at first, and gradually increase the amount of time spent indoors. Misting frequently will also help to ease the transition to drier air. Also note that herbs grown indoors require the same growing conditions as when outdoors: full sun and dryish soil for some, moist conditions and indirect light for others (refer to Table FEB-1, page 40).

Winter hardy herbs, such as chives, tarragon and mint, can be cut back, potted up and brought indoors any time between September and November, before the ground freezes solid. They seem to do better if given a period of cold; either delay digging as long as possible, pot them up and leave them outside until they have had a month of freezing or near freezing temperatures, or put them in cold storage for a month.

Chives should be cut back hard, given their cold spell, then treated to warmth, light, moisture and fertilizer. Their burst of new growth is much more prolific than the tired growth of late summer. Dig up mint by the spadeful if it is growing beyond its bounds, and pot up some stolons, putting an inch (2.5 cm) of soil over them. Pot up catnip for feline pets and some beebalm for pet rabbits.

### Preventive Measure

To avoid bringing insects indoors, inspect the plants carefully and keep them away from other houseplants until it is clear that they are free of pests. Forceful sprays of water, or spraying with insecticidal soap, will dislodge unwelcome critters. The soil can also be drenched with insecticidal soap, or use 1 tablespoon (15 ml) of bleach to a quart of water (1.1 l). Pour in the solution until it runs out the bottom, wait one-half to one hour, then pour clear water through until it runs out the bottom. This can be repeated two or three times two weeks apart if there is evidence of insect activity.

## Harvesting Roots and Fixatives

Roots, such as those of angelica and sweet flag or calamus root (*Acorus calamus*) are harvested late in the season after they have plumped out with stored food for the winter. Orris root is harvested earlier when irises are divided (see page 306). Valerian root—used as a fixative for potpourris—is usually not dug until it is two years old. It smells quite unpleasant when wet, but drying takes the offensive odour away. To dry roots, wipe off the soil and split those that are 3/4 inch (2 cm) thick or more. Dry with some gentle artificial heat, or leave them in a homemade drier (see page 295) for a couple of weeks until they snap cleanly. Grind or chop them finely and add them to potpourris as described for orris root on page 260. Horseradish roots are usually harvested in their second year as well, as the one-year-old roots are rather small. The roots can be left in the ground as long as possible, then mulched as for carrots; left in the ground over the winter and dug as required; or dug and stored in the cold room the same way as other root crops.

To make horseradish relish, peel the roots and then grate or process them in a blender. Add 1/2 cup (125 ml) of vinegar and 1/4 teaspoon (2 ml) of salt for every 1 cup (250 ml) of grated root. Mix thoroughly, pack the relish in sterilized jars, seal tightly and store in the refrigerator.

To start horseradish from root cuttings, insert pieces that are 2 to 6 inches (5 to 15 cm) long into loose, well drained soil. Bury them in 6 to 12 inch (15 to 30 cm) deep holes (depending on how heavy or light the soil is), and space them about 12 inches (30 cm) apart.

## *Fall Planting and Dividing*

Herbs that need lifting and dividing, or must be moved for some reason, should be attended to as soon as possible. Disturbing them less than six weeks before the ground freezes increases the risk of losing them over the winter—even with plenty of time some losses are likely. If you have to move them late, dig them up with a large ball of soil, water them in well, and mulch the soil around them immediately after planting. Mulching will keep the ground from freezing for a little longer and give the roots more time to settle in. Immediately after planting, apply a thick layer of straw or oak leaves over the roots but not over the crowns of the plants; add more to cover the plants as well after the ground has frozen solid. This late mulching helps prevent frost heave and winter injury among plants with newly established roots.

Bulbous herbs can be planted in late summer or autumn. Saffron comes from the stigmas of *Crocus sativus*, a lovely little autumn blooming crocus planted in August or early September (see page 312). Bear's garlic, or *Allium ursinum*, is the rampion that Rapunzel's mother had to have from the witch's garden. It has leaves like lily-of-the-valley, starry white flowers on 18 inch (45 cm) stalks, and grows well in damp woods. It is grown from a bulb and is best left to multiply until there is enough to harvest in subsequent years. Nodding onion (*Allium cernuum*) has pink flowers and slim, pinkish-skinned bulbs. It is a wild plant found on rocky bluffs, in meadows and in open woods across Canada and the northern United States. Wild onions tend to have a stronger flavour than domestic onions, so use a little less in your cooking.

## *Flowers*

### *Bringing Plants Indoors and Taking Cuttings*

Tender perennial flowers, such as geraniums, fuchsias, coleus, impatiens and wax or fibrous begonias, should be brought in before they are exposed to and killed by frost. There are two ways to treat such plants to continue the supply next spring; the method to use depends on the state of the plants when they are brought indoors, whether they are brought in early or late in the fall, and on the growing conditions that can be provided through the winter.

One method is to take cuttings in the autumn. Cut back the plants as soon as you bring them into the house, repot, water and fertilize them, and then take cuttings when there is sufficient new growth (usually in November). Fuchsias have a natural rest period in early autumn, which fits in well with this regime, and cuttings taken in November will produce full plants in time for Mother's Day. This method also works well for impatiens and wax begonias if temperatures are warm and there is sufficient space; however, impatiens cuttings seem to root readily at any time of year.

Cuttings can be started using the summer's growth when the plants are cut back, but this older growth sometimes does not root as well as the young. Success depends on how vigorously the plants were growing before they were brought indoors, which depends in part on how early or late they were brought in and on how much fertilizer and other care they received during the summer. Cutting plants back in August will yield vigorous growth for cuttings this month or next.

The second, more common way to reproduce tender perennials is to take cuttings in late winter after the plants have rested. Let the plants continue to grow indoors in the autumn so that their flowers can be enjoyed; stop fertilizer applications in October, or sooner if the plants start to flag; and gradually reduce watering until the plants enter dormancy or a resting phase in November. How cool the house is will determine whether fuchsias and geraniums become completely dormant and lose their leaves, or keep their leaves and just tick over through the winter. Those that drop their leaves can be stored in their pots in a cool place that stays above freezing, with or without light. Keep them barely moist but do not fertilize them.

In January, cut back the plants, repot them, start watering lightly and put them in bright light. Start fertilizing as soon as new growth appears, and take cuttings when there is sufficient new material. Fuchsia cuttings taken in February will produce full plants which are ready to go outdoors in June.

If the garden geraniums are only just beginning to bloom, bring them indoors before the first frost and pot them up in 5 inch (125 mm) pots. If you let the soil surface dry out between waterings, give them full sunshine and a minimum temperature of 50°F (10°C), they will flower magnificently well into winter.

Tender perennials that grow from tubers and corms (see Table MAR/APR-3, page 88) can be left growing in the garden until the tops are nipped by frost, but the "bulbs" must then be dug up and overwintered indoors at above freezing temperatures. If frosts come early, see page 389 for care and storage after digging. Before frost strikes, bring in agapanthus, nerine, caladium and other bulbs that were grown in pots and keep them growing indoors for a while longer.

If petunias, portulaca, ageratum and a variety of other annuals are cut back, potted up, watered and fertilized they will bloom through the winter. Feverfew, browallia, Boston yellow daisy, heliotrope and petunia can be started from cuttings, and this is a good way to increase the supply of a particularly good colour of petunia. Marguerite started from cuttings in September will yield larger plants for bedding out in the spring than plants started from cuttings in February. Remove any flower buds from the cuttings and proceed as described on page 62.

Attend to window boxes, outdoor furniture and tools in September (see pages 416 and 420) if October and November are too inclement for outdoor work.

## Propagating and Moving Perennials

Perennial flowers can be moved while the soil is still warm if there is enough time for roots to grow and become established before the ground freezes. As with herbs, the earlier you move plants, the more likely they are to survive the winter. If there is not enough time left, note down the changes you want to make next spring. Some perennials can be potted up and forced indoors over the winter (see pages 415-416).

As a general guideline, flowers that have finished blooming can be moved, including ones that bloomed early in the spring (see Table APR/MAY-3, page 138). Those that failed to bloom, or that show signs of dying in the middle of the clump, need to be dug up and divided. Those that are not divided, but are simply transplanted with the root ball intact, stand a better chance of surviving the winter. If there is a pressing need to move flowers in bloom, cut off the flower stalks first.

Work rough compost or well rotted manure into the planting holes, or scratch it into the soil between plants to improve the growing conditions of plants that are not being moved. Adding some bonemeal every four years encourages blooming.

Autumn is the best time to move true lilies; if the stalk is accidentally broken off a whole year's growth is not lost as it would be if the growing tip were damaged or broken in the spring. Wait until the foliage turns yellow if you can as this indicates that this year's nutrients have been transferred to the bulb, which makes for better blooms next year. It is good to work compost into the planting hole, and fishmeal, fish bonemeal or bonemeal are all right if they do not touch the bulb. Do not use manure because it can lead to fungal diseases. Mark newly planted and existing lilies with stakes to avoid damaging their tender shoots in the spring, as they are late to appear.

Peonies rarely need dividing, and when moved they may take several years to become established and start blooming again.. They can be moved in either the spring or autumn, but many gardeners are convinced that they take longer to bloom if disturbed in the spring. Peonies do poorly where winters are warm, however, and autumn planting would exacerbate this.

In either case, they should be put 3 feet (1 m) apart in a deep bed of enriched soil, but avoid manure. Each division should have at least five eyes or buds so that it will not take so long to start blooming again. Cover the eyes with only 1 or 2 inches (2.5 to 5 cm) of soil—a greater depth may prevent them from blooming at all in subsequent years.

### Focus on Plants

Some lilies have tiny bulbils, like little black beads, growing on the stem in the axils of the leaves. These can be used to propagate more lilies. To increase bulbil production, sacrifice the blooms one year and cut out the flower bud very early.

Bulbils can be gathered when the stem turns yellow. Plant them in slightly mounded soil—for good drainage—1 to 2 inches (2.5 to 5 cm) deep and about 5 inches (12 cm) apart. Cover them with more soil after frost kills back everything, and add a deep winter mulch after the ground has frozen (see page 414).

Lilies can also be propagated from the stem bulblets clustered along the stem beneath the soil level, although not all varieties produce them. These bulblets can be removed and planted in a nursery the same way as tiny bulbils, and will grow to blooming size in a couple of years.

Plant bulblets and bulbils indoors in the autumn to ensure a higher rate of survival over the winter. They will need six to twelve weeks of chilling in the refrigerator or cold room sometime during the winter for top growth to start next spring.

Lily bulbil

Stem bulblet

## Extending the Fall Repertoire

If there are gaps in the autumn perennial bed, some standbys to consider include hardy chrysanthemums, asters or Michaelmas daisies, goldenrod, various sedums, pansies, helenium or sneezeweed, and low growing *Campanula carpatica*. If asters appear stunted with yellowed leaves and deformed flowers, they probably have aster yellows and should be removed immediately and burned or discarded, not composted.

Some hardy shrub roses bloom late into autumn; those that finish earlier add colour with their hips. Colchicum and true autumn crocuses (see page 312), planted as soon as they arrive if ordered by mail, give a splash of colour, tender perennials such as acidanthera bloom right up until the first frost, and *Anemone coronaria* continues to bloom even after freezing temperatures arrive. Sternbergia is barely hardy even in zone 6, and blooms just before the ground freezes. It needs a sunny, dry summer in well limed soil and winters that are not wet, so it is usually grown indoors.

Annual flowers that are frost tolerant extend the season of bloom beyond the first light frosts, and some, such as sweet alyssum, will self sow, making them perennial additions to the flower bed.

There may be a few flowers that have just reached the peak of perfection and can be dried. To dry Chinese lanterns, strip off the leaves when the papery sheaths turn orange, and hang the plants upside down to dry in a warm, airy place out of direct sunlight. Strawflowers are best picked just as the outer petals fully open, while the flower centre is still tight. They can be cut for drying right up until they are killed by frost.

## Bogs as an Asset

Autumn rains make boggy places in the garden visible. You can dig them over and incorporate more soil and organic matter to raise the soil level and improve the drainage. They can be enhanced, however, or a new boggy area created on purpose, to make a suitable habitat for moisture loving plants. Many of the plants below grow wild and have a wide distribution:

- blue flag
- cardinal flower
- cotton grass
- fringed orchid
- Jack-in-the-pulpit
- Joe-Pye weed
- marsh marigold
- monkeyflower
- swamp milkweed
- sweet flag
- turtlehead
- water plantain
- yellow flag

To enhance or create a bog, dig out the soil in a low lying area to a depth of 10 to 12 inches (25 to 30 cm), lay down a liner of flexible polythene or butyl rubber, punch some holes in it, and back fill the area with soil heavily enriched with peat moss. A deep soaking during dry periods will keep the bog going if it is not naturally wet enough.

A wide variety of plants do not tolerate standing water but they will thrive in very moist soils, turning a problem area into an asset. The following will generally survive better if they are planted in the spring, but the ground can be dug and prepared now (see also bulbs on pages 360-362).

| | | |
|---|---|---|
| astilbe | goatsbeard (Aruncus) | ornamental rhubarb |
| beebalm | hosta | primroses |
| crested iris | Japanese iris | Siberian iris |
| fringed loosestrife | meadowsweet | swamp rose mallow |
| globeflower | mint | Virginia bluebell |

## Spring Bulbs

### Order of bloom and planting locations

Many spring blooming bulbs that are planted at this time of year. They need excellent drainage, otherwise they will simply rot away. Use raised beds and plenty of organic matter if the soil is very moist. Some will tolerate moisture in the spring, but all seem to cope best with warm, dry summers.

Daffodils, crocuses, tulips and many others can be planted in flower beds, under trees and shrubs, or in the lawn, but some bulbs are better suited to certain conditions. Because many bloom before trees leaf out, they can be planted where they will get full or partial sunshine in the spring when they are actively growing, and partial or full shade during the summer months when they are resting. Focus your planning by considering the order of bloom and by deciding where in the garden early spring or late spring interest is desired.

Snowdrops are usually the earliest to bloom. They prefer moist conditions and partial shade, such as under shrubs and trees; they do all right in grass, but do not multiply as quickly. Plant them where they can easily be seen from indoors.

Tiny species of crocus, such as C. *tomasinianus* and C. *chrysanthus*, bloom at about the same time. They are ideal for intimate viewing and stand up to rain and foul weather better than the large Dutch hybrid crocuses. Both species and hybrids do well in grass but multiply more quickly under shrubs where there is less competition for nutrients, moisture and space.

Yellow eranthis or winter aconite blooms very early as well. It often takes three years to become established and is hardy only in milder zones. It grows best in rich soil in deciduous woods or similar growing conditions and should be planted where it can be weeded and tended.

Bulbous irises come into bloom a little later. *I. reticulata* and *I. histroides* often need to be planted yearly to make a good showing. Each bulb seems to bloom only every two or three years, if it survives. They thrive where there is excellent drainage and dryness in the summer. The large Dutch irises are not winter hardy but make superb pot plants in the winter.

Glory-of-the-snow (*Chiondoxa*), in soft blue or pink, striped squill (*Puschkinia*) in pale blue, and Siberian squill (*Scilla sibirica*) in deep blue, bloom next. Both squills grow in lawns, multiplying slowly, but Siberian squill will self seed prolifically under trees and shrubs or in flower borders. Siberian squill is such a deep blue that it needs to be planted in large numbers or in an intimate setting to show up well.

The little wandflower (*Anemone blanda)* is reliably perennial in zone 6 once it establishes itself. Most gardeners have better luck treating it as a tender perennial and planting it in the spring. It performs well in flower beds and rockeries, in grass, and under trees and shrubs.

Grape hyacinths, another minor bulb, bloom much later, about the same time as daffodils (narcissus). *Muscari botryoides* is a good shade of blue, but it self seeds so readily that it is best planted where it can spread freely.

### Focus on Plants

Crocuses, squills, wandflowers and other small bulbs are often called the minor bulbs, but they are minor only in size as most plants reach 4 inches (10 cm) in height. In a small or intimate setting, one or two dozen bulbs may be enough, but think in fifties, hundreds or more when planting in larger areas. Those planted under trees and shrubs often look better growing up through a low-growing ground cover such as blue phlox (*P. divaricata*), sweet woodruff, aubrieta, arenaria, low growing campanulas, perennial candytuft, cliff green (*Pachystima*), foamflower, ferns, saxifrage or Virginia bluebells. These covers help to protect the blossoms from muddy rain splashes. The bulbs also do well in rock gardens, but they should not be placed near plants that need summer watering.

They can be grown in perennial beds, although taller, later blooming bulbs tend to be favoured there. Plant the minor bulbs in large drifts around the base of hostas, daylilies, ferns, crane's bill, lady's mantle (*Alchemilla mollis*), astilbe, Siberian iris, artemisia and baby's breath, if these plants are in places that are likely to be observed in early spring. The bulbs will bloom before the perennials make much top growth, and later their dying leaves will be hidden by the growing perennials.

Crocus peeping through a bed of sweet woodruff.

## Table SEP/OCT-2 Planting Locations for Hardy Spring Blooming Bulbs

| Plant (Approximate Order of Bloom) | Suitable Planting Locations: Sun | Lawn | Meadow | Flower Bed | Rockery | Shrub Border | Pond Side |
|---|---|---|---|---|---|---|---|
| Snowdrop (*Galanthus* spp.) | - | x | | x | | x | x |
| Winter Aconite (*Eranthis*) | + - | | | x | | x | |
| Crocus | + - | x | x | x | x | x | |
| Iris, bulbous | + - | x | | x | x | x | |
| Glory-of-the-Snow (*Chiondoxa*) | + - | | | x | x | x | |
| Siberian Squill (*Scilla sibirica*) | + - | x | | x | | x | |
| Striped Squill (*Puschkinia*) | + - | x | | x | x | x | |
| Wandflower (*Anemone blanda*)* | + - | | x | x | x | x | |
| Tulip | | | | | | | |
| - species | + | | x | x | x | x | |
| - *kaufmanniana* | + | | x | x | x | x | |
| - *greigii* | + | | x | x | x | x | |
| - *fosteriana* | + | | x | x | | x | |
| Snakeshead Fritillary | + - | | x | x | x | x | x |
| Crown Imperial Fritillary | + - | | x | x | | x | |
| Daffodil | | | | | | | |
| - miniature | + - | | x | x | x | x | x |
| Grape Hyacinth (*Muscari*) | + - | x | x | x | | x | |
| Daffodil | | | | | | | |
| - standard | + - | | x | x | | x | x |
| Hyacinth | + - | | | x | | x | |
| Tulip | | | | | | | |
| - tall varieties, hybrids | + | | | x | | x | |
| Snowflake (*Leucojum* spp.) | - | | x | x | | x | x |
| Hyacinthoides (*Scilla campanulata*) | + - | | x | x | x | x | |
| Camassia | + - | | x | x | | x | x |
| Allium | + - | | x | x | x | x | |

* = hardy only in zone 6
x = suitable planting location
+ = 8 hours of sunshine daily
- = 4 to 8 hours of sunshine daily

Species tulips bloom soon after most of the minor bulbs and are reliably perennial, unlike some of the taller, later blooming tulips. Some, such as *T. tarda* and *T. urumiensis*, multiply rapidly. They do well in lawns, under trees and shrubs, in flower borders, and in rockeries provided unwanted tulip seedlings are removed. *Kaufmanniana* hybrid tulips are low growing, making them good candidates for windy positions. *Greigii* tulips come up year after year and are good in meadows as well as flower borders and rockeries. *Fosteriana* tulips are not quite so reliably perennial but are better than later blooming tulips.

After the small tulips, species and miniature daffodils come into bloom. White arabis, a low growing perennial often used in rockeries, sets off the yellow tones of daffodils very well. These small gems, such as 'Hawera,' seem ideal for woodsy settings and are superb in rock gardens.

While grape hyacinths are in bloom, usually in May, fragrant single early tulips and long blooming, double early tulips flower, along with daffodils. The large, fragrant hyacinths bloom at about the same time. Some people find them too stiff looking for an informal garden, and they are difficult to establish in cold regions. All of these bulbs are suitable for forcing indoors over the winter.

### Focus on Plants

Daffodil is the common name for narcissus, which is the botanical name. The names can be used interchangeably, but jonquils are a subgroup of narcissus. Daffodils can be planted in rough grass, in woods, among perennials, under trees and shrubs, or in lawns as long as the leaves are not cut down for at least six weeks after they have finished blooming. They come in yellow, pale yellow, white, yellow and white, yellow and orange, white and orange, and unusual shades of pink. Some daffodils bear one flower per stem, others carry several. Some particularly fragrant ones are 'Cragford,' 'Cheerfulness,' 'Yellow Cheerfulness,' 'Geranium,' 'Pheasant's Eye,' 'Suzy,' 'Hawera' and 'Quail.' The double daffodils do not stand up to wet springs, but they can be forced indoors as can all the other daffodils.

In perennial beds, plant daffodils in groups of five, seven or more, or in drifts that weave in between the clumps of perennials. They can be planted behind or among the perennials mentioned on page 357 as these will grow up and hide the dying foliage. They are also attractive next to plants with blue flowers such as Virginia bluebells, Jacob's ladder (*Polemonium*), brunnera, forget-me-not and periwinkle (*Vinca minor*).

### *Focus on Plants*

To propagate your favourite daffodils, try the technique known as chipping. In the autumn or after the leaves have died back in the summer, cut off the neck section and the roots (be careful not to damage the basal plate) and remove any loose, brown tunic. With the basal plate uppermost, cut the bulb vertically into eight to sixteen chips (segments), each with a piece of basal plate. If you have a steady hand, large chips can be further divided by twin scaling: divide the chips into pairs of scales by peeling the layers, using a sharp knife to cut through the basal plate.

Soak the chips or twin scales in fungicide (0.2% benomyl solution) for fifteen to thirty minutes, and then put several chips or twin scales into plastic bags half filled with eleven parts vermiculite to one part water. Seal the bags, leaving an airspace above the vermiculite, and store them in a dark place at about 68°F (20°C) for twelve weeks. After small bulbils have developed on the basal plate between the pairs of scales, plant each half of twin scales or chips individually in 3 inch (75 mm) pots and grow them cool. In the spring as soon as the soil is workable, plant the bulbils 2 inches (5 cm) deep in a nursery bed and grow them on for three or four years until they reach blooming size.

Bulbs suitable for growing in rough grass include all of the small early tulips, snowdrops if the soil is moist, snakeshead fritillary (*Fritillaria meleagris*), the taller crown imperial, wandflower, camassia, grape hyacinth and snowflakes (*Leucojum* spp.). Snowflakes are difficult to establish and do not do well under trees and shrubs, perhaps because it is too dry for them.

Allium, or ornamental onions, grow in rough grass and nearly any other place in the garden one might like to try. They usually do not bloom until June, and are available in a range of colours and sizes. Hyacinthoides are late blooming and come in shades of pink, white or blue. They will tolerate grass, but do better in rich soil with perennial flowers such as hosta.

There is a wide variety of later blooming tulips—tall and stately and with unusual flower shapes—that can be planted in perennial beds or on their own. Many are not reliably perennial, although Darwin hybrids may last fairly well—most types need to be planted each autumn, particularly in cold regions. They can be planted among any of the perennials mentioned so far, as well as with columbine, basket-of-gold alyssum, doronicum, globeflower, pulmonaria and both kinds of bleeding hearts. They can also be planted in beds for annual flowers; some gardeners rip them out and discard them before the annuals are planted. Try to cluster related colours of tulips together; group white, pink, rose and burgundy, combine a series of yellows, oranges and orange-reds, or try yellow and white together. For a more striking effect, plant all of the bulbs of each colour together, rather than mixing colours.

#### *Planting bulbs*

Do not plant tulips or any other bulbs where the soil stays cold and wet for a long time in the spring, such as in deep shade or on the north side of buildings. The bulbs are likely to rot before they bloom. As well, plant them no closer than 12 to 18 inches (30 to 45 cm) from foundations.

Some bulbs thrive in moist conditions near water, however. Snowdrops (*Galanthus* spp.), snowflakes (*Leucojum* spp.), colchicum (which is autumn blooming), snakeshead fritillary, camassia and all kinds of daffodils do well in these conditions. Make sure the bulbs are above the water line, not sitting in water. It is fine if the water dries out in the summer because the bulbs go dormant at this time.

In spite of working out the time of bloom for various bulbs, they may not perform according to plan. The sequence in the first year is often quite different from that in subsequent years—bulbs need to migrate to their preferred depth in the soil and get well established, and those in warm, sunny positions bloom sooner than the same kind in cool, semi-shady places.

When buying bulbs, choose those which are firm and heavy without any soft spots. Bargain bulbs that are lightweight have dried out and are beyond ever growing again. Bulb sizes indicate the circumference in centimetres—a size 12 bulb is 12 centimetres around. Within the same type of bulb, the larger sizes usually produce larger and taller flowers.

Do not purchase bulbs labelled "Bulbs From Wild Source." Many of the minor bulbs are collected each year from the wild and are in danger of becoming extinct. They can be propagated from seed or by division, so look for the label "Bulbs Grown From Cultivated Stock."

Large bulbs such as daffodils and tulips are planted 4 to 6 inches (10 to 15 cm) apart, and the minor bulbs 2 to 3 inches (5 to 8 cm) apart, so purchase enough to adequately cover the area. A more effective showing is created by planting large areas of a few different kinds of bulbs, rather than small patches of a lot of different bulbs. Daffodil bulbs often come with two or three "noses"; they bloom better if these are not separated into individual bulbs.

After purchasing bulbs, immediately store them in open containers at 35 to 40°F (2 to 4°C), the temperature of most refrigerators. If for some reason a few do not get planted, they can be potted up and "forced" into bloom indoors. This cold time in the refrigerator counts as part of the cold requirement when forcing bulbs (see page 405). Those that were forced last winter should be planted outdoors this autumn, if they were not planted out in the spring.

Bulbs can be planted either by making individual holes, or by digging out a large area, planting the bulbs and then backfilling. Either approach will work in grass; just peel back the sod, dig the ground and enrich the soil, plant the bulbs pointed end up, scratch up the underside of the sod to loosen the soil, then pat it back into place and water. Cover bulbs with soil to a depth twice their diameter—4 to 6 inches (10 to 15 cm) for large bulbs and 2 to 3 inches (5 to 8 cm) for small bulbs. Use the shallower depth if the soil is a heavy clay (but make sure it drains well). Bulbs such as daffodils do not seem to need lifting as often when planted deeply, and tulips tend to last a little longer. It is also possible to plant bulbs in layers on top of each other, such as grape hyacinths over daffodils, to obtain a sequence of bloom in one area.

Avoid using manure to enrich the soil, unless you dig it in six months in advance. Compost is excellent, and fish bonemeal can be worked in as well (1/2 oz/yd$^2$ or 15 g/m$^2$). Regular bonemeal was a good source of nitrogen at the turn of the century, when bones were not steamed to remove the

**Green Thumb Tip**

Casual groupings of bulbs look best in most gardens, although straight lines can be used in formal settings. Throwing bulbs up in the air and planting them where they land is one way to create a casual look, but a lot of the minor bulbs will be lost this way. Instead, plant large numbers of minor bulbs in a spiral pattern, with the bulbs close together in the middle and gradually getting further apart as the spiral expands. Planting in drifts or teardrop shapes also works; plant the bulbs so that they are close together in the wide part of the drift and gradually get further apart in the tail. Use only one kind of bulb in each drift or spiral, but the groups can overlap at the edges.

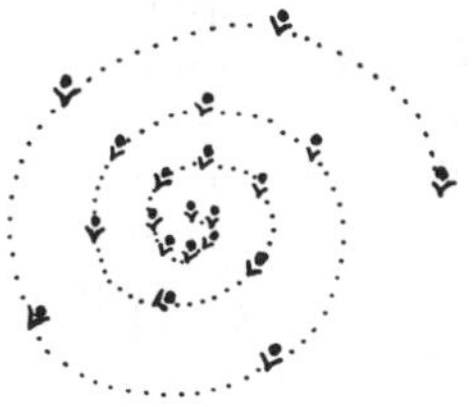

**Green Thumb Tip**

If you have a lot of spring flowering bulbs to plant, put the smaller ones in the ground first. This works out roughly to planting them in the order they bloom. Tulips can be planted as late as November in mild areas, but sooner is better. The soil does not freeze to the depth tulips are planted until late in the season, but those bulbs planted in the upper levels need enough time to grow roots before the ground freezes at the surface. If a few bulbs poke up green leaves, just throw on more soil. After the ground has frozen, the bulbs can be mulched to prevent frost heave in zones where snow cover is unreliable.

gelatin—the part which contains most of the nitrogen. Fish bonemeal has more nitrogen than plain bonemeal and therefore is a better fertilizer, unless a fertilizer containing nitrogen is added along with the bonemeal.

If planting in individual holes, break up the underside of the soil plug that has been removed, mix the amendments and fertilizer with the soil, put a little of the mixture in the hole, add the bulb, finish filling the hole with the mixture, and replace the sod. It is important that each bulb sit squarely on soil, not be perched over a gap. If the soil is reasonably rich, skip this and simply scratch fertilizer into the surface of the soil over the entire area. Remember, though, that phosphorus is nearly immobile in soil, so try to place bonemeal fairly close to the roots but not touching the bulbs.

After the bulbs are planted, water them in well to make sure the soil is in close contact with the bulbs, and to supply the moisture needed by the roots that start growing soon after planting. If rodents have eaten bulbs in the past, put a layer of fine wire mesh over the bulbs before covering them with soil.

Bulbs that are planted in small raised beds or in containers are more vulnerable to damage from extreme cold than those planted in regular beds or lawns. Insulated containers are best (see page 439), and all should be mulched deeply with 12 inches (30 cm) or more of cover as soon as the ground freezes (see page 413), or put into cold storage (see page 405).

## Fruits

Tree fruits should be ripening nicely, although some may drop prematurely. Planting soft fruits, storing the crop and preparing the ground for winter are pleasant and satisfying autumn chores.

### Cover Crops and Planting

Cover crops can be sown on new ground cleared for soft fruits such as strawberries and currants. Sod that was turned last fall, cultivated in the spring and planted with buckwheat, and then turned again in August, will be ready for sowing winter rye, annual ryegrass, or other cover crops (refer to Table AUG-2, page 299). Sow at least four weeks before the first frost is expected.

Fruits can also be planted in the autumn, but this should be done six weeks or more before the ground freezes. Of course, planting raspberries and other fruiting plants early increases their chances of getting established properly and surviving the winter. Rhubarb can be dug up and divided, or prepare the ground now and move it early in the spring (see Focus on Plants, page 148). In milder zones where snowcover is unreliable, mulch the new plantings well once the ground freezes.

## Harvest, Storage and After Harvest Care

Sound fruits, with no nocks or bruises, can be stored in a cold room for anywhere from a week or two to several months (see Table SEP/OCT-3, below). Cool them as quickly as possible after picking. They should not be washed until just before they are used. Store them upright, the way they hung from the plant, and make sure the trays and boxes are scrubbed clean.

Ripe plums will sometimes split on the tree after a rain, so it might be wise to do a picking if a storm is predicted. Those which are to be preserved should be picked slightly before they reach full maturity. Ripe cherries may also split after a rain, but try to leave them on the tree to ripen fully. Pick them with the stem left on, using scissors if necessary, and use them quickly as they do not last long in storage. They do freeze very well, however, when stemmed, pitted and sugared.

After the harvest, shorten the laterals on sweet cherries to three buds, and cut the fruiting laterals on sour cherries back to the replacement shoots. Remove any dead wood on plums and cherries. Plums and other fruits trained in a fan form should have the new laterals tied into place and strong vertical shoots either cut out or tied in a more horizontal position.

Handle peaches and apricots with the utmost tenderness, putting them in shallow containers lined with cotton batting or something similar. They do not ripen well once picked, so pick them only when the flesh near the stem gives under light pressure from the fingertips; they should easily pull off the branch. Pick apricots with the stalk left on. After the harvest is complete, cut those shoots that bore fruit back to the replacement shoots on each branch (see page 237).

Grapes are ready when the sugar content seems high. Taste the fruit, rather then relying on colour alone, because they do not sweeten after harvest. A touch or two of frost will not hurt them and seems to hasten sweetening. Those to be used for wine making and eating fresh should be picked at full maturity, and those for jellies picked slightly before full maturity. Cut the entire cluster from the vine—including 2 inches (5 cm) of woody stem on either side of the bunch to form a handle—and remove the grapes only when you are ready to use them. Harvest elderberries by picking the entire cluster. Clusters do not ripen all at the same time, so make several pickings.

* see also Freezing (page 316) and Drying (page 317)
+ do not store blueberries in metal containers
Maintain relative humidity at 85 to 90%
Based in part on Agriculture Canada Publication 1478/E.

## Table SEP/OCT-3 Storage of Fresh Fruits*

| Fruit | Temperature | Storage Life |
|---|---|---|
| Apple | 30 to 32°F (-1.1 to 0.0°C) | |
| - early | | up to 1 month |
| - mid season | | 2 to 3 months |
| - late | | 3 to 6 months |
| Apricot | 32°F (0.0°C) | 1 to 2 weeks |
| Blackberry | 32°F (0.0°C) | 2 to 3 days |
| Blueberry + | 32°F (0.0°C) | up to 1 week |
| Cherry | | |
| - sweet | 32°F (0.0°C) | 2 to 3 weeks |
| - sour | 32°F (0.0°C) | 2 to 4 days |
| Cranberry | 36 to 40°F (2.2 to 4.4°C) | 2 months |
| Currants | 32°F (0.0°C) | 2 to 4 days on cluster |
| Elderberry | 32°F (0.0°C) | 1 week on cluster |
| Gooseberry | 32°F (0.0°C) | 2 weeks stems in |
| Grape | 32°F (0.0°C) | 1 month on cluster |
| Melon | | |
| - Cantaloupe, Muskmelon | 32 to 45°F (0.0 to 7.2°C) | 2 weeks |
| - Honeydew | 45 to 50°F (7.2 to 10°C) | 2 to 3 weeks |
| - Watermelon | 36 to 40°F (2.2 to 4.4°C) | 2 to 3 weeks |
| Mulberry | 32°F (0.0°C) | 2 to 3 days |
| Peach | 32°F (0.0°C) | 2 weeks |
| Pear | 30 to 32°F (-1.1 to 0.0°C) | |
| - Bartlett | | 2 to 3 months |
| - winter varieties | | 3 to 5 months |
| Plum | | |
| - Japanese | 40°F (4.4°C) | 2 to 4 days |
| - other | 32°F (0.0°C) | 4 to 6 weeks |
| Quince | 30 to 32°F (-1.1 to 0.0°C) | up to 1 month |
| Raspberry | 32°F (0.0°C) | 2 to 3 days |
| Rhubarb | 32°F (0.0°C) | 2 to 3 weeks |
| Saskatoon, Indian Pear (*Amelanchier* spp.) | 32°F (0.0°C) | up to 1 week |
| Strawberry | 32°F (0.0°C) | 5 to 10 days |

Pick pears at the first blush of colour. Pears and apples can be individually wrapped in a square of tissue paper or newspaper. Sort apples into groups for long-term storage (no nicks or blemishes), short-term storage (some scab, which may develop cracks over time) and immediate use or processing (nicks, bruises and signs of insect damage). Up to 5 pounds (2 kg) of apples can be stored in a perforated clear plastic bag, but pears tend to suffer from internal rot when stored in plastic bags. Remember to store fruits in the upright position. Early season apples will not keep as long as late season apples. Crabapples tend to shrivel if stored more than a few weeks; storage in perforated plastic bags helps to extend their storage life. After the leaves fall, tie the new tiers of espaliered apples and pears into the horizontal position.

Bog cranberries picked from wild plants can be stored clean and dry in the freezer for use later in sauces. Large and small cranberries (*Vaccinium macrocarpon* and *V. oxycoccus*) are abundant in many areas. They make a fine cordial (see page 318) when mixed with equal parts of sugar and brandy along with some whole cloves and a short piece of cinnamon stick. Highbush cranberry (*Viburnum trilobum*), often grown as an ornamental plant, does not produce berries with the same taste as bog cranberry, and the shrubs can grow to be 10 feet (3 m) high. The berries, however, do make excellent sauces for meat and poultry.

Nuts will probably not be ready for picking until late September or sometime in October. Start harvesting them as soon as they begin dropping to the ground, before mice and squirrels get them. Spread a cloth on the ground and shake the tree to harvet those that cannot be reached. Dry them in shallow layers in a dry, airy place, and store them dry and cool but above freezingz—not in a moist cold room.

## Autumn Care and Pest and Disease Control

Remember to cut out the raspberry and blackberry canes that bore fruit, and the oldest black currant canes (see page 314). Tie this year's new growth of blackberry canes together loosely for protection from winter winds.

Renew bands of Tanglefoot on trees bothered by such insects as fall canker worms, bruce spanworms and winter moths (see page 106). After a few autumn frosts, fall canker worms leave the pupal stage and their summer home in the ground, and wingless females crawl up the trunk to lay eggs.

canker worm

Spray a light horticultural oil on pear and apple trees that were badly affected by pear psylla. Spray a copper fungicide, Bordeaux mixture or 2% lime sulphur on affected plants just before the leaves fall to help control peach leaf curl, anthracnose, leaf blights, canker and cane blight. Rake up and burn, bury or discard leaves from trees and shrubs affected by leaf diseases; do not compost them. Cut out small branches which are badly affected with canker (which appears as sunken areas) and cut out diseased areas on large branches until clean wood is reached. Spray these areas as described above for canker. Remember to dip the pruning shears in disinfectant and water after each cut (see page 91).

Keep picking up fruit drops every couple of days to get rid of overwintering insects and disease organisms. Several factors other than insects cause the premature drop of apples and other fruits late in the season (see page 315).

Sometime this month or next, cultivate the ground under fruiting trees and shrubs that were affected by such insects as apple maggots, codling moth, currant sawflies and currant fruit flies. This will turn up adult and larval forms that overwinter in the soil. Cultivate as deeply as possible without harming the roots, perhaps to a depth of 2 to 3 inches (5 to 8 cm). Leave the soil bare for two weeks, cultivate again, then apply a 6 inch (15 cm) mulch of straw, marsh hay or oak leaves. Keep the mulch away from the trunks of trees so that mice do not have a hiding place close to the bark. Coarse compost can be spread first (but not manure), then spread a layer of cardboard or pads of newspaper before the mulch goes on to keep down the weeds next spring. Instead of the straw, a 4 inch (10 cm) layer of shredded bark can be used, or a fall cover crop can be sown instead. A deep mulch applied in the summer may serve as an alternative to autumn cultivation. If insects overwinter in mulch instead of soil, they are more vulnerable to cold temperatures and may not survive.

### Hardwood Cuttings

Autumn is a good time to propagate black currants and other fruits (see Table JUL-3, page 275). To take hardwood cuttings of black currants, cut off pencil thick, 8 to 12 inch (20 to 30 cm) long pieces of this year's growth. This can be done once the leaves start to colour in the autumn until winter sets in. Some gardeners, however, successfully take cuttings before the buds burst in early spring (see page 103).

Cut just below a bud at the bottom, cut off any unripened wood at the tip just above a bud, and remove any remaining leaves. Slice off a thin sliver of bark and wood vertically near the base. Prepare more cuttings than necessary because not all of them will root. From this point, there are several options. In zone 6, the cuttings can be inserted in a trench of soil mixed with coarse sand or perlite either outdoors in a sheltered location or in a cold frame. Add leaf mould to very sandy soils. Insert them 6 inches (15 cm) apart to two-thirds their length, and at a 45⁰ angle to help reduce the amount they are heaved out by frost. (If this is done in the spring they are inserted vertically). Tamp the ground firmly to make sure they are well anchored. When the ground freezes, bury them under 12 inches (30 cm) of straw, oak leaves or marsh hay to further protect them and reduce frost heave.

Rooting outdoors in the winter is usually not successful in colder regions. Instead, tie the cuttings into bundles of six or eight and bury them under 12 inches (30 cm) of sand or sandy soil, or store them in a cold room. The bases of cuttings are usually cut at an angle and the tops cut horizontally so that the bases can be readily identified in the spring. In early spring, dig them up or bring them out of storage, separate them, and root them outdoors (as described above) or in pots (see below).

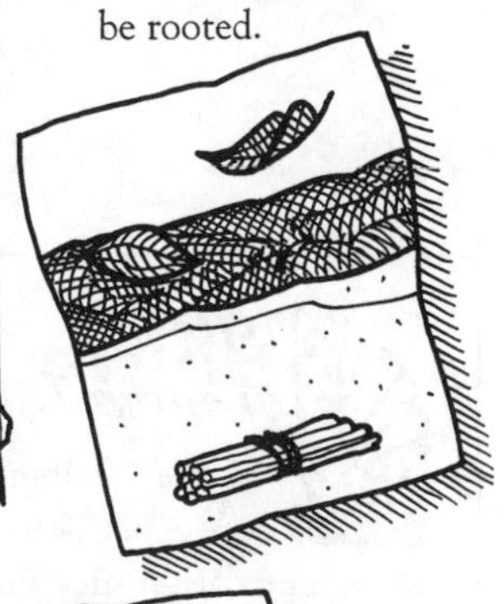

Cut hardwood cuttings at an angle to identify the bottom of the cutting and then bury under sand to store them for the winter. In early spring they can be rooted.

Alternatively, in any region, cuttings can be rooted in pots. Poke deep holes in a rooting medium of moistened peat moss plus perlite or peat-based potting soil plus perlite. Use one pot for each kind of cutting. Dip the base of each cutting in rooting hormone and drop one into each hole so that two-thirds of the length is buried. Firm the rooting medium around each cutting and water carefully. After the pots have drained, put the entire pot with cuttings into a plastic bag and keep the pots in a coolish environment, above freezing (50 to 60°F or 10 to 15°C), in bright light but out of direct sunlight. Instead of placing the pots in plastic bags, they can be placed outside in a cold frame or in a sheltered location until the temperatures start dipping below freezing. Store them in a cold room over the winter, then bring them gradually into light and warmth in late winter or early spring (see page 103).

Treat cuttings of red currants in a similar way, but make them 12 to 15 inches (30 to 38 cm) long, and remove all but the top four buds after the unripe tip has been removed. Gooseberries are treated in much the same way, but leave all of the buds on because the cuttings seem to root better that way. The lower buds can be removed once rooting has occurred to give a clean, unbranched leg. It also helps to dust rooting hormone on the lower part of the cutting.

Elderberries can be propagated from hardwood cuttings which are 12 to 15 inches (30 to 38 cm) long. Remove all but the top three buds after the unhardened tip has been removed. Grape cuttings should be 10 to 12 inches (25 to 30 cm) long, or use eye cuttings (see page 103).

Gooseberries and other soft fruits (refer to Table JUL-3, page 275) root very easily when layered (see pages 149-151). Any plants that are layered should be left undisturbed for twelve to eighteen months. After this period, cut them from the parent plant in the spring and set them in a nursery bed or plant them in a permanent location.

Raspberries and blackberries are propagated from vigorous young shoots. This can be done in the autumn, but more will survive if they are dug up in the spring. It is not a good idea to propagate apple and other fruit trees from cuttings because they will not have the dwarfing and hardiness characteristics of the root stock. Peach trees and others started from seed will not be true to the parent, but it is fun if there is space to grow experimental trees.

## Woody Ornamentals

### Planting and General Care

Many woody ornamental plants are affected by the same diseases and insect pests as fruit trees and benefit from the same remedial measures, but only if there have been significant problems in the current growing season.

Potted deciduous trees and shrubs can still be planted as they will make good root growth in the still-warm soil, and bare root stock can be planted in October or even November if there is still a good six weeks before the ground freezes solid. Woody plants such as roses and other shrubs and trees are best moved after they lose their leaves. Encourage roses to go into dormancy by leaving faded roses on the plant to mature into rose hips.

**Green Thumb Tip**

If the weather co-operates, keeping roses and other deciduous shrubs on the dry side will encourage proper hardening of the wood before hard frosts arrive. On the other hand, coniferous and broad-leaved evergreens, such as rhododendrons, should be watered deeply and regularly right up until the ground freezes, if autumn rains are lacking.

Broad-leaved and coniferous evergreens do not fare well when planted in the autumn, particularly if planted in windy locations. If there are some still not planted, they might do better stored in an unheated garage with some daylight or with ten hours of artificial light each day. Put them under shelter just before the ground freezes hard.

Before the ground freezes hard, apply a 12 inch (30 cm) mulch of straw, oak leaves or marsh hay under evergreens to delay freezing a little longer. This will enable the plants to continue taking up water for a little longer, which reduces winter drying and wind burn.

### Propagation

#### Cuttings and seeds

Many deciduous ornamental shrubs root readily from hardwood cuttings (refer to Table JUL-4, page 282). Prepare them in the same way as fruiting shrubs (see pages 366-368). The length of a cutting depends mainly on the length of new growth made in the current season. Broad-leaved evergreens can be started from semi-hardwood or hardwood cuttings from mid August through November (see pages 280-281 for details). Cuttings of coniferous plants are taken in November or later (see page 419).

Sometime in September or October, the seeds of many trees and shrubs mature. Starting woody plants from seed may seem like a slow method of propagation, but most trees, other than willows and poplars, do not root easily from hardwood cuttings, while seeding works for a wide variety of conifers and deciduous trees.

Seeds are usually best sown fresh, after they have air dried for a few days. Oak seeds, for example, must be planted within two months of harvest. Other seeds can be stored cool and dry for one year (see page 8 for storage conditions). Some seeds are stratified (refer to Table JUL-4, page 282) before they are planted: mix them with moist peat moss and sand and store them in a plastic bag in a refrigerator or cold room for three to five months. Sowing them fresh and then exposing them to cold temperatures is also a method of stratifying and is the method most often used to break dormancy, particularly for large seeds.

Plant fresh seeds outdoors in a prepared seedbed or in pots. Either leave the pots or flats outside in a protected location until just before the ground freezes hard to expose them to cold nights and freezing temperatures, or store them in a refrigerator or cold room for three to five months to simulate winter before bringing them into warmth and light.

Locate a nursery bed where it will receive regular attention throughout the growing season. Even if the seeds are not yet ready for sowing, prepare the soil. Cultivate 9 to 12 inches (23 to 30 cm) deep and work in some organic matter, creating a slightly raised bed. Adjust the pH if required (see pages 377-378), but the natural pH of local soils is fine for native plants.

Broadcast the seed over the area very generously. Conifer seed sown at one hundred seeds per square foot will probably yield only three dozen seedlings in three years. Cover the seed to two times its depth with sand, and mulch the bed after the first hard frost with straw, shredded bark or very old sawdust. Small one-year-old seedlings should also be mulched for the winter. Seedlings are transplanted when they are two years old to five per square foot (900 $cm^2$), or fewer for large seedlings such as oak.

When warm weather arrives in the spring, gradually remove the mulch and keep the seed bed moist. During the first summer, shade the young

## Green Thumb Tip

In most cases, tree seeds have to be extracted from a cone or some other protective covering. The cones of most conifers, such as spruce and pine, can be dried at room temperature for a few weeks until they open. Jack pine, red pine and black spruce may require a little more heat to open. Balsam fir cones, however, fall apart while still on the tree when the seed is mature. Rub off the wings of the seeds, except for those from fir and cedar trees.

Leave the wings on maple seeds (some mature in June or July), but separate the pairs of these and ash seeds. Squash berries to remove most of the flesh and wash the seeds by rubbing them in warm water. If you would rather not fuss, you can plant small berries whole, but germination may take longer. Air dry all seeds by spreading them in a single layer on waxed paper in a warm, dry location. Leave oak and chestnut seeds in the shell, but remove the spiny outer capsule on chestnuts. Discard any nuts with tiny worm holes. Soak pulpy magnolia seeds until fermentation starts and the solution is frothy. Beat the mixture to remove the pulp from the seeds, then wash in a bit of detergent and water.

seedlings with cheesecloth or a lath structure. Apply fertilizer only after the first true leaves appear; start with a mild solution and increase it gradually to full strength.

Very fine seeds, such as those of rhododendrons, pieris, azaleas and heathers, are best sown indoors. Use a mix of perlite and peat moss in 4 inch (100 mm) pots, with 1/4 inch (6 mm) of seived sphagnum moss on the surface. Dust the seed over this, add a very light dusting of seived moss, and cover the pot with clear plastic to keep the seedbed moist. Keep the pot in light, and increase the light to sixteen hours per day once the seeds have germinated. Pot them on when they produce the first true leaves, and fertilize with a mild solution. Plant them outdoors once the weather is warm and settled next summer, keeping them shaded and protected as for other seedlings. See pages 397-398 for autumn care of young propagated material.

## Lawns

### General Care

Lawn chores can be carried out between now and November, or December in mild areas. Repairs can still be made (see page 325) and there may still be time to sow seed, as long as about six weeks remain before the first expected fall frost. Any lawns seeded last month should have bare patches sprinkled with more grass seed; bare areas usually fill in with weeds, not grass. Some lawns may require lime and fertilizer, but do not add these as a matter of course. Only spread lime each spring and/or autumn until a pH of around 6.5 is reached (see page 378 for application rates). This can be tested crudely using purchased soil test kits or pH test kits, or by having the soil analysed. Once the appropriate pH is attained, lime only once every three years.

If you are going to apply a fall ferilizer, spread it two weeks after the lime has been applied, or after a good rainfall, so that the lime binds with the soil and not with the fertilizer. Use fertilizers which are low in nitrogen but high in phosphorous and potassium. The idea is to promote good root growth and increase disease and pest resistance, not to encourage top growth. Being concerned about when fertilizers of various nutrient proportions are applied is not a problem with organic fertilizers because they release their nutrients slowly over a long period of time and the plants take from the soil what they need when they need it. Fishmeal (7-9-4) or other organic fertilizers such as a 7-7-7 formulation will do nicely, or use finished compost as a top dressing.

## Aeration and Top Dressing

Not all lawns need aeration, nor do those that need it require it every year. Aeration is carried out where soil is compacted as this can lead to poor grass growth and result in weed, disease and insect problems. All lawns benefit from aeration, but it is only really needed if the soil remains waterlogged after rain; there is rapid browning in dry weather (which is also caused by shallow soils); there are bare patches and areas of heavy foot traffic; there is poor grass growth and competition from moss and weeds; or insects and diseases have been a problem.

Carry out the process when the soil is damp. On small areas, aeration can be done once a year by inserting a garden fork at intervals and working it back and forth, but this is not very effective. There are hollow tine forks available for aerating which are more effective, making aeration once every three years sufficient. Large areas are best done with an aerating machine. The light weight models that are usually available for rent are not worth the money; it might be better to hire a lawn care company to do it once every three years, or more often if problems persist.

Aeration can be done in the spring, if preferred, but it is better done in the autumn as weeds are not germinating and the plugs of soil left lying on the surface of the lawn will break down over the winter with frost action. If you prefer, the plugs can be crumbled and raked in as a top dressing or added to the compost pile.

Top dressing is simply the application of soil, sand and organic matter to the surface of established lawns. It is not essential, but greatly helps lawns growing on heavy clay soils, on light sandy soils or on soils lacking organic matter. It will also gradually add depth to soils that are too shallow for good lawn growth (aim for 6 inches or 15 cm eventually), and is particularly beneficial where summers are dry.

With plenty of organic matter, lawns are better able to withstand drought, nutrients are held in the soil better, there are fewer problems with soil compaction, and earthworm populations—which are good for thatch control and soil aeration—are high.

Spread the top dressing mixture over the lawn and scratch it in with the back of a rake so that the layer added is 1/4 to 1/2 inch (6 to 12 mm) thick. This is best done after aeration, if this is carried out, or give the lawn a good hard raking before spreading the top dressing. The grass should show through clearly and not be buried under clumps of material.

The edges of lawns can be tidied up with a sharp spade (see page 152), but

### Green Thumb Tip

Traditionally, the material used for top dressing has been a mix of peat moss, good garden soil and sand. Increasingly, gardeners are using compost instead of peat moss, or using compost alone. Use finished compost which is less than 7/16 inch (10 mm) in diameter, not the big, chunky kind that has not broken down very much yet. Some gardners mix in perennial ryegrass seed with the topdressing.

On heavy clay soil, use one part compost, two parts soil and four parts sand; for sandy soil use two parts compost, four parts soil and one part sand; and for regular soils use one part compost, four parts soil and two parts sand.

this may be a waste of effort as grasses produce a lot of root growth and side shoots at this time of year. Trimming should be done as late in the autumn as possible so that there is little or no regrowth.

## Indoor Gardening

Be careful not to overwater indoor plants when days are cloudy or overcast. There are still plenty of warm and sunny days, however, and plants can dry out all too quickly. Any shading that was put on the windows in June should be removed about the middle of September to allow full light penetration.

### Vegetables and Herbs

A variety of leafy greens and annual herbs can be started indoors in September, or treated as repeat sowings of plantings made in August. Chinese cabbage, cos and leaf lettuce, radicchio, Swiss chard, beet greens and collards will provide plenty of variety in the coming months. They thrive in the shorter, cooler days of autumn and grow faster than their outdoor counterparts.

Outdoor chives, kale and other plants (refer to Table JAN-2, page 24) can be dug up in October or November and heeled in in a cool greenhouse or sun porch (see pages 344 and 350). Peppers and eggplants can also be dug up before frost strikes and potted up as for herbs (see page 350), but they prefer warmer conditions. They are actually perennials and will continue to produce well into the autumn. They can be kept going for more than one year, although they will need a winter pause in growth. This rest can easily be provided: stop fertilizing and reduce watering in late autumn or early winter for about three months. Cut the plants back lightly in late winter and start them into growth again by watering lightly and providing warmer temperatures. Start fertilizing when new growth appears.

Rooted layered pieces of perennial herbs such as rosemary, thyme and sage can be cut from the parent plants and potted up. Sow annual herbs such as coriander, dill, summer savory, bush basil and sweet marjoram, and plant a few radishes to add zing to winter salads. Celery and celeriac are long-term crops, but will be very welcome several months from now.

Provide seedlings and mature plants with good ventilation and fertilize regularly. Pot on tomato cuttings and seedlings as well as peppers, eggplants and cucumbers started in the summer, and grow them as warm as possible with sixteen hours of light each day.

### *Warm Flowers*

After gloxinia, achimenes, zephyranthes, white calla and other tender bulbs have finished blooming, stop fertilizing them and gradually reduce watering. They can be stored in their pots (refer to Table OCT/NOV-1, page 390). Tuberous begonias potted now should be in bloom for Valentine's Day. Fading browallia plants are best thrown out, but take cuttings first to start new plants (see pages 61-62).

Sow salpiglossis and petunia, which are related to each other, and pot up, cut back and fertilize tender perennials brought in from outdoors, such as petunia, wax or fibrous begonia and impatiens (and see page 350 for details on bringing plants indoors).

### *Cool Flowers*

Bring primroses in from outdoors at the last possible moment, perhaps making use of a cold frame. They need lots of cool nights, but do not let them freeze. Many kinds of annual flowers sown this month will bloom in the winter and early spring, including winter-flowering sweet pea, annual chrysanthemum, larkspur, calendula, wallflower, more schizanthus, feverfew, winter-flowering snapdragon, Chinese forget-me-not (*Cynoglossum*), nasturtium and African daisy (*Dimorphotheca*). Many seed companies will honour orders from their catalogues in the autumn and winter as readily as they d in the spring.

Four hours of extra light at the end of the day, or two hours of light around midnight (see Green Thumb Tip, page 32), will encourage pansies, larkspur, annual chrysanthemum, feverfew, marguerite, nasturtium and schizanthus to bloom early. Provide half of the calendulas with warmer tempertures to extend the period of bloom. Calendulas for cut flowers are best started from the tallest varieties, but shorter ones make attractive pot plants.

Pot on seedlings when they have developed their true leaves, and again when the pots are full of roots. Pinch pansies, and pinch schizanthus tips and side shoots when they are small. Pinch schizanthus again three weeks later to make them full and bushy (see Table FEB-4, page 56, for other flowers that benefit from pinching). They can be potted on to 3 inch (75 mm) pots and eventually to 5 to 7 inch (125 to 175 mm) pots by February. Fertilize annual flowers every two to three weeks with a fertilizer for flowering houseplants, such as 10-30-10.

Try potting annuals for winter blossoms.

Month-by-Month

# October/November

- dig new areas
- analyse soil
- clean up vegetable garden
- store tender bulbs
- protect evergreens
- reduce mowing time!
- start indoor worm compost
- pot up spring bulbs

- save leaves, leaves and more leaves

Expanding or digging new areas in the garden is invigorating work on cool, crisp autumn days. This is also a good time of year to lay sod for new lawns and to carry out fall maintenance on the lawn mower. Chilly days are not so good for the composting process, but an indoor worm compost can easily be started to continue composting through the winter. Some vegetables can be potted up and brought indoors to extend the harvest, and spring flowering bulbs can be potted up for winter bloom. Tender bulbs should be dug up and stored indoors under the right conditions until spring, and certain roses in the outdoor garden may need special care to make it through the winter.

# October November

### Ornamental

*A shrub, bush, or small tree that is transplanted at least twice in any calendar year.*

*Beard and McKie*

## Breaking New Ground

Autumn is the ideal time to prepare soil for next year's planting, whether for a new lawn, in the vegetable garden, for a new asparagus or flower bed, where the hedge or shrub border is going to be planted, or where the soft fruits are going. If plants arrrive in early spring and cannot be settled in right away because the soil is not ready to receive them, they may suffer some dieback or die completely. Seeds can also be sown sooner if all that is required is a little raking in the spring.

### Types of Soil

The first step when digging a new area in the garden is to determine the type of soil, how well it drains, its nutrient content and the pH value. Deciding how to deal with the sod is the next step, unless it is a brand new property. Depending on how much time is available, the soil can be made free of grass and ready for planting this fall, next spring, or a year from next spring. The final step is to incorporate plenty of organic matter. Again, this can be done quickly or be extended over the next year and a half, depending on the soil type, plant requirements, and the quality of preparation desired by the gardener.

According to Henry Beard and Roy McKie, "there are basically three kinds of soil: sandy, clay, and loamy-muddy. How can you tell which type you have? Ask one of your children or a neighbor's child to come over and play in your yard. Inspect the results. Is it a castle, a tasteful little ashtray, or a messy mud pie? That's really all there is to it" (1982, p. 79).

Clay soils are wet, slow to drain, slow to warm up in the spring and they hold nutrients well but do not release them readily. Sandy soils tend to be very dry, quick to drain, quick to warm up in the spring and poor at holding nutrients. Loam is moist, drains well, warms up moderately quickly in the spring and holds nutrients well in forms readily available to plants. Fortunately, both clay and sandy soils can be improved to the quality of loam soil by adding organic matter.

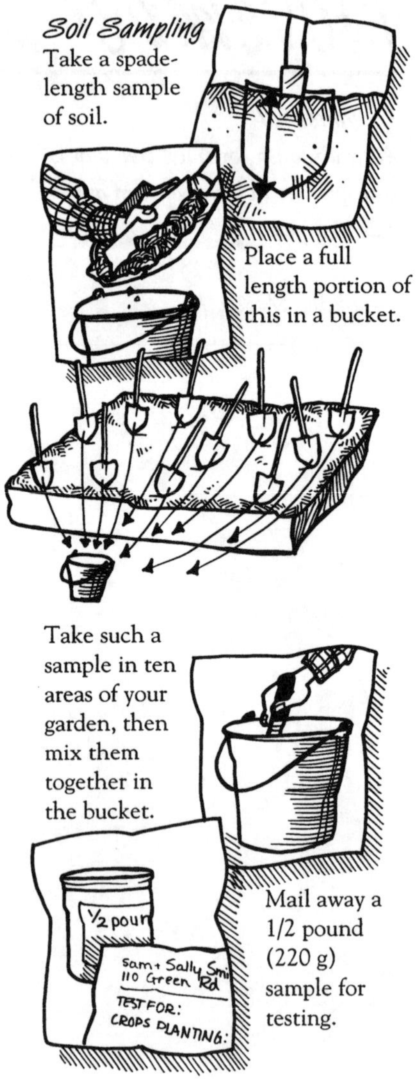


## Drainage

If there is water within 12 inches (30 cm) of the soil surface when a hole is dug, or if water is lying on the surface several days after it has rained, the drainage is poor. To be certain of the drainage capacity, dig a hole 2 to 3 feet (60 to 90 cm) deep, note whether there is a layer of really hard soil (called hardpan), and fill the hole with water. If it drains immediately the soil is too sandy; drainage in one-half to one hour is good; and if water is still there after twenty-four hours, there is a definite problem. The soil itself may drain well, but a layer of hardpan may impede drainage unless it is broken up. Soils that are slow to drain are low in fertility and plant growth is poor because the soil stays cold and airless. The micro-organisms that break down organic matter into humus require warmth and air.

Adding plenty of organic matter will help sandy soils hold water, and clay soils drain. This is often all that is required. Raising the level of the soil by mounding it or making raised beds is the next step to take to improve drainage. Make beds slightly below ground level in sandy soils.

Where drainage is very poor, it may be necessary to dig 3 foot (90 cm) deep trench drains at the bottom of a slope or on either side of a flat property. Fill the bottom half with stones and rubble and the top half with soil. If the problem is really severe, a permanent herring bone pattern of drainage pipes will need to be installed, but call in an expert for this.

## Soil Analysis and Amendments

To determine the nutrient content and pH of the soil, take a soil sample and either test it with a purchased soil testing kit or send the sample away to a soil lab. Once every five years is frequent enough (see page 163 for a discussion of nutrients). Purchased kits give barely adequate estimates of the nutrient content, but satisfactory estimates of pH levels. Very simple kits are available that test only the pH.

To obtain a soil sample, take a spade and push it into the soil at ten different locations throughout the area in question. Each time, take a little soil from the full blade length of the spade, from top to bottom, and put it in a bucket. Mix the soil collected, and then remove 1/2 pound (225 g) of

### *Preventive Measure*

Drainage problems can be severe with clay soils. The water in clay is under great pressure and it may go uphill if that is the easiest route, often right into a person's basement. Solid clay pipes laid below the frost line on a slope away from the house may be required instead of the usual perforated plastic pipe laid a foot or two deep in gravel. This will ensure that water is led away in the only direction possible. The exit downhill must be free, such as into a French or dry well which is several feet deep. From the dry well run perforated plastic pipe in a gravel bed that ends eventually in a rubble trench as described above. The exit from the clay pipe into the dry well must be higher than the entrance to the plastic pipe. Clay is so fine that silting is a problem; the entrance to and exit from the clay pipe, and the dry well, must be cleaned yearly to prevent blockage from silt buildup.

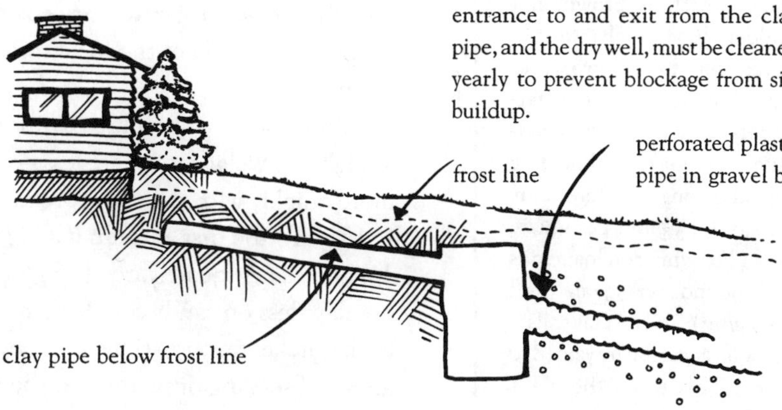


mixed soil for testing. Repeat this procedure in other parts of the garden if the soil has been treated differently in the past, but keep the mixtures separate so that they can be tested separately. Be sure to follow kit directions carefully. If sending the sample away to be tested, include your name and address and state that you want the soil tested for nutrient and organic content and pH. State what crops (vegetables, fruits, flowers, grass or shrubs) will be planted and ask to be advised on the necessary soil amendments.

### *pH adjustment*

Soil acidity or alkalinity is measured as pH levels. Soil microbial activity is dependent on the pH, which affects the rate of decomposition of organic matter, which in turn makes nutrients available for plant growth. The wrong pH causes low fertility because some nutrients, such as phosphorous, are in forms that are unuseable by plants while other nutrients, such as calcium, potassium and magnesium, leach out faster. Earthworms, which mix and aerate the soil, will leave acidic soils.

Most soils tend towards acidity. Signs of acidic soil with a pH less than 6.0 include moss on the surface, poor plant growth, vegetation that does not decay, and a predominance of such weeds as sheep sorrel, plantain and dock.

### Green Thumb Tip

There are several ways to raise the pH. The usual way is to add garden lime (which is brown, not builders' lime which is white). Spread it in the fall two weeks before manures or other fertilizers are added. The maximum amount that should be spread at one time on sandy soils is 1/2 pound per square yard (270 g/m$^2$); on loam soils is 1 pound per square yard (540 g/m$^2$); and on clay soils is 1½ pounds per square yard (810 g/m$^2$). This raises the pH 1 point, from 5.5 to 6.5. On larger areas, 1 pound per square yard (540 g/m$^2$) converts to 110 pounds per 1000 square feet (54 kg/100m$^2$). Raising the pH one full point is considered a big change; spread small quantities more frequently if a greater change is required.

It takes at least six months for lime to reduce acidity, so wait and test the soil again before spreading more. Once the right pH is reached, spread lime once every three or four years to maintain it, using only one-third to one-half of the quantities above. Lime is also used as a soil amendment to lighten the texture of clay soils; it causes fine clay particles to bind together into larger particles, resulting in larger air spaces between the particles.

Occasionally soil is alkaline (a pH above 7.0), particularly in very dry climates and overlying some rock formations.

For lawns, flowers and vegetables, aim for a pH of 6.5 (6.2 to 6.8), although a pH of 5.8 on naturally peaty soils is fine (and see below, page 384, under vegetables). Most fruits get by with a slightly more acidic soil of pH 6.0 to 6.5, and blueberries prefer an even lower pH. The pH range that trees and shrubs will tolerate varies according to the type. Native plants are adapted to the pH of the local soils and should be used as much as possible in landscaping.

Wood ashes can be added to raise the pH, but they must be used carefully. Weight for weight, they are less neutralizing than lime but they react much more quickly with the soil. Spread them at a rate of 1 pound per square yard (540 g/m$^2$) the first autumn if a big change in pH is needed, and at a rate of 1/4 pound per square yard (135 g/m$^2$) each year thereafter as required (more on clay, less on sandy soils). Some gardeners prefer wood ashes because of their quicker reaction time, but they must be spread a minimum of two weeks ahead of seeding or planting if they are used in the spring so that crops are not harmed.

Crushed oyster shells (chicken feed grade), crushed eggshells and mussel mud (crushed mussel shells) can also be mixed into the soil to raise the pH. These also provide calcium to plants, as do lime and wood ashes, and they are rich in potassium and micronutrients. They need to be spread less frequently than lime because they have a neutralizing effect that lasts for many years. There is little need for concern about them harming earthworms.

It is difficult to lower the pH. If the soil is alkaline and the pH has to be lowered, apply sulphur or ferrous sulphate at a rate of 1/4 pound per square yard (135 g/m$^2$). Ammonium sulphate can also be used but do not use aluminium sulphate. Some gardeners content themselves with growing acid-loving plants such as blueberries in individual tubs of peat enriched soil that is further ammended with sulphur.

### Organic matter

All types of soil benefit from additions of organic matter. Not only does it improve drainage, hold moisture and reduce erosion, but it also adds nutrients and helps hold nutrients already present in the soil. As a rough measure of organic content, count earthworms. On a humid day there should be, ideally, about ten earthworms per square foot in the top 7 inches (18 cm) of soil, if there is a sufficient supply of organic matter.

## *Green Thumb Tip*

Use rotted manure, rough compost, mushroom compost, seaweed, rotted straw, very old sawdust, spoiled hay, leaf mould or shredded leaves to add organic matter to the soil. Eel grass (*Zostera marina*) is fine, but be careful not to add too much salt marsh hay (mainly *Spartina patens*) unless is is old and rotted. It is difficult to add too much, but more than 30% organic matter by volume can lead to waterlogging and poor aeration, so aim for 25 to 30%. If nothing is to be planted in the soil until next spring, fresh manure can be used. Try to obtain manures mixed with straw bedding or sawdust. Fine compost which breaks into pieces less than 7/16 inch (10 mm) in diameter is best used for top dressing lawns, or store it under cover over the winter and use it throughout the garden in the spring. Pound for pound, leaves have twice the nutrient content of manure in terms of phosphorous, calcium, magnesium and trace elements. Seaweed is rich in calcium and micronutrients, including zinc, copper, boron, cobalt and molybdenum. If compost contains a variety of materials, it may contain slightly more plant nutrients than rotted manure. Mushroom compost has about the same nutrient content as rotted manure and has the added benefit of producing a crop of mushrooms when it is added to the soil. Avoid using peat moss (see Green Thumb Tip, page 115).

### *Incorporating sod*

Sod adds valuable organic matter to the soil when the growth above ground and the root system below are incorporated in the soil, or at least composted and added later. Incorporating sod is a challenge; however, there are several methods to try. If light has been excluded by covering the grass (see page 118) all the plant growth will be killed and the sod can be turned into the soil right away. If the plants are still green, the sod can be skimmed off the surface, chopped up, and buried deeply as the soil is being dug. Both of these methods work if the aim is to plant next spring, or even this autumn. If topsoil is being added, it is a good idea to roughly dig and break up the sod, or even flip the sod upside down, before burying it under the additional soil.

During the growing season, while the grass is green, another method is to let the grass grow about 6 inches (15 cm) long, cut it as short as possible, and then rake it to one side. Spread lime if it is required, spread the grass clippings over the area, and spread a thick layer of manure or mushroom compost if they are available. Till these into the soil; the high nitrogen content of the grass clippings and manure or mushroom compost will help to break down the sod more quickly. This area will be ready for planting in two to six months, depending on how warm the weather is and on how much nitrogen is in the soil.

## *Green Thumb Tip*

There is another, somewhat slower method of soil preparation that is superb for improving soils low in organic matter.

FALL 1 - Spread lime in the autumn, if required, and plough the sod. In small areas, simply dig up chunks of sod and turn them upside down.

WINTER 1 - Leave the soil like this over the winter, allowing frost action to help break up the chunks.

SPRING 1 - Cultivate shallowly or dig over the surface several times and work in plenty of organic matter (see page 379) to one spade's depth. Plant buckwheat after all danger of frost is past.

SUMMER 1 - When half of the buckwheat is in flower cut it down. Cultivate the area several times again and work in more organic matter, to two spade's depth if necessary, depending on the crop that will be grown.

FALL 2 - Plant annual rye or some other fall cover crop (see Table AUG-2, page 299) to protect the soil over WINTER 2.

SPRING 2 - Dig up the fall cover crop and work in more organic matter if desired. At this stage the bed is ready for planting.

This method adds organic matter without having to bring in manure, and does an excellent job of getting rid of grass and weeds.

## *Soil Depth, Digging and Mulching*

To properly dig in organic matter, for root crops or where the soil is low in nutrients, incorporate it throughout the entire rooting depth, rather than putting it in a trench or digging it into the top few inches. Research has shown that soil moisture and air content are optimal for root growth when organic matter is mixed throughout the full rooting depth of the crop being grown.

To double dig, skim off a strip of sod and set it to one side, then dig a 15 inch (38 cm) wide trench the depth of one spade and set the soil to one side. Next break up the soil in the bottom of the same trench to one spade's depth, using a fork or crow bar if necessary. Skim off the next strip of sod, chop it up with the spade, and work the sod as well as a 4 inch (10 cm) layer of organic matter into the lower level of the first trench. Add the soil from the

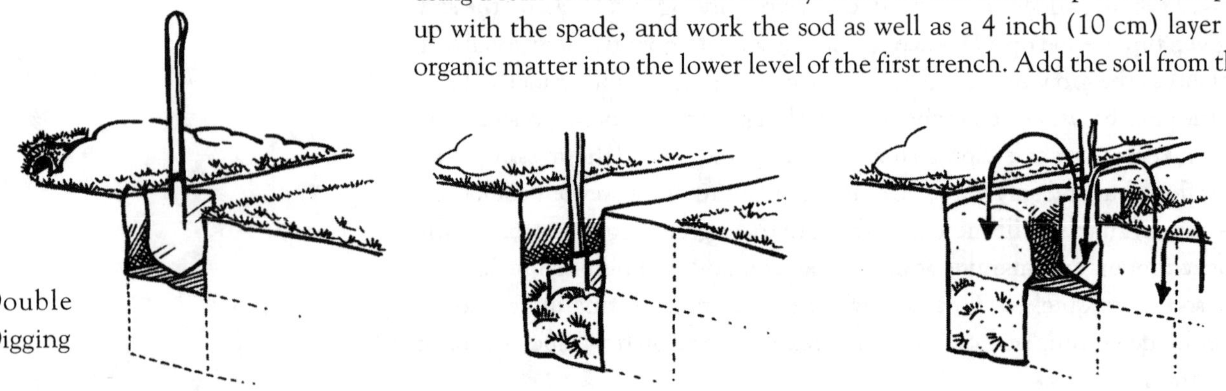

Double Digging

upper level of the second trench, removing any perennial weeds and rocks and mixing in another 4 inch (10 cm) layer of organic matter. Proceed in this manner until the end of the area to be dug is reached. Use the sod and soil from the first trench to fill in the last trench.

To single dig, skim off the sod and incorporate organic matter throughout the top layer of the soil to one spade's depth. Sod that is only shallowly buried may regrow, so it is best to compost the sod in this situation.

After the soil has been prepared, mulching the area for the winter helps to maintain the soil structure created. Covering the soil with leaves, seaweed or straw, for example, will protect especially vulnerable sandy soils that can be compacted by pounding winter rains. In areas where snow cover is deep and reliable, mulching is not necessary, although it can still be done. Very heavy clays are best left uncovered over the winter so that frost action can work on the clods.

A root guard is helpful if digging flower beds and vegetable gardens next to trees and shrubs. Dig a trench about 12 inches (30 cm) deep and insert a 12 inch (30 cm) wide strip of galvanized metal along the edge of the bed adjacent to the tree or shrub roots. Of course, one does not want to cut too many roots in doing this, but it will help to prevent any more roots from growing into the bed in the future.

## Raised Beds and Containers

Using raised beds, or purchasing topsoil, is sometimes necessary where there is little or no soil. Soil for annual flowers and shallow rooted vegetables such as lettuce needs to be only 8 inches (20 cm) deep, although 12 inches (30 cm) is better. Soil should be at least 12 inches (30 cm) deep for perennial flowers, bulbs, vegetable root crops and large plants such as Brussels sprouts, but 20 inches (50 cm) is better, especially for fruiting shrubs. Most tree roots go no deeper than 12 inches (30 cm), but the extra depth acts as a nutrient and moisture reserve.

Senior citizens and gardeners working from a wheelchair or stool can work most easily in beds that are raised to 30 inches (75 cm). Raised beds that are to be combined with seating are best at 14 to 16 inches (35 to 40 cm) high, and 16 to 18 inches (40 to 45 cm) wide.

Bottomless containers are best, placed directly over the soil. In effect they become raised beds. The height of the container in this case is not important. What matters is the depth of useable soil available to the plants. If these are not possible, containers with bottoms should be even deeper than the

### Green Thumb Tip

For vegetables, fruiting shrubs or perennial flowers, try to double dig (see above) the area to a depth of two spades, or 18 to 20 inches (45 to 50 cm) deep. If that is too difficult or onerous, aim for at least 12 inches (30 cm) deep. Dig individual planting holes for trees and shrubs rather than a large area (see pages 146-147). Single digging to one spade's depth is fine for shallow rooted crops. Aim for a minimum depth of 6 inches (15 cm) for lawns and 8 inches (20 cm) for annual flowers and shallow rooted vegetables. Add topsoil ammended with organic matter and lime (if it is required) if the depth is inadequate for what you plan to grow.

minimum depths suggested above to ensure a sufficient reserve of moisture. Whether the soil is sandy or mostly clay, plan on working in plenty of organic matter, even if so-called "topsoil" is purchased to fill beds.

There is lively debate among gardeners about the merits and demerits of raised beds. A combination of both raised and flat beds is probably a good idea, if conditions allow. Soil warms up more quickly in the spring in raised beds—which is beneficial in short season areas and coastal regions—but it dries out faster in the summer. Working in organic matter and mulching will help to preserve moisture in the soil. There may be a few occasions each season when a raised bed helps to protect plants from a ground frost. If you are keen to plant some early vegetables, you can use raised beds, or warm up the soil early using various methods (see page 117). On bedrock, where you are forced to bring in topsoil, raised beds may be the only choice. Where summers are hot and dry, beds that are slightly below ground level will hold moisture better. Drainage must be good, however, for this method to be effective.

For large area crops, such as potatoes, corn and squash, raised beds are probably too much effort, so plant them on flat ground. A less onerous alternative is to build up the soil into raised rows or mounds; this will allow the soil to warm more quickly than when left flat.

Raised and sunken beds may need to be edged, unless they are low or shallow. To edge a standard raised bed, use 2 by 6 lumber in beds less than or equal to 4 feet (1.2 m) in width. Leave paths, about 2 feet (60 cm) wide, between the beds and add the soil from the paths to the raised beds. Fill in the paths with a thick layer of newspaper covered by sand, leaf mats or shredded bark to keep the weeds down. For higher beds use two or three levels of boards held in place with stakes, or use landscape ties.

**Green Thumb Tip**

The individual size of a vegetable, flower or soft fruit bed depends in part on how much is to be planted. A width of no more than 4 feet (1.2 m) will allow easy access from either side—you will not need to step on the bed—but some flower growers prefer a width of 5 feet (1.5 m) so that they can include varying heights of plants. This applies both to raised beds, sunken beds and traditional beds at ground level. Soil compaction caused by stepping on the soil reduces root growth and hence total productivity. As well, only the growing ground is cultivated and manured, not the paths, so that waste and effort is reduced. Disabled gardeners find that narrower beds are more convenient as they can reach across the bed without having to lean on the soil.

## Vegetables

### Fall Care

Aside from digging, there is little to do in the vegetable garden in the autumn other than harvesting, clearing and mulching. Bring in pumpkins and winter squashes if a hard freeze threatens, and try to protect them from light frosts on other nights. Immature squashes do not ripen properly once cut, and they are quicker to spoil, so try to keep them going on the vine as long as possible without exposing them to chilling damage.

Spread row covers or put out cold frames to protect late season crops. Mulch hardy bunching onions before the ground freezes, and spread a light mulch of straw or pea vines over kale. Wait until the tops die back before mulching carrots and other root crops that are being left in the ground over the winter, but mulch before the ground freezes. Try to have all garlic planted by the first expected frost date, or as soon as possible afterwards, so that it can grow roots and get established before the ground freezes hard.

#### Cleaning up

As crops are harvested, plant debris can be turned into the soil or left on the soil surface to act as a mulch; added to the compost pile; or burned, buried or put in the garbage if diseases have been a problem.

Coarse materials such as corn stalks and Brussels sprout stems should go on the bottom of a new compost heap, or be chopped and mixed with the rest of the pile. The remains of rhubarb, tomato and potato plants can be added to the pile as well. Even though they are poisonous if eaten, they are harmless when composted and the rotted debris can be freely used next spring in the vegetable garden. Large quantities of rhubarb leaves may slow the composting process, but this is not a problem if they are mixed throughout the pile.

Cut down asparagus fronds to 1 inch (2.5 cm) above ground level after they have turned yellow and remove them from the area to reduce overwintering populations of asparagus beetle and disease organisms. Clean out old mulch as well, if asparagus beetles have been a problem, because the adults overwinter in garden trash. Sprinkle a little garden lime on the soil—about once every three years—to keep the pH near neutral, but do not spread any manure until the spring.

If you prefer long spears in the spring, mound 2 to 3 inches (5 to 8 cm) of soil over the stubs of the fronds. Remove all weeds and grass that have invaded the bed and then apply a fresh, shallow mulch around the plants

**Preventive Measure**

There are several reasons for removing plant debris. Insect pests such as carrot rust fly larvae and corn borers are removed from the site, and viral and fungal disease organisms, such as clubroot, are reduced in number. Clearing crop residues, weeds and grass also removes egg laying sites for such insects as cutworms, and reduces the hiding places for cucumber beetles, flea beetles, onion maggots and tarnished plant bugs.

now or in the spring. This will keep down weeds and preserve moisture next growing season. Young crowns can be mulched with a deep layer of straw after the ground is frozen to help them through their first winter or two.

> **Preventive Measure**
>
> If you dig the soil to manage insect problems, work it anytime before the ground freezes to a depth of 6 to 8 inches (15 to 20 cm), leave it bare for two weeks, and then cultivate again to a depth of 2 or 3 inches (5 to 8 cm). This helps to turn up various life stages of such insects as potato beetles, flea beetles, wireworms, June bugs, grasshoppers, onion maggots and brassica root maggots. They will either die of exposure or be eaten by birds.

### *Digging and soil amendments*

It is best to avoid digging where autumn rains are common. Ideally, leave soil undisturbed, with a winter cover crop or winter mulch to protect it from compaction and erosion. All that will be needed in spring is perhaps a little loosening with a fork or U-bar digger. If, however, the soil does not drain well at the subsoil level (e.g. due to heavy clay or a layer of hardpan), or if it is low in organic matter, or if the soil has too little air (e.g. clay) or too much air (e.g. sand), then autumn digging can be useful. Incorporating bulky organic matter throughout the rooting depth of the crop helps address a range of problems and improves plant growth.

Digging can help destroy overwintering insect pests, improve the structure of some soils, and prepare the soil for early spring planting of such crops as lettuce, spinach and peas. Mulching soil after digging reduces erosion and compaction. All that is needed in spring is to pull aside the mulch, perhaps rake a little to reduce clumps, and sow seeds or set in transplants.

The soil is too wet to work if it sticks to your boots. Where heavy autumn rains occur, clay soils needing improvement should be dug early in the autumn before they get too wet; light soils can be dug as late as October or November. Refrain from walking on freshly dug beds to avoid compacting the soil. Four-foot (1.2 m) wide beds are a useful working width.

Autumn digging that includes the incorporation of manure or coarse, unfinished compost has other benefits, too. Many crops grow too vigorously or with distorted roots if grown in freshly manured soil; adding manure six months before planting gives plants the benefits with none of the problems. In freshly manured soil, sweet potatoes will grow rampant vines and distorted tubers, cabbages may split, Brussels sprouts will be crowded and loose, and carrots and other roots may be forked.

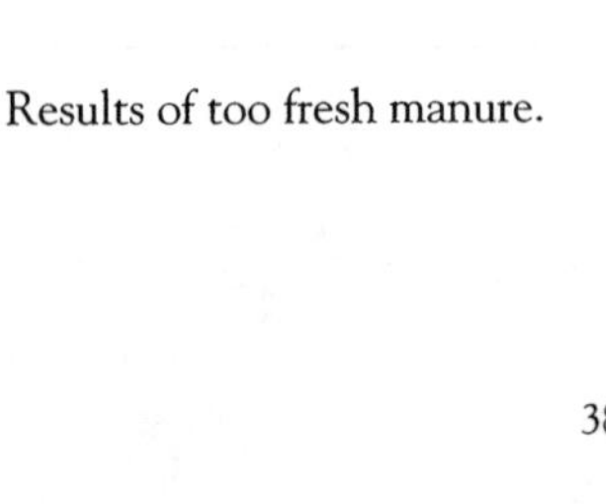

Results of too fresh manure.

Coarse, lumpy compost can be incorporated into the soil and will continue to break down, or spread it as a winter mulch instead. Do not leave manure lying on the surface over winter. Mix it into the soil to ensure that the nutrients are not lost through winter rains and spring runoff.

If soil requires liming, apply the lime two weeks before manure is added, because chemical reactions between the two will release nitrogen as ammonia gas. Wood ashes can be dug into the soil in the autumn, or a minimum of two weeks before planting in the spring. Save them in a covered container over the winter if collecting a supply for spring use. In a crop rotation plan, spread lime where the potatoes have just been harvested, so that potatoes are never planted in freshly limed soil.

A well-prepared soil rich in organic matter does not require digging. If the soil needs improvement, single digging to a depth of 8 to 10 inches (20 to 25 cm) can be used to incorporate organic matter throughout that depth. Initially, and once every five years, some gardeners like to double dig (pages 380-381). Most soils will maintain good structure over many years provided care is taken not to compact soils, particularly late in the year. If the soil is very sandy or if summer droughts are a problem, double dig more often to incorporate organic matter to help crops cope better with water shortages, and to improve growing conditions for deep-rooted crops.

If you must dig, use a fork or spade. A fork is better on stony or heavy soils and is better for digging perennial weeds because they are less likely to chop up roots and underground stems that can regenerate. Avoid mechanical cultivators. They pulverize the soil, leaving a fine tilth, and the idea is to leave fist-sized chunks over winter. If used for all cultivation, they can create a layer of hardpan at their depth of working. Avoid walking on prepared soil.

### Preventive Measure

There is some evidence that working leaves into the soil helps to depress root maggot populations, so put them where brassicas will be planted next year. Whether it is the leaves themselves exerting some influence, or the act of digging that destroys the insects, is not clear. It is certainly a good way, however, to use up some of the leaves which are dropping everywhere.

### *Weeding and winter mulching*

Make sure that annual weeds are dug out before they go to seed, and remove any that have already set seed before they drop too many. Dig out perennial weeds as thoroughly as possible. Those with tap roots are fairly manageable, but those with creeping roots or stems can be troublesome and persistent. Some perennial weeds also set seed, making them rogues extraordinaire. For severe weed problems that are unmanageable and harmful to crops despite persistent digging and faithful hoeing throughout the growing season, the best approach may be to use a herbicide containing the active ingredient glyphosate. Apply it during warm weather in May or June, when there is plenty of top growth and the weeds are growing actively.

If there is not enough time to sow a cover crop (see pages 298-299), cover the cleared and dug ground with a winter mulch of straw, leaves or seaweed. Unless huge amounts of seaweed are used year after year, there is no need to rinse off the salt. If salt is a concern, spread the seaweed on the driveway before a rain to rinse it. Anything that protects the soil from the impact of rain and prevents nutrients from being lost is worth the effort of applying. An added advantage is that planting can happen earlier in the spring; simply pull back the mulch and rake the bed, or loosen the top 4 inches (10 cm) of soil before raking if need be.

## Herbs

### General Care

Tender annuals will be killed back by frost, but many herbs will continue to yield enough leaves for fresh use well into the autumn, particularly if they are protected by a cold frame before the hard frosts and cold weather come. Raise the lid a few centimetres on sunny days to provide good air circulation and prevent overheating. Continue to pot up other herbs to overwinter indoors (see pages 349-350), and see Flowers below (page 387) for the care of young herb plants.

Lemon balm can be propagated from root cuttings (see page 137). As it is not reliably winter hardy, starting a few plants from root cuttings in pots indoors will ensure a supply of plants next spring, although it is also very easy to start from seed.

After the leaves have faded, cut back angelica stalks and those of other perennial herbs, unless they are wanted for winter interest (see below). Because herbs are rarely bothered by insects, it is not necessary to clear out herb gardens or patches each autumn. The stalks can be left to form a natural mulch and to trap blowing leaves. Dig out weeds and grass to reduce your workload in the spring. Add fresh mulch between plants if desired, but wait until the ground freezes before applying a deep winter mulch over the crowns of plants (see November, page 413). Beds where annual herbs were grown can be dug over and treated the same way as vegetable beds (see page 384).

**Preventive Measure**

It is important to remove all foliage if plants have been affected by any diseases, such as black spot in roses, powdery mildew in phlox and botrytis in peonies. Rake up any dropped leaves and old mulch under diseased plants, and burn or discard both.

## Flowers

### General Care and Seed Stalks

It is still too early to apply a deep winter mulch on flower beds, but weeds and grass can be dug out and faded flower stalks and foliage removed.

If insects and diseases were not a problem, faded seed stalks can be left in place for their decorative value in the winter, or used for dried flower arrangements. Birds also appreciate the seed heads of many grasses, herbs and flowers (see page 153). The more attractive ones are:

| | | |
|---|---|---|
| angelica | filipendula | lupine |
| astilbe | foxglove | mallow |
| blue lace flower | fritillaria | nigella |
| canterbury bells | gasplant | peony |
| chervil | hibiscus | Queen Anne's lace |

Seed heads come in a variety of shapes and sizes.

| | | |
|---|---|---|
| Chinese lantern | hollyhock | rhododendron |
| chive | honesty | rue |
| clarkia | iris | saponaria |
| delphinium | Joe-Pye weed | sedum |
| dill | larkspur | snapdragon |
| fennel | liatris | sweet cicely |
| | lily | yucca |

Leave them in place until they become flattened or miserable looking. Certainly they should be cleared away when the first bits of green poke through the soil in the spring. Leave lily stalks in place, or mark the position of lilies and balloon flowers with stakes. Pull up spent annuals, unless they are wanted for their seed stalks or for self-seeding purposes.

Fork in manure or compost where annuals were grown, but wait until spring to add it to perennial flower beds. It is difficult to work in the manure among the plants, and nutrients are lost during winter rains and spring runoff if it is left on the surface. If it is added in the autumn, at least scratch it into the top 1 to 2 inches (3 to 5 cm) of soil.

It is almost too late to move perennials around, even in milder zones. They will probably not have enough time to establish their roots before the ground freezes, particularly young plants with small root systems. If plants must be moved for some unavoidable reason, mulch the ground around them immediately after planting. This will keep the ground from freezing for a while longer and enable the roots to keep growing. Mulch them deeply, covering the crowns of the plants as well, after the ground has frozen solid (see November, pages 413 and 415).

### Preventive Measure

If there have been severe insect problems, such as columbines being devoured earlier in the season by sawfly larvae, carefully cultivate around the affected plants. This may help to destroy overwintering insects, even if only the top 2 inches (5 cm) can be cultivated. Leave the soil bare after the first cultivation. Repeat in two weeks, then between the plants apply a fresh mulch of shredded bark or chopped leaves and grass clippings to protect the soil over the winter. A deep mulch applied around the plants in the summer may also help; insects that overwinter in mulch instead of soil are more vulnerable to the cold.

## Protection of Special Needs Perennials and Tender Roses

The safest way to protect a few special or vulnerable perennials is to pot them up and put them in cold storage for the winter. A cold room or unheated garage that does not drop below freezing is ideal, and there is no need for lighting because the perennials will be dormant through the winter. There is probably no need for watering, either, except to prevent the soil from becoming bone dry.

Young perennials started from seeds or root cuttings, as well as young lilies started from scales, bulblets or bulbils, will also need protection for the winter. Those in pots should be moved indoors to cold storage. Do not attempt to keep them growing all through the winter because most need a period of cold and dormancy before they will make good growth in the spring. Any that are in nursery beds can either be potted up and put into cold storage, or protected outdoors. After everything is killed back by frost, add an extra 2 inches (5 cm) of light soil or sand over the bed. After the ground freezes hard, apply a deep winter mulch (see November, pages 413 and 414). This is quite a reliable form of protection.

Continue to plant daffodils and other spring blooming bulbs (see September/October, pages 356-362). Try to have them all in the ground by the time night frosts are frequent to give the roots time to grow before the ground freezes. The longer planting is delayed, the greater the risk of losing bulbs over the winter. Those that are planted late should be mulched thickly immediately afterwards. This will keep the ground from freezing for a little longer and give the roots more time to grow.

### Focus on Plants

Hardy shrub roses require no special care in the fall, but hybrid teas, climbers and roses in pots need attention. Bring soil from another part of the garden and mound it in a foot hight (30 cm) cone around the base of hybrid teas when temperatures start dropping regularly below freezing at night. Cut off any long canes after the leaves drop to prevent the wind from whipping them around in the winter and disturbing the cone of soil.

Flower buds on climbing roses have already been formed for next year's bloom, so the canes must not be cut back. Only in the mildest regions do climbers survive winters well; elsewhere they must be lowered to the ground and mulched. After the leaves have faded, bury the tops in a trench after lowering them to the ground, and mound soil around the base as described for hybrid teas. Hardy shrub roses used as climbers, such as 'Henry Kelsey,' 'John Cabot,' 'Aïcha,' 'William Baffin,' and 'Leverkusen' do not require any special attention. For both hybrid teas and climbers, mulch the ground deeply after the ground has frozen (see November, pages 413 and 415).

For patio roses in pots and roses pruned to standard form, one of three things can be done to help them survive the winter. 1) Dig a trench and bury the roses pots and all, or standard roses complete with root ball, on their sides under 1 foot (30 cm) of soil after the leaves have yellowed or fallen off. 2) Pot up the roses and place them in cold storage over the winter after the leaves have yellowed or fallen. 3) Bring them indoors and treat them as house plants while they are still green; stop fertilizing in October or November and gradually reduce the water supplied until the plants enter a resting phase. Increase watering in late winter or early spring, prune, and start fertilizing once new growth shows.

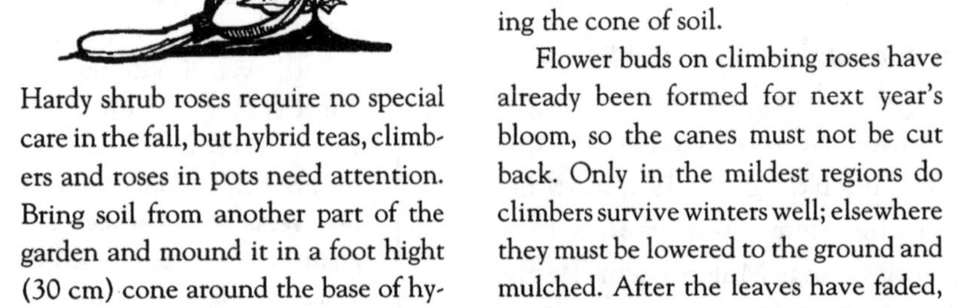

### Storing Tender "Bulbs"

Plants growing from tender "bulbs," including tubers, corms and rhizomes, will be killed back sooner or later by frost. They should be dug up soon afterwards and stored for the winter. Depending on the type, they will require various levels of moisture and warmth (refer to Table OCT/NOV-1).

Dahlias require cool, moist storage. Cut them back to 6 inches (15 cm) above ground level after frost kills the tops. Dig them up carefully, let them dry for a few hours turned upside down on the ground, brush off any loose soil, dust them with sulphur to control fungal problems, and store them in barely moistened wood shavings or vermiculite at 41°F (5°C). Some gardeners include dried artemisia in an effort to repel hidden insects.

Mirabilis is usually treated as an annual but it is actually a tender perennial. Dig the tuberous roots after the tops have been blackened by frost and store them in the same way as dahlias. Cannas are cut back to ground level and treated the same as dahlias, but stored with sand or soil around the roots at a warmer temperature.

Tuberous begonias, caladiums and calla lilies require drier storage conditions. They should have the tops left on after they are dug, and be placed in a warm, dry place out of direct sun for one to two weeks. After drying, break off the tops and fibrous roots, dust the bulbs with sulphur, and store them in dry sand, perlite or vermiculite. They also store well in individual paper bags in with potatoes. Label everything by type and colour. Those that were growing in pots can simply be left in the pots and stored at the appropriate temperature range.

Tuberose is stored at 68°F (20°C) or warmer. If these conditions cannot be met, discard tuberose because it will not bloom next season if stored cooler. *Anemone blanda* (de caen and St. Brigid varieties) is marginally hardy in zone 6 and will self sow in shady places, so it does not need to be lifted and stored, but *Anemone coronaria* is tender in all zones. Some gardeners treat anemones as annuals and buy new ones every spring, particularly as they do not keep well over the winter. Be certain to buy nursery grown stock, however, because the wild populations are dwindling due to overharvesting.

Many bulbs, such as gladiolus, acidanthera, freesia, tigridia, zephyranthes and crocosmia (montbretia), are stored moderately warm and dry. Cut these off just above ground level after frost blackens the tops and try to dig them up on a warm, sunny day. Those that have been bothered by thrips or mites can be dipped in water at 110°F (43°C) for 20 minutes to kill the pests. Dry the

## Table OCT/NOV-1 Storage Conditions For Tender Bulbs

| Plant Name | Method of Storage | Temperature Range | Rest Period |
|---|---|---|---|
| Achimenes | Pd,D | 10-15ºC | winter |
| Acidanthera | Pd,D | 5-10ºC | fall or winter |
| Agapanthus | Ps | 5-10ºC | fall or winter |
| Alstroemeria (Peruvian Lily) | Ps | 10-15ºC | anytime |
| Amaryllis | Ps | 10-15ºC | fall or winter |
| Anemone | Pd,D | 5-10ºC | anytime |
| Babiana | Pd,D | 5-10ºC | summer |
| Begonia, Tuberous | Pd,D | 5-10ºC | anytime |
| Caladium | Pd,D | 13-16ºC | anytime |
| Calla Lily (*Zantedeschia*) | Pd,D | 10-15ºC | anytime |
| Canna | L - U | 5-15ºC | winter |
| Crinum | Pd | 5-10ºC | fall or winter |
| Crocosmia | Pd,D | 5-10ºC | fall or winter |
| Dahlia | S | 5ºC | winter |
| Elephant's Ear | Pd,D | 13-16ºC | winter |
| Eucharis (Amazon Lily) | Ps | 15-20ºC | winter (with a pause in summer) |
| Eucomis (Pineapple Lily) | Ps | 10ºC | winter |
| Freesia | Pd,D | 5ºC | anytime |
| Galtonia (Cape or Summer Hyacinth) | Pd,D | 5-10ºC | winter |
| Gladiolus | Dd | 5-10ºC | fall or winter |
| Gloriosa (Glory Lily) | D | 15ºC | fall |
| Gloxinia | Pd,D | 15ºC | fall or winter |
| Haemanthus | Ps | 10ºC | fall or winter |
| Incarvillea (Hardy Gloxinia) | Ps | 5-10ºC | winter |
| Iris, Dutch | Pd,D | 5-10ºC | summer or fall |

| Plant Name | Method of Storage | Temperature Range | Rest Period |
|---|---|---|---|
| Ismene (*Hymenocallis*) (Spider Lily) | S - U | 18-20°C | fall |
| Ixia (Corn Lily) | Pd,D | 5-10°C | summer or fall |
| Lachenalia | Pd, | 5-10°C | spring or summer |
| Lily - # | Ps | 2-5°C | fall, winter or spring |
| Lycoris | Ps | 5-10°C | summer |
| Mirabilis | S | 5°C | winter |
| Nerine (Guernsey Lily) | Ps | 10°C | spring or summer |
| Oxalis | Pd,D | 5-10°C | anytime |
| Ranunculus (Persian Buttercup) | S | 5-10°C | fall or winter |
| Sparaxis(Harlequin or Wandflower) | Pd,D | 5-10°C | summer or fall |
| Sprekelia | S | 10-15°C | fall or winter |
| Tigridia | D | 5-10°C | fall or winter |
| Tuberose | S | 20°C | fall or winter |
| Vallota (Scarborough Lily) | Ps | 10°C | fall or winter |
| Zephyranthes (Fairy Lilies) | Ps | 10-15°C | fall or winter |

D = store bulbs in mesh bags, nylons, paper bags, dry sand, perlite or vermiculite
L = store bulbs in damp sand or soil
Pd = store dry in pot out of sight
Ps = keep plant in pot with potting soil slightly moistened; keep in light if there is foliage present
S = store bulbs in barely moistened wood shavings, sawdust or vermiculite
U = store bulb upside down
# = lilies vary in hardiness depending on climatic zone; they can be stored for winter protection or for indoor culture

5°C = 41°F    15°C = 60°F
10°C = 50°F    20°C = 68°F

"bulbs" as quickly as possible over a screen or in flats in a warm, dry place for seven to ten days. Next, remove the tops, soil and loose husks, dust the "bulbs" with sulphur, and store them in shallow, open boxes, in net bags or in nylons (see Table OCT/NOV-1, above). Cormels on gladiolus corms, and other "babies," can be discarded or saved for planting next spring to increase stocks.

Some bulbs, such as agapanthus and nerine, are stored in barely moist conditions. They are usually left in their pots because they are late blooming. Keep them growing by watering and fertilizing regularly until the foliage starts to fade. The leaves may never die back, but the bulbs should be slowed in their growth after flowering is finished by withholding fertilizer and watering only enough to keep the potting soil from becoming bone dry.

Gladiolus corms

### Preventive Measure

Excellent drainage and a soil that is not overly rich are essential for lilies. Avoid adding manure as it seems to promote disease. Working it in six months before planting may help, but using compost or leaf mould is safer. Mix in a small handful of bonemeal or fish bonemeal as well.

## Planting Lilies and Scaling Bulbs

This is a good time to plant lily bulbs, or at least to prepare the ground. Mail order bulbs often do not arrive until late October, or even November sometimes, and they should be planted immediately. To keep the ground from freezing while waiting for the bulbs to arrive, apply a thick mulch of straw or oak leaves over the prepared planting area. Some gardeners, particularly in colder zones, prefer to purchase lily bulbs in the spring and to plant them as soon as the soil is workable.

Lilies are superb with rhododendrons as they enjoy the same soil conditions and bloom in the summer after the rhododendrons are finished. They can also be grown among widely spaced perennials, overplanted with annuals, put in front of evergreens, and small ones can be planted in rock gardens. They vary in height from 2 ½ feet (75 cm) to over 4 feet (1.2 m) and come in a full range of colours, from brilliant reds, oranges and yellows to the softest pinks, creams and peaches. The bloom time can be extended from late June to September, depending on the types of lilies chosen; the short asiatics bloom first, followed by taller trumpets and orientals late in the season. These later types are not reliably hardy in colder zones and are often grown in pots that can be put in cold storage for the winter.

All lilies do best in full sun or partial shade, but require partial shade at noon where summers are hot. Trumpet-shaped lilies face the sun and track it through the day as it moves across the sky, so keep this in mind when planting if you want their blooms to face the viewer.

Plant lilies in holes 12 to 18 inches (30 to 45 cm) apart covered with 3 to 8 inches (8 to 20 cm) of soil (see Table MAR/APR-3, page 88). Water thoroughly after planting so that the soil makes good contact with the bulbs and roots start growing quickly. If, however, the soil stays compacted when you squeeze it in your hand, do not add any more water. If mice and squirrels have eaten lily bulbs in the past, plant bulbs in small-mesh galvanized wire baskets. After the ground has frozen, a thick mulch may be applied, particularly in areas where snow cover is unreliable.

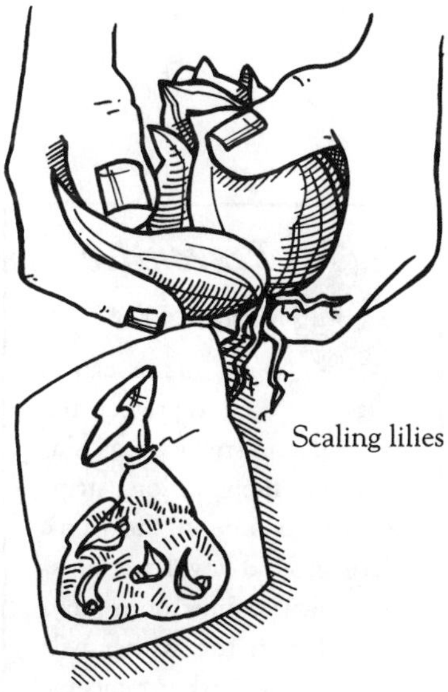

Scaling lilies

The usual causes when bulbs fail to grow in the spring are poor drainage, frost heave and late planting. Occasionally, bulbs planted in the autumn will not appear until spring a year and a half later. If bulbs cannot be planted right away, store them in the refrigerator in open paper bags.

Bulbs can be scaled before planting to increase supplies—this is particularly attractive with expensive bulbs (see page 354 for other methods of propagating lilies). Pull off four to eight firm scales from each plump bulb and place them in damp sphagnum, peat moss or vermiculite inside closed plastic bags. Store at 70°F (21°C) for several weeks until little bulblets form on the scales. Plant the bulblets either attached to the scales or separated. Use any regular potting soil with good drainage or with extra sand or perlite added. Store them in the refrigerator or cold room for six to twelve weeks to simulate winter. Bring them into warmth and light in late winter or early spring and plant them outdoors in a nursery bed as for bulbils and bulblets (see page 354) as soon as the soil is workable.

## Fruits

Preparing soil for spring or autumn planting, getting the orchard and soft fruits ready for winter, continuing propagation efforts, and taking strawberry and rhubarb plants indoors for a winter treat are the main activites at this time.

### Planting, Propagation and Autumn Care

Soft fruits such as strawberries, raspberries and currants grow best in soil that is rich in organic matter and free of weeds and grass. Preparing the soil as described above under Breaking New Ground (pages 375-382), whether for planting next spring or, better yet, the following year, will ensure the healthiest start for all fruits. Strawberries seem to do better in raised beds because of the improved air circulation and drainage. Raised beds are essential for blueberries if they are grown on heavy clay soils.

Fruiting shrubs that have lost their leaves can be moved to a new location, if required. Bare root shrubs ordered through the mail can also be planted; the survival rate over the winter is often very high, but be prepared for some losses. Applying a deep mulch immediately after planting delays freezing of the soil and gives roots more time to get established. Raspberries seem to do better if planted in the spring. If planted now, mulch them well after the ground freezes (see pages 413 and 417) to prevent poorly rooted shrubs from being heaved out of the ground in the late winter and early spring.

To propagate blueberries, dig carefully around the roots to obtain pieces for root cuttings (see page 137). Hardwood cuttings of currants and other fruiting shrubs (see page 366 and Table JUL-3, page 275), can be taken into November.

Grapes grown in severe climates and trained in a fan or oblique side arm shape (see page 101) should be lowered to the ground and protected in the same manner as climbing roses (see page 388). Lower the branches on espaliered fruits to horizontal as part of their training and tie them to the wires.

Mice are sometimes a problem in orchards. They are attracted by the fruit drops and sheltering mulch. Make sure there is a clear space around each trunk to keep mice away, and cut the grass and flowers short to make it a less effective hiding place and easier for owls and hawks to catch mice and voles. Where deer are a persistent problem in the winter, electric fencing is the only reliable solution (see page 186).

Rake up diseased leaves and burn or discard them rather than adding them to the compost pile. Continue to pick up fruit drops and consider cultivation to reduce overwintering insect pests (see page 384). The pupal stage of apple maggots, for example, can stay in the ground for up to five years. Be careful not to harm roots, particularly under shallow rooted plants such as gooseberries and currants. Apply a light mulch after the second cultivation to protect the soil over the winter, but do not apply manure until spring.

Do not bother cultivating where insects have not been a problem, but do pull out weeds and grass under all the tree fruits and soft fruits. Top up the mulch only if the ground is bare in places. Coarse, unfinished compost can be spread, and shredded leaves make a good mulch in the autumn. Apply a thick winter mulch over strawberries after the ground has frozen (see page 413).

### Preventive Measure

Tree guards can be used to protect trees from mice and reduce sunscald. They are flexible, long strips that wind around the trunk from ground level upwards. Bark that is warmed on a sunny, mild day in the winter will sometimes split when temperatures drop below freezing at night. On the other hand, apple, pear, beech, birch, hawthorn and poplar trees are susceptible to canker, which is exacerbated by tight tree guards that make the bark dry slowly. Painting trunks and major branches with slightly thinned, white interior latex paint is an effective way to reduce sunscald on these and other trees.

## Fruit production problems

Fruit trees that grow vigorously but fail to produce fruit are frustrating. Before losing all hope, decide if any of the following factors might be the cause and what action can be taken. Vigorous root stocks bear fruit later than dwarfing and less vigorous root stocks (be patient); pruning too hard during dormancy induces vegetative growth at the expense of flower bud production (prune more lightly, or try summer pruning instead); too much nitrogen stimulates vegetative growth (reduce or eliminate manures or nitrogenous fertilizers); and lack of nutrients, particularly phosphorous and potassium, reduces flowering and fruiting. Other reasons for little or no fruit production include: poor pollination because of cold or wet weather, or lack of a pollinating tree (see pages 43-44); low bee population (see page 187); too much shade; and frost damage to blossoms or very young fruits (see pages 43 and 188).

## Woody Ornamentals

Woody plants can be moved in the autumn in certain situations, and others may need attention to prepare them for winter. Some people despair over what to do with all the leaves that fall, but others are only too keen to garner all they can.

### Planting, Moving and Autumn Care

Even though leaves are changing colour and dropping, roots continue to grow actively until the ground finally freezes. This makes autumn an ideal time to plant and transplant trees and shrubs, and plants can often be obtained at bargain prices as nurseries clear their stock. In very windy situations, it is better to plant in the spring when there is a full growing season ahead; constant wind rock in the autumn can make it difficult for roots to establish properly before the ground freezes. This is particularly important for evergreens, which may suffer from winter drying. You can still take advantage of autumn sales, however, and put plants in cold storage for the winter then plant in the spring. Evergreens can be kept in an unheated garage with natural light; use a cold room for deciduous stock.

Autumn is a good time to plant hardy shrub roses. Because they are usually planted about 4 inches (10 cm) deeper than they grew in the nursery, there is little likelihood of frost heave. Even without a mulch, they seem to survive winter with great ease. If any are of borderline hardiness, they are more likely to be lost in their second or a subsequent winter. Less hardy roses and shrubs tend to continue growing very late in the season; this results in a lot of winter dieback, but when they are dug for shipping and planting in the autumn, they are forced into dormancy and so survive winter quite nicely.

If there is a woody plant in the garden that leans, and no amount of staking and roping straightens it, the best course is to replant. Simply dig up the plant and set it back in the ground in an upright position.

When moving any plant, dig out as far as the drip line on small trees and shrubs, and 1 foot (30 cm) out from the trunk for every 1 inch (2.5 cm) of trunk diameter on large trees (See page 143). These measures will clearly indicate which plants can actually be moved without bringing in heavy equipment. Manure should not be added to planting holes as it will stimulate top growth late in the season, but compost and other organic matter can be worked in. Top dress with manure in the spring. Add a deep layer of mulch over the root zone after planting is completed to give the roots time to get established before the ground freezes (see pages 413 and 417).

On fine autumn days, you might be tempted to do some pruning. Only dead, damaged and diseased wood should be pruned at this time of year, however. Extra branches left in place over the winter help to shelter the remaining wood.

It is still all right to take hardwood cuttings—this can continue throughout the autumn (see pages 366-368). Hardy shrub roses seem to respond well to this type of propagation, but they can also be started from seed. Remove the seeds from the hips and then stratify them to break dormancy, treating them in the same way as tree seeds (see page 369).

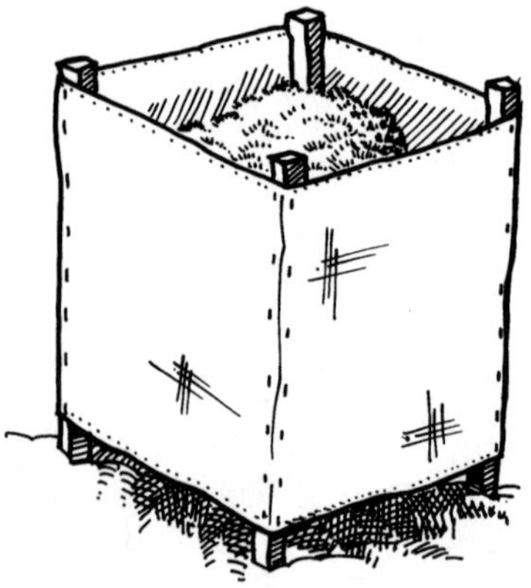

Protect shrubs with burlap barriers.

## Winter Protection of Evergreens

Evergreens are planted mainly to provide winter interest in the garden. It makes no sense, then, to wrap them up so that they look miserable and forlorn through the winter. Wrapping in plastic is a sure way to kill evergreens, both coniferous and broad leaved. Wrapping them in burlap is not much better. There is a better way to protect evergreens that have turned brown in previous winters.

Firstly, plant Oregon grape (*Mahonia*), rhododendrons, hollies and other broad-leaved evergreens where they will be sheltered from winter winds. It also helps to plant them where they receive sun in the summer and shade in the winter.

Secondly, make sure that the soil is well watered before the ground freezes solid. Even with plenty of rain, shrubs next to the house will need additional water to compensate for the drier conditions. Put a 1 foot (30 cm) thick mulch over the soil around the plant at least as far out as the drip line *before* the ground freezes. Use straw, oak leaves, pine needles or any organic material which will not compact easily. Mature, well established plants seem to get by without this treatment, although there are occasional winters that will harm even those plants.

Thirdly, if some form of protection from winter wind is required, erect a screen on the windy side of the plant. Use three wooden stakes with burlap stretched between them to form a wall that will filter the wind, or use four stakes to form an open-topped box. Make both as tall or taller than the plant. This might be necessary for any evergreen's first winter or two. Some gardeners erect burlap walls on the street side of hedges to help protect them from salt spray, snow blowers and street clearing.

Evergreens often lose a lot of needles at this time of year. There is no cause for concern as long as those dropping are the older needles, towards the centre of the tree or shrub. Each needle lives about two years, and this loss is natural. The same applies to broad-leaved evergreens. Some rhododendrons change colour in the autumn, but this is nothing to worry about. PJM rhododendrons, for example, turn a rusty, mahogany colour as cold weather approaches. Some conifers and heathers change colour, too, but this only enhances their appearance in the winter.

## Propagation of Broad-Leaved Evergreens

Rhododendrons and other broad-leaved evergreens can be started from cuttings, with or without a heel (see Table JUL-4, page 282). Use wood that grew this year, with three to four sets of leaves. The length of the cutting depends on the type of plant. Cut just below a leaf, or take a 1 inch (2.5 cm) heel of last year's wood along with the cutting. Remove the lower leaves, and shorten long leaves by cutting off up to one-half of each leaf. Wound the cutting at the bottom end by scraping the bark on each side (on only one side for lepidotes). Dip the end in a fungicide and then in a strong rooting hormone. Insert the cuttings carefully in a moist mix of peat moss and perlite or sand. Keep the cuttings misted using a propagation unit (see pages 442-443), or put the cuttings, pot and all, in a plastic bag. Keep them in light shade out of direct sunlight. Heathers can be started the same way, with cuttings which are only a couple of inches (5 cm) long.

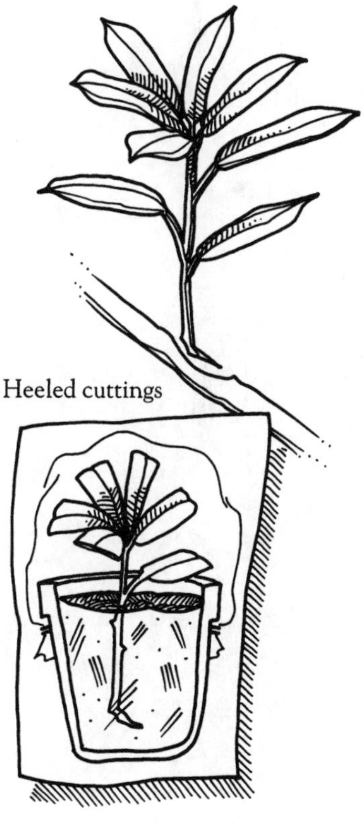


## Care of Other Propagated Pieces

Softwood and semi-hardwood cuttings that were rooted earlier in the season, young shrub and tree seedlings, root cuttings, rooted plants from air layering and other plant pieces propagated during the current year, need extra protection to see them through their first winter. If they are still in pots, they can be transplanted to larger pots (see page 281 for the appropriate pot shape and pot sizes) and put into cold storage for the winter. Use a cold room, a very cool basement or an unheated garage that hovers close to freezing in the winter. They will not require light because they will be dormant. Some gardeners in zones 5 and 6 have luck plunging young plants in pots in the ground outdoors, pot and all, but this is not always successful even with cold frame protection. Removing plants from their pots and planting them directly in the ground in cold frames at this time of year is also risky.

All pieces, including those plunged in the ground in pots, must be mulched deeply after the ground is frozen (see November, page 413). A 2 inch (5 cm) layer of light soil, sand or very old sawdust should be spread first, soon after the first really hard frost of the season.

One-year-old cuttings and seedlings that were planted in nursery beds in the spring, and any other young woody plants in the nursery, should have an inch (2.5 cm) of soil added over the bed before the ground freezes. One-year-old cuttings still in their pots are best transplanted to larger pots (see page 281) and moved into cold storage for the winter.

## The Great Leaf Bonanza

Deciduous trees drop leaves in quantities that wise gardeners bless. Rather than raking them up and bagging them neatly to await garbage day, set them aside to add in layers to the compost pile next summer. They will break down faster if mixed with kitchen and garden refuse and not left in a pile by themselves. Some bags can be left open for the winter, where snow and rain can get at the leaves and pack them down. In the spring, these thick mats of leaves can be laid down over layers of newspaper to form a superb, natural looking mulch around shrubs, trees and soft fruits.

Save oak leaves for winter mulching. They do not pack down and thus trap and hold insulating air throughout the winter. Other leaves can be shredded and used to top up mulch in flower beds and any other permanent plantings, or can be bagged and kept dry for use next spring when mulching materials are in demand. A lawn mower run back and forth over piles of dry leaves does a superb shredding job. If mowing and leaf chopping are combined and the results caught in the mower bag, an excellent mulching material is created for use this fall after weeding and fall clean-up is completed. Put it around plants, not on top of them.

Leaves can also be heaped in a pile and left to break down naturally over the next couple of years. The process will be faster if they are shredded first or if grass clippings and other green plant materials are mixed in. Either way, the resultant leaf mould is excellent for mulching or as a soil amendment.

Leaves can also just be left where they drop. This forms the most natural mulch under trees and shrubs and bypasses the compost route. Leaves that lay in heavy, wet clumps on the lawn, or over the crowns of herbs and perennial flowers, should be removed as the underlying plants may be killed. Clean leaves out of roof gutters so that water runs freely off the roof.

## Lawns

Even though top growth has slowed down, grass roots and side shoots are growing actively at this point. There is still time to dethatch (see page 325), aerate (see page 371), top dress (see page 371), and repair bumps and hollows (see page 325) if this has not been done yet. It is too late for seeding, but sods can certainly be laid.

Join beds, to form fewer, larger beds with no isolated pieces, to make mowing easier.

### Reducing Lawn Area

To reduce maintenance time, run grassed areas into each other for faster mowing. Try to replace corners with curves so that the mower does not have to be backed up and manoeuvred around difficult places. As new beds are dug for flowers, fruits and vegetables, try to join up existing, isolated beds to form fewer, larger beds. There will be fewer edges to trim around beds, and the awkwardness of mowing between boundaries will be reduced.

Consider replacing grass with low care ground cover plants or low growing shrubs wherever there are isolated bits of lawn, such as between a sidewalk and the house, or between the driveway and sidewalk (see page 201 for ground cover plants to grow in shade). Slopes that are steeper than one unit high for each three units wide should be planted with ground covers, not grass, so that unsafe mowing is avoided.

If eliminating grass in areas where a mulch will be laid, such as around trees and shrubs, there is no need for deep digging. The sod can be stripped and composted, or simply dug and turned upside down. Cover the area with pads of newspaper and a mulch such as shredded bark, leaf mats, pine needles or leaf mould.

If the slope is more than 1:3 (rise :run) then plant with a no mow ground cover.

### Laying Sod

Starting a lawn by laying sod is quicker and easier but more expensive than starting from seed. Even if most of the lawn is seeded, sods are better for

### Green Thumb Tip

Order all of the sod you need at one time. Various lots may have slightly different grass mixtures, which show up as different colours in the lawn. Order about 5% more than what is needed to cover the area to allow for wastage. Good sod will be a uniform thicknes of 1 to 1½ inches (2.5 to 4 cm), it will look recently cut, and plenty of white roots will be present. When a sod is lifted at one end with both hands and gently shaken, it should not tear or fall apart. Inspect the sod as soon as it is delivered and complain immediately if it is not satisfactory. Sod can stay in rolls if it will be laid within three days, but unroll it and put it in a shady spot if it will be laid more than three days after delivery. Water the sod if necessary.

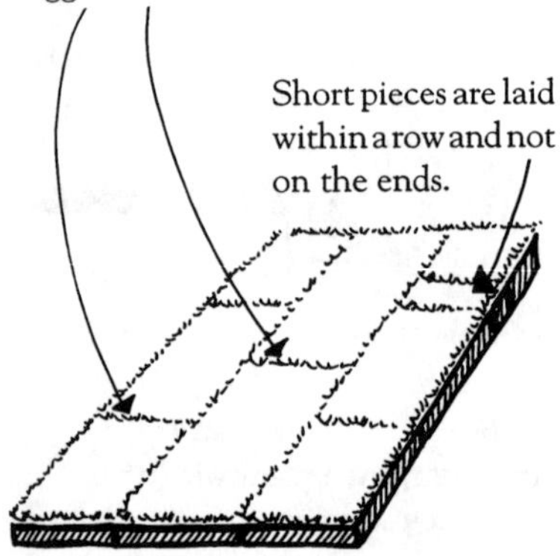


covering slopes. Keep in mind, though, that steep slopes and small, isolated areas should be planted with some other ground cover.

Sod can still be laid after it is too late to seed—up to four weeks before the ground freezes. The area to be sodded should have 5 inches (12 cm) or more of good topsoil in place, with manure or compost mixed in. This will save endless problems in later years with weeds and stress during dry times. Alternatively, prepare the ground as already described above (pages 375-381), plant cover crops to improve the soil, and lay sod next spring. The last step before sodding is to rake and level the soil as described on page 324 for seeded lawns.

Lay the first row closest to the pile of sods, and gently tamp it into place with a board that has a long stick or handle attached. If there are hollows or bumps, add or take away soil from underneath. Pull out weeds as each piece is laid, but complain to the supplier if there are a lot of weeds and good quality sod was ordered. Lay down boards to avoid walking on the sods and the unsodded ground. If using a wheelbarrrow to move sods, lay down boards for the wheel to run on.

Lay the second row of sods firmly abutted against the first row, with the joins staggered much like bricklaying. If only a short piece is needed at the end of a row, move a larger piece into the end position and use a small piece to fill in the gap further in from the edge.

When you have finished laying, use a board to mark straight edges, or a hose to mark curved edges, and trim off the excess sod. Use a lawn rake or broom to brush a mixture of soil, sand and fine compost into the cracks. Water the new lawn thoroughly once a week until the sodded edges have knit together, unless there is at least 1 inch (2.5 cm) of rain each week.

With autumn sodding there may not be any need to mow, but lawns sodded in the spring should not be mowed until the sod edges have knit and the grass is 3 to 4 inches (8 to 10 cm) high. Encourage grasses to send out runners by not letting sodded or seeded lawns flower.

## Mower Maintenance

Keep mowing established lawns as long as the grass continues to grow— this may be until November in mild areas. The last cut of the season can be a bit shorter than usual to compensate for any very late growth.

Dig out the owner's manual for your mower before making the last cut, and follow the directions for end of season care. Maintenance shops make much of their profit from people who neglect to give their mowers this attention.

Run four-stroke, gasoline powered mowers until the engine warms up, say fifteen to twenty minutes, and then keep it running until all of the gasoline is used up, perhaps running it back and forth over piles of leaves if all of the grass is cut.

If there is a fuel filter, clean or replace it. Next, disconnect the spark plug. Put the mower on blocks and reach underneath to open the crank case drain plug. All of the dirty oil must be removed. Warming the engine stirs up all the impurities; these are drained out with the oil. Clean or replace the air filter. Clean the spark plug, and adjust the width of the plug gap. This is no small feat! Check the owner's manual for the correct width.

Turn the mower on its side (regardless of the type), and scrub out the gubbins and old grass clippings with a stiff brush and soapy water. Dry the area and then wipe all of the exposed metal parts with an oily rag or spray with WD-40. Remove the blade and sharpen it. If you do not know how to balance it, have the blade sharpened professionally. Complete the oil change by adding a really good quality oil, usually half a litre of 10W-40, and reconnect the spark plug. The final step is to store the machine in a perfectly dry place for the winter.

## Indoor Worm Compost

Autumn is a good time to start indoor composting with worms. Indoor composts enable gardeners to deal with kitchen scraps and to keep composting all winter. It will provide a rich soil amendment for indoors or outdoors and a generous supply of compost worms next spring to get the outdoor pile off to an early start before the outdoor worm population has had time to build up.

A simple composting system can be set up using a large plastic garbage bin or other large container. Compost worms need a minimum temperature of 45°F (7°C) to multiply, so put the bin where it will not get cold. Before filling the bin, arrange some sort of drip tray underneath to collect any seepage; this can be used as liquid manure.

Drill a ring of 1/2 to 3/4 inch (12 to 18 mm) drainage holes in the sides of the bin at 3 and 6 inches (7 and 15 cm) from the bottom. Fill it to a depth of 6 inches (15 cm) with gravel and sand, and add 3 inches (7 cm) of water in the bottom to provide humidity for the worms. Lay shingles or thin boards on top of the sand/gravel with 1/2 inch (12 mm) gaps between them that allow liquids to pass through. Fill one-fifth of the remaining space in the garbage bin with peat moss—this serves as the worms' permanent home. Drill a dozen tiny holes in the lid for ventilation. Now add about a 6 inch (15 cm) layer of kitchen waste and a supply of compost worms.

The worms prefer a slightly alkaline environment, so do not include citrus peels, vinegary foods or pickles in the compost. As worms need protein, include scraps of meat, bread, cheese and waste milk—things which should not go in the outdoor pile (although bread is okay). Be careful to start with small quantities of scraps until the worm population builds up. Eggshells tend not to be broken down, but they can be kept in a separate, open container. Crush them finely when the container is full, and use them outdoors in the spring as a soil amendment (see page 378) and to help manage slugs (see page 170).

When adding kitchen waste, either add it in a different place each week, leaving it on the surface or burying it in a hole, or spread it over the entire surface and mix it in to help aerate the mass. It may be necessary to sprinkle the pile occasionally with water to keep things moist, but it is more likely that too much moisture will build up. If the mixture threatens to become slimy, add sprinklings of peat moss or dry leaves with each fresh load of kitchen waste. Try to avoid adding liquids to the collecting container in the kitchen.

After three to six months, the compost and worm castings will have a dark colour and uniform texture and be ready to harvest. To separate out the worms, dig out the contents and make little piles. The worms, in an effort to get away from the light, will go to the middle of each of these piles, thereby doing the sorting themselves. The compost can be mixed with potting soil for indoor plants, or used in the outdoor garden as a soil amendment. An indoor compost started this month or next should give a finished product and a large supply of worms by next April or May, in time for the gardening season.

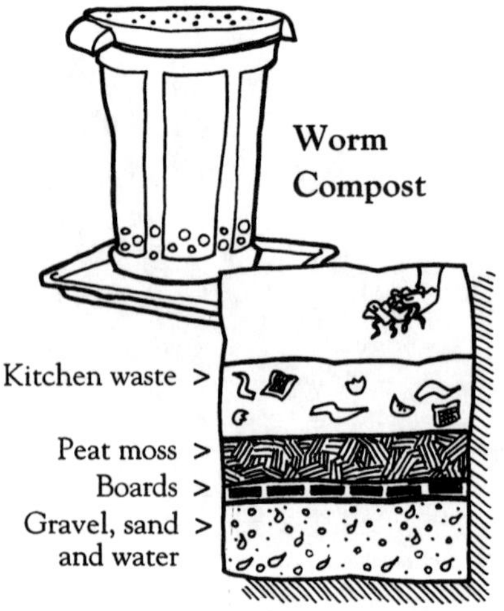


### Worms

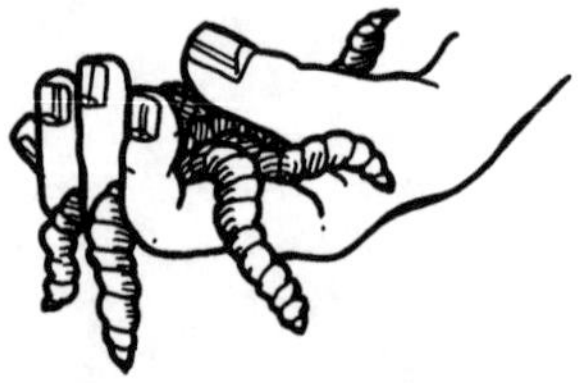

Rather than going to the expense of purchasing worms, dig through an established compost pile and bring out clumps of the slim, red wrigglers (do not use earthworms). One can simply add shovelfuls of compost, but this method may bring in other creatures along with the worms, some of which may be worm predators.

## Indoor Gardening

### Soil Sterilization

If soil is to be used indoors in the winter, it is a good idea to dig up some now. The easiest way to make sure it is free of weed seeds and disease organisms, or at least to reduce them, is to solarize the soil in the heat of summer (see page 299).

The other method is to heat the soil in an oven—a very stinky but very effective process. Bake it in a foil covered pan until a meat thermometer in the soil reaches the temperature needed to eliminate a particular problem.

| | |
|---|---|
| nematodes | 120°F (50°C) |
| damping off disease | 130°F (55°C) |
| most disease causing bacteria and fungi | 150°F (65°C) |
| soil insects, most plant viruses | 160°F (70°C) |
| most weed seeds | 175°F (80°C) |
| stubborn weeds and viruses | 212°F (100°C) |

A 1% solution of acetic acid (vinegar), applied at a rate of 1/2 gallon per square foot (2.5 l/1000 cm$^2$) will kill various fungi. None of these measures are effective if the pots used are not also clean. Soaking them in a 10% bleach solution for a few minutes will kill troublesome disease organisms.

## Vegetables and Herbs

It is easy to grow fresh greens in the winter in a cool greenhouse or other growing area, and butterhead and leaf lettuces, spinach and watercress make quick growth. Bolting is not a problem because days are getting shorter. Provide additional lighting for twelve hours each day. Fruiting crops of tomatoes, peppers, eggplants, summer squash, zucchini and cucumbers do better with fourteen to sixteen hours. Blossoms are likely to abort if there are less than nine and a half hours of light each day. They prefer warm temperatures, ideally 70 to 75°F (21 to 24°C) during the day and no less than 65°F (18°C) at night.

To start watercress, germinate the seeds on moist paper towel; it takes about ten days at 60°F (15°C). Plant the sprouted seeds in pots or flats filled with one-third soil and two-thirds sand, or with a regular potting soil mixed with perlite or sand. Space plants 8 inches (20 cm) apart, and keep the medium very wet, either by watering regularly or by setting the containers in water.

Bunching onions, scallions, summer savory and chervil can be started and will help perk up winter cooking. Sow other annual herbs (see Table JAN-2, page 24) if none were started in the previous two months, or sow extra for gifts to give in the winter. Grow basil in warm conditions in individual pots, but pinch out the growing tips regularly to produce bushy plants. The little spicy globe basil makes an attractive pot plant. Sow dill and coriander densely in pots and harvest them while young. A little extra lighting at the end of the day may be in order as days get shorter, but do not exceed fourteen hours.

Moulds and mildews can be a problem, so make sure that plants are not overwatered. Ventilation is important, too, not just on sunny days but on cloudy days as well. The upper part of the greenhouse or sunroom will be warmest, so put tomatoes and other heat loving plants there. Continue to fertilize plants regularly.

### Fruits

Prune back grapes and passion fruit after the leaves drop (see November, pages 428-430). This will allow more light into the greenhouse, which will also increase the temperature. Strawberry plants can be brought in from outdoors. To initiate flowering, they need cold temperatures followed by warmth, or a period of long nights and short days followed by a period of short nights and long days. Everbearing and dayneutral strawberries do not require a temperature or light regime to induce flowering.

After three or four weeks of nights below 50°F (10°C) outdoors, dig up two-year-old strawberry plants and pot them up: one plant per 5 inch (125 mm) pot; two per 8 inch (200 mm); three per 10 inch (250 mm); or four per 12 inch (300 mm) pot. Alternatively, plant them in a strawberry barrel (see page 438). Keep the plants warm, between 63 and 72°F (17 and 22°C). If it is difficult to provide this regime, give them less than twelve hours of light each day for three or four weeks, and then provide extra lighting for a total of sixteen to eighteen hours each day until flower buds show.

Rhubarb crowns can be planted in a large box of moist sand or soil. Keep them cool for two to three months, either outdoors or in a cold room or by delaying digging, and then expose them to warmth and light. Instead of digging up an entire clump, slice out a substantial chunk from the crown while it is still in the ground, and fill in the hole with enriched soil.

Cycle of Growth

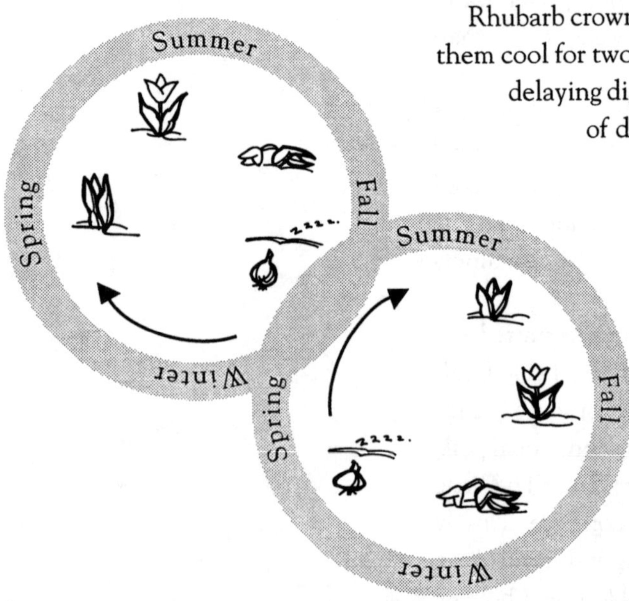


### Flowers

Bulbs have a regular cycle of growth that includes leafing and flowering (or sometimes flowering before leafing), gradual dieback and then dormancy. Whether it is daffodils, amaryllis or gloxinia, the cycle is the same. What varies is the time of year that each event occurs. Dormancy may occur in the summer or winter, depending on the type of "bulb," it can be lengthened or shortened, or it may be shifted to a different time of year, but the pattern of leafing and flowering, followed by gradual dieback and then dormancy, remains constant. Throughout the period of growth and flowering, it is important to water and fertilize regularly. Keep this up for as long as the leaves are green. During dormancy, watering is reduced or discontinued and fertilizing stopped.

### *Forcing spring bulbs*

Daffodils naturally leaf out and flower in the spring, die back in the summer, and then become dormant. The timing of this cycle can be manipulated so that they flower indoors in February instead of outdoors in May. Shorten the dormant period and start them into growth in the winter instead of the spring. Shifting the natural cycle is called "forcing," although "gentle encouragement" is a more accurate term.

Division 4 daffodil, ruffled variety.

To force daffodils and other spring bulbs, plant them in moist potting soil with extra sand or perlite added. Use pots which are at least 4 inches (10 cm) deep with drainage holes and water the bulbs after planting. Allow them to drain well, and then put the pots somewhere cold, either in a refrigerator, cold room, or unheated basement or garage. The temperature should be less than 48°F (9°C), but above freezing. Bulbs do not have to be kept in the dark, as was once thought. Some gardeners in milder zones find that digging a pit outdoors, putting the pots in it and piling straw or oak leaves on top to insulate the bulbs works well.

Keep them cold for three months or more while their roots grow and leaves start up, watering only enough to keep them damp (usually this is not necessary if they are buried in a pit), and then expose them gradually to warmth and increased light to simulate spring and bring them into flower (see January, page 31). Hold some pots in cold storage for longer and bring them out at different times to extend the season of bloom over many weeks. Continue to water and fertilize until the leaves turn yellow, then plant them outdoors. Plant them either right away in the spring, or leave them dry in their pots and plant them outdoors in the autumn. They will not force well another year.

Use both regular sized and miniature daffodils, and try division 4 and division 8 daffodils—the bi-coloured and ruffled ones. Some bulbs, such as the latter two types, do not stand up to outdoor weather very well or are too tender to survive most winters, but they are lovely indoors. Other bulbs suitable for forcing include crocuses (Dutch hybrids force better than species), early flowering tulips, Siberian squill, hyacinth, grape hyacinth, snowdrops, allium and glory-of-the-snow.

Position bulbs in the pots so that they are packed in close but not touching each other. Plant allium with the tips just showing and daffodils with the necks just peeking above the soil line. Most other bulbs are covered with a thin layer of soil. Ten to twelve crocuses or other tiny bulbs can be planted in a 5 or 6 inch (125 or 150 mm) pot. Plant only one kind of bulb in each pot and only one colour. Yellow crocuses, for example, bloom before purple ones, so mixing them makes a poor showing in a pot.

Six daffodils can be packed into a 6 inch (150 mm) pot by planting in two layers; fill a pot one-third full of potting mix, plant three bulbs, add more potting mix, position three more bulbs in a staggered layer above the first, and finish filling the pot so that there is a 1/2 to 1 inch (12 to 25 mm) gap between the top of the soil and the rim of the pot. The tips of the second layer of bulbs should be peeking through the soil.

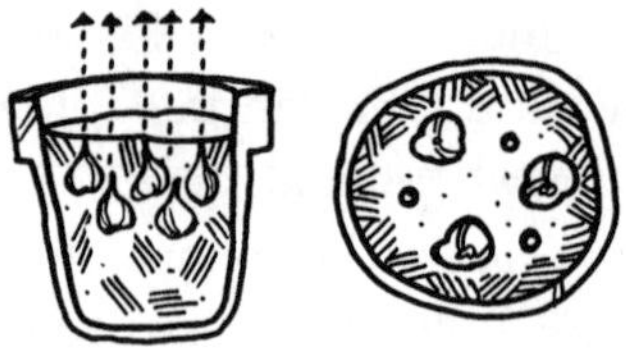

side view top view

Use only early varieties of tulips, and plant them so that the flat side of the bulb faces the outside of the pot. The first leaf grows on that side and will hang gracefully over the pot's rim. The number of bulbs per pot depends on the type of tulip and size of bulb. For single early tulips, plant six bulbs per 5 inch (125 mm) pot; nine per 6 inch (150 mm) pot, or twelve per 7 inch (175 mm) pot. Plant double earlies and Darwin hybrids six bulbs per 6 inch (150 mm) pot; eight per 7 inch (175 mm) pot, or eleven per 8 inch (200 mm) pot. The bulbs of species tulips are quite small, so more can be planted per pot.

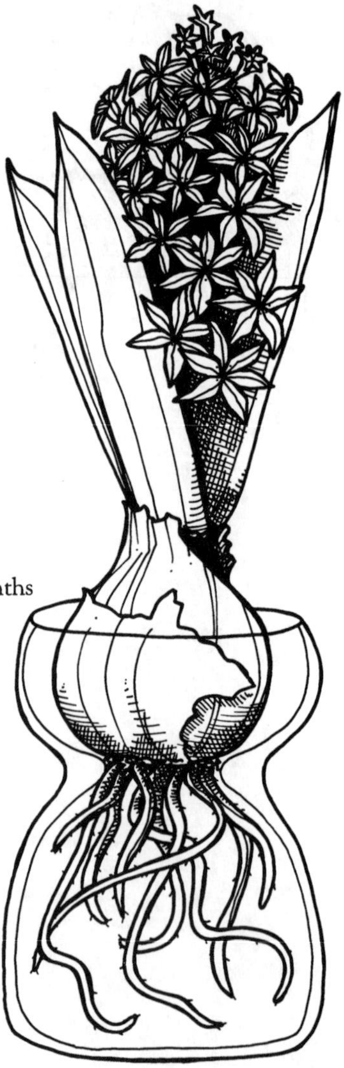

Hyacinths can be grown over water.

Triumph tulips can also be forced, but do not bring them into warmth and light until February. As a general guideline, bring the bulbs out of cold storage for forcing in roughly the order that they bloom—minor bulbs first, followed by early tulips, daffodils and late tulips.

Chinese sacred lily, paperwhite narcissus and soleil d'or do not require a period of cold. They seem to do better, however, if given ten days in cold storage as this gives the roots a chance to start growing before the leaves emerge. They will bloom about three weeks after planting if the temperature is warm, but will take up to six weeks in a cool environment. The growth will be stockier and less likely to fall over, however, in cool conditions.

To extend the season of flowering, hold several bulbs in the refrigerator before planting them, or pot up the bulbs but leave them in cold storage for several weeks. Use wide pots so that they are less likely to tip over when the flowers are fully grown.

Hyacinth bulbs can be purchased pre-cooled. They can be potted up and grown on the cool side, but ten to fourteen days in cold storage after planting seems to produce better subsequent growth. They will bloom approximately four weeks after being put in warmth and light. Some people like to grow them in water. To do this, brush the base of the bulb clean and set it in a narrow glass or special hyacinth glass in the dark. The water level should be just below the base of the bulb, and the roots will grow into the water. Move it into the light when the flower cluster is about 3 inches (7.5 cm) tall.

### Growing lilies

True lilies, not daylilies, can also be potted up, stored cold, and then forced into bloom; or they can be potted up, given no cold storage, but grown cool as soon as they have been potted. Alternatively, the bulbs can be held in the refrigerator for up to eight weeks and then planted and grown cool, or held eight weeks, planted, and put in cold storage for a couple of months. All of this is done to manipulate the season of dormancy so that the plants bloom when wanted (see Table DEC-2, page 461). Be extremely careful not to overwater the bulbs at any stage because they are prone to rot.

The length of time it takes for lilies to come into bloom depends on the type and time of year, and on whether they are grown in warm or cool conditions. The large oriental lilies can easily take four to five and a half months from potting to blooming. *Lilium speciosum rubrum* and trumpet lilies, planted around October 1, could be in bloom for Valentine's Day. The small Asiatic lilies force much faster; planted in mid November, an early asiatic could bloom for Valentine's. The length of time to bloom, however, varies with the time of year (see Table DEC-2, page 461). Since lily bulbs can be shipped in both the spring and fall, there is plenty of scope for manipulating dormancy and flowering.

Most lilies are best planted in deep pots with 2 or 3 inches (5 to 8 cm) of soil over the top of each bulb (see Table MAR/APR-3, page 88). This will help to hold the stem upright and will allow rooting along the underground portion of stem. An exception is Madonna lily (*L. candidum*), which is covered with only 1 inch (2.5 cm) of soil. Unlike spring flowering bulbs, lilies can be grown in the same pot for several years. They will settle into a natural rhythm of blooming, although they can still be manipulated somewhat by holding them in cold storage for longer periods than is natural.

### *Warm flowers*

Dormant armaryllis bulbs are often sold at this time of year. They take seven to nine weeks to come into bloom after being planted, so can be ready for December celebrations. Their natural bloom time, however, is in the spring. Untangle the roots and soak them in tepid water for three to four hours. Then plant each bulb in a pot 1 inch (2.5 cm) larger than the bulb, with the upper one-third of the bulb exposed above the soil line, and water lightly. If the house is very cool, keep the amaryllis somewhere warm or put it in a hot box as used for starting seeds (see page 20).

If an amaryllis that has been growing through the summer is now fading and the leaves are turning yellow, stop fertilizing and watering it. This will allow the bulb to rest for two or three months. If the leaves are still green, however, simply remove any yellowed leaves. Continue to water sparingly, but stop fertilizing for three months. Top dress with fresh soil and start it carefully into growth in late winter (see January, page 30).

Gradually dry off and store such bulbs as crinum, agapanthus, ismene, haemanthus and nerine after they have finished flowering (see Table OCT/NOV-1, pages 390-391). Alternatively, nerine can also be started into growth at this time of year.

Roses growing indoors can be encouraged into dormancy by eliminating fertilizer applications and reducing watering. Except for climbers, cut roses back to 8 to 10 inches (20 to 25 cm) above the soil level and put them into cold storage. Alternatively, if you want roses in December, cut plants back lightly, keep them in bright sunlight, and continue to water and fertilize them.

As hydrangeas lose their leaves, cut them back to the lowest pair of buds on each stem, and then give them a complete rest at 45 to 50°F (7 to 10°C) until January.

### *Cool flowers*

There is another group of bulbs that can be planted in the autumn and brought immediately into growth, but at cool temperatures. These include freesia, babiana, ixia and sparaxis—all members of the iris family. Miniature gladiolus (G. *nanus*, G. *byzantinus*) belongs to the same family, but it is best planted in December, January or February.

Most of these bulbs are sold only in the spring, to bloom in the summer and fall. By holding them dry through the spring and summer, however, their period of dormancy is greatly extended. They can then be planted anytime from August to December to bloom in the winter and spring (see Table DEC-2, page 461). Many species from the iris family are best potted in porous, somewhat sandy soil and watered only moderately until growth starts. Initially, keep the potted bulbs cool (45°F or 7°C) and in bright light until the middle of November, then bring them into warmth. If brown tips on the foliage develop, the plants were either overwatered in the early stages of growth, or underwatered in the late stages. Fertilize three or four times, three weeks apart, until colour shows on the buds. Gradually reduce watering after flowering is over and allow the foliage to die back completely. The bulbs can be stored bone dry in their pots and forced again, but they benefit from being replanted in fresh soil every year or two.

Another member of the iris family, the large flowered Dutch irises, are beautiful grown in pots. Keep the potted bulbs cold for two months (unless pre-cooled bulbs were purchased), then grow them cool at 45 to 50°F (7 to 10°C) until flower buds begin to develop. At that point, grow them warmer at around 55°F (12°C). They must not be allowed to dry out as this will cause the buds to fail to develop properly, and the temperature in the later stages must not drop below 50 to 55°F (10 to 12°C) at night or the flowers will be blasted (fail to open properly and wither). They seem to take a long time to come into flower, but the exotic blooms are worth the wait.

Bulbs from other families which can be planted in the autumn include oxalis, cape cowslip or Lachenalia, alstroemeria, ranunculus and anemone. Plant ranunculus with the claw ends down, 2 inches (5 cm) deep, 3 or 4 per 6 inch (150 mm) pan. Anemones should be crowded into pans of light soil to develop a good root system, which leads to the production of flower buds. Be careful not to overwater as they may develop crown rot or fail to bloom. Grow these cool at first, around 50°F (10°C), but raise the temperature somewhat in January. Anemones can also be started from root cuttings (see page 137). Keep a sharp eye out for aphids on anemones.

There are a myriad of annual flowers to choose from for winter and early spring bloom indoors. Most should be planted by now, but winter flowering sweet peas, annual chrysanthemums and forget-me-nots can be sown again. Most annual flowers grow well in cool temperatures. They do best with plenty of light but not too much water or fertilizer as both can cause legginess. Primroses also grow well in cool temperatures, but they should not be seeded after October 15; if planted later little or no bloom will result. Combining seeding and potting up of various types of bulbs will produce a wealth of colour in the coming months.

Month-by-Month

# November

- put on winter mulch
- dig perennials for forcing
- propagate conifers
- get tetanus shot
- prune greenhouse grapes
- start fern spores

- feed birds!

- clean tools

- protect fruit trees and others for winter

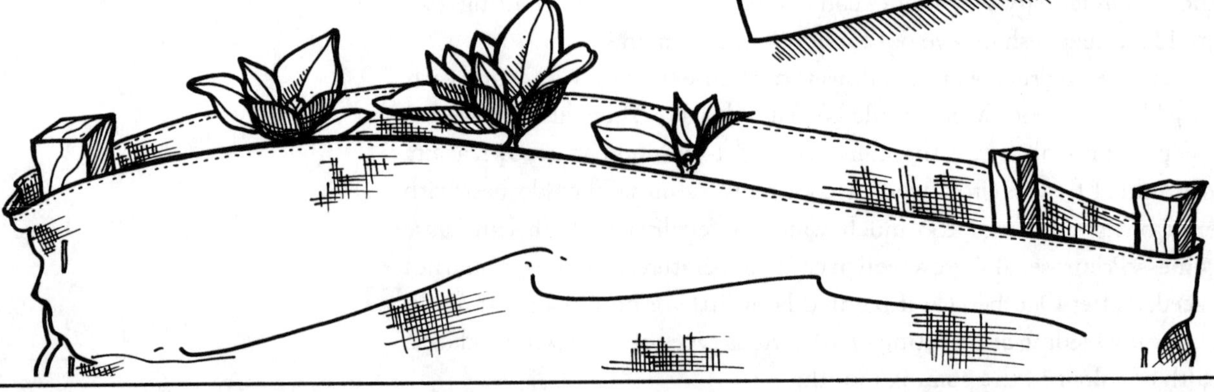

In many regions plants stop growing this month, although in mild areas some late season vegetables and a few brave flowers may persist. There are plenty of odd jobs which will keep you busy, however, such as winter mulching, tool care, evergreen propagation and, of course, indoor plant care.

# November

### Hardy

*A plant is said to be hardy if it remains alive in a nursery long enough to be sold.*

*Beard and McKie*

## Winter Survival

Six factors which affect the winter survival of plants—both woody and herbaceous (those that die back to ground level)—are the level of plant dormancy when winter arrives, sudden temperature changes, soil drainage, exposure to wind, frost heave and premature dormancy changes in plants during mild spells in the winter.

A mild autumn followed by a sudden severe drop in temperature will sometimes kill plants immediately because they have not had time to become fully dormant. Those that continued to grow late into the season—generally non-native and borderline hardy plants—are particularly vulnerable. This is usually mistaken for midwinter damage because the results are not apparent until the following growing season. During the winter, a sudden drop in temperature is also harder on plants than a gradual drop; plants in full dormancy are better able to withstand severe cold than the same plants earlier or later in the dormant period.

Various types of plants are likely to die over the winter if the soil in which they grow drains poorly. Puddles of ice over their roots or over their crowns spell almost certain death. Harsh winter winds, when combined with low winter temperatures, can lower the chill factor to temperatures below the hardiness level of certain plants. By protecting plants from wind or placing them in a sheltered position, their chances of survival will be increased. Keep the ground frozen with mulches during midwinter thaws in regions where snow cover is unreliable to prevent frost heave and reduce the chance of plants coming out of dormancy too soon. If conditions are harsh or variable in your area, you may want to select reliably hardy plants at the outset to increase the winter survival rate in your garden.

## Mulching

Any trees, shrubs, lilies and spring blooming bulbs that were planted late can be mulched before the ground freezes; this will give plants more time to grow roots. Evergreens also benefit from early mulching. Mulch can be laid to slow the freezing of the soil if planting of any of these things is going to be delayed for some reason.

### Preventive Measure

Mulching is done either before the ground is frozen—to keep the ground from freezing for a while longer—or after the ground is frozen—to keep it frozen throughout winter and early spring. Mulching immediately after the ground freezes also helps to protect the crowns and roots of plants from severely cold temperatures. This application is not essential in regions where the snow arrives early, is deep and lasts throughout winter.

Candidates for mulching after the ground is frozen include tender perennial flowers and herbs, strawberries and plants experiencing their first winter. It is essential that plants be fully dormant before mulch is laid over their crowns. This stage will be reached in November in most regions, but will occur as late as December in mild areas.

Mulching after the ground is frozen helps in three ways. Firstly, repeated freezing and thawing can cause young plants with small root systems to be heaved out of the ground. A mulch helps to keep the ground frozen, thus eliminating the freeze-thaw cycle. Secondly, plants may start to come out of dormancy during a mild spell if they are not mulched. They are then less able to withstand the rigours of the subsequent cold spell. Thirdly, mulch acts as a layer of insulation, keeping the temperature of the roots of woody and herbaceous plants, and the crowns and flower buds of herbaceous plants, higher than the surrounding air temperature. This difference may be essential if plants are only marginally hardy.

## Vegetables

Cold frame and row cover vegetables, and those covered with a light mulch before the ground freezes, often survive several weeks longer than their unprotected counterparts, even after the first snowfalls. There are some vegetables that survive late into the season in mild zones without protection. Kale, broccoli, Brussels sprouts, cabbage, Swiss chard and corn salad, for example, sit quite happily through cold spells, although they do not do much, if any, active growing—it is more a case of outdoor cold storage.

Corn salad can be frozen solid in the garden and still be useable. Cut it on a mild day at ground level, or pick a few leaves. A light mulch of straw will enable it to survive even later into the season. Cook frozen Brussels sprouts immediately after picking them.

Hardy bunching onions and young asparagus crowns can be mulched deeply after the ground is frozen, particularly if snow cover is unreliable in your region.

Before the ground freezes, harvest parsnips and other root crops and store them in the cold room. Mulch them deeply before the ground freezes if they are to be kept in the garden over the winter (see page 342). Inspect other vegetables that were stored in the cold room earlier in the season. Anything showing signs of spoilage should be removed immediately and either used up or discarded. Recondition chilled potatoes at room temperature for two weeks to take away the sweet taste (see page 345).

### Preventive Measure

The best winter mulches are those that trap air. Apply a 12 inch (30 cm) deep layer of straw, salt hay or oak leaves, or multiple layers of coniferous branches or anything else that will not become sodden or compacted. Coarsely shredded bark will do and pine needles are fine if enough are available. The final, settled depth should cover the crown of herbaceous plants with a minimum of 2 inches (5 cm) of mulch, but thicker is better. Clay soils which heave need a thicker mulch than lighter soils. Hay is usually too full of weed seeds to make a good mulch, and fine hay will sometimes pack down to a dense mat with no insulating value. A wide area of mulching is more effective than little patches of mulch applied here and there.

If cold frames are used for additional protection, put them in place before the winter mulch is applied. Wooden lath lids are preferable over glass as frames are less likely to overheat on sunny days or cave in under heavy snow loads. Frames with glass lids should face north or be put in a shaded location; those in the sun may need to be opened a crack on sunny days to prevent overheating. Additional insulation a foot (30 cm) thick can be piled around the outside of the frame, or mound soil all around the sides.

## Herbs

Any borderline hardy herbs should either be dug up and potted to spend the winter indoors, or mulched after the ground freezes. If puddles linger around them after a rain, use some soil from another part of the garden to change basins into slight mounds. If a lot of soil has to be added to keep water from collecting around a plant, make a note to dig it up and replant it at a higher level next spring. At the time of replanting, work in organic matter to raise the level of the bed and improve drainage.

Sodden masses of leaves should be removed from the crowns of plants, but they can be left lying between and among the plants. Leaves which are compacted are not effective as a winter mulch, so add a thick layer of oak leaves (which do not compact) or straw over the bed, covering the crowns of the plants as well, after the ground has frozen. This is only necessary if herb plants have been lost in previous winters. To keep the mulch from blowing away, lay chicken wire or a few coniferous branches on top, perhaps after the Christmas tree is dismantled.

## Flowers

Perennial flowers require much the same care as herbs. Removing sodden masses of leaves from the crowns of perennials and making sure that drainage is good will help to ensure their survival. Make sure that there is no standing water around rockery plants because they require excellent drainage, particularly in the winter. Even a few sodden leaves on the crown of a tiny rockery gem can spell disaster. After the plants are dormant, sift sand over the crowns and resting buds to cover them in a mound shape so that snow and rain cannot sit on the crowns and cause rotting.

### Mulching

It is not necessary to mulch perennial flowers for the winter unless plants are very small or recently planted, or the snow cover is unreliable and the ground is subject to repeated freezing and thawing. Some perennials, however, are barely hardy or more vulnerable to uneven winter temperatures. The following could be mulched no matter what the winters are like (see page 413):

anemone
asarum (wild ginger)
balloon flower
centranthus
chrysanthemum
coral bells (*Heuchera*)
delphinium
epimedium (barrenwort)
eupatorium (Joe-Pye weed)
evening primrose (*Oenothera*)
false sunflower (*Heliopsis*)
geranium (cranesbill)
golden glow (*Helianthus*)
helleborus
hosta
incarvillia
lamb's ear (*Stachys*)
lobelia
meadow rue (*Thalictrum*)
mullein (*Verbascum*)
shasta daisy
stoke's aster (*Stokesia*)
tradescantia (spiderwort)
tufted pansy (*Viola cornuta*)
veronica

Mullein (*Verbascum*) is barely hardy in zone 6 but, as long as the first planting has time to set seed, self sown seedlings will bloom the following year and mullein will appear fairly reliably each spring. The true *Geranium* (cranesbill) is not the same as the garden geranium (*Pelargonium*); the garden geranium must be taken indoors each autumn.

If there are any perennials about which you are particularly concerned, the safest route is to pot them up and place them in cold storage for the winter (see page 387). When they are planted out next spring, they will have a whole season to get well established before they face their first winter outdoors.

Young perennials and those started from seeds, root cuttings, bulbils or bulblets, must be given extra protection if they are to be left in a nursery bed over the winter. After they have been covered with more soil (see page 388), apply a deep winter mulch after the ground has frozen (see page 413). A cold frame will provide extra protection and can be filled with oak leaves or straw as soon as the ground is frozen. Additional insulation can be piled around the outside. As a variation on this theme, place smaller inverted boxes, weighted down with a stone, over individual plants. This does not provide as reliable protection as a cold frame, but it certainly reduces wind chill over the crown of the plant.

Tender roses that were hilled with soil or buried in trenches (see page 388) should be thickly mulched as soon as the ground freezes. Cut back long canes (except climbers) to just above the soil mound. Do not worry about careful pruning cuts, just make them slanted so that moisture runs off easily. Proper thinning and shaping can take place in the spring when the soil is removed.

Spring blooming bulbs and lilies, planted recently, seem to do better if a deep mulch is applied just before the ground freezes. If applied too soon, the bulbs may be stimulated to send up their leaves. If a few leaves do emerge, just throw on some soil from another part of the garden; the bulbs should still bloom next spring. Adding a mulch after the ground freezes is also helpful as it protects the bulbs somewhat from the extreme cold of winter.

### Green Thumb Tip

Even with autumn care, some perennials will be lost over the winter. Nature has a way of ensuring survival, however, and a careful search around the dead parent in the late spring or early summer will sometimes reveal a few seedlings. Be careful not to disturb the soil; keep it well weeded with only the lightest of mulches until any seeds produced have had a chance to germinate. This cycle seems to happen fairly frequently with rockery plants.

## Forcing Perennials

If it is altogether too late to plant bulbs in your area, they should be potted up, put in cold storage, and either forced indoors for winter bloom (see page 405) or held in cold storage until the pots can be put outdoors in the spring. Window boxes full of spring bulbs can also be stored this way. If stored unplanted over the winter, both lilies and spring blooming bulbs will shrivel up and dry out, losing all of their vitality and failing utterly if subsequently planted. After forcing indoors, they can be planted outside permanently.

For fun, dig up a few perennials for winter forcing indoors and plant them in good-sized pots. Because they will have already been exposed to freezing temperatures and weeks of chilly weather, many will have entered dormancy. Store them cold for another month or two, either in a cold room or unheated basement, and then bring them into warmth and light for a burst of bloom in the late winter or early spring (see January, page 32).

• Perennials that force well include:

| | | |
|---|---|---|
| arabis | catnip | Jacob's ladder |
| armeria | columbine | pansy |
| aubrieta | creeping phlox | primrose |
| basket-of-gold alyssum | dianthus | veronica |
| bleeding hearts | garden phlox | violet |
| camassia | hepatica | Virginia bluebells |

• Other perennials which can be forced but must first have the flower stalks removed during the summer as soon as they appear include:

| | | |
|---|---|---|
| achillea (yarrow) | delphinium | shasta daisy |
| butterfly weed | gaillardia | wallflower |
| coreopsis | | |

Coreopsis and gaillardia require extra lighting in the winter to encourage blooming (see January, page 32).

Perennials that can be propagated from basal shoots or division (see Table APR/MAY-3, page 138), can also be dug up after they have died back in the autumn, treated to cold as described above, brought into light and warmth in January, and then cut up and divided—or basal shoots can be taken—in order to start several new plants. These can be planted out next spring and will grow and bloom at the normal times in the garden, gaining several months in propagation and growing time.

## Window Boxes

Some gardeners bring window boxes in for the winter, but this is not necessary. These and other planters can be left in place and brightened up with branches of evergreens and berried plants. Any of the conifers look attractive, especially if there are a few cones to add to the arrangement (see pages 454-455 for other possibilities).

If your planters and boxes are not decorated, now is a good time to empty them of soil, scrub them clean, and repaint or refinish them. Emptying them also ensures that you aerate the soil and enrich it with compost or fertilizer before plants are put in next spring.

Window boxes require a lot of attention between winter maintenance and summer watering and care. Consequently, they are sometimes the first thing that gardeners no longer bother with when they wish to reduce the amount of time and energy they spend on the garden. Older gardeners, however, often find them more manageable than many other gardening chores.

## *Fruiting Plants and Woody Ornamentals*

### *Winter Protection and Planting*

Strawberries and young rhubarb plants should be mulched with a thick layer of straw after the plants have become dormant and the ground has frozen—that is usually sufficient care to see them through any winter. The preparation of woody plants for the rigours ahead, however, is a little trickier.

Ideally, fruiting trees and shrubs were planted where they are not exposed to harsh winter winds, and where the soil drains well. Ideally, also, the autumn was dry enough and cool enough to allow plants to become dormant. Those that continued to grow late in the season and did not harden off properly will have dead branch tips next spring. This is not necessarily a problem, however. Raspberries routinely have dead branch tips each spring; these are easily pruned off without any harm to the plant or its fruit production. High humidity also decreases hardiness, particularly in the spring. Although there is nothing gardeners can do about the weather, some measures can be taken to help fruiting trees and shrubs survive winter.

Coming out of dormancy too soon is probably the greatest cause of winterkill. It is more likely to happen to plants that are borderline hardy because they only need a little mild spell in the winter. Really hardy plants require longer periods of warm weather to come out of dormancy, so they probably do not require any special attention. Early bloomers, however (see February, page 43), may have their flowers destroyed by spring frosts; keeping them dormant a little longer in the spring may help prevent this.

Sometimes nothing can be done to avert winterkill, but mulching may reduce the number of losses. By keeping the soil frozen until spring has truly arrived, there is less chance that the plants will come out of dormancy prematurely. In addition, a thick mulch will protect roots from extreme cold during periods when there is no snow on the ground. It is often the roots that die over the winter, not the woody portion above ground. After the ground has frozen, apply a thick mulch (see page 413) at least as far out as the drip line, to ensure that the root zone is completely covered.

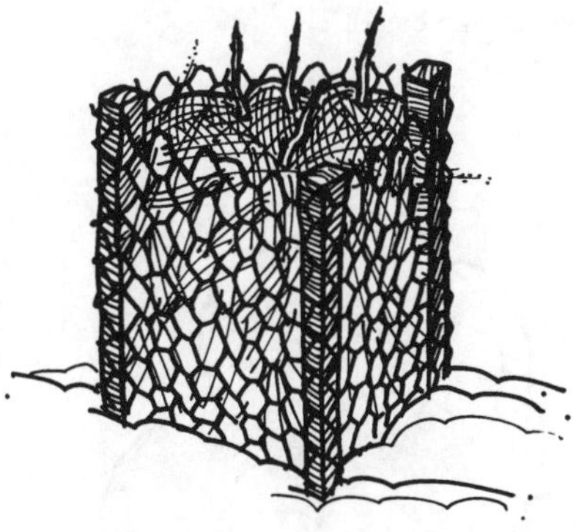

Place chicken wire around shrubs and fill with oak leaves or straw.

Protecting the above-ground portion from winter wind may also help small fruiting and ornamental shrubs to survive. Plants can be protected by a burlap barrier on the windy side, or be boxed in with burlap, as for evergreens (see page 396). Protection can also be provided by putting a ring of chicken wire around the plant and then filling the space with oak leaves or straw. All that this does is create a dead air space around the plant, but this may be enough to keep the temperature above the killing level. If planted in a sheltered position, plants are less in need of this extra fuss each fall. There are always a few gardeners, however, who want to grow tender specimens and who are willing to go to great lengths to push plants to the limits of their hardiness.

Mulch around shrubs in containers.

Potted trees can be placed in a bag of leaves.

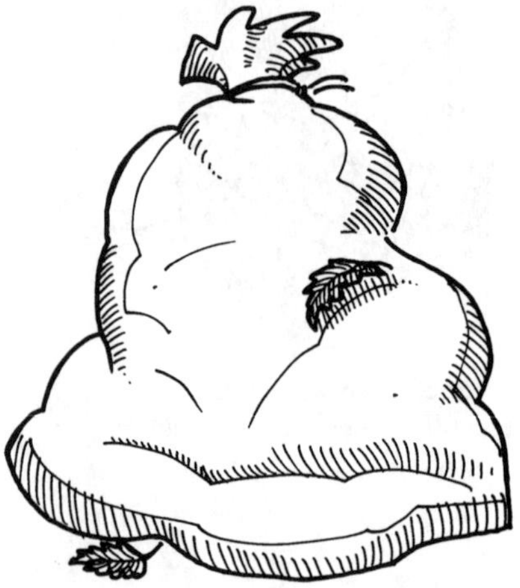

Young woody plant material that was propagated during the last few months needs extra protection. All of it should first be covered with a layer of light soil after hard frosts arrive (see page 388). After the ground is frozen, spread straw, oak leaves or other winter mulching material over the bed, being careful not to break any branches. If a cold frame is used, fill it with mulch and then pile additional mulch or soil around the outside, if extra protection is desired.

Coniferous and broad-leaved evergreens may require protection and preparation for winter, but this must be done before the ground freezes (see October/November, page 396).

Trees, shrubs and vines in containers may need attention before winter sets in. Those in containers that are insulated around the sides on the inside (see page 439) may survive the winter outdoors. Those in uninsulated containers, however, are much more vulnerable to freezing injury or death because the soil freezes quickly from all sides, rather than gradually from the top down. Depending on the situation, it may be possible to insulate containers from the outside. Pile a 1 foot (30 cm) thick mulch all around the sides and on top, or mound soil around the sides. If they are small enough, put each container inside a large bag of dry leaves. If you cannot insulate those containers with plants, move them indoors into cold storage, or put them in an unheated garage. Coniferous and broad-leaved evergreens require light during the day, but deciduous plants can be stored in darkness if required.

If bare root deciduous stock is being planted late in the season, water the plants in well, and immediately apply a deep, thick mulch to keep the ground from freezing for a little longer. Plants with poorly established root systems suffer the most from frost heave in the spring; the thick mulch will also help to reduce this problem. On the other hand, bare root plants which have been set out late in the season without any special care often survive remarkably well, probably because the plant was fully dormant to begin with. Frost heave is still a problem, however, where winter snow cover is unreliable.

## *Propagation of Coniferous Evergreens*

After some good hard frosts, yew, juniper and cedar (*Thuja*) can be propagated from cuttings. This can even be done in December. Take spruce cuttings in February or March from juvenile branches.

Take 10 inch (25 cm) long cuttings of this year's growth, with a heel of old wood at the bottom (see page 281). Remove the lower branchlets, wash the cutting in fungicide, dip the end in rooting hormone, and insert the bare portion of the stem in a mixture of sand and peat moss. Now comes the tricky part. It is essential that the cuttings have bottom heat (72°F or 22°C), but that their tops be kept cool and humid, in light but out of direct sunshine. Use a heating cable buried in sand, or some other source of localized heat, and either mist the tops frequently, or set up a propagation unit (see pages 442-443).

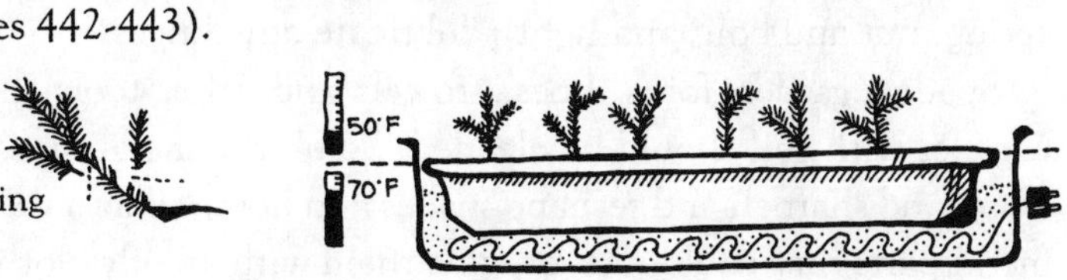


Coniferous cutting with heel.

Leave the cuttings in their pots for a long time after rooting has occurred to give the brittle roots time to toughen up before being transplanted to larger pots. It may well be next autumn or the following spring before they are ready to be moved to other quarters (see pages 397-398).

## *Fertilizing and Pruning Trees*

The late autumn is the best time to fertilize trees in stressful urban conditions. They should be fertilized regularly, before the ground freezes. Healthy trees in natural situations, not stressed by drought, injury and salt, and with a natural mulch of their own dropped leaves each year, do not require this attention. Top dressing with rotted manure or compost each spring eliminates the need for autumn fertilizing for all trees.

Each year, if it is required, use about 5 pounds of 10-6-4 or 7-7-7 fertilizer per inch diameter of the trunk at knee height (890 g/cm). Use a crowbar to punch 8 to 12 inch (20 to 30 cm) deep holes, 18 inches (45 cm) apart, just outside the drip line of the tree. For large trees, punch another circle of holes 2 to 3 feet (60 to 90 cm) inside the first circle. Pour an equal amount of fertilizer into each hole, fill with soil, and then water the ground thoroughly.

Trees such as maples that ooze a lot of sap when they are pruned in the spring, can be pruned in November (see page 90 for the method). There is a greater risk of bud injury from winter temperatures if pruning is done during December, January or February.

### *Preventive Measure*

Salt is very hard on plants, particularly along urban streets (see page 33 for preventive measures). Evergreens in particular often suffer badly from salt spray and road salt. Some of the more resistant types include: Colorado spruce, red cedar (eastern red juniper), European larch, yew, Austrian pine, jack pine, Japanese black pine and false cypress (*Chamaecyparis*). When noting winter wind patterns and other factors in order to plan next year's planting, remember that all evergreens exposed to salt fare better if planted on a raised berm. This will keep salt runoff from flooding their roots and reduce the chance of salt spray browning their lower needles. Salt in the soil is best dealt with in early spring (see April/May, page 151).

## Tool, Gardener and Soil Care

### Tool Care

When everything is done that can be done outdoors, take time to clean, sharpen and repair your gardening tools. Hedge clippers, secateurs, pruning saws, lawn mower blades and other cutting tools should be sharpened. Stores that provide this service are much less busy now than they will be in the spring. Wipe or spray parts which may rust with a rust inhibitor.

Use a pair of pliers and a screwdriver to dismantle shears, loppers and pole clippers. Start with the lock nut and bolt, and then remove the spring. Scrub each part with an old toothbrush dipped in kerosene to remove the sap which has built up over the season. Put multi-purpose grease on the spring, nut and bolt, and lightly lubricate any hinges.

Spades, garden forks, hoes, trowels and other tools that come into contact with soil should be cleaned. Scrub the metal surfaces with steel wool, and sharpen and reshape spades and hoes. Spray a rust inhibitor on metal parts that could rust, or wipe them with an oily cloth.

Clean wooden handles of all tools, lightly sand any rough spots, and then rub them down with pure linseed oil. If you prevent the handles from becoming brittle, they are less likely to break. A bright coloured paint could be applied instead of oil; this makes small tools easier to spot in the garden, but paint tends to flake and wear off rather readily. A plain wooden handle that is well rubbed with hand labour and linseed oil, and stored indoors when not in use, should remain smooth and splinter-free.

Scrub out wheelbarrows, clean up rusty areas, and either apply a rust inhibitor or paint with a good metal paint. Plastic wheelbarrows, of course, are easier to maintain in this regard. Check to see that the wheel is running smoothly, and pump up the tire now or in the spring.

To keep watering hoses in good condition, drain and store them before temperatures dip low enough to freeze the water in the hose. Use a bucket if necessary to water shrubs late in the season.

Store all tools and equipment in a dry place for the winter. The same applies to garden furniture. Make any repairs and paint or stain furniture before putting it into storage. Clean and fumigate bird houses, then leave them in place for the winter, or mount them as soon as possible in the late winter or early spring.

### Tetanus

Gardeners need to take care of themselves by keeping their tetanus immunizations up to date. Once every ten years is the recommended frequency, so check to see if you need an update. Gardeners are at risk because of the type of injury that can result in tetanus. Deep, dirty puncture wounds are the culprits—it is not unusual for gardeners to stab themselves with a dirty garden fork or sharp stone in the soil. Surface scratches are not a worry, but deep pricks or wounds that carry dirt into the body are definitely cause for concern.

According to a study done in Britain, it is older gardeners who are most at risk. This may be partly because they are less likely to have their tetanus shots up to date.

### Oil Spills

If you are faced with the misfortune of having heating oil spilled in your yard, there are several steps to take. Oil companies at fault are usually prepared to remove the contaminated soil, but make certain that they replace it with good quality topsoil. This is not done routinely so be sure to insist on it.

If any plants are affected, remove contaminated soil from the roots, rinse them off thoroughly using soapy water followed by clear water, and replant them immediately in clean soil. If oil was sprayed onto the above-ground portion of the plant, it too should be cleaned. Cleaning and replanting should also be paid for by the offending oil company, but some gardeners prefer to provide this care themselves. Come to an agreement with the company before taking any action, and state at the time of the accident that the affected plants are to be replaced if they fail to leaf out and make new growth next spring.

## Feeding Birds

There are two approaches that can be taken to feeding birds: either grow plants that provide food, and that perhaps provide cover and nesting sites as well, or set out food in the form of fat, grains, seeds and nuts at feeding stations.

### Plants for Food and Cover

The type of bird that is likely to be attracted depends in part on whether the garden is an opening in a fairly dense cover of trees and shrubs, or a bit

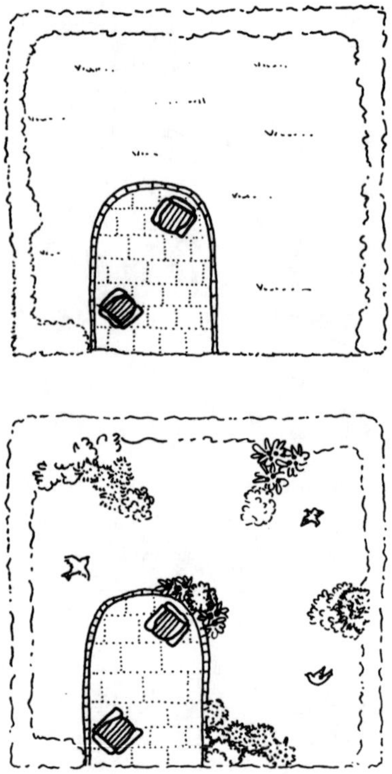

Birds are attracted to open areas and fingers of vegetation.

of woodland in an otherwise open area of lawns or meadows. Either situation is desirable because what birds seem to like best is a forest "edge." Ideally, there should be a transition zone between a flat, open area and trees. Shrubs in varying heights that bridge these two extremes are attractive both from a garden design point of view and from a bird's point of view. Steps can be taken in a wide open area or a full cover situation to provide a transition edge or improve an existing one. Even if there is next to no room to plant another tree or shrub, there may be room to fit in a vine or two to increase the variety of plants.

If the plant cover is very dense, and you are determined to attract birds, it might be wise to remove some of the shrubs and perhaps a tree or two. Driveways, parking spaces, decks, patios and seating areas also count as open space, as do any lawn areas, so it may be better to extend these areas by removing adjacent shrubs rather than creating entirely new open areas. An irregular edge with fingers of vegetation in the open area and fingers of openness creeping into the vegetation, are highly attractive.

If, on the other hand, more trees and shrubs can be planted to provide an island of plants in an otherwise open area, or to increase the irregularity of the forest edge, there is plenty to choose from. Native plants are the best choice, but there are some non-native plants that are also attractive to birds. Any one plant may provide only cover and a nesting site to some birds, only food to others, and both food, cover and a nesting site to yet other species.

### Focus on Plants

Some trees, shrubs and vines to consider for birds are:

*fruiting tree, shrub or vine

Ash
Beech
Birch
* Bittersweet
* Blackberry
* Blueberry
* Cherry
* Crabapple
* Currant
* Dogwood
* Elderberry
Elm
* Firethorn (*Pyracantha*)
* Grape
* Hardy Kiwi
* Hawthorn
Hemlock
* Holly
* Honeysuckle
Juniper
Maple
* Mountain Ash
* Mulberry
Oak
Pine
* Plum
* Raspberry
* Rose
* Russian Olive (*Eleagnus*)
* Saskatoon (Serviceberry, Indian Pear)
* Sea Buckthorn
Spruce
* Sumac
* Viburnum - many species
* Virginia Creeper
* Winterberry (*Ilex verticillata*)

### *Feeding Stations*

Many gardeners have a lot of success attracting birds to feeding stations. Unlike bird houses, which need to be firmly attached to something, feeders can hang and there can be many in even a small garden. It is necessary to make a commitment if birds are going to be fed through the winter as they come to rely on feeders. Food must be supplied frequently and in small amounts to reduce wastage and prevent spoilage.

There are three basic types of food that birds appreciate, depending on the species: fat, including meat and suet; grains; and seeds and nuts. In addition, a supply of grit (coarse sand or finely ground oyster shells) should be made available as this aids digestion. Some birds appreciate bits of fruit. Baked goods are not recommended because they spoil readily, but a bit of pie crust now and again is okay.

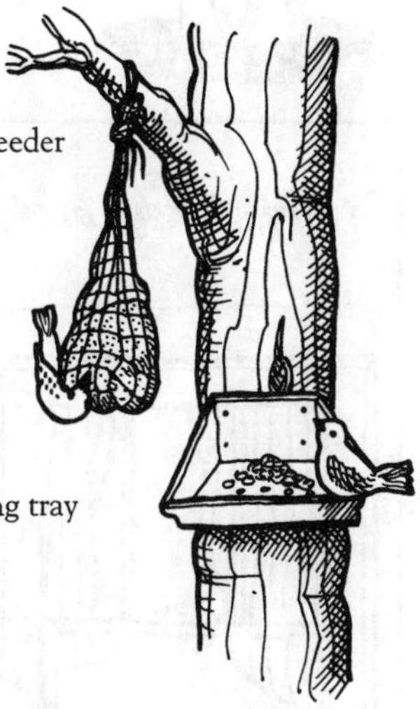


The type of feeder to use depends on the type of food being offered. To offer large chunks of suet, solidified bacon drippings, shortening and leftover cheese, use feeders that hang from trees and other locations. Locate them where they are visible from the house, although some shy birds will appreciate more hidden feeding places. Put the food in some sort of shallow container and cover the opening with plastic netting rather than wire mesh. A mesh bag will also work well. As the suet is eaten, the remaining amount should continue to press against the netting face. Woodpeckers can hang upside down from a suet feeder and obtain the suet from the underside. Since most other birds are unable to feed hanging upside down, this method prevents other birds from taking all the suet.

Tiny bits of meat and small pieces of suet, moist dog food, cheese and shortening can be put out on a stationary feeding tray. These foods are particularly important in the winter months as they provide more of the calories that birds need to keep warm. Use them with caution or avoid them altogether in the summer as they easily turn rancid or bad in the heat.

A variety of grains, seeds and nuts can also be spread out on feeding trays. Seed eating birds with thick, stubby bills are very adept at cracking seeds. Approximately half of the mix can be sunflower seeds, somewhat less millet, and the rest cracked corn and other grains and nuts such as whole oats, wheat, peanut pieces and canary seed. Walnuts and other large nuts can be cracked open and left out for the birds to clean. A variety of fresh, frozen or dried fruit cut into small pieces can also be offered on a tray, along with the other foods. When feeding birds that prefer just one type of seed, there will be less scratching and wastage if only one kind is presented.

Hopper type feeder

Instead of using trays, many people prefer to put expensive seeds and nuts, such as thistle seed, in hopper type feeders. They dispense the food as it is eaten, resulting in very little wastage. Hopper shapes vary and may be spherical, tubular or box shaped. Most styles have several holes from which birds can feed and they are usually hung rather than anchored firmly.

Bird fanciers have come up with many creative ways to offer food. Some use peanut butter to provide a high energy, fatty food, and mix in a variety of grains and seeds. Grains and seeds can also be mixed into melted suet. Pine cones stuffed with suet or peanut butter are fun for children to prepare for birds, and sunflower seeds can be stuck in as well. For more ideas, look to *How to Attract Birds* (Ortho Books, 1983), which is full of excellent information on all aspects of attracting birds.

**Here...birdy, birdy.**

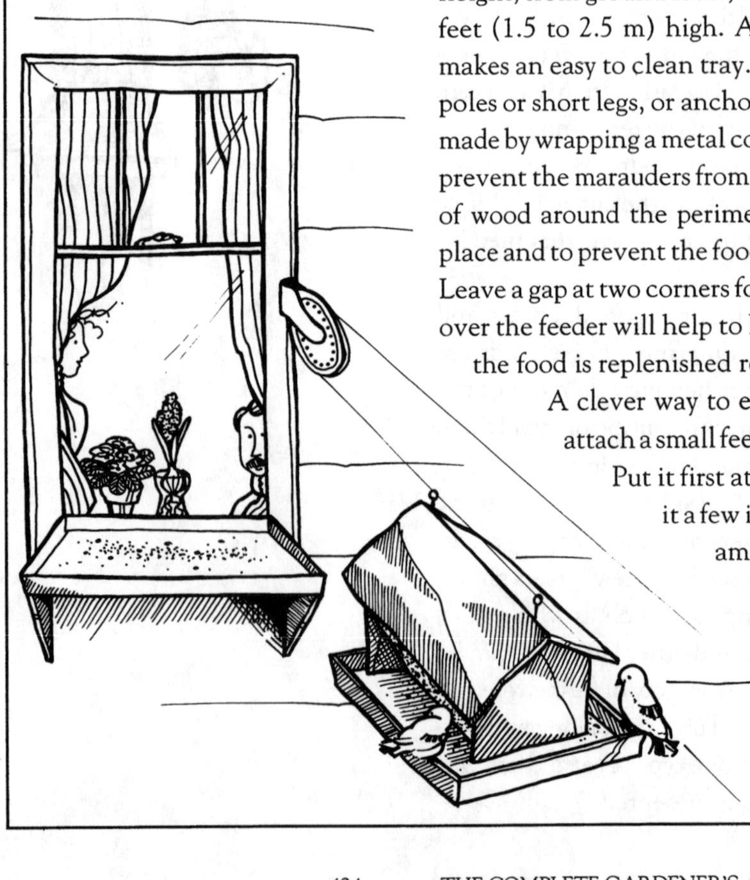

According to *How to Attract Birds* (Ortho Books, 1983), trays can be any height, from ground level, to a few inches (8 to 15 cm) above, to 5 to 8 feet (1.5 to 2.5 m) high. A piece of marine plywood at ground level makes an easy to clean tray. Higher platforms can be hung, attached to poles or short legs, or anchored to windowsills. A squirrel guard, simply made by wrapping a metal cone around a pole or post (see page 322), will prevent the marauders from taking all of the food. Attach a narrow strip of wood around the perimeter of any platform to provide a perching place and to prevent the food from spilling off and blowing away readily. Leave a gap at two corners for drainage and easier cleaning. A small roof over the feeder will help to keep the food dry, but this is not essential if the food is replenished regularly.

A clever way to encourage birds to a windowsill feeder is to attach a small feeder to a clothesline that runs to the window. Put it first at some distance from the window, and move it a few inches closer each day. Gradually reduce the amount of food in the moveable feeder and put more in the windowsill tray as the distance closes.

## *Indoor Gardening*

### *Microclimates*

Understanding the microclimates in a sunroom or greenhouse and taking advantage of different microclimates in the home can help you grow crops more effectively. The air next to the glass can be quite cool compared to further back, but the light is also best near the glass. Air becomes warmer behind the glass towards the roof, so plants needing plenty of light but tolerating different degrees of cold or warmth can be placed at different levels next to the glass. Plants that flower and produce fruit require the most light; hardy annual flowers could go lower down and tomatoes and peppers higher up. Alternatively, these temperature gradients can be reduced or eliminated, if desired, by cir-culating the air with a fan.

The coolest, shadiest place is on the floor. Dormant or resting foliage plants, such as ferns, could be placed there. Dormant tubers in pots can go under shelves, but place them on their sides so that water cannot drip into them. The middle of the sunroom, top to bottom and front to back, is bright and cool in the winter and is a good place for leafy crops such as lettuce, spinach and other greens. They might also be fine on the floor, provided it is not too shady.

Plants needing more warmth should be placed towards the back, but of course there is less light there. Again, it is warmer towards the top than the bottom of the room or greenhouse. Foliage plants are the most suitable for these positions and can be positioned according to their need for warmth.

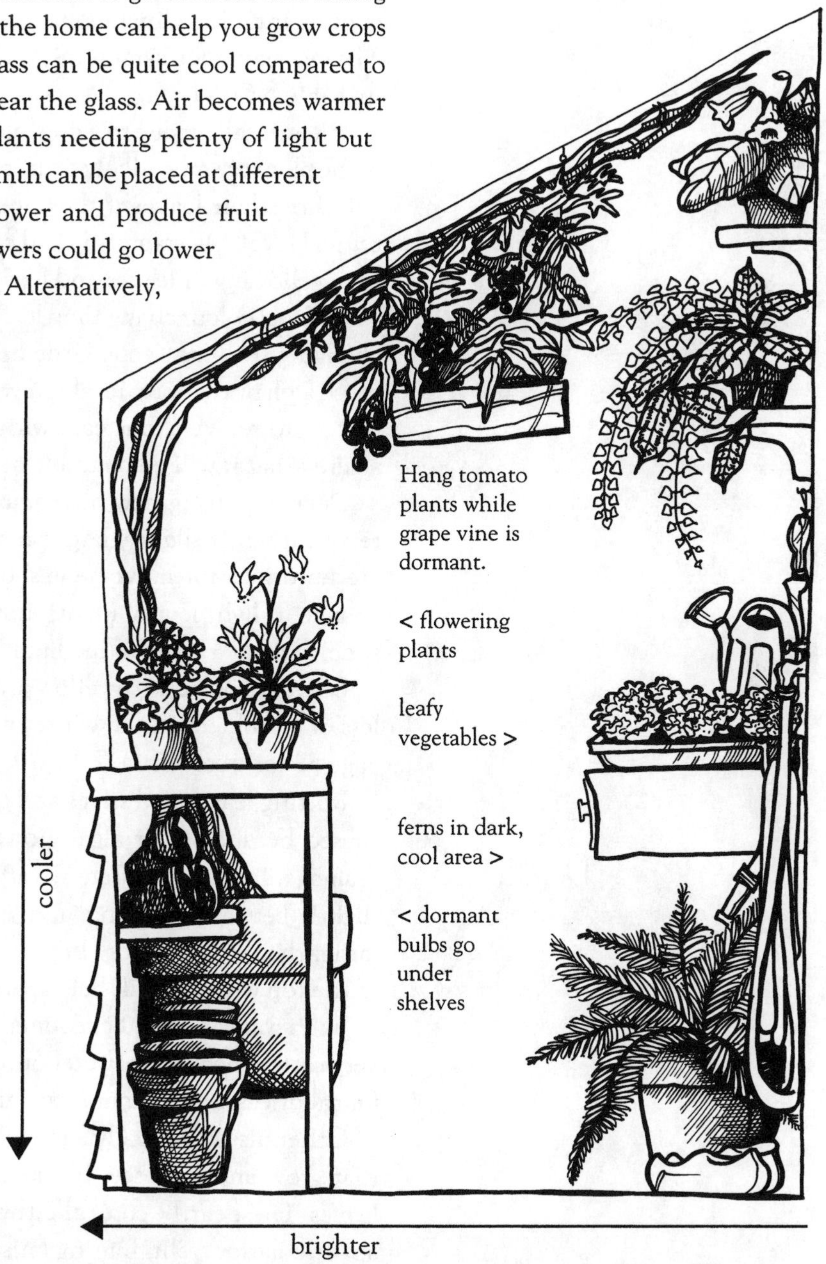

### *Cultural Problems*

Sometimes plants do not grow very well; the difficulties can usually be traced to the growing conditions, and mainly to temperature, light, water and fertilizer. Moving plants around within the greenhouse to take advantage of different microclimates may help with temperature and light problems. The most common symptoms, and their underlying causes, are summarized in Table NOV-1.

If leaves fall off due to aging, older leaves close to the bottom and centre of the plant are more likely to drop off than young leaves at the tips. Azaleas will drop their leaves if they are allowed to dry out even once below a critical level. Overwatering and cold draughts are often followed by an all-over yellowing of leaves and leaf drop.

Gradual colour change and leaf drop is probably a natural response to the changing seasons. Keeping the house cooler than usual in the winter may cause a plant that previously stayed green in the winter to go dormant. Do not try to revive it; instead, withhold fertilizer and water sparingly. Rest assured that it will come to life again in the spring.

Delay repotting new plants, unless it is obviously necessary, and then repot into only slightly larger containers (see pages 64-65). Weeping figs are notorious for movement shock—it is usually caused by too rapid a change in light levels. Plants moved from a shady place to a bright place should spend a week in medium light.

Leaves stippled with yellow are usually hosting red spider mites. This is less of a problem in the winter when growing conditions are cooler (see page 82 for treatment).

Rotting leaves and stems and green slime on pots or the soil surface are caused by diseases or algal growth brought on by overwatering or poor drainage. Immediately remove affected foliage. Let the soil surface dry out slightly between watering, and water from the bottom by filling a saucer, rather than from the top. Improving air circulation and filling pots almost to the top with soil will help reduce the incidence of fungal diseases.

Extra watering may be required on sunny days, even in the winter, but be very careful not to overwater during dull, overcast days. Rotting roots and fungal diseases are common at this time of year.

Other diseases usually show up as distinct spots on leaves, moist spots that grow and coalesce, blackening of the stem, or fuzzy mould on the leaves. These can be controlled by removing affected leaves, improving the air circulation, eliminating misting for several weeks, improving soil

## *Table NOV-1 Common Cultural Problems with Indoor Plants*

| Symptom | Possible Causes |
|---|---|
| • lower leaves dry up and fall off | normal aging, too little light, too much heat, underwatering |
| • sudden leaf fall without initial wilting or discolouration | sudden change in temperature or light, cold draft |
| • leaf fall preceded by overall yellowing | overwatering, cold draft |
| • leaf fall on new plants | shock from moving, change in light levels |
| • leaves that curl and fall | too little heat, cold drafts, overwatering |
| • change in leaf colour | paint fumes, cold temperatures |
| • wilting leaves | dryness, waterlogging, insect damage, dry air, too much heat, too much light (wilting occurs at noon), plant is pot-bound |
| • brown leaf tips, brown or yellow margins | bruising, dry air, too much or too little light, too much or too little heat, overfertilizing, potassium deficiency |
| • crisp, light brown spots on leaves | underwatering |
| • soft, dark brown spots on leaves | overwatering |
| • hard, brownish black spots on leaves | too much sun |
| • white or straw-coloured patches on leaves | water splashes, watering with cold water, aerosol damage, pest or disease problems |
| • spindly growth, pale small leaves | too much warmth and moisture for existing light levels, too little fertilizer |
| • plants grow slowly or not at all | overwatering, underfertilizing, too little light |
| • variegated or coloured leaves turn green | too little light or too much fertilizer |
| • lack of flowers | lack of maturity, too little light, overfertilizing, wrong day length |
| • flower buds drop | turning or moving plant, dry air, too little light, underwatering |
| • flowers last short time | dry air, too little light, too much heat, underwatering |
| • rotting leaves and stems, green slime on soil | overwatering, poor drainage |
| • distinct spots on leaves, moist spots that grow, blackening of stem, fuzzy mould on leaves | poor air circulation, excessive misting, poor soil drainage, overwatering, too warm or too cool |

drainage, keeping the soil a little drier, and either reducing or increasing the air temperature. In the winter it is usually cool temperatures that are the problem, but watch for overheating in some areas of the greenhouse or sunroom. Before reusing a pot that contained a diseased plant, scrub it clean and soak in a 10% bleach solution for a few minutes.

## Vegetables

The only things worth planting at this time of year are radishes, cress, and butterhead and looseleaf lettuce. Radishes mature in about six weeks, so they could be ready for midwinter celebrations. Watercress can be harvested by cutting back the plants to 4 inches (10 cm) above the soil line. New plants can be started from some of the cuttings, or sow more seed. In very cold greenhouses or where additional lighting is unavailable, late season seeding is usually not successful.

Continue to fertilize any plants that are still actively growing; in a cold greenhouse most plants will be growing very slowly, if at all. Maintain good air circulation to keep plants healthy and free of disease. Use a fan if necessary to keep the air moving gently. Crops take longer to reach maturity in the winter because of shorter days, lower light levels and cooler temperatures, but keep artificial light to around twelve hours a day to prevent bolting. Additional lighting is not necessary for broccoli, leeks and other plants that have been brought in from the garden. Tomatoes, peppers, eggplants, cucumbers, zucchini and summer squash do better with longer hours—up to sixteen per day—and they must have warm temperatures.

Mushrooms are grown in the dark. Purchase mushroom spawn and sprinkle it over rotted horse manure mixed with straw, or over rotted compost. Keep the mixture moist but not soggy, and between 50 and 75°F (10 and 24°C).

## Fruits

Prune grapes after they have dropped their leaves. Passion fruits can also be pruned, even if just some of the leaves turn yellow and drop off. This will help to let more light into the greenhouse or room, which will increase the temperature indoors.

Grapes that are grown on vertical supports indoors can either be pruned in any of the ways suggested for outdoor grapes (see pages 100-101), or more simply using one of two basic shapes, with variations. These latter shapes are particularly useful for grapes grown against glass. Anchor horizontal number

10 support wires spaced 8 to 10 inches (20 to 25 cm) apart. The grapes are trained behind these wires and the clusters of grapes will hang down.

The simplest form is a single central stem trained to whatever height is desired (and manageable!), with laterals (side branches) spaced on alternate sides of the stem. The first year, allow the young grape vine to grow as tall as possible, training it vertically. When the leaves fall, cut it back to the topmost good bud. The second year, continue to train it vertically, but now laterals will arise. Select alternate laterals spaced 15 to 18 inches (38 to 45 cm) apart and train them along the wires. Cut off any extra laterals flush with the stem. The central stem may be allowed to continue growing for another season, and more alternating laterals selected, if there is enough space. Otherwise, keep the top cut back to its maximum height. The established laterals are cut back every spring to two buds; the new growth on them produces the grapes.

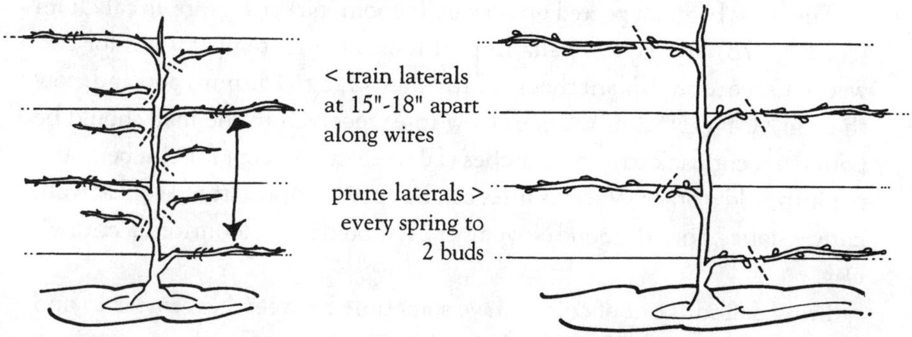


The second form has a very short central stem and two or more lateral arms, either directly opposite each other or all arising from the same side. Allow the central stem to grow upwards the first season. After the leaves fall, cut it back to the topmost good bud. The second year, when laterals arise, train the two or three chosen laterals, spaced 2 feet (60 cm) apart, along the wires. Cut back the central stem to just above the topmost lateral as soon as the laterals have been selected and are growing well. This will direct growth along the laterals. Cut out any extra laterals. When the leaves fall, cut back the lateral arms to the last strong bud so that their growth can continue for the full length of the allotted space. From each of these secondary laterals, train a system of tertiary laterals, spaced 15 to 18 inches (38 to 45 cm) apart, vertically. Each spring, cut back these tertiary laterals to two good buds and train the vigorous new growth, from which the grapes will arise, vertically behind the wires.

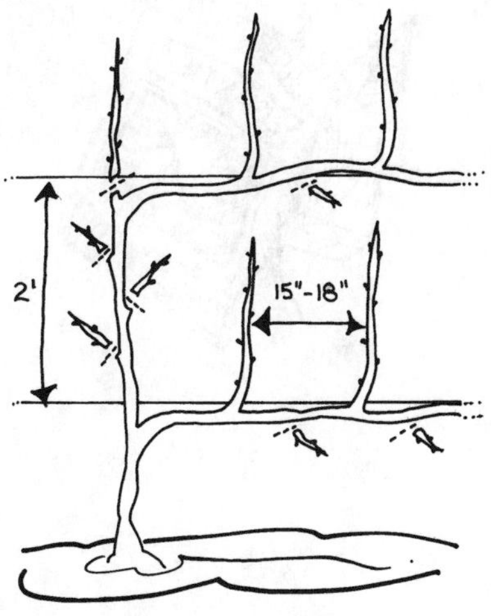


Tertiary laterals are trained vertically from one side.

Passion fruit can be trained in much the same way as grapes, but its growth is much more exhuberant. As with grapes, cut back passion fruit laterals to two buds on the previous year's growth. These branches can easily grow several yards (metres) in just a few months.

## Warm Flowers

There is a little seeding to do in November. Statice and petunia can be started, and lisianthus sown now will bloom in June to make a lovely, long lasting cut flower. Gerbera can be started from seed; it is rather expensive as it works out to about 50 cents per seed for a package of twenty. To ensure germination, leave the seed uncovered after sowing—light triggers germination—and keep the starting medium at 75°F (24°C), or as close to that as possible. It should germinate in eight to ten days, and then be grown partially shaded and cool at 60°F (15°C).

Tuberous begonia potted up now will bloom in April. Start up caladium (see page 78) and yellow calla in peat moss at high temperatures for two weeks. Once rooted, plant them in 5 to 6 inch (125 to 150 mm) pots and grow them at 60°F (15°C) or warmer. New roses received in the mail should be potted up, cut back to 8 to 10 inches (20 to 25 cm) except for climbers, and put into cold storage. Various lilies can be potted up and stored cold as well. Early Asiatics, potted around November 25, should be in bloom for Valentine's Day.

Bring daffodils out of cold storage sometime between November 15 and 25 and grow them at 55 to 60°F (12 to 15°C) to bloom for Christmas. Grow tulips a little warmer at 65°F (18°C). Take cuttings of the new growth on fuchsias, if they were cut back a couple of months ago; these will be large plants in full bloom by Mother's Day. Mist tuberose on sunny days, and fertilize it and other bulbs, such as amaryllis, once new growth starts.

Chinese sacred lily, soleil d'or, paperwhite narcissus and specially prepared hyacinths planted this month will be in bloom by late December (see page 406).

## Cool Flowers

As already suggested, certain garden perennials can be potted up, put into cold storage, and forced into growth in midwinter for an early bloom (see pages 415-416). Another little beauty is lily-of-the-valley. The pips can be dug and stored at 32°F (0°C) or less for a month or two, thawed out and planted—they will be in bloom in another three weeks. Alternatively, they can be dug up, planted 8 to 10 per 5 inch (125 mm) pot in a peat and sand mix, and stored cold until you are ready to force them. They will bloom five or six weeks after being brought into warmth.

You can still sow forget-me-not, gypsophila, larkspur, stock, candytuft and winter-flowering sweet pea (see Table DEC-2, p. 461). Sow snapdragons and calendula on November 15 and 30—the two sowings will bloom about a month apart. Provide extra light (see page 32) for flowers still not in bud. Be careful not to overwater anemones as they will not flower, and pot up rooted marguerite cuttings, more freesias, and larkspur seedlings. Fertilize freesias and other plants started into growth when you first notice new green foliage, and continue to fertilize any plants that are coming into bud. Be careful to supply freesias and others in the iris family with a steady, even supply of moisture without overwatering.

## Ferns from Spores

Growing ferns from spores is a slow but fascinating process. The spores (see page 310) are usually sown in the late winter, but they can be started earlier when there is not much else to be planted. It is essential to start with sterile containers and growing media.

To spread the spores evenly, hold them in a piece of folded paper over the surface of smoothed, moist moss and gently tap the hand holding the paper with the other hand. Do not cover the spores with more moss because they need light to germinate. Immediately replace the glass cover or plastic lid and put the brick, clay pot or plastic container in a bright but not sunny place, such as on a north facing windowsill or 5 to 10 inches (13 to 25 cm) under fluorescent lights. Do not remove the cover at any time. If the moss seems to be drying at the edges, add more cool or tepid water to the pan or plastic container holding the growing medium, or add it to the bottom if an aquarium is being used. Add a few drops of a damping off preventative to the water (see page 50).

After a month or two, a green film will show on the surface of the growing medium. These are the tiny prothallia, an intermediate stage from which the ferns will eventually grow. Some gardeners think the brick has been contaminated with moss and throw it out, but have patience. Continue to keep the moss moist, and after another three to four months, tiny ferns will be visible. It is fun to use a magnifying glass to keep watch over the development. At this stage, the glass should be lifted a crack at first and then gradually propped open more to increase the amount of drier air

### Green Thumb Tip

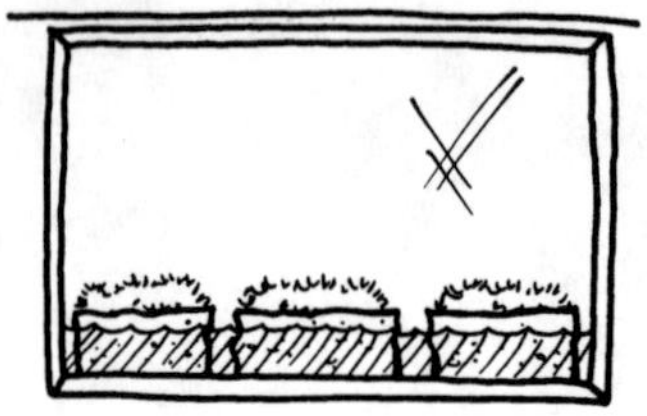

The traditional method for growing ferns from spores is to soak a brick in water for several hours, and then bake it for thirty minutes at 325°F (160°C). Clay pots can be sterilized the same way and filled as described below for plastic containers. Spread sterile, shredded sphagnum moss or peat moss on the brick and pass some through a seive to make the top layer very fine. Lay the brick in a pan with sides at least 1 inch (2.5 cm) higher than the top of the moss, and put hot water in the pan to below the level of the moss. Cover the pan with a sheet of glass until the brick has soaked up enough water to make the moss moist. A speedier way is to spread a sheet of newspaper over the moss and pour boiling water over it. The paper keeps the fine surface from being disturbed. Continue to add water to the pan until no more can be soaked up by the brick. Keep a sheet of glass or clear plastic over the top of the pot at all times to prevent contamination, or put several pots or bricks in an old aquarium with a glass lid on top.

Small, covered plastic refrigerator containers used for food storage also work well. Wash them in very hot water and fill them one-third full of wet vermiculite that has been rinsed with boiling water. Add boiling water to the same depth and then fill the rest of the container to within 1/2 inch (12 mm) of the top with seived sphagnum moss, peat moss or leaf mould, all of which have been moistened with boiling water. Place newspaper over the surface if more boiling water must be added. If using moss or leaf mould from outdoors, wet it and then sterilize it in the oven at 250°F (120°C) for one hour before moistening it with boiling water and adding it to the container. Smooth the surface and let it cool to room temperature before planting the spores, keeping it covered at all times.

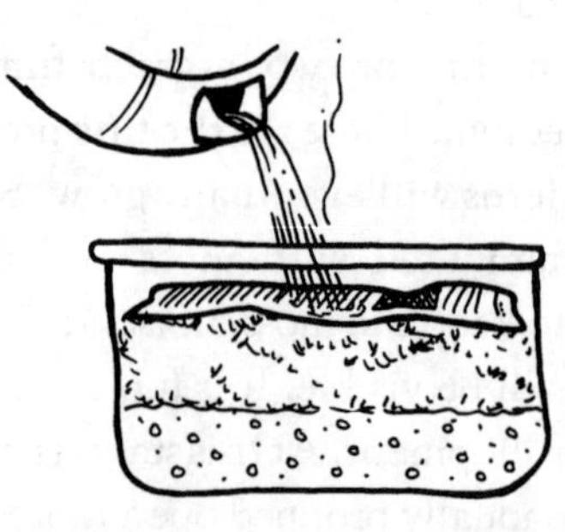

that the ferns are exposed to. Continue to be vigilant against damping off disease (see pages 20 and 50). Use clean tweezers to thin out the ferns if they are crowded.

When the ferns are 1 to 1 ½ inches (25 to 38 mm) high, separate them carefully and plant them in a flat of African violet potting soil or a peat based potting soil. A glass or clear plastic cover will help to keep them moist, but they do need air. It may be better to mist them regularly, or to open the cover a crack. Continue to keep them in a lightly shaded place.

When the tiny ferns have grown new fronds, transplant them to individual 2 ½ inch (60 mm) pots in a light, peat based soil mixture. Include leaf mould to more closely simulate the natural growing conditions. To avoid compacting the soil when watering, keep the pots in a tray and put some water in the tray. Do not add any more water than can be absorbed in an hour.

About two months later, tip a fern out of its pot to see if the roots have reached the edge of the soil. Repot them all into larger pots when this happens and water them with a little weak fertilizer. If it is early in the summer, they can be set outdoors in a shaded cold frame, if they are hardy ferns, but do not rush this. They can readily be potted on into 3 inch (75 mm) and then eventually into 4 inch (100 mm) pots or larger, and will probably be at least a year and a half old or more before they are ready to be planted in the ground. They will need to be protected during their first winter in the same way as young perennial flowers (see pages 387-388).

The *Handbook on Ferns* (1969) from the Brooklyn Botanic Garden Record is an excellent reference for information on all aspects of growing and using ferns, and includes descriptions and drawings of forty-three North American ferns.

Month-by-Month

# December

• what does "rugosa" mean?

• get a spade for Uncle or someone special

• plan flowers for cousin's wedding in June
• light pruning for winter decorations
• build bird house, cold frame, strawberry barrel, planter, sundial, propagation unit and cold room

At this time of year hard core gardeners turn their attention to indoor activities such as sowing flowers and vegetables for winter use and ordering seed catalogues. There are garden and greenhouse building projects to attend to, tools to purchase and a host of garden dreams to be dreamt. It is also fun to think up gardening type gifts for special occasions, and there are always a few tasks that can be done outdoors.

# December

### Hoe

*Gardening tool whose name derives from the fact that when its blade is stepped on, its handle delivers a sharp rap to the gardener's brow, at which point he [or she] cries "Ho!", or "Oh,________!" or "Holy________!"*

*Beard and McKie*

## Outdoors

### Winter Gardens

In some gardens a few persistent pansies may still be in bloom. Even without flowers, however, there can be considerable plant interest in the winter garden. Ideally, the most interesting views should be visible from inside the house or be near the driveway, sidewalk or door.

Leaving herbaceous stems in place, whether of perennial flowers, herbs or grasses (see page 386), will add height and interest to the landscape. A covering of hoare frost or a sprinkling of snow adds contrasts in colour and texture. They can be left in place until they become flattened or tattered; they should certainly be removed by the time that early spring bulbs peek through. Trees and shrubs are like exclamation marks emerging through a blanket of snow, and their shadows add patterns and movement to the garden.

Coniferous trees and shrubs add colour and shape to winter landscapes. A variety of upright and spreading plants, as well as variations in texture, will increase the interest. A dense, dark yew contrasts sharply with a light and lacy false cypress, and an upright juniper stands out against a spreading companion. A few evergreens, such as golden coloured false cypress and some of the blue or gold junipers, add interesting colours to a snowy scene. Some of the evergreen heaths and heathers turn colour in the autumn and are reddish orange or silvery grey through the winter.

Plants with interesting shapes, bark or flower buds also add interest. Red osier dogwood, Cornelian cherry (*Cornus mas*), star magnolia, berberis, kerria, pieris, burning bush, flowering quince, weeping trees, Oregon grape (*Mahonia*), birch and cotoneaster are all worth considering. Corkscrew hazel is a study in twisted branches, very appealing to some gardeners but considered artificial and unattractive by others. Staghorn sumac is architecturally interesting and its red fruit clusters stay on for quite a long time.

Crabapples and various *Viburnum* species, such as highbush cranberry and nannyberry, also hold their fruits well into winter, until the birds get them (and see November, pages 421-422, for plants attractive to birds). Canada holly looks especially attractive in front of evergreens.

Some groundcover plants have evergreen or semi-evergreen leaves. They include periwinkle (*Vinca minor*), ivy, bugleweed, *Dianthus* species, bergenia, candytuft (*Iberis*), wintercreeper (*Euonymus fortunei*), Christmas fern, blue fescue and Japanese spurge (*Pachysandra*). Yucca is a striking plant in the winter due to its unusual evergreen leaves.

Some plants are at their most attractive stage in the late winter or early spring. Pussy willows spring to mind, as do witch hazel and daphne. Because of the way they bloom bravely through late season snowfalls, crocuses can fairly be considered part of the winter garden. The species crocuses bloom one to two weeks ahead of the large Dutch hybrids. Snowdrops have earned their name for the way they push through crusts of melting snow. Certainly a winter garden is not the same as a summer garden, but it can have its own measure of beauty and appeal.

## General Plant Care

If you are using a snowblower, be careful not to cover evergreens and other woody plants with the snow they spew out, and avoid direct contact of the machine with trees and shrubs. When shoveling walks and driveways, put the snow on perennial beds and herb gardens to act as a winter mulch. Snow often blows clear at the corners of buildings, so pile snow around the base of shrubs or over perennial beds in these locations as well.

During any outdoor activities, try to stay off the lawn as much as possible until the ground is fully frozen—sodden soil is prone to compaction. Look for hollows where ice, snow or water accumulate, and make a note to repair these next year as they are often sites where snow mould and other fungal diseases develop.

If there are any plants that have already started to heave out of the ground due to frost action, add more soil over the roots rather than pushing them back into the ground—the latter could tear the roots. After the soil is added, put on a thick mulch as described in November (pages 411-415 and pages 417-418), as soon as the ground is frozen.

## Building Projects

It is fairly easy to build cold frames, strawberry barrels, propagation units, bird houses, sundials and a planter or two. There may also be more time in the winter to construct a cold room for fruit and vegetable storage. Check the local library for books on garden furniture and other garden construction projects.

### Cold Frames

There are many styles of cold frames, but the essential features are the same: a box with a sloping lid of glass or other material that will admit light, and a lid that can be opened for ventilation. Cold frames are useful not only for extending the gardening season in the spring and fall, but also for use in the summer and winter as a shelter for plants. It can double as a miniature lath house for cuttings and young plants if a lath lid is substituted for the glass one. Cold frames can also be insulated with 1 or 2 inch (2.5 to 5 cm) thick rigid urethane insulation if the frame is to be used at extreme ends of the gardening season. Protect this with a layer of thin wood, shingles, metal or tarpaper.

The area of ground that a cold frame covers can vary considerably, but aim for larger rather than smaller sizes. A frame 4 feet (1.2 m) long by 3 or 4 feet (1 to 1.2 m) wide would fit comfortably over a raised bed 4 feet (1.2 m) wide. The single window frames from a double hung window are rather small if used alone, but two of them side by side make a good sized cold frame. A good working size to aim for is 3 by 6 feet (1 by 1.8 m). This is large enough to reduce temperature swings and be roomy for plants, but small enough to be reasonably portable. Cold frames that will be installed permanently against the south side of the house or another building can be made larger.

Plastic for the lid is less expensive than glass and is less easily broken in hail storms, but it discolours and transmits less light as it ages and has to be replaced every two or three years. Plexiglass or acrylics can be used, but they are more expensive than glass. Lids with double layers of glass provide more insulation, or a piece of plastic sheeting can be stretched over a single pane of glass. If growing plants during very cool conditions, insulation can be put in place over the lid each night.

To make the seal between the lid and the top of the frame as tight as possible, cover the frame edge with weather stripping or a strip of used carpet underpad. Any gaps anywhere in the frame should be caulked. Ventilation and air movement is provided by propping the lid open on mild days. There are also automatic ventilation devices that can be installed.

The height of the frame will depend on the height of the crop that will be grown in it and the building materials available. Three-quarter inch (18 mm) exterior grade plywood will provide strength and durability. Deep frames that are used for hot beds (see page 348) must be at least 2 feet (60 cm) high at the front and even taller at the back, and frames used for peppers and eggplants during the growing season have to be slightly taller than the plants at maturity.

It is possible to make stackable, customized cold frames to suit various purposes. Low frames are all that are required in the spring for early crops, but the units can be stacked to make fewer but taller units for tall crops. They are created by making a bottom unit, say 6 or 8 inches (15 or 20 cm) high all around, and one or more similar units to raise the height. A sloping unit is also made to put on the top. Peg legs that fit into the unit below will make the stacking secure. The flat units can be used separately without the sloping lid, covered instead with cheesecloth or agricultural fabric, and used to protect plants from insect attack.

Increasingly, environmentally conscientious gardeners are shying away from using pressure-treated wood, preferring to rebuild their cold frames periodically instead. Often it is only the bottom edge that rests on the ground which needs to be replaced, but even this is less of a problem if cold frames are used on raised beds edged with lumber. They last longer if they are painted and are stored somewhere dry for the winter. To maximize the amount of light reaching the plants during the spring and autumn, the interior should be painted with a glossy white, exterior grade paint. This will reflect light more evenly onto the back of the plants than a silver paint or aluminum foil, which can cause hot spots.

## Strawberry Barrels

You can use a full or half barrel to make a strawberry barrel. The only equipment required is a drill and a 1 ½ inch (38 mm) diameter speed bore bit, or a hole saw to make 2 inch (50 mm) diameter holes.

Drill three, 1 ½ or 2 inch (4 or 5 cm) holes in the bottom for drainage. On the side of the barrel, 6 to 8 inches (15 to 20 cm) above the bottom, drill more holes of the same size spaced 10 to 12 inches (25 to 30 cm) apart. Drill more holes 6 to 8 inches (15 to 20 cm) above these, staggered between the holes in the first row. Continue in this manner, putting the last row of holes 6 to

### Green Thumb Tip

The appropriate slope of the lid depends on how the frame is to be used. A shallow slope of 7 to 15° to admit light and also allow rain to run off is sufficient if the frame will be protecting young plants and cuttings during the summer and winter. To maximize sunlight admittance and warmth in the early spring and late autumn, a slope of 30 to 45° is best. This would make the back of the frame extremely tall, so a peaked roof might be better unless it is built against a house. If the slope is very steep, with the back of the frame very high relative to the front, the box will heat up too much and there will be a loss of growing space relative to the amount of material used to make the frame. Make the back of a peaked roof an opaque, openable hatch to make plant care easier.

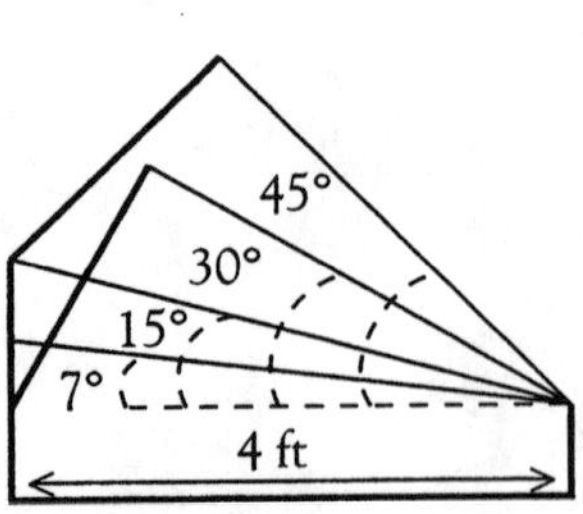

8 inches (15 to 20 cm) below the top. Mount the barrel on castors so that it can be turned easily to give all plants access to full light.

When it is time to plant the barrel, either in the spring or with plants dug up from the garden in the autumn, put a 1 inch (2.5 cm) layer of coarse gravel in the bottom. Fill the barrel to the level of the first holes with enriched soil or potting mix and put a single strawberry plant in each hole. Make sure that the roots are well spread out and watered in.

Continue in this manner, but insert a watering system before the barrel is one-third full. This need be nothing more than a well perforated pipe which is 3 to 4 inches (7 to 10 cm) in diameter placed upright in the centre of the barrel. When the barrel is full of plants and soil, finish off by planting the top of the barrel. At watering time, fill the pipe until the soil is thoroughly moistened but not wet.

Strawberry Barrel

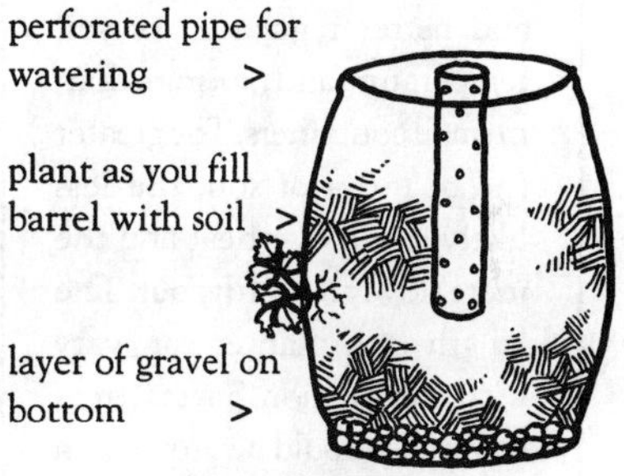

## Containers and Planters

Wooden containers in a variety of sizes and shapes can be built now for use as window boxes, planters and raised beds in the spring. Ersatz stone planters can be built using readily available materials and are particularly good for alpine plants.

Winterkill is often a problem with containerized woody plants. It helps to line the container inside with below grade rigid urethane insulation, so that the root ball freezes gradually from the top down, rather than suddenly from all sides.

If containers are to have bottoms, be sure to put in drainage holes of 3/4 inch (18 mm) diameter every 6 to 8 inches (15 to 20 cm) along the bottom. Add short legs or castors underneath or put the planters on blocks so that air circulates and the wood stays drier. Legs are not necessary for window boxes, but some people like to attach a tray underneath to catch the drops (and see the wick watering system described on pages 223-224).

Stone-like planters for rockery plants and annual flowers can be made of two parts Portland cement, three parts dry sphagnum peat moss and three parts perlite or vermiculite (see Brooklyn Botanic Garden Handbook *Miniature Gardens* (1976), for detailed instructions). Perlite gives a rougher, more stone-like finish. The planters can be coloured with concrete colouring powders—use 1/2 cup (125 ml) for every quart (1.1 l) of Portland cement. Use rock colours if a more realistic look is wanted, but there are many colours to choose from, or use none at all. Such containers are not as heavy as they might seem; a box 2 feet square by 8 inches deep (60 by 60 by 20 cm) is

### Green Thumb Tip

Very large containers for trees and shrubs should be at least 30 inches (75 cm) high and 40 inches (120 cm) across. This will provide stability in winds and better regulation of soil temperature and moisture than in small containers. The greater the quantity of soil, the less likely it will overheat and the more slowly it will dry out. The length of a planter can vary with the situation. Several trees or shrubs should be grown in a long planter rather than a series of individual containers.

A container should be at least as wide or wider than the depth. Containers for annual flowers and shallow rooted vegetables and herbs need be only 8 to 12 inches (20 to 30 cm) deep, and at least as wide. Perennial flowers and deep rooted vegetables require a soil depth of 12 to 20 inches (30 to 50 cm). The container itself does not need to be that deep if part of the soil depth includes the earth below the container. Planters with the soil mass in contact with the earth will maintain soil moisture for longer periods, and plant roots will be able to grow downward. A planter combined with seating is most comfortable if 14 to 16 inches (35 to 40 cm) high, with the seat part being 16 to 18 inches (40 to 45 cm) wide.

reasonably easy to lift and move around. They also stand up to frost quite well and can be made stronger by moulding them around chicken wire.

The shape of any bowl, pot, tub or dishpan can be used to form the general shape of the container. This is modified by placing the bowl or tub upside down and covering it with damp sand in the desired form. Create rock-like shapes for more natural looking containers. Shape a trench around the base using sand, making it about 1 inch (2.5 cm) deep and 1 to 2 inches (2.5 to 5 cm) wide to

form a rim for the planter. Place an old, wet sheet over the sand mold and cover it closely with chicken wire, being careful not to disturb the sand. Remove the wire shape and sheet and then cover the sand with a large sheet of plastic. Have on hand several pieces of wooden dowel or piping, 1/2 to 3/4 inch (12 to 18 mm) in diameter for making the drainage holes.

Mix the peat moss and perlite or vermiculate thoroughly so that there are no lumps in the peat moss; mix in the colouring powder at this stage if it is used. Then mix in the dry Portland cement thoroughly. Add water a little at a time, stirring well after each addition, until the mixture is moist and workable but not wet or sloppy. More can be mixed as you carry out the molding process if there is not enough to finish the job.

Cover the mold with a 1/2 inch (12 mm) thick layer of the mixture, making sure that the trench which was formed around the base is filled. Place the wire shape over the concrete covered mold so that the edge is embedded in the concrete filled trench. Its shape will not fit exactly but do not worry.

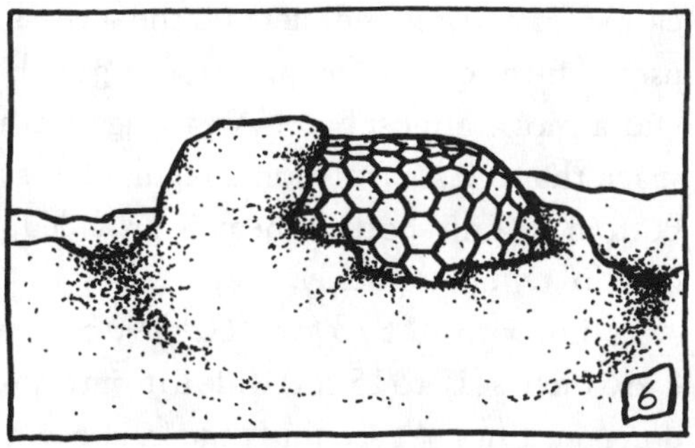


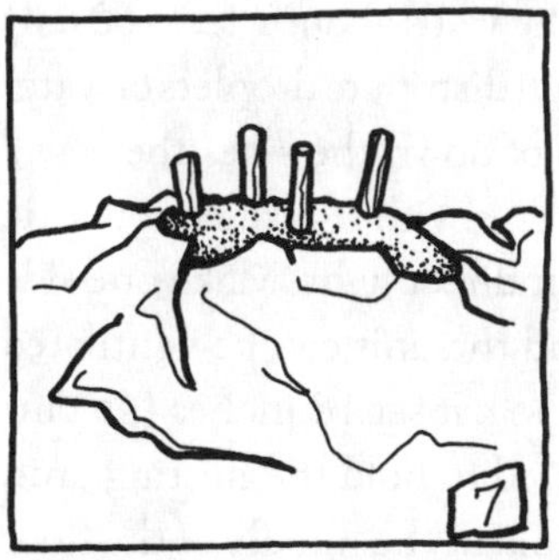


Add more concrete, working it through the mesh so that it makes direct contact with the first layer. The total thickness should be 1 inch (2.5 cm) on the sides and up to 2 inches (5 cm) on the base. A rim can be added around the bottom of the planter to raise the drainage holes off the ground. Push the pieces of dowels or pipe into the bottom of the planter until they touch the plastic-covered sand mold.

Fold back the remaining edges of the large sheet of plastic, up and over the sides of the container but not covering it completely. The concrete should stay in place while it sets. If there is a risk of the concrete slumping, pack moist sand around the sides, patting it into place over the folded plastic. Let the container dry for the next twelve to twenty-four hours, until it will not dent when pressed hard but is still scratchable. Remove the dowels and level off the bottom of the planter with a flat board or scraper. At this stage, cover the planter with plastic and leave it to dry for two weeks.

After two weeks, remove the plastic and take the container off the mold. Let it air dry for another two weeks, and punch through the drainage holes with a sharp point. Leave the planter outside for a month, if there is likely to be rain. Otherwise, soak the planter in a large container of water for two weeks, changing the water every two or three days. Plants do not like to be near fresh concrete.

Making "stone" troughs and planters may sound rather bizarre, but the method is easy and the results are useful and realistic looking.

## *Propagation Units*

Softwood and other cuttings can be rooted without a propagation unit, but caring for cuttings is easier and the success rate is usually higher if a unit is used. The essentials for quick rooting are bottom heat, light (see page 62), and a moist atmosphere. A propagation unit is essentially an enclosed space that releases mist on a regular basis and has a source of heat at the bottom. If only bottom heat is provided, it can be used to get seeds to germinate more quickly.

A unit with a 2 by 3 foot (60 by 90 cm) wooden floor, edged with a board 4 to 6 inches (10 to 15 cm) wide to form a box, will comfortably house several dozen cuttings. At seeding time in late winter and spring it will hold three 11 by 21 inch (28 by 52 cm) seed flats. Make the walls about 2 feet (60 cm) high and add a flat roof above that. A flat roof will distribute droplets of water more evenly over the rooting surface, instead of down the sides the way a sloping roof would. Frame in the unit and cover it with translucent plastic or frosted glass, so that cuttings get bright but indirect light. Make one side hinged so that plants can be easily reached and the unit can be ventilated when the plants are being hardened off. A cross bar set 18 inches (45 cm) above the floor will add stability and can be used to hold the misting unit.

Thread a hose into the interior through a hole in the middle of the floor about 12 inches (30 cm) from one end of the unit. This will make it easy to fit two flats on one side and one flat on the other side of the hose. Take the end of the hose up to the cross bar, thread it through a hole and add a mist nozzle to it.

Propagation Unit

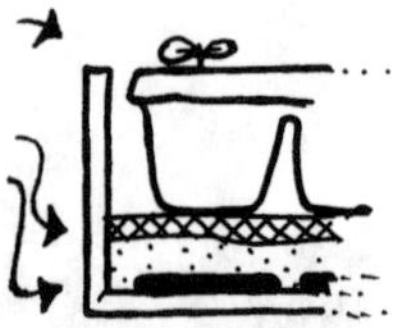

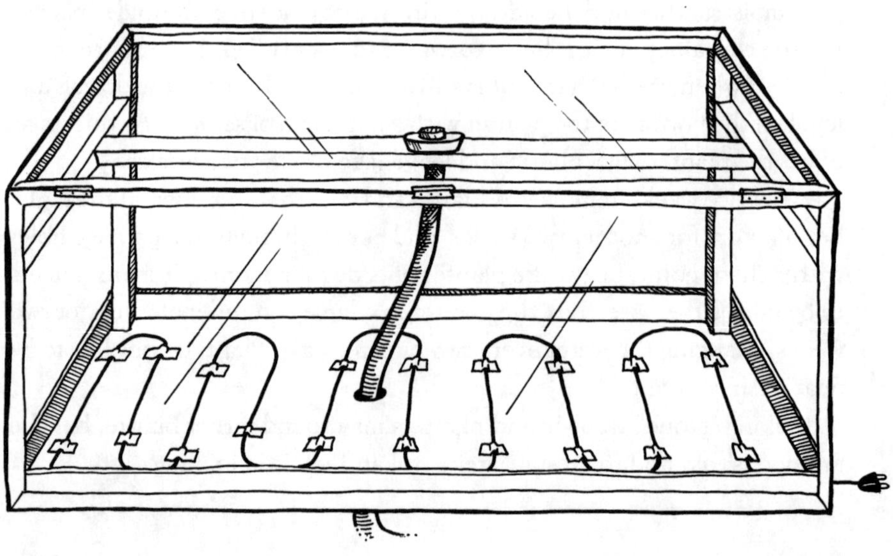

Some misters produce such a fine spray that they can be left on throughout the day, but most need to be automatically (using a timer) or manually turned on and off intermittently. Interestingly, cuttings exposed to continuous mist rarely, if ever, develop rotting and other fungal problems. It seems that the continuous misting washes off spores before they have a chance to develop.

There are several types and wattages of heating cable that can be used to provide the bottom heat. Follow the particular directions that come with the cable, but the usual method is to cover the bottom of the unit with parallel rows of cable spaced 4 to 4¾ inches (10 to 12 cm) apart. Fasten it with electrical tape or insulated electrical staples. If external conditions will be very chilly when the unit is used, use a longer line and attach it to the surrounding board 1/2 inch (12 mm) above the base so that the ends and sides of the growing area are kept warm.

The thermostat bulb should be on the floor, 3 to 6 inches (8 to 15 cm) from the wall, and the cable itself should not touch the thermostat. Most cables come with a thermostat pre-set at about 70°F (21°C), but some models are available with a thermostat that can be manually set. Cover the entire base and heating cable with 1 inch (2.5 cm) of loose sand and cover that with metal or plastic screening. Top this with vermiculite to the level of the surrounding board, and set pots with their cuttings into the vermiculite. Newspaper or peat pots work well. Remove the vermiculite if using the unit to start seeds and set the flats or pots directly on the screen over the sand.

## Bird Houses

By encouraging birds to make a home in your yard, you will be gaining help in insect control while having the pleasure of watching birds go through their various daily activities.

The size and shape of a bird house or nesting box, and the size and placement of the entrance hole, determine the type of bird that will be attracted (see Table DEC-1 and pages 322-323 regarding setting up boxes). Swallows, for example, prefer a hole that is a somewhat flattened oval; starlings will not use a hole that is less than 1½ inches (3.8 cm) in diameter and house sparrows will not use one that is less than 1⅛ inches (2.8 cm).

A bird house should be a plain, simple shape, painted or stained in a quiet colour such as grey, green or brown. The interior can be painted flat black. Stain should be applied before the house is put together. Use 3/4 to 1 inch (18 to 25 mm) thick wood to construct it; this thickness will help to insulate the bird house against hot weather. Redwood, cedar and cypress are the best woods to use, but exterior grade plywood will suffice. Use spiral nails or screws to join the pieces.

*How to Attract Birds* (Ortho Books, 1983) provides clear guidelines on how to build a bird house. Except for purple martin houses, which are built in eight compartments, they should be built singly for only one pair of nesting birds. The roof should be a single slope, overlapping the sides and front by 1 ½ inches (38 mm) or more. One side should be hinged to allow for easy cleaning (a hinged roof may leak when it rains). The back should extend beyond the roof, walls and floor to make mounting easier.

On the underside of the roof extension at the front of the house, 1 inch (2.5 cm) back from the edge, score a 1/8 inch (3 mm) deep drip line to channel off water. Drill three, 1/4 inch (6 mm) holes in the sides near the top for ventilation. They should be above the level of the entrance hole to avoid drafts. Drill three more 1/4 inch (6 mm) holes in the bottom for drainage. Do not add a perch to the outside, but cleats or 1/8 inch (6 mm) deep cuts can be made on the inside of the wall below the entrance hole. A mounting hole in the back wall, opposite the entrance hole, will make mounting easier, or drill mounting holes in the top and bottom of the back wall above the roof and below the floor.

Home for the Birds

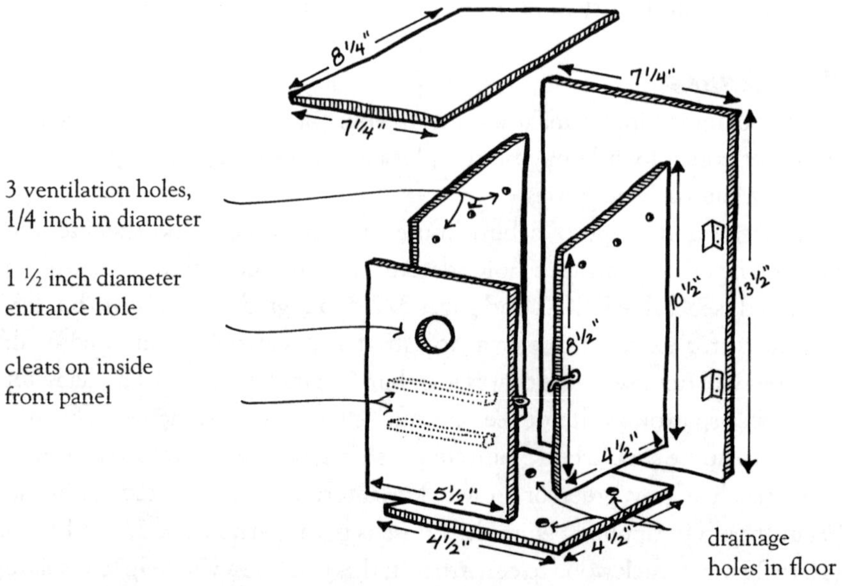

## Table DEC-1 Dimensions of Bird Houses

—measured in inches (cm)

| Bird | Floor inches (cm) | Average Wall Height inches (cm) | Diameter of Hole inches (cm) | Entrance Height Above Floor inches (cm) |
|---|---|---|---|---|
| Barn Swallow * | 6 x 6 (15 x 15) | 6 (15) | | |
| Chickadee | 4 x 4 (10 x 10) | 8 to 10 (20 to 25) | 1 ⅛ (2.8) | 6 to 8 (15 to 20) |
| Downy Woodpecker | 4 x 4 (10 x 10) | 8 to 10 (20 to 25) | 1 ¼ (3.2) | 6 to 8 (15 to 20) |
| Eastern Bluebird | 5 x 5 (12 x 12) | 8 (20) | 1 ½ (3.8) | 6 (15) |
| Eastern Phoebe * | 6 x 6 (15 x 15) | 6 (15) | | |
| House Wren | 4 x 4 (10 x 10) | 6 to 8 (15 to 20) | 1 to 1 ¼ (2.5 to 3.2) | 4 to 6 (10 to 15) |
| Northern Flicker | 7 x 7 (18 x 18) | 16 to 18 (40 to 45) | 2 ½ (6.4) | 14 to 16 (35 to 40) |
| Nuthatch | 4 x 4 (10 x 10) | 8 to 10 (20 to 25) | 1 ¼ (3.2) | 6 to 8 (15 to 20) |
| Red-headed Woodpecker | 6 x 6 (15 x 15) | 12 to 15(30 to 38) | 2 (5) | 9 to 12(23 to 30) |
| Robin * | 6 x 8 (15 x 20) | 8 (20) | | |
| Screech Owl | 8 x 8 (20 x 20) | 12 to 15 (30 to 38) | 3 (7.6) | 9 to 12 (23 to 30) |
| Song Sparrow * | 6 x 6 (15 x 15) | 6 (15) | | |
| Tree Swallow | 5 x 5 (13 x 13) | 6 (15) | 1 ½ (3.8) | 1 to 5 (2.5 to 13) |
| Winter Wren | 4 x 4 (10 x 10) | 6 to 8 (15 to 20) | 1 to 1 ¼ (2.5 to 3.2) | 4 to 6 (10 to 15) |

* nesting shelves

Based on information in *How to Attract Birds*, Ortho Books (1983).

### Sundials

A sundial made specifically for your latitude will keep time more accurately than most purchased models. There are several types (see Waugh, 1973), but the horizontal dial is easy to construct and the one familiar to most gardeners.

There are several aspects to building a horizontal sundial that will ensure accuracy in telling time. One is to make sure that the gnomon—the bit that stands up and casts the shadow on the hours—is perfectly vertical to the sundial face and is set at the angle of latitude where the sundial will be used. As well, the sundial face must have the hours marked according to the angle of latitutude. When setting up the sundial in the garden, the face must be perfectly level and the gnomon must be aligned with solar or true north—not magnetic north. It sounds complicated, but the steps are straightforward when taken one at a time.

The face can be made of any material that will stand up to weather and can be marked in some way, such as wood, concrete or metal. The gnomon can be made of such materials as wood or sheet metal. Before marking on the hours, draw the dial face on a large piece of paper according to the latitude at which you live.

Draw two parallel lines, AB and CD, for the top and bottom of the face. Draw a perpendicular line, FG, from the midpoint (F) of AB to the midpoint (H) of line CD and continue the line well above CD. Think of this as the noon hour line. Construct a line, FL, such that the number of degrees in angle HFL is equal to the exact latitutde of your garden. Draw a perpendicular, SH, from FL to point H. Measure the length of SH and mark point T on the line GH such that HT is the same length as SH. Construct a line parallel to AB and CD through point T.

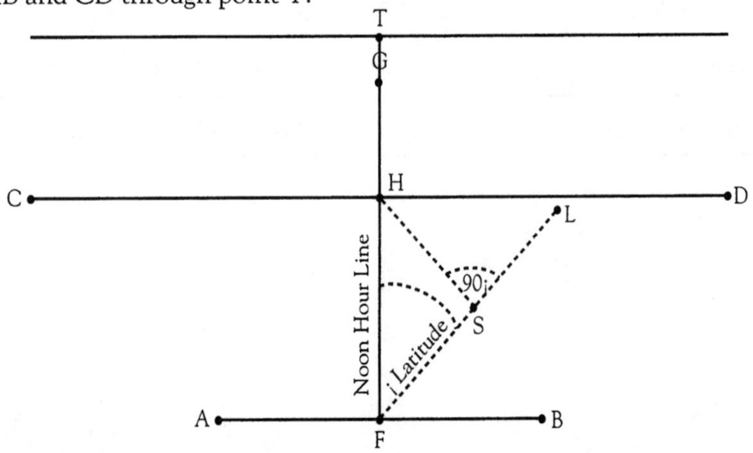

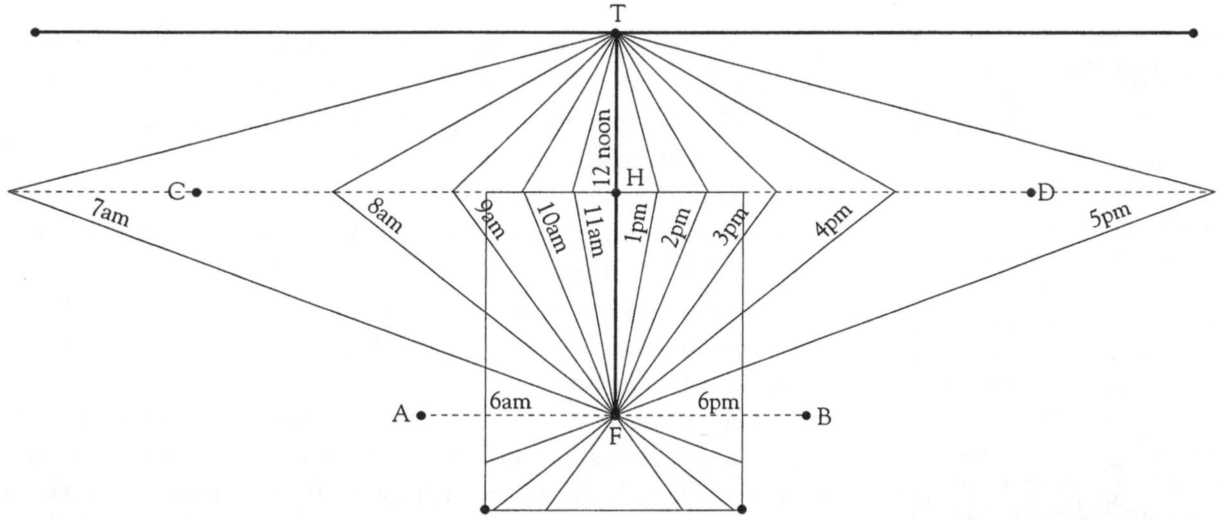


Only lines AB and FH appear on the final dial face, but now you are in a position to draw the hour lines. Use a protractor at T to mark off 15° lines. Where they intersect CD indicates the hours, left to right, from 7 a.m. to 5 p.m. (Add one hour to take daylight savings into account, such that the 6 a.m. line, for example, is labelled 7 a.m., and the 1 p.m. line points to true north.) Connecting each of these points to point F creates the actual hour lines that will be marked on the face of the dial. If the gnomon is more than 1/16 inch (2 mm) thick, separate the dial face at the noon hour line by the thickness of the gnomon before marking in the remaining hours. Extend the 3 p.m., 4 p.m. and 5 p.m. hour lines to produce the hour lines for 3 a.m., 4 a.m. and 5 a.m. Extend the 7 a.m., 8 a.m. and 9 a.m. hour lines in the same way to produce the equivalent evening hours. If the dial face is large enough, mark the half hours and perhaps even the quarter hours.

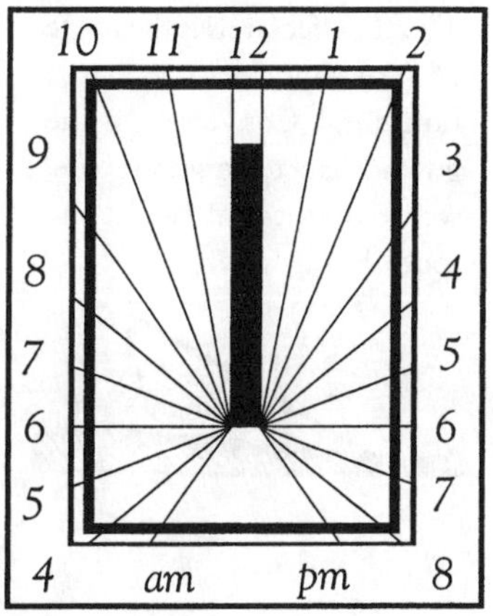


For a rectangular face, drop perpendiculars from where 9 a.m. and 3 p.m. intersect line CD. If a round dial face is preferred, draw a circle centred on point F. More pleasing proportions will be achieved if the circle is moved upwards on the face by centring it on a point slightly above F on line FH. It is essential, however, that the front of the gnomon remains centred on point F on the 6 o'clock (7 o'clock DST) line.

In true sundial tradition, the face is usually decorated in some way. Popular designs in the past have been the signs of the zodiac, seeds, leaves, flowers, stems, the four seasons, tortoises, mottoes and family coats of arms.

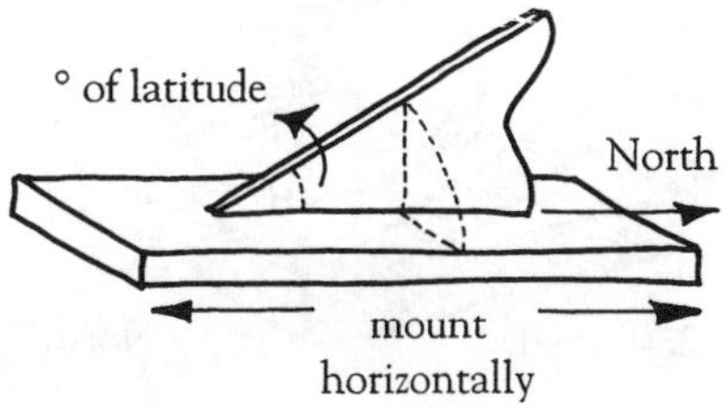


Make the angle of the gnomon the same as the degrees latitude. The upper side is straight, since it casts the shadow for reading the time, and the under

## Sundial Tip

If a purchased horizontal dial is incorrect for your garden, correct the angle of the gnomon by tilting the sundial face when installing it on its pedestal. A sundial with the gnomon at too low an angle for the new latitude, having been made initially for a more southerly garden, would need to have the dial face wedged up at the north end, equal to the difference of the two latitudes. This, in effect, raises the angle of the gnomon relative to true horizontal. Conversely, if the gnomon is at too high an angle, wedge up the dial face at the south end.

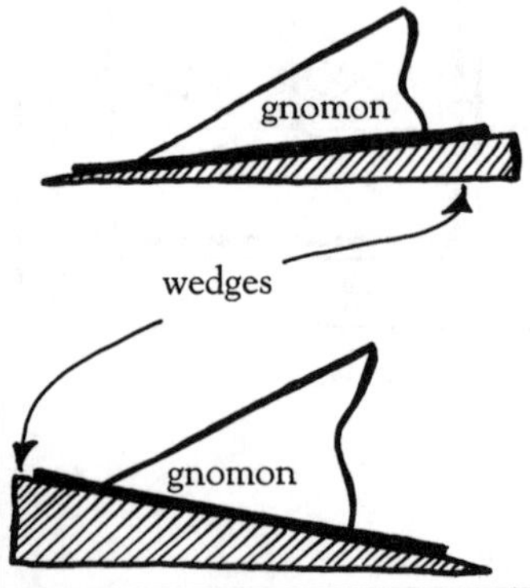


Equatorial Sundial

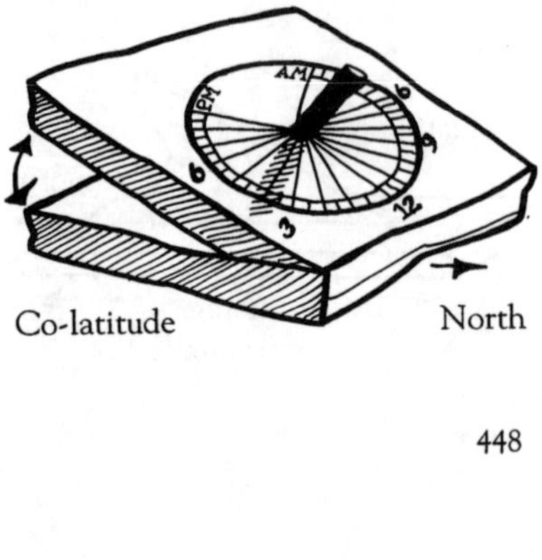


side is usually curved in some way to distinguish its shadow from the upper side. When attaching the gnomon, make sure it is perfectly vertical to the dial face. The gnomon must also point to true north, not magnetic north, when the sundial is placed in the garden. One way to find true north is to add (or subtract) the magnetic declination for your site (phone the local weather office or ask for help at the public library). Another method is to line up two vertical stakes with the North Star on a clear night. A third method is to drive a perfectly vertical, six foot stake into the ground and mark the direction of its shadow at exactly midway between sunrise and sunset (check a newspaper for the times).

To maintain the face at true horizontal and the gnomon pointing to true north, the sundial must be firmly anchored when it is put in the garden (once the ground thaws!). Use a concrete pedestal (form it using a sono tube, a heavy cardboard tube used in construction) or make a pedestal of bricks or stone on a concrete footing. To make final adjustments easier, place a layer of concrete on top of the bricks or stone and set four bolts into the concrete before it dries. Point the noon hour line (1 p.m. DST) of the sundial face to true north before marking and drilling four holes in the face to match the bolts, and then finely adjust it to horizontal using washers or double nuts.

A simpler sundial is the equatorial dial. The face is a full circle with the hours marked off in even, 15$^0$ increments, and the face itself is angled to match the co-latitude (90$^0$ minus the latitude of your garden). The gnomon, a slender pole such as a piece of dowel, is centred in the middle and points to solar north. When marking the radiations on the face, the noon hour line (1 p.m. DST) points to solar north, 6 a.m. (7 a.m. DST) points west (because the rising sun in the east casts the shadow of the gnomon to the west), and 6 p.m. (7 p.m. DST) points east. If there is enough room on the dial face, half hours and quarter hours can be marked.

Although the face is round, it is easiest to mark it on a square piece of wood or metal so that the angle at which the face is set is more stable. The equatorial sundial works in the northern hemisphere from March 21 to September 21; in the other half of the year, sunshine falls on the underside. To use such a sundial in the winter—after brushing away the snow—mark hours on the underside as well, with 12 noon pointing north, 6 a.m. pointing west, and 6 p.m. pointing east. In this case, attach a gnomon on the under side as well as on the upper surface. Calculate the length of the under gnomon so that it serves as a resting point for the upper face when it is at the correct angle (co-latitude).

### *Flower Press*

A flower press is easy to make and worthwhile for anyone who presses more than a few flowers. Use two pieces of 1/2 inch (12 mm) plywood, each 12 by 18 inches (30 by 45 cm). Drill a hole in each corner, 1/2 inch (12 mm) from the long edge and 2 inches (5 cm) from the ends, to fit four long bolts. These are held in place with wing nuts and washers when the flowers are being pressed. To use the press, flowers and leaves are arranged carefully between single sheets of blotting paper, which are sandwiched between pads of newspaper. The layers can be built up as thickly as the bolts will accommodate. Screw the wing nuts securely, and check their tightness each day while the plant material is drying.

### *Cold Rooms*

A cold room is invaluable for storing fruits and vegetables in relatively fresh condition, and for holding various bulbs, perennial flowers, shrubs and cuttings in cold storage during dormancy.

A cold room can be built in one corner of a basement, under a porch or under a bay window, among other places. A space which is 10 by 10 feet (3 by 3 m) provides enough room for most families for food storage, but make it larger or smaller to suit your particular needs. A window or vent to outdoors is essential for cooling and air circulation.

A simple space can be blocked in with 2 by 4s, leaving room for a door. Put vapour barriers outside the insulation on the warm side of the walls facing the rest of the basement, and on the ceiling facing the warm floor above. Insulation is then added to the inside of the cold room. Place plywood or hardboard sheathing on both sides of the newly constructed walls, and on the ceiling if a finished look is desired. Outside walls will not need to be insulated unless the basement is mostly above ground level. Make a door with 1½ inch (38 mm) wood framing, insulating it and covering it with 1/4 inch (6 mm) plywood. It should fit the opening snugly with the help of weather stripping.

An automatic, semi-automatic or manual ventilation system is essential. Automatic ones are more expensive, but manual ones increase the chance of losses due to human error. It is devastating to discover that most of the carefully stored fruits and vegetables have been destroyed by frost because the vent door was left open or blew open too far in a storm.

Make shelves and bins of slatted construction to ensure good air circulation. The lowest shelves or bottom of bins should be raised 4 inches

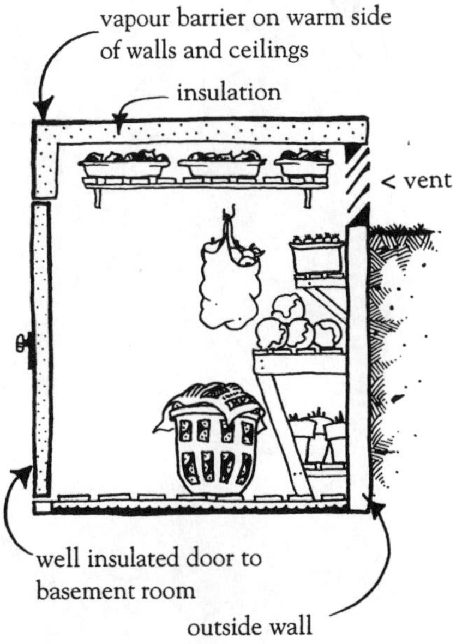

(10 cm) above the floor to protect them from water sprinkled on the floor to maintain humidity. Walls and shelves can be left plain or painted, but painted wood is easier to scrub clean each year. Put on two coats of outdoor grade paint after a primer has been applied.

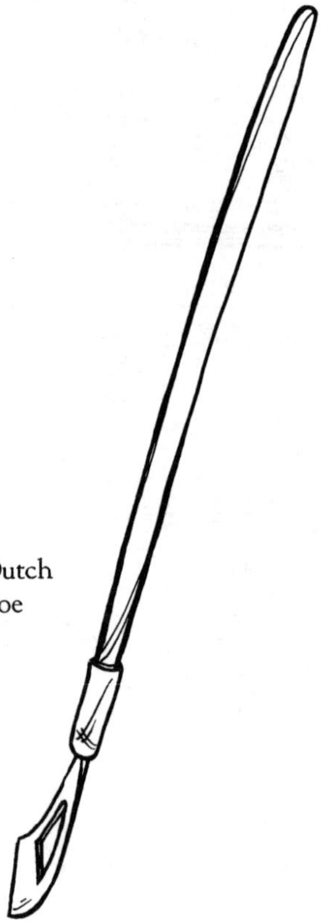

Dutch hoe

## Tools

The choice of a comfortable tool is a very personal one, so be cautious if selecting a tool for someone else. The weight of a spade or the spread of the handles on a pair of secateurs may feel right to one person but quite wrong to another. There are general guidelines, however, when purchasing tools.

Buy the best tools that can reasonably be afforded, but the most expensive is not necessarily best. For a small person, a lightweight tool that has to be replaced fairly often may be more appropriate than a heavier tool that will last a lifetime. Depending on the choice available, one may find really good quality tools that are both light and durable.

Do not automatically reject a plastic grip on spades and forks. A few ounces (grams) less weight can make the difference between a tool that has the right heft and one that feels too heavy. It is often worth investing in two tools of each type if the preferences between two gardeners in the family are different, particularly if the tools are used frequently.

When selecting spades and shovels, look for metal shanks that extend some way up the handle and are wrapped around it. These are much stronger than tools that have the handle inserted into a small piece of metal, or those that rely on tang and ferrule construction. The same principle applies to small hand tools such as trowels.

The length of the handle is important, too. Some people prefer a short digging spade with a D-shaped grip whereas others, perhaps those with back problems, prefer a long handled spade that entails less bending. Others with back problems like a short handle and learn to bend at the knees with every lift of the spade. A long handled shovel or pitch fork enables the user to throw longer distances.

Shovels with a cup-shaped blade are either rounded, which is good for moving dirt, sand and sawdust, or they are pointed, which is good for digging. A small and narrow blade lifts less dirt, so select the blade size according to the size and strength of the gardener. A flat, square-nosed blade is ideal for cutting and digging heavy soil and for removing sod. It will also produce straight-sided, flat-bottomed trenches.

Garden rakes usually have tang and ferrule construction to attach the handle to the head; make sure they are firmly connected. The row of short metal teeth are at right angles to the handle and are good for raking soil to make it smooth and to remove lumps and small stones. They can also be used to dethatch small areas of lawn, although there are dethatching rakes with cutting edges that are more effective. An S-shaped handle produces less strain on a gardener's back, but this is mostly noticed when the rake is pulled, not pushed.

Leaf or lawn rakes are very light with long, flexible tines—made of steel, bamboo or polypropylene—that are fine for raking leaves and grass clippings but useless on soil or for dethatching. Steel tines should return to their original shape when bent; bamboo tines can be soaked overnight in soapy water if they are brittle; polypropylene tines will not rust or break, but select a heavy duty model.

Select a hoe on the basis of its intended use. A hoe with the blade set at a right angle to the handle is meant for chopping and digging, whereas a proper cultivating hoe has a narrow blade that can be sharpened and it is set at a wide angle to the handle. Its flat blade rests almost parallel to the ground and is used to decapitate weeds in a sweeping rather than a chopping motion, which is also easier on the gardener's back.

Gardeners with large properties may want to purchase a rotary tiller. Those with the tines in front of the wheels have a tendency to run away from the gardener, but they are fine for light to medium work. Tillers with the tines behind the wheels tend to dig in and stay in one place. They can perform heavy duty work, such as tilling soil covered in vegetation.

Secateurs, or pruning clippers, should have a sharp cutting edge that bypasses a curved, non-cutting blade. The kind of clippers that have a sharp blade that comes down to meet a flat anvil are not good for most pruning jobs. Unless the blade is kept very sharp they tend to crush branches rather than cut them cleanly, and this in turn leads to poor healing and a greater risk of disease. They are fine for pruning conifers, however, but one pair of by-pass shears is sufficient for all pruning jobs including conifers. Be sure to choose a model that comfortably fits the size of your hand.

Curved by-pass shears are the most useful and will cut hardwood branches up to 1/2 inch (12 mm) in diameter. Straight by-pass shears with narrow blades are useful for cutting flowers or for getting into tight corners to cut softwood shrubs. Select secateurs with vinyl coated handles as these give a good grip. Look for a safety lock to close the blades when they are not

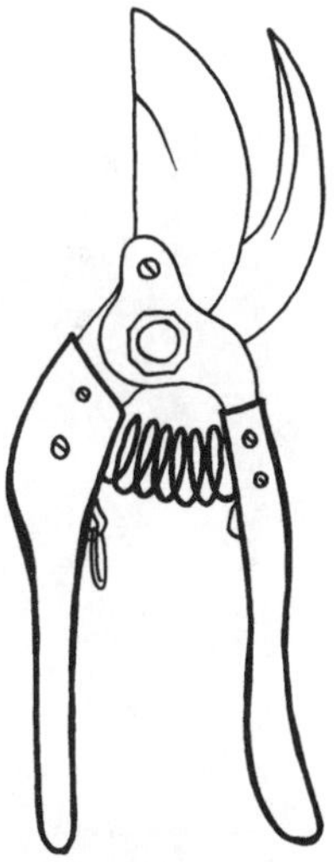

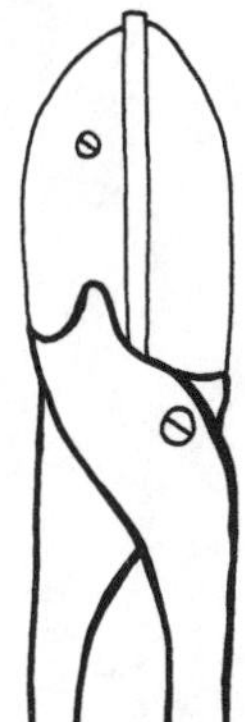

Secateurs with curved sharp blades are best for pruning as the flat blades that cut to an anvil tend to crush branches.

in use; you should be able to release the lock with the hand holding the shears. A holster worn at the waist is very useful.

To cut wood that is greater than 1/2 inch (2 cm) in diameter, use long handled loppers as they provide more leverage. Wide blades will generally cut thicker wood than narrow blades. They come in light, medium and heavy weights, and can cut increasingly larger branches as they get heavier.

Wood thicker than 1 ½ inches (4 cm) in diameter requires a pruning saw with a curved blade. Saws are available in various lengths with a range of seven to twelve teeth per inch (2.5 cm). The more teeth, the finer the cut will be. For most home gardeners, look for a small size about 14 inches (35 cm) long with seven to eight teeth per inch (2.5 cm). Avoid those with varying lengths of blades that can be inserted and removed from the handle; they are usually of weak construction and do not function well on the job. For overhead work, select a combination pole saw and clipper.

Check for weight and a smooth cutting action when purchasing hedge clippers. The heaviest, most expensive pairs are just dandy for people who are tall and muscular, or who need them for thick-stemmed hedges, but they are awkward and unmanageable for small people and unnecessary for soft-stemmed hedges. The user needs to be able to wield them with a good snap as each cut is made, and there should be no heavy dragging action as the blades close on each other. Look for clippers with secure and durable joins between the blades and handles. Some people prefer blades with wavy edges; they help to trap branches when cutting, but they are difficult to sharpen. A notch in the blade of some models is designed to hold thick stems for cutting.

There is a myriad of tools to choose from. To avoid unnecessary purchases and tools of poor quality, wait until there is a need for a particular item, and then select the one that best suits the gardener.

## Garden Gifts

Whether for birthdays, anniversaries, or some other occasion, it can be satisfying to give gardening gifts such as products from the garden, gardening books and gadgets, or even an offer to help someone else in their garden.

Food gifts are attractive and almost always welcome, especially on feast days. Some preparations which make good gifts include chutneys, pickles, jams, jellies, herbal products, baked goods, fruit cordials, candied flowers—the list is endless.

Jo Ann Gardner in *The Old-Fashioned Fruit Garden* (1989) offers many fruit recipes, including red currant meat sauce, pie, sass (a New England colloquial word for fruit sauce) and snub (a fruit drink), and red currant-raspberry ice, tart and jelly. There are also black currant sticky buns, juice, ice cream, jelly rolls, wine and mead. Elderberries can be used in numerous concoctions, many of which make unusual gifts such as cordial, custard pie, green grape jelly, orange jelly, sass and wine. If you are using elderflowers, recipes for fritters, pancakes, wine and peppermint tea can be added to the list. A nice touch is to include the recipe with the item you give.

Other fruit gifts might be "How to Grow" booklets on strawberries or blueberries, and a gift certificate for the matching plant or a promise of some plants from one's own garden. An offer of a variety of rooted cuttings from fruit shrubs in the spring would be greatly appreciated by a gardener who is just getting established.

A pot of herbs makes a pleasant introduction to herb gardening, or make some pesto or basil flavoured spagetti sauce and include the recipe and a potted basil plant. Several glass jars of home grown dried beans, along with some recipes and dried herbs, is a pretty gift for anyone who has not grown their own beans, or give just the beans to spark the artistic talents of an older child.

If you have an established garden, you could promise to pass on a selection of your perennial flowers when you are dividing plants next spring, or you might offer an afternoon's digging, mowing or several hours of odd jobs to an older person who finds heavy work too strenuous. A pot of forced bulbs, even if only the green tips are showing, makes a long lasting gift that can be planted in the garden in the spring. It is fun for children to watch the stages of growth, and it may be especially appreciated by someone who is house-bound. Dried flower arrangements and potpourris bring a breath of summer.

Older gardeners or anyone with arthritis might appreciate foam-rubber knee pads or a foam kneeling pad; a light-weight wheelbarrow or garden cart to help with carrying plants and other items; a light weight garden stool; a sturdy apron with lots of pockets so that extra trips to fetch things can be avoided; extra large gardening gloves with padding inside; foam padding on tool handles; small size garden tools; and a batwing sweater that is easy to get in and out of for outdoor work on cool days. A very generous offer would be to turn regular growing beds into raised beds—the width should be limited so that reaching the middle is easy.

An outdoor composting unit is another possible gift idea. An indoor worm composter may or may not be appreciated (see page 401)! Purchase or build a plant stand with fluorescent lights for the indoor gardener. A sunbonnet with a wide brim and a generous piece of cloth to cover the neck, or a modified men's cap complete with added neck cloth, will protect loved ones from the sun. Long sleeved cover ups, made of patterned fabric so that the dirt does not show, are also good for blocking the sun's rays while gardening.

There are plenty of little garden gizmos to choose from and some not so little: special purpose water nozzles; soil testing kits (lots of fun for a budding chemist); air or soil thermometers; maximum-minimum thermometers; bird feeders and a package of bird food; automatic watering timers; light and moisture meters; soil heating cables; packages of fertilizer. It is great fun to cruise through a garden centre to look at all of the gardening gadgets.

Other good small gifts are nursery and seed catalogues. Wrap up a bundle of old favourites and tie it with a ribbon, or send the recipient's name and address to seed and nursery companies so that he or she is added to their mailing lists. To discover other seed companies, look in the January and February issues of gardening magazines; they often have lists of seed and nursery companies. The reference section in a local library may have a shelf of catalogues to browse through and get addresses from. That is also the place to look for sources of rare and exotic seeds. Many gardeners greatly enjoy curling up in a corner with seed and nursery catalogues and dreaming away the winter hours. Children like to cut up old catalogues because of their colourful pictures.

A gift subscription to a gardening magazine or horticultural journal gives year round pleasure. Check the local library if you are unfamiliar with the various magazines. They make great reading even if no subscription is actually started. The library or civic recreation department can provide information on local garden clubs and horticultural societies, should you want to take out a membership for yourself or another person. Books on all aspects of gardening are welcomed by both novices and experienced gardeners. *Chickens in your Backyard* by Rick and Gail Luttmann (1976) might also get a gardener interested in live help with pest management.

### Potpourri

If containers of potpourri are put out to decorate and scent the house, they may need a little boost to release their scent. Stirring them up or putting them near a source of heat may help, and a few drops of brandy will revitalize a fading mixture.

## Winter Decorations

In the winter, gardeners turn to evergreens and plants with berries (see page 422) for decorative plant material, either for indoor use or for window boxes. Some branches stay in good condition better than others, depending on the species, but making sure they have absorbed as much moisture as possible after being cut from the parent plant will help all branches stay fresh looking.

There is a greater risk of winter injury when plants are pruned in December and January, but a little light pruning for decorations can usually be tolerated. Prune on a mild day above freezing, and put the cuttings into water as soon as possible. Water uptake is improved if the lower end of the branch is slit with a sharp knife. The branches should be allowed to stand in water for twelve to twenty hours before being removed and tied into position. The entire branch can be submerged in water for several hours to ensure that the maximum amount of water has been taken up.

The needles of yew stay attached for a very long time, making it an ideal plant with which to decorate, but be aware that the needles and berries are poisonous. Evergreen holly and ivy grow in only the mildest regions, but deciduous holly (winterberry, black alder or Canada holly, *Ilex verticillata*) will survive in zone 3. It carries its orange-red fruit well into winter and adds a marvelous spark of colour to decorations. Boxwood, juniper, spruce and pine can also be used.

If you buy wreaths, but want to add individual touches to them, tuck in some pieces of holly, or use Canada holly berries. Wrap florist wire around pine cones and wire them into place. Simply adding a few pieces of a different kind of conifer, such as pine added to spruce, will also create interest.

There is nothing like a Christmas tree to scent a house. Cutting down a conifer on one's own property will ensure a fresh Christmas tree. If purchasing one, test for freshness first by tugging on the needles: if they stay firmly anchored, the tree will hold its needles longer after it arrives home. Keep the tree outdoors in a shaded location until you are ready to erect it in the house.

If purchasing flowering plants for decoration, look for those that are mostly in bud with only a few flowers open. They will provide colour for a much longer period. With poinsettias, it is a little more difficult to tell whether or not the flowers are still closed. Look carefully in the centre of the red (or pink or white) bracts at the little yellow flowers. Open flowers look fuzzy and closed flowers look more like smooth balls.

Be careful that poinsettias and other plants

### Preventive Measure

To keep a tree fresh, mix up some "tree juice." Use 1 gallon (4.5 l) of hot water, 1 cup (250 ml) of sugar and 2 tablespoons (30 ml) of bleach. Let this cool. Cut off 1 or 2 inches (3 to 5 cm) at an angle from the bottom of the trunk and then stand the tree immediately in the tepid "juice." Be sure to top up the liquid daily so that the tree is always standing in liquid; keeping the tree as moist as possible will reduce the fire hazard.

Poinsettia

do not get chilled as they may respond by dropping their leaves. Plants should not be left in the car, for example. Once home, keep poinsettias in a well lit spot away from drafts and keep them reasonably warm. Wait until the soil is moderately dry before watering them again. Keep new plants separate from other plants in the house until it is clear that they have no insect or disease problems. Dipping the stems of poinsettias in 90% rubbing alcohol (isopropyl type) for ten minutes immediately after cutting them will help poinsettias last longer—for eight to ten days—in a cut flower arrangement.

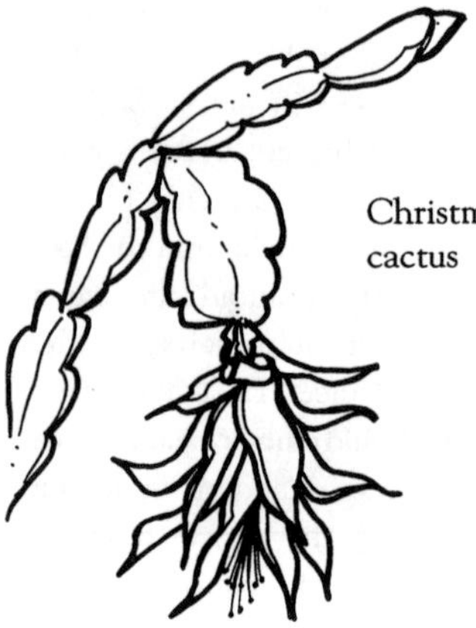

Christmas cactus

If Christmas cactus is purchased or must be moved, do it while the buds are miniscule and do not change its orientation towards the light. Larger buds turn to grow in the direction of the light, which is what causes them to drop off when moved. Christmas cactus, cyclamen and azaleas last longer in cool temperatures, and azaleas must never be allowed to dry out.

## The Meaning of Plant Names

It is not unusual for some gardeners to freeze at the sight of a Latin plant name. Many names, however, are used as everyday names for plants, even though they are Latin or Greek words. Think of *Iris*, *Crocus*, *Trillium*, *Aster*, *Narcissus* and *Phlox*. Many names have meanings that are not difficult to interpret, such as *canadensis* (in Canada), *odorata* (scented) and *triloba* (with three lobes).

Each plant name has two parts: the genus and the species. All of the plants that are close relatives belong to the same genus, such as *Allium* for the onion group. Within the group, the different species names distinguish the individual members: *Allium sativum* (garlic), A. *ampeloprasum* (elephant garlic and leeks), A. *schoenoprasum* (chives), A. *tuberosum* (garlic chives, also known as Chinese chives), A. *fistulosum* (bunching onions) and A. *cepa* (common bulb onions). After the genus name is given once, subsequent references to it are identified by the first letter, as in A. for *Allium*.

Some plant names have a third name after the genus and species name. If no quotation marks are used, the third name indicates a natural variety of the species; if single quotation marks are present, the third name indicates a variety created by humans, called a cultivar. Thus, *Betula pendula crispa* is a natural, cut-leaved variety of silver birch, whereas B. *pendula* 'Youngii' is a cultivar (Young's weeping birch). When plants of different species are hybridized, the name has 'x' in it. Thus, *Rosa x harisonii* (Harison's yellow rose) is thought to be a hybrid of *R. spinosissima* and *R. foetida 'Persiana.'*

The genus name is often derived from the name of a famous person, plant explorer (in the 19th century, plant enthusiasts, many from Britain, explored in the middle east and eastern countries for new plants), scientist, or friend of the person doing the naming. The species name is usually very descriptive and is used to describe leaf or flower colour; the place where the plant originated; the plant's size or shape; stem and branch characteristics; the usual habitat or growth habit (whether annual, biennial or perennial); characteristics of the leaf; and characteristics of the flower. *Kerria japonica* is a plant from Japan named after William Kerr, the head gardener at Kew Gardens in England around 1800. *Rhododendron ferrugineum* is the rhododendron with leaves that are rust coloured on the underside.

Examples of **colour** names are:

*alba* white
*argentea* silvery
*aurantiacum* orange
*atrovirens* very green
*caerula* blue
*cardinalis* scarlet
*carnea* flesh coloured
*cinerea* ash coloured
*cruentus* blood red
*cyanus* dark blue
*ferruginea* rust coloured
*glauca* blue-green
*lutea* yellow
*maculatum* spotted
*niger* black
*purpurea* purple
*ruber, rubra* red
*rubicunda* red
*sanguineum* blood red
*sempervirens* evergreen

Plant names that identify their **geographic origin** include:

*alpina* in the Alps
*atlantica* in the Atlas mountains
*australis* in the southern hemisphere
*borealis* in the northern hemisphere
*brasiliensis* in Brazil
*canadensis* in Canada
*europaea* in Europe
*gallica* in Gaul (France)
*germanica* in Germany
*japonica* in Japan
*occidentalis* in the Occident
*orientalis* in the Orient
*pennsylvanica* in Pennsylvania
*virginica* in Virginia

A few names that indicate **habitat** or **growth habit** include:

*annuus* annual
*arenarius* in shady areas
*autumnalis* autumn
*campestre* on plains
*hiemalis* winter
*maritima* on the seashore
*montana* in the mountains
*muralis* on walls
*nivalis* near snow
*perennis* perennial
*pratensis* in fields
*saxatile* among rocks

*Armeria maritima*, the common thrift, sea pink, is an example.

Some words that describe a plant's **shape** or **size** are:

*arborea* tree shaped
*caespitosa* growing in clumps
*excelsior* taller
*fastigiata* columnar
*fragilis* fragile
*fruticosa* shrubby
*helix* in a spiral
*horizontalis* horizontal growth
*humilis* low-growing
*nanus* dwarf
*pendula* weeping
*pumila* very small
*repens* creeping
*robusta* strong

**Stem, branch** and **leaf characteristics** are defined by words such as:

*acaulis* stemless
*aculeatus* prickly
*alatus* winged
*elatior* tall
*glutinosus* sticky
*hirsuta* hairy
*nudicaule* bare stemmed
*oxycantha* very prickly
*radicans* with adventitious roots
*rugosa* rough or wrinkled
*sarmentosa* climbing
*spinosa* spiny
*spinosissima* very spiny
*verrucosa* warty

*Euonymus alatus* (winged euonymus or burning bush), with its corky wings on the branches, and rugosa roses, with their wrinkly leaves, come to mind as examples.

**Leaf shape** is an important characteristic for distinguishing plants from one another. Two types of terms are used: one type compares the leaf in question to a known leaf (*buxifolia* means boxwood leaved, or leaves like boxwood); the other type describes the actual form of the leaf (*dentata* means toothed leaf). Some examples of both are:

*acerifolium* maple leaved
*acuminata* pointed
*alnifolia* alder leaved
*latifolia* wide
*lyrata* lyre shaped
*macrophylla* big leaf

*angustifolia* narrow
*buxifolia* boxwood leaved
*carpinifolia* *Carpinus* leaved
*cordifolia* heart shaped
*crassifolia* thick
*crenata* notched
*dentata* toothed
*heterophylla* variable
*integrifolia* simple
*lanata* wooly
*myrtifolia* myrtle leaved
*platyphylla* wide leaf
*prunifolia* *Prunus* leaved
*quercifolia* oak leaved
*rotundifolia* round leaf
*serrata* toothed
*tricuspidata* with three points
*trifoliata* with three leaflets
*triloba* with three lobes

*Alternifolia* means that the leaves are arranged alternately on the stem. Some plant names, such as floribunda roses, describe **characteristics of the flowers** (many roses per stem) and other terms include:

*barbatus* bearded
*bracteatum* bracted flowers
*floribunda* floriferous
*globerata* clustered flowers
*grandiflora* big flowers
*pauciflora* few flowers
*racemosa* clustered flowers
*semperflorens* everblooming
*spicata* s piked blooms
*verticillata* whorled

Sometimes the people who named plants were so taken with the **aesthetic qualities** that they described them as:

*amoena* charming
*gloriosa* superb
*gracilis* fine
*nobilis* noble
*spectabilis* remarkable
*vulgaris* common

In some cases it was the **use of the plant** or some other property that those naming plants thought meritted attention. Such words include:

*amara* bitter
*catharticus* purgative
*esculenta* edible
*foetida* smelly
*graveolens* scented
*odorata* scented
*officinalis* medicinal
*saccharum* sugar
*sativus* cultivated
*scoparius* used in brooms
*tinctoria* used in dyeing

The next time a Latin plant name springs to your attention, see if any meaning can be gleaned from the name and what relation it has to characteristics of the plant.

## Indoor Gardening

### Fruits, Vegetables and Herbs

Bringing fresh produce to the table gives great pleasure to both the gardener and the guests. Rhubarb and chicory can be forced into growth after they have had a couple of months of cool temperatures (see January, page 27). Gardeners living in regions where winter comes early have an advantage and can expect an earlier treat than those living where cool conditions started only this month.

A variety of greens, vine ripened tomatoes, radishes, onions and fresh herbs can make a salad fit for gourmets. Planting in the dead of winter in a cool greenhouse is not always successful, but seeds started in earlier months will continue to produce for many weeks. In warm conditions, anything from the autumn schedule (see Table JAN-2, page 24) can be sown if they were not seeded earlier. Cress takes four or five weeks to mature in the shorter days of winter. Fertilize all growing plants regularly, and provide a minimum of twelve hours of light each day if growth seems to have stopped altogether.

### Warm Flowers

Salpiglossis, a relative of petunia but a much taller plant, can be seeded this month if warm growing conditions can be provided. Extra light will bring it into bloom sooner. Gloxinia can be started from seed, but it will take longer to reach blooming size than tubers that are potted up this month.

White calla lily needs considerable warmth to start into growth, but regal lily and *L. speciosum rubrum* can be potted up and started into growth slowly in cool temperatures. If there are plenty of roots and green tips showing, early spring flowering bulbs can be brought out of cold storage.

### Cool Flowers

Lilies and spring blooming bulbs can also be grown in cool temperatures, although they will take much longer to come into flower, and more freesias and other members of the iris family (see page 408) can be potted up. Ranunculus brought into growth does best at a temperature of 50°F (10°C) at first, but this can be gradually raised. Give it light shade and avoid overwatering. Dutch iris, ixia, sparaxis and other bulbs can also be grown a little warmer once growth is established, and they should have been fertilized three or four times by the time they come into bud. Be careful to never let them dry out, but reduce watering a little after the buds have formed.

## *Table DEC-2 Potting, Forcing, Cutting and Sowing Dates for a Succession of Bloom Indoors*

| Blooming Date | Flower | Potting (p), Forcing (f) or Sowing (s) Date | Temperature, Remarks |
|---|---|---|---|
| **January** | Browallia | s-August 1 | warm |
| | Calendula | s-July | cool |
| | Dutch Iris | p-October | cool |
| | Forget-me-Not | s-September | cool |
| | Freesia *et al.* | p-August | cool |
| | Gerbera | s-September—16 months prior to occasion | warm |
| | *Lilium regale*, *L. speciosum* | f-August | warm; cold from spring |
| | Marigold | s-September | cool |
| | Pansy | s-July-August | cool; extra light |
| | Primrose | s-May | cool |
| | Snapdragon | s-August | cool |
| | Sweet Pea | s-August-September | cool |
| **February** | Amaryllis | p-October | warm |
| | Anemone | p-September | warm |
| 14th | Begonia | p-September 15 | warm |
| | Calendula | s-September | cool |
| | Calla Lily | p-September | warm |
| 14th | Daffodil | f-January 15 | warm; cold from October |
| | Feverfew | s-July | cool; extra light |
| | Forget-me-Not | s-October | cool |
| | Freesia *et al.* | p-September | cool |
| 14th | Hyacinth | f-January 1 | warm; cold from October |
| | Larkspur | s-September | cool |
| 14th | Lily-Asiatics | p-November 25 | warm |
| 14th | Lily-of-the-Valley | p-January 24 | warm |
| | Pansy | s-July-August 1 | cool; extra light |
| | Perennials | f-November | cool, then warm; cold from autumn |
| | Petunia | s-September | warm |
| | Primrose | s-June, August | cool; *Malacoides* blooms sooner than other types |
| | Salpiglossis | s-September | warm |

| Blooming Date | Flower | Potting (p), Forcing (f) or Sowing (s) Date | Temperature, Remarks |
|---|---|---|---|
| | Snapdragon | s-August | cool |
| | Stock | s-July | cool |
| | Sweet Pea | s-September | cool |
| 14th | Tulip | f-January 1-15 | warm; cold from October |
| **March** | Anemone | p-September | cool |
| | Aster | s-August | cool; extra light |
| | Calendula | s-August-September | cool |
| | Calla Lily | p-September | warm |
| | Centaurea | s-September 15 | cool |
| | Chrysanthemum, annual | s-September 1 | cool; extra light |
| | Daffodil | f-February | warm or cool; cold from October or November |
| | Feverfew | s-July | cool; extra light |
| | Forget-me-Not | s-November-December | cool |
| | Freesia *et al.* | p-October | cool |
| | Gypsophila | s-November | cool; extra light |
| | Hyacinth | f-February | warm or cool; cold from October or November |
| | Larkspur | s-September | cool |
| 1st | Lily-Asiatics | p-December 10 | warm |
| 17th | | p-January 1 | |
| 28th | | p-January 15 | |
| | Pansy | s-July-August | cool; extra light |
| | Perennials | f-December | cool, then warm; cold from autumn |
| | Petunia | s-November | warm |
| | Primrose | s-July | cool |
| | Schizanthus | s-August 20 | cool |
| | Snapdragon | s-September-October | cool |
| | Sweet Pea | s-October | cool |
| | Tulip | f-February | warm or cool; cold from October or November |

| | |
|---|---|
| cold from | = pot up and put into cold storage from season given until the forcing date, when pot is brought into warmth and light |
| *et al.* | = and others in the iris family |
| W.F. | = winter flowering |
| N.B. Asiatic Lilies | = early flowering varieties |

| Blooming Date | Flower | Potting (p), Forcing (f) or Sowing (s) Date | Temperature, Remarks |
|---|---|---|---|
| **April** | Amaryllis | p-February | warm |
| | Aster | s-December 1 | cool; extra light from December 10 |
| | Begonia | p-November 1 | warm |
| | Calendula | s-November 15 | cool |
| | Candytuft | s-November 20 | cool |
| | Centaurea | s-December | cool |
| | Chrysanthemum, annual | s-September | cool; extra light |
| | Clarkia | s-January 25 | cool |
| | Daffodil | f-March | cool or warm; cold from November or December |
| | Feverfew | s-November-December | cool |
| | Forget-me-Not | s-November-December | cool |
| | Freesia *et al.* | p-November-December | cool |
| | Gladiolus, dwarf | p-January | warm; bottom heat |
| | Hydrangea | f-January | cool or warm; cold from autumn |
| | Larkspur | s-November | cool |
| | *Lilium candidum* | f-January | cool; cold from autumn |
| | *L. regale* | p-January | cool or warm |
| | *L. speciosum* | p-December | cool or warm |
| 12th | Lily Asiatics | p-February 1 | warm |
| 24th | | p-February 15 | |
| | Lily-of-the-Valley | f-April | warm; cold from autumn; 3 weeks to bloom |
| | Lisianthus | s-August 15 | warm |
| | Marigold | s-February | cool |
| | Perennials | f-January | cool, then warm; cold from autumn |
| | Poppy | s- January | cool |
| | Primrose | s-March-April | cool |
| | Rose | f-January | cool, then warm; cold from autumn |
| | Snapdragon | s-November | cool |
| | Stock | s-November | cool |
| | Sweet Pea | s-January | cool |
| | Tulip | f-March | cool or warm; cold from autumn |

| | |
|---|---|
| cold from | = pot up and put into cold storage from season given until the forcing date, when pot is brought into warmth and light |
| *et al.* | = and others in the iris family |
| W.F. | = winter flowering |
| N.B. Asiatic Lilies | = early flowering varieties |

| **Blooming Date** | **Flower** | **Potting (p), Forcing (f) or Sowing (s) Date** | **Temperature, Remarks** |
|---|---|---|---|
| **May** | Aster | s-December 15 | cool; extra light from December 24 |
| 15th | Begonia | p-December 1 | warm |
| | Browallia | s-December 1 | warm |
| | Calendula | s-November 30 | cool |
| | Calla Lily | p-September | warm |
| | Candytuft | s-December | cool |
| | Chrysanthemum, annual | s-October | cool |
| | Clarkia | s-December | cool |
| | Feverfew | s-December | cool |
| | Freesia *et al.* | p-January | cool |
| | Fuchsia | c-November | warm |
| | Geranium | c-September | warm |
| | Gladiolus, dwarf | p-January | warm |
| | Gloxinia | p-January | warm |
| | Godetia | s-December | cool |
| 15th | Hydrangea | f-January | cool, then warm; cold from autumn |
| | Larkspur | s-November | cool |
| | *Lilium candidum* | f-March 15-30 | cool; cold from autumn |
| 4th | Lily-Asiatics | p-February 26 | warm |
| 20th | | p-March 15 | |
| | Lily-of-the-Valley | f-May | cool; cold from autumn; 3 weeks to bloom |
| | Marigold, African | s-January 1 | cool; remove side buds |
| | Nemesia | s-December | cool |
| | Pansy-W.F. | s-December | cool |
| | Petunia | s-December | |
| | Rose | f-January | cool, then warm |
| | Salpiglossis | s-December | warm; extra light |
| | Snapdragon | s-January-February | cool |
| | Statice | s-November | warm |
| 15th | Stock | s-December-February | cool; extra light |
| | Sweet Pea-W.F. | s-January | cool |
| 20th on | Zinnia | s-April 1 | warm |

| Blooming Date | Flower | Potting (p), Forcing (f) or Sowing (s) Date | Temperature, Remarks |
|---|---|---|---|
| **June** | Calla Lily | p-September | warm |
| | Candytuft | s-December | cool |
| | Feverfew | s-December | cool |
| | Freesia *et al.* | p-February | cool |
| | Fuchsia | c-January | warm |
| | Gerbera | s-November | warm |
| | Gladiolus, dwarf | p-February | warm |
| | Gloxinia | p-February | warm |
| | | s-December | warm; 15 hours light |
| 5th | Lily-Asiatics | p-April 1 | warm |
| | Lisianthus | s-November-December | warm |
| | Nemesia | s-December | cool |
| | Salpiglossis | s-December | warm |
| | Scabiosa | s-December | cool |
| | Stock | s-February | cool |
| | Sweet Pea | s-February | cool |
| 1st-10th | Zinnia | s-April 15 | warm |
| 10th-20th | Zinnia | s-May 1 | warm |
| **June and July** | Aster | s-March 10 | cool; extra light |
| | Aster | s-March, late | cool; no light |
| | Fuchsia | c-March 1 | warm |
| | Gypsophila | s-April | cool |
| | Snapdragon | s-February | cool |
| | Sweet Pea | s-Match | cool |
| **August** | As for July and September | | |
| **September** | Gerbera | s-February | warm |
| | Snapdragon | s-March | cool |
| | Statice | s-February | warm |
| | Sweet Pea | s-June 15 | as cool as possible |
| **October** | Aster | s-April | cool |
| | Calendula | s-June | cool |
| | Forget-me-Not | s-June | cool |
| | Lily-of-the-Valley | p-October 1 | warm; 3 weeks to bloom |

| | |
|---|---|
| cold from | = pot up and put into cold storage from season given until the forcing date, when pot is brought into warmth and light |
| *et al.* | = and others in the iris family |
| W.F. | = winter flowering |
| N.B. Asiatic Lilies | = early flowering varieties |

| **Blooming Date** | **Flower** | **Potting (p), Forcing (f) or Sowing (s) Date** | **Temperature, Remarks** |
|---|---|---|---|
| | Marigold | s-July | cool |
| | Nasturtium | s-July | cool |
| | Statice | s-March | warm |
| | Sweet Pea | s-June 15 | as cool as possible |
| | Tiger Lily | f-June | cool; store cold from spring |
| **November** | Calendula | s-July | cool |
| | Chrysanthemum, annual | s-April | cool |
| | Forget-me-Not | s-July | cool |
| | Lily-of-the-Valley | p-November | warm; 3 weeks to bloom |
| | Marigold | s-August 1 | cool |
| | Nasturtium | s-August | cool |
| | Pansy | s-July | cool; extra light |
| | Sweet Pea | s-June 15 | as cool as possible |
| | Tiger Lily | f-July | cool; store cold from spring |
| **December** | Amaryllis | p-October | warm; 7 to 9 weeks to bloom |
| 25th | Begonia | p-July 25-August 1 | warm |
| | Calendula | s-July | cool |
| 25th | Daffodil | f-November 15-25 | warm; cold from mid-August |
| | Forget-me-Not | s-August | cool |
| | Freesia *et al.* | p-August | cool |
| | Gerbera | s-August-September | warm |
| | Gloxinia | p-August 1 | warm |
| 25th | Hyacinth | f-November 25 | warm; cold from mid-August |
| 25th | *Lilium speciosum* | p-July 7 | warm |
| | Marigold | s-August 1 | cool |
| | Nasturtium | s-September | cool |
| | Pansy | s-July | cool; extra light |
| | Paperwhite | p-November-December | cool or warm; 3 to 6 weeks to bloom |
| | Schizanthus | s-August | cool; pinch to October 15 |
| | Snapdragon | s-July 1 | cool |
| | Stock | s-July | cool |
| | Sweet Pea | s-August | cool |

There are a number of annual flowers that can be sown in December; their growth will be quick when days start to noticeably lengthen in February. Nemesia, candytuft, godetia and clarkia grow best in dryish soil without much fertilizer. Stock sown now should be in bloom in April, and many others will bloom not long after, including annual phlox, calendula, scabiosa, centaurea, feverfew, winter flowering pansy and annual chrysanthemum. Watch for powdery mildew and provide good air circulation and wide spacing among plants or pots. Asters seeded on the 1st and 15th of the month will bloom earlier if they are given extra light until they are in bloom. A difference of two weeks in the seeding date in the winter translates into a difference of several weeks in blooming time because of the effect of increasing day length on the seedlings.

### Timing of Flowering

Planning ahead will ensure that a variety of flowers are in bloom for a special occasion, such as a graduation in May or a wedding in June. If one has access to both warm and cool growing conditions, an even greater variety can be grown. Of course, the more that is grown, the better the chances of having at least something in bloom for the big day, whatever the occasion. Exact timing is dependent on temperature and lighting levels (see January, page 32, regarding extra lighting). Timing is also dependent on the time of year that growth takes place. For example, snapdragons planted in September take longer to come into bloom than those planted in March, and early blooming Asiatic lilies take anywhere from nine to twelve and a half weeks to bloom, depending on whether they are planted in April or November.

As the date of the occasion nears, increasing the temperature or lowering it can hasten or retard crop maturation. Flowers that bloom a little ahead of time can be held in lighted, very cool conditions to keep them fresh for a while longer.

## Conclusion

Whether one begins gardening out of necessity or pleasure, there usually comes a time in the life of a gardener when one becomes comfortable with plants and develops an appreciation and understanding of the natural processes involved in growing them. As one gains experience and learns to work with nature, gardening becomes less of a struggle and more a mellowing and flowing with the insects and weather that come our way. Extending the growing season by moving indoors in the winter seems to be a natural continuation that is becoming more popular. Hopefully, as the years go by, more children will see their parents and grandparents gardening and will pick up by word of mouth and direct apprenticeship much of the lore that is in books such as this.

# References


Agriculture Canada. 1978. *Home storage room for fruits and vegetables*. Publication 1478/E. Ottawa: Communications Branch.

Ball, Jeff and Liz Ball. 1989. *Landscape Problem Solver*. Emmaus, PA: Rodale Press.

Beard, Henry and Roy McKie. 1982. *A Gardener's Dictionary*. New York: Workman Publishing.

Bleasdale, J.K.A., P.J. Salter and Others. 1991. *The Complete Know and Grow Vegetables*. New York: Oxford University Press.

Brooklyn Botanic Garden Record. 1969. "Handbook on Ferns." Handbook #59, *Plants & Gardens*, Vol.25 No.1.

Brooklyn Botanic Garden Record. 1976. "Miniature Gardens." Handbook #58, *Plants & Gardens*, Vol.24 No.3.

Brooklyn Botanic Garden Record. 1982. "Trained and Sculptured Plants." Handbook #36, *Plants & Gardens*, Vol.17 No.2.

Brooklyn Botanic Garden Record. 1990. "Herbs & Cooking." Handbook #122, *Plants & Gardens*, Vol.45 No.4.

Carr, Anna, 1979. *Color Handbook of Garden Insects*. Emmaus, PA: Rodale Press.

Coleman, Eliot. 1989. *The New Organic Gardener*. Camden East, ON: Old Bridge Press.

Creasy, Rosalind. 1988. *Cooking From the Garden*. Vancouver/Toronto: Douglas & McIntyre.

Fettner, Ann Tucker. 1977. *Potpourri, Incense, and other Fragrant Concoctions*. New York: Workman Publishing Company.

Gardner, Jo Ann. 1989. *The Old-Fashioned Fruit Garden*. Halifax, NS: Nimbus Publishing.

Garland, Sarah. 1979. *The Herb and Spice Book*. London: Frances Lincoln Publishers.

Grenier Simmons, Adelma. 1988. *Country Wreaths from Caprilands*. Emmaus, PA: Rodale Press.

Hall-Beyer, Bart and Jean Richard. 1983. *Ecological Fruit Production in the North*. Trois-Rivieres: Jean Richard.

Hardin, James W. and Jay M. Arena. 1974. *Human Poisoning from Native and Cultivated Plants*. 2nd edition. Durham, NC: Duke University Press.

Howie, Virginia. 1978. *Let's Grow Lilies*. Burlington, VT: George Little Press.

Jacobs, Betty E.M. 1988. *Flowers that Last Forever*. Pownal, VT: Storey Communications.

Luttman, Rick and Gail Luttman. 1976. *Chickens in your Backyard*. Emmaus, PA: Rodale Press.

Mulligan, Gerald A. 1987. *Common Weeds of Canada*. NC Press, in co-operation with Agriculture Canada and the Canadian Government Publishing Centre, Supply and Services Canada.

Ortho Books. 1983. *How to Attract Birds*. San Francisco: Chevron Chemical Company.

Osborne, Robert. 1991. *Roses for Canadian Gardens*. Toronto: Key Porter Books.

Patent, Dorothy Hinshaw and Diane E. Bilderback. 1982. *Garden Secrets*. Emmaus, PA: Rodale Press.

Rahn, James J. 1979. *Making the Weather Work for You*. Charlotte, VT: Garden Way Publishing.

Richardson, Noel. 1990. *Winter Pleasures*. Toronto: Whitecap Books.

Richardson, Noel. 1991. *Summer Delights*. Toronto: Whitecap Books.

Riotte, Louise. 1975. *Carrots Love Tomatoes*. Pownal, VT: Storey Communications.

Riotte, Louise. 1983. *Roses Love Garlic*. Charlotte, VT: Garden Way Publishing.

Rubin, Carole. 1989. *How to get your lawn & garden off drugs*. Ottawa: Friends of the Earth.

Szczawinski, Adam F. and Nancy J. Turner. 1978. *Edible Garden Weeds of Canada*. Ottawa: National Museums of Canada.

Waugh, Albert E. 1973. *Sundials: Their Theory and Construction*. New York: Dover Publications.

Willison, Marjorie. 1989. *Marjorie Willison's Successful Landscape Design*. Halifax, NS: Nimbus Publishing.

Yepsen, Roger B. Jr. (ed.). 1984. *The Encyclopedia of Natural Insect & Disease Control*. Emmaus, PA: Rodale Press.

# Index

V

## W



## X